JAPAN'S COMPUTER AND
COMMUNICATIONS INDUSTRY

Praise for *Japan's Computer and Communications Industry*

'Fransman's authoritative analysis . . . should clear away many of the myths and mis-understandings which have bedevilled discussion about Japanese industrial success. His book should be essential reading, not only to students of Japan, but to anyone interested in the competitiveness of firms and nations.' *Sir Geoffrey Owen, former editor, Financial Times*

'While the largely self-contained case studies offered by this authoritative volume deserve attention by themselves, interested readers will find even greater reward from the composite picture they present of Japan's search for economic advantage from information technologies.' *Arno Penzias, Vice President Research, Bell Laboratories*

'I have not read any book comparable to this one in depth, accuracy, and comprehensive analysis on the Japanese information and communications industry. This is the book for everyone who wants to understand this industry.' *Michiyuki Uenohara, Executive Advisor, NEC*

'Martin Fransman's book is a major achievement, which combines mastery of the detail of the development of major Japanese IT firms with the latest concepts emerging from the evolutionary theory of the firm.' *Keith Pavitt, SPRU, University of Sussex*

'A TOUR DE FORCE. A methodologically rigorous, theoretically sophisticated, and thoroughly documented study. . . . This pioneering book is essential reading for anyone who wishes to understand the nature of Japanese firms generally and the direction of Japanese information technology specifically.' *Glen S. Fukushima, former Director for Japanese Affairs, Office of the United States Trade Representative*

'This book . . . takes us well beyond much of the current management hype about the "uniqueness" of the Japanese way into a detailed analysis of the technical and institutional evolution of [the computer and communications industry]. [Its] "realistic" theory of the firm and how it makes decisions . . . will bring joy to those institutional and evolutionary economists who labour to find sound historical evidence to support techno-economic path dependency. . . . It provides a salutary corrective to current simplistic views of the Japanese government's national innovation policy and takes a stage further the pioneering work of Chalmers Johnson by looking in detail at the changing role, particularly of MITI, in the development of the firms in these sectors. The book is comprehensive and extremely readable.' *Michael Gibbons, Director, SPRU, University of Sussex*

'This is an impressive and highly valuable book on Japanese industry. . . . The lessons that can be drawn from this book are extremely relevant for economists, policy makers, and managers who are concerned with issues related to the growth and dynamics of high technology industries and the factors behind firm performance, adaptation, and long-term survival.' *Franco Malerba, Deputy Director, CESPRI, Bocconi University*

Japan's Computer and Communications Industry

The Evolution of Industrial Giants and Global Competitiveness

MARTIN FRANSMAN

OXFORD UNIVERSITY PRESS

1995

Oxford University Press, Walton Street, Oxford OX2 6DP

Oxford New York
Athens Auckland Bangkok Bombay
Calcutta Cape Town Dar es Salaam Delhi
Florence Hong Kong Instanbul Karachi
Kuala Lumpur Madras Madrid Melbourne
Mexico City Nairobi Paris Singapore
Taipei Tokyo Toronto
and associated companies in
Berlin Ibadan

Oxford is a trade mark of Oxford University Press

Published in the United States
by Oxford University Press Inc., New York

British Library Cataloguing in Publication Data
Data available

Library of Congress Cataloging-in-Publication Data
Fransman, Martin.
Japan's computer and communications industry : the evolution of
industrial giants and global competitiveness / Martin Fransman.
Includes bibliographical references and index.
1. Computer industry—Japan   2. Telecommunication equipment
industry—Japan   I. Title.
HD9696.C63J3154   1995   384'.06'552—dc20   95–22268

ISBN 0–19–823333–7

1 3 5 7 9 10 8 6 4 2

Typeset by BookMan Services, Oxford

Printed in Great Britain
on acid-free paper by
Biddles Ltd.,
Guildford and King's Lynn

For Tammy, Judy, Karen,
and Jonathan

PREFACE

This book is about the evolution of the technologies, forms of organization, firms, industries, government policies, and institutions that have shaped the Japanese information and communications (IC) sector, arguably the most important sector in the Japanese economy. This sector has not been as outstanding globally as the Japanese motor car or consumer electronics sectors, but it has been far more successful than, say, the Japanese chemical and pharmaceutical sectors. This book explains why.

An enormous number of debts have accumulated in the preparation of this book, which has taken some nine years and more than 600 personal interviews to complete. While not all those who should be acknowledged can be acknowledged here, mention must be made of some who have been important in the writing of this book. To begin with, I owe a debt to a number of thinkers who have provided the inspirational fuel that has kept this project going. These thinkers are united in their greater commitment ultimately to explaining the complexities and subtleties that are part and parcel of the process of change in the real world than to the formal elegance of their arguments. These thinkers include older generations—such as Adam Smith, Alfred Marshall, and Joseph Schumpeter—as well as contemporary intellectuals like Alfred Chandler, Ron Dore, Chris Freeman, Brian Loasby, Dick Nelson, Edith Penrose, Nathan Rosenberg, David Teece, and Oliver Williamson. While many of their ideas are to be found threaded through this book, I remain responsible for the interpretations provided.

Many other academics have also been important in the making of this book. They include my colleagues at the Research Center for Advanced Science and Technology (RCAST), University of Tokyo, where on two occasions, in 1988 and again in 1992, I held the NTT Visiting Professorship of Telecommunications. Special mention must be made of the late Professor Takanori Okoshi as well as Professors Yoichiro Murakami, Kei Takeuchi, Takeshi Hiromatsu, Fumio Kodama, Hiroyuki Sakaki, and Yasuhiko Arakawa, and the many non-Japanese visiting professors, like James Merz, who shared their insights into the Japanese science and technology system with me. On both occasions, Ikuko Suganuma provided efficient help as well as friendly support. Masashi Shirabe, a postgraduate attached to RCAST, gave invaluable assistance in wading through the daunting archives of the Ministry of Communications, and through the histories of the Japanese IC companies and other material on the sector, in an ultimately rewarding attempt better to understand the crucial 1920s and 1930s, which played such an important role in laying the foundations for controlled competition and the sector in general. (In view of the sections of this book devoted to NTT, it is worth noting that NTT itself had nothing to do with appointments to the NTT Chair at RCAST.) Also at Tokyo University, mention must be made of Professors Hiroshi Inose and Takahiro Fujimoto, both of whom on a number of occasions provided stimulating and suggestive discussions. The same was true of the late Professor Yasusuke Murakami and of Professor Shumpei Kumon (formerly of Tokyo University, now Director of GLOCOM).

I am similarly indebted to many other academics. They include Professors Mark Fruin from the University of British Columbia, Seichi Kawasaki now at Nagoya University, Tsuruhiko Nambu from Gakushuin University, Ikujiro Nonaka from Hitotsubashi University, Hiroyuki Odagiri from Tsukuba University, and Jon Sigurdson from Lund and Stockholm Universities.

A special debt and warm thankyou must be extended to the many people from the Japanese and Western companies in this sector who were extremely generous in the time and information that they gave me. Most importantly, by sharing their understanding and insights with me, they provided an invaluable source of learning about the complexities of this sector (imperfect though my knowledge remains). Most of them have become close and valued friends. Although I came away from each one of my interviews with the feeling of a richer understanding, it is unfortunately not possible to thank everyone here. Nevertheless my deep gratitude must be expressed to the following. In NTT I must thank Dr Iwao Toda, Mr Noboru Miyawaki, Mr Jun-Ichiro Miyazu, Mr Teruaki Ohara, Dr Ken'ichiro Hirota, Mr Kazuo Asada, Mr Fukuya Ishino, Mr Ichiro Yamanouchi, Mr Koichiro Hayashi, Dr Hiromasa Ikeda, Mr Kunihiro Kato, Mr Hiroshi Ishikawa, Mr Chiaki Hishinuma, and Mr Hiroharu Kimura; in NEC I am grateful to Dr Koji Kobayashi, Dr Michiyuki Uenohara, Mr Toshiro Kunihiro, Mr Daizaburo Shinoda, Mr Kiyoshi Emi, Mr Keiichi Shimakura, Mr Kazuo Kiji, and Mr Hiroshi Okazaki. In Fujitsu, my appreciation goes to Mr Motojiro Shiromizu, Mr Shigeru Sato, Mr Masaka Ogi, Dr Hirobumi Takanashi, Dr Kunihiko Asama, Mr Sukeyoshi Sakai, and Dr Masayuki Abe. In DDI I am grateful to Dr Sachio Semmoto and Mr Sanshiro Fukada. I am also grateful for the assistance that I have received through the Institute for Japanese–European Technology Studies (JETS) at the University of Edinburgh from the Ministry of International Trade and Industry (MITI), the Department of Trade and Industry (DTI), NEC, Fujitsu, and the Lothian Regional Council, all of whom have sponsored JETS. Most importantly, all of them have provided rich sources of information which have constituted a crucial input for this book. As I trust the reader will recognize, their support has not unduly coloured the analysis, interpretations, or criticisms made in this book.

I must also thank the following for the important insights they have provided: from Advanced Telecommunications Research Institute (ATR), Dr Kohei Habara; from AT&T Bell Laboratories, Dr Arno Penzias and Dr Mel Cohen; from AT&T Japan, Mr Glen Fukushima; from BT Japan, Mr Tony Cox; from Cable and Wireless Japan, Mr Keith Handley; from Canon, Mr Ryuzaburo Kaku; from Corning Japan, Mr Peter Booth; from Dataquest Japan, Mr Kenshi Tazaki; from Digital Equipment Corporation, Mr Martin Rosenblith; from Ericsson

Japan, Mr Morgan Bengtsson; from Furukawa Electric, Dr Hiroshi Murata; from Hitachi, Dr Yasutsugu Takeda, Dr Yutaka Kuwahara, and Dr Akira Tonomura; from IBM Japan, Mr Hiyoshi Yokogawa; from ICI Japan, Mr Desmond O'Shea; from IDC, Mr Hideo Suetsugu and Mr Barry Moul; from the Institute for Future Technology, Dr Ken'ichiro Hirota; from InfoCom Research, Mr Takahiro Ozawa, Mr Hirofumi Takahashi, and Mr Nobuki Hori; from Japan Aviation Electronics, Mr Takeshi Takahashi; from Keizai Doyukai (the Japan Association of Corporate Executives), Mr Masaru Hayami; from Matsushita, Dr Tsunehara Nitta and Dr Tohru Fukui; from the Ministry of International Trade and Industry, Dr Shunso Ishihara, Mr Masami Tanaka, Mr Katsuo Seiki, Dr Chihiro Watanabe; from the Ministry of Posts and Telecommunications, Mr Kazuhiro Suda and Mr Masao Hirai; from Motorola Japan, Mr Ian McCrae and Dr Robert Orr; from Northern Telecom Japan, Mr Roger Moore; from Philips, Professor Hans Dinklo; from Siecor International, Mr Yuji Aoyagi; from Siemens, Professor Heinz Teichmann, and from Siemens Japan, Dr Stefan Speidel; from Sony, Mr Toshiyuki Yamada and Dr Seiichi Watanabe; from Sumitomo Electric, Dr Tsuneo Nakahara; and from Toshiba, Dr Sei-ichi Takayanagi, Mr Yoshihiko Wakumoto, and Dr Ken-ichi Mori.

Last but not least I must thank some of those whose help has been essential for this long-lasting project. Lynne Dyer at JETS has been unfailing in her good spirits, her outstanding accuracy, and her constant support. Simon Collinson and Nils Tomes, also at JETS, have provided critical comments, good advice, and a friendly environment. My kindred spirit, Shoko Tanaka, has often been a candle lighting the way, giving both emotional support and the benefit of her attentive and critical mind. My parents, Dee and Elie, and my sister and brother, Denny and Terry, have also been unfailing in their encouragement. To my family— Tammy, Judy, Karen, and Jonathan—to whom this book is dedicated, must go my deepest gratitude for bearing with the best of spirits both the ups and the downs that have gone with writing it, for providing sympathetic ears, and for putting up with all times when I have been far too grumpy and should have been more available. Without their support, this book would certainly not have been completed.

M.F.

Edinburgh, June 1995

CONTENTS

LIST OF FIGURES

LIST OF TABLES

LIST OF ABBREVIATIONS AND TECHNICAL TERMS

AFIS Automated Fingerprint Identification System

APT ATT-Philips Telecommunication

ASIC Application specific integrated circuit

ATE Automatic Telephone & Electric

ATM Asynchronous transfer mode

BNR Bell Northern Research

BOCs Bell operating companies

BT British Telecom

C&C Computers and Communications

CCITT Comité Consultatif International Télégraphique et Téléphonique

CGCT Compagnie Générale de Constructions Téléphoniques

CGE Compagnie Générale d'Électricité

Circuit switching The switching of circuits for the exclusive use of the connection for the duration of a call

CIT Compagnie Industrielle des Téléphones

CNET Centre National d'Études des Télécommunications

Codec Coder/decoder (A device for converting analog modulation signals into digital modulation and vice versa)

Crossbar switch A switch with a matrix of mechanical crosspoints having electro-mechanically operated activation means common to crosspoints in the rows and columns

Crosspoint A set of physical contacts that operate together to extend the path of a connection through a particular stage of a space-division switching network

DAII Industrial and International Affairs Directorate

DDI Daini Denden

DEC Digital Equipment Corporation

DGT Directorate General of Telecommunications

Digital switching Switching of discrete-level information signals

DINA Distributed Information Processing Network Architecture

DIPS Dendenkosha Information Processing System

DRAMs Dynamic random access memories

ECL Electrical Communications Laboratories

ESS Electronic switching system

ESSEX Experimental Solid State Exchange

ETL Ericsson Telephones Ltd.

FETs Field effect transistors

GEC General Electric Co.

GPT GEC-Plessey Telecommunications

HEMTs High electron mobility transistors

INS Information Network System

ISDN Integrated services digital network (An integrated digital network in which the same digital switches and digital paths are used to establish connections for different services, for example, telephony, data, facsimile)

ISE International Standard Electric Corporation

ISS International Switching Symposium

ITT International Telephone and Telegraph Corporation

ITU International Telecommunication Union

IVD Inside vapour deposition

JECC Japan Electronic Computer Company

JEIDA Japan Electronic Industries Development Association

JTECH Japanese Technology Evaluation Program

KDD Kokusai Denshin Denwa Co.

LAN Local area networks

LCT Laboratoire Central de Télécommunications

LEDs Light-emitting diodes

LMT Le Matériel Téléphonique

LSI Large-scale integration

LSSGR Local access and transport area switching systems generic requirements (a Bellcore standard for switching)

MBE Molecular beam epitaxy

MCVD Modified chemical vapour deposition

MIA Multivendor Integration Architecture

MIT Massachusetts Institute of Technology

MITI Ministry of International Trade and Industry

MOS Metal oxide silicon

MPT Ministry of Posts and Telecommunications

NCCs New Common Carriers

NECI NEC Research Institute

NHK Nippon Hoso Kyokai

NPA National Police Agency (Japan)

NTT Nippon Telegraph and Telephone Public Corporation

OECD Organisation for Economic Co-operation and Development

OH Hydroxyl

OVD Outside vapour deposition

Packet switching In packet-switched networks, information sent from a calling terminal is stored in the network and then assembled into a block of variable length. These blocks are then encapsulated into 'packets' which contain additional information in a 'header' used inside the network for routeing, error correction, flow control, etc. Having been stored, the packets are then forwarded to the called terminal.

PAM Pulse amplitude modulation

PBX Private Branch Exchange (A switching system owned or leased by an organization and generally installed on its premises, which provides lines for internal communications between local extensions and a smaller number of lines to the public network)

PC Personal computer

PCI Peripheral Component Interconnect

PCM Pulse code modulation (If an analog waveform is sampled so as to produce a PAM signal, the magnitude of each pulse in the PAM signal can be represented by a binary word. The process is called pulse code modulation and the resulting string of binary words is a PCM signal. The process includes the function of regenerating an analog waveform from a PCM signal)

PDAs Personal digital assistants

PHS Personal handy phone system

PIPS Pattern Information Processing System

RBOC Regional Bell Operating Company

RDSS Radiodetermination satellite services

RISC Reduced instruction set

SEL Standard Electrik Lorenz A.G.

Space-division The separation in the space domain of a plurality of transmission channels between two points

Space-division switching The switching of inlets to outlets using space-division techniques

SPC Stored program control

STC Standard Telephone and Cables

STE Société des Téléphones Ericsson

Switching The establishment, on demand, of an individual connection from a desired inlet to a desired outlet within a set of inlets and outlets (for as long as is required for the transfer of information)

TDM Time-division multiplexing

TI Texas Instruments

Time-division The separation in the time domain of a plurality of transmission channels between two points

Time-division switching The switching of inlets to outlets using time-division (multiplexing) techniques

TT&T Thai Telephone and Communications Company

VAD Vapour phase axial deposition

VANs Value added networks

VHSCS Very High Speed Computer System Project

VLSI Very large-scale integrated circuits

I don't think economics is going to change rapidly
until all graduate students are exposed . . . to field
methods that study how decisions are actually made in
the firm.

HERBERT SIMON

Where is the wisdom we have lost in knowledge?
Where is the knowledge we have lost in information?

T. S. ELIOT

1

Introduction

Overview

The products and technologies of the information and communications (IC) industry have transformed our world. They include the computer and associated software; telecommunications switches, which connect and network telephones, computers, faxes, and video conferencing systems; transmissions systems, including optical fibre which can carry broadband multimedia information; and the devices needed in these kinds of products, such as microprocessors (computers on a chip) and memories.

Most of these products and technologies were initially invented and innovated in Western countries. However, by the 1990s some of the largest companies in the world in the three main segments that constitute the IC industry—computers, telecommunications equipment, and semiconductor devices—were Japanese. In computers, four of the ten largest companies in the world were Japanese: Fujitsu, NEC, Hitachi, and Toshiba; in telecommunications equipment, two were Japanese: NEC and Fujitsu; in semiconductors, six out of the top ten were Japanese: NEC, Toshiba, Hitachi, Fujitsu, Mitsubishi Electric, and Matsushita. NTT, the major Japanese telecommunications carrier, was by far the largest company in the world in terms of market value. In 1994 NTT's market value was $129 billion, followed by the Royal Dutch/Shell Group with $92 billion. NTT's total sales were about the same as AT&T's.

This book deals with five sets of questions relating to the Japanese IC industry. First, the explanation of the success of the Japanese IC companies: why and how were they able to catch up with their Western rivals (and in some cases overtake them)? Second, the anomaly of the Japanese IC companies: why is it that, although they are among the largest in the world, they remain primarily dependent on the Japanese market and have not succeeded in dominating many IC markets outside Japan? Third, the distinctiveness of the Japanese IC companies: why are they universalist system producers with competences in computers, semiconductors, and telecommunications equipment, while their US counterparts are far more specialized and lack capabilities in telecommunications equipment? Why have Japanese IC companies not performed as well globally as their Japanese counterparts in motor vehicles and consumer electronics?

The fourth set of questions relates to the role of the Japanese government: how important has the Japanese government been—particularly the Ministry of Communications before the war and NTT afterwards and the Ministry of

International Trade and Industry (MITI)—in accounting for the success of the Japanese IC companies? The fifth and final set deals with the future: will the Japanese IC companies become increasingly competitive internationally?

A major premiss of this book is that, to answer these five sets of questions, it is necessary to understand the evolution of the Japanese IC industry. The reason is simply that, at any point in time, the characteristics of the companies that make up the Japanese IC industry are contingent on what went before. For example, during the decade following the late 1940s, the Japanese IC companies were able successfully to enter the new markets of semiconductors and computers largely as a result of the competences they had already accumulated before the war in developing telecommunications systems such as switches. But why in Japan were there four major telecommunications equipment companies—NEC, Fujitsu, Hitachi, and Oki—while in the USA there was only one, Western Electric, the subsidiary of AT&T? The answer to this question requires an understanding of the form of organization referred to in this book as 'controlled competition', which was perfected in Japan in the 1920s and 1930s as a way of organizing the development and production of telecommunications equipment for the Japanese network.

However, although an understanding of the evolution of the Japanese IC industry captures the 'path-dependencies' which are an important part of the answers to the five sets of questions posed above, it is equally important to understand the 'path-independencies', the ruptures with the past, which have also been crucial in shaping the Japanese IC industry. Examples include the way in which Fujitsu, a relatively weak supplier of telecommunications equipment compared with NEC, transformed itself into the largest Japanese computer company which became the second largest in the world; the transition of the Japanese copper cable companies into some of the largest producers of optical fibre in the world; and NEC's emergence as the dominant Japanese producer of personal computers.

The analysis of the evolution of the Japanese IC industry in this book draws on the pioneering work of writers such as Alfred Marshall, Joseph Schumpeter, Edith Penrose, Alfred Chandler, Richard Nelson, Sidney Winter, Nathan Rosenberg, Christopher Freeman, Ronald Dore, and David Teece. However, a point of departure lies in the insistence that, in order to understand the evolution of companies and the industries they comprise, it is necessary to create a 'theory of the firm' capable of grasping the development of *real firms* in the *real world* as they evolve in *real time*. This insistence had led to the development of an approach to the firm which emphasizes the *ex ante* decisions that are made in firms as they create and respond to new technologies, new forms of organization, and other changes in their environment. As will be seen, this approach stresses the importance of the *beliefs* that are constructed in the firm under conditions of 'interpretive ambiguity', and which guide the firm's decisions.

In the remaining part of this introductory chapter, the distinctiveness of the Japanese IC companies is examined. How do they compare with the Japanese motor vehicle and consumer electronics companies? Next, controlled competition is analysed, that unique form of organization which evolved in Japan for the development and production of telecommunications equipment. Controlled competition involved a long-term, obligational relationship between the Ministry of Communications (and later NTT) and a closed group of supplying companies. What impact did controlled competition have both on the structure of individual Japanese IC companies and on the Japanese IC industry as a whole? The theoretical approach adopted for analysing the evolution of the Japanese IC industry, paying particular attention to the theory of the firm which lies at the heart of the analysis, is presented in Appendix 1.

In Chapter 2 the combination of circumstances that gave birth to controlled competition in the 1920s and 1930s is examined. Why in Japan did the telecommunications carrier (the Ministry of Communications) decide it needed four major suppliers of equipment, while in the USA from the beginning AT&T relied on vertical integration? As is shown later in the book, this decision of the Ministry of Communications, perpetuated after 1952 by NTT, was to have significant consequences for the Japanese IC companies and IC industry.

The postwar IC industry was transformed by the new electronics paradigm which emerged with the advent of the transistor (which, as shown in Chapter 3, was itself developed in an attempt to improve telecommunications switching). While in the USA only two of the major ten companies that produced vacuum tubes successfully made the transition to transistors and integrated circuits, in Japan all the main IC companies succeeded. The Japanese IC companies went on to develop more sophisticated electronic devices such as microprocessors and dynamic random access memories (DRAMs). The Japanese telecommunications equipment companies developed electronic switches and then digital and ATM (asynchronous transfer mode) switches. Furthermore, they entered the market for computers and related software. Other Japanese companies, which began as copper cable producers, became major producers of optical fibre cable.

Why were these Japanese companies able successfully to assimilate the waves of new technology and to use them to improve their products and enter new markets? In order to analyse this question rigorously, three crucial components of the IC industry were selected for detailed study: telecommunications switches, computers and related software, and optical fibre. The distinctive feature of the analysis involves examining how the Japanese companies responded in *real time* (that is, *ex ante*) to the new technologies as they emerged. This analysis reveals the 'fuzziness' or interpretive ambiguity that usually surrounds the decisions that are made in connection with new technologies. Most analyses of the process of technical change are *ex post*, with the result that they eliminate this central aspect involved in the creation of and response to new technologies.

Two examples, examined in detail in this book, illustrate the fuzziness involved. It was only in the late 1950s that the Japanese companies came to believe that there was an important potential market for computers, with the result that the first computers created in Japan were developed not in the companies but in government laboratories. By this time IBM, under the new leadership of Thomas Watson Jr, was well on the way to establishing its global dominance of the computer industry. In the mid-1970s, NTT, NEC, and Fujitsu believed that the state of device technology was such that digital switching would not become cost-effective until the 1980s. Northern Telecom held contradictory beliefs, however, with important consequences for the structure of the switching industry, as shown in Chapter 3.

The real-time analysis also shows that the response to new technologies involved not only the Japanese companies. Organs of the Japanese government also became embroiled in the process, as bureaucrats responded in ways they believed to be most appropriate. Accordingly, the analysis ends up with an explanation, based on the real-time processes, of the co-evolution of technologies, companies, industries, and government institutions.

In Chapter 3 the Japanese telecommunications switching industry is analysed. How did NTT and its family of suppliers respond to the four main generations of switches that evolved in the postwar period (electromechanical crossbar switches, electronic space-division switches, time-division digital switches, and asynchronous transfer mode (ATM) switches)? Particular attention is paid to the failure of NEC and Fujitsu to penetrate the US market for digital switches from the late 1970s. Why did they fail when Northern Telecom, entering at around the same time, succeeded? Why was Fujitsu (followed closely by NEC) the first company in the world to offer a commercial next-generation ATM switch? Why did leading companies such as ITT, Philips, and GTE drop out of the switch market while the Japanese companies remained in? Why did the British companies, leaders in switching in the early postwar period, lose their competitiveness in switching while their French counterpart, Alcatel, became the largest telecommunications equipment company in the world? In the mid-1980s, NTT added Northern Telecom to its group of suppliers jointly to develop the next-generation ATM switch under controlled competition. How did this Western company cope, co-operating in Japanese fashion with Japanese companies which remained rivals in global telecommunications equipment markets? These are some of the questions answered in Chapter 3.

Chapter 4 contains an analysis of the evolution of the Japanese computer industry from the 1950s to the mid-1990s. This analysis goes beyond the major existing accounts of the Japanese computer industry, which focus exclusively on mainframe computers and stop in the late 1980s, to examine personal computers, microprocessors, and software in Japan. Why were the Japanese computer companies never able to make much headway against IBM outside Japan in mainframes? Why did Fujitsu and Hitachi decide to follow the 'IBM road' while NEC chose a fundamentally different path, concentrating instead on distributed networks of smaller computers? Why is it that, although NEC developed Japan's first microprocessor (computer on a chip) only five months after the world's first microprocessor was announced by Intel in 1971, by the mid-1990s NEC only had around 1 per cent of the global market for

32-bit microprocessors compared with Intel's 73 per cent? Why are Japanese companies globally dominant in memory semiconductors, but hold only a minute fraction of the world market for microprocessors which use the same process technology as memories? Why do Japanese companies dominate the world market for microcontrollers (simple kinds of microprocessors, used largely in consumer electronics products) while they have not performed well in microprocessors?

Why is Japan alone among all the major industrialized countries in terms of its reliance on customized (as opposed to packaged) computer software? Why do US companies hold 70 per cent of the Japanese market for packaged software even though Japanese companies dominate the Japanese market for computers? Why is it that the major Japanese computer companies began exporting packaged software only in 1994? What role did NTT play in the development of the Japanese computer industry? In the mid-1980s NTT did a significant about-turn. Previously it had worked with the Japanese computer companies in attempting to narrow IBM's lead. From the mid-1980s, however, it changed tack, incorporating both IBM and Digital Equipment (DEC) in a co-operative attempt to develop a new multi-vendor computer architecture for computers to be used in its telecommunications operations. How did IBM and DEC adjust to working co-operatively with their main Japanese rivals, which remained strong competitors in global computer markets? These are some of the puzzles tackled in Chapter 4.

Chapter 5 provides a real-time analysis of the evolution of the optical fibre industry in Japan. Major early research in optical fibre was undertaken in Britain, and the first technical breakthrough was achieved by Corning in 1970 which won for the company the commanding patents in this field. However, in 1976 and 1978 Japanese companies were able to break world records, producing fibre with the lowest loss rates. How were they able to achieve this success? How did Japanese companies manage to achieve world-class competences in optical fibre, and how did they come to dominate the Japanese market for this product? How does the indigenously developed Japanese approach to the production process for optical fibre compare with that used by the leading US companies? How did Sumitomo Electric manage to establish an important bridgehead into the US market for optical fibre, and with what longer-run effect?

The analysis of the optical fibre industry in Japan also illustrates the usefulness of the *unified approach* to the firm adopted in this book. According to this approach, a common concept of knowledge can be used to analyse both the firm's interior and its exterior, that is its environment. This approach emphasizes the importance of the beliefs of the optical fibre companies regarding both the technologies that should be used and the markets that it was hoped would emerge for this product.

While the three previous chapters focus on the evolution of entire industries— i.e. telecommunications switches, computers and software, and optical fibre—Chapter 6 analyses the evolution of a single firm, NEC, the largest

Japanese telecommunications equipment company and in the early 1990s the only company in the world to be in the top five in terms of sales in the three key IC markets for computers, semiconductors, and telecommunications equipment. In this chapter a major issue relates to the co-evolution of a company's technological competences and its *internal forms of organization*. How was NEC able to transform itself from a company specializing in telecommunications equipment to one with distinctive competences also in computers and semiconductors? What forms of organization did the leaders of NEC construct in order to co-ordinate its activities in these three complementary yet diverse areas of technology and business? How does NEC organize its R&D in order to create the technologies needed for its approximately 10,000 products? How do NEC's specialist R&D organs create the technologies that will be needed for the company to survive in the long term? How did NEC become the world leader in automatic fingerprint identification systems? Why did NEC adopt a more decentralized, segmented, form of corporate organization more than twenty years before its far larger counterparts—such as IBM and AT&T—decided that a similar form of organization was essential for their survival?

Chapter 6 also delves into the complexities of *corporate vision*. What role is played in a company's evolution by its 'vision' or set of beliefs regarding what must be done to achieve its ojectives in the future? How did NEC develop its 'C&C vision', its beliefs regarding the convergence of computer and communications technologies? Why did NEC suffer from 'vision failure' which led to its tardiness in developing digital switches sufficiently quickly to take advantage of the opening of the US market? What were the costs and benefits of NEC's close relationship with NTT? How important was the Japanese government in accounting for NEC's long-term performance? What role was played by NEC's strategic alliances and by its form of corporate governance? These are some of the questions examined in Chapter 6.

In Chapter 7 attention is turned to Japan's major telecommunications carrier, NTT. Earlier chapters reveal the key influence of NTT (and its predecessor, the Ministry of Communications) in shaping the structure of both the Japanese IC companies and the Japanese IC industry. This chapter analyses the major winds of change currently blowing around NTT which will change the company's structure and role over the next decade. How has NTT dealt with its new competitors? What impact has competition had so far on NTT's performance? How was NTT able to avoid the threat of divestiture which it faced in 1990? Will the company be able to do the same again in 1995/6? Why is Japan the only major country still to insist on separating domestic telecommunications operations from international operations, and thus segmenting the activities of NTT and KDD? To what extent has NTT been able to globalize its operations? Will NTT be able to compete with other major carriers like AT&T and BT that have already made a major commitment to offer global services? Will NTT, increasingly pressurized by competition, be forced to abandon its technology-led vision with important implications for the shape of the Japanese

IC industry? Why has NTT been so strongly regulated by the Ministry of Posts and Telecommunications (MPT)? Has MPT scored an 'own goal' by insisting on restricting NTT to such an extent, or are there good reasons for its constraints on NTT? These are a few of the issues analysed in Chapter 7.

Chapter 8 is devoted to an examination of NTT's major competitor, DDI. The major puzzle tackled in this chapter is how DDI, with its 30 engineers, can possibly hope to compete in the longer term with NTT and its 8,200 scientists, engineers, and technicians in R&D alone. Does DDI's reliance on the market as a source of new technology and equipment constitute a sufficient response to NTT's controlled competition? How has DDI managed to grow as rapidly as it has and what are its strengths compared to NTT? These questions are examined in the chapter.

Chapter 9 is the concluding chapter. It begins with a comparison of the Japanese IC companies and, on the one hand, the Japanese motor vehicle and consumer electronic companies and, on the other, comparable Western IC companies. The performance of the Japanese IC companies is then examined. How well have they done in terms of technological performance, competitiveness in global markets, and financial performance? How are the global competitive strengths and weaknesses of the Japanese IC companies to be explained? Are these companies likely to increase their global competitiveness in the future? How important has the Japanese government been in accounting for the performance of the Japanese IC companies? What does the future hold for NTT? Will NTT be able to deal with the challenges of increasing competition in Japan, threatened divestiture, and the globalization of its activities? The discussion of these questions brings the book to a close.

The Issues Covered

This book is about two closely related sets of issues. The first is the long-term growth of the Japanese information and communications industry; the second is the method that is most appropriate to analyse the dynamics of long-term industrial change.

Why the Japanese information and communications industry? There are several reasons. The first is that generalizations made about Japanese industry have been unduly influenced by the motor vehicle and consumer electronics industries. While they make an important contribution to Japanese gross domestic product, and an even more significant contribution to Japanese exports, the special circumstances of these industries, unique to each of them, makes it invalid to generalize readily from their experience to other Japanese industries.

The second reason (which is related to the first) is that in the 1980s there was a tendency in Western countries to overestimate 'Japanese' success. The fires of enthusiasm were fanned by popular books of the 'Japan as Number One' and 'The Japanese Threat' genre. With the advent of recession in Japan in the early

1990s, however, and the fall of some of Japan's major companies—such as Fujitsu and NEC—into loss-making positions, this tendency has produced an equal and opposite counter-tendency. This is evident, for example, in the *Newsweek* front cover that confidently stated, regarding Japan, that 'The System Has Crashed—Its High-Tech Edge Fades'. In fact, both tendency and counter-tendency are over-exaggerated. A rigorous study of the Japanese information and communications industry shows that, while there are (and have for a long time been) important strengths in this industry, there also are fundamental weaknesses.

The third reason is that the information and communications industry is arguably the most dynamic and strategically important in the Japanese economy. This industry provides what is perhaps the most important single innovation produced in the postwar period: the computer, and the software required to use it for a multitude of purposes. Furthermore, this industry provides the nerve system for the communication of information—in the jargonized (and distorting) terminology of the 1990s, the Information Superhighway. The strategic significance of this industry alone provides sufficient justification for an inquiry into its long-term dynamics and its strengths and weaknesses.

The Japanese Motor Vehicle and Consumer Electronics Industries

In order to appreciate the performance of the Japanese IC industry, it is necessary first to consider the performance of two other growth sectors of the Japanese economy. Both the motor vehicle and the consumer electronics industries have been important engines of growth for the Japanese manufacturing sector and the economy as a whole. In the early 1990s, the manufacturing sector made by far the largest contribution to Japanese gross domestic product, contributing about one-third. The transport machinery industry alone (mainly cars) was responsible for 15 per cent of the output of this sector. The electrical machinery industry (including consumer electronics) contributed 17 per cent, bringing their combined contribution to about a third of manufacturing output.

More astounding still, in the early 1990s just four industries—non-electrical machinery, electrical machinery, transport machinery, and precision machinery—accounted for 75 per cent of total Japanese exports (responsible for one side of Japan's trade surplus, the other side being imports). As shown in Table 1.1, transport machinery provided 25 per cent of Japan's total exports, while electrical machinery accounted for 24 per cent, and non-electrical machinery, 22 per cent. The same table shows that just five product groups (rows 4–8), which fall into three areas—i.e. motor vehicles and parts, consumer electronics, and electronic components—are responsible for almost one-third of total exports.

The causes of the rapid growth of the Japanese motor vehicle and consumer electronics industries, however, are to some extent specific to each of these industries. Although there is not space here to elaborate, these causes can be briefly summarized. As Takahiro Fujimoto has recently emphasized, superior Japanese motor vehicle product development performance—on which Japanese

Table 1.1 *Japan's Exports by Value, 1980 and 1991 (¥ bn)*

	1980	% of total exports	1991	% of total exports
(1) Total exports	29,382	—	42,360	—
(2) Machinery and equipment exports	18,412	62.66	31,868	75.23
of which:				
(*a*) Machinery excl. electrical	4,091	13.92	9,362	22.10
(*b*) Electrical machinery	4,222	14.37	9,934	23.45
(*c*) Transport equipment	7,772	26.45	10,485	24.75
(*d*) Precision instruments	2,327	7.92	2,087	4.93
(3) (2)/(1)		62.66		75.23
Specific products				
(4) Passenger cars	3,648	12.42	6,017	14.20
Parts of motor vehicles	456	1.55	1,524	3.60
(5) Tape recorders, TVs, and radio receivers	1,795	6.11	1,684	3.98
(6) VCRs, etc.	444	1.51	774	1.83
(7) Electronic integrated circuits	—	—	1,112	2.63
(8) Electron tube, etc.	523	1.78	2,003	4.73
(9) [(4)+(5)+(6)+(7)+(8)]/(1)		23.37		30.96
(10) Medical and pharmaceutical	67	0.23	147	0.35

Source: Japan Statistical Yearbook, 1992.

international competitiveness in motor vehicles significantly depends—was due largely to a number of organizational innovations that were made since the 1950s. These innovations include the just-in-time method of production, the system of 'black box parts' suppliers, capabilities in co-ordinating and overlapping the activities involved in product and process development, the ability of product development engineers to undertake a wide range of tasks, and of product managers to effectively champion concepts and co-ordinate project activities. Fujimoto stresses, however, that the radical improvements in performance that these crucial innovations resulted in were at first unintended and unforeseen. Rather, they emerged as piecemeal and iterative solutions to other problems, and their effectiveness was recognized only with hindsight.[1]

In the case of the Japanese consumer electronics industry, the following causes

[1] Personal communication with Takahiro Fujimoto. See also, *inter alia*: T. Fujimoto, 'The Origin and Evolution of the "Black Box Parts" Practice in the Japanese Auto Industry', Research Institute for the Japanese Economy, Discussion Paper Series, Faculty of Economics, University of Tokyo, 1994; 'Reinterpreting the Resource-Capability View of the Firm: A Case of the Development-Production Systems of the Japanese Auto Makers', Research Institute for the Japanese Economy, Discussion Paper Series, Faculty of Economics, University of Tokyo, 1994; K. B. Clark and T. Fujimoto, *Product Development Performance: Strategy, Organization, and Management in the World Auto Industry*, Harvard Business School Press, Boston, Mass., 1991.

may be identified as having been particularly important. The first was the rapid accumulation by Japanese companies in the early postwar years of competences in the new electronics paradigm, coupled with an ability to innovate. This facilitated not only a rapid assimilation of Western technologies, but also the development of innovative products such as Sony's transistorized radio, the second in the world to be developed, and its transistorized television—the world's first fully transistorized set—produced in 1960. Secondly, in the early postwar years consumer electronics production in Japan was aided by relatively low factor prices, particularly for skilled and semi-skilled labour.

Thirdly, unlike in the case of many Japanese information and communications products, such as telecommunications switches and proprietary computing systems, Japanese consumer electronics products, produced for the Japanese market, could be readily and at relatively low cost adapted for Western markets. Finally, Japanese consumer electronics companies, again unlike their counterparts in the IC industry, were greatly assisted by the rapid collapse of their US competitors. Of these, the most dramatic was RCA, the company established in 1919 by AT&T, General Electric, and Westinghouse to develop radio-based technologies and products. By the 1960s, RCA held a dominant share of almost 50 per cent of the US colour television market. However, owing largely to the company's failed attempt to remain in the computer industry and to its move into competence-unrelated markets, RCA's position in consumer electronics collapsed. In 1985 RCA was sold to General Electric. By the mid-1970s, Japan accounted for over half of world production of colour TVs and three-quarters of world exports.[2]

The Japanese Information and Communications Industry

In contrast, the position of the Japanese information and communications industry is significantly different. As shown in Figs. 1.1–1.3, Japanese companies feature prominently among the world's top ten largest companies in the three main segments of the IC industry, namely computers (information technology), telecommunications equipment, and semiconductors. In computers, four of the top ten companies are Japanese (Fujitsu, NEC, Hitachi, and Toshiba); in telecommunications equipment, two of the top ten are Japanese (NEC and Fujitsu); and in semiconductors, six of the ten are Japanese (NEC, Toshiba, Hitachi, Fujitsu, Mitsubishi Electric, and Matsushita).

Impressive though this at first sight seems, a rather different picture emerges if we examine the competitive position of Japanese companies in the largest and most intensely competitive market in the world, namely the USA. Table 1.2, from a report by a McKinsey executive, shows the position of these companies in various markets. Selected US markets are divided into three categories: those where Japanese companies have a 'high' relative position (that is, where one or

---

[2] For further detail on RCA, see Ch. 4.

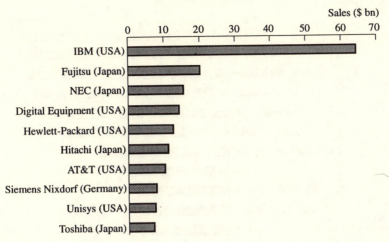

Fig. 1.1 The ten largest information technology suppliers in the world, 1992
Source: Datamation.

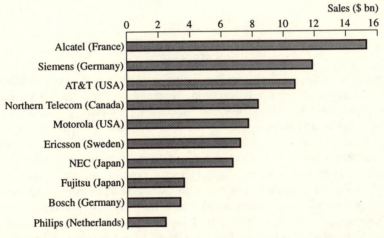

Fig. 1.2 The ten largest telecommunications equipment companies in the world, 1992
Source: Dataquest.

more Japanese companies are the leading competitors), a 'medium' position (where Japanese companies share a strong position with US and/or European companies), and a 'low' position (where Japanese companies are not among the leaders in the USA). Japanese companies are in a 'high' position in only four markets: consumer electronics (where the reasons for Japanese competitiveness have just been briefly discussed), cameras, semiconductor memories, and semiconductor manufacturing equipment.

Next, we consider how Japanese companies perform in the three main segments of the information and communications industry, i.e. semiconductors, computers, and telecommunications equipment.

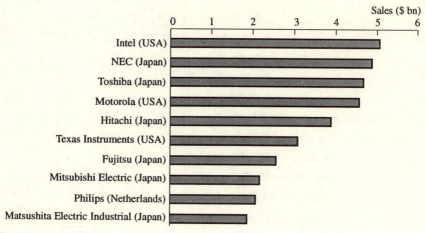

Fig. 1.3 The ten largest semiconductor manufacturers in the world, 1992
Source: Dataquest.

Semiconductors

In two sub-segments of the semiconductor industry, i.e. memory semiconductors and semiconductor manufacturing equipment, Japanese companies are in a 'high' position. Although the semiconductor industry got its start in the USA, with the invention of the transistor in 1947 and the integrated circuit in 1959, a position that was bolstered with the invention in 1970 of the dynamic random access memory (DRAM), used widely in computer memories, Japanese companies managed to master semiconductor product and process technology and to make the necessary investment in plant and equipment, with the result that they now hold a dominant position in memory semiconductors.

However, the undoubted strength of Japanese companies in semiconductors must be qualified. The first qualification arises from the speed and relative ease with which Korean companies such as Samsung established strong global market positions in memories in the early 1990s. This clearly demonstrates that the Japanese companies have not developed a distinctive competence that is very difficult to emulate.

The second qualification comes from the paradox presented by the co-existence of Japanese strength in memories and Japanese weakness in microprocessors. As shown in Table 1.2, Japanese companies have a 'low' position in the USA in microprocessors. This is a puzzle, since the same process technologies are used in the production of both memories and microprocessors. Furthermore, although the first microprocessor was announced by Intel in 1971, only five months later NEC produced Japan's first comparable microprocessor. However, by 1992, while Intel held 73 per cent of the global market for 32-bit

Table 1.2 *The Comparative Strength of Japanese Companies in Selected US Markets, 1990*

Relative position of Japanese MNCs	Industry segment	Leading competitors		
		Japanese	USA	European/Other
High One or more Japanese MNCs are the leading competitors in the US market	• Consumer electronics (TV, VCRs, CD, HiFi/Stereo)	• Matsushita (JVC, Panasonic, Quasar) • Sony • Sanyo • Mitsubishi • Several others	• Zenith • Bose • Harman	• Thomson (GE, RCA)* • Philips
	• Cameras	• Canon • Nikon • Minolta • Asahi (Pentax)	• Kodak • Polaroid	
	• Semiconductor memories	• Toshiba • NEC • Hitachi	• Texas Instruments • Motorola	
	• Semiconductor manufacturing equipment	• Canon • Nikon	• Applied Materials • Varian	
Medium Japanese MNCs share strong position with US and/or European companies	• Cars and light trucks	• Toyota • Honda • Nissan • Several others	• GM • Ford • Chrysler	• Daimler-Benz • BMW • Volvo • VW/Audi • Several others
	• Medium-class trucks	• Isuzu • Nissan • Hino	• GM • Ford • Navistar	• Daimler-Benz • Volvo
	• Farm and construction equipment	• Kubota • Komatsu/Dresser	• Deere • Ford	• Kloeckner-Humboldt Deutz

Table 1.2 (cont.)

Relative position of Japanese MNCs	Industry segment	Leading competitors		
		Japanese	USA	European/Other
	• Machine tools	• Fanuc • Yamatake-Honeywell • Komatsu • Okuma	• Allied • Caterpillar • Tenneco (Case) • Harnischfeger • Litton • Cross & Trecker • Cincinnati Milacron • Ingersoll-Rand	• Fiatallis • Asea Brown Boveri • Thyssen (Hueller/Hille) • Coman
	• Telecommunications equipment (consumer and industrial)	• NEC • Toshiba • Matsushita	• Rockwell • AT&T	• Northern Telecom • Siemens • Ericsson
	• Plain paper copiers	• Canon • Several others	• Xerox • Kodak	
Low Japanese MNCs not among leaders in US market	• Mainframe computers	• Fujitsu/Amdahl* • Hitachi/EDS	• IBM • Unisys	• Bull HN (Groupe Bull, NEC, Honeywell)*
	• Personal computers	• Toshiba(lap-top only) • NEC (lap-top only)	• IBM • Apple • Compaq	
	• Microprocessors and related ICs	• Hitachi • NEC	• Intel • Motorola • Texas Instruments • AMD	
	• Large home appliances	• Mitsubishi	• GE • Maytag • Whirlpool	• Electrolux/White*

	Japanese	US	European
• Small home appliances	• Matsushita (microwave only) • Sharp (microwave only)	• Allegheny (Oster, Sunbeam) • Hamilton Beach • Black & Decker • NAACO (Procter-Silex) • Gillette (Braun)	• Krups • Samsung • Lucky-Goldstar
• Automotive components and supplies	• Nippondenso • Bridgestone/Firestone*	• TRW • Rockwell • Eaton • Bendix • Goodyear	• Bosch • Michelin/Uniroyal-Goodrich* • ITT Teves • Pirelli
• Steel	• NKK/National*	• USX • Bethlehem • LTV • Inland • Armco	
• Scientific/analytic instruments	• Hitachi • Shimadzu	• Tektronix • Perkin-Elmer • Hewlett-Packard • Varian • Millipore(Waters)	• Siemens • SmithKline Beecham (Beckman Instruments)
• Electrical equipment and general machinery	• Toshiba • Hitachi	• GE • Westinghouse • Emerson • Ingersoll-Rand • Reliance	• Asea Brown Boveri • Siemens
• Medical imaging equipment	• Toshiba	• GE	• Siemens • Philips

* US position increased through acquisition.

Source: H. De Nero, 'Creating the "hyphenated" corporation', *McKinsey Quarterly*, 4 (1990): 154–5.

microprocessors, NEC's share (the largest by a Japanese company) came to a mere 1.1 per cent. Clearly, the Japanese weakness in microprocessors needs to be explained. (This is done in Chapter 4 on computers.)[3]

The Japanese 'high' position in both semiconductor manufacturing equipment and cameras is not coincidental. This is apparent from the fact that the same companies, Nikon and Canon, dominate in both markets. The reason is the optical competences that were accumulated by the camera companies from the 1930s, when government interventions, aimed largely at developing military equipment, were used to encourage these competences. As things turned out, optical technologies also became dominant in the semiconductor production process. Through incremental improvements, these technologies were extended for use in the production of submicron circuits, thus delaying the application of alternative technologies such as electron beams and X-rays. As shown in Chapter 4, companies like Nikon were also major beneficiaries from MITI's VLSI Project from 1976 to 1980, which bonded semiconductor equipment and manufacturing companies in mutually beneficial supplier–user innovation relationships. Optical competences also contribute to Canon's 'medium' position in plain paper copiers and to its strength in producing the 'laser engines' which are incorporated, with software, into laser printers. Canon has an alliance with Hewlett-Packard, the world's largest producer of laser printers, with Canon providing most of the laser engines. (The concept of competences is central in the theory of the firm developed in Appendix 1. The case of Japanese optical competences, and the different products and markets in which these competences have been exploited, provides a good example of the usefulness of this concept.)

Computers

Two preliminary observations may be made about the Japanese computer industry. The first is that, as noted in Table 1.2, Japanese companies occupy only a 'low' position in the USA in computer markets; that is, they are not among the leaders. This is the case for mainframe computers, personal computers, and microprocessors (computers on a chip, already discussed). The second observation is that the major books that have been written on the Japanese computer industry deal with a period ending in the late 1980s. However, after that date it became apparent that there were fundamental structural changes that were radically altering the shape of the computer industry. This was dramatically illustrated when, at the beginning of 1993, IBM, dependent on

---

[3] The major book on Japanese semiconductors does not provide an explanation for Japanese relative weakness in microprocessors. Nor does it explain why Japanese companies dominate globally in microcontrollers, which are simple forms of microprocessors also containing embedded software. This book suggests that Japanese weakness in microprocessors is due to weakness in software capabilities, but it then goes on to provide evidence that Japan has relatively strong software capabilities (and notes that in the early 1980s NTT produced microprocessors equalling those of Intel); see D. I. Okimoto *et al.*, *Competitive Edge: The Semiconductor Industry in the U.S. and Japan*, Stanford University Press, Stanford, Calif., 1984, pp. 45–50.

mainframes but finding its sales undermined by open-systems architectures and distributed systems of smaller computers, announced the largest loss in corporate history. However, as noted in Chapter 4, the Japanese computer industry has been built in IBM's image. A re-analysis of the Japanese computer industry is therefore essential, and this is undertaken in Chapter 4.[4]

The global position of Japanese companies in the computer industry portrayed in Fig. 1.1 must be substantially qualified. This is necessary since by the late 1980s the major Japanese computer companies were making about 80 per cent of their sales in Japan. While they therefore benefited from the rapid rate of growth of the Japanese postwar economy, their ability to sell their computer systems in foreign markets was significantly lower than their Japanese counterparts in motor vehicles and consumer electronics. In some cases their overseas sales were partly a reflection of their foreign acquisitions. This is true in the case of Fujitsu's acquisition of significant holdings in Amdahl in the USA and ICL in the UK. It is also true, though to a lesser extent, of NEC's holding in Bull of France.

The position of Japanese companies in personal computers (not dealt with in the books on the Japanese computer industry just referred to) is revealing. As discussed in Chapter 4, the first personal computer announced in the USA in 1975 was very much of a backroom affair, produced by players who were off the main stage and out of the spotlight. Japan's first personal computers were produced in 1976 and 1977. But they were made and sold by large integrated electronics companies such as Hitachi, Sharp, and NEC. True, by 1990 NEC was the fourth-largest producer of PCs in the world, with a global market share of 5.7 per cent. However, this was due primarily to the company's strength in Japan, where, for reasons analysed in Chapter 4, it was able to capture over 50 per cent of the market.

Further qualifications are necessary in the case of computer software, which now accounts for the bulk of the costs of information-processing systems and applications. As Chapter 4 shows, studies of the Japanese software industry reveal that software quality and productivity performance equal that in the USA. However, Japanese companies have not been able to apply their software competences successfully to the lucrative global market for packaged computer software. US companies hold 70 per cent of this market in Japan. In 1994 NEC received less than 1 per cent of its revenue from the sale of packaged software and its exports of packaged software were negligible. In 1994 Fujitsu made its first export of packaged software. The reasons for this anomaly are given in Chapter 4.

---

[4] Four of the most detailed books on the Japanese computer industry are: M. Fransman, *The Market and Beyond: Information Technology in Japan*, Cambridge University Press, 1993; K. Flamm, *Targeting the Computer: Government Support and International Competition*, Brookings Institution, Washington, DC, 1987; K. Flamm, *Creating the Computer: Government, Industry, and High Technology*, Brookings Institution, Washington, DC, 1988; M. Anchordoguy, *Computers Inc.: Japan's Challenge to IBM*, Harvard University Press, Cambridge, Mass., 1989.

However, Japanese companies have been far stronger globally in some of the key components of computing systems. These include memories (discussed earlier), flat panel displays (including thin film transistor liquid crystal displays), lasers, and laser 'engines' for laser printers. Does this mean that Japanese competences have been well adapted to the mass production of 'commoditized' components, but not to complex software-intensive computer systems? This question too is analysed in Chapter 4.

What do all these qualifications imply for the success of the industrial policies of the Japanese Ministry of International Trade and Industry (MITI)? It is likely (as again is indicated in Chapter 4) that policies relating to the information-processing sector were the most important of all of MITI's industrial policies. Certainly, in the early 1970s, when the Japanese computer industry was threatened by IBM's System 370 family of mainframe computers, MITI cobbled together the most expensive programme it had ever initiated in order to support this industry. In Chapter 4, and again in the concluding chapter, the success of MITI's industrial policy in the computer industry is appraised.

Telecommunications Equipment

Fig. 1.2 shows that the Japanese presence in the global telecommunications equipment market is smaller than in the computer or semiconductor markets. There are only two Japanese companies in the top ten in the telecommunications equipment market—NEC and Fujitsu—and they are in the seventh and eighth places, respectively. But again, further qualification is necessary.

In 1982, the USA recorded a surplus of $275 million on international trade in telecommunications equipment. By 1987, however, with the divestiture of AT&T and the freeing of the regional 'Baby Bells' to purchase non-AT&T equipment, the surplus had turned into a deficit of $2.5 billion. This almost cancelled the US surplus of $2.8 billion on computer trade. $2.2 billion of the US telecommunications equipment deficit was with Japan. From 1980 to 1987, Japan's share of the total OECD telecommunications equipment market doubled from 17 to 34 per cent.

However, this rosy picture of Japanese performance in global markets for telecommunications equipment obscures significant weaknesses. These were highlighted in the late 1980s in a study carried out by the prestigious Japanese Technology Evaluation Program (JTECH) supported by the US National Science Foundation. The report of the JTECH panel on telecommunications technology in Japan disaggregated the position of Japanese companies in the major world telecommunications markets. This showed that Japanese companies held a 'dominant' position in only two equipment markets: cordless telephones and facsimile. Their position was 'strong' in a further six markets: microwave equipment, key telephone systems, paging devices, communications components, fibre optics, and cellular telephones. However, in the key markets for complex telecommunications equipment, particularly digital PBXs (private branch exchanges) and digital central office switches, their position was only 'moderate'.[5]

Indeed, when NEC and Fujitsu attempted to enter the US market for digital central office switches in the early 1980s, they failed. In 1992 AT&T was dominant in the US market for central office switches with a 48 per cent share. This compared with 38 per cent for Northern Telecom, the Canadian company which entered the US market for digital central office switches at about the same time as NEC and Fujitsu. NEC, the highest Japanese company, came seventh with a mere 0.2 per cent.

Why did Japanese companies fail in the USA in the central office switch market? Why did Northern Telecom succeed? Why did ITT, a major player in this market with excellent technological competences, exit? How does the major Japanese telecommunications equipment company, NEC, compare with its Western rival, Ericsson? Will the Japanese companies be more successful, as they hope, in the next-generation broadband asynchronous transfer mode (ATM) switch? These are the kinds of questions analysed in Chapter 3.

The International Competitiveness of Japanese Industries

In the light of the strengths and weaknesses of the Japanese information and communications industry just discussed, how does the international competitiveness of this industry compare with that of other Japanese industries? Table 1.3 is designed to throw light on this question. In the table the foreign sales ratio (ratio of foreign sales to sales in the Japanese market) serves as a rough indicator of an industry's international competitiveness. The higher the foreign sales ratio, the greater the international competitiveness of the firm. The averages give some idea of the international competitiveness of the industry.[6]

As Table 1.3 shows, the Japanese IC companies have a significantly lower foreign sales ratio than their counterparts in consumer electronics and motor vehicles. Furthermore, their sales ratio is also much lower than that of IBM, Siemens, and Alcatel. The table, therefore, corroborates the data in Table 1.2, which suggests that Japanese companies are relatively weak in global information and communications markets.

---

[5] Japanese Techology Evaluation Programme, *Telecommunications Technology in Japan* (Panel Report), Science Applications International, La Jolla, Calif., 1986.

[6] While useful, this indicator must be treated with caution. For example, both Toyota and Matsushita, the largest companies in the Japanese motor vehicle and consumer electronics industries respectively, have lower foreign sales ratios that their nearest competitors, Nissan and Sony. This, however, is not an indication of lower international competitiveness. Rather, it is a reflection of the larger company's stronger hold over distribution and sales outlets in Japan. Part of the strategic response on the part of the smaller rivals was to give high priority to foreign sales.

Table 1.3 *Foreign Sales Ratios for Selected Companies, Early 1990s*

Company	Foreign as % of total sales
Western companies	
IBM	61
Siemens	40
Alcatel	67
Average	*56*
Japanese companies	
Consumer electronics	
Matsushita	49
Sony	74
Average	*62*
Motor vehicles	
Toyota	36
Nissan	41
Honda	62
Mitsubishi	48
Mazda	58
Average	*49*
Information/Communications	
NEC	23
Fujitsu	33
Hitachi	24
Toshiba	30
Average	*28*

Source: Japan Company Handbook; company annual reports.

The Competences of Japanese and US Information and Communications Companies

Figs. 1.1–1.3 point to an important structural difference between the major Japanese IC companies and their US counterparts. These figures show that some Japanese companies feature strongly in all three of the main sub-segments of the IC industry, i.e. computers, telecommunications equipment, and semiconductors.

More specifically, NEC and Fujitsu are included in the top ten in all three of these markets. Hitachi has a strong position in computers and semiconductors, and sells telecommunications equipment although it is fairly weak in this market. However, none of the US companies are in the top ten in all three of these markets. IBM, for example, remains the overwhelmingly dominant computer company in terms of size of total sales. However, although in 1984 IBM made an attempt to accumulate telecommunications competences with its acquisition of Rolm, a PBX maker—in the belief that the convergence of computer and communications technologies made competences in both areas strategically important—this attempt was soon aborted. Rolm was later sold to Siemens. Furthermore, IBM does not feature strongly in semiconductor markets, although it is a large in-house producer of semiconductors.[7]

AT&T is in the top ten in telecommunications equipment and computing and is also a large in-house producer of semiconductors. Since the late 1980s it has increasingly been selling semiconductors externally. However, its position in computers is the result of its hostile acquisition of NCR. (Owing to its consent decree with the US Justice Department, AT&T was prevented from entering the commercial market for general-purpose computers.) By the early 1990s, however, AT&T admitted that it was not yet getting enough of the synergies between communications and computing that were an important motivation for its acquisition of NCR.

Motorola is the other US company with strong positions in two of the three sub-segments of the IC industry. Motorola, however, is not a broad supplier of telecommunications equipment as are companies such as AT&T, Alcatel, Siemens, Ericsson, NEC, and Fujitsu. Its strength in telecommunications is due largely to its competences in radio-related telecommunications equipment such as mobile base stations and phones. These competences were accumulated since the company's founding in the 1920s when it developed house and car radios. It does not have strengths in switching. In semiconductors, its strength is primarily in microprocessors.

In strong contrast, NEC, Fujitsu, and Hitachi have strong competences in computers, semiconductors, and telecommunications equipment. In other words, the Japanese companies have a significantly different combination of competences compared with their US counterparts. Furthermore, they believe strongly that in the future, with the increasing integration of ever-broader information systems, this combination of competences will give them an international competitive advantage.

This raises two questions. First, how is their different combination of competences to be explained? Second, is there any evidence that these competences are likely to give them a competitive advantage in the future? The second question is deferred to the concluding chapter of this book. The answer to the first question depends on a unique co-operative form of organization perfected in Japan in the 1920s and 1930s. One of the earliest forms of co-operation between a large user and large, competing suppliers, it is referred to in this book as 'controlled competition'.

---

[7] It was only in the early 1990s that IBM began to sell microprocessors externally. Its reason for failing to do so earlier was to protect the company's mainframes from the producers of compatibles. One of the main costs of refusing to enter the external markets for microprocessors, however, was that IBM lost competitiveness in design, although it did develop good process technologies. Its decision to allow Intel to produce all the microprocessors for its PC, and not to develop simultaneously in-house second sourcing of microprocessors, has been heavily criticized. When in the 1990s IBM developed its challenge to Intel's microprocessors with its PowerPC, it had to do so with design assistance from Motorola, although the alliance with Motorola and Apple in the PowerPC project was also motivated by marketing considerations.

Controlled Competition

Controlled competition is the form of organization that evolved in Japan in the 1920s and 1930s in order to aid the development of complex telecommunications equipment. The essence of controlled competition is a co-operative relationship between a large procurer and user of equipment and a closed group of suppliers which compete in outside markets. The procurer and user was the Japanese Ministry of Communications (Teishinshō) until 1952 and thereafter, NTT. The main members of the closed group of suppliers until 1985 were NEC, Fujitsu, Hitachi, and Oki.

Controlled competition is an alternative form of organization to vertical integration on the one hand, and arm's-length market relationships on the other. As will shortly be seen, in the USA vertical integration evolved as the major form of organization for the development of telecommunications equipment, with important long-run consequences for the collection of competences embodied in the main US information and communications companies.

Under controlled competition, telecommunications equipment is developed jointly by NTT and the closed group of supplying companies, which assume sole responsibility for manufacture. On the one hand, each supplier co-operates with NTT and the other suppliers in jointly developing equipment. On the other hand, there is a degree of competition between the suppliers in selling the jointly developed equipment to NTT. However, this competition is not of the 'winner takes all' variety. Rather, it involves *controlled* competition in so far as, contingent on reasonable performance as judged and monitored by NTT, each supplier can expect to receive a sizeable share of NTT's order.

The *incentive properties* of this form of organization are of interest. NTT gains in several ways by opting for this form of organization rather than the alternatives. First, it is able to specialize in the competences necessary for researching, developing, and running the telecommunications network, leaving the competences required for manufacture to the suppliers. Secondly, since the suppliers also sell equipment and other products in other markets, both in Japan and abroad, NTT benefits from the innovation and economies of scale and scope that the suppliers enjoy. NTT also gains from the variety of ideas and approaches followed by different suppliers. Thirdly, NTT avoids the possibility of being 'held hostage' by any one supplier by ensuring that they all provide alternative sources of supply. Fourthly, NTT is able to use its market power as the largest single customer of its suppliers, and its substantial research competences, to ensure that it gets what it wants. As the companies acknowledge, they have little option but to give NTT what it demands.

From the suppliers' point of view, the main incentive is the possibility of selling substantial amounts of equipment on a regular basis to NTT. Furthermore, since the suppliers are virtually guaranteed steady sales at reasonable profit margins, provided they abide by NTT's rules of the game, they have an incentive to accumulate so-called 'transaction-specific assets', that is assets such as equipment and human skills which are of particular use in their transactions with NTT but which are worth substantially less if they are put to alternative use. Under conditions of arm's-length competition, it is likely that, because of the resulting uncertainty, there would be a significantly lower incentive to accumulate transaction-specific assets. One example of these assets is the specialized divisions that each of the main suppliers have established which are dedicated to the supply of NTT. Furthermore, the suppliers to some extent have an incentive to share technology and information with the other suppliers since they are reasonably sure of getting a sizeable portion of NTT's business. This incentive is constrained, however, by the competition that exists between the suppliers in non-NTT markets.

Under controlled competition, NTT rewards co-operative behaviour and good performance, and punishes poor performance, by somewhat increasing or decreasing a supplier's share of its orders. This gives the supplier some time to correct behaviour and performance. It also increases the degree of certainty that the supplier enjoys, relative to arm's-length competition where winner of a tender takes all. However, where the supplier either would not, or could not, deliver the goods, NTT has exercised its credible threat of exclusion. A case in point, as shown in Chapter 4, was NTT's decision to exclude Oki from its joint development of DIPS computers from 1968, working only with NEC, Fujitsu, and Hitachi.

However, it is one thing to analyse the efficiency properties of a form of organization, but quite another to explain how the form emerged in the first place. How did controlled competition emerge? This question is examined in Chapter 2.

The Effects of Controlled Competition

The main effect of controlled competition was that, by the end of the Second World War, it gave Japan four major companies that had accumulated competences in producing complex telecommunications equipment: NEC, Fujitsu, Hitachi, and Oki. As shown in detail in Chapter 4, these companies used the competences they had *already* accumulated in telecommunications as a springboard to enter the emerging fields of semiconductors and computers. When the first computers were developed in Japan in government laboratories and were transferred to Japanese companies, and when MITI established its first co-operative projects to develop computer competences in Japanese companies, it was no accident that NTT's suppliers—Hitachi, NEC, and Fujitsu—quickly assumed the leading role. It was their capabilities, honed originally in telecommunications, that gave them a head start. Although MITI also included Toshiba and Mitsubishi Electric in most of its projects, they remained in a weaker position relative to the members of NTT's 'family'. (Oki after the war was the weakest of NTT's suppliers and was never able to strengthen its position.)

After 1968, as detailed in Chapter 4, the position of the three suppliers was strengthened through the DIPS computer project established by NTT. NTT's procurement and technological input helped, so that, after IBM introduced its System 370 family of computers, it was Hitachi, Fujitsu, and NEC that managed to remain in the mainframe market, while RCA, General Electric, Toshiba, Mitsubishi Electric, and Oki exited.

Controlled competition therefore is the main factor explaining how the leading Japanese companies came to have competences in all three areas of information and communications, i.e. computers, communications, and semi-conductors. However, while controlled competition emerged in Japan in the 1920s and 1930s in response to the specific conditions that existed in the country at that time, it was later adapted to serve other purposes. More specifi-cally, after NTT was part-privatized in 1985, the company opened its joint development projects and its procurement to a wider range of suppliers. The new suppliers included Japanese companies that were not part of NTT's traditional 'family' of suppliers, as well as Western companies, e.g. Northern Telecom, IBM, and Digital Equipment. How did these Western companies, unaccustomed to Japanese obligational relationships, fit in to NTT's system of controlled com-petition? This question is examined in Chapters 3 and 4 on telecommunications switching and computers.[8]

In the USA, however, fundamentally different forms of organization and political circumstances shaped the evolution of a very different information and communications industry. Particularly important were the conditions in the telecommunications industry. While, as we have seen, in Japan the tele-communications industry served as the incubator for the development of competences not only in telecommunications equipment, but also in computers and semiconductors, in the USA there was a more rigid division between telecommunications and computing.

This division may be traced back to the emergence of vertical integration in AT&T. In the USA, from the time that Alexander Graham Bell co-operated with instrument-maker Thomas Watson in producing the first telephone sets, it was the same organization that both developed the telecommunications network and developed and manufactured the equipment that it required. This pattern was firmly established in 1880, when the American Bell Telephone Company purchased Western Union's telephone supplying subsidiary, the Western Electric Company of Chicago. According to an 1882 agreement, American Bell restricted itself to purchasing all its telephone equipment from Western Electric, while the latter agreed to limit its activities to supplying American Bell and its licensees. As a result of this form of organization, in the USA only one major all-round producer of telecommunications equipment emerged, namely Western

---

[8] Controlled competition in Japan worked in a fundamentally different way from the form of or-ganization in the UK, which at first sight looks similar, i.e. the relationship between the British Post Office and the equipment suppliers GEC, Plessey, and STC. This difference is analysed in Ch. 3 on telecommunications switching, where the different evolutionary paths of the switching industry in the two countries is explored.

Electric/AT&T. (Motorola, as we have seen, was more narrowly specialized in radio-based communications, while companies such as GTE were confined to the small telecommunications services market which was independent of the AT&T system.)

It is unsurprising that companies with competences in developing telecommunications equipment moved into computers the way the Japanese companies did. More surprising is that this did not happen in the USA. As the official book, *A History of Engineering and Science in the Bell System*, observes, 'It is no accident that Bell Labs was deeply involved with the origins of both analog and digital computers, since it was fundamentally concerned with the principles and processes of electrical communication. Electrical analog computation is based on the classic technology of telephone transmission, and digital computation on that of telephone switching.'[9]

However, in the USA it was the 1956 'consent decree' between AT&T and the Justice Department which constrained the 'natural' extension of competences from telecommunications into computing. It did this by preventing AT&T from entering the field of general-purpose commercial computers as part of the *quid pro quo* for the company's monopolization of telecommunications services. This decree, therefore, together with vertical integration in telecommunications, bequeathed a fundamentally different structure to the US information and communications industry compared with that of its Japanese counterpart. At the same time, this meant a totally different combination of competences in the major US and Japanese IC companies.

But how effective was controlled competition, not only in providing for the needs of NTT and the Japanese telecommunications network, but also in facilitating the accumulation by the Japanese supplying companies of internationally competitive competences? This question is analysed in detail in Chapters 3, 4, and 5 in the case of telecommunications switches, computers, and optical fibre. In Chapter 6 the impact of NTT and controlled competition on the evolution of NEC is examined.

The Firm and Industry in the Evolutionary Process of Economic Change

The analysis of the Japanese IC industry presented in this book draws on a theoretical approach that I have developed for the study of the evolution of firms and industries. This approach, in turn, uses the pioneering work of contemporary writers such as Alfred Chandler, Ronald Dore, Christopher Freeman, Richard Nelson, Edith Penrose, Nathan Rosenberg, David Teece, and Sidney Winter, and earlier writers such as Alfred Marshall and Joseph

---

[9] S. Millman (ed.), *A History of Engineering and Science in the Bell System: Communications Sciences (1925–1980)*, AT&T Bell Laboratories, Indianapolis, 1984, pp.351–2.

Schumpeter. A summary of the approach is presented in Appendix 1, and also in my companion volume, *Visions of the Firm and Japan.*

How to Read this Book

This is a complex book, in terms of both the breadth and the depth of its coverage. The book covers a good proportion of the information and communications industry. The methodology employed has required a detailed analysis of the co-evolution of technologies, firms, national institutions, and industries as they emerge in real time, paying particular attention to the context within which the beliefs that underlie key decisions are formed. Parts of the book, particularly the chapter on optical fibre, the section on NEC's development of its automatic fingerprint identification system, and NTT's co-operative development of the ATM switch, contain detailed accounts of the processes involved in the development of new technologies. This has been done not simply to provide technical background and history, but also to show that technical change involves the same process of *belief construction* as occurs when the firm appraises its environment in order to formulate its vision and strategies. In the first case, the beliefs relate to a technical landscape; in the second, they relate to the firm's external environment. (A companion volume, titled *Visions of the Firm and Japan*—also published by Oxford University Press—provides a more detailed analysis of the theory of the firm used in the present book as well as further material on Japan.)

The benefit of this methodological approach is a detailed explanation of why and how the Japanese IC industry assumed the form and performed in the way it did. The cost is a good deal of complexity. In order to assist readers in dealing with this complexity, each chapter contains an overview, which summarizes the major points made and how they fit into the overall themes of the book. Readers will then be able to decide whether to delve into the complexities of the particular chapter and if not will not lose the thread of the argument.

It is also worth noting that each chapter is relatively self-contained. This means, for example, that those interested only in computers or switches or optical fibre or NEC or NTT will be able to read the relevant chapters without missing too much. The introduction and conclusion analyse the Japanese IC industry as a whole.

2

Origins of the Companies and Controlled Competition

CHAPTER OVERVIEW

The chapter begins by tracing the links between the emergence of the major Japanese IC companies and the development of first telegraph and then telephone services in the country. The particularly important role of the government-owned telegraph factory, established in 1868, is analysed. Some of the major companies were started by individuals who acquired their first knowledge of the IC industry in this factory. From 1889, with the establishment of the first telephone service in Japan, the IC companies diversified their activities into telephone-related equipment.

In 1885 the Ministry of Communications (Teishinshō) was established, assuming responsibility for telegraph and later telephone services from the Ministry of Industry (Kobushō). While the Ministry developed and managed the Japanese communications networks, from the beginning it left the manufacture of the necessary equipment to a small group of privately owned companies. However, a close co-operative relationship evolved between the Ministry and its suppliers, including the transfer of senior personnel from the former to the latter who went on to play important roles in the companies.

Although several Japanese companies produced the telecommunications equipment that was needed, by the 1920s one—NEC, partly owned by Western Electric, the in-house supplier to the Bell System—became increasingly dominant. By the early 1930s, however, although NEC remained in a strong position, its share of the Japanese telecommunications equipment market declined significantly and it faced far stronger competition from the other major suppliers, Oki, Fujitsu, and Hitachi. It is from this time that 'controlled competition' can be said to have become institutionalized in Japan. (See Chapter 1 for an account of the way in which controlled competition works.) In stark contrast, in the USA vertical integration characterized the telecommunications industry, with Western Electric as the only major producer of equipment.

The conjuncture of circumstances that gave birth to controlled competition between the late 1920s and early 1930s is examined next, showing the roles played by depression, financial crisis, and nationalism. While controlled competition was one of the outcomes of this mix of forces, another was a reduction in Japanese dependence on foreign technology and a boost to indigenous technological competences. In analysing this process, particular attention is paid to the changes that occurred in NEC and to the development of automatic switching in the country.

The Development of Telegraph and Telephone
Services in Japan

It was in the 1860s that telegraph services were first introduced into Japan. In 1868, the first year of the new post-Tokugawa Meiji regime, the Japanese Ministry of Industry established a government-owned telegraph factory which aimed at supplementing imported telegraph equipment with domestically produced products.

On 10 March 1876 in Boston, Alexander Graham Bell first demonstrated the operation of the telephone. The following year, two telephone sets were imported into Japan to be reverse-engineered in the Ministry of Industry's telecommunications factory. By 1885, when the Ministry of Communications was established, 252 telephone sets had been produced. These were installed in the principal ministries, such as the Cabinet Office and the Ministries of Finance, Foreign Affairs, and Home Affairs, and in the residences of senior officials. They were, however, for communication only between two points.

In July 1888 the Ministry of Communications sent one of their senior engineers, Saitaro Oi, to the USA, where he studied the Bell System, and to Europe. On Oi's return to Japan in 1889, a telephone service was established covering the Tokyo–Yokohama area. In 1890 the first telephone exchange was introduced in Japan, providing for 155 subscribers in Tokyo and 42 in Yokohama. By December 1890 the number of subscribers was 260; this climbed to 2,872 by March 1896.

The domestic rate of telephone diffusion, however, was constrained by the high cost of the service and the limited network externalities that had been achieved, namely the small number of existing subscribers, which acted as a disincentive for new subscribers to join. Nevertheless, demand for telephones increased steadily, encouraged both by internal and external events. Japan's victory in wars with China in 1894 and Russia in 1904 served to stimulate economic growth in Japan and to create opportunities for communications-related involvements by the Ministry of Communications and the emerging Japanese communications companies in China and Korea.

For example, after Russian influence in the region had been eliminated, and Korea had become a Japanese protectorate, the Korean government signed an agreement with Japan giving the latter control of Korean communications services. Similarly, in 1908 a treaty was concluded with China which gave Japan control over the telegraph system which had been installed by the Japanese army in southern Manchuria during its war with Russia. Japanese communications companies simultaneously expanded their activities in these regions. NEC, for instance, established offices in Seoul in 1908 and in Dalien, Liaotung Peninsula, in 1909.

To cope with the steadily rising demand for telephones, the Ministry of Communications initiated a number of investment programmes aimed at improving the telecommunications infrastructure. The first of these was a seven-year plan beginning in 1896 with an expenditure of ¥12.7 million. This programme involved the establishment of a long-distance telephone link between Tokyo and Osaka and marked the first step from a purely local network to toll calling. The second and third programmes lasted from 1907 to 1913 and from 1916 to 1921, and helped the Japanese suppliers to weather serious economic recessions in 1912 and 1920.

The Birth of the Major Companies

As noted above, in 1868 the Japanese Ministry of Industry established a government-owned factory to produce telegraph equipment.[1] A famous Japanese inventor already in his seventies, H. Tanaka, was invited to develop the equipment in this factory. Tanaka gathered together a talented group of engineers. It was some of the members of this group who subsequently established the private companies that came to form the core of the emerging Japanese IC industry.

In 1875 Tanaka himself left to establish Tanaka Seisakusha, a company that in 1904 became Shibaura Engineering. In 1939 Shibaura merged with the Tokyo Electric Company to form *Toshiba*. The origins of the Tokyo Electric Company go back to 1890 with the founding of a company, Hakunetsusha, by I. Fujioka, a professor at the Imperial College of Engineering in Tokyo. (The Imperial College of Engineering was established by a Glasgow engineer, Henry Dyer, in 1871. In 1886 the college became the Engineering Department of Tokyo University.) In establishing Hakunetsusha, Fujioka was assisted by S. Miyoshi, who was one of the engineers in Tanaka's group in the Ministry of Industry's telegraph factory. In 1899 Hakunetsusha became the Tokyo Electric Company.

Another one of Tanaka's group was K. Oki, who left to establish his own company, Meikosha, which later became *Oki*. At the turn of the century Oki was the largest supplier of telecommunications equipment, and by the time of the Second World War it was second only to NEC.

The increase in demand for communications equipment in Japan in the late 1890s very soon attracted the attention of foreign companies. In 1896 Western Electric, which had already sold equipment to Japan, sent a representative to the country in order to explore the feasibility of establishing a joint venture. In view of its experience with nationalism in Europe, Western Electric had decided that it would operate through joint ventures rather than wholly owned subsidiaries. The only company in Japan at the time that seemed to be a possible partner was Oki. However, preliminary discussions with Oki were unsuccessful, and Western Electric then proposed a joint venture with Kunihiro Iwadare, its former sales agent in Japan.

---

[1] For this early history, see the companion volume, M. Fransman, *Visions of the Firm and Japan*, Oxford University Press, 1995.

Since Iwadare was not licensed to supply telephone equipment to the Ministry of Communications, he entered into an agreement with Takeshiro Maeda, who had received a licence from the Ministry. Iwadare and Maeda subsequently purchased the firm established by S. Miyoshi (who, as noted earlier, worked with Fujioka in establishing Hakunetsusha), which had gone bankrupt; they used this purchase to establish a limited partnership in 1898. In 1899, with the introduction of the so-called revised treaties with Western countries that allowed foreigners to own shares in Japanese firms, Nippon Electric (*NEC*) was established, 54 per cent owned by Western Electric. The main equipment produced was telephones and switchboards. In addition, equipment was also imported from Western Electric and General Electric, which were also represented in Japan by Iwadare.

Fujitsu also owes its origins to government activities. In 1896 Furukawa Mining established Furukawa Denko (Furukawa Electric Company) to supply electrical wire to the Ministry of Communications. With the expansion of the Ministry's expenditure on telecommunications, Furukawa Electric decided in 1921 to begin making manual switchboards and telephones. Furukawa Electric's entry into this industry was facilitated by the transfer to the company of Dr M. Tonegawa, Director of the Ministry of Communications' laboratories, and some of the engineers who worked under him.

In 1923 Furukawa Electric concluded an agreement with Siemens with the purpose of gaining access to the latter's switching technology. This resulted in a joint venture, Fuji Denki (Fuji Electric). In the same year Fuji Electric became an official supplier to the Ministry. In 1935 Fuji Electric spun-off a subsidiary, Fuji Tsushinki (Fuji Telecommunications), to specialize in the production of Siemens switches. In 1967 Fuji Tsushinki changed its name to Fujitsu.

The company that was later to be absorbed by *Hitachi*, Toa Denki Seisakusho (East Asia Electric Machine Manufacturing Company), was also encouraged by the 1916 expansion programme to enter into the production of telephones. Toa Denki was founded in 1918 by K. Munesue, formerly Director of the Electricity Bureau of the Ministry of Communications. The original aim of Toa Denki was to produce telephone sets. In 1922 Toa Denki became an official supplier to the Ministry for magneto and common-battery types of telephones, and in 1926 for magneto and common-battery types of manual switchboards. In the same year, the company was given managerial assistance by G. Ayukawa, an influential figure in Japanese industry at the time who later became President of the Manchurian Railway Company.

The origins of Hitachi go back to 1908, when Namihei Odaira, an entrepreneurial engineer, established the Kuhara Mining Company. Hitachi began as the electrical machinery repair shop of Kuhara Mining at its Hitachi mine. After Kuhara Mining moved its corporate headquarters to Tokyo in 1918, Hitachi Limited was established (in 1920) as an electrical machinery company.

In 1934 Toa Denki merged with Kokusan Kogyo, a company manufacturing iron and steel parts, whose president was G. Ayukawa. Three years later, in 1937, Hitachi acquired Kokusan Kogyo. Since then the Hitachi brand name, rather than Toa Denki, has been used for its telecommunications products.

Growing Competition among Japanese Equipment Manufacturers

In 1920 the postwar boom turned into inflation and depression. The downturn was further reinforced by the Washington Naval Conference in 1921–2, which allocated three battleships to Japan for each of the five for the USA and Britain. This badly affected Japanese heavy industry. Labour disputes and strikes broke out in many parts of the country, and in 1922 conditions deteriorated further with a stock exchange crash that threatened several banks. Although the telecommunications equipment companies were to some degree insulated from this depression by the Ministry of Communication's telephone expansion programme, the Ministry itself came under increasing budgetary pressure as a result of the downturn.

Matters were made even worse with the Great Kanto Earthquake on 1 September 1923, which killed about 140,000 people and left about 3.4 million homeless. The Central Telephone Office in Tokyo and twelve other offices were destroyed and many cables and telephone sets were damaged. While these events were a setback, they unexpectedly resulted in a more rapid modernization of the Japanese telecommunications network. Faced with the destruction of much of the fixed capital in the Kanto area, the decision was taken to implement more rapidly the plans that were made before the earthquake to introduce automatic telephone switching and radio broadcasting. As we shall see, this provided an important boost to the equipment suppliers and to their level of technological competence.

The onset of economic depression in Japan, however, coincided with a significant rise in nationalism. In the industrial area this was evident in the establishment in 1926 of the Domestic Product Promotion Committee (Kokusan-shinko Iinkai) by the predecessor of the Ministry of International Trade and Industry (Shokoshō). Nationalist sentiment was extremely strong in the Ministry of Communications. In 1929 the Ministry issued the 'Directive for the Use of More Domestic Telecommunications Products' (Denkitsushin-kiki kokusanka taiko), which, as will be seen, had a major impact on the Japanese equipment manufacturers.

Japanese nationalism, however, not only was a matter of political ideology but also contained an economic dimension connected with Japan's dependence on foreign companies and the corresponding high cost of imports of foreign technology and equipment. This emerges clearly in the case of the development of domestic capabilities in automatic switches, which will be examined below. The nationalist movement substantially transformed the relationship between the Japanese telecommunications equipment manufacturers and the foreign companies that supplied them with technology.

This is illustrated in the case of NEC. As in the cases of Fujitsu and Hitachi already discussed, close links had been forged between the Ministry of Communications and NEC. This is seen, for example, in the career of Saitaro Oi, who, as mentioned earlier, was sent in 1888 by the Ministry of Communications to study the telecommunications systems of the USA and Britain: in August 1919 Oi left the Ministry and joined NEC as a member of its board of directors.

Similarly, in 1924 Yasujiro Niwa, formerly an engineer in the laboratory of the Ministry of Communications, joined NEC and in 1927 became the head of its Engineering Department. Niwa was particularly enthused by the nationalist-inspired move to reduce Japanese dependence on foreign technology and introduced several important reforms in NEC designed to strengthen the company's technological capabilities. These included the establishment of factory-level R&D, as opposed to the central laboratory that was the pattern in Western Electric, and the yearly recruitment of young engineers from prestigious Japanese universities. In December 1926, Iwadare, one of the founders of NEC, vacated his position as Managing Director and became Chairman of the Board. He was replaced by Genichiro Ohata, who joined NEC in 1920 from the Ministry of Communications and had been a member of the board since 1923.

The nationalist movement of the late 1920s, however, created a dilemma both for NEC and for the Ministry of Communications with which it had such close ties. The reason for the dilemma was that NEC remained a majority-owned subsidiary of Western Electric. This dilemma increased greatly in intensity when, in July 1930, the Ministry of Communications issued an unpublished decree on national production which stipulated that 'domestic production', to which the Ministry would give preference, was to be defined as output from companies that were at least 51 per cent Japanese-owned. Did this imply the emergence of a nationalist-inspired conflict of interest between the Ministry of Communications and NEC as the majority-owned subsidiary of a foreign company? And how was the 'dilemma' resolved? In true Japanese style, the parties sought a pragmatic resolution of the dilemma which would safeguard both their interests. The result was that the dilemma was satisfactorily side-stepped. How was this accomplished?

In reality, the 'dilemma' was not as stark as it appeared on the surface to be. While the Ministry of Communications was committed to an increasingly strong nationalist line, in pursuit of both financial and political objectives, it also had an interest in maintaining, and indeed strengthening, the technological capabilities of NEC. This was because NEC remained its most important supplier of telecommunications equipment.

On NEC's side, the Japanese part of the joint venture was by no means adverse to any steps that would strengthen the company's capabilities. Although NEC was heavily dependent on Western Electric's technology, there were an increasing number of young engineers in the company who had received excellent engineering training at the top Japanese universities and who wanted to extend their and their company's mastery of the imported equipment and technologies they were working with. Furthermore, the close links that existed between the Ministry of Communications and NEC, cemented by the transfer of staff from the former to the latter, helped to consolidate the common interest that existed and made a compromise acceptable.

The compromise that was eventually accepted revolved around the close relationship that had already been established between NEC and the Sumitomo group. In 1919 International Western Electric, a wholly owned subsidiary of Western Electric formed in 1918 to run the company's overseas interests, discussed with Iwadare of NEC the possibility of establishing a joint venture to produce electrical cables. Since at this stage NEC was operating at full capacity and Iwadare was concerned (in more modern terminology) to concentrate on the company's core competences, he proposed that a joint venture be negotiated with Sumitomo Densen Seizosho (now called Sumitomo Electric Industries Ltd). Sumitomo Densen was the electrical cable manufacturing unit of the Sumitomo *zaibatsu* (which originated at the end of the sixteenth century, based on copper smelting and refining). According to the deal that was eventually struck in 1920, NEC acquired 25 per cent of Sumitomo Densen's shares, in return giving the company 5 per cent of its shares; and all NEC's rights to Western Electric's duplex cable technology were transferred to Sumitomo Densen.

In the late 1920s, the link that had been forged with the powerful Sumitomo *zaibatsu* was to prove useful in providing a way out of the dilemma created by the Ministry of Communication's efforts to procure equipment only from majority-owned Japanese companies. In 1925 International Telephone and Telegraph Corporation (ITT) took over International Western Electric and its affiliated companies. Under this agreement, International Western Electric was renamed International Standard Electric Corporation (ISE) and became a subsidiary of ITT. This made NEC an affiliate of ISE. Through various agreements, NEC retained its access to Western Electric's technology.

In 1929 discussions began between Sosthenes Behn, the President of ITT, and Sumitomo representatives regarding the transfer of NEC's management to Sumitomo. In view of the political climate prevailing in Japan at this time, this was an option that Behn favoured. Eventually agreement was reached in May 1932. This involved a transfer of some of ISE's shares in NEC to Sumitomo together with the transfer of an equal number of Sumitomo Densen shares to ISE. In this way, ISE's shareholding in NEC was decreased from 59 to 50 per cent, while the Sumitomo groups's holding in NEC increased from 5 to 14 per cent. At the same time, NEC was entitled to receive continuing technical and managerial support from ISE.

In this way, with the full knowledge of the Ministry of Communications, a way was found for NEC to continue in its role as the major supplier of telecommunications equipment to the Ministry, despite the company's continuing technological dependence on ISE. As the political situation deteriorated further in the period leading up to Japan's entry into the war, however, ISE was forced to further reduce its shareholding in NEC while the Sumitomo group became the largest shareholder in NEC. Nevertheless, after the war, in July 1950, ISE regained the 32.8 per cent holding in NEC which it held on the eve of Japan's entry into the war.

In its handling of the NEC case, the Ministry of Communications had shown that it was willing to act pragmatically while insisting, for nationalistic reasons, that overall legal control of the company be moved into Japanese hands. Sumitomo's legal control of NEC at this stage, however, did not change the latter's dependence on Western Electric's technology, which continued despite the increasing attempts made by people such as Niwa in NEC to strengthen the company's technological capabilities. Nevertheless, the Ministry took the view that it was important for Japan to increase its technological self-reliance, and for this reason it encouraged where it could the development of Japanese capabilities.

The Case of Automatic Switches

The case of automatic switches is of particular interest because it shows in detail how domestic technological competences were accumulated in Japan during the interwar period. This process of domestic competence accumulation also indicates the important role played by the Ministry of Communications, first in negotiating the import of foreign technology on terms that ultimately proved favourable to Japan, and secondly in taking steps to ensure that Japanese companies, instead of remaining dependent on foreign sources of technology, developed their own competences. While the case of automatic switches illustrates well the kinds of difficulties that all developing countries face in importing technology while attempting to increase indigenous technological competences, it also provides a textbook example of how governments in these countries might cope with these difficulties.[2]

Import of Foreign Technology

In 1922 the Ministry of Communications imported the first automatic switching system into Japan, a Strowger-type switch with a capacity of 10,000 lines that was purchased from the Automatic Telephone Manufacturing Co. (ATM) of the UK. This switch was imported so that the Ministry's engineers could examine the system and learn more about it. In April 1923 it was installed in the Talien Central Office in Liaotung Peninsula in China. NEC assisted with

---

[2] For a survey of the issues associated with the import of technology and the development of domestic technological competences in the developing country context, see M. Fransman, *Technology and Economic Development*, Wheatsheaf, Brighton, 1986.

the installation, and as a result the company became the sole agent for ATM products in Japan.

After the Great Kanto Earthquake in September 1923, the Ministry, facing the destruction that had occurred of telecommunications equipment including switches, decided to introduce automatic switches. To this end, in choosing from among the different technologies and systems that were available, the Ministry examined six different types of automatic switches that were currently in use elsewhere in the world. This examination was facilitated by the learning and knowledge that had already accumulated in the Ministry's engineering and research divisions with the earlier investigation of ATM's switch. As a result of the examination, in 1924 the Ministry narrowed the choice to two switches. The first was the Strowger-type switch made by ATM and another company, Automatic Electric Inc. (AEI). The second switch was made by Siemens-Halske. These switches at the time were the most widely used in the world.

In making its choice, the Ministry faced a dilemma. The choice of one system for the entire country would produce important benefits in terms of the standardization of training of engineers and technicians and of maintenance. It would also eliminate the problem of the incompatibility of different switching systems within the same network and would increase the flexibility of the Ministry's technical staff. On the other hand, the choice of one system raised the danger of the Japanese network becoming a hostage to the foreign company controlling that particular proprietary switching technology. This would mean that a high price would have to be paid for the switching technology.

This dilemma polarized debate within the Ministry of Communications between the Engineering Bureau, which, with technical considerations uppermost in mind, favoured a single system, and the Accounting Bureau, which was more concerned with the financial aspects and wanted to use competition, both among foreign companies and among Japanese suppliers, as a policy tool to keep down the costs of telecommunications equipment. In the event, the policy line of the Accounting Bureau triumphed and the Ministry decided to introduce both automatic switching systems. Accordingly, in 1924 a Strowger system was imported from the company ATM through NEC for use in the Tokyo area. The value of this contract was ¥8.15 million, a substantial sum for the Ministry at that stage. At around the same time, a Siemens system was purchased for the Yokohama area. This system was 12 per cent cheaper than the Strowger system, already illustrating the benefits of a degree of competition between the foreign suppliers of switching systems. Later the Siemens system was introduced into Osaka and Kobe while the Strowger system was used in Tokyo, Nagoya, and Kyoto. In 1925 Fuji Denki took over from the Siemens Schukert Tokyo Company the right to import and sell Siemens-Halske telecommunications equipment and parts.

Although competition between the foreign companies supplying these two systems served to bring down the price to some extent, the Ministry realized, as the governments of many developing countries later came to realize, that by 'unpackaging' the system the price could be further reduced. Accordingly, while the original orders were for entire systems from the foreign supplier, the Ministry later divided the automatic switch into about ten sub-systems which could be assembled in Japan and negotiated separately with the suppliers for each sub-system. In this way, the price of the imported technology was lowered even more.

The success of the Ministry in lowering prices is shown in Table 2.1. As can be seen, the payment for automatic switches as a proportion of the total payment to foreign companies for telecommunications equipment fell from 61 per cent in 1925, the first year the switches were imported, to 34 per cent in 1929. In view of the severe recession that affected the Japanese economy from 1927, which had serious negative implications for the Ministry's budget, the improvement in the terms on which this foreign technology was acquired was most welcome.

Table 2.1 *Payment to Foreign Companies for Automatic Switches by the Ministry of Communications, 1925–1929*

	Total payment to foreign companies by Teishinsho (¥ '000)	Total payment for automatic switches (¥ '000)	Proportion (%)
	(1)	(2)	(2)/(1)
1925	16,345	9,951	61
1926	12,947	8,435	65
1927	5,701	1,832	32
1928	3,065	1,526	50
1929	2,379	809	34

Source: NTT, *Twenty-Five Years of Japan's Automatic Telephone Switches* (in Japanese), NTT, Tokyo, 1953.

Increasing Domestic Competences in Automatic Switching

Despite its success in bringing down the price of imported automatic switches, the Ministry felt that it was necessary simultaneously to strengthen the competences of the Japanese suppliers in the area of automatic switching. Co-operating closely with the Ministry, NEC, while importing automatic switches from ATM, proceeded simultaneously in 1924 to develop its own Strowger-type switch with technical assistance from Western Electric. In 1929, at a time as we have seen when domestic production was accorded high priority by the Ministry, NEC installed the first domestically developed automatic switch in a central office in Tokyo. A year later Oki delivered its first domestically produced automatic switch.

Toa Denki (later to become part of Hitachi) decided in 1927 to begin developing its own switch. This development received strong encouragement from the Ministry of Communications which allowed Toa Denki to reverse-engineer the automatic Strowger-type switch that had been procured via NEC from the American company Automatic Electric Inc. (AEI), and which was installed in the Tokyo Central Telephone Office. In 1930 the Ministry approved Toa Denki as a supplier of automatic switches. In 1934 Toa Denki delivered its first automatic switch for use in the Atami exchange.

In 1932 Fuji Denki (which later spun-off Fujitsu) proposed to the Ministry that it would assemble automatic switches domestically using parts imported from Siemens. The Ministry, however, strongly opposed this proposal and threatened to purchase Strowger-type switches for the Osaka–Kobe area, which until then had used the Siemens-Halske switch, unless Fuji Denki moved to purely domestic production. This threat resulted in tough negotiations between Fuji Denki and Siemens. The outcome was that Fuji Denki got agreement from Siemens to begin domestic production, and in 1934 the company provided domestically produced Siemens-Halske-type switches for Yokohama–Tsurumi and Osaka–Fukushima. In this way, spurred by both depression-induced budgetary constraints and nationalist sentiment, the Ministry of Communications succeeded in improving the terms on which it acquired foreign switching technology while at the same time improving the technological competences of the Japanese equipment suppliers.

The Institutionalization of Controlled Competition

Controlled competition—the Japanese form of organization for the development of telecommunications equipment, analysed in Chapter 1—became institutionalized during the late 1920s and early 1930s. In turn, it came to be an important influence on the shape and evolution of the entire Japanese IC industry.

What conjuncture of circumstances led to the institutionalization of controlled competition? Earlier in this chapter reference was made to two of the factors that were important precipitating influences. The first was the financial crises from 1927 onwards. These crises, through the pressure they put on government budgets, provoked attempts to reduce government costs. In the case of the Ministry of Communications, this translated into efforts to reduce the costs of procuring the equipment needed to run and modernize the telecommunications network. As was shown, one way of reducing these costs was to strike better deals with the foreign companies that supplied such equipment. Another way was to increase the technological competences of domestic equipment suppliers while at the same time increasing the competition between them, in order to hold prices down and increase quality.

The second factor provided the ideological glue that would hold these policies together. This was the growing tide of Japanese nationalism that swept through various ministries from the late 1920s. The Ministry of Communications was a hotbed of nationalism, and this was evident in its various pronouncements aimed at encouraging domestic production and the reduction of technological dependence on foreign suppliers. Although the Ministry's policies remained highly pragmatic, as was seen in its delicate handling of NEC, the nationalism of the times provided a significant impetus for increasing the accumulation of indigenous technological competences.

If financial crisis and nationalism were two important forces driving the institutionalization of controlled competition, so was the belief that an efficient form of organizing the development of telecommunications equipment necessitated a degree of competition between several alternative suppliers. Although this belief contradicted that formed in the USA, where the vertically integrated Bell System obtained its equipment from its wholly owned subsidiary Western Electric, it was a belief that had already served the Japanese system well; as mentioned above, from the beginning the Ministry of Industry and then the Ministry of Communications relied on several suppliers for its telegraph and telephone network equipment.

Nevertheless, although the belief regarding the necessity for having several suppliers was longstanding, it was transformed under the combination of circumstances of the late 1920s and early 1930s. More specifically, the belief, which became enshrined with the institutionalization of controlled competition, stipulated that the Ministry should have the option of procuring the equipment needed from several suppliers, each with sufficient strength to compete effectively with the others. The main benefits of this arrangement were that the Ministry could not be 'held hostage' by one dominant supplier and, furthermore, that the Ministry would benefit from the variety of products and technologies generated by the different suppliers with their different sets of competences. The problem, however, was that in the mid-1920s the Ministry *was* heavily dependent on one supplier, namely NEC, the partly owned subsidiary of the world's dominant telecommunications equipment company. As shown in Table 2.2, in 1927 almost three-quarters of the Ministry's total purchases of telecommunications equipment came from NEC.

Under the new circumstances that emerged in the late 1920s, the Ministry set about trying to change its supplier situation. In view of its dominance, NEC would obviously have to remain an important supplier. It was this realization, together with the close personal links that had been forged between the Ministry and NEC, that explains the pragmatic negotiations that took place between the two over the reduction of the US parent's ownership in NEC, as documented earlier. Nevertheless, the Ministry resolved to reduce NEC's dominance relative to the other suppliers. The measures that the Ministry took transformed the supplier situation from one characterized by overwhelming dominance by a single supplier to one characterized by controlled competition. Henceforth there would be a more even sharing of the procurement among the major Japanese supplying companies, an evenness that increased markedly after the war.

Table 2.2 *Value of Ministry of Communications' Purchases of Telecommunications Equipment, 1926–1931*

	1926	1927	1928	1929	1930	1931
NEC						
Value (¥ '000)	14,757	8,029	3,079	3,878	1,862	1,341
% of total	68.4	72.4	60.8	63.1	62.6	54.5
Oki						
Value (¥ '000)	3,619	2,226	928	1,369	581	510
% of total	16.8	20.1	18.3	22.3	19.5	20.7
Hitachi						
Value (¥ '000)	260	153	163	323	171	150
% of total	1.2	1.4	3.2	5.3	5.8	6.1
Fujitsu						
Value (¥ '000)	2,415	271	586	151	191	294
% of total	11.2	2.4	11.6	2.5	6.4	11.9
Anritsu						
Value (¥ '000)	576	413	307	425	168	166
% of total	2.4	3.7	6.1	6.9	5.7	6.7
TOTAL						
Value (¥ '000)	21,567	11,092	5,063	6,146	2,973	2,461
%	100.0	100.0	100.0	100.0	100.0	100.0

Source: NTT, *Twenty-Five Years of Japan's Automatic Telephone Switches* (in Japanese), NTT, Tokyo, 1953.

One indicator of the change in the Ministry's policy is evident in Hitachi's procurement share shown in Table 2.2. Hitachi was particularly important for the Ministry's nationalistic policies, since Hitachi was the only major company that did not rely largely on the purchase of foreign technology for its equipment. This fitted in well with the Ministry's 'national production' policy. As the table shows, Hitachi's share of the Ministry's purchases increased from 1.2 per cent in 1926 to 6.1 per cent in 1931. The other gainers (though not to the same extent) included Anritsu, Oki, and Fujitsu. It was NEC, however, that was the big loser. By 1931, only 55 per cent of the Ministry's purchases came from NEC. The change is all the more dramatic when viewed from the perspective of the proportion of NEC's total sales going to the Ministry of Communications: while in 1925 this proportion was 84 per cent, by 1931 it had decreased to 33 per cent. An even better indication of the Ministry's determination to reduce its dependence on NEC is provided by the proportion of the Ministry's expansion budget, used to finance new purchases, going to NEC. This is shown in Table 2.3. As this table shows, in 1925 NEC's share was 38 per cent; by 1931 it had fallen to 11 per cent. By the early 1930s, therefore, controlled competition had become institutionalized in Japan in a form that would remain recognizable for its continuity until the present day.

Table 2.3 *NEC's Sales to the Ministry of Communications (MoC), 1925–1931*

	Total expansion budget (MoC)	NEC sales to MoC	Share (%)
1925	37,000	13,945	37.8
1926	48,620	16,041	33.0
1927	47,000	13,027	27.7
1928	40,770	8,481	20.8
1929	30,950	6,500	21.0
1930	21,051	1,862	8.8
1931	11,859	1,341	11.3

Source: NTT, *Twenty-Five Years of Japan's Automatic Telephone Switches* (in Japanese), NTT, Tokyo, 1953.

Conclusion

In 1949 the Japanese government, in consultation with the Supreme Commander for the Allied Powers (SCAP), disbanded the Ministry of Communications and created two new ministries, the Ministry of Postal Affairs (Yuseishō) and the Ministry of Telecommunications (Denki Tsushinshō). Simultaneously, the government established the Advisory Council for the Reconstruction of Telegraph and Telephone Networks to consider an appropriate framework for the postwar telecommunications sector in Japan.

The Advisory Council published its final report in March 1950, recommending that the Japanese telegraph and telephone networks should be run by a public corporation, rather than as a direct government monopoly. In 1952 a large part of the Ministry of Telecommunications was transferred to the newly created Nippon Telegraph and Telephone Public Corporation (NTT). Unlike the Japanese National Railways, which had to compete in some areas with private railways, NTT was given a monopoly over telegraph and telephone services. The Ministry of Postal Affairs was renamed the Ministry of Posts and Telecommunications (MPT) and given regulatory responsibility in some telecommunications areas.

NTT's first President was Takeshi Kajii. Kajii was Director of the Engineering Bureau of the Ministry of Communications until 1938, when he became Managing Director of NEC. In 1943 he became President of NEC, the same year that NEC was designated under the government's Munitions Company Law of October 1943 as a munitions company under the jurisdiction of the military-run government. Kajii was made the officer responsible for production under this law. In January 1946 he was purged by the Allied authorities and resigned as president of NEC. In 1952 he became the first president of NTT.

Although the metamorphosis of the Ministry of Communications into NTT took place at the formal level, at the more substantive level there was a far greater degree of continuity. More specifically, the main characteristics of controlled competition, which evolved in the 1920s and 1930s under the tutelage of the Ministry of Communications, continued after 1952 with only minor change. As will be seen in the rest of this book, these characteristics were to remain the defining feature of the Japanese telecommunications system even beyond NTT's part-privatization in 1985, when foreign telecommunications suppliers began to be incorporated into the system.

3

The Evolution of the Japanese Telecommunications Switching Industry

CHAPTER OVERVIEW

The chapter begins with an examination of the transition from electro-mechanical crossbar switching to electronic space-division switching. The introduction of the latter in Japan is compared with that of the world leader, AT&T. How far behind were the Japanese? How did they manage to catch up?

Attention is then turned to the development of digital time-division switching which, together with events in the USA, created new market opportunities for the world's major switching companies. How did the responses to the new technologies and markets of companies like AT&T, NTT, Northern Telecom, NEC, and Fujitsu compare? How was Northern Telecom able to succeed in the US market, and why did the Japanese companies fail?

NTT's co-operative development of its two digital switches, the D60 and D70, is then analysed. How did the form of organization for this development—controlled competition—work? What were the costs and benefits for NTT and its suppliers, NEC, Fujitsu, Hitachi, and Oki? How did NTT go on to use these switches to help develop one of the most modern digitized telecommunications networks in the world?

In the following section, the importance of competences, the company's concept of the company, and national innovation systems are examined. This examination involves a detailed comparison of ITT, NEC, Fujitsu, Ericsson, Philips, and Motorola. The influence of national systems of innovation is analysed by comparing the Japanese and US systems analysed earlier with those of France and Britain. Why did the French system produce the largest central office switching company in the world, Alcatel, while in Britain the leading companies' switching activities were in effect absorbed by Siemens?

What have been the effects of corporate competences, structure, and strategy on corporate performance in the case of central office switching companies? How strong have the earliest corporate entrants been compared with later comers? These questions are examined on the basis of the major companies.

The final section contains an analysis of the decision-making process involving NTT's co-operative development of the next-generation ATM (asynchronous transfer mode) switch. What were the main determinants of the crucial decisions? In developing this switch, NTT transformed controlled competition so as to include Western companies. How did they respond to Japanese trust-based obligational relationships, co-operating with Japanese companies which were simultaneously competitors in global markets?

Introduction

The central office telecommunications switching industry in Japan raises several important questions and puzzles. How were Japanese companies, significantly behind their Western counterparts at the end of the war, able to catch up in switching technology? What role did NTT's system of controlled competition play in the catch-up process? By the early 1990s, there were seven major global competitors producing central office telecommunications switches. Japan was the only country to have two representatives among these seven—NEC and Fujitsu—while all the other countries had one. Why? In the late 1970s, NEC and Fujitsu, like their Western competitors such as Canada's Northern Telecom, attempted to take advantage of the window of opportunity presented by new digital switching technology to enter the US market. However, while Northern Telecom succeeded, NEC and Fujitsu failed. By 1992, Northern Telecom held 39.6 per cent of the US central office switching market compared to 41.3 per cent for AT&T; NEC, the largest Japanese contender, held 0.7 per cent. Why did the Japanese companies fail? From the late 1980s, NTT established the world's largest consortium to develop the next-generation ATM (asynchronous transfer mode) switch which will be used to switch multimedia signals such as voice, data, fax, and video. In the early 1990s Fujitsu became the first company to market a commercial ATM switch followed closely by NEC. Why?

Further questions are raised from the perspective of the global central office switching industry. How did AT&T, by far the most dominant player in switching in the USA until the early 1980s, lose such a significant proportion of this market to Northern Telecom? Why, as shown in Table 3.1, did major switch producers such as ITT, Philips, Plessey, and GTE drop out of the switch market? How did France's Alcatel become the world's largest central office switch producer? Why did Britain, with some of the strongest switching companies in the world prior to the war, lose an independent presence in this key telecommunications equipment market? What role is played by corporate strategy and structure in explaining corporate competitive performance in this market?

Table 3.1 *Major Competitors and Drop-Outs in Telecommunications Switching, 1990s*

Major competitors	Drop-outs
Alcatel	ITT
AT&T	Philips
Northern Telecom	GTE
Ericsson	Plessey
NEC	Stromberg-Carlson
Siemens/GPT	
Fujitsu	

From an *ex post* perspective, three major changes have occurred in the post-war years: the succession of four major generations of technology; a significant increase in the concentration of the global industry as investment and R&D costs have risen (from around fifteen major producers in the 1970s to seven in the early 1990s); and a gradual liberalization of some of the main markets for central office switches. However, from the real-time, *ex ante* perspective pursued in this book, several other important features of the evolution of the global central office switching industry become apparent.

To begin with, significant interpretive ambiguity surrounded the introduction of each new generation of switching technology. It took between ten and twenty years from the invention of the major technologies to the introduction of the first technically viable switches. Then it took another five to ten years before the new generation of switches was able to compete economically with the previous generation. During this time, there were significantly different beliefs—between countries and companies as well as within companies—regarding whether and when the new generation of switches would become both technically and economically superior. These beliefs, in turn, influenced the decisions made in companies regarding the timing of their entry into the new technologies. In the present chapter, the different beliefs of companies such as AT&T, Northern Telecom, NTT, NEC, and Fujitsu are analysed in detail, along with the competitive consequences of these beliefs.

However, it was not only different beliefs regarding the new technologies and markets, formed under conditions of interpretive ambiguity, that drove the strategic choices of the companies. Also crucial were the companies' 'concept of the company', that is their beliefs regarding the kinds of activities that were appropriate for their companies. The present chapter analyses the different concepts of the company which shaped the strategies of companies such as ITT, NEC, and Ericsson and which in turn influenced the structure of the central office switching industry that emerged in the 1990s. In short, the real-time analysis in this chapter illuminates the 'fuzziness' that surrounded most of the key decisions that shaped the evolution of the global switching industry. These decisions were made not in the light of clear, unambiguous predictions regarding the consequences that would follow, but rather on the basis of tentative beliefs and hopes, some of which turned out, with the benefit of hindsight, to be false.[1]

---

[1] This chapter is based heavily on numerous detailed interviews with many of Japan's leading experts in the field of switching, in NTT, NEC, Fujitsu, Hitachi, and Oki. Of these people, I am particularly grateful to K. Hirota, H. Inose, K. Habara, H. Ikeda, M. Shiromizu, I. Toda, T. Kunihiro, H. Ishikawa and C. Hishinuma. Dr K. Hirota was especially helpful in helping me to reconstruct the early postwar history of switching in Japan. None of them, however, bears any responsibility for faults regarding fact or interpretation. The present chapter also draws heavily on the valuable source reference by R. J. Chapuis and A. E. Joel, *Electronics, Computers And Telephone Switching*, North-Holland, Amsterdam, 1990. Joel, from Bell Laboratories, is one of the acknowledged fathers of modern switching.

From Electromechanical to Electronic Switching

The four main postwar generations of switching technology are:

1. Crossbar
2. Space-division
3. Time-division digital
4. ATM

The Transistor and Switching

In electronic space-division switching, electronic components such as the transistor and later the integrated circuit replaced the electromechanical components of the earlier generation of switches. (See the List of Abbreviations and Technical Terms at the front of the book for an explanation of the technical terminology.) Indeed, it was the search for new devices to be used in switching that was one of the important factors motivating the research that led to the invention of the transistor.

The transistor was invented in 1947 in Bell Laboratories by John Bardeen, Walter Brattain, and William Shockley. All three had backgrounds in quantum mechanics and solid-state physics. However, the context within which they applied their scientific knowledge was also an important influence on their invention. This context was provided by Bell Laboratories' mission to improve the company's telecommunications network. For example, Shockley's initial appointment to Bell Laboratories was explicitly motivated by the desire to improve telecommunications equipment. Shockley was employed by Bell in 1929 when he left the Massachusetts Institute of Technology having completed his Ph.D. on the behaviour of electrons in a crystalline structure. He was recruited by the Director of Research at Bell Laboratories, Mervin J. Kelley, who assigned him to the Solid-State Research Department. Shockley has referred to 'Kelly's stimulus for new devices useful in [the] telephone business' as an important influence in his own research that led to the transistor.[2]

Amos Joel, one of the fathers of modern switching, who also worked at Bell Laboratories, has elaborated on the desire to bring about improvements in both telecommunications transmissions and switching technology which served to orient the research that led to the transistor. Joel notes that Kelly, who was later to become President of Bell Laboratories, 'was very much aware of the promising prospects of solid-state physics and of research on semiconductors. Even more than the need for the "crystal amplifier" intended to replace the vacuum tube in transmission equipment, Kelly envisaged an electronic device in which a semiconductor would replace the relay as the basic element in automatic telephone exchanges'. Joel, accordingly, concludes that 'electronic switching,

---

[2] W. Shockley, *Electronics and Holes in Semiconductors, with Applications to Transistor Electronics*, Van Nostrand, New York, 1950 (emphasis added).

even before World War II, had been one of the main objectives . . . of Bell Labs research on semiconductors'.[3]

Despite the switching-related motivations for the research that led to the transistor in 1947, by the close of the 1940s leaders in the switching industry remained sceptical regarding the feasibility of electronic switching. The expectations were summarized by C. Jacobaeus, at the time Executive Vice-President of Ericsson:

[At] the end of the 1940s, the telephone industry began setting [up] laboratories—albeit on a small scale—for studying in more detail the possibility of introducing electronic components as essential building bricks in switching engineering. Relatively few people really believed that electronics would come to play an important role in telephone exchanges. In industry at that time the electronic laboratory activities in switching were in the nature of an insurance against unpleasant surprises.[4]

Part of the reason for the scepticism regarding the viability of electronic switching was the advanced crossbar electromechanical switches that were developed by leaders such as AT&T and Ericsson in the early postwar period. However, even in the early 1960s, crossbar engineers in AT&T still had a vision of the future of switching that excluded the viability of electronic switching. 'At this time many electromechanical switching system development engineers never conceded the advantages of electronic switching and found it hard to believe that it could then compete with their technology.'[5]

The Development of Electronic Space-Division Switching

Research began in Bell Laboratories on electronic space-division switching in 1948 at the same time as improved crossbar switches were being developed. In the mid-1950s, this research led to the introduction for the first time of the concept of stored program control into the field of switching. This concept was developed by John von Neumann in 1945 and 1946 in his ideas for a stored program-controlled computer. Stored program control (SPC) 'has been widely recognized as the single most important contribution to electronic switching'.[6] It introduced software into computing and brought about a technological convergence between the fields of communications and computing.

In 1960 the first electronic SPC switch was put on trial by Bell Laboratories. This led, in 1965, to the first commercial electronic SPC switch, the No. 1 ESS,

---

[3] Chapuis and Joel, *Electronics*, 128 (emphasis added).

[4] Quoted ibid. 43.

[5] Ibid. 158.

[6] Ibid. 154. According to Chapuis and Joel, 'The interplay of technology developments between the computer and telephone industries [up to the early 1950s] may be very roughly summarized as a two-way affair: *telephone switching provided the logics* for computers, while *computers provided the memories* for electronic switching. . . . The software concept of "stored programs", a familiar one in the computer industry, constituted by the mid-1950s the most important contribution of computer technology to electronic telephone switching' (ibid. 44).

jointly produced by Western Electric and AT&T. In 1958 AT&T had estimated that it would cost $25 million to develop an electronic SPC switch and would take five years.[7] In the event, the No. 1 ESS, including the total system development costs, cost $500 million to develop and took seven years.[8]

The development of electronic space-division switching is summarized in Fig. 3.1.

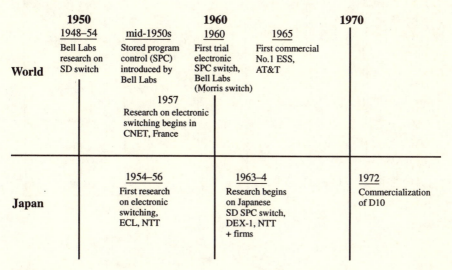

Fig. 3.1 Evolution of telecommunications switching: from crossbar to electronic space-division (SD) switching

Electronic Space-Division Switching in Japan

Research on electronic switching began in Japan in 1954 (see Fig. 3.2).[9] However, it was only in 1963 that NTT and its suppliers made a significant commitment of resources to the development of electronic SPC switches. It was in this year that Bell Laboratories announced their forthcoming No. 1 ESS, signalling AT&T's intention to make widespread commercial use of its new electronic switch. In 1963 NTT, in consultation with the heads of NEC, Fujitsu, Hitachi, and Oki, set up the largest co-operative project ever established in its Electrical Communications Laboratories (ECL). Fully one-third of all ECL's researchers were allocated to this project. In 1972, seven years after AT&T's

---

[7] Ibid. 153.

[8] J. Brooks, *Telephone: The First Hundred Years*, Harper & Row, New York, 1975, pp. 278–9. See also Chapuis and Joel, *Electronics*, 153.

[9] I am extremely grateful to Dr K. Hirota, former head of ECL's Musashino Laboratory, who compiled Fig. 3.2 for me showing the history of the development of Japan's major switches.

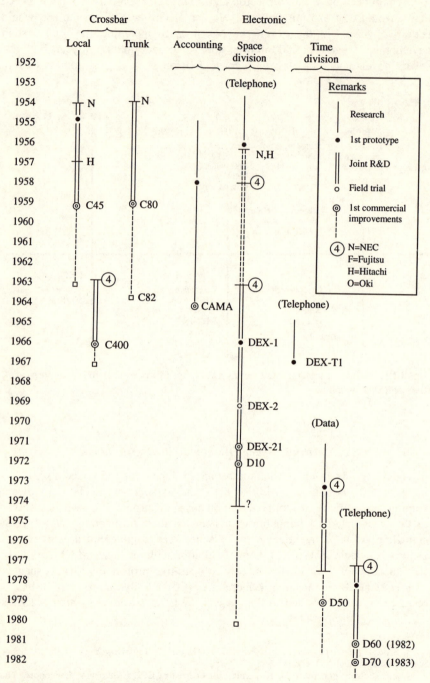

Fig. 3.2 Japan's switching technology, 1952–1982

introduction of its No. 1 ESS, this project resulted in the commercialization of the D10, NTT's equivalent of the No. 1 ESS.

While Britain and France introduced their first SPC space-division switches soon after AT&T, other European countries were slower. For example, in Sweden Ericsson introduced its comparable AKE 12 in 1968, two years before the Japanese D10 first appeared; and in Germany the Siemens EWS 1 first made its appearance in 1973, three years after the D10. Judged against this background, the Japanese lag was not too significant. However, having mastered SPC space-division switching and caught up with the international leaders, the Japanese were soon hit by a new shockwave. As Koji Kobayashi, then President of NEC, recalled, in the mid-1970s 'NEC was selling crossbar switching equipment and space-division electronic switching equipment. . . . In May 1976 I received a shock. Northern Telecom announced the development of a digital switching system at a seminar they were holding at Disney World in Florida.'[10]

The Japanese response to digital switching technology is examined in the following sections.

Digital Switching and New Market Opportunities

Digital Switching Technology

Digital switching involves a combination of two associated technologies: pulse code modulation (PCM) and time-division multiplexing (TDM). Although there were earlier precedents, both technologies were invented in France at the time of the Second World War. However, it took a further twenty years before digital switching was realized practically.

Pulse code modulation was invented in 1938 by the British researcher, Alex A. Reeves, in ITT's Laboratoire Central de Telecommunications (LCT) in France. (In 1925 ITT took over Western Electric's international operations. LCT was established in France in 1927 as a precondition for ITT's sale of automatic switches for the French network. In addition to LCT, ITT also ran a laboratory in Belgium, the Bell Telephone Manufacturing Company, and in the UK, namely STL, which belonged to STC.) There were important precedents for PCM, the earliest of which went back to 1874 when the Frenchman Emile Baudot invented a PCM-like system for the transmission of telegraph signals.

PCM is a method for converting analog speech information into digital signals. It involves sampling the speech signal and quantifying it in the form of binary pulses. As shown in Fig. 3.3, in the early 1960s PCM transmission systems began proliferating. It was the spread of these digital transmission systems that facilitated the subsequent development of digital switching systems.

---

[10] K. Kobayashi, *Rising to the Challenge*, Harcourt, Brace, Jovanovich, Tokyo, 1989.

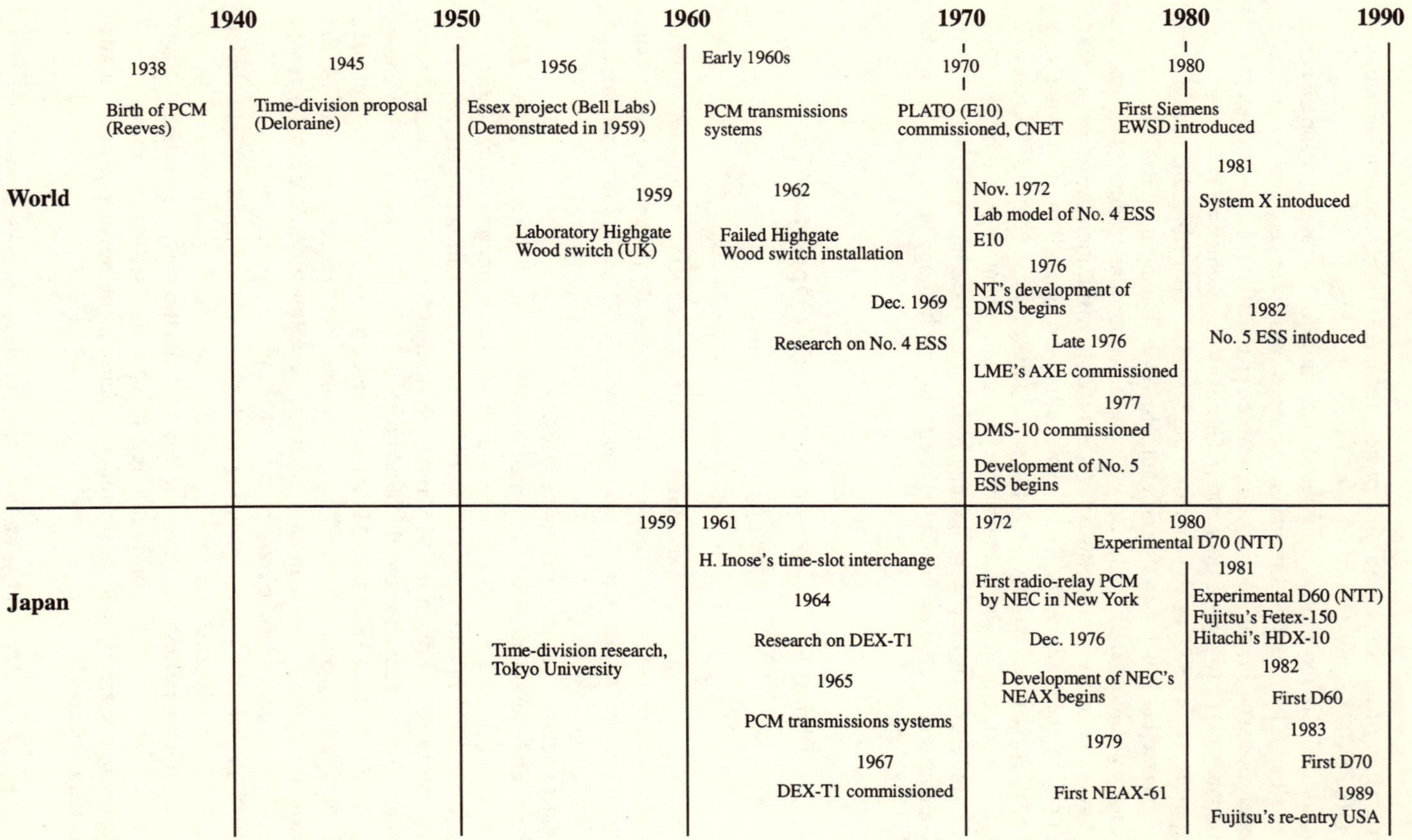

World

- 1938 — Birth of PCM (Reeves)
- 1945 — Time-division proposal (Deloraine)
- 1956 — Essex project (Bell Labs) (Demonstrated in 1959)
- 1959 — Laboratory Highgate Wood switch (UK)
- Early 1960s — PCM transmissions systems
- 1962 — Failed Highgate Wood switch installation
- Dec. 1969 — Research on No. 4 ESS
- 1970 — PLATO (E10) commissioned, CNET
- Nov. 1972 — Lab model of No. 4 ESS, E10
- 1976 — NT's development of DMS begins
- Late 1976 — LME's AXE commissioned
- 1977 — DMS-10 commissioned
- Development of No. 5 ESS begins
- 1980 — First Siemens EWSD introduced
- 1981 — System X introduced
- 1982 — No. 5 ESS intoduced

Japan

- 1959 — Time-division research, Tokyo University
- 1961 — H. Inose's time-slot interchange
- 1964 — Research on DEX-T1
- 1965 — PCM transmissions systems
- 1967 — DEX-T1 commissioned
- 1972 — First radio-relay PCM by NEC in New York
- Dec. 1976 — Development of NEC's NEAX begins
- 1979 — First NEAX-61
- 1980 — Experimental D70 (NTT)
- 1981 — Experimental D60 (NTT), Fujitsu's Fetex-150, Hitachi's HDX-10
- 1982 — First D60
- 1983 — First D70
- 1989 — Fujitsu's re-entry USA

Timeline axis: 1940 — 1950 — 1960 — 1970 — 1980 — 1990

Fig. 3.3 The evolution of digital switching

The idea of time-division multiplexing (TDM) was first put forward by Maurice Deloraine in a US patent application filed in 1945. TDM is a technique in which message channels are interleaved in time for transmission over a common channel. Time-division implies that speech information is sliced into a sequence of time intervals (or 'time slots'). Each time slot corresponds to a sample of the speech information. In most time-division systems these samples have been the subject of a quantization and, in the case of PCM systems, of digital coding of the quantified values.[11] After ITT was formed by Sosthenes Behn and the company took over Western Electric's interests in Europe in 1925, it was Deloraine whom Behn appointed to direct research at the laboratory that was to become the LCT.

There were several reasons for the long time-lag in implementing digital switching technologies. The first was the slow evolution of the complementary technologies that were necessary, not only for digital switching to become technically viable, but also for it to compete economically with space-division switching. For example, pulse modulation required considerable bandwidth, and it was only with the development of ultra-high frequency (UHF) radio transmissions from the 1930s that such bandwidth became available. (The first radio link for digital transmissions in the USA was built by NEC in 1972 linking Brooklyn and North Staten Island.) Furthermore, for digital switching to become both technically and economically feasible, advances were necessary in electronic devices, both logic devices and memories. The second reason for the delay in implementing digital switching was the rapid progress that was being made in space-division switching. This is considered in the following section.[12]

The First Digital Switching Systems

Several important points emerge from a comparison of Figs. 3.1 and 3.3, which trace the evolution of electronic space-division and digital time-division switching, respectively. The first is that the digital switching techniques of pulse code modulation and time-division multiplexing were invented *before* research began in Bell Laboratories on electronic space-division switching. It was the research done at the LCT under Deloraine, which built on his 1945 patent, that first showed how to combine PCM transmission with digital time-division switching. In 1956 the first laboratory model of a digital time-division switch was produced

---

[11] These definitions of PCM and TDM come from Chapuis and Joel, *Electronics*, 22 and 295.

[12] PCM provides another example of experimental applied advances preceding theoretical advances. Chapuis and Joel note that 'it has to be realized that it was practical laboratory work and experimental achievements, far more than theoretical considerations, which motivated the invention of PCM by Reeves [in 1938]' (*Electronics*, 294). It was 'only in mid-1943 . . . that the group of Bell Laboratories engineers learned of Reeves' patent and realized its true value. . . . After discussion in internal memoranda within Bell Laboratories, scientific studies of the theory behind the PCM concept . . . gave rise to a whole welter of publications' (pp. 297–8). These included Claude Shannon's 'A Mathematical Theory of Communication' (July 1948), which gave birth to information theory.

by Bell Laboratories under its ESSEX project (Experimental Solid State Exchange). This switch used solid-state devices.

However, while the ESSEX switch demonstrated the technical feasibility of the time-division concepts, and although this switch stimulated research on digital switching, the concepts themselves 'were far in advance of their time and development of the system was not pursued'.[13] Four years after the start of the ESSEX digital switching project, the first commercial space-division switch was demonstrated: the Bell Laboratories Morris switch, introduced in 1960. This delay in the development of digital switching was due largely to the slow progress being made in developing the necessary electronic components. Furthermore, attention focused on the space-division switches that would cater sooner for the increased demand for switches arising from the greater demand for telephones. Indeed, it was in the area of transmissions that digital technologies first took hold; only some ten years later did digital switching begin to make significant progress. In the early 1960s the T1 digital transmission systems developed by Bell Laboratories, which soon established their economic viability *vis-à-vis* pre-existing systems, began rapidly to diffuse.

CNET's Plato Switch (later E10)

The interdependence of transmissions and switching meant that the spread of digital transmissions systems stimulated the further development of digital time-division switching. In January 1970 the world's first digital switch was put into service in France, the Plato (later versions of which became known as the E10), developed by CNET, the laboratory established in 1944 by the French telecommunications administration.[14]

AT&T's No. 4 ESS

One month earlier, in December 1969, AT&T announced that it would begin work on its digital time-division switch, which in time would become the No. 4 ESS. As Chapuis and Joel indicate, the immediate motivation for this work was the need for a switching system that would more efficiently integrate with the digital transmissions systems that had been widely adopted (the T1 systems).[15] In undertaking this search, four design teams were established in Bell Laboratories to explore the different approaches that were available. Of the four alternatives, one was based on modified space-division switching while another depended on PCM time-division switching.

Chapuis and Joel point to the great uncertainty that at this stage confronted the choice of digital time-division switching: 'At the time, great enthusiasm for a time-division approach [came] only from a small, and generally less vocal, group of engineers.'[16] One of the reasons for their lower profile was the

---

[13] Chapuis and Joel, *Electronics*, 56.   [14] Ibid. 219, 223, 319.
[15] Ibid. 334.   [16] Ibid.

dependence of time-division switching on electronic devices that had not yet been developed to an adequate level. When by December 1969 the studies of the design teams were completed and a choice had to be made regarding the future switching system that would be developed, the digital time-division proposal won, but only by a whisker. Indeed, it was only because of the prior installation of the complementary digital transmissions systems (the T1 systems) that the scales were tipped in favour of the time-division switch:

> By December 1969... the PCM time-division approach was found to be slightly less costly than the competing designs. After many comparative technical and economic studies in which the PCM time-division approach seemed to show a slight projected economic advantage, its choice for development was recommended by W.H.C. Higgins, Bell Labs. Vice-President of switching. *The favorable and rapid growth of T1 carrier [transmissions systems] added to the formal studies and tipped the scales toward the time-division choice.*[17]

In November 1972 the first laboratory model of the No. 4 ESS was completed. In 1976 AT&T announced the world's first stored program control digital time-division switch, the No. 4 ESS, and by the end of this year there were four of these switches in service in the Bell network. Since it was mainly long-distance transmission lines that were digitized, the No. 4 ESS was a long-distance (toll) switch. As will be seen shortly, however, AT&T was far slower to introduce its local digital switch, the No. 5 ESS, a factor that had serious negative competitive consequences for the company. The first laboratory No. 4 ESS appeared only seven years after AT&T's first widely used commercial stored program control space-division switch, the No. 1 ESS (see Fig. 3.1). However, with software comprising a burgeoning proportion of the development cost of the No. 4 ESS, this digital switch cost four times more to develop than the No. 1 ESS.[18] Moreover, just as it took a considerable amount of time for the electronic space-division switch to establish its economic viability over the electromechanical crossbar switch, so the digital time-division switch took significant time to dominate space-division switching.

Northern Telecom and the US Market

Northern Telecom was not one of the first-comers in the digital switching market, although, as Fig. 3.3 shows, it was an early-comer. However, by 1988 Northern Telecom held 42.0 per cent of the North American market (including Canada) for digital switches. This compared with AT&T's 42.6 per cent market share.[19] On the other hand, as will be shown later in this chapter, the Japanese companies NEC and Fujitsu attempted to enter the US digital switch market a few years after Northern Telecom and failed; in 1988 NEC, the Japanese

---

[17] Ibid.
[18] Ibid. 337.
[19] *Northern Business Information*, 1989; *World Switching Market*, 1988.

company with the largest share in the North American market, held only 0.1 per cent of the market. How is Northern Telecom's spectacular success to be explained?

'Interpretive Ambiguity' and Digital Switching, pre-1979

The innovations that drive long-term economic growth are mainly the result of decisions made in companies. These companies include both those that make the initial innovations and those that adopt them. How are these decisions made? How do companies appraise the environments within which they operate, deciding what kinds of innovation will bring them success in these environments and when such innovations should be introduced? These questions are at the heart of the process of technical change and economic growth and are the substance of much of the rest of this chapter.

At the outset, it is necessary to stress that there was a significant degree of uncertainty and therefore 'interpretive ambiguity' regarding the prospects for digital switching. This uncertainty and ambiguity were present from the time that the first inventions were made relating to digital switching and lasted at least until 1979. Thereafter, as will be seen, an international consensus emerged that digital time-division switching had become both technically and economically superior to space-division switching. During this period of interpretive ambiguity, however, several crucial changes occurred in the fortunes of the companies and countries involved, which were to have important implications for the characteristics of the global switching industry and market.

I have already mentioned the ambiguity that surrounded AT&T's decision in 1969 to go ahead with the R&D that would lead to the No. 4 ESS. The situation regarding the perceived prospects for digital switching in the 1970s is summarized by Chapuis and Joel:

In the 1970s, almost all the countries interested in electronic switching for public exchanges hedged their bets, looking closely at both analog space-division and digital time-division switching systems. In those days, digital switching systems were regarded as requiring long-term research of a rather fundamental nature and unlikely to produce any short-term [benefit]. Consequently, they were usually the preserve of research centers. . . . With a few exceptions such as L.M. Ericsson, Bell Northern [i.e. Northern Telecom], some of ITT's European companies and some Japanese companies, virtually all switching manufacturers concentrated solely on developing space-division switching systems.[20]

The uncertainty that existed in the mid-1970s regarding digital switching is underlined by the switch procurement decisions that were made in France in 1976. In this year the French chose two space-division switches under a large international call for tender for an initial supply of one million lines to modernize their network. The switches chosen were ITT's Metaconta and

---

[20] Chapuis and Joel, *Electronics*, 313.

Ericsson's AXE, although the choice was bound up with the politically motivated restructuring of the French telecommunications industry master-minded by the Directorate General of Telecommunications. (NEC under this tender offered its D10 space-division switch in alliance with CIT Alcatel.) Significantly, this decision to procure space-division switches was made at a time (1976) when in France there were more than 100,000 subscriber lines in 68 exchanges using the E10 digital time-division switch (originally developed by CNET as the Plato—see Fig. 3.3). Clearly, at this stage the French did not yet feel that digital switching was economically viable.

Furthermore, in Germany it was only in 1979 that the Deutsche Bundespost decided to renounce space-division switching in favour of digital time-division switching. In view of the uncertainty that still existed in the late 1970s regarding the relative advantages of the two switching systems, Chapuis and Joel refer to the 'great era of hype' that emerged when companies such as Northern Telecom began advertising their new digital switches, and the 'competitively inspired technical inaccuracies' that were created to attempt the 'disparagement of space-division systems by calling them "analog"'.[21] In fact, it was only at the Paris meeting of the International Switching Symposium (ISS) in June 1979— the main forum where the industry's experts met to discuss technical and commercial trends—that 'a world consensus in favour of digital switching was reached'.[22]

The uncertainty that therefore existed at this time regarding the medium-term future of digital switching provides a crucial part of the context within which the corporate decisions that will shortly be analysed were made.

Northern Telecom's Entry into Digital Switching

Northern Telecom was originally established in 1895 as Northern Electric, the manufacturing subsidiary of Bell Canada. In 1906, 44 per cent of Northern Electric was acquired by Western Electric. In 1956, however, when AT&T and its manufacturing subsidiary Western Electric signed a Consent Decree with the US government in order to end the antitrust case against them, Western Electric agreed not to sell equipment outside AT&T. As a result, Western Electric gradually sold its interests in Northern Electric to Bell Canada, ending its stake in Northern Electric in 1962.

The Consent Decree also prevented Western Electric from undertaking joint research with Northern Electric, and in 1972 all technical transfer from Western Electric to the Canadian company ceased. Meanwhile, in order to strengthen their R&D capabilities, in 1971 Bell Canada and Northern Telecom (the renamed Northern Electric) established Bell Northern Research (BNR) as a jointly owned R&D subsidiary. Virtually all of Bell Canada's switching systems were purchased from Northern Telecom. However, as will be seen, the

---

[21] Ibid. 380.   [22] Ibid. 327.

Canadian market remained relatively small, and as the R&D costs involved in the development of digital switches rose, Northern Telecom recognized the crucial need to export switches in order to cover these and other sunk investment costs.[23]

According to the father of modern switching, Amos Joel, Northern Telecom provides 'one of the best examples in switching of being at the right place, at the right time, with the right products'.[24] But why was it Northern Telecom—rather than ITT, or NEC, or Fujitsu—that was in the 'right place, at the right time, with the right products'?

Availability, quality, and cost of components
A key determinant of the timing of the viability of digital switching was the availability, quality, and cost of some of the needed electronic components such as processors, memories, and the so-called BORSCHT circuit, which provided the interface functions required between an analog line and a time-division digital switch. Chapuis and Joel, for example, discuss the difficult techno-economic decisions that faced the designer of digital switches in the period 1965–75, referring to 'the choice of which components would be used in the exchange, a difficult stage [in the design process] as it meant submitting the system to the test of its economic viability. Integrated circuits had only just come onto the market, but at what price!'[25]

A great deal of uncertainty at this stage, therefore, accompanied both the design, and the assumptions regarding the timing of the viability, of digital switches. Under these circumstances, there was a significant degree of interpretive ambiguity regarding the future of digital switching. Different individuals in the same company, as well as in different companies, could and did hold different beliefs regarding the viability of digital switching. Under such conditions, there was no way of judging which of the contradictory beliefs were 'rational' and which were not. To quote the father of modern switching again, the 'early entrants in this [digital switching] market [entered] because they *believed* in the future of digital microelectronics and not because they were expecting an immediate economic advantage in telecommunications'.[26] Conversely, however, as we shall see, some of their competitors, such as the Japanese companies, arrived, on the basis of similar information, at contradictory beliefs.

Construction of favourable beliefs
Northern Telecom is a prime example of a telecommunications company that relatively early on constructed a set of favourable beliefs regarding the impli-

---

[23] This background information on Northern Telecom draws on L. Waverman, 'R&D and Preferred Supplier Relationships: The Growth of Northern Telecom', paper presented to the International Telecommunications Society (ITS) Conference, Venice, 1990, mimeo.
[24] Chapuis and Joel, *Electronics*, 356.
[25] Ibid. 320.
[26] Ibid. 343 (emphasis added).

cations of developments in microelectronics for the viability of digital switching. This is evident from the following quotation from a January 1969 Bell Northern Research Systems Engineering Report:

The feasibility of integrated [i.e. PCM and TDM] switching has been experimented in many countries and the successful results that have been obtained everywhere show, without a shadow of doubt, that such a system is technically viable. [But] digital switching in the present situation can hardly compete with conventional [i.e. space-division] switching systems. In the best cases, the advantages of this change would be too small to justify the effort of the modification. However, the near availability of large scale integrated circuits will change the competitive position in favour of digital switching *within 5 years probably, and definitely not later than 10 years.*

In addition, the development of pulse code modulation [PCM] transmission systems which is now well underway in most industrialized countries will eliminate the need for interface equipment, and therefore will give integrated switching a decisive advantage over conventional systems, both from the economic and technical viewpoints.[27]

However, although these beliefs were evident in Northern Telecom's central research laboratories, Bell Northern Research (BNR), as early as January 1969, it took significantly longer for them to be accepted by the company's senior management. Indeed, it was only by early 1975 that 'a task force with representatives from Northern Telecom, BNR, and Bell Canada was appointed to develop strategies to introduce a complete line of [digital] central office switching systems'.[28] Regarding this timing, it is worth recalling that, as can be seen in Fig. 3.3, in 1972 Alcatel launched its E10 digital switch, the first working digital switch, and Bell Laboratories completed the laboratory prototype of its No. 4 ESS digital switch.

Development and production
In 1976 BNR began development of a small local digital switch, the DMS10. This switch made extensive use of integrated circuits and was one of the first to use microprocessors. However, this advanced use of microelectronics was to produce an economic payoff only a decade later. BNR/Northern Telecom

recognized where the major costs lay in these small digital switching systems. It was in the BORSCHT circuit [which provided the interface function between the analog line, at this time widely used with local switches, and the time-division digital switch]. . . . Northern Telecom's management understood that the technologies that would make these systems economical were in sight for the future but were not available currently. This management was willing to set its sights on this distant target and recognize that the products would not be economically viable in the immediate future. This also meant that the prices for these systems were set with market entry in mind, rather than initial profit. In fact, the DMS10 product line was not considered profitable until 1985.[29]

In October 1977 the DMS10, Northern Telecom's first digital central office

[27] Quoted in Waverman, 'R&D', 13.
[28] Chapuis and Joel, *Electronics*, 349.
[29] Ibid. 350.

switch, was installed in Fort White, Florida. Since this office served Disney World, it gave the company an important publicity opportunity.

Marketing Northern Telecom's DMS10

Even before the first DMS10 was installed, Northern Telecom waged a substantial publicity campaign beginning in 1976 under the banner 'Digital World'. To some of the *cognoscenti* in the industry with a more subtle understanding of the relative technical merits that were being marketed under this banner, the publicity campaign was to a significant extent a matter of 'hype'. According to two industry experts, 'Perhaps overshadowing the actual development of [the DMS10] was the . . . sales sendoff that the entire product line received. . . . it was the beginning of the "hype" which has accompanied time-division digital switching.'[30] However, hype or not, the announcement of Digital World was to have a dramatic impact not only on potential customers, but also on some of Northern Telecom's competitors which were still delaying their introduction of digital switches.

AT&T's Competing No. 5 ESS

By the late 1980s, Northern Telecom's share of the US market for digital lines more or less equalled that of AT&T at about 40 per cent each. However, Northern Telecom's success was due as much to the appropriateness of its own vision regarding the future of digital switching as it was to the 'vision failure' of its main competitor in the US market, AT&T. More specifically, it was AT&T's failure to develop its No. 5 ESS in time that gave Northern Telecom its crucial window of opportunity to enter this market. But why did AT&T fail in this way, particularly since it was the first in the world to develop a stored program control toll (i.e. long-distance) time-division digital switch, the No. 4 ESS?

'Failure' is a word used by Bell Laboratories' Amos Joel, with reference to AT&T's No. 5 ESS. However, Joel argues that this failure was not the result of lack of interest: 'AT&T's failure to bring a local time-division central office system onto the market [in the 1970s] was not from a lack of interest in the problem. In 1969 H. S. McDonald of Bell Laboratories proposed an interesting new architecture for local [switches] using VLSI technology.'[31]

Why then did AT&T fail? Joel identifies several reasons.[32] The first was the

---

[30] Ibid. 349.

[31] Ibid. 379.

[32] Since extensive use has been made of Chapuis and Joel's work in this chapter—the 'bible' for the history of telecommunications switching—it is worth stressing that this is essentially a technical book, written by engineers for engineers. Many issues of interest to an economist or other social scientist concerned with the process of technical change are dealt with as *obiter dicta*, scattered among more technical discussions. The account in the present chapter draws on many of Chapuis and Joel's comments in order to provide my own interpretation of the process of technical and economic change in the global switching industry. Their comments are of particular interest since both authors were active participants in creating the new switching technologies, and since Joel's statements represent

difficulty of establishing the economic superiority of a proposed new digital local switch over the already-installed space-division systems. As we saw, this was a problem that also confronted the decision to begin developing the No. 4 ESS. However, the latter was a toll switch, and most of the lines connecting with such switches were already digitized, thus reducing the costs of interfacing with a digital switch. In the case of local switches, on the other hand, such as the DMS 10 and the future No. 5 ESS, digital lines constituted less than 20 per cent of terminations. 'Internal records at Bell Laboratories show that many studies were made in an attempt to capitalize on the No. 4 ESS design as well as other proposals to find a design that would compete economically with the highly successful No. 1 and 1A ESS space-division systems then being produced in a large quantity.' However, Joel the engineer, having been confronted frequently with the task of having to justify proposed projects *ex ante* in terms of expected economic return, goes on to note (rather ruefully) that, 'It is often difficult to show new designs to be more economical than proven existing designs that have been refined and produced over a period of time.'[33]

The second reason, however, followed from the nature of AT&T's 'selection environment' at the time: 'Under the monopoly situation that then existed in the Bell System market, there was no need to rush an uneconomical design into production to assure continuing prestige in the industry.' However, just as technologies are subjected to unexpected changes, so are selection environments. Joel continues: 'Unfortunately, the events of the early 1980s [i.e. the divestiture of AT&T] made a complete change necessary from this perspective.'[34] Even before the installation of Northern Telecom's first DMS10 in October 1977, the company began to attack the US market. Its first target was the independent service providers outside the Bell System. Unconnected to AT&T and Western Electric, the independents were sometimes fertile ground for new innovations and some of them had begun buying digital switches. Although Northern Telecom was early into this market, it was not the first. Indeed, Stromberg-Carlson, a small equipment maker which had long sold to the independents, had its local digital switch in service in this market before Northern Telecom.[35] Nevertheless, the 'digital hype' already referred to, together with the purchases of digital switches beginning to be made by the independents, had significant consequences for the Bell System's interest in these switches. 'Regulators [began] asking why independent telephone companies, but not the BOCs [Bell operating companies], were buying time-division digital systems.'[36] This helped to stimulate demand from the BOCs for digital switches, which aided Northern Telecom's efforts.

a perspective from within the context of Bell Laboratories and AT&T. It must be noted, however, that it is not necessarily the case that these authors would accept the present interpretations.

[33] Chapuis and Joel, *Electronics*, 379.
[34] Ibid. 379–80.
[35] Ibid. 350.
[36] Ibid. 351.

Under the growing pressure for a local digital switch, and lacking its own product, AT&T eventually agreed to co-operate with Northern Telecom in modifying the DMS10 so that it fitted in with the BOCs' requirements. The historical connection that had existed between AT&T and Western Electric on the one hand and Bell Canada and Northern Electric on the other no doubt facilitated this agreement. (An interesting counterfactual question to ask is whether a company that lacked these historical ties but had a suitable local digital switch—such as Ericsson or Alcatel—could have been given the same assistance from AT&T.) AT&T evaluated the DMS10 and requested design changes to adapt it to the Bell network. Northern Telecom complied with the requests, and at the beginning of 1980 AT&T recommended to the BOCs that they purchase the new version of the DMS10. By 1983 the BOCs had purchased more than 100 DMS10s. This constituted about 15 per cent of Northern Telecom's total sales of the DMS10, helping the company to achieve a more efficient scale of production than could have been achieved on the basis of the Canadian market alone.

It must be stressed, however, that it was not simply luck that aided Northern Telecom's entry into the BOC market. Northern Telecom had to commit itself to a substantial investment so as to modify its switch (most of the cost going to software re-engineering). It has been estimated that the redevelopment costs necessary to enter the US market were as much as $100 million per year. While Northern Telecom made this commitment, other large companies such as ITT and Fujitsu (the latter until around 1983) did not. (Subsequently, Bell Communications Research (Bellcore)—the post-divestiture R&D subsidiary of the former BOCs which was hived off from Bell Laboratories—has come to provide support for the modification of equipment. It does this by publishing the technical requirements that must be met by switching companies wishing to supply the seven former BOCs. Since the 1980s, this has aided other companies such as NEC, Fujitsu, and Siemens to make a bid for this market.) After the DMS10, Northern Telecom went on to develop a family of switches which included the DMS200 transit switch and the DMS100 large local switch for use in large metropolitan areas. In 1982 and 1983, that is before its divestiture, AT&T authorized the use of these two switches by the BOCs. In making this authorization, AT&T was in part responding to regulatory pressure to open the market for telecommunications equipment in the run-up to divestiture.

In early 1977 Bell Laboratories had began to work on what was to become the No. 5 ESS local digital switch. In 1979 AT&T authorized funding for the development of the switch. In March 1982 the first No. 5 ESS was installed. Although AT&T was relatively slow to produce this switch—by 1982 Alcatel's E10 had already been on sale around the world for twelve years!—its response was influenced by the early development of digital switches by the independent manufacturers of digital switches such as Alcatel, Northern Telecom, Ericsson, and Stromberg-Carlson. According to Chapuis and Joel, 'Had it not been for the foresight and pressure brought about by the presence and apparent success of independent manufacturers in this field, AT&T might not have entered into the post-divestiture era, starting in 1984, with a competitive product well underway.'[37] Nevertheless, AT&T's failure with the No. 5 ESS cost the company dear. Although the DMS10 became profitable only in 1985, it was shortly thereafter, as already noted, that Northern Telecom gained approximately the same share of the North American digital switching market as AT&T. Not until 1986 did the number of No. 5 ESS lines exceed that of DMS10 lines.

Japanese Companies in the US Market

Japan's Entry into Digital Switching[38]

As can be seen from Figs. 3.2 and 3.3, NTT began joint research on its first digital time-division switch, the DEX-T1, in 1964. (The T1 in the name of this experimental switch referred to the PCM transmissions systems, originated in Bell Laboratories, which Japan had adopted.) Although Bell Laboratories had begun research on its ESSEX digital switching project in 1955 and had demonstrated a prototype in 1959, NTT's DEX-T1 project was relatively early in international terms. Indeed, it was in December 1969, some five years after the DEX-T1 project began, that Bell Laboratories started its R&D on what would become the No. 4 ESS.

The DEX-T1 project was 'applied-fundamental' research in so far as it involved an experimental implementation of the digital switching principles of pulse code modulation and time-division multiplexing. However, in the early 1960s important fundamental research on time-division switching was being carried out in Japan. A notable example is the research by Professor Hiroshi Inose of the University of Tokyo.

Between 1945, when Deloraine put forward his time-division proposal (discussed above), and the late 1950s, by which time Bell Laboratories' early research on PCM digital multiplexing had been completed, the outlines of digital time-division switching were beginning to form. However, some of the key concepts relating to the working of a time-division switching system were still unclear. As Chapuis and Joel put it, even after publication of the results of the ESSEX project, 'switching engineers were left somewhat in the air as to the workings of the exchange's switching network at which the PCM multiplexes terminated'.[39] It was the attempt to clarify these workings that led, in these authors' words, to 'the birth of the first offspring of digital switching' concepts.

---

[37] Ibid. 381.

[38] The following sections on the evolution of digital switching in Japan depend largely on numerous detailed personal interviews with the country's leading personalities in the field of switching from NTT, NEC, Fujitsu, Hitachi, Oki, and Tokyo University. I am extremely grateful to these individuals for all the time and information that they gave me, though they are not responsible for the contents or interpretation of these sections.

[39] Chapuis and Joel, *Electronics*, 310.

Inose is one of the two sets of researchers to whom 'the honour of having delivered [these "offspring" concepts] must go' as a result of his concept of 'time slot interchange'. This concept was the subject of a famous patent taken out by Bell Laboratories in the names of Inose and J. P. Runyon (since Inose did some of his research at the time in Bell Laboratories, where he was on leave from Tokyo University). It was to have an important impact on the conceptualization of time-division digital switching.[40]

As can be seen from Fig. 3.2, the DEX-T1 project was started about a year after NTT began co-operative research and development of the space-division DEX-1, which led ultimately to the commercial D10 space-division switch. The aim of the DEX-T1 was to test the feeling of NTT's Electrical Communications Laboratories' (ECL) switching leaders that the time was not yet ripe for the commercial implementation of digital switching.

The DEX-T1 project involved co-operation between ECL and NEC. The leader of the project in NEC was Mr Toshiro Kunihiro, whose counterpart in ECL was K. Hanawa. Kunihiro's background is of particular interest since it shows the close interconnections that were beginning to emerge between switching and computing at this time. More specifically, for companies like NEC, Fujitsu, and Hitachi, it was the competences that they had already accumulated through their involvements in communications activities such as transmission carrier systems and electromechanical switching that facilitated their entry into the emerging computer and semiconductor technologies of the late 1940s and 1950s.

Kunihiro joined NEC in 1952. His university research interest was in electronic switching, but in Japanese companies at this time such switching was only of academic interest. For his first few years in NEC he worked on quality control for a mechanical switch of old design. Thereafter, he moved on to work on the development of the new crossbar switch that NEC was developing jointly with NTT (see Fig. 3.2). This experience, together with his earlier interest in electronic switching, led him on to an interest in computers. In the late 1950s he went to the University of Illinois, one of the few US universities which at that stage accepted foreign students to study computing. There he joined several other Japanese who would go on to play an important role in the Japanese computer industry, such as Professors Aiso and Moto-oka. After returning from the USA, Kunihiro did R&D work in NEC on time-division switching—as noted in Fig. 3.3, from 1955 the computer-originated concept of stored program control was being applied to electronic switching. When the DEX-T1 project with NTT began, Kunihiro was put in charge on NEC's side.[41]

The DEX-T1 prototype was completed in 1967. It showed that, although time-division switching was technically feasible, largely as a result of the costs of the electronics involved, such switches could not compete economically with the

---

[40] Author's interview with Professor Hiroshi Inose. It was in 1957 that Professor Inose went to Bell Laboratories.
[41] Author's interview with Mr Toshiro Kunihiro.

space-division switches that were currently being developed. Accordingly, in 1967 the time-division research of NTT was halted and attention was focused fully on space-division switching. This was in line with what was happening both in the USA and Europe, as noted earlier in this chapter. A similar decision was made in connection with a parallel project that NTT undertook with Fujitsu. This project, using serial PCM technology, resulted in the KOH 40A exper-imental digital switch.

Although these projects on digital time-division were temporarily suspended, having served the immediate purpose of establishing the technical but not the economic feasibility of digital switching, they were to have significant, although at the time unforeseen, consequences for NEC and Fujitsu. As will be seen shortly, when about a decade later these companies were both thrown at unexpected speed into the digital era, they were able to draw on the valuable competences that they had already begun to accumulate in digital switching through the DEX-T1 and KOH 40A projects.

NEC's Entry into Digital Switching

As can be seen from Fig. 3.3, it was in 1972 that Alcatel launched its commer-cial E10 digital switch, and in the same year the first laboratory version of Bell Laboratories' No. 4 ESS was completed. In early 1975, BNR, Northern Telecom, and Bell Canada formed their working group charged with developing digital switching systems.

Later in 1975, as part of its evolving strategy in the field of digital communi-cations, the President of Northern Telecom, Robert C. Scrivener, approached Dr Koji Kobayashi—then President of NEC—to propose a strategic alliance in this field. Northern Telecom had already taken the strategic decision to make a decisive entry into digital switching. And NEC—as noted in Chapter 6 below— had already established internationally competitive competences in the area of digital transmissions. (Indeed, it was NEC that built the first radio link for digital transmissions in the USA in 1972.)

In an interview, Dr Kobayashi provided a personal account of the proposal: 'Scrivener said he accepted that NEC was the strongest in the world in digital transmission. So he proposed, "Why don't we exchange technology—digital switching from Northern Telecom to NEC; and digital transmission from NEC to Northern Telecom?" '[42] Kobayashi turned down Scrivener's proposal. The reasoning behind his rejection is important, primarily because it provides a clear account of Kobayashi's concept of NEC as a corporation and of the competences it would need in order to grow in the future. This concept will be starkly contrasted later with that of ITT's Harold Geneen; ITT, as will be seen,

---

[42] This account of NEC's response to the digital age in switching is based on the author's sev-eral detailed interviews with Dr Koji Kobayashi and on a number of interviews with Mr Toshiro Kunihiro. It also draws on numerous interviews with NTT's leaders in switching at the time. The quotations in the following paragraphs come from interviews with Dr Kobayashi.

was the most dramatic drop-out of the switching industry in the postwar period. Kobayashi's reasoning also provides the prelude to NEC's entry into digital switching.

This reasoning was based on Kobayashi's vision of the convergence of computer and communication technologies. From the 1950s, this convergence had increased with the emergence of common solid-state electronics technologies and with the application of stored program control to switching. However, from the 1970s, convergence was significantly boosted by the diffusion of digital switching which created a common digital 'currency' for both computing and communications. In Kobayashi's view, in order for NEC to take advantage of convergence, it was necessary for the company to develop its competences in both computing and digital switching. NEC's competitive advantage in the future, he thought, would come from the *fusion* of computer and communications technologies, rather than from their separate development. Accordingly, NEC should not follow companies like IBM or Northern Telecom, which were involved in only one of these areas (IBM in computers and Northern Telecom in communications).

In Kobayashi's words,

Almost ten years before [I saw Scrivener], I had decided that I would not follow IBM's way in computers. Impossible. IBM was only involved in computers while we were involved in computers and communications. Other companies like Fujitsu and Hitachi were imitating IBM [and producing IBM-compatible computers, without stressing the link with communications]. But since our main business was communications, it was impossible for me to follow IBM.

According to Kobayashi,

When Scrivener came to see me, I had the idea of convergence in my mind. But I did not yet have the concrete concept of C&C [the vision of the convergence of computers and communications, which Kobayashi first proposed publically in 1977]. At that time I was not very confident about the future for digital switching. But I had already decided that there was a fundamental difference between Northern Telecom and NEC. Northern Telecom was not in the computer business. We were already deeply committed to computers. Computers and digital switches converge. Therefore the requirements of each company, and some of the markets of each company, were quite different.

If NEC had agreed to Scrivener's proposal, it would have come to depend on Northern Telecom for digital switching technology. NEC would therefore have become a 'hostage', constrained by the directions in which Northern Telecom was developing digital switching technology. 'It was very risky to depend on Northern Telecom. We needed to develop digital switching technologies that would suit both our communications and our computing needs. I did not know in what direction Northern Telecom was intending to go. I knew roughly the direction of NEC. So I told Scrivener that we would develop our own digital switching that would suit us. I think Scrivener understood because he is a businessman.'

However, despite his earlier interaction with Scrivener, Kobayashi was nevertheless 'shocked' when in May 1976 Northern Telecom announced its Digital World concept at Florida's Disney Land, thus launching the 'digital hype' discussed earlier.[43] As he later recalled, 'Although I should have foreseen what was coming, when the announcement broke I couldn't help feeling that Northern Telecom had stolen a march on us.'[44]

But why was Northern Telecom able to 'steal a march' on NEC? This question is all the more intriguing since, as we have seen, NEC began research on digital switching with its work on the DEX-T1 in 1964, significantly earlier than Northern Telecom's first research in this area. There are several answers to this question. The first followed from the influence that NTT had on NEC's communications strategies since it was the latter's largest customer. In Kobayashi's words, 'Because NTT was our biggest customer, we could not make the decision ourselves regarding entry into digital switching. We had to follow the policy of NTT. At this stage NTT had not yet decided to begin R&D on digital switching.'[45] (NTT's delay in opting for digital switching will be analysed below.)

However, this was not the only reason, and as will shortly be seen, NEC was not simply passively following NTT. A further reason was that NEC's earlier experience with the DEX-T1 had taught the company's switching engineers that the cost of the electronics involved in time-division switching made these switches economically uncompetitive relative to space-division switching. A more specific reason was that the BORSCHT circuit, which at the time provided the interface functions between the analog line and the time-division switch, was particularly expensive. This was the case with the *codec* which formed a part of the BORSCHT circuit (the coding/decoding device which converted analog speech to digital samples for a specific time-channel and back again to analog signals).

In the opinion of NEC's switching engineers, therefore, these costs rendered digital switching unviable at this juncture. In other words, in the situation of interpretive ambiguity that existed at this time regarding the implications of eletronics technology for digital switching, NEC's engineers took a decidedly bearish view. Certainly, their expectations regarding the future progress of electronics in this area were significantly more pessimistic than those of Northern Telecom's colleagues in BNR quoted earlier.

In the mid-1970s, however, NEC's leader in switching R&D, Toshiro Kunihiro, read a paper about the development of a single semiconductor codec chip which had the potential to lower the cost of the BORSCHT circuit significantly. 'This was like a bolt out of the blue for me', he recalled in an interview, 'and it quickly changed my mind about the viability of digital switching.'[46]

---

[43] According to Kobayashi, in May 1976 'an event occurred that came as a real shock to me' (K. Kobayashi, *The Rise of NEC*, Basil Blackwell, Oxford, 1991, p. 119).

[44] Ibid. 120.

[45] Author's interview with Dr Kobayashi.

[46] Author's interview with Mr Kunihiro.

While this helped to increase the economic viability of digital switching, NEC had other reasons for wanting to respond favourably to the new window of competitive opportunity that was opening with the increased economic viability of digital switching. While NEC had successfully mastered crossbar technology and had even established an international competitiveness in this area, it had been making less progress in space-division switching. Although the company had jointly developed the D10 space-division switch with NTT and its other suppliers and was doing good business selling this switch to NTT, it was facing strong competition in this field in export markets. As Koji Kobayashi, President of NEC at the time, recalled:

In 1962 NEC had built one of the world's leading crossbar switching equipment plants at Sagamihara, second only to Western Electric's Hawthorne Works. In view of this plant's supply capacity we realized that if our business was to grow in the future we would need to seek markets abroad. The plan to rely on exports to expand our switching business resulted in a huge success in the US for our crossbar switching equipment. But we were unable to achieve the same rate of success with the space-division electronic switching system that we developed next [based on the D10] because of strong competition from Western Electric's No. 1 ESS in the US and from ITT's Metaconta 10C and Ericsson's AXE systems elsewhere in the world. In this respect we were perhaps fortunate that the era of space-division switching systems was unexpectedly brief.[47]

As Toshiro Kunihiro noted, digital switching presented NEC with the opportunity to catch up rapidly with the world's leading switch companies: 'Even the traditional suppliers like Ericsson, AT&T and Siemens were like newcomers in this field. This presented a very rare opportunity for NEC.'[48] Furthermore, in view of the 'digital switching hype' that Northern Telecom had helped to inject into the US switching market—particularly as noted earlier among the carriers that were independent of the Bell system—NEC America was beginning to receive strong market signals for a digital switch.

Nevertheless, Kobayashi at first resisted the pressure that was being put on NEC headquarters to begin development of a digital switch: 'Although our US sales office, NEC America, suggested that it would be wise for NEC to start selling digital equipment soon, I resisted their advice, believing that such a move would be premature in view of the situation in Japan, where NTT was sticking with space-division switching.'[49] However, the pressure soon became too strong to resist: in the USA before too long, 'No one was interested in buying unless we had digital switching. When the request came again from NEC America that we immediately develop a digital system, we had no alternative but to swim with the tide.'[50]

Having finally decided to commit itself to digital switching, NEC wasted no opportunity to move ahead rapidly. In December 1976, only four months after Northern Telecom announced its Digital World concept from Disney Land, NEC

[47] Kobayashi, *The Rise of NEC*, 121.   [48] Author's interview with Mr Kunihiro.
[49] Kobayashi, *The Rise of NEC*, 120.   [50] Ibid. 121.

began developing its digital switch for the US and international markets. In time this switch would become the NEAX-61.

With digital switching now a top priority for NEC, Toshiro Kunihiro was given the resources that he and his team needed. Furthermore, they were able to draw on the stock of knowledge the company had already accumulated in digital switching through the earlier experience in developing the DEX-T1. In addition, the team was able to utilize NEC's competences in semiconductors, an area in which the company was making substantial investments in the latter 1970s. Two and a half years later, in May 1979, NEC's first NEAX-61 was installed in the USA, sold to Continental, one of the independents.

How competitive was the NEAX-61? To answer this question we can do no better than turn to the views of a fair-minded competitor, John Meurling of Ericsson (one of the designers of Ericsson's AXE switch). Regarding the NEAX-61, Meurling concluded that 'In all fairness, one has to concede that NEC has done a good job. The system was first presented in 1977. By 1979, a multi-processor configuration was on offer. . . . NEC . . . has certainly found a position among the three current leaders in switching.'[51]

NTT's (Relatively Late) Commitment to Digital Switching

NEC's first NEAX-61 was installed in the USA in May 1979. (Northern Telecom's first DMS10 was installed one and a half years earlier, in October 1977.) In competitive terms, this was a significant delay.

We have seen that a major reason for NEC's hesitation in making the commitment to digital switching was NTT's delay in moving to this technology. Indeed, in view of the pressure coming from NEC America, NEC began developing its NEAX-61 digital switch a full year before NTT began joint development of its equivalent digital switches. This had extremely important consequences for NEC. It meant that for the first time NEC would have to enter the world market for a switch *before* having had the opportunity first to test, debug, and improve the switch through learning in the Japanese market. Furthermore, it meant that NEC would have to carry the costs of developing and maintaining two quite different switching systems, one for the international market and one for the Japanese market. In all other cases—such as cars, consumer electronics, machine tools, and cameras—successful Japanese exporters had first made use of the domestic market as a 'learning springboard' to facilitate their entry into Western export markets. In the case of digital switching, NEC, Fujitsu, Hitachi, and Oki were denied this opportunity.

This, however, raises a crucial question regarding the effectiveness of the Japanese innovation system in telecommunications: Why was NTT relatively slow to move to digital switching? Through intensive interviewing of the key

---

[51] J. Meurling, *A Switch in Time*, Telephony Publishing Co., Chicago, 1985, p. 168.

decision-makers in NTT, NEC, Fujitsu, and Hitachi, the following explanation can be pieced together.

A preliminary point, however, must be made. NTT's 'relative lateness' must be put into perspective. It was in December 1977 that NTT finally began joint development of its digital D60 and D70 switches. While this was a year after the beginning of NEC's development of the NEAX-61, and while Alcatel's E10 and the first laboratory model of AT&T's No. 4 ESS appeared in 1972, other crucial decisions to commit to digital switching technology were made at about the same time as NTT's. For example, as discussed earlier, AT&T's decision to develop its local No. 5 ESS digital switch was also made in 1977. Furthermore, it was only around 1978–9 that the Deutsche Bundespost made its decision to 'go digital'. So, although NTT's decision came relatively late, it was not that late compared with other major decisions. Having said this, however, the fact remains that NTT was *relatively* late, with important consequences for the international competitiveness of the Japanese telecommunications equipment suppliers. This relative lateness therefore requires explanation.

There were several factors. The first was that, in the climate of interpretive ambiguity that existed regarding the future implications of electronic developments for digital switching, NTT's engineers remained fairly pessimistic compared with their counterparts in companies such as Alcatel, Northern Telecom, and AT&T (at least as far as the No. 4 ESS was concerned). There were a number of reasons for their pessimism. NTT's transmission engineers were pessimistic about the rate at which digital transmission systems would be installed. To the extent that lines remained analog, however, and the electronics remained underdeveloped and expensive, the interfacing electronic circuits would remain prohibitively costly. NTT's switching engineers, on the other hand, were largely preoccupied with driving down the costs of their space-division switch, the D10, which, it must be remembered, was commercialized only in 1972. (It is important to understand that a significant proportion of the benefit derived from a new switch comes from the learning and incremental improvements that occur *after* the switch is first commercialized. In the view of NTT's engineers, the doubtful benefits of digital switching at this stage were more than outweighed by the benefits that could be had by improving the D10.)

Furthermore, interpretive ambiguity implied that it was possible to interpret the information available so as to support different, contradictory, conclusions. While Northern Telecom's interpretation was bullish regarding the medium-term future for digital switching, NTT's was bearish. And there was no shortage of information to 'support' NTT's pessimistic interpretation, even though at the same time Northern Telecom could draw on information regarding the progress being made in electronics (relating to integrated circuits and microprocessors) to 'support' their more optimistic position. This is exactly what interpretive ambiguity is!

For example, a leading NTT switching engineer went with NEC engineers to France in 1975 to support the latter's application under France's invitation to tender for a large number of switching systems (as discussed earlier). In the event, the French opted for space-division, rather than digital time-division, switches, even though the French digital E10 had already been commissioned and a significant number were in operation in France at the time. The NTT engineer examined some of these digital systems and this confirmed his views, and those of his colleagues in NTT, that digital switching was not yet economically competitive with space-division switching. Their belief was that progress in the electronics would be made slowly and that therefore the decision to 'go digital' could be delayed.[52]

Even when Northern Telecom announced its Digital World concept, the NTT engineers remained unconvinced. In an interview, one of NTT's leading switching engineers explained:

When Northern Telecom announced their first digital switching system, they explained that its chief advantage was that it had digital program control and that this would allow the network to make the transition from analog to digital. However, this change in itself is irrelevant from the customer's point of view. The customer doesn't know whether signals are being transmitted and switched in analog or digital form, and what is more doesn't care. The customer is only concerned with the quality and cost of the service. We knew that at this stage digital systems did not offer better quality and/or cost. Indeed, in view of the state of development of the electronics technology, digital technology would if anything be more costly than space-division technology![53]

These beliefs of one of NTT's leading switching engineers are corroborated by Amos Joel. As noted earlier, Joel also expressed the view that for a few years following 1976 Northern Telecom benefited from the 'digital hype' which, while it favoured digital switching systems, did not correspond to additional technical or economic benefits relative to the alternative space-division technology. The NTT engineer later admitted in an interview with the author that 'In retrospect, my mistake was that I underestimated the downsizing and the improvement in cost that would be brought about by LSI technology. What I should have done was to begin earlier with developing a digital switch for telephony. Instead I started with a digital data switch [which became the D50].'[54] However, incorrect though his earlier beliefs turned out to be, under the circumstances of interpretive ambiguity that existed at the time, they were not then unreasonable.

The Failure of Japanese Companies in the USA

The first NEAX-61 was put into service in California in 1979. Fujitsu was slower than NEC to develop its first digital switch, the FETEX-150. However, Fujitsu too, responding to the same market forces in the USA as NEC, decided to develop a digital switch for the international market independently of NTT. Fujitsu's development of what would become the FETEX-150 was started about

---

[52] Author's interview with leading NTT switching engineer.
[53] Ibid.
[54] Ibid.

a year after NEC began on the NEAX-61 and at about the same time that NTT started its joint development of the D70. The first FETEX-150 was installed in 1981 in Singapore. Hitachi's first digital switch, the HDX-10, was first put into service in Sri Lanka also in 1981. Oki, the fourth equipment supplier to NTT, developed its KB270.

In the USA, however, the Japanese companies had limited success. To begin with, it was only NEC and Fujitsu that made serious efforts in this market (Hitachi and Oki restricting their attention to developing countries). After 1979 NEC continued to supply small numbers of its NEAX-61, mainly to the independent carriers. Fujitsu, however, made the decision to abort the US market shortly before its first digital switches were to be installed there in March 1982.[55] It was only in 1989 that Fujitsu decided to re-enter the US market[56] (although as will later be seen, Fujitsu has since made a significant commitment to this market, becoming the first company to offer a commercial next-generation ATM switch in the USA). By the late 1980s, as noted earlier, NEC held only a meagre 0.1 per cent of the US digital switch market.

Why did the Japanese companies fail in the US market? One factor that undoubtedly played a role was the knock-on effect for the Japanese companies of NTT's relatively late entry into digital switching. As was seen from Dr Kobayashi's statements, this helped to delay NEC's entry, since NTT was by far NEC's biggest customer for switches. If NEC and Fujitsu had had competitive digital switches available in the US market at the same time as Northern Telecom, they would undoubtedly have been in a much better position.

However, some important qualifications are necessary to these conclusions. First, there was nothing inevitable about NEC's and Fujitsu's decisions to follow NTT in making a relatively late entry into digital switching. Indeed, as was seen, both companies, under the influence of market pressure from the independents in the USA, ultimately decided to 'go it alone' and develop their international switches independently of NTT's joint development of digital switching. They could have made this decision earlier.

Secondly, even if the two Japanese companies had had competitive digital switches available in the US market at the same time as, or even somewhat before, Northern Telecom, it is not clear that they would have been able to break into this market the way Northern Telecom eventually did. We saw earlier that AT&T, partly under pressure from its regulators, played an important role in assisting Northern Telecom to modify its DMS10 so as to suit the requirements of the Bell operating companies. It is possible that AT&T's and Western Electric's historical ties with Bell Canada and Northern Telecom (then Northern Electric) facilitated this assistance, even though formal ties had been severed by the time AT&T's help was given. It is worth recalling in this connection that Stromberg-Carlson (a small switch company producing mainly for the independents, later taken over by Plessey) was selling its digital switch in the

[55] Chapuis and Joel, *Electronics*, 346.   [56] Ibid. 347.

US market before Northern Telecom, but failed to make the same degree of progress. It is perhaps relevant that in the late 1980s all four of the top digital switch suppliers in the US market were North American-based: AT&T with 42.6 per cent of the market, Northern Telecom with 42.0 per cent, GTE (another supplier to the independents) with 10.4 per cent, and Stromberg-Carlson with 2.9 per cent. The fifth supplier was the French company Alcatel, with 1.2 per cent; NEC came sixth with its 0.1 per cent. It is by no means obvious, therefore, that the Japanese companies would have succeeded at this stage even if they had had competitive digital switches.

Finally, it must be noted that NEC and Fujitsu faced difficulties in providing adequate software support to the users of their digital switches in the USA. Toshiro Kunihiro of NEC was quoted as saying that 'The telephone companies [in the USA] are worried about our ability to support them. The problem does not lie in our software design capability, but in really understanding what our customers [in the USA] need. That is the single biggest challenge our company faces.'[57] (It was seen that AT&T was a crucial source of information for Northern Telecom regarding the needs of the Bell operating companies, enabling the necessary changes to be made to the DMS10.) The problem of software support was one that NEC and Fujitsu would have faced even if NTT had not been relatively late to enter digital switching.

For all these reasons, it may be concluded that the causes of the failure of the Japanese companies in the US market are complex, making it difficult to apportion 'blame' in a straightforward way. The progress that the Japanese companies have made in the USA since the latter 1980s is examined later.

The Differing Beliefs of Northern Telecom and the Japanese Companies

The notion of interpretive ambiguity, as used in this book, refers to that situation where the relevant set of information is capable of supporting different, possibly contradictory, beliefs. The problem arises from the incompleteness of the set of information and the consequent ambiguity that arises in the process of constructing beliefs based on this information. The problem does not follow from the *quantity* of information relative to the ability of individuals and organizations of individuals to process this information, as is the case in the concept of 'bounded rationality'.[58]

In the present case, the set included information on the concepts involved in digital switching and on the state of the technologies that at the time were believed to be necessary to implement these concepts in the form of working digital switches. The set of information was most obviously incomplete in so far

---

[57] Interview with Guy de Jonquieres, *Financial Times*, 5 December 1990.
[58] See the companion volume to this one, M. Fransman, *Visions of the Firm and Japan*, Oxford University Press (forthcoming), for a detailed discussion of interpretive ambiguity, bounded rationality, and related issues.

as it provided little guidance regarding the improvements that would be made in the future to these technologies and the timing of these improvements. Under these circumstances, as has been seen, Northern Telecom's engineers and the Japanese engineers constructed contradictory beliefs regarding the anticipated rate and timing of technical improvements. As a result, their expectations regarding the timing of the viability of digital switching differed.

Can anything be said regarding why they constructed the beliefs that they did? The general answer is that, under conditions of interpretive ambiguity, beliefs are not formed in a deterministic manner. Accordingly, it is always possible for different beliefs to be constructed. Having accepted that there is no determinism operating in the construction of beliefs, however, it is worth noting that Northern Telecom's engineers and the Japanese engineers formed their beliefs under different 'background circumstances'. While these background circumstances did not determine their beliefs, they influenced their content.

What were these background circumstances? In Northern Telecom's case the following were important. First, Northern Telecom had not been particularly successful with its space-division switch, the SP-1. This meant that the company did not have a very strong vested interest in pre-digital switching technology. Secondly, Northern Telecom realized early on (see above) that the limited size of the Canadian market for switches made it necessary to find export markets. With the rising R&D and investment costs of developing next-generation switches, the importance of exports became greater. Taken together, these two background circumstances posed an acute dilemma for Northern Telecom: how would the company be able to penetrate export markets where hitherto it had no presence? The proposed solution to this dilemma was to use the opportunity created by the emerging viability of digital switching technology to launch a daring assault on the US market (and to accept a chance of failure). Under these background circumstances, Northern Telecom went on to construct largely positive views regarding the medium-term viability of digital switching.

The Japanese decision-makers, on the other hand, constructed their beliefs regarding the future of digital switching within a quite different set of circumstances. To begin with, they had only several years before completed their space-division D10 and were beginning to 'travel down the learning curve' of incremental improvements. Furthermore, the D10 offered all the services that were required at the time and, moreover, in a cost-effective way. While exports had long been important for the Japanese switch manufacturers (partly a consequence of the four suppliers having to share the NTT market), their sales to the rapidly growing Japanese market were far more important. Although, as was seen, ultimately it was the demands for digital switching from the export market that forced NEC and Fujitsu to 'go digital', in the interim there was less pressure on them to move in this direction. Accordingly, until about mid-1976 the Japanese view was that they could safely remain with space-division technology for a while longer.

These differing sets of background circumstances influenced, but did not determine, the respective beliefs that were constructed, Northern Telecom taking a more optimistic view and the Japanese a more pessimistic view regarding the medium-term future for digital switching. Different beliefs could have been formed, but the Japanese decision-makers interviewed, with the benefit of hindsight, were unanimous in their view that they should have moved more quickly into digital switching.

The Digitization of the Japanese Network

Controlled Competition and the Development of the D70 and D60

From the time of the International Switching Symposium (ISS) held in Kyoto in October 1976, attitudes in NTT began to change regarding the timing of the introduction of digital switching. Part of the reason was the attention devoted at this meeting to AT&T's No. 4 ESS, which led NTT's leading switching engineers to realize that digital switching would soon have to be taken very seriously. A little over a year later, in December 1977, NTT began joint R&D on two digital switches with its suppliers, NEC, Fujitsu, Hitachi, and Oki. These switches would become the D70 local switch and the D60 toll switch.

The Objectives of the Participants

As shown earlier in this book, NTT had a long tradition of co-operation with its suppliers on which to draw, going back to the days of the Ministry of Communications. NTT's main objective in developing the new digital switches was to improve the quality of its network in order to better the quality of its services. Both NTT and its predecessor, the Ministry of Communications, had always believed that it was necessary for them to be actively involved in the research and development of new, costly, and complex equipment. As the operator of the network and the body in touch with the customers through the services which it provided, NTT believed that it knew best what it required. Furthermore, as we have seen, NTT was not only a user of telecommunications equipment but a particularly sophisticated user, with substantial R&D competences in its Electrical Communications Laboratories (ECL). This sophistication enabled NTT to keep abreast of technological trends and to give direction to its suppliers regarding its needs. With a massive procurement budget, NTT had the market power which provided a strong incentive for its suppliers to offer the inputs and co-operation that were needed for the development of innovative equipment.

How Did Controlled Competition Work for the D70 and D60?

The form of organization that NTT used for the development of the digital switches was very similar to that used for the D10 space-division switch. Joint committees were established, under the leadership of ECL engineers, to work out the details regarding both the overall design of the switch and the design of the switch's sub-systems. Once the overall design was agreed, individual companies were assigned to work on the sub-systems. This was done through a process of discussion and negotiation with NTT officials, taking into account the comparative strengths of the supplying companies. At least two companies, and sometimes more, were allocated to the development of each sub-system. In this way, even at the design stage, NTT was able to 'multi-source', reducing the danger of being dependent on only one supplier while taking advantage of the competences of at least two of them.

The ultimate objective was for each of the suppliers to supply NTT with complete, substitutable switches. In this way, NTT would end up with four alternative sources of supply, from NEC, Fujitsu, Hitachi, and Oki. The criterion of substitutability of their switches meant that there was a degree of competitive pressure on each of the suppliers, although (as will be shown below) NTT's procurement rules meant that this competition was controlled; hence 'controlled competition'.

The major advantages of this co-operative R&D included avoiding duplication and benefiting from the specialization and comparative strengths of each of the co-operating companies. In order to reap these advantages, a process of technology transfer between the companies was necessary. For example, rather than all the companies developing a processor for the switch, one company could develop the processor and sell it on an OEM basis to the other companies, or transfer the technology (in the form of circuit diagrams, etc.) to help them develop their own processors. Where a company brought its own technology into the project, it was entitled to charge a royalty to the other companies to which the technology was transferred. Each company followed its own strategy in deciding when to 'make' and when to 'buy' from another participant, taking into account that all four suppliers, while co-operating with NTT, were competitors in the export switching market.

NTT had particularly strong views regarding the software (which could account for as much as 70 per cent of the development cost of a digital switch). It was NTT's belief that it had to own the key software so that it had maximum flexibility in making subsequent changes to the software, for example in order to introduce new services. NTT was determined not to have to negotiate separately with its suppliers whenever it needed software changes. Accordingly, although software tasks were commissioned to the participating suppliers, NTT insisted on paying for and owning the software. To further strengthen its position in this strategically important area, NTT also ensured that its own engineers played a large role in developing the software that was needed. In this way, NTT also guaranteed that it would retain internally, and enhance, crucial software competences.

When all the sub-systems were completed, NTT assumed responsibility for integrating them into a prototype working digital switching system. This was done in ECL, where exhaustive tests were then carried out on the switch to debug it and ensure its reliability. The suppliers have great respect for the rigour with which NTT's engineers test jointly developed equipment. Indeed, these tests and the learning platform they provide constitute one of the most important benefits flowing from the co-operative R&D.

Financing the R&D

Generally speaking, the individual supplier assumed financial responsibility for its own costs in the joint development. The exception was when NTT contracted for the supplier to produce a specific input, such as software; in this case the supplier was paid by NTT. Until the part-privatization of NTT in 1985 and the introduction of the so-called 'track system' for procurement, the *quid pro quo* for a company taking part in co-operative R&D was that it would get a reasonable share of NTT's subsequent procurement of the jointly developed equipment. This would compensate the supplier for the resources that it allocated to the co-operative project and provide it with a reasonable rate of return. Although NTT has never released information on the rate of return that it allows its suppliers on sales of various equipment to NTT, the return is obviously high enough to ensure the continuing long-term commitment of the suppliers. (As will be seen later, the expected overall size of the procurement and rate of return involved has been sufficient to secure the commitment to NTT of such Western equipment suppliers as Northern Telecom, IBM, DEC, Ericsson, Siemens, and Corning, in addition to Japanese companies.)

However, privately, Japanese manufacturers have told me that the return that they get is not nearly as generous as that which Siemens is allowed by the Deutsche Bundespost. Each year NTT lowers the procurement price so as to take advantage of the post-project incremental innovation process which occurs as the manufacturers begin producing the equipment on a large scale. Each supplier is required to provide NTT with cost data for the equipment. Procurement prices are calculated on the basis of the lowest-cost supplier.

According to its pre-1985 *de facto* procurement rules, NTT's procurement of the jointly developed equipment was shared among the co-operating suppliers on the basis of both their contribution to the joint project and the performance of their equipment. The intention behind this rule was to obtain maximum co-operation while providing an incentive for further innovations. In reality, however, although this was never made explicit by NTT, the tacit understanding was that any 'merit points' given to an individual supplier to reward its performance would result in only a small increase in that company's proportional share of the total procurement of the equipment in question. NTT retained the right to vary the proportion significantly, or even to exclude an errant supplier, thus keeping a 'credible threat' to help maintain performance. But by sharing procurement more or less evenly among the co-operating suppliers, NTT ensured their co-operation and goodwill while providing them with the relatively certain expectation of revenue. In turn, this encouraged the suppliers to accumulate 'transaction-specific assets', such as human skills and specialized equipment used for NTT's specific requirements but having little value in non-NTT transactions.

The following data, given me by one of the suppliers, shows the share of the Japanese market for digital switches by supplier for 1988 (sales to NTT constituting the vast majority of this market in this year). Hitachi had the largest share, with 26.1 per cent, Oki was second at 25.5 per cent, NEC third at 25.0 per cent, Fujitsu fourth at 22.8 per cent, and Northern Telecom had 0.6 per cent. (Northern Telecom was the first non-Japanese company to become a major supplier of switches to NTT after its part-privatization in 1985 when it supplied its DMS switches.)

Since there were five companies co-operating in producing these digital switches, it might be surmised that each paid one-fifth of the total development cost that otherwise would have been incurred had they developed the switch alone. This is not the case, however, for three reasons. First, there are the co-ordination costs involved in getting five independent companies to agree and implement their agreements. Second, there are the costs of transferring technology from one company to another, particularly tacit knowledge. Third, in practice there was a fair degree of overlap as a result of the strategic decisions of the companies to develop core parts of the switch themselves so as to try and ensure future competitiveness in export markets. How significant were these three costs? According to a leading NEC switching engineer whom I interviewed, each supplier probably paid about 40–50 per cent of the total development cost that would have arisen if it had developed the switch itself.[59]

Commercial Production

As shown in Fig. 3.3, in 1980 the first experimental D70 was completed and the following year the first experimental D60. In 1982 and 1983, the first D60 and D70 respectively were commercially introduced.

How good are the D70 and D60? I put this question to a senior employee in Ericsson who had had personal experience in Japan with these switching systems. He replied: 'They are well-engineered and well-suited to the Japanese telecommunications network. However, they have both "belt and braces". They obviously have not been designed primarily with commercial considerations in mind.' My own interviews revealed that NTT's prime concern was the requirements of its own network. In designing the switches little attention had been paid to the requirements of potential export markets, a concern that was far more important for the suppliers.

---

[59] Other advantages and disadvantages of controlled competition are examined in M. Fransman, 'Controlled Competition in the Japanese Telecommunications Equipment Industry: The Case of Central Office Switches', in C. Antonelli (ed.), *The Economics of Information Networks*, North-Holland, Amsterdam, 1992, pp. 253–76.

Is digital switching an example of Japanese failure in a high-tech industry? This question was answered in the affirmative by the prestigious *Nikkei Communications* in a detailed and highly critical report on NTT's R&D programme[60] and also by the authoritative Japanese Technology Evaluation Programme (JTECH) Panel Report on Telecommunications Technology in Japan.[61] The criticisms made in these two publications can be distilled into four 'allegations'. However, since these 'allegations' have been analysed in detail elsewhere,[62] the arguments will not be repeated here. Suffice it to say that my own conclusion is that, while there are important criticisms that can validly be made regarding Japanese performance in the field of digital switching, it is not clear that the Japanese 'failed' in this area up to the early 1990s. Furthermore, these two reports were written before NTT's co-operative R&D project to develop the next-generation broadband multimedia ATM (asynchronous transfer mode) switch, which is discussed below.

Japanese INS and ISDN: Creating Japan's Information Superhighway

By the mid-1980s the technologies had been perfected which, when combined, would facilitate the evolution of Japan's Information Superhighway. Optical fibre and microwave-based digital transmissions, together with digital switching and communications and information processing, made possible the integration of voice, data, and images services provided through the same network.

In the early 1980s, however, there were three independent communications networks in Japan: the telephone network, to which was linked a facsimile system; a digital data network, which provided circuit switched and packet switched services (see the List of Abbreviations and Technical Terms for the terminology); and a telex network. The demand for facsimile services had increased rapidly, eroding the demand for inferior telex services. The digital data network had been built up on the basis of the D50 digital data switch that NTT jointly developed after the D10 and before it went on to develop the D60 and D70. The increased demand for the networking of computers in Japan, although lagging behind the demand in Western countries (particularly for personal computers), lay behind the expansion of the digital data network.

Facsimile

It is worth adding a little about facsimile, since this was one of the new

---

[60] *Nikkei Communications*, 3/12 (1990).

[61] Japanese Technology Evaluation Programme (JTECH), *Telecommunications Technology in Japan*, Panel Report, Science Applications International, La Jolla, Calif., 1986. (The JTECH programme was supported by the US National Science Foundation and the US Department of Commerce.)

[62] M. Fransman, 'Japanese Failure in a High-Tech Industry? The Case of Central Office Telecommunications Switches', *Telecommunications Policy*, 16: 259–76 (1992).

non-telephone services for which there was great demand in Japan. Facsimile provided an important motivation for the creation of an integrated digital network which, among other things, would provide digital facsimile services together with the possibility of media conversion.

Like digital switching, the conceptual origins of facsimile go back to the nineteenth century. The basic idea of electrically transmitting an image over a distance is, therefore, by no means new. Indeed, the first fax patent was taken out in 1843 and its first commercial use was in 1865. From the beginning, it was realized that fax would be useful for the transmission of writing. The famous American inventor, Thomas Edison, was motivated to try to improve fax technology by his prescient realization that it would be particularly useful for the communication of Chinese characters (including Japanese, which uses many Chinese characters). Even today, the large number of characters involved makes Chinese or Japanese language processing complicated and has been one of the major factors behind the relatively slow diffusion of personal computers and computer networks in Japan.

The first Japanese fax was developed in 1928 by Yasujiro Niwa, a senior engineer in NEC who was involved in research and development in the Ministry of Communications. Owing to a perceived lack of profitability in faxes, Western companies failed to put much resource into this area. But, as Edison had predicted, Japanese companies became interested as the enabling technologies made faxes increasingly technologically and economically viable. A major facilitating role was played by NTT, which by the 1970s had the world's largest fax research capability. When NTT harmonized the fax standards of the competing Japanese companies and co-operated with them in providing fax services through the telephone network, the fax facility began to diffuse rapidly in Japan. With Japan as a springboard, Japanese companies moved quickly and successfully into global markets. By the late 1980s, Matsushita Graphic Communications Systems, with 60 per cent of the market in Japan, had acquired 40 per cent of the world market. Other Japanese companies also held strong positions in the global fax market.[63]

From INS to ISDN

The idea of integrating voice, data, and image telecommunications services in the same network in Japan was first put forward by NTT's Yasuda Kitahara in his concept of the Information Network System (INS). He proposed INS at the Third World Telecommunication Forum held by the International Telecommunication Union (ITU) in Geneva in September 1979. NTT began to implement INS by developing a model system for experimental purposes in the

---

[63] For a brief discussion on the development of facsimile, see J. Coopersmith, 'Facsimile's False Starts', *IEEE Spectrum* (February 1993), 46–9. For a discussion of Japan's Information Network System (INS), see Y. Kitahara, *Information Network System: Telecommunications in the Twenty-First Century*, Heinemann, London, 1983.

Mitaka–Musashino area, part of greater Tokyo, in September 1982. The D60 and D70 digital switches played a key role in this network.

NTT's experience with its INS was used as the basis for its contributions to the international discussions under the auspices of the Comité Consultatif International Télégraphique et Téléphonique (CCITT), aimed at producing global standards for the provision of integrated services. These discussions resulted in agreement on ISDN (integrated services digital network), a set of standards which Japan incorporated into its network. By the beginning of the 1990s, Japan was able to provide ISDN services to 90 per cent of its customers.

The Company's Concept of the Company

It is not only the firm's concepts and beliefs regarding its environment (including its markets and technologies) that matter, but also the firm's concepts of itself: its concepts of the corporation.[64] Here too, there can be significant differences between firms. This can be seen by comparing some of the major telecommunications companies.

We have already seen how NEC's concept of the firm influenced its decisions regarding its entry into digital switching. The difference between NEC's concept and that of ITT, the company that remained NEC's largest shareholder until the early 1970s, is worth elaborating upon to illustrate the importance of the firm's concept of itself and the role that this plays in the process of competition.

ITT

ITT's Digital Switch: System 12

Until 1986, ITT was one of the world's major switch producers. As noted earlier, it became a prime player in the international telecommunications equipment market when, in 1925 under Sosthenes Behn, it took over Western Electric's international operations. These operations were particularly strong in Europe, where Western Electric, on the basis of its superior competences, had established extensive activities in countries like Belgium, France, the UK, and even Germany, where Siemens reigned supreme. In the early 1980s, ITT's subsidiaries in these and other European countries produced about 40 per cent of the total value of switches sold in Europe.

In the area of digital switching, however, ITT was a relative late-comer. Nevertheless, the company was determined to use its lateness to its strategic advantage, seizing the opportunity to introduce the latest technical advances into

---

[64] The idea of the firm's concept of itself, which fits in closely with my own notion of 'vision', was suggested to me in a discussion with Alfred Chandler.

its digital switching system, System 12. Expert switching engineers referred to System 12 as 'brilliant'.[65] Moreover, ITT's efforts were not confined to the technical field. The company also established 'excellent marketing and sales activities for the system, lauding its new concepts'.[66]

The best indication of ITT's commitment to digital switching is the sum it invested in developing System 12. By March 1985, the company had spent over $1.1 billion on the development of this digital switch, making it 'one of the most expensive initial switching developments ever undertaken'.[67] Although some of the original concepts for System 12 came from the USA (and of these, some had come from several switching engineers who joined ITT from Bell Laboratories),[68] the system was developed largely in Europe. However, with the divestiture of AT&T, ITT intended marketing System 12 in the US Regional Bell Operating Company (RBOC) market. By the beginning of 1986, ITT had spent $200 million on adapting System 12 for the RBOC market.[69]

ITT's Concept of the Company

As the foregoing paragraphs indicate, ITT made as strong a commitment to digital switching as its rivals Northern Telecom, AT&T, NEC, Ericsson, and Siemens. A crucial difference, however, was that ITT had a fundamentally different concept of the company from that of its rivals. Moreover, the origins of this concept went back to the 1970s when, under the presidency of Harold S. Geneen, ITT began toying with the conglomerate concept. The significance of this concept may be illustrated by comparing it with NEC's concept of the company.

The difference in the concept of the corporation propounded by ITT and NEC from the 1970s is well illustrated through the words of Dr Koji Kobayashi, who in the early 1970s was President of NEC. As President, he had to visit ITT's headquarters in New York in order to report on NEC's operating results. Running a company that was also heavily involved in telecommunications equipment, Kobayashi was naturally very interested to understand ITT's view of its own future. He was aware that under 'Geneen's leadership, ITT had begun to adopt a special growth strategy that was producing striking results. Journalists referred to this corporate concept as the *conglomerate.*'[70]

What guidance did this concept of the company suggest for ITT, a company based on communications and information? Kobayashi recalls his discussions with Geneen:

How . . . was [Geneen] planning to cope with the increasing importance of information, I asked. His response was that the only answer was the conglomerate. I could not fathom the logic in that approach. ITT had already acquired Avis Rent-a-Car and was proceeding to take over hotels [including the Sheraton group] and food businesses. I was at a total loss to understand how this was a response to the information age.[71]

[65] Chapuis and Joel, *Electronics*, 569.   [66] Ibid. 418.   [67] Ibid. 419.
[68] Ibid. 415–16.   [69] Ibid. 419.
[70] Kobayashi, *The Rise of NEC*, 48–9.   [71] Ibid. 49.

How did Geneen explain ITT's strategic approach?

Geneen explained it to me this way. When information from all over the world reaches people's eyes and ears, they will want to travel and see for themselves, so the hotel business will boom. When they stay at a hotel, they will have to eat, so the food business will prosper. Whether they are there for business or for pleasure, they will need transportation: that is where the car rental business comes in. . . . Accidents may happen, so the insurance business will grow.[72]

Kobashi's response to Geneen indicated his and NEC's totally different concept of the company:

though Geneen was certainly proving that this was a management strategy for high growth and good returns, I did not feel it was a direction I wanted NEC to take. . . . I was clearly aware that we were going our separate ways into totally separate worlds. NEC took the orthodox route, perhaps. We decided to become a 'billion dollar company' through internal growth built on our own traditional technological base. Even the limits of business diversification were gradually defining themselves. The criterion for pioneering new spheres was not just their potential profitability; they must share similar technologies, customers, and markets with our existing operations. Our entry into the computer field might be called diversification, but it was based on an area that was inextricably tied to our main line of business.[73]

Metamorphosis

In 1979, Rand V. Araskog succeeded Geneen as head of ITT but continued with the latter's concept of the company. In February 1986, despite ITT's huge investment in developing its System 12 digital switch and adapting it to the US market, Araskog made the decision to withdraw from this market. The immediate reason was disappointing sales, but a more fundamental reason was Araskog's concept of the company. (We saw earlier, for example, that Northern Telecom was willing to wait for up to a decade before beginning to make a profit on its DMS series.)

For technical 'old hands' such as Joel and Chapuis, ITT's decision was yet one more indication of the supremacy of the 'financial authorities' over the technicians. Although ITT's System 12 was technically 'brilliant', it was unable to survive Araskog's concept of the company. Joel and Chapuis note rather wryly that in the mid-1980s, 'However great the capital and reserves of the industrial switching groups, their financial authorities tended always to the view that the pace of progress imposed by research, development and the marketing of their products was starting to reach a dangerous threshold.'[74] In their view, ITT's decision with System 12 supports one of the general conclusions of their seminal book on the history of switching: 'The success of a switching system is determined less by the technical merits of the engineers who design and develop

---

[72] Ibid.   [73] Ibid. 49–50.   [74] Chapuis and Joel, *Electronics*, 419.

it, than by the industrial and financial power of the groups which produce and market it.'[75] As the present book shows, at least as important as the industrial and financial power of the group is its concept of the company.

Araskog's concept of the company led him even further. In June 1986, Araskog and his board took the decision to sell some 70 per cent of ITT's telecommunications interests—including the rights to System 12—to France's Compagnie Générale d'Électricité (CGE). Since 1970, CGE's subsidiary, Alcatel, had held a dominant position in telecommunications in France, in 1983 merging with the telecommunications part of the French group Thomson. In March 1992, under its concept of the company, ITT's metamorphosis—from a telecommunications company to one without any interests in telecommunications equipment—was completed. ITT announced that it would sell its 37 per cent stake in Alcatel for £3.6 billion, thus relinquishing completely its former core competences and business. ITT's remaining interests were in three main fields: the ITT Sheraton Corporation; manufacturing, mainly auto-parts and defence; and financial services and insurance.

The rationale behind ITT's concept of the company was that the company, aided by the financial possibilities provided by the capital market, should, in the interests of its shareholders, move into those areas where expected rates of return are most attractive. According to this concept, and unlike NEC's concept, the company need not be constrained by its current competences in research and development, production, marketing and sales.

How well has this concept served ITT and its shareholders? While this counterfactual question cannot be answered definitively, some general indications are relevant. In a remarkable article in May 1994, *Business Week* examined this question. According to the writer of the article, 'For years, investors watched in dismay as ITT's stock languished while Araskog and his lieutenants were lavishly compensated.' From 1979, the year Araskog took over, to the end of 1991, the writer noted, ITT's share price lagged behind Standard & Poor's 500-stock index by 36 per cent.

Then in 1991, under pressure from ITT's activist shareholders, the board decided to link executive pay to the company's share price. The results for the executives were unequivocal: 'Araskog's job remains plum by most corporate standards. . . . ITT's boss currently receives an annual salary of $1.6 million and a yearly bonus that should equal that amount. Last year [1993], he also received options worth more than $22 million. . . . Even after his retirement in October, 1996, Araskog is guaranteed a $400,000 annual consulting contract through 2001 and a nomination to ITT's board each year until 2003.'

It appears that this package of incentives had the effect of focusing Araskog's attention. According to a former top executive quoted in the article, Araskog 'spent a great deal of time focused on the price of the stock and how that related to bonuses and stock options'. Furthermore, the incentives seem to have

<hr>

[75] Ibid. 328.

had the desired impact on ITT's share price. 'It worked like a charm: ITT's stock is up 46% . . . in the span of two years. And the [company] now finds itself held up as a model of corporate governance by shareholder groups.'

However, it also appears that the 'valuation' of ITT by the stock market, as measured by the company's share price, contradicts its performance by other measures: 'ITT's newfound popularity with investors doesn't reflect much of a fundamental turnaround in its businesses.' How could this discrepancy come about? The answer, according to the writer, is that 'Araskog has focused largely on boosting ITT's stock, pursuing a strategy aimed at arousing investor interest more than engineering a real turnaround in operating results.' An example of ITT's 'creative accounting' is given: 'In 1993 . . . ITT stopped including less impressive results from Sheraton's 230 franchised properties in its annual report, while it added in the revenues, ocupancy rates, and average room rates of its 149 more desirable leased and managed hotels, which were never included before. The result: Sheraton now reports revenues of $3.2 billion rather than the $784 million that would have been reported under the previous accounting methods.'

Despite the rise in it's share price, 'by many other measures, ITT remains a laggard. [In 1993] its revenues dropped 1% . . . its return on assets has dropped . . . return on total capital has fallen . . . and the operating margins for four of ITT's seven divisions remain far below prerecession levels.' In striking constrast to NEC, which has practically maintained its R&D spending despite the severe recession in Japan and the significant fall in its revenue and profits, 'Since 1990 ITT has cut research and development spending by 19% . . . and slashed capital spending by 32%.' The writer accordingly concludes that, 'Despite ITT's poor performance, [Araskog has] become one of the most richly compensated CEOs in Corporate America.'[76]

One last set of statistics is worth mentioning. NEC was founded in 1899 as a company 54 per cent owned by ITT's predecessor. NEC became just one of the large number of subsidiaries that ITT owned around the world. By 1993 ITT's sales amounted to $22.8 billion; in the same year NEC had sales of $30.6 billion.[77]

NEC and Fujitsu

In strong contrast to ITT, NEC and Fujitsu, under the influence of a different concept of the company, made a long-term commitment to the liberalizing US market, taking the losses that were unavoidable in the interim. Both companies realized that this necessitated building up competences *in the USA* that would

[76] 'While ITT Lumbers its Stock Has Legs: How CEO Araskog Keeps Investors Coming Back for More', *Business Week*, 30 May 1994, 44–7.
[77] On 13 June 1995 Araskog announced that ITT would be broken up into three separate companies, one dealing with insurance, one with defence and electronics, and one with hotels and entertainment.

allow them to evaluate the needs of their customers, modify and adapt their switches to suit these needs, and support their customers in maintaining and upgrading their switches as they operated their networks and offered new services.

NEC began strengthening its links with those carriers it had already begun to supply. Particularly important for NEC was its links with one of the Regional Bell Operating Companies (RBOCs), US West. NEC had already sold them pre-digital switches and had followed this up by supplying its digital NEAX-61. Similarly, NEC supplied its digital switch to Continental, one of the independents. In 1987 NEC established a Switching Technology Center in Dallas, and this was followed in 1989 by NEC's Advanced Switching Laboratory in the same location. This US base helped NEC to have its digital switches approved by Bellcore (under the latter's local access and transport area switching systems generic requirements (LSSGR)), a precondition for selling to the RBOCs. By 1991, NEC had 300 software engineers working on switching in the USA.

Fujitsu, having decided in 1982 temporarily to abort its switching efforts in the US market, re-entered it in 1989. In Fujitsu's view, the next generation of switches, ATM (asynchronous transfer mode) switches, offered a new 'window of opportunity' for successful entry into the lucrative USA. (ATM switches are discussed in more detail below. They offer broadband multimedia switching facilities and will be essential in the running of the Information Superhighway.) In 1991 Fujitsu became the first company in the world to offer commercially an ATM switching system for the high-speed, two-way transmission and routing of voice, video, and data simultaneously. Fujitsu announced that by March 1995 it would begin manufacturing ATM switches in the USA in order to be nearer its customers in this market, thus overcoming the company's earlier weakness. Fujitsu sold trial ATM switches to MCI (AT&T's main long-distance competitor), Bell South, Nynex and another two of the RBOCs. NEC sold its trial ATM switch to a small long-distance carrier in the USA.

Philips and Motorola

Philips was established in 1891 by Gerard Philips, a young engineer, in partnership with his father Frederik Philips, a wealthy tobacco merchant and banker. The company began producing small light bulbs and incandescent lamps. On the basis of these competences, the company later moved into other lighting products, radio, vacuum tubes, and after the war transistors and semiconductors, other consumer products such as television and VCRs, computers, and telecommunications. In 1914 the company hired a physicist, Gilles Holst, to lead its research effort. This eventually led to the establishment of the Philips Research Laboratories. These laboratories became world-renowned and made some important contributions, including the development of new magnetic materials such as ferroxcube and ferroxdure. Together with Sony, Philips developed the compact disc.

In its early years, Philips was threatened by the more sophisticated German companies which had been founded earlier. Indeed, in 1893/4 the company suffered heavy losses as a result of German competition. It was the Second World War, however, resulting in Germany's defeat and the temporary immobilization of Siemens, that gave Philips the opportunity to enter the field of telecommunication switches. The company's first switching system was a Siemens-type step-by-step system to replace those in the Netherlands that had been destroyed during the war. Subsequently, the company used its competences in electronics to help with its development of electronic switching systems.

With the advent of the digital era in the 1970s, Philips developed its own digital switch, the PRX-D. However, when the continually rising costs of switching R&D became apparent, and when Philips failed to be selected as a major supplier of digital switches for the German network at the end of the 1970s, the company decided to abandon its own digital switching programme. Instead, it opted for an alliance with AT&T. Essentially, this meant adapting the latter's No. 5 ESS for European conditions. While AT&T would supply the technology, Philips would provide the network of European contacts that would give AT&T entry into the relatively closed European market. Beginning in January 1984, the two companies set up ATT–Philips Telecommunication (APT), a 50–50 joint venture.

The strategic alliance, however, was not successful. On the one hand, Philips was unable to deliver on significant European market access in the face of competition from strong European telecommunications equipment companies such as Alcatel, Siemens, and Ericsson. On the other hand, Philips' ability to continue its commitment to telecommunications was put under increasing pressure as it faced strong competition, particularly from Japanese consumer electronics companies such as Sony and Matsushita. In 1988 Philips reduced its share in APT to 40 per cent and in 1989, to 15 per cent. In 1990 Philips withdrew from APT totally. In Europe's telecommunications equipment market, worth about $40 billion in 1994, AT&T has remained a 'second-tier player' with an estimated 4 per cent of the market for central office switches and 5 per cent of the market for transmission equipment.[78]

ITT's withdrawal from switching and telecommunications equipment was driven by a concept of the company that encouraged it to pursue opportunities which it thought would be more profitable, even if they were in competence-unrelated areas. However, Philips' exit from switching was determined more by the financial pressures that arose from its lack of success in the broad range of technologies and markets in which it had chosen to compete. Although Philips had attempted to undertake competence-related diversification, it had over-extended itself by moving into too many areas in which it lacked a strong international competitiveness. Once its core business of consumer electronics

---

[78] 'AT&T Is No Smooth Operator in Europe: Its Old Strategy Bombed So It's Looking to the $160 billion Services Market', *Business Week*, 11 April 1994, 16.

came under strong threat from Japanese competition, Philips was forced to reign in, abandoning those areas, like switching, in which it was comparatively weak. By the early 1990s, Philips was left with four main product divisions: lighting, consumer products, components and semiconductors, and professional products and systems. Like Sony and Matsushita, Philips moved more strongly into 'consumer software', notably through PolyGram with its interests in pop music.

If ITT and Philips are companies that decided to abandon the competences they had accumulated in switching (though for different reasons), Motorola is an example of a firm that took the decision never to acquire switching competences even though these were 'complementary assets' to which it needed access. Motorola's evolution has been based largely on radio-related competences. The company's communications products (which in 1993 accounted for 26 per cent of sales, compared with 31 per cent for semiconductors and 28 per cent for general systems products) are still primarily radio-related.

Motorola was founded in 1928 by Paul V. Galvin. Its first product was a 'battery eliminator', which allowed consumers to use radios directly from household current instead of from the large batteries that were supplied with the first models. In the 1930s the company's fortunes were boosted when it successfully commercialized car radios. In the 1940s Motorola entered the semiconductor field, becoming one of the largest producers of microprocessors (though it failed to displace Intel's dominance). In the mid-1970s the company abandoned colour TV in the face of strong Japanese competition.

About 54 per cent of Motorola's current sales are in wireless communications. This includes sales of mobile communications equipment, including radio base stations and mobile handsets. However, since Motorola lacks switching competences, it has been forced to ally itself with switch producers in order to obtain switches for mobile communications. At first Motorola worked with DMS, a relatively small US switch producer. But as rivals such as Ericsson (helped by the early launch and widespread use of mobile communications in Scandanavia) increased market share in mobile communications in the USA partly at Motorola's expense, the company decided that stronger competences in switching were needed. Accordingly, in the early 1990s Motorola established strategic alliances with Northern Telecom in North America, NEC in Japan, and Siemens in Europe.

Ericsson

Like Philips, Ericsson's concept of the company led it to concentrate increasingly on those competences in which it had the strongest international competitiveness. In Philips' case this was, generally speaking, lighting and consumer electronics; in Ericsson's it was telecommunications equipment. As shown in Fig. 3.3, Ericsson was an early-comer in the field of digital switching, although, like Northern Telecom, not a first-comer. Ericsson's AXE digital switch was 'evolved' from its earlier space-division switch rather than completely redesigned from scratch. This was achieved at about the same time as Northern Telecom brought out its DMS family of digital switches.

Unlike Northern Telecom, however, Ericsson, accepting the widespread belief in the strategic importance of the convergence of communications and computers, decided to move into information technology. As a result, Ericsson began producing minicomputers and personal computers. In the mid-1980s, however, the company's financial performance declined significantly, partly because of poor results from its Data Systems subdivision. In response, under the leadership of Lars Ramqvist, Ericsson launched a 'return to basics' programme, under which in January 1988 it sold its computer interests to the Finnish company, Nokia (a company whose computing interests were subsequently acquired by the British computer company, ICL, which itself is 80 per cent owned by Fujitsu). At the same time, Ericsson sold its office equipment division.

As part of its restructuring, Ericsson concluded an important strategic technology alliance with Texas Instruments. Under this agreement, TI supplies Ericsson with the electronic devices that it needs for its digital switches, including the crucial processors. It was the decision to depend on a long-term relationship with this outside supplier of electronic components that facilitated Ericsson's exit from computers, since the company no longer needed the electronics competences contained in its computer activities for its 'core' business area of telecommunications equipment.

Does Ericsson's decision to opt for a long-term market relationship as a means of acquiring the electronics competences it needs put it at a disadvantage *vis-à-vis* its competitors like NEC, Fujitsu, and AT&T, which have substantial in-house competences in electronics? This is a question to which we will return later when comparing the competitiveness of Ericsson and NEC in digital switching.

Ericsson was fortunate in that its 'return to basics' programme coincided with the company's strong performance in international telecommunications equipment markets. By the late 1980s, for example, more than 40 per cent of the world's approximately two million fully automatic cellular mobile telephones were linked to Ericsson's mobile communications systems.

The National Innovation Systems of France and Britain

France: the Emergence of Alcatel

The 1970s and 1980s saw significant changes in the French telecommunications industry, including the emergence of Alcatel, together with AT&T the largest telecommunications equipment company in the world. How did these changes come about?

From the end of the war until the early 1970s, telecommunications services in France lagged behind those of the leading European countries. In the early

1970s there was a sense of crisis, as political expression was given to frustrations over the quality of services and the time delay for new subscribers to be connected. It was this crisis that led to a radical restructuring of the entire French telecommunications industry.

In the early 1970s the French telecommunications equipment industry was dominated by three groups. The first was Compagnie Industrielle des Téléphones (CIT), which later became CIT-Alcatel. It was the telecommunications equipment subsidiary of Compagnie Générale d'Électricité (CGE). At first, because of its relatively weak position in switching and the French administration's need for standardization, CIT-Alcatel depended on licences for its switches. As time went on, however, CIT-Alcatel increased its own competences in telecommunications equipment and switching. In so doing it was assisted by the government-owned laboratory CNET. CNET was established in 1944, modelled after Bell Laboratories, and fell under the control of the Directorate General of Telecommunications (DGT) of the French Ministry of Posts, Telegraph, and Telephones. From 1954 onwards, CNET gained a far wider degree of autonomy and increasingly became involved in more fundamental research, including switching. While research was done in CNET, industrial application was undertaken by CIT-Alcatel. It was CNET's research that led to the development of the Plato (which later became the E10), the world's first time-division switching system.

The second group consisted of three ITT subsidiaries: Compagnie Générale de Constructions Téléphoniques (CGCT), Le Matériel Téléphonique (LMT), and Laboratoire Central de Télécommunications (LCT). Earlier ITT had made the strategic decision to decentralize its activities in Europe so as to be able to respond more effectively to the differing demands of the telecommunications authorities of the European countries which were the main procurers of equipment. In addition to its French subsidiaries, ITT also had major subsidiaries in Britain (Standard Telephone and Cables—STC), in Germany (Standard Electrik Lorenz A.G.—SEL—which was the second major source of supply to the Deutsche Bundespost after Siemens), and in Belgium (Bell Telephone Manufacturing Co.). The third 'group' was L. M. Ericsson's French subsidiary, Société des Téléphones Ericsson (STE).

From 1974, with the election of a new president, French industrial policy gave priority to restructuring the telecommunications industry as part of a programme to improve the French telecommunications infrastructure and services. This gave considerable political clout to the Industrial and International Affairs Directorate (DAII) of the Directorate General of Telecommunications. In 1975, as noted earlier, the French government announced a huge tender for an initial supply of switches for one million lines. Although the E10 digital time-division switch was already being installed in France, it was felt that digital switching was not yet cost-effective and so the decision was made to install space-division switches.

In line with its industrial policy, the DGT was determined to see a greater degree of French control over the supply of telecommunications equipment.

Accordingly, it linked its procurement of switches to a restructuring of the ownership of the telecommunications equipment companies in France. Under the agreement that was eventually reached, the DGT made ITT's Metaconta space-division switch the chosen system for the French network. Ericsson's AXE-10 switching system was selected as the second source for the network.

There was, however, a *quid pro quo* with which ITT and Ericsson had to comply. As part of its policy, the DGT had decided that it wanted to cultivate a second French competitor to compete with the major French telecommunications equipment supplier, CIT-Alcatel. Rather than choose one 'national champion', the idea was to have two French competitors who would also face competitive pressures from other international suppliers. Thomson-CSF, a French company involved in areas such as defence and consumer electronics, was selected as the second competitor. Thomson-CSF had played a relatively passive role in telecommunications equipment hitherto, relying on licences and a market-sharing agreement with CIT-Alcatel. Under the agreement orchestrated by the Directorate General of Telecommunications, Thomson-CSF bought ITT's LMT company. ITT retained CGCT, which produced the Metaconta. Thomson-CSF also took over Ericsson's STE subsidiary. This meant that Thomson-CSF would produce the AXE-10, the second switch for the French network, Ericsson receiving its satisfactory return from the deal through its sale of proprietary rights to the switch.

However, the rising R&D costs that emerged with digital switching (discussed in detail earlier), together with other pressures in the European and global electronics industry, combined to create further changes in the structure of the French telecommunications industry. In 1983 Thomson gave up its telecommunications interests to CIT-Alcatel. Furthermore, as mentioned above, in 1986, in the wake of its own corporate restructuring, ITT sold some 70 per cent of its telecommunications interests to CGE, the parent of CIT-Alcatel. As a result of this agreement, CIT-Alcatel took over ITT's System 12 digital switch. Finally, in 1992 ITT sold its 37 per cent stake in CIT-Alcatel back to CGT. In this way, heavily influenced by the French government's 'concept of the company', Alcatel became, with AT&T, one of the two largest telecommunications equipment companies in the world.

Britain: the Early Bird Loses the Worm[79]

An unkind critic of the British effort in telecommunications switching might categorize the experience as one of 'death by misadventure'. How unkind would such a critic be?

[79] This section draws on a number of sources, including Chapuis and Joel, *Electronics*; a valuable paper which concentrates on switching technology development in the UK and Sweden by A. Molina, 'Building Technological Capabilities in Telecommunications Technologies: Development and Strategies in Public Digital Switching Systems', paper presented to the *International Telecommunications Society Conference*, Venice, 1990; R. Harris, 'Electronic Telephone Exchanges:

If the outcome was 'death', it is certainly the case that there was also life before death, and thriving life at that. Britain entered the postwar period with extremely strong capabilities in switching, among the strongest in the world. On the basis of its wartime experiences in electronics, such as those that produced the code-breaking Colossus digital computer in 1943, after the war Britain was able to make an early start in developing electronic switching. The research on electronic switching conducted by people such as Thomas H. Flowers and his colleagues at the Dollis Hill Research Centre of the General Post Office quickly became world-renowned.

Despite this early vitality, however, by the late 1980s British switches, which had held strong positions in international markets before the war, had all but disappeared from these markets. System X, Britain's digital switching flagship, had failed to make an impact outside the UK despite having been designed with the export market in mind. Even more significantly, the independence of Britain's telecommunications equipment industry—which in the area of switching by the late 1980s was reduced to a single company, GEC—had become seriously compromised as this company merged its telecommunications equipment interests with those of the far more powerful and globalized Siemens.

If, unkind or not, this is to be called 'death', the question is: Why, with such a strong start, was this the outcome? In answering this question, the general point that must be made immediately is that the problem was *not*—in the parlance of the current passing terminological fad—one of a lack of 'technological foresight', that is failure to appreciate the importance of forthcoming technologies. Indeed, as will be seen, a reasonably strong case can be made that, if anything, the problem was one of 'too much foresight', in so far as the British quickly came to believe in the future importance of electronic switching and moved rapidly to position themselves to take advantage of this new technological wave. As it turned out, their problem was not the inertial one of waiting too long before making the commitment to the new technology, but rather one of being over-optimistic regarding the rate at which this electronics-based technology would become superior to the old electromechanical technology.

The problem, in other words, was largely one of *timing* rather than foresight. As will be seen, however, it was further complicated by other factors. These included the general economic and financial well-being of the country, the greater priority that the British equipment manufacturers attached to their own short-term financial performance than to technological and product commitment, and mistaken judgements made by the British Post Office regarding technological trends and the institutional requirements necessary for co-operative interfirm research and development.

An Introductory Review of Development', *POEEJ*, 59/3 (1966), 211–19; R. Harris and J. Martin, 'The Evolution of Switching Systems Architecture', *POEEJ*, 74 (1981), 187–93; J. Hills, *Information Technology and Industrial Policy*, Croom Helm, London, 1984; K. Morgan, 'Breaching the Monopoly: Telecommunications and the State in Britain', Working Paper Series on Government–Industry Relations, no.7, University of Sussex, 1987.

To summarize a highly complex set of events (at the cost of some over-simplification), the British, with a strong prewar international position in Strowger-type switches, attempted to leapfrog one generation of switches—namely crossbar switches—and jump straight into electronic switching. That they landed on their faces rather than their feet was arguably the outcome of their attempt. From an analytical point of view, however, the important question is not so much why the outcome as why they made the mistakes they did and whether things might have been different.

The optimism that existed in Britain in the early postwar years regarding the future viability of electronic switching stands in strong contrast to the pessimism on the same topic expressed in many of the other leading countries which was noted earlier in this chapter. To some extent, the optimism was a spinoff (undesirable, as it later turned out to be) of the high-quality research being done in the country. Chapuis and Joel go so far as to state that 'Flowers' expertise greatly influenced the U.K. Post Office in its [development and] procurement of switching equipment.'[80]

At any rate, this optimism persuaded the Post Office to put most of its eggs in one basket and make an early strong commitment to developing electronic switching. This decision entailed not only making an early commitment to the new electronic switching, but also deciding to foreclose on the main technological alternative, namely electromechanical crossbar switches. Unlike other countries—such as the USA, Germany, France, and Sweden—Britain chose for a long time to remain out of crossbar switching. And when in the late 1960s crossbar switches were first developed in the country—and then only on a small scale—this was the result of a fallback defensive posture in the wake of the failed effort in electronic switching. In retrospect, it seems clear that if all the eggs had not been put in the same electronic basket and if some had been kept for another crossbar basket (whether it relied on domestic development or on imports), Britain may have been able to move forward, slowly but more effectively, into electronic switching.

In the event, however, this was not to happen. In 1956 the Post Office established the Joint Electronic Research Committee, charged with developing an electronic switch which would replace the country's ageing Strowger switches. Under the co-ordinating leadership of the Post Office, the Committee included the country's five switch producers: Siemens Edison Swan, later to become Associated Electrical Industries (AEI), Automatic Telephone & Electric (ATE), Ericsson Telephones Ltd (ETL), the General Electric Co. (GEC), and ITT's subsidiary, Standard Telephone and Cables (STC).

The work of the Committee resulted in the development of an analog time-division switch based on pulse amplitude modulation (PAM), which became known as the Highgate Wood exchange. As shown in Fig. 3.3, the laboratory version of this switch was completed in 1959 and the switch was installed in the

---

[80] Chapuis and Joel, *Electronics*, 63.

Highgate Wood exchange in December 1962. However, although one of the first examples of a time-division switch, the Highgate Wood exchange failed to perform effectively, largely as a result of heat dissipation problems caused by the large number of thermionic valves that it used. In Chapuis and Joel's words, it 'turned out as a *monstre sacré*'.[81]

The immediate effect of the Highgate Wood *débâcle* was to establish the unviability, in both technical and economic terms, of electronic switching in the short to medium term. But this meant that the UK did not have a suitable switch with which to replace its ageing Strowger-type switches since, as noted, it had failed to insure its position by developing crossbar switches at the same time as pressing ahead with electronic switching. And, as in other parts of the world, the demand for telephone services was rising rapidly and becoming a politically sensitive issue.

The Post Office's response to this dilemma was to achieve the worst of all worlds: it locked Britain into old technology; it rendered the move into electronic switching conservative and hesitant; and it put severe strain on the co-operative relationship with the switch suppliers. The response of the Post Office was essentially threefold. First, as a stop-gap measure until the mid-1960s, the Post Office opted for the old tried and tested technology, namely the prewar Strowger-type technology. Incredibly, the last Strowger switch was supplied to BT (the successor of the Post Office) in 1985. It was supplied from the same factory line that had begun in 1912! However, while this was a pragmatic response under the Post Office's tight financial constraints, it worried the suppliers. The reason was that they knew that it was crossbar technology that was increasingly being demanded in export markets. Without a domestic base in crossbar switches, they would not be able to compete in this technology in export markets.

Secondly, the Post Office—in the knowledge that, despite Highgate Wood, the future belonged to electronic switching—pursued a cautious approach in continuing with the development of electronic switches. In 1963 the Joint Electronic Research Committee had decided to develop two electronic switches, a large and a small exchange. However, perhaps overreacting to the negative fallout over Highgate Wood (and perhaps also influenced by the financial pressures of a stop–go British economy), the Committee took an overly conservative position in choosing the technologies it would use for these exchanges. Both used manually programmable wired-logic control based on reed-relays, as opposed to the more flexible stored-program control (SPC). As shown in Fig. 3.1, SPC was first introduced by Bell Laboratories in the mid-1950s, the first trial SPC electronic switch was installed by these laboratories in 1960, and in 1965 Bell Laboratories' first commercial SPC space-division electronic switch— the No. 1 ESS—was installed. In the UK, however, not until 1976 did the Post Office start the field trials for its first experimental SPC local switch, known

---

[81] Ibid. 63.

as Pathfinder. Clearly, in electronic switching the British were going more cautiously down a more conservative technological road. Ironically, this was the same country that a decade earlier had launched itself most enthusiastically into the electronics era, in advance of most other countries.

The Joint Electronic Research Committee had reasonable success with its small electronic switch (called the TXE2) which was first put into service in 1966. This switch, through technology agreements, was soon produced by all the Post Office's suppliers. However, much slower progress was made with the large switch, the TXE4. This prompted the Post Office's third response, under pressure to meet the rapidly increasing demand for telephones. The response was belatedly to support crossbar switches for large exchange purposes. In 1968 the first crossbar switches were put into service in the British network. This led the suppliers—Plessey, GEC, and STC—to commit themselves to crossbar technology by making the necessary investments in production facilities. However, while the commitment to crossbar switching, although late, provided an interim solution to the telephone supply issue, at the same time it helped to lock the UK into a technology that was rapidly becoming obsolete.

While supplying crossbar switches to the Post Office, STC took the most progressive stance by simultaneously pressing on with its development of the TXE4 electronic switch, eventually producing an improved version. This benefited STC, which was able to announce in 1976 that its share of the UK's main exchange market had increased to 35 per cent from 20 per cent in the late 1960s. However, having made their investments in crossbar facilities and still not seeing much progress in the UK in introducing advanced electronic switching, GEC and Plessey stuck more conservatively with crossbar technology. Instead of giving the lead in researching, developing, and procuring the new technologies—which at this stage, as shown in Figs. 3.1 and 3.3, were SPC space-division and PCM time-division switching—the Post Office, under extreme political pressure exerted by GEC and Plessey, made a conservative compromise. In the early 1970s the Post Office decided to increase its purchases of crossbar switches from GEC and Plessey from £45 million to £350 million. At the same time, £180 million was allocated to the TXE4 electronic switch programme.

The failure of the British to move ahead and develop the new switching technologies was both cause and effect of serious division between the suppliers and the Post Office on the one hand, and between the suppliers themselves on the other. In the 1960s the Post Office operated a Bulk Supply Agreement which, similar to the Japanese controlled competition system analysed earlier, provided for co-operative research and development tied to procurement. However, by the late 1960s the Post Office felt that it was not getting the co-operation it wanted from its suppliers. The suppliers, as was seen, opposed the Post Office's procurement of Strowger switches and objected strongly to the reduced prices that it tried to impose. In response, the Post Office took action which was severely to upset the delicate balance of trust, obligation, and stability that (as the Japanese example analysed in detail earlier so clearly illustrates) is necessary for co-operation in research and development.

In 1969 the Post Office ended the Bulk Supply Agreement, opting instead for an arm's-length relationship with its suppliers and greater competition between them. However, this move from co-operation to competition backfired. To begin with, it produced problems of incompatibility between the equipment supplied by the different companies, which were costly to resolve. Furthermore, competition between the suppliers destroyed the trust needed for co-operation at just the time when the new digital switching technology was to raise R&D costs to such an extent that for many companies interfirm co-operation was the only way of remaining in the switching market. This was to have serious negative effects when the Post Office later launched its co-operative programme to develop its digital time-division switch, System X.

Further problems emerged from the rivalry between the supplying companies. The 1960s saw an increase in market concentration in the UK switching industry through a bout of mergers and acquisitions. In the early 1960s, Plessey took over both ATE and Ericsson Telephones. In 1968 GEC took over AEI. This left three suppliers: Plessey with 41 per cent share of the UK market, GEC with 36 per cent, and STC with 21 per cent.[82]

Frustrated regarding the co-operation that it felt it was not getting from its suppliers, the Post Office in October 1969 ended the Bulk Supply Agreement, which as noted tied co-operative research and development to procurement, and moved towards an arm's-length relationship with its suppliers together with increased competition between them. But this, of course, increased the rivalry between the suppliers, making them more reluctant to share information. The deterioration in the spirit of co-operation became evident after 1974, when the Post Office, realizing that it was essential that resources be pooled in order to develop costly digital switching, tried to revert once more to a co-operative form of organization with its suppliers in order to develop System X. As Chapuis and Joel somewhat bemusedly note, 'It . . . took no less than 7–8 years of prior deliberation, followed by discussion, before the necessary cooperation agreements for developing System X could be concluded.'[83]

During this time a great battle developed between GEC and Plessey over who would control the development of the all-important main processors for System X. These processors were perceived to be central to the competences that would be needed to develop not only System X but also future digital switches for the export market. While Plessey probably had stronger competences in this processor area, having developed similar processors for the Ptarmigan military communications system, GEC was a larger company and politically more powerful. Eventually GEC secured its designation as the main processor developer. Unlike the Japanese form of controlled competition analysed earlier, where at least two suppliers were required to

---

[82] Hills, *Information Technology*.   [83] Chapuis and Joel, *Electronics*, 397.

take responsibility for the development of each sub-system including its devices, the Post Office left only one supplier in control of each sub-system. Thus, while GEC took control of the processor utility sub-system, Plessey was responsible for the digital switching sub-system, and STC for the message transfer sub-system. This left more bargaining power in the hands of the individual suppliers.

The effectiveness of co-operative R&D of System X was also affected both by the general economic circumstances of the country and by the willingness of the managers of the supplying companies to make the financial commitment to the project. In view of Britain's patchy economic performance and the dependence of the Post Office on the government's budgetary decisions, this meant at times a stop–go procurement of telecommunications equipment. In turn, this made financially oriented managers of the kind who under Lord Weinstock managed GEC wary of making significant long-term commitments to projects as expensive as digital switching.

Summarizing the vicious cycle that the British switching industry had got itself into, Chapuis and Joel conclude that:

Britain's industrialists were wary of any initiative that might involve them in the sort of investment needed to develop a new technological generation of switching systems. Their manager's ambition was simply to retain the slice of the Post Office's order cake traditionally allotted to their companies, with the result that the innovations recommended by their excellent research engineers were inevitably swept under the carpet. Starved of competitive products, export markets closed one after another to the detriment of both the British economy and its balance of payments.[84]

The first System X local exchange was installed in September 1981, significantly later than most other digital switches. Although System X was specifically designed with the export market in mind in addition to the Post Office's requirements, it failed to make headway in these markets.

From the early 1980s, the British System in telecommunications changed drastically. In 1981 the Telecommunications Act was passed, separating the postal function and creating British Telecom (BT). In 1982, in the light of an internal report which showed that there would be excess capacity in the switching industry if three suppliers produced at minimum efficient scales of production, STC was excluded from the System X programme. Concentrating on the TXE4 switch, STC had not made a full commitment to System X. This prompted ITT to sell a majority of STC's shares to British investors, retaining only a 24 per cent stake. Thereafter, STC acquired the British 'national champion' computer company, ICL, motivated by the convergence between communications and computing. Later, STC, having abandoned switching, was acquired by Northern Telecom, and Fujitsu acquired an 80 per cent share of ICL with Northern Telecom retaining about 17 per cent in ICL.

In 1984, under the Conservative government's privatization programme,

[84] Ibid. 395–6.

BT was privatized. In 1985 GEC launched a hostile takeover bid for Plessey. This eventually resulted in the formation of a joint venture, GPT, which pooled both companies' telecommunications equipment interests. In September 1988, GEC and Siemens jointly paid $3.1 billion for Plessey, including its 50 per cent share in GPT. In view of Siemens' greater size and global importance in telecommunications, this meant that British telecommunications equipment interests came under the significant influence of the German company.

Meanwhile, freed of any obligation to consider the 'national good' in British telecommunications and electronics, BT devoted itself to its concept of the company, which was to act in its shareholders' interests as it saw them. With its hands freed, and no doubt in the light of its less than successful experiences in the co-operative research and development of telecommunications equipment, BT increasingly opted for the international market as a way of obtaining the equipment it needed.[85]

Finally, several comments are in order comparing the telecommunications equipment industries in the UK and Japan. In both countries, as we have seen, co-operative research and development between the user—the country's main telecommunications carrier, namely BT and NTT—and its several equipment suppliers was pursued. In the UK, however, this form of organization on the whole failed, while in Japan it is arguable (see above) that it succeeded. Why this difference?

Perhaps the most striking difference between the UK and Japanese cases was the manifest inability of the British Post Office to assert its dominance over its suppliers. In sharp contrast, NTT (and its predecessor the Ministry of Communications) was from the beginning able to establish its dominant role. At first sight this difference presents something of a puzzle. Since both the Post Office and NTT had significant market power as a result of their substantial procurement of equipment, why was it only the latter that was apparently able to realize this power?

There are a number of components to the answer to this puzzling question. First, in the Japanese case NTT benefited on the whole from getting both the technology foresight and the timing issues right. As was seen, NTT tended to be a little behind the international leaders in developing the successive generations of technology. This lag was costly in the case of digital switching since it contributed to the late entry of NEC and Fujitsu which ended up having to support two digital switches. Nevertheless, NTT was able to move forward steadily from technology generation to generation, giving effective leadership to the supplying companies while taking advantage of their competences. In the UK, on the other hand, the untimely leap into electronic switching, the subsequent backtrack, and the lack of a viable crossbar option injected

---

[85] This subsection provides the crucial background to understand the role that BT went on to play in the 1990s, as analysed in the chapter comparing AT&T, BT, and NTT in the companion volume, Fransman, *Visions of the Firm*.

considerable tensions into the interfirm co-operative form of organization that was being used.

Secondly, NTT's position was also strengthened by the steady and rapid growth of the postwar Japanese economy, which translated into large and growing orders for telecommunications equipment. In the UK, on the other hand, economic growth and government fiscal decisions meant that at times the domestic 'pie' was not as attractive to British suppliers, who were very much fixated on their short- to medium-term financial performance and the returns they were getting in other areas such as the defence sector.

Thirdly, NTT was also assisted by the remarkable degree of continuity and stability in its controlled competition form of organization with its suppliers. As we saw earlier, this form of organization was perfected in the late 1920s and early 1930s and remained essentially unaltered until 1985 when NTT was part-privatized. This meant that a set of routines had been established and, most importantly, had worked to the mutual benefit of all those involved. In the UK, on the other hand, particularly as the vicious cycle began for the reasons mentioned, there was discontinuity and instability which disrupted the co-operative form of organization. To make matters worse, the Post Office clearly demonstrated that it did not understand the delicate dynamics of co-operation when it ended the Bulk Supply Agreement in 1969 and opted instead for a competitive form of organization. By the time it realized that it would have to revert to co-operation in order to develop the costly System X digital switch, much of the trust and mutual obligation on which effective co-operation rests had been destroyed.

Taken together, these three points account for the very different experiences of co-operative research and development in telecommunications equipment in the UK and Japan.

Corporate Long-Term Performance

The Market for Switches and Corporate Performance

According to Schumpeter, firms are not independent entities, but rather are interdependent parts of the broader process of economic change. In the case of switches, we have seen that until the liberalization era, which began particularly in the USA, Japan, and the UK in the mid-1980s, those national innovation systems that contained one or more major telecommunications equipment supplier were relatively insulated. Their insulation resulted from restrictions on trade; in short, the national telecommunications carrier tended to procure equipment from nationally based suppliers (which in some cases included national subsidiaries of foreign companies, such as ITT's subsidiaries in France, the UK and Germany).

However, in the pre-liberalization era, even these national innovation systems were not totally insulated. To begin with, we have seen that there were highly effective international flows of information connecting different national systems. To some extent these information flows were institutionalized; for example, the International Switching Symposia (ISS) brought together managers and engineers from the switching community to exchange information and share ideas regarding developments in switching. To some extent the flows were less formal, such as the technical journals of Bell Laboratories and the other major national laboratories, which served as important international sources of technical information.

But the interdependence of carriers, suppliers, and national innovations sytems was effected also through the operation of markets. Two markets were particularly important, even in the pre-liberalization era. The first was the market constituted by the 'independents' in the USA, that is the smaller carriers which were independent of AT&T's Bell System. We saw that this market had a significant effect in terms of its influence on the rate of innovation and diffusion of new switching technology, not only in the USA, but also internationally. The second market was 'the rest of the world', namely those countries, in both the developed and developing world, that did not have their own major nationally based suppliers of telecommunications equipment. It was in these markets that the world's major telecommunications equipment suppliers competed vigorously with one another. The process of competition in these markets helped to ensure that the switching activities that took place in each of the major supplying companies were to some extent dependent on what happened in the other competing companies. An illuminating indicator of the interdependence that existed is provided by the evolution of a dominant design configuration for digital switches.[86]

While the interdependence of firms and national innovation systems was to some extent market-mediated, the market also provides an indication of the relative performance of the competing firms. In the rest of this subsection, the performance of the major equipment companies will be analysed through an examination of their market share in the various markets. In the following subsection, several hypotheses will be examined which attempt to explain the performance observed.

Table 3.2 shows the top seven companies in the global and US central office switching markets in terms of cumulative lines shipped. There is a strong

[86] An excellent insider's account of the process of competition in the international switching markets is provided by Meurling's story (*A Switch in Time*) from Ericsson's point of view. From the mid-1980s, a dominant design configuration emerged for digital switches. From this time there was 'a general consensus amongst the switching industry as to the best design of switching exchanges regardless of their size or place in the public network. This consensus also applied to . . . PBXs. . . [F]rom now on all new systems had to have stored-program control and digital switching networks. There was also a consensus as to the type of exchange architecture: it had to be modular as regards both hardware and software [which helped to make the systems "future proof" by making it easier to introduce new features] and decentralised in that microprocessors were used throughout' (Chapuis and Joel, *Electronics*, 563).

Table 3.2 *Cumulative Line Shipments of Central Office Switching Equipment (thousands of lines), up to 1992*

	USA	%	Worldwide	%	Rank
AT&T	47,076.0	41.3	54,200.0	18.6	3
Northern Telecom	45,222.0	39.6	59,100.0	20.3	2
AG Communication Systems (GTE)	12,253.0	8.8	17,200.0	5.9	7
Siemens	5,390.5	4.7	32,800.0	11.3	5
Ericsson	1,749.6	1.5	40,300.0	13.8	4
Alcatel	1,628.5	1.4	66,700.0	22.9	1
NEC	781.4	0.7	21,000.0	7.2	6
TOTAL	114,101.0		291,300.0		

Source: Dataquest (June 1993).

correlation between the top six switching companies and the top six tele-communications equipment companies (shown in Chapter 1). Exactly the same companies occupy the top six positions in both these lists. However, while Northern Telecom is fourth in terms of equipment, it is second in terms of switching (reflecting its strong competences in switching but relatively weak competences in transmissions and customer premises equipment such as phones and faxes). The table also shows that the top three switching companies in terms of worldwide line shipments—Alcatel, Northern Telecom, and AT&T—together accounted for almost 60 per cent of total shipments.

It is also evident from Table 3.2 that AT&T and Northern Telecom dominated the US market. While the former had 41.3 per cent, the latter had 39.6 per cent, implying that these two companies together held about 80 per cent of the total US market. The third company, AG Communication Systems, which held about 9 per cent, consists largely of the former GTE, which previously was the biggest supplier of switches to the independents in the USA (mainly to the GTE operating companies). (In 1987 GTE decided to concentrate on services and give up the production of network products such as switching and transmission systems. Accordingly, it sold its PBX (private branch exchange) operations to Fujitsu and its switching interests outside the USA to Siemens. In 1988 GTE formed a joint alliance with AT&T to take care of its customers who had purchased its switches in the USA.)

It is clear from the table that it is North American companies that have overwhelming dominance of the US market. The three European companies—Siemens, Ericsson, and Alcatel—held only 7.6 per cent of this market, the latter two holding only about 1.5 per cent each. NEC, the biggest Japanese switching company in the USA, held a miniscule 0.7 per cent of the market.

Table 3.2 also shows the great relative importance of the US market for AT&T and Northern Telecom. Indeed, 87 per cent of AT&T's switching lines were sold in the USA. Recently, AT&T's Network Systems Group has increased its efforts

Table 3.3 *Shipments of Central Office Switching Equipment to the USA (thousands of lines), 1991 and 1992*

	1991	1992	% change, 1991–2	1991 Market share (%)	1992 Market share (%)
AT&T	5,136.0	6,585.0	28.2	45.0	48.2
Northern Telecom	4,531.0	5,191.0	14.6	39.7	38.0
Ericsson	678.0	749.6	10.6	5.9	5.5
Siemens	523.0	705.5	34.9	4.6	5.2
AG Communication Systems	454.0	353.0	– 22.2	4.0	2.6
Alcatel	45.0	50.5	12.2	0.4	0.4
NEC	37.0	29.4	– 20.5	0.3	0.2
TOTAL	11,404.0	13,664.0	19.8	100.0	100.0

Source: Dataquest (June 1993).

in export markets. Although, as seen earlier, AT&T has not made much of a breakthrough in Europe, it is concentrating efforts in countries such as China. As for Northern Telecom, 77 per cent of its sales of switches are in the USA, and it is worth noting from the table that this company's worldwide shipment of switching lines was 9 per cent higher than AT&T's.

While Table 3.2 shows cumulative lines shipped, Table 3.3 shows sales of central office switches in the USA for 1991 and 1992, providing a more recent picture of competitiveness as evident in market share data. We can see that in 1991 and 1992 the gap between AT&T and Northern Telecom was greater than that indicated by cumulative shipments. Also, the gap appears to be widening somewhat in AT&T's favour, with the latter holding 48 per cent of the market compared with Northern Telecom's 38 per cent. Of the other companies, Siemens is the only one that has increased its share slightly. The three European companies held an 11 per cent share of the US market in 1992 (compared with 7.6 per cent for cumulative lines).

In the main Western European countries with national telecommunications equipment suppliers—countries that have generally been slower than the USA to liberalize the procurement of foreign equipment—the market is dominated by the national suppliers. As Fig. 3.4 shows, the USA and Western Europe accounted for about 60 per cent of the total world market for digital central office local lines, leaving about 40 per cent for the rest of the world.

Figure 3.5 provides a breakdown for the rest of the world. As can be seen, Japan accounts for 16 per cent of the 'rest of the world' market. Table 3.4 shows the share of the Japanese market for central office switches (cumulative lines) held by the main Japanese suppliers in 1990. NEC held the largest share of 39 per cent, followed by Fujitsu with 26 per cent, Hitachi with 19 per cent, and Oki with 16 per cent. By 1993, Northern Telecom, the major Western new entrant into the Japanese switch market, held about 8 per cent with its DMS switches.

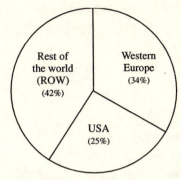

Total=55.4 million lines

Fig. 3.4 The worldwide central office market: shipments of digital local lines, by region, 1992

Note: Segments do not add to 100% because of rounding.

Source: *Dataquest* (August 1993).

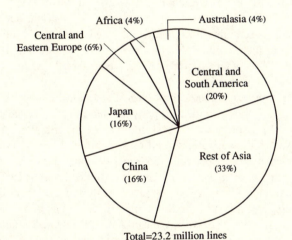

Total=23.2 million lines

Fig. 3.5 Rest-of-the-world central office market: shipments of digital local lines, by region, 1992

Note: Segments do not add to 100% because of rounding.

Source: *Dataquest* (August 1993).

It is clear from these data that the major switch markets in the USA, Western Europe, and Japan are dominated by equipment companies from these particular regions. To a large extent, the reasons are both historical (regional companies already have their switches installed in region-specific networks to which they have adapted their switches) and political. A particularly important question in so far as international competitiveness is concerned relates to how well

Table 3.4 *The Central Office Switching Equipment Market in Japan, 1990*

Company	Market share (%)
NEC	39.0
Fujitsu	25.8
Hitachi	19.1
Oki	16.1

Source: Infocom.

these major companies have done in 'the rest of the world' where there is a more level competitive playing field. Data answering this question are provided in Fig. 3.6.

As can be seen from Fig. 3.5, Asia (including Japan, China—each accounting for 16 per cent of the market—and the rest of Asia) is by far the most important part of the market, accounting for 65 per cent of the total 'rest of the world' market. How well have the major equipment companies done in Asia?

Fig. 3.6 shows that Alcatel has the biggest share of this market, accounting for almost 30 per cent. Next come NEC and Fujitsu, with about 15 and 12 per cent, respectively. After them come Siemens and Ericsson, with about 10 and 5 per cent, respectively. The others include AT&T, Northern Telecom, and the Japanese companies Hitachi and Oki.

Central and South America is the second largest segment of the 'rest of the world' market, as Fig. 3.5 shows, with a 20 per cent share of this market. As for individual companies, Ericsson has done best in this market, with about a 30 per cent market share. Next follow Alcatel and NEC, with about 20 and 10 per cent, respectively. Siemens had about 9 per cent and Fujitsu about 4 per cent. Alcatel's strong showing in both these market segments is notable. So is AT&T's and Northern Telecom's absence from the five top places in these markets (both being included in the 'others' category). In relative terms, Ericsson has done very well in Central and South America and fairly well in Asia. NEC and Siemens have done rather well in both Asia and Central and South America. Fujitsu has done fairly well in both markets.

Ericsson versus NEC

In order to provide a more detailed analysis of international competitiveness (as measured by market share), two of the major contenders in the world market are examined—NEC and Ericsson. The data are provided in Appendix 6 on a country-by-country basis.[87] The regions identified in Table A6.1 are somewhat different from those in Figs. 3.4 and 3.5.

In the world as a whole, Ericsson has performed significantly better than

---

[87] I am very grateful for these data provided by senior executives from Ericsson and NEC.

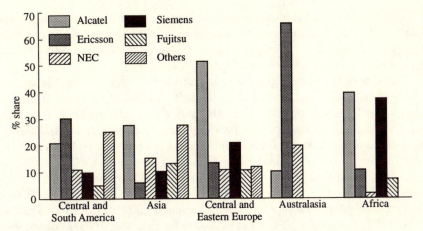

Fig. 3.6 Rest-of-the-world central office market: suppliers of digital local line market share, by region, 1992

Source: Dataquest (August 1993).

NEC. In terms of numbers of local lines for their respective digital switches—Ericsson's AXE and NEC's NEAX-61 switches—Ericsson's installed capacity for 1990 was 3.06 times as large as NEC's; in terms of number of transit (long-distance) lines, Ericsson's installed capacity was 3.07 times as large. However, in terms of number of switches installed, Ericsson's figure was only 1.36 times as large as NEC's, indicating that on average Ericsson's switches have significantly greater capacity.

How have Ericsson and NEC competed in regional terms? In Asia–Oceania, NEC's strong region but Ericsson's weakest (see above), the two companies are neck-and-neck. Ericsson's local lines installed are only 1.04 times larger than NEC's. However, NEC's transit lines installed are 1.10 times larger than Ericsson's. In this region NEC has 1.83 times as many exchanges installed as Ericsson, again suggesting the smaller average capacity of NEC's NEAX-61.

For NEC, the Asia–Oceania region was by far the most important. It accounted for more than half of the company's worldwide local lines installed, or 63 per cent, and about half of its worldwide transit lines, or 50 per cent. Europe–Middle East–Africa accounted for 9.3 per cent, and North and Latin America 27.5 per cent, of NEC's worldwide installed local lines. In terms of transit lines, Europe–Middle East–Africa provided only 0.8 per cent of NEC's worldwide lines, while North and Latin America provided just under 50 per cent of worldwide lines. (Differences are due to rounding.)

For Ericsson, Europe–Middle East–Africa was the company's most important regional market, accounting for 63.5 per cent of its total number of local lines installed, and 60 per cent of transit lines. For local lines, Asia–Oceania came next, providing 21.6 per cent of worldwide local lines. North and

Latin America provided 14.9 per cent of local lines. In terms of transit lines, North and Latin America was the second most important regional market for Ericsson, accounting for 25.4 per cent of worldwide lines; while Asia–Oceania accounted for 14.6 per cent of worldwide transit lines.

Which were the most important countries for Ericsson and NEC in each of these regions? The top five countries for NEC outside Japan in terms of local lines were: Malaysia, New Zealand, Thailand, China, and the USA. Ericsson's top five countries outside Sweden for local lines were: the UK, Australia, Italy, Korea, and Spain. Countries that were important markets for both Ericsson and NEC and were strongly contested by both companies include: China (680,000 local lines for NEC versus 254,000 for Ericsson; 80,000 transit lines for Ericsson versus 42,000 for NEC); Malaysia (1,052,000 local lines for NEC versus 780,000 for Ericsson; 82,000 transit lines for NEC versus 53,000 for Ericsson); Thailand (814,000 local lines for NEC versus 220,000 for Ericsson; 166,000 transit lines for NEC versus 22,000 for Ericsson); Argentina (193,000 local lines for NEC versus 51,000 for Ericsson; 145,000 transit lines for NEC versus 18,000 for Ericsson); Brazil (781,000 local lines for Ericsson versus 76,000 for NEC; 181,000 transit lines for Ericsson versus 55,000 for NEC); Colombia (426,000 local lines for Ericsson versus 106,000 for NEC; 89,000 transit lines for Ericsson versus 23,000 for NEC); USA (617,000 local lines for NEC versus 111,000 for Ericsson; 440,000 transit lines for NEC versus 73,000 for Ericsson); Venezuela (105,000 local lines for Ericsson versus 44,000 for NEC; 22,000 transit lines for Ericsson versus 4,000 for NEC).

Although it is not necessarily an adequate indicator of international competitiveness, in those countries where both Ericsson and NEC have made significant sales of digital switches, NEC seems on the whole to have done somewhat better. This is suggested by the figures given in the paragraph above.

Structure and Strategy

The extent to which the international competitiveness of the major telecommunications equipment companies, as revealed and measured by their market share in the different global markets, can be explained by the structure and strategy that they have developed obviously depends on one's definition of 'structure and strategy'. In the present context, 'structure and strategy' refers to two distinct characteristics of a company: its *coherence*, and its degree of *vertical integration*. Both coherence and vertical integration are the result of the decisions made by the company in the light of its explicit or tacit vision (that is, its set of guiding beliefs).

Coherence and Vertical Integration

David Teece and his associates have defined 'coherence' in the following way:

A firm exhibits coherence when its lines of business are related, in the sense that there are certain technological and market characteristics common to each. A firm's coherence increases as the number of common technological and market characteristics found in each product line increases. Coherence is thus a measure of relatedness. A corporation fails to exhibit coherence when common characteristics are allocated randomly across a firm's lines of business.[88]

Coherence, however, must be distinguished from vertical integration. A firm's vertical integration increases the more it develops and produces the inputs that it requires for its outputs. Accordingly, a firm that exhibits a high degree of coherence may reveal a low degree of vertical integration; and vice versa.

Some examples from the companies that have been examined in this chapter will clarify the distinction between coherence and vertical integration. Both Ericsson and NEC are significantly more coherent than ITT, as is clear from the information provided earlier. But Ericsson is significantly less vertically integrated than NEC, which produces its own electronic devices, including processors and memories, and also computers. Ericsson, on the other hand, depends on its strategic alliance with Texas Instruments for many of its crucial devices.

The major companies analysed in this chapter are categorized in Fig. 3.7 according to their degree of coherence and vertical integration. The companies that have remained as serious contenders in the international telecommunications equipment market appear in bold type. The other companies have either exited from this market or do not have a presence in the four regional markets—Western Europe, USA, Japan and the rest of the world. The position of the companies in the figure relates to the time when the companies were actively involved in telecommunications equipment. Most of the companies, of course, are still actively involved.

In view of the large number of products, technologies, and markets that these companies are (and have been) involved in, there is room for possible disagreement regarding where the companies have been located relative to the two axes. Accordingly, the rationale will be briefly mentioned here. ITT lies at one extreme, in the south-east quadrant. It is a company that has been neither coherent nor vertically integrated. The concept of the company which has driven its development has emphasized opportunities for profit rather than technological or market relatedness. In the north-east quadrant are Philips and GEC. Neither company is very coherent, though both are more coherent than ITT, which, as was seen, is/was involved in hotels, finance, car rental (and even biscuits). While Philips has become more coherent as a result of its profits squeeze and consequent restructuring in the 1980s, in the years when it developed its own switches it was involved in a wide range of products and technologies which were not always closely related. Apart from telecommunications, these included lighting, consumer electronics (such as TV,

---

[88] D. Teece *et al.*, 'Understanding Corporate Coherence: Theory and Evidence', *Journal of Economic Behavior and Organization*, 23 (1994), 4.

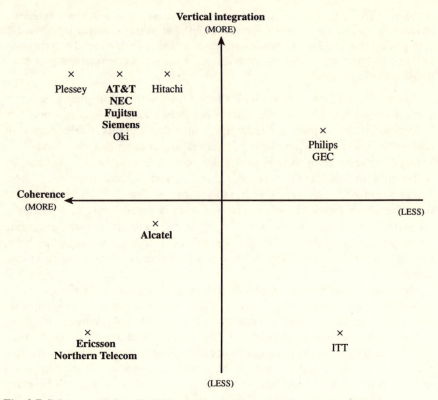

Fig. 3.7 Coherence and vertical integration of telecommunications equipment companies

Note: Companies in bold type have major involvements in *all* the global major market regions.

VCR, and audio), consumer 'white goods' such as washing machines and dishwashers, consumer electrical goods such as hairdryers, computers, and semiconductors. GEC is involved in areas such as defence, telecommunications, semiconductors, and heavy electrical equipment. The involvement of Philips and GEC in semiconductors makes them fairly vertically integrated as far as telecommunications equipment is concerned.

At the other extreme, the north-west quadrant contains the majority of the companies. These include four of the top six equipment and switch companies, namely AT&T, Siemens, NEC, and Fujitsu. This quadrant also includes the two remaining Japanese equipment and switch companies, Hitachi and Oki, neither of whom are actively involved in all four of the regional markets in the world. Finally, there is Plessey, which merged its telecommunications interests with GEC in GPT, a company that was later merged with Siemens' telecommunications activities.

With the exception of Plessey, all these companies are more or less equally vertically integrated in terms of telecommunications equipment. All the companies (again with the exception of Plessey) produce their own semiconductors, and all have significant computer competences. However, their degree of coherence is somewhat different. Hitachi is shown as a little less coherent than the others on the grounds that it is also, in addition to semiconductors and computers, involved in consumer electronics and electrical goods (like Philips), and in heavy electrical equipment. Plessey is shown as more coherent with its (previous) involvements in defence, semiconductors, and telecommunications.

Finally, in the south-west quadrant are to be found the remaining three of the six major international equipment and switching companies—Alcatel (incorporating, it must be said, important parts of the former ITT), Ericsson, and Northern Telecom. These companies are less vertically integrated than those in the north-west quadrant since they lack significant in-house semiconductor competences as well as competences in computers (that is, designing, developing, and manufacturing computers). However, Ericsson and Northern Telecom are more coherent than Alcatel, which more recently has acquired the heavy electrical equipment activities of Alsthom.

Equipped with this categorization of the 'structure and strategy' of the companies, we are now in a position to examine two hypotheses.

HYPOTHESIS 1 (the Coherence Hypothesis): The more coherent a firm's activities, all other things equal, the better its long-run performance.

How well does this hypothesis stand up against the evidence? Fig. 3.7 seems to give strong evidence in support of this hypothesis. (In this context, 'long-run performance' is defined in terms of long-run market share rather than financial or other measures of performance.) All the successful firms are to the west of the vertical axis (that is, are 'more' rather than 'less' coherent), while all the unsuccessful firms—firms that have either exited from this market or failed to become major global players—are to the east (that is, are 'less' coherent). It may therefore be concluded that coherence seems to be a necessary condition for success. This conclusion is supported by the substantial rise in R&D costs in the digital switching era noted earlier—with costs as high as $1 billion. These costs, which are also a feature of other areas such as semiconductors, make it difficult for firms to support too many unrelated products and technologies.

However, Fig. 3.7 also shows that coherence, although perhaps necessary, is not sufficient for success. This is to be expected, since there are many other factors that influence success apart from coherence.

HYPOTHESIS 2 (the Vertical Integration Hypothesis): The more vertically integrated a firm's activities, all other things equal, the better its long-run performance.

This hypothesis, it is worth noting, is at the centre of one of the most influential beliefs in the information and communication industry, a belief over which there is still no consensus in the industry. It may be termed the 'convergence belief', i.e. the belief that the technological convergence of computers and communications equipment implies that firms with competences in both areas will be able to establish a competitive edge relative to companies with competences in only one of these areas. It is this belief that originally motivated IBM to attempt to enter the telecommunications area with its acquisition of the private switch company Rolm (which it later sold to Siemens), which encouraged AT&T to acquire NCR, and which leads the Japanese companies to argue that in the long run they will be highly internationally competitive in the IC industry.

What light does Fig. 3.7 throw on this hypothesis in so far as it relates to the telecommunications equipment industry? The striking feature of the figure is that three of the six most successful firms are in the south-west quadrant, which indicates a relatively low degree of vertical integration. These firms are Alcatel, Ericsson, and Northern Telecom. Regarding the 'convergence belief', it is worth noting that none of the latter companies has significant involvements in the design, development, or manufacture of computers. With regard to vertical integration, it must also be noted that none of these companies is an important designer, developer, or producer of semiconductors. (It was pointed out earlier, for example, that Ericsson depends on a strategic alliance with Texas Instruments for its main customized semiconductor needs such as the processors for its switches. In other words, Ericsson's strategy has involved substituting a long-term market relationship for vertical integration, a strategy that does not appear to have disadvantaged the international competitiveness of the company in telecommunications equipment.)

It may be concluded, accordingly, that there is no evidence to support hypothesis 2.[89]

National Innovation Systems and Corporate Performance

While coherence has had an important impact on corporate long-term performance as measured by market share, the national innovation system under which a firm operates has also been significant. More specifically, the beliefs, ideology, and *modus operandi* of a company's national innovation system have constituted an important determinant of its long-run performance. This is clearly evident in the case of Alcatel, which, as was seen earlier, achieved its status as the largest telecommunications equipment company in the world as a result of

---

[89] The effect of vertical integration on long-run performance is to a significant extent affected by the firm's forms of organization. In an attempt to improve the speed of response and performance of their business units, vertically integrated companies such as AT&T, NEC, and IBM have attempted to decentralize decision-making power to these units. However, this has to some extent made it more difficult for them to realize the complementarities or synergies that are potentially available from vertical integration. The way these companies have attempted to resolve this organizational dilemma is examined by the present author in 'Different Folks, Different Strokes: How IBM, AT&T and NEC Segment to Compete', *Business Strategy Review*, Autumn 1994.

its acquisition of ITT's equipment interests. In turn, this was the direct result of the industrial policy of the French government. The Japanese innovation system in telecommunications, with its emphasis on controlled competition, is largely responsible for the fact that Japan is the only country in the world to have two representative companies in the global top ten—NEC and Fujitsu—although in both cases corporate strategy has also been a crucial determinant. The way in which the Japanese system operates also accounts for the continued presence of Hitachi and Oki in the switching market even though they are not major global players. Their continuing share of the NTT switching market allotted to them by controlled competition has kept them in the business. It is of interest to compare the fate of Plessey—in many ways comparable to Oki in terms of size and involvements in both telecommunications and semiconductors—with that of Oki. In the British innovation system, capital-market-facilitated mergers and acquisitions, together with BT's disinclination to continue developing and procuring equipment from national companies, meant that Plessey disappeared from the scene, swallowed by GEC and Siemens. In Japan, on the other hand, Oki, by far the weakest of the four Japanese equipment suppliers, has continued to be an important supplier to NTT.

In the USA, a very different innovation system in telecommunications, with its centre of gravity in the former Bell system and a small fringe constituted by the independents, meant that only one company survived as a major player in the global equipment market, namely AT&T. Furthermore, the size of the US market, together with the regulations that governed the old AT&T, resulted in AT&T having very much of a domestic focus. It is only since the 1990s that AT&T has begun to try to establish an international presence in telecommunications equipment (as well as in services and computers).

The size of the domestic market in which the national innovation system is based has also been significant in the cases of Ericsson and Northern Telecom. As was seen earlier, the small size of the domestic market, together with the rising costs of remaining in the switching business, meant that these two companies from an early stage emphasized the importance of the export market. In turn, this necessitated the achievement of international competitiveness, undoubtedly an important factor behind their market share in the world's major markets. On the other hand, a small domestic market in the Netherlands was not sufficient to facilitate Philips' continuation as a major player in telecommunications equipment. In the case of Philips, it was clearly company-related factors—specifically, its relative lack of coherence and the strong competition it faced from Japanese companies in its core consumer electronics businesses—rather than the operation of its national innovation system that determined its fate in the telecommunications equipment industry.

We conclude, therefore, that the effects of both a company's national innovation system and its chosen structure and strategy must be taken into account in accounting for its long-term performance.

The Present as History in Switching

The list of the world's top telecommunications equipment companies offers further food for thought. To begin with, it suggests a critique of the 'voluntarism' inherent in any argument that emphasizes corporate strategy as the main determinant of long-term corporate performance. While there certainly is evidence that strategy is an important determinant of performance (as the above analysis of coherence showed), there is more to long-term performance than choice of an appropriate strategy. This is suggested by the longevity of all the major companies on the list. It is also suggested by the close historical ties that link many of the companies on this list. Indeed, a closer examination of the top companies shows that they can be grouped into three 'families' (Fig. 3.8).

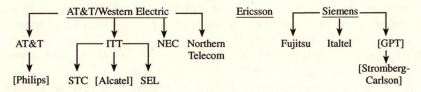

Fig. 3.8 Major switching 'families'

Note: [ ] Indicates strategic alliance/merger/acquisition.

But 'family', with its notion of genes being passed on to subsequent generations, is not the right analogy. Corporate 'genes'—more accurately, competences—have been passed on to other companies, as is shown in the figure. But these competences have intermingled with the recipient company's other competences, and together the resulting amalgam of competences has influenced its long-term performance. A better analogy comes from the biotechnology notion of recombinant DNA, suggesting the combining of the competences received with the company's pre-existing competences.

To make this discussion more concrete, let us examine the groups of companies more closely. It is clear from Fig. 3.8 that the main cluster of companies is around AT&T/Western Electric. As we saw earlier in this chapter, AT&T/Western Electric's technological competences were 'passed on' to ITT, which after 1925 took over Western Electric's international activities. Similarly, they were passed on to NEC, which was originally a Western Electric majority-owned subsidiary. Western Electric's technological competences were also transferred to Northern Telecom's predecessor, Northern Electric. Through ITT, a second generation of 'Western Electric-originating competences' were passed on to several other companies. The most important of these was Alcatel, which acquired ITT's French operations. But ITT also passed on its competences to its subsidiaries in other countries, including STC in Britain and SEL in Germany. Finally, through its relatively short-lived joint venture with Philips—APT—AT&T passed on some of its competences.

Significantly, four of the top six companies in telecommunications and switching are included in the AT&T/Western Electric cluster: AT&T, Alcatel, Northern Telecom, and NEC—companies that at one stage or another received important technological competences from AT&T/Western Electric. This suggests that the competences, accumulated slowly over a long period of time, have been a crucial determinant of long-run performance as measured here.

Indeed, there are only two other clusters, and in the second case the 'cluster' consists of only one company, Ericsson. The first case is the cluster around Siemens. It includes Fujitsu, which, as shown in the last chapter, was originally established as the telecommunications subsidiary of Fuji Electric, a joint venture between Furukawa mining and Siemens. Italtel, the Italian state-owned equipment company, was originally a subsidiary of Siemens, established in Milan in 1921. As noted earlier, through its alliance with Britain's GEC, Siemens has to some extent combined its telecommunications competences with those of GPT. GPT also owns the former Stromberg-Carlson, one of the larger independent switch makers in the USA. This resulted from Plessey's earlier acquisition of Stromberg-Carlson.

The final 'cluster' consists of Ericsson. In 1975, as part of the agreement for selling its AXE10 space-division switch to France, Ericsson was required to sell its subsidiary in France to Thomson-CSF. These activities were later acquired by Alcatel when it took over Thomson's telecommunications operations. So indirectly, Ericsson also made some contribution of competences to Alcatel. Ericsson also has a joint venture with Thorn-EMI in Britain in order to sell its AXE digital switch to BT as a second supplier complementing the sale of System X.

From Fig. 3.8, therefore, it is clear that the past—indeed, the distant past—is significant in the current performance of telecommunications equipment corporations. Accordingly, unlike the computer industry, where several newcomers—e.g. Apple, DEC, Compaq, and Dell—have achieved a significant share of particular computer market segments on the back of commoditized microprocessors, the telecommunications equipment industry is dominated by the 'old-timers'. This is also true in the case of the private switches (PBXs) used within organizations, the growth of which may in some ways be compared to the growth of distributed computing networks. For example, the top four suppliers of PBX lines to the USA in 1992 were AT&T, Northern Telecom, Rolm/Siemens, and NEC, with market shares of 28, 27, 15 and 7 per cent respectively. Here too, therefore, the old-timers dominated.

The Japanese Broadband Information Superhighway

NTT's Vision

Like its major counterparts in other countries, NTT has a set of general beliefs—in looser terminology, a vision—which guide its activities. What are these beliefs, and how is NTT attempting to implement them?

NTT's general beliefs are summarized by the term VI&P—visual, intelligent, and personal. The vision is one of a future world where everyone will be connected to networks that will provide them with the kind of information they want at a low cost. The networks will be both fixed, optical-fibre-based networks and wireless, radio-based networks which, in the current jargonized terminology of the telecommunications industry, will provide information 'anywhere, anytime'. The information that will be provided over these networks will come in a variety of different forms, including voice, data, and images such as those in fax and video. In present parlance, 'multimedia' services will be provided.

The 'V' in NTT's VI&P indicates the belief that in the future NTT's subscribers will be able to receive (and, equally importantly, will *want to receive* at the prices charged) services such as interactive video conferencing and video-on-demand, where the images received are life-like in that they are in real time, with full movement, and possibly even three-dimensional. The belief that customers will demand services such as these at the going prices is an integral part of the interrelated set of beliefs that constitute NTT's vision. However, it is a belief that is usually not made explicit. It is also a belief that, currently, is subject to significant interpretive ambiguity.

The services provided will be personal in that they will allow person-to-person communications. The most ambiguous of the three terms used by NTT in expressing its vision is intelligent. What are 'intelligent' services? The term has 'high-tech' undertones—as in the research area of artificial intelligence—and its use expresses not only the belief that these services can be provided and will be demanded in the future, but also the intention to *persuade* customers to buy these services. According to NTT's documentation, intelligent services include communication with automatic translation into other languages.

How was NTT to realize its vision? In April 1988 NTT had introduced ISDN (integrated services digital network), the first carrier in the world to do so. ISDN provided integrated voice, data, and image services over the same digital network. However, while the digital network gave transmission speeds up to several dozen times faster than the former analog network, VI&P services such as high-definition motion picture communication require speeds up to 10,000 times faster. Furthermore, the leap in the quantity of information contained in VI&P services requires not only faster transmission speeds but also greater bandwidth. It was accordingly necessary to move to broadband communications based on optical fibre transmission. In order to switch the greatly increased amount of information arriving at faster speeds, improved methods of switching were needed. This led to the advent of ATM (asynchronous transfer mode) switching.

ATM Switching

Early research into ATM switching was undertaken in the 1970s in places such as Bell Laboratories and France's CNET, laboratories that had also pioneered digital switching.[90] However, although this research began as early as the 1970s, it will come as no surprise to the persistent reader of this chapter to learn in a 1994 issue of *Business Week*, providing an overview of the main technologies shaping the information revolution, that 'today ATM is not mature enough or cost-effective enough to put in the network'.[91]

The switching function is only a part of a larger and more complex technological system, namely the telecommunications network. The evolution of ATM switching has been influenced both by technical changes that have occurred in other parts of the interdependent network and by improvements that have taken place in the technologies that are embodied in the ATM switch itself. For example, the introduction of optical fibre into the communications network (analysed in detail in Chapter 5) led to a significant reduction in transmission errors. In turn, this allowed the transport network to be dedicated entirely to information transfer, leaving the terminals to handle most flow and error control. Advances in semiconductor technology allowed switches to process protocols and perform switching functions automatically and economically with a reduced need for software control. Enabling technical advances such as these facilitated the emergence of ATM switching.

In the era of digital switching there have been two basic switching principles: circuit switching and packet switching. In circuit switching, a connection is made on demand between two or more terminals (such as telephones, faxes, or computers), allowing for the exclusive use of the circuit until the connection is terminated. In circuit-switched networks the signals are sent at pre-specified bit (binary digit) rates, with the result that these networks cannot effectively handle variable bit rate transmission. In some cases, however, such as the sending of messages or collections of data, it is more efficient to send the information in variable 'bursts' of signals. Packet switching emerged to deal with these needs. In packet-switched networks, information sent from a calling terminal is stored in the network, and then assembled into a block of variable length (typically ranging from a few hundred to a few thousand bits). These blocks are then encapsulated into 'packets', which also contain additional information (in a so-called 'header') which is used inside the network for routing (that is, transporting the data from the source to the destination), error correction, flow

---

[90] An account of the development of ATM in CNET and the implications of ATM for France Telecom is to be found in D. Primot, 'France Telecom: Options for ATM', Theseus Institute, Sophia Antipolis, 1992, mimeo.

[91] *International Business Week*, 13 June 1994, 59.

control, etc. Having been stored, the packets are then forwarded to the called terminal.

However, both circuit and packet switching have limitations which make them unsuitable for the switching of broadband multimedia information. More specifically, circuit switching cannot easily deal with the variable bit rate transmission that is necessary for integrated multimedia information such as voice, data, and video signals. On the other hand, because packet switching requires the handling of transmission protocols through software control, significant limitations are imposed on transmission speeds. As we have seen, the transmission of the vast amount of information contained in multimedia signals such as video necessitates faster transmission speeds. Furthermore, packet switching, because of the delays involved in the store-and-forward procedures in this kind of switching, is not suitable for continuous information, such as voice information.

Asynchronous transfer mode switching (ATM) was developed in order to deal with these limitions. ATM is a transfer mode which digitizes information of various media having different transmission speeds, such as voice, data, and video, and breaks them into blocks of a set length called 'cells' for transmission within a network.

An ATM switching system is illustrated in Fig. 3.9. The ATM terminal (source) shows the incoming information from voice, data, or video being broken up into predefined cells. 'Labels' or 'headers' are then added to the cells which give the destination for the information contained in the cell. The cells are then transferred at high speed to the ATM network. Here the cells are routed according to the cell headers. They are then sent to the ATM terminal (destination), where the cell header is examined, the cell disassembled, and the information sent through the terminal to the user–receiver in the form of voice, data, or video.

The main reason for the high speed and efficiency of the ATM switch is its simplicity. Because all the cells are of the same predetermined fixed length (consisting of 53-byte blocks), the protocols, which define the way in which the information signals are transmitted, are simplified. This simplification enables the ATM switch to take advantage of the progress in VLSI semi-conductor technology so that the transmission can take place on a hardware rather than software basis. This allows the cells to be treated in a uniform manner at all the stages of the operation: at the terminals, by the transmission equipment, and by the switching systems responsible for communications. In turn, this makes high-speed, broadband multimedia switching possible.

The Development of ATM Switching by NTT

The beliefs contained in NTT's VI&P vision served to orient the company's activities to the future in an uncertain world. There was a further set of beliefs which shaped the evolution of NTT's ATM switch. The first of these was the

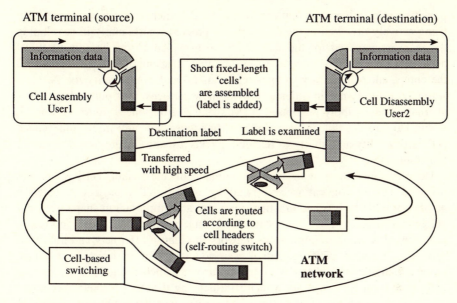

Fig. 3.9 The mechanism of an ATM switch
Source: NTT.

belief that NTT should play a leading/initiating role in developing the ATM switch, which it needed to help realize its VI&P vision. ATM technology was already beginning to be developed, not only in the research laboratories of the leading carriers and equipment suppliers, but also by computer and semiconductor companies. These companies were eager to take part in the first applications of ATM technology, such as the connection of local area networks (LANs) used, for example, for the networking of computers. NTT, however, believed that it should not wait for the time when equipment vendors would have ATM switches ready for sale; rather, NTT should take the initiative and lead its suppliers in developing the ATM switches it needed. It was this kind of thinking that led NTT to spend $2,547 million on R&D in 1993, some 4.5 per cent of its revenue.

Why not let the equipment suppliers take the lead—and the risk—in developing ATM switches? According to NTT's belief system, there were two reasons. The first was that if NTT were to wait it would lose the opportunity to be one of the world's leading carriers introducing the most advanced services. According to NTT views, the equipment suppliers tend to be uncertainty-averse, only seriously developing equipment when they feel sure of making a profit. But since NTT can hold out the promise of large procurement sales in the future, it can entice equipment suppliers into developing advanced equipment such as ATM earlier than they would otherwise do.

In the case of switching, there was also a more practical reason for playing a proactive role in the development of the ATM switches that were needed. By being actively involved in the development process—particularly in developing the software required for the services to be provided by the broadband ISDN network—NTT would be able to ensure that it accumulated and controlled the competences necessary to operate, maintain, and even modify the switch's software in the future in order to provide new services. If it pursued the other alternative, and simply purchased ATM switches from one or more vendors, it would have to depend on them for modifications. Not only might this reduce NTT's flexibility and ability to respond quickly by introducing new services, it might also be costly.

Detailed interviews with a large number of the senior NTT managers involved in the conception and planning of the ATM project revealed a number of other beliefs and practices that were also important in shaping the development project. First, in establishing this project, NTT was motivated primarily by a desire to improve its network in order to offer new and improved services. A senior NTT executive was adamant that a desire to compete more effectively with the new common carriers which since 1985 have been competing with NTT was *not* a factor influencing the ATM project. Secondly, the decision to go ahead with the ATM project was made without rigorously comparing the costs and benefits to NTT of developing the ATM switch with its suppliers instead of buying the switch on the market from vendors. The belief referred to earlier—that NTT should lead the market rather than be led by it—underlay the decision to launch the ATM project without a full cost–benefit analysis of the 'develop/buy' alternative. (This decision was therefore made in a way that contradicts the assumption made in transaction costs economics, that, in deciding whether to 'make' or 'buy', decision-makers compare both alternatives and choose the cost-minimizing one.) We will return to this issue later.

There was a further set of beliefs that influenced the evolution of NTT's ATM switch. These beliefs were carried over from NTT's past experience with what in this book is termed 'controlled competition'. According to these beliefs, it was desirable that NTT co-operate closely with a closed group consisting of a small number of equipment suppliers. (The way in which controlled competition operated in the development of the digital time-division switch was analysed earlier in this chapter.)

Changing external circumstances, however, put severe pressure on these beliefs. Since the 1920s first NTT's predecessor, the Ministry of Communications, and then NTT had worked with a fixed group of Japanese companies—the so-called Den Den Family, consisting of NTT together with NEC, Fujitsu, Hitachi, and Oki. Changes within Japan (examined in detail in Chapter 7), together with pressure being put on Japan by its trading partners to open the Japanese market—particularly to the USA—meant that it was impossible for NTT to maintain the Den Den Family.

How did NTT and the other Japanese interests involved (such as the Ministry of Posts and Telecommunications) respond to these pressures? In the area of immediate relevance, namely R&D and procurement of equipment, a new procedure was introduced. Under the so-called Track Three provision (see Chapter 7 for further details), NTT was required to advertise internationally, in an open and non-discriminatory way, when it wished to develop co-operatively equipment that was not yet available in satisfactory form on the market, and to invite applications to join from potential partners. Under this provision, it is worth noting, NTT was able to keep the main components of its belief structure intact. To begin with, it was still able to take the lead in developing new equipment. Furthermore, it was able to establish a co-operative relationship with a small group of suppliers. The main difference was that this group would now include both Western equipment companies as well as new Japanese entrants.

Participants in the ATM Project

Following its traditional practice, NTT began by carrying out its own research. Accordingly, in 1986 it started doing research on ATM switching. By October 1989, it had developed a fully fledged experimental ATM switching system. On 12 April 1990, NTT officially invited partners for its ATM project. The deadline for applications was 20 August 1990, and on 9 January 1991 NTT announced the companies that had been selected.

The ATM project was divided into two distinct sub-projects: the ATM Node System (involving switching) and the ATM Link System (involving the transmission). The participants chosen for the ATM Node System were Fujitsu, Hitachi, NEC, Northern Telecom, Oki, and Toshiba. The participants for the ATM Link System were AT&T, Fujitsu, Hitachi, Mitsubishi Electric, NEC, and Siemens.

Beliefs, Strategic Choices, and Dilemmas[92]

> I don't think economics is going to change rapidly until all graduate students are exposed . . . to field methods that study how decisions are actually made in the firm.[93]

The economist assigned to analysing the issues involved in deciding on ATM switching, drawing on his or her conceptual toolkit, is likely to think that the matter is relatively straightforward. Essentially, the carrier (in this case NTT) has a choice between two options. The first—which may be termed the 'develop' option—is for NTT to develop the ATM switch itself, with or without the supplier/s who will then manufacture the switch (since NTT does not have

---

[92] This subsection is based on a number of detailed interviews with senior staff closely involved in the planning, design, and development of NTT's ATM switch from NTT itself and the suppliers involved in the ATM project.

[93] Comment by H. Simon in H. Simon *et al.*, *Economics, Bounded Rationality and the Cognitive Revolution*, Edward Elgar, Aldershot, 1992, p. 22. Simon was awarded a Nobel Prize in 1978.

manufacturing competences). The second option—termed the 'buy' option—is for NTT to stipulate the specifications it requires and then invite vendors to tender for the procurement of the switches. The choice is made on the basis of a cost-minimizing calculation, taking account not only of the costs of designing, developing, manufacturing, installing, and maintaining the switch, but also the costs of the transactions that are necessary in order ultimately to get the switches in place and operating. (The transaction costs might include, for example, the costs of establishing whether the vendor is reliable, has the necessary capabilities, and will be available to provide the post-purchase services that are necessary to maintain the switch.[94]) The option that has the lowest cost will be chosen.

Such an economist would soon discover, however, that alas, things are not so simple. To begin with, even if choice were confined to only these two options, considerable problems will arise regarding the information that is necessary for a cost-minimizing calculation to be made. Even if the unrealistic assumption is made that all the information necessary is already available, for a product as complex as an ATM switch, and with the large number of potential vendors, the costs of acquiring the information, processing it, and making the cost-minimizing calculation will be substantial.

But of course, much more important, as the economist would soon discover, is the fact that most of the crucial information is not only unavailable, but cannot even be calculated (at any cost!) with the degree of accuracy needed in order to make a cost-minimizing choice between the two options. The reason, simply, is that, at the time NTT was confronted with this choice, ATM still consisted mainly of a number of concepts and experimental systems. And, as we saw above in connection with the development of earlier generations of switches, the international switching industry has no successful track record of predicting the development costs of new switching systems. Nor can we expect them to succeed in view of the irreducible uncertainty that attaches to the evolution of future technologies. In the light of such uncertainty, and the interpretive ambiguity that this necessarily implies, 'rational' cost-minimizing calculations and choices are impossible. Accordingly, my own findings that none of the telecommunications companies interviewed—including NTT, BT, AT&T, DDI, MCI, NEC, Fujitsu, and Hitachi—attempted to make such calculations should come as no surprise.[95]

How, then, did NTT proceed in making the key decisions regarding the development of the ATM switch? It made its decision to develop not on the basis of a comparison with the 'buy' alternative, but in the light of its general belief

[94] For an account of transaction cost economics, see O. E. Williamson, *Markets and Hierarchies: Analysis and Antitrust Implications: A Study in the Economics of Internal Organization*, Free Press, New York, 1975; and O. E. Williamson, *The Economic Institutions of Capitalism*, Free Press, New York, 1987.

[95] See M. Fransman, 'Whether To Develop Yourself Or To Buy, That Is The Question: An Analysis of the Develop/Buy Decision in NTT, AT&T, BT, DDI, and MCI', paper for the Telecommunications Advancement Foundation, Tokyo, 1994.

structure. As indicated earlier, this belief structure held that it was necessary for NTT to take the lead, in advance of the equipment vendors, in developing complex new technologies. It is worth pointing out, however, that the guidance of choice by belief rather than cost-minimization (as our economist referred to earlier would prefer to have it) should not be regarded as either 'irrational' or 'non-rational'. In view of the problems raised by the cost of information acquisition and processing, by uncertainty, and by the resulting interpretive ambiguity, making decisions such as this one on the basis of guiding beliefs may be the only reasonable way of proceeding.

However, the necessary precondition, of course, is that the beliefs themselves must be reasonable. They must not be obsolete, and they must be 'in tune' with reality. That it is often not possible to 'test' or 'prove' that beliefs are reasonable and in tune, and that interpretive ambiguity often attaches to the very beliefs that are used to deal with interpretive ambiguity regarding the requirements of the firm's circumstances, is an unfortunate fact of life. Often, however, the firm has no option but to proceed on the basis of the beliefs it has constructed. Nevertheless, the firm constantly receives feedback from its environment (which affects factors such as its sales, market share, and profits), and it is this feedback against which the firm's beliefs are constantly being tested. In some cases, the selection feedback from the firm's environment will over time establish to the satisfaction of most that the firm's beliefs are inappropriate and will have to be modified if the firm is to survive. This is precisely what happened with IBM when its leaders finally came to the conclusion in 1991 that they had to modify their beliefs concerning the role of the mainframe in their business. In Chapter 7 and in the concluding chapter, we will deal with the question of whether NTT's beliefs regarding R&D and procurement are becoming obsolete in the light of the changing circumstances of the 1990s. Here, however, the main concern is with the decisions that NTT made regarding the development of its ATM switch.

Having decided that it would take the lead in developing the ATM switch in co-operation with a small group of vendors, NTT then confronted a further complex choice. The 'develop' option itself was divided into several further options, depending on the division of labour between NTT itself (as the user of the switch) and the vendors (as the producers). These options ranged from NTT being very actively involved in all of the tasks, leaving only the manufacture of ATM entirely to the vendors, to NTT being only minimally involved (only deciding on the functions it required from the switch and the specifications needed for the switch to be compatible with the network), leaving everything else to the vendors. (It is worth noting in passing that it is the latter option that NTT's competitors have chosen, on the basis of their (very different) beliefs. See Chapter 8 for the case of DDI. It is also worth observing that the existence of these further subchoices makes considerably more complicated any attempt to use a cost-minimizing methodology, since a greater number of options have to be evaluated.)

NTT came up with a list of five options that it had in operating in a multi-vendor environment:

1. Procure equipment from more than one vendor, all of whom are allowed to decide specifications as they like.
2. Determine common external interfaces and function requirements, allowing considerable differences among vendors' specifications.
3. Determine common software interfaces, letting vendors decide a large portion of hardware and software specifications.
4. Determine software specifications, letting vendors decide a relatively small portion of hardware specifications.
5. Determine both hardware and software specifications.

How did NTT decide which of these five options was best for its purposes? According to its general beliefs, discussed earlier, the first two options were unacceptable since they posed the difficulty of NTT having to depend on its vendors when modifying the switch in order to develop different functions and services; for strategic reasons, NTT did not want to be in such a dependent position. Although option 3 posed similar problems of dependence, the degree of dependence would be somewhat less than under the first two options.

While option 5 would overcome most of the problems of dependence by leaving both the design of the switch, as well as the competences to modify the switch, in NTT's hands, it raised other problems. In particular, this option would limit NTT's ability to take significant advantage of the vendor's hardware competences (for example, the design of the processors for the switch). Since NTT has never become involved in the manufacture of telecommunications equipment or computers, it has a comparative disadvantage in this area relative to the vendors. While option 5 was chosen in the late 1970s for the co-operative development of the D60 and D70 digital switches, the competences of the vendors had increased significantly since then. Although option 4 would allow NTT to take greater advantage of the vendor's competences than option 5, it suffered from a similar weakness.

In the light of the options, NTT ultimately decided on a compromise, somewhere between options 3 and 4. This is shown in Fig. 3.10. The software architecture of the ATM switch is depicted in terms of four modules or 'layers', separated from each other and from the hardware by an interface. The first layer controls the hardware while the second controls the logic functions for the switching. The third layer controls the calling. It is the fourth layer, also referred to in the figure as the 'intelligent layer', which controls the services that are provided by the switch. The aim of the S3 interface is to separate the fourth layer from the implementation carried out in the other three layers (also referred to in Fig. 3.10 as the 'transport layer'). The separation (or modularization) of the fourth layer allows changes to be made to the switch in order to provide new services without having to modify the other three layers.

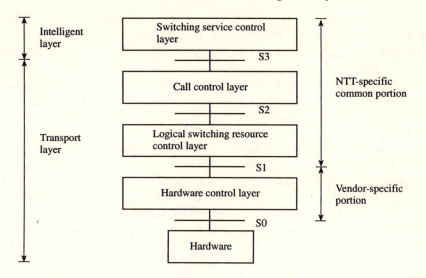

S0: Hardware interface
S1: Multi-vendor interface concealing the hardware and its
     architecture
S2: Interface to provide logical switching resource for call
     control layer
S3: Interface so that intelligent layer can efficiently enhance
     advanced service control functions independently from the
     implementation of the transport layer

Fig. 3.10 The division of labour between NTT and vendors in developing the ATM switch

S0, hardware interface; S1, multi-vendor interface concealing the hardware and its architecture; S2, interface to provide logical switching resources for call control layer; S3, interface enabling intelligent layer efficiently to enhance advanced service control functions independently from the implementation of the transport layer.
Source: NTT.

As the right-hand of the figure illustrates, NTT decided to keep control of the second, third, and fourth layers, leaving control of the hardware and the first hardware control layer to the vendors. The S1 interface, not only separating the first from the second layers, but also dividing responsibility between NTT and its vendors, had to be worked out co-operatively, taking into account the specific details of the vendor's hardware and software portions.

Modifying Controlled Competition for ATM

Having decided on the strategic parameters for developing the ATM switch, NTT confronted two further problems. The first was how to work co-operatively with suppliers who, while co-operating with NTT, were at the same time intending to compete vigorously in the global market for ATM switches. The second was how to take maximum advantage of the suppliers' technological competences. In the case of both the D10 space-division and the D60 and D70 digital time-division switches discussed earlier, NTT had worked with NEC, Fujitsu, Hitachi, and Oki in determining both the hardware and the software specifications (that is, option 5 above). In order to do this, the hardware and software were broken up into a number of 'modules'. These modules were developed jointly by NTT and at least two of the suppliers, under the leadership of NTT.

This mode of organization, however, was inappropriate for developing the ATM switch. To begin with, given the strong competences of the suppliers in hardware and related software, it was unnecessary for NTT to 'reinvent the wheel' and spend resources developing components and systems (such as the processors for the switch) that had already been developed by the suppliers. Furthermore, since new competing suppliers had been chosen to participate in the project—namely Northern Telecom and Toshiba—(and procurement would have to be shared among a larger number of suppliers), it was now more difficult to persuade the suppliers to share information.

NTT resolved these problems in two ways. First, it arranged joint meetings in order to reach a consensus on the common multi-vendor interface with which all the suppliers' ATM switches would have to be compatible—namely the S1 interface in Fig. 3.10. Secondly, NTT arranged *separate* meetings with each of the suppliers in order to discuss the related hardware and software details. At these meetings secret company-specific technical information could be discussed, since NTT guaranteed that such information would not be passed on to the other competing suppliers. Having agreed on the common S1 interface, the suppliers could go ahead and develop their own ATM switches on the basis of their own company-specific technologies. Since all their switches would be compatible with the S1 interface, and therefore compatible with the software developed for the remaining three layers above this interface (see Fig. 3.10), the suppliers' switches would be perfectly substitutable, leaving NTT free to choose as it wished from among the suppliers.

Having agreed on the S1 interface, the next job was for the suppliers to produce their ATM switch prototypes with NTT playing the co-ordinating role. NTT undertook to pay the costs of the prototype development. On the basis of the prototype ATM switch, NTT could then proceed to develop the rest of the software that was needed—the 'NTT-specific common portion' referred to in Fig. 3.10. When this task was completed, the suppliers would become 'qualified designated suppliers', which would enable them to apply when the time came for NTT to call for tenders for ATM switches. According to the Track Three procedures, any vendor from around the world can apply to become a qualified designated supplier. In this sense, NTT's procurement is genuinely open. However, clearly, there are significant entry costs involved. Although any potential vendor is in principle free to make the investments necessary to qualify as a supplier of ATM switches that will meet NTT's specifications, those vendors that have taken part in the joint development of ATM switches with NTT are at an obvious advantage, with NTT having paid the cost of prototype development and as a result of the learning they have undergone. The likely outcome, therefore, is that there will be 'small numbers competition' at the procurement stage. Certainly, the expectations of the suppliers participating in the ATM project is that they will more or less equally share NTT's procurement according to their own efforts, costs, and performance.

Implementation of ATM Switching

By October 1989, NTT had developed a fully fledged experimental ATM switching system. In October 1991, this ATM system was unveiled at the International Telecommunication Union's (ITU) Telecom 91 in Geneva. After gradually introducing ATM switching into its network, NTT's plan is to replace the current narrow-band digital network with a large-capacity broadband ATM trunk line network by around the year 2000.

In 1991, on the basis of research and development done inside their companies while participating in NTT's joint project, Fujitsu and NEC unveiled their own ATM switching systems. In 1991 Fujitsu became the first company in the world to offer commercially an ATM switching system for the high-speed, two-way transmission and routing of voice, video and data simultaneously. Fujitsu sold trial ATM switches to MCI (AT&T's main competitor), and to four of the Regional Bell Operating Companies, including BellSouth and Nynex. NEC also sold its trial ATM switch in the USA. Both companies announced that their US facilities would manufacture and support their ATM switches sold to American customers. In this way, they hoped to avoid their earlier weakness when they were unsuccessful in entering the US market in the early 1980s with their first digital switches.

Conclusion

This chapter has analysed the co-evolution of technologies, companies, and national innovation systems in the context of telecommunications switching. The technologies are the four main generations of switching technology that have emerged since the Second World War: electromechanical crossbar switches, space-division switches, digital time-division switches, and asynchronous transfer mode (ATM) switches. The companies included both those that entered the 1990s as winners—e.g. AT&T, Alcatel, Ericsson, Northern Telecom, Siemens, NEC, and Fujitsu—and those that dropped out, including ITT, Philips and GTE.

While most attention has been paid to the evolution of the Japanese Innovation System in telecommunications, and in particular to the evolution of its key form of organization—controlled competition—comparative analyses were also provided of the American system centred around AT&T, and the French and British systems. While the French innovation system produced Alcatel, one of the two largest telecommunications equipment companies in the world which incorporated much of the former ITT, the British system—the case of the early bird losing the worm—ended up with a merger of the telecommunications interests of its major company, GPT, and Siemens.

As mentioned in this and previous chapters, the Japanese system of controlled competition evolved from the 1920s and 1930s as a form of organization adapted to the task of assisting Japan to catch up with its technologically more advanced Western counterparts. There is more than a touch of irony, therefore, when in the early 1990s NTT used controlled competition to establish the largest co-operative ATM research and development programme in the world, incorporating the very Western companies that this form of organization was originally intended to catch! The companies included in the two ATM sub-projects were Northern Telecom, AT&T, and Siemens. Other major Western telecommunications have been included in some of NTT's other Track Three projects; among these are Ericsson, which is involved in the development of mobile communications equipment, and Corning, which is involved in the area of transmissions.

Although representing an important break from the past, NTT has discovered, initially to its own surprise, that there are important advantages to be had from modifying its traditional form of organization to include Western companies. For example, my own interviews have revealed that NTT has learned a great deal in the area of software and human interfaces from Western companies such as Northern Telecom and Ericsson. On the other hand, advantages such as these have to be balanced against the higher searching, negotiating and co-ordinating costs that NTT has had to face in order to open its co-operative research and development and procurement to foreign companies.

The last word, however, should be given to the Western companies that have decided—lured by the hope of large sales—to enter into NTT's controlled competition. How have they managed to cope with a co-operative form of organization with all the trappings—such as obligational, trust-based relationships, and consensual forms of decision-making—that many believe are uniquely Japanese? In conducting a large number of interviews with the major Western companies involved with NTT in controlled competition, I was surprised to discover the extent to which their behaviour and expectations were the same as those of their Japanese corporate counterparts. Both Western and Japanese companies appreciated the benefits of a co-operative relationship with a major sophisticated user, although they were also similarly aware of the disadvantages. In the words of a senior executive from Northern Telecom, the Western telecommunications company which more than any other Western company has been incorporated into the new 'NTT Family',

We wish we had more interaction with our users in other global markets like we have with NTT in Japan. NTT is willing to work with you to help you improve, rather than saying 'we will find someone else' when they are not happy with what they get from us. They will not easily drop you and go elsewhere. We have learned a great deal, particularly in areas such as quality improvement and hardware such as electronic devices. On the other hand, NTT has benefited from our expertise in areas such as software. In general, it has been a very rewarding group learning process.[96]

[96] Author's interview with executive from Northern Telecom.

4

The Evolution of the Japanese
Computer Industry

CHAPTER OVERVIEW

What was the influence on the Japanese computer industry of the dominant company in the global computer industry, IBM? This chapter begins
with an analysis of IBM's 'architecture of the mind', showing how IBM
dominated not only global computer architectures, but also beliefs about
what computing was all about. A major theme in the present chapter is the
influence, until the early 1990s, of IBM's architecture of the mind on the
shape of the Japanese computer industry.

What were the major factors that influenced the entry of Japanese
companies into the computer industry in the 1950s? This is the next
question examined, with particular attention being paid to the role of the
telecommunications industry and the Japanese government. The fundamentally different factors motivating entry by the major Japanese computer
companies is stressed.

How did the Japanese companies manage to survive IBM's Systems
360 and 370, which drove powerful companies such as General Electric and
RCA to exit from the computer industry? This question is analysed in the
following sections, with special emphasis on the responses of the Japanese
companies themselves, of MITI, and of NTT. NTT's role in the Japanese
computer industry is examined in detail, showing its special interests in this
industry and the importance of the DIPS family of computers which it developed co-operatively with Fujitsu, NEC, and Hitachi. An explanation is
also provided for the survival of these three companies in the mainframe
market, while Toshiba, Mitsubishi Electric, and Oki exited. The contrasting
case of RCA is compared.

Why, having devoted significant energy to helping Fujitsu, NEC,
and Hitachi catch up with IBM, did NTT in 1988 decide to include both
IBM and Digital Equipment (DEC) in its new multi-vendor computer
architecture project? This question is considered, illustrating the new
conditions that began emerging in the Japanese computer industry
from around this time. How did the US companies adapt to the long-term,
obligational relationships that characterize NTT's controlled competition
with its suppliers? This question is answered through an examination of
DEC's relationship with NTT.

Frustrated by IBM's continuing dominance, MITI officials, in consultation
with the major Japanese computer companies, made several attempts through
the 1980s to break out of the IBM mould. These included some well-known

co-operative R&D projects, such as the VLSI, Supercomputer, and Fifth Generation Computer projects. How successful, in retrospect, were these projects? This question is analysed, examining the longer-run effects of these projects.

The microprocessor was perhaps the most important agent of change which undermined IBM's architecture of the mind. Why are Japanese semi-conductor companies weak in the global microprocessor market? Why are they strong simultaneously in microcontrollers and memories? These issues are the next to be analysed, with emphasis given to the importance of the differing characteristics of semiconductor market demand in the USA and Japan. The influence of the personal computer industries in the two countries is also examined.

In the early 1990s, fundamental change began altering the structure of the Japanese computer industry. What were the main forces for change and what were their effects? The penultimate section of this chapter answers this question to show that the Japanese computer industry, hitherto distinguished from Western counterparts by proprietary computer systems and unique patterns of software creation and use, is increasingly being harmonized with the rest of the global computer industry. The implications of this trend for the Japanese software industry are discussed. The new opportunities presented by harmonization for the Japanese computer companies are examined, paying particular attention to their new entry in the mid-1990s into the global market for packaged software.

The concluding section ties together the threads in this chapter regarding the main causes of the development of the Japanese computer industry. How effective was the Japanese government—particularly MITI and NTT—in facilitating this development? An examination of this question brings the chapter to a close.

Introduction

By the early 1990s, four of the world's ten largest computer companies were Japanese. True, IBM, despite its difficulties, still towered above all the others, with sales of about $65 billion. However, the Japanese companies Fujitsu and NEC were in second and third places, with sales of about $20 billion and $17 billion respectively. Hitachi was in sixth place with about $11 billion, and Toshiba came tenth with about $9 billion.

Two broad questions arise from this league table which are examined in this chapter. First, given that the Japanese companies were weak relative to their Western counterparts at the end of the war, how were they able to get to their current positions? Secondly, why do the individual Japanese companies hold the positions they do in the global pecking order? Although the overall performance of the Japanese computer companies in terms of size is undoubtedly impressive, they nevertheless raise several important puzzles and paradoxes. It is essential to analyse these in order to understand the Japanese computer industry and its major companies.

Puzzles and Paradoxes

Seven such puzzles and paradoxes are analysed in this chapter.

1. *While Japanese computer companies are prominent in the global top ten, they are still mainly oriented to the Japanese domestic market.* The Japanese computer companies have been unable to establish their dominance in global markets the way their Japanese counterparts in areas such as consumer electronics and motor vehicles have. By around 1990, roughly 80 per cent of the worldwide computer revenues of Fujitsu, NEC, Hitachi, and Toshiba came from the Japanese market.

2. *While Japanese computer companies are in the top ranks of the global computer market, they don't feature at all in the global market for computers-on-a-chip (i.e. microprocessors).* In 1971 Intel invented the world's first microprocessor. Just five months later, NEC developed Japan's first micro-processor. However, by 1992 Intel held 73 per cent of the global market for 32-bit microprocessors in terms of sales; Motorola came second with 8.5 per cent and AMD third with 8.0 per cent; fourth was NEC with just 1.1 per cent.

3. *While Japanese companies are very weak in the global market for microprocessors, they are very strong in the global market for microcontrollers (which are simpler but technically similar to microprocessors).* NEC, for example, is the world's largest producer of microcontrollers.

4. *While, as noted, Japanese companies perform poorly in microprocessors, they are dominant in the global market for semiconductor memories (such as dynamic random access memories, DRAMs), which rely on the same underlying technologies and processes.* In 1992, for example, Japanese companies held 45 per cent of the US market for MOS (metal oxide silicon) memories and 57 per cent of the market outside the USA.

5. *Japanese computer companies are among the largest in the world and are big sellers of computer software. Furthermore, studies show that the productivity and quality of their software is comparable with that of US companies. Yet they are extremely weak in the global market for packaged software.* One of the few quantitative comparisons of Japanese and US software projects concluded that 'Japanese software projects perform at least as well as their US counterparts in basic measures of productivity, quality (defects), and reuse of software code.'[1] However, the major Japanese computer companies do not feature in the largest software market, the global market for packaged software. In the early 1990s, when Bill Gates of Microsoft was asked about the Japanese challenge in his software market, he answered, 'What Japanese?' In the year ended March 1994, for example, NEC earned only $152 million—

---

[1] M. A. Cusumano and C. F. Kemerer, 'A Quantitative Analysis of US and Japanese Practice and Performance in Software Development', *Management Science*, 36 (1990): 1384. An important forthcoming study comparing software productivity and quality in leading Japanese and UK companies is being undertaken by the Institute for Japanese–European Technology Studies (JETS) at the University of Edinburgh.

less than 1 per cent of its annual sales—from packaged software. 'Its software exports have been marginal.'[2]

6. *In computers, Japanese companies have a strong international competitiveness in 'commoditized components' but have been unable to establish a dominance in the major 'architectural domains' in the field of computing.* In 'commoditized components'—such as dynamic random access memories (DRAMs), flat panel displays (such as thin-film-transistor liquid crystal displays used in computer screens), lasers, and 'engines' for laser printers—Japanese companies have established strong international competitiveness. However, in the 'architectural domains' that dominate the commanding heights in the field of computing—such as operating systems for personal computers and networks of personal computers or architectures for microprocessors—they have not presented a serious challenge to companies such as Microsoft, Novell, and Intel.

7. *By the late 1980s academic analysts were concluding that the Japanese computer companies had caught up with IBM and were posing the major challenge to the US computer companies. However, by the early 1990s analysts were increasingly arguing that the Japanese had largely got it wrong.* An example of the latter view is one of the more sophisticated of the books that have appeared since IBM announced the biggest loss in corporate history at the beginning of 1993. The book, by Ferguson and Morris, concludes that 'Japanese *computer* companies are not the primary threat to American [computer] firms. . . . the single-minded, 30-year-long focus on IBM's position in mainframes has left the Japanese [computer] industry overcommitted to a commodity manufacturing and a mainframe strategy.'[3]

The Co-evolution of Technologies, Companies, and the National Innovation System

The conceptual framework for this chapter, like the associated chapters on telecommunications switches and optical fibre, involves the analysis of the co-evolution of technologies, companies, and the Japanese innovation system. New technologies, created largely by companies and universities, create new opportunities for companies and foreclose on old options. Companies, conceived of as collections of competences, react to these opportunities and foreclosures in the light of the beliefs that guide their visions. But they are also influenced by, as much as they influence, the other institutions (such as government) which together comprise the national innovation system. In the process, new technologies are created, and in this way technologies, companies, and the national innovation system continue to evolve.

The aim of this chapter is to outline the main dimensions of the co-evolution of technologies, companies, and the innovation system in the case of the Japanese

---

[2] *Nikkei Weekly*, 18 July 1994: 8.
[3] C. H. Ferguson and C. R. Morris, *Computer Wars: How the West Can Win in a Post-IBM World*, Times Books, New York, 1993, 220, 230.

computer industry. In doing so, explanations will be provided for the seven puzzles and paradoxes listed above.

The Importance of Vision: IBM's Architecture of the Mind

The evolution of the global computer industry, as well as Japan's computer industry, can be analysed in terms of the transition from one dominant vision of how information should be processed to a very different vision regarding information processing. These two visions may be thought of metaphorically as successive patterns generated by a kaleidoscope.

The first pattern, or vision, resembles a *large continent consisting of numbers of mainframe computers* surrounded by *smaller and less influential islands of smaller computers*, first minicomputers, and then personal computers and workstations. But then a change occurs, and the positioning of the elements in the kaleidoscope alters, revealing a fundamentally different pattern—the second vision. The continent of mainframes has shrunk considerably in size (although it is still there) relative to the islands, which have become far more numerous. Each island is now more powerful, both in absolute terms and relative to the mainland, than it was before. And the islands are now increasingly *connected* to one another by communications systems that can transport huge quantities of information, rapidly and cheaply.

What has caused this transition, this kaleidoscopic change from one pattern to another, fundamentally different pattern? The answer is: the evolution of some of the elements that generated the first pattern—particularly the electronic devices, including microprocessors and memories. As the performance of these devices steadily increased, so 'downsizing' occurred as users increasingly substituted distributed networks of smaller computers for many (but not all) of their mainframes. This gradually forced a realignment of the other elements, in the process generating a fundamentally new pattern and vision.

Two related events were responsible for the generation of the first pattern and its associated vision. The first was IBM's rise to a position of dominance from the mid-1950s. This dominance was the result of the far greater commitment of resources that the company made, compared with its competitors, which turned it into a research-driven company. This increased commitment coincided with the passing of leadership from Thomas J. Watson Sr to Thomas J. Watson Jr. In 1954 IBM was the fourth largest US seller of digital computers, with total sales of all products of $461 million compared with RCA's $941 million, Sperry Rand's $696 million, and Bendix Aviation's £608 million. In 1956 IBM hired Emanuel R. Piore, who had been chief scientist at the Office of Naval Research, as Director of Research. IBM's R&D expenditure, which had been running at about 15 per cent of net income, jumped to about 30 per cent. By 1963, on the eve of IBM's introduction of its System 360 family of computers, IBM's data processing revenues were the highest in the US computer industry: its data processing revenue of $1,244 million compared with $145 million for Sperry, $85 million for Control Data, and $74 million for Philco in fourth place.[4]

The second event responsible for the generation of the first vision was IBM's System 360. This family of smaller to larger mainframe computers allowed companies to upgrade their computing capabilities as the need arose while maintaining software compatibility between their machines. From IBM's point of view, System 360 allowed the company to standardize both its hardware and software, thus significantly cutting costs.

These two related events thrust IBM into a position of dominance in the computer industry, in the process creating a world in its own image. It was a world that IBM had structured, a world that the other players (including the Japanese) had little alternative but to accept, seeking to position themselves as best they could against their more powerful adversary.

In asserting its dominance, however, IBM not only created a new computer architecture; more importantly, it created an architecture of the mind, a vision of what computing was all about. As we shall see, it was a vision that the main Japanese companies, with one important exception, and the Japanese government policy-makers, bought into. Ironically, it was also a vision that later came to trap IBM as the company viewed the world through its perspective. IBM's increasingly inappropriate vision slowed its ability to respond and adapt as the kaleidoscope inexorably rolled on, generating the new patterns and visions that would come to shape the computer industry in the 1990s. Thus, although in the 1970s it had developed what was arguably the first personal computer, IBM, constrained by its outmoded vision, did not understand the new world of distributed networks of smaller computers that was in the making. And, as Bill Gates of Microsoft—the company that came to dominate the operating system architectural domain for personal computers—later observed, 'Personal computing was qualitatively a very different thing than the computing that came before.'[5]

In order to explain the evolution of the Japanese computer industry to its present state, it is necessary to understand first the dominance of the 'IBM Vision', and then the transition to the new vision of the 1990s and beyond. The few notable detailed analyses of the Japanese computer industry are limited by their focus on the 'IBM Vision', thus missing the important changes that were in the process of ushering in the New World. The story of the Japanese computer industry, accordingly, must be updated.[6]

---

[4] These figures come from K. Flamm, *Creating the Computer: Government, Industry, and High Technology*, Brookings Institution, Washington, DC, 1988.

[5] Bill Gates, quoted in *Business Week*, 27 June 1994: 37.

[6] These analyses of the Japanese computer industry include M. Fransman, *The Market and Beyond: Information Technology in Japan*, Cambridge University Press, 1990 and 1993. They also include Flamm's *Creating the Computer* (see fn. 4 above) and K. Flamm, *Targeting the Computer: Government Support and International Competition*, Brookings Institution, Washington, DC, 1987. In addition, there is M. Anchordoguy, *Computers Inc.: Japan's Challenge to IBM*, Harvard University

The Japanese Computer Industry in the 1950s:
Company Entry on the Back of Government Research

Roots in the Japanese Telecommunications Industry

To understand the evolution of the Japanese computer industry, it is crucial to understand that this industry is rooted in the Japanese telecommunications industry. And the soil that was the telecommunications industry influenced the form that the computer industry over time assumed.

The best illustration of this is the fact that the three main Japanese computer companies—Fujitsu, NEC, and Hitachi—all have competences in telecommunications, while none of the top US companies have. This is true of IBM, Digital Equipment (DEC), Hewlett-Packard, and Unisys, which in 1992 were first, fourth, fifth, and ninth largest in the world in terms of sales. In the early 1980s IBM made an abortive attempt to add telecommunications competences to its collection of computer competences with its short-lived acquisition of Rolm, a company involved in private branch exchanges (PBXs). AT&T, the seventh largest computer company, is the only partial exception to this generalization with its hostile acquisition of NCR. But AT&T itself has admitted that it has not yet succeeded in realizing the synergies between telecommunications and computing that were the objective of this acquisition. Whether the Japanese companies in the future will be able to turn their different combination of competences to their competitive advantage is an important question to which we shall return in the concluding chapter to this book.

It is unsurprising, however, that enterprises with a background in older telecommunications competences should extend these into the new area of computing. Indeed, it is far more surprising that this did *not* happen in the USA. As observed in the official *A History of Engineering and Science in the Bell System*,

It is no accident that Bell Labs was deeply involved with the origins of both analog and digital computers, since it was fundamentally concerned with the principles and processes of electrical communication. Electrical analog computation is based on the classic technology of telephone transmission, and digital computation on that of telephone switching. Moreover, from its very inception, Bell Labs found itself with a rapidly growing load of design calculations, performed partly with slide rules but mainly with

Press, Cambridge, Mass., 1989. All these books, it has to be said, were written in the 'IBM mould', reflecting both the time and the prevailing thinking when they were researched. They also reflect the thinking of decision-makers in the Japanese Ministry of International Trade and Industry (MITI) as well as in the Japanese computer companies, particularly Fujitsu and Hitachi. However, they are weak on topics such as the emergence of microprocessors and personal computers both globally and in Japan. And they do not contain a detailed analysis of the Japanese software industry and its idiosyncracies, particularly the unique dominance in Japan of customized over-packaged software, a phenomenon that is only now beginning to change. They do not deal adequately with the seven 'puzzles and paradoxes' that are identified at the beginning of this chapter.

desk calculators. The magnitude of this load of routine computation and the necessity of carefully checking it indicated a need for new methods.[7]

Why then did the Japanese telecommunications companies move into computers whereas the US telecommunications companies did not, leaving it to firms such as those involved in business machines to enter the new computer industry? There are two components to the answer to this question. The first is that from 1882, when the American Bell company restricted itself to purchasing all its telephone equipment from Western Electric (which the company had acquired from Western Union in 1880), AT&T had been a vertically integrated company. In view of its emerging monopoly over telecommunications, this meant that the USA only had one major telecommunications equipment supplier. (The few small US equipment suppliers that supplied the independent carriers outside the Bell system, such as GTE, generally kept out of the computer industry.)

The second component is the 1956 'consent agreement' which AT&T reached with the US Department of Justice as part of the settlement of an antitrust case brought by the latter. Under this agreement, AT&T was excluded from commercial computer activities unrelated to its communications business. While this meant that AT&T dropped out of the commercial general-purpose computer market, it continued its work on computers for communications and military purposes. The company also carried on researching in software, and its notable achievements in this area included the UNIX operating system and C software language.

Japan's First Commercial Computers

Until the mid-1950s, the significant degree of uncertainty associated with both computer technologies and the commercial viability of computers meant that Japanese companies paid little attention to computers. As a result, the first serious computers developed in Japan were developed in government laboratories, and to a lesser extent in universities, rather than in Japanese companies. Later the technology was transferred from these laboratories to the main Japanese electronics companies, to become their first commercial computers.[8]

The crucial government laboratories in the case of computers were the Ministry of International Trade and Industry's (MITI's) Electrotechnical Laboratories (ETL) and NTT's Electrical Communications Laboratories (ECL). Both these laboratories, however, descended from the activities of a government factory established originally by the Ministry of Industry in 1868 to develop domestic telegraph equipment and later taken over by the Ministry of

---

[7] S. Millman (ed.), *A History of Engineering and Science in the Bell System: Communications Sciences (1925–1980)*, AT&T Bell Laboratories, Indianapolis, 1984, 351–2.

[8] An account of the development of the Japanese computer industry is to be found in Ch. 2 of Fransman, *The Market and Beyond*, which provides further details on many of the points summarized in the earlier parts of this chapter.

Communications. This factory, and the associated government laboratories that were eventually set up, were to have a remarkable impact on the Japanese information and communications industry. For example, they served as an 'incubator' for the Japanese entrepreneurs and technicians who later went on to establish and develop the forerunners of companies such as Toshiba, NEC, Fujitsu, and Oki.[9] Moreover, in the late 1950s ETL and ECL developed the ETL series and the Musashino series of computers which were transferred to NEC, Fujitsu, Hitachi, Toshiba, Mitsubishi Electric, and Oki.

How did the Japanese companies themselves react to the advent of the computer as a commercially viable product? The response of each of the companies was quite different, depending on its specific combination of competences and market strengths, its past history, and its beliefs and vision regarding the opportunities presented by its selection environment. This is illustrated by the case of Fujitsu, the company that by the early 1990s had only IBM in front in terms of total sales.

Fujitsu's Entry into Computers: Constructing a Vision for the Postwar Period

By the mid-1950s, Fujitsu had already produced its first computer—significantly, not with its own resources, but with funding obtained from MITI designed to facilitate the development of new industrial products.[10] However, there was still significant interpretive ambiguity regarding the future for Fujitsu in the field of computers. Important uncertainties related to the company's ability to acquire the necessary new technologies, to the future size and growth of the computer market in Japan, and to the competition that Fujitsu would face in this market.

Furthermore, NTT's practice of 'controlled competition', analysed in detail elsewhere in this book, meant that Fujitsu already had a relatively certain and stable market in its sales of telecommunications equipment to NTT, even though the company was significantly behind NEC, the main supplier of such equipment. Under these conditions of interpretive ambiguity, it was hardly surprising that different Fujitsu leaders came to hold different beliefs regarding the company's future direction. As Taiyu Kobayashi, who became Chairman of the Board of Fujitsu in 1981, recalled, 'more than half of the directors preferred a more cautious course of action which dealt with known quantities. Rather than attempting some unknown [i.e. developing computers] . . . if we stuck to contract work for NTT, it had the advantages a long and steady relationship offers, as well as the prospect of assured profitability.'[11]

---

[9] Further details on the Japanese entrepreneurs originally trained in this government laboratory are to be found in 'Theory of the Firm and Explaining the Growth of "Real" Firms: The Case of Japanese Information and Communications Companies', in M. Fransman, *Visions of the Firm and Japan*, Oxford University Press, forthcoming. This is a companion volume to the present book.

[10] See Fransman, *The Market and Beyond.*

[11] Taiyu Kobayashi; quoted in Fransman, *The Market and Beyond.*

There was, however, a group of engineers already in Fujitsu, including Kobayashi, which had been involved in the development of the company's first computers and which wanted to see computers becoming a priority for Fujitsu. However, as a result of the vision of the majority of directors, Kobayashi remembers, 'Regardless of the merits of our plan [to develop computers in Fujitsu], because we were still viewed with the bias accorded a stepchild, we could expect a predictably sour response.'[12]

A major change was required within Fujitsu before the company's prevailing vision—albeit a vision contested by a minority of directors—could change in favour of computers. As it turned out, this change came about at the right time, although fortuitously. In 1959 Wada, overburdened by his responsibilities as President of both Fuji Electric and Fujitsu, asked Kanjiro Okada to become President of Fujitsu. Before the war, Okada had been President of the Furukawa company but had been ousted in a realignment. As early as 1955, Okada, who had been moved to a cement company in the Furukawa group, Ube Industries, had come to believe that computers had an important future for Japanese companies. Kobayashi recollected his visit in this year to discuss computers with Okada: 'What excited me was that Okada had listened to our presentation, nodding from time to time as if in agreement, and had shown a great enthusiasm for computers.'[13]

It was Okada who was responsible for the emergence of a new vision in Fujitsu, a vision that put computers at the centre of the company's future. When he became President of Fujitsu in 1959,

Okada disregarded the advice of the directors set in their old ways. He quickly picked a number of young men like our computer group and assigned them to important positions in the company. Although it was a radical recasting of the company, I do not think our [computer] business could have been transformed so quickly had he not done so. . . . From the point of view of the people directly involved it was strong medicine and only possible because of Okada.[14]

However, the adoption of this new vision did not bring about the end of Fujitsu's problems. The company still had to cope with a selection environment that severely restricted its access to the emerging markets for computers. At this time government markets, and especially NTT, were particularly important since a large private market for computers had not yet emerged. Kobayashi explained the difficulty that Fujitsu confronted:

NTT is one of Fujitsu's main customers—primarily for telephone switching equipment. We also . . . tried to sell them computers. . . . however, they had an unwritten policy [part of NTT's controlled competition] that worked against us: Regardless of how hard we strove, as a manufacturer late to the market we were not able to displace NEC which was there first. A friend of mine at NTT told me, 'If you want to obtain a lion's share of the orders from us, you will have to become the undisputed leader so well known in markets

[12] Ibid. 44.   [13] Ibid. 43.   [14] Ibid. 45.

outside NTT's sphere of influence, that everyone will be asking why we are not buying Fujitsu's equipment.'[15]

Facing difficulties such as this in accessing new computer markets, and being relatively weak in telecommunications equipment compared with NEC, Okada and his supporters in Fujitsu believed that it was important for the future well-being of the company rapidly to build strong competences in computing. It was this competence-creating decision and related subsequent decisions that in 1968 led to Fujitsu overtaking NEC and Hitachi as the leading Japanese computer producer, second at the time only to IBM Japan.

Entry of the Other Japanese Computer Companies

The strategy that Fujitsu derived from the beliefs underlying its vision entailed seizing the opportunity presented by the advent of computers to compensate for its weakness in telecommunications and establishing a strong distinctive competence in computers. NEC, however, was in a quite different position compared with Fujitsu in view of its strength in telecommunications equipment (see Chapter 6). As the commercial demand for computers began to grow, NEC also began to see opportunities in computers. However, from the late 1950s NEC began to develop a very different vision regarding the role of computing in its company. Essentially, NEC saw computers as *complementing* its strength in telecommunications equipment, rather than as a distinct set of technologies, products, and markets. This provided the basis for NEC's 'C&C Vision', based on the convergence of computers and communications. It was this vision that shaped a fundamentally different approach to computing in NEC compared with Fujitsu and Hitachi. Moreover, as in the case of AT&T, NEC's competences in telecommunications facilitated the company's entry into computers. More specifically, NEC's first computers were developed by some of the company's transmissions engineers who worked in its Tamagawa Plant.

The situation of Hitachi was different again. Hitachi was weaker than either NEC or Fujitsu in telecommunications equipment, but was a far larger player in consumer electrical and electronic goods and was also a major competitor in heavy electrical equipment. For Hitachi, the American companies RCA and General Electric (GE), which had become involved in computers and produced similar products to those of Hitachi, served as role models. Hitachi too made the strategic decision to enter the field of computers in the mid-1950s and early on established a prominence in this area in Japan.

Toshiba—unlike NEC, Fujitsu, and Hitachi—was not one of the charmed circle of privileged equipment suppliers to NTT. In other respects, however, its product range was closest to that of Hitachi. Its decision to enter the computer market in the latter 1950s was also probably influenced by the example of GE,

---

[15] Ibid. 46.

its long-time ally and supplier of technology. Mitsubishi Electric's position was similar to that of Toshiba—it was not a member of NTT's family of suppliers, and it too was involved in heavy electrical equipment and consumer electrical and electronic goods. However, it was not as large as Toshiba or Hitachi, and there is some evidence that its decision to enter the field of computers was influenced by the demand for computers in the Mitsubishi Group in the face of government restrictions on imported computers.[16]

Oki was the smallest member of the NTT family. It was primarily a telecommunications equipment company, and its decision to enter the computer market was influenced by the decisions of NEC, Fujitsu, and Hitachi.

The Early 1960s: Developing Computer Competences through Technology Imports

By the late 1950s a consensus had emerged in Japan that the new electronics paradigm in general, and computers in particular, were of increasing strategic significance. Working through its consultative committees in co-operation with industry, MITI had the enabling legislation in place to support the development and diffusion of the new electronics technologies. In 1958, through MITI's initiative, the Japan Electronic Industries Development Association (JEIDA) was established serving as the link between the ministry and the emerging electronics and computer companies.[17]

By the early 1960s there was a growing commercial demand for computers both in Japan and abroad. However, it was readily apparent to all concerned in Japan that a large technology gap in computers existed relative to Western countries and that this gap was growing. There were three responses to this gap. The first entailed the establishment of technology agreements with some of the major US companies involved in computers. These agreements are summarized in Table 4.1. Hitachi, the company at the time with the largest market share among the Japanese companies, was the first to sign an agreement—with RCA in May 1961. This was followed over the next two years by Mitsubishi Electric, NEC, and Oki, which signed agreements with TRW, Honeywell, and Sperry Rand respectively. Toshiba was the last of the major companies to enter into an agreement, with General Electric in October 1964, some three and a half years after Hitachi's agreement. (Unlike earlier US entrants into the commercial computer market—e.g. IBM, Sperry Rand, and RCA—General Electric, despite its involvement in

---

[16] 'when companies in the Mitsubishi group applied in 1961 to import over 30 IBM 1401 computers, MITI scolded the group: "There are too many applications to import IBM 1401s from the Mitsubishi group." MITI advised Mitsubishi officials either to use computers of other Japanese companies or to make their own, "even if only for Mitsubishi group firms". Mitsubishi chose to make its own machines' (Anchordoguy, *Computers Inc.*, 32–3).

[17] For a more detailed account of the measures taken by MITI in the latter 1950s, see Fransman, *The Market and Beyond*.

Table 4.1 *Technology Agreements between Japanese and US Computer Companies*

Japanese company	US company	Date
Hitachi	RCA	May 1961
Mitsubishi Electric	TRW	February 1962
NEC	Honeywell	July 1962
Oki	Sperry Rand	September 1963
Toshiba	General Electric	October 1964

military-related computers, and with its wide range of other activities, was rather slow to enter this market, doing so only in 1963.)

It was around 1960–1 that Fujitsu became fully committed to computers. By this time, however, the other Japanese computer companies had already entered into negotiations with prospective American technology partners. Fujitsu also actively pursued the possibility of a technology link with an American firm. As Taiyu Kobayashi recalled, 'Like many other Japanese businesses at the time, we gave serious consideration to introducing advanced European and American technology. It was, of course, the easiest method of obtaining such technology.' In view of the negotiations that had already been started by the other Japanese companies, Fujitsu made overtures to IBM.

It turned out, however, that when negotiations to introduce IBM technology were conducted, IBM flatly refused to consider technology transfers unless they were given 100 percent capital participation. This was 'IBM's world policy'. Of course there was no way that Fujitsu was going to become a wholly-owned subsidiary of IBM. This meant that independent development was now the only route open . . . although that path was not an easy one.[18]

To assist the company's efforts, Fujitsu Laboratories was established in 1962 through the merger of a number of R&D sections from several different divisions. This was the first Japanese laboratory to specialize in computer research and development.

The second response involved an increased commitment of R&D and investment in computers by the Japanese companies. This complemented the third response, which comprised a range of supportive measures undertaken by MITI, including co-operative research programmes involving most of the Japanese companies, the establishment of an organization to finance the purchase of Japanese-made computers (the Japan Electronic Computer Company, JECC), and protective tariffs.[19]

---

[18] Kobayashi, quoted in Fransman, *The Market and Beyond*, 45–6.
[19] Measures taken by MITI in the early 1960s are discussed in more detail in Fransman, *The Market And Beyond*. Also see Flamm, *Targeting the Computer*, 254–5, tables D-4 and D-5, for details on the liberalization of foreign investment and imports relating to the Japanese computer industry and Japan's tariff rates on computers and integrated circuits.

IBM Ups the Stakes: System 360

By as early as 1956, IBM was supplying 70 per cent of the world value of computers sold. In 1957, IBM's sales exceeded $1 billion for the first time. Underlining its international competitiveness, in 1960 20 per cent of IBM's revenues came from foreign sources, although the rapidly growing US market accounted for the bulk of its sales. By 1964, the year in which IBM introduced its System 360 family, this foreign proportion had increased to 29 per cent.

In the early 1960s, however, IBM was facing several important problems. Its computers had become dominant in world markets. The 1400 series had become the world standard in medium-size mainframes and the 650 small business computer was the world's first mass-produced computer. The large mainframe 700 series dominated the market in this category. At this time IBM was producing six different lines of computers, all of which were incompatible. However, IBM's competitors—e.g. Sperry, Control Data, Philco, Burroughs, RCA, and GE—following and learning from the leader, were beginning to make inroads into its markets. Equally important, software was beginning to limit the overall growth of the computer market. Software was becoming a greater proportion of the cost of computer systems, and users were reluctant to pay the high price of upgrading their software when they changed to incompatible new or larger systems.

In 1961 a task force was established in IBM to deal with these difficulties. It came up with a radical and daring solution: to develop a new advanced family of *software-compatible* computers, even though this would 'cannabalize' sales of some of IBM's existing computers. The result was the System 360 series of compatible computers, which not only served to reassert IBM's dominance, but also established the dominant belief regarding what computing was about—that is, IBM's architecture of the mind.

The Integrated Circuit

Technically, System 360 depended to a significant extent on the use of hybrid integrated circuits. The first integrated circuits were invented independently in 1959 by Jack Kilby at Texas Instruments and Robert Noyce at Fairchild Semiconductor.[20] (An integrated circuit consists of multiple interconnected circuit components on a single silicon chip.) In 1962 NEC built the first experimental Japanese integrated circuit based on planar technology that it acquired from Fairchild. In the mid-1960s MITI forced NEC to sub-license this technology to other Japanese companies. This measure, together with a small grant to help Japanese companies develop integrated circuits, helped to diffuse the technology in Japan.

---

[20] See Jack S. Kilby, 'Invention of the Integrated Circuit', *IEEE Transactions on Electronic Devices*, ED-23 (1976): 648–9.

By the mid-1960s, a dominant design configuration for general-purpose mainframe computers had been established based on the von Neumann sequential processing architecture. In order to improve performance and cost—and therefore competitiveness—attention increasingly focused on electronic devices. As will be seen later, an important emphasis in Japanese co-operative research programmes in the field of computing was placed on electronic devices. By the late 1960s integrated circuits became the dominant technology for computer processors, and they were soon increasingly used for computer memories.

The Japanese Response to System 360

In the wake of the introduction of System 360, the Japanese computer companies, like their American counterparts which also competed with IBM, took steps to upgrade their computer lines. In Hitachi, NEC, and Toshiba this process was assisted by their agreements with RCA, Honeywell, and GE respectively.

In the autumn of 1965, Fujitsu, which had no computer technology agreement with a major Western company, began to modify its mainframe series. In 1968 this resulted in the FACOM 230-60, an integrated circuit-based computer influenced by System 360. The FACOM 230-60 was regarded in Fujitsu as a 'strategic turning point' for the company. While in 1965 Fujitsu was third to NEC and Hitachi, which were in first and second places, by 1968 Fujitsu had moved to first place as a result of the success of the FACOM 230-60. The first sale of a FACOM 230-60 was to Kyoto University, a sale at a concessionary price that left Fujitsu with little profit. Soon after there were further sales. Early customers included NTT (which apparently—see Taiyu Kobayashi's statement quoted earlier—had become convinced that Fujitsu had accumulated the necessary competences in computing) and the Dai-Ichi Kangyo Bank, which has close financial ties with Fujitsu and the Furukawa group of companies. In 1968, computer revenues for the first time exceeded revenues from communications products in Fujitsu.

One of the main design shortcomings of the original System 360 was that it did not allow for time-sharing, that is the interactive use of the mainframe by several users. By the mid-1960s time-sharing had become increasingly popular, and later versions of System 360 soon introduced time-sharing capabilities. Time-sharing was one of the main objectives of the co-operative R&D project which MITI introduced in 1966–72 as one of its responses to System 360, the Very High Speed Computer System Project (VHSCS). In 1966, MITI's consultative committee with industry, the Electronics Industry Deliberation Council, had concluded that computers were one of the most important determinants of Japan's long-term economic growth. Accordingly, the Council recommended that MITI take steps to promote the computer industry. The VHSCS Project was one of the main policy measures undertaken by MITI to achieve this objective.

The VHSCS Project was under the overall technical co-ordination of MITI's research institute, ETL. The companies that participated in this project were Hitachi, Fujitsu, and NEC—which developed the hardware for a time-sharing computer similar to IBM's time-sharing mainframe, the IBM 360/67 introduced in 1965. Toshiba and Oki, the remaining two participants which were still relatively weak in computing, developed peripheral equipment. One of the principal features of the VHSCS Project was its concentration on electronic devices. In order to develop specific devices, MITI encouraged a process of specialization among the participating companies. Thus, for example, NEC specialized in the development of memories, while Hitachi—which, with its lead in the Japanese computer market at the time, became the lead company in the project—developed high-speed logic devices.

The VHSCS Project has been widely credited with the development of technologies that subsequently made important contributions to the commercial computers of the participating companies. For example, Hitachi's 8700/8800 system used VHSCS technology, as did improvements to Fujitsu's 230 series. NTT's DIPS computers (discussed in more detail below) also embodied VHSCS technologies. But important questions arise regarding the nature and extent of the 'co-operation' that MITI was able to elicit from the participating companies—which, after all, were strong rivals in the Japanese computer market.

What kind of 'co-operation' occurred between the competing Japanese companies within the VHSCS Project? My own research into this question showed that relatively little knowledge-sharing took place between them. While a division of labour was agreed upon, with ETL serving as the neutral co-ordinator, the work was done inside each company, with no joint research and development being undertaken in the same facilities. My investigation showed that none of the patents resulting from the VHSCS Project were joint patents held by the employees of more than one of the participating companies, indicating the limited extent of knowledge-sharing. By the late 1980s, only 10 per cent of the patents had been licensed out, and this was to only two companies. This points to the 'catching-up' nature of the VHSCS Project rather than to any advancement of the global technology frontier.[21]

Useful though it was, the importance of the progress made under the VHSCS Project was to be thrown into doubt when, as will be seen, IBM introduced its System 370 in 1970. But before then, NTT too was to get into the time-sharing act.

NTT Re-enters: DIPS Computers from 1968

In the late 1960s, there were six Japanese producers of mainframe computers: Hitachi, Fujitsu, NEC, Toshiba, Mitsubishi Electric, and Oki. (Matsushita briefly

---

[21] See Fransman, *The Market and Beyond*, ch. 2.

flirted with computers but unlike RCA soon exited from this area.) By the late 1970s the number was reduced to three: Fujitsu, NEC, and Hitachi. In the early 1990s it was these three companies that were included in the global top ten in terms of sales, together with Toshiba which came tenth, largely as a result of its sales of lap-top computers. It was by no means 'coincidental'[22] that it was Fujitsu, NEC, and Hitachi that came to dominate the Japanese computer industry and to be among the largest computer companies in the world.

To begin with, as we have seen, it was the competences that Fujitsu, NEC and Hitachi had *already* accumulated in the field of telecommunications which, as in the case of AT&T, facilitated their entry into the computer industry in the first place. Toshiba, strong before the war in electronic devices and radio largely as a result of its alliance with General Electric, was relatively weak in the development of electronic systems. It was only in 1964 that Toshiba seriously entered the field of computing through its link with GE, which the year before had made the strategic decision to move from military-related computing into commercial computing. Toshiba's relative weakness was evidenced in the role that it played in MITI's VHSCS Project from 1966, where it specialized with Oki in the development of peripherals rather than the mainframe itself. Despite its strength in the earlier part of the twentieth century in telecommunications equipment, Oki in the postwar period had become by far the weakest of the four main suppliers of equipment to NTT. It was similarly weak in computing. Mitsubishi Electric, like Toshiba, was weakened by its lack of telecommunications capabilities. It was further disadvantaged by its US ally in computing, TRW, which never came to play a prominent role in commercial computers.

Furthermore, Fujitsu, NEC, and Hitachi were significantly advantaged by the long-term relationship that they enjoyed with NTT. Not only in the late 1960s and early 1970s did this relationship provide an important source of technology; throughout the whole postwar period it provided a crucial stable and growing source of demand for their computers. In order to understand the success of these three companies in the field of computing, therefore, it is necessary to examine their relationship with NTT.

NTT and Computers

Analysts have frequently cast NTT and MITI in the role of co-conspirators in

---

[22] '*Coincidentally*, the three survivors [in the Japanese mainframe market in the 1970s, i.e. Fujitsu, Hitachi, and NEC] were all participants—as independent manufacturers—in the design and construction of the DIPS series of timesharing mainframe computers' (Flamm, *Targeting the Computer*, 134; emphasis added). 'NTT has transferred much of the fruit of its internal research efforts . . . to this family of suppliers [i.e. NEC, Fujitsu, and Hitachi] that, *coincidentally*, includes the principal forces in the Japanese computer industry' (Flamm, *Creating the Computer*, 187–8; emphasis added).

the quest to challenge IBM. This judgement is misleading, even though, when their interests and views coincided, NTT and MITI did co-operate closely. In fact, ever since its inception in 1952, NTT has been a relatively autonomous organization, both *vis-à-vis* the ministry under whose jurisdiction it formally falls and with which it often seriously conflicts—that is, the Ministry of Posts and Telecommunications (MPT)—and the ministry whose interests are closest, namely MITI. This relative autonomy is important to understand in grasping how the Japanese innovation system in computing worked.

By the late 1960s, NTT had developed an important commercial interest in computers. While in the latter 1950s the computer was largely an experimental plaything for NTT's researchers, eager, like their counterparts in other parts of the world, to explore the possibilities of the new electronics technologies, by the late 1960s new commercial opportunities were being created by the fusing of computing and communications technologies. More specifically, computers provided NTT with the possibility of providing new data processing services to its customers through its telecommunications network.

The widespread use of digital computers in NTT began in 1964 with the development of a billing system. At the same time, the possibility of a computer-based telephone directory service was examined. However, the real-time processing and large data-base management requirements that were necessary were beyond NTT's current capabilities. The next major application of computers began in 1968 with the development of an on-line computing system for small local banks which could not afford their own systems. With this service, NTT in 1968 established a new division solely dedicated to data communications.

Before 1968, data communications research was housed together with switching research in NTT's ECL. This made sense, with the development in ECL in the mid-1960s of space-division and digital time-division switching which had some technological affinity with computing (as discussed in detail in Chapter 3). In 1968, however, with the prospect of data communications services becoming increasingly important for NTT, the Data Communications Research Division was established, containing three laboratories and initially fifty researchers. The establishment of this division coincided with NTT's strategic decision to begin co-operative development of its own large-scale computer for use in data communications services. This computer was called the DIPS computer (Dendenkosha Information Processing System).

Why did NTT decide to develop its own computer rather than rely on the market for procuring its requirements? It is clear that the decision had little to do with a patriotically motivated desire to strengthen 'Japanese' competences in computing. Indeed, until this time NTT was doggedly self-interested in the decisions that it made in the field of computers, strongly resisting pressures from MITI to give priority to the infant Japanese computer companies.

'It is crazy for you to pressure NTT in its selection of a computer,' an NTT official once warned MITI's Nakagawa. 'We will take you to court!' NTT did not succumb to MITI's pressure. As late as 1971, NTT was using 172 [computing] systems, 109 of which were foreign; of these, 75 were [from] IBM. NTT favored foreign computers in the 1960s because, as the provider of telephone services and other communications infrastructure to the entire nation, it could not afford the substantial social costs inherent in using inferior domestic computers.[23]

Why, then, did NTT in 1968 decide to develop its own computer in co-operation with the manufacturers of these 'inferior domestic computers'? The reason was that, to provide on-line data communications services, NTT would require large mainframes. If it relied on the market for its needs, this would inevitably result in dependence on IBM, the major global supplier of these computers. Such dependence on a near-monopolistic supplier, in turn, would be translated not only into higher costs of procuring computing inputs, but also to less flexibility for NTT to develop its own data communications services on the basis of its own computing capabilities. On the other hand, the development of the DIPS computer would contribute substantially to the accumulation of computer-related competences in NTT, which would provide a source of growth in the future.

The reluctance to be overly dependent on any particular supplier was hardly new to NTT. As shown in the Chapter 2, it was precisely the desire to reduce its dependence on particular suppliers that led the Ministry of Communications (NTT's prewar predecessor) to begin to develop its 'controlled competition' form of organization in the late 1920s. It is in the light of NTT's desire to secure a satisfactory procurement situation that the statement made by Honoki Minoru, Director of NTT's Data Communications Division (which emerged from the activities of the Data Communications Research Division), in 1973 must be seen:

Behind NTT's aggressive entry into data communications [research and development] was, frankly, a view of it as a policy to counter IBM. If our computer makers had only been a bit stronger, it would have been okay for NTT not to do the DIPS project. But five or six years ago, our national [computer] technology and IBM's were on different levels. Because of this, NTT had to take the lead and do it [i.e. develop computers for use in data communications].[24]

The DIPS Project

How did NTT apply its time-tested 'controlled competition' form of organization in developing the DIPS computer co-operatively with Fujitsu, NEC, and Hitachi, and what effect did the project have on these companies?

The decision to develop DIPS was made by NTT in 1968. The following year ECL completed an experimental model, the DIPS-0, which in trials demonstrated the feasibility of a larger project. In 1969 NTT announced that

---

[23] Anchordoguy, *Computers Inc.*, 31.   [24] Ibid.

it would co-operatively develop the DIPS-1 data communications computer, and in July the same year a joint research contract was concluded with Fujitsu, NEC, and Hitachi. (Oki was excluded by NTT from the DIPS project on the grounds of its weakness in computers.) In 1971, the prototype DIPS-1 was completed.

In making its decision to offer on-line data communications services on the basis of mainframes procured from its family of Japanese suppliers, NTT faced two difficulties. The first was that the Japanese companies were still relatively weak in large mainframes. Secondly, in view of Hitachi's and NEC's alliances with different US companies and Fujitsu's development of its own computing system, the Japanese suppliers used different operating systems. For NTT this posed the problem of the costs that would arise if software were not portable across the different computers from the different companies. Furthermore, incompatible computing systems would raise the costs of training computer operators.

To cope with these difficulties, NTT decided to develop a new DIPS operating system jointly with the three suppliers. In order to do so, a new organization was created under ECL's leadership. Three hundred and fifty researchers from ECL's total complement of 1,200 joined this organization together with other personnel from NTT's Data Communications Division and employees from Fujitsu, NEC, and Hitachi. The basic and functional designs of the operating system were developed by NTT jointly with the three companies, with NTT having the final say in the decision-making. NTT retained proprietary rights over the operating system. Once the operating system was completed, facilities were established in NTT's Yokosuka laboratories where NTT, together with the three suppliers, jointly developed the applications software required for particular uses. These included a motor vehicle registration system, an inventory control service for small companies, a scientific calculation service, and a service for members of the national banking system, all developed between 1970 and 1973. Later projects included weather forecasting and air traffic control.

While the DIPS project involved the creation of a common operating system for all the suppliers, NTT was able to rely on the three companies for the supply of the hardware compatible with this operating system. Accordingly, hardware specifications were left up to each company. In practice, Fujitsu, Hitachi, and NEC adapted their existing mainframes for use as DIPS computers. On the one hand, this meant that NTT was able to 'free-ride' on the hardware already developed by the companies and to benefit from any improvements they made. On the other hand, the companies were able to incorporate innovations made under the DIPS project into the computers that they sold outside the NTT system. For example, Fujitsu's 230-75 mainframe benefited from high-speed logic circuits developed under the DIPS-1 project. Some of the advances made in MITI's VHSCS Project were also incorporated into DIPS computers.

IBM's Bombshell: System 370

No sooner was NTT's DIPS-1 project off the ground when IBM dropped its latest bombshell—System 370, which gave IBM a great leap forward and led several of its major competitors to exit from the computer industry. Ironically, however, System 370 at first appeared to IBM to be a damp squib. When System 370 was eventually announced in 1970, after several years of development, the USA and world economies were in recession and IBM's sales rate decreased significantly. So serious was the situation perceived to be that in the summer of 1971 IBM established a task force with a brief similar to that which was set up a decade earlier and which led to System 360. The work of the later task force resulted in a strategic plan that was every bit as bold as the one ten years earlier. Code-named Future Systems, the plan was to leapfrog over the next generation of mainframes (which IBM would have expected to introduce around 1975) through the development of radically advanced technologies.

(As will be seen later, near panic broke out in Japan when the Japanese got wind of the very large-scale integrated circuits (VLSIs) that were planned under the Future Systems project. In response, first NTT and then MITI established Japanese VLSI projects. Unexpectedly, however, there was more than a slip twixt cup and lip for IBM—the overly ambitious Future Systems project failed and was abandoned in 1976, the very year in which MITI began its VLSI project. Furthermore, the ramifications of the unsuccessful Future Systems project were to reverberate through IBM, causing the company to cling in an increasingly reactionary way to its current System 370 technology, in the process stunting the generation of new technologies and products that were being developed in the company, such as reduced instruction set (RISC) microprocessors and computers.)

System 370 was able to provide improved features, such as virtual memory and increased performance, by drawing on the incremental innovations that were being made in areas such as integrated circuits. Despite IBM's initial pessimistic sales forecasts, with the end of the recession, sales of System 370 computers rapidly increased. For IBM's competitors, System 370 signalled the significant increase in R&D and associated investment that was necessary to remain competitive in the commercial computer market. Some of IBM's main rivals were unwilling to make the necessary commitment. This was the case for General Electric and RCA.

Despite the company's plunge into commercial computing in 1963 and its acquisition of the French computer company, Machines Bull, the following year, GE remained something of a reluctant participant. Its decision to exit, made finally in April 1970, coincided with the introduction of System 370. GE sold its computer division to Honeywell although it remained in computer services. RCA's decision to drop out came just over a year later, in September 1971. Its computer operations were sold to Sperry Rand. TRW similarly decided to leave the computer market.

The Japanese Response to System 370

In 1969 MITI identified the 'knowledge-intensive industries' as being crucial to Japan's long-term growth. In 1971, in the wake of the introduction of System 370, MITI-drafted legislation was passed allowing the Ministry to propose plans for the development of the electronics and machinery industries (which included the development of 'mechatronics', the fusion of electronics and machine technologies).

Essentially, there were four major related responses in Japan to System 370 which were intended to promote the development of the domestic computer industry: subsidization of computer research, development and sales; co-operative R&D programmes; 'rationalization' of the industry through closer government-encouraged interfirm co-ordination; and NTT's DIPS-11 project.[25]

Subsidization and Co-operative R&D Programmes

Through its close consultations with the major Japanese computer companies, MITI realized that, if Japanese companies were to survive the stage of rapidly increasing research, development, and investment costs in the computer industry, government funding was going to be necessary. The inevitability of the coming liberalization of international trade, which would reduce the price and increase the availability of imported computers in Japan, made the matter all the more urgent. Accordingly, subsidies that directly or indirectly benefited the Japanese computer companies were stepped up. These included, for example, loans extended by the Japan Development Bank (which worked in close co-ordination with MITI) to organizations such as the Japan Electronic Computer Company, which subsidized the purchase of computers made by Japanese companies, and the provision of accelerated depreciation allowances.

Furthermore, MITI launched two co-operative R&D programmes. The first, and by far the larger, was the Mainframe Computer Project (often referred to as the 3.5 Generation Project), 1972–6, which aimed at the development by Japanese companies of a new family of computers that would rival System 370. The project included research on logic devices, memories, input/output terminals, and software. In addition, funding was provided for the development of applications systems in eight fields, including hospitals, education, and pollution prevention. As in the VHSCS Project, through consultation with the Japanese computer companies, R&D tasks were allocated to the companies, which did the related work in-house.

The second co-operative project was the Pattern Information Processing System (PIPS) Project, 1971–80. The aim of the project was to develop computer technology for the recognition and processing of pattern information such as characters, pictures, objects, and speech. The project also provided for the development of electronic devices to support these capabilities, such as a

---

[25] See Fransman, *The Market and Beyond*, for further details.

one-chip 16-bit microprocessor and a parallel image processor. The participating companies were the computer companies—Fujitsu, NEC, Hitachi, Toshiba, Mitsubishi Electric, and Oki—together with Matsushita, Sanyo, and Hoya Glass.

Although significantly smaller than the 3.5 Generation Project in terms of the funding it received, the PIPS Project, devoted more to longer-term research, did more to advance Japanese research in new directions. For example, the first Japanese word processor, developed by Dr Mori of Toshiba, emerged from research which spun off from the PIPS Project. My own research revealed that the PIPS Project resulted in 365 patents, compared with only 39 patents for the VHSCS Project, indicating the greater degree of long-term research in the former project. However, as in MITI's earlier co-operative R&D projects, there was little sharing of knowledge between the participating companies. Only 7, or 1.9 per cent, of the 365 patents were held jointly by researchers from more than one of the participating companies, and in all seven cases the companies were non-competing.[26]

Closer Interfirm Co-ordination

MITI's policy-makers believed strongly that one of the main sources of weakness in the Japanese computer industry (as in other industries such as motor vehicles) was the number of competing companies. The six major competitors were Fujitsu, NEC, Hitachi, Toshiba, Mitsubishi Electric, and Oki, although, as we have seen, the first three, with their backgrounds in telecommunications, were significantly stronger from the beginning than the others. However, in the USA— Japan's role model—IBM's overwhelming dominance seemed to point to the importance of economies of scale, scope, and vertical integration. In 1972, for example, IBM's research and development accounted for no less than 46 per cent of the total R&D expenditure of the entire US computer industry! To policy-makers in MITI, viewing the world from the perspective of IBM's architecture of the mind, this suggested that Japanese companies should merge if possible, or at the very least should co-ordinate their activities far more closely.

In the light of these beliefs, MITI exerted considerable pressure on the Japanese companies. Since the latter refused to contemplate merger, a compromise was agreed involving a coupling of the six computer companies. Fujitsu and Hitachi were paired jointly to produce the new M-series of IBM-compatible mainframes. Fujitsu had already come to the strategic decision that it should follow the IBM-compatible path. Although Fujitsu's FACOM 230-60 had given the company the lead among the Japanese companies in the domestic market, the machine was not doing well overseas.

By 1968 Fujitsu had decided, in Taiyu Kobayashi's words, that, 'unless we could, without modifications, run the same software created for IBM systems on our computers built around the same architecture, we would never be able to compete in the international market'.[27] By a stroke of luck, Fujitsu was able to

---

[26] Ibid.   [27] Quoted ibid.

link up with Gene Amdahl, one of IBM's top designers who had played a major role in the design of System 360 and who, after falling out with IBM in 1969, had left to form his own company. Unable to raise the necessary funding from the American capital markets, in 1972 Amdahl reached an agreement with Fujitsu that eventually gave Fujitsu control of the company. As Kobayashi observed, 'Fujitsu saw tremendous potential in joining hands with Dr Amdahl who knew so well the strengths, weaknesses, and overall situation of IBM.'[28]

Following the exit from the computer industry in 1971 of RCA—Hitachi's technological ally—Hitachi had also made the strategic decision to become IBM-compatible. Their common strategic direction therefore provided the basis for the intended co-operation between Fujitsu and Hitachi.

NEC's strategic thinking, however, was fundamentally different from that of Fujitsu and Hitachi (as is analysed in detail in Chapter 6 below). The beliefs that underlay NEC's vision were constructed on the basis of the company's position as the largest Japanese telecommunications equipment supplier. When in the latter 1950s NEC decided to enter the commercial computer market, it quickly came to see computers as part of broader information and communications systems (C&C systems, in the company's language). Accordingly, NEC's vision regarding the role of computers differed significantly from those of IBM, Fujitsu, and Hitachi. While the latter saw computing—in line with IBM's architecture of the mind—as dominated by and organized around large mainframes, NEC preferred to envision distributed networks of smaller computers joined by communications systems. Dr Koji Kobayashi, who played a major role in the construction of NEC's vision, later recalled his view in the 1960s that it was inconceivable that NEC should follow Fujitsu and Hitachi down the IBM-compatible road. The reason was that IBM was solely a computer company, whereas NEC had already accumulated competences in both communications and computing; accordingly, NEC's computing needs were fundamentally different from those of IBM.[29]

One of the reasons for the compatibility between NEC and its technology partner, Honeywell, was that the latter's larger computers complemented NEC's concentration on smaller computers. (In the 1960s and 1970s Honeywell, with significant government military funding, increasingly concentrated on military-related computers.) In 1970, when GE pulled out of commercial computers, its computer division along with its computer architecture were acquired by Honeywell. Since GE was Toshiba's technological ally, this created the basis for an NEC–Toshiba pairing. Accordingly, these two companies got together, as a precondition for Japanese government funding, to develop the IBM-incompatible line of ACOS computers. Finally, Mitsubishi Electric and Oki, the weakest of the Japanese computer companies, co-operated to produce the COSMOS series of computers.

In effect, however, these pairings produced minimal co-operation between

---

[28] Ibid.   [29] Quotation by Koji Kobayashi, given in Ch. 6 below.

the companies which, being strong rivals particularly in the Japanese market, continued to go their own way in developing their computer lines.

NTT's DIPS 11

In the light of System 370, NTT felt that it had to upgrade its DIPS series. Accordingly, in 1973 NTT began co-operative research and development with Fujitsu, NEC, and Hitachi on the DIPS-11 Project. In 1975 this resulted in the DIPS-11/10 and DIPS-11/20 and in 1976 in the DIPS-11/30. After 1979 further models were developed as part of the DIPS-11/5 series. In 1985 NTT announced the DIPS-11/5E series as successors of the 5 series.

The Importance of Government Funding

How important was funding from the Japanese government for the development of the Japanese computer industry? Information that will help to answer this question is given in Table 4.2.

The first point to make is that the figures in the table—calculated from data given in Anchordoguy[30]—must be interpreted with extreme caution. Some of them are inconsistent with information provided elsewhere,[31] and some (such as total subsidies to the computer industry, or R&D undertaken by this industry) are inherently difficult to measure accurately. With this word of caution, let us try to determine what the figures in Table 4.2 reveal about the role of government funding.

It is clear from the table that total subsidies and tax benefits provided by the Japanese government (row (3)) were important for the Japanese computer industry. (Subsidies in row (3) include NTT's expenditure on the R&D of DIPS computers—also shown separately in rows (1) and (2)—and include the implicit subsidies given in loans by the Japan Development Bank directly or indirectly to the computer industry at below-market rates of interest.)

Row (6) shows total government subsidies and tax benefits to the computer industry as a proportion of this industry's investment in plant and equipment and R&D. As can be seen, government subsidies and tax benefits were extremely important in 1968, amounting to 75 per cent of the industry's investment in these items. The reason for the high figure is NTT's DIPS-1 project, which began in this year. NTT's expenditure on developing the DIPS-1 in 1968 came to 36 per cent of the industry's investment in plant and equipment and R&D. It will be recalled that the DIPS project was NTT's response to IBM's System 360, released in 1964. The proportional significance of total government subsidies and tax benefits gradually decreased until 1971, when it amounted to 43 per cent. From 1972 to 1974 it increased again, amounting to 69 per cent in the

---

[30] See Anchordoguy, *Computers Inc.*
[31] See Fransman, *The Market and Beyond*, for a discussion of some of the inconsistencies between data from Flamm and Anchordoguy.

Table 4.2 *The Financing of the Japanese Computer Industry, 1968–1975*[a] (¥bn)

	1968	1969	1970	1971	1972	1973	1974	1975
(1) DIPS-I Project	7.500	7.500	7.500	7.500	—	—	—	—
(2) DIPS-II Project	—	—	—	—	—	1.670	1.670	1.660
(3) Total subsidies[a] and tax benefits (from government)	15.595	17.685	22.141	26.844	25.017	41.132	42.839	50.729
(4) Computer industry investment in plant and equipment	8.600	10.900	21.300	22.300	14.700	18.500	24.800	27.800
(5) Computer industry investment in R&D	12.200	24.000	29.700	40.200	33.000	45.100	37.700	52.800
(6) (3)/[(4)+(5)] (%)	75.0	50.7	43.4	43.0	52.5	64.7	68.5	62.9
(7) (1) or (2)/[(4)+(5)] (%)	36.1	21.5	14.7	12.0	—	2.6	2.7	2.1

[a] For assumptions, see text.

Source: calculated from data given in M. Anchordoguy, *Computers Inc.: Japan's Challenge to IBM*, Harvard University Press, Cambridge, Mass., 1989.

latter year. This increase reflects the response to System 370 and includes MITI's expenditure on the 3.5 Generation Project (1972–6) as well as the smaller expenditure on the PIPS Project (1971–80).

The Importance of the DIPS Projects

Row (7) of Table 4.2 shows NTT's expenditure on research and development of the DIPS computers as a proportion of the investment of the Japanese computer companies in plant and equipment and R&D. As can be seen, the proportion gradually decreases from a high of 36 per cent in 1968, the year the DIPS programme began, to a low of just over 2 per cent in 1975.

However, this considerably understates the importance of the DIPS programme for the major Japanese computer companies, Fujitsu, NEC, and Hitachi. To begin with, NTT's expenditure on DIPS benefited only these three companies. However, the figures given for computer industry investment in rows (4) and (5) include *all* the Japanese companies, that is also Toshiba, Mitsubishi Electric, and Oki (and perhaps some investment by the consumer electronics companies such as Matsushita). Accordingly, NTT's expenditure on the research and development of DIPS as a proportion of the investment of Fujitsu, NEC, and Hitachi must be significantly higher than the proportions indicated in row (7).

However, against this must be set the fact that, while the non-DIPS computers of Fujitsu, NEC, and Hitachi certainly benefited from the DIPS programme as indicated above, some of NTT's R&D expenditure on DIPS cannot be justifiably regarded as a subsidy to the Japanese computer companies. For instance, it was shown that an important part of the DIPS-1 project involved the development of an operating system for the DIPS computers. While the three companies may have learned something from developing this operating system, it was significantly different from that used in their own commercial computers; its main purpose was to provide NTT with inter-operability between the computers from the three companies.

Nevertheless, it must be emphasized that the figures for DIPS given in the table refer only to the research and development of DIPS. The three computer companies derived additional benefit from their *sale* of DIPS computers to NTT. While there is some evidence that only 22 DIPS-1 computers were bought by NTT,[32] the figure for the different DIPS-11 series must have been substantially higher. This is not reflected in Table 4.2, where the lower per annum expenditures given for DIPS-11 compared with DIPS-1 are an indication of the development that had already been made under the DIPS-1 project (most importantly, the development of the operating system) which was carried over to the DIP-11 project. (It is also possible that, if all the time and resources of all of NTT's staff involved in the DIPS projects were properly costed, the figures

---

[32] See Anchordoguy, *Computers Inc.*, 55.

given in Table 4.2 would turn out to be underestimates. This may account for the higher figures that have sometimes been given for NTT's R&D expenditure on DIPS.[33])

Did Fujitsu, NEC, and Hitachi receive further hidden subsidies from NTT through the latter's purchases of DIPS computers at 'above-market prices'? This politically fraught question is inherently difficult to answer without accurate information which has not been released. For the record, however, a senior NTT official, closely involved in the DIPS programme, whom I interviewed stated that the price paid to the three firms for DIPS computers was at least 30 per cent less than the market price of equivalent IBM computers. (As a large procurer, however, NTT would be expected to have been able to purchase IBM computers at a discount below this 'market price'.)

US Government Assistance to its Computer Industry

How do the data in Table 4.2 compare with the situation in the USA? Although the figures are not directly comparable, Flamm shows that from 1949 to 1959 the US government funded 68 per cent of IBM's total R&D, 87 per cent of Sperry Rand's, 52 per cent of General Electric's, and 46 per cent of RCA's.[34] In 1975 and 1976 the US federal government funded 26 and 25 per cent of total US expenditure on computer R&D. If Bell Labs is included in federal government funding, Flamm estimates that these figures rise to 35 and 34 per cent.[35]

Putting these figures together with those in Table 4.2 suggests that Flamm is correct when he concludes that

While it is true that Japanese authorities heavily subsidized computer development in the 1970s, these efforts have never approached the relative share of all R&D funds supplied by the US government in the 1950s and 1960s. . . . Moreover, the Japanese government's relative role in financing computer research declined significantly in the late 1970s. Today [i.e. late 1980s] government directly funds *less* of Japan's industrial computer research and development than is the case in the US or Europe.[36]

The Remaining Contestants

The efforts made by the major Japanese computer companies, together with the support they received from MITI and NTT's projects, bore fruit. By the middle to late 1970s, the leading Japanese companies had succeeded in closing the technology gap with the world's leaders. By 1974, 'Fujitsu introduced a clone

---

[33] According to *Kagaku Shimbun* (22 February 1990), for example, NTT spent a total of ¥40 billion on R&D for DIPS-1 and ¥50 billion on DIPS-11.
[34] Flamm, *Targeting the Computer*, 96, table 4-1.
[35] Ibid. 102, table 4-4.
[36] Ibid. 177.

of the extremely successful IBM 370 series, Fujitsu's [M series], which was faster than IBM's machine. Hitachi followed and by the end of the decade IBM Japan's share of the Japanese market had shrunk to 27 per cent. In 1979 Fujitsu passed IBM as the nation's leading manufacturer of computers.'[37]

However, while Fujitsu, NEC, and Hitachi entered the 1980s as would-be challengers of IBM, the measures taken by the Japanese government were insufficient to sustain all the Japanese companies that had entered the computer race. In the event, Toshiba, Mitsubishi Electric, and Oki dropped out.

Why was it Fujitsu, NEC, and Hitachi that remained? To elaborate on what was said earlier, two factors were of particular importance. The first was the competences that these companies had already accumulated even before the Second World War in developing electrical and electronic systems in the field of communications. As we saw earlier, it was similar competences that facilitated AT&T's entry into computers, although the 1956 consent decree with the US Justice Department prevented the company from exploiting its competences in the field of general-purpose commercial computers. The competences that they had accumulated meant that, from the very beginning, Fujitsu, NEC, and Hitachi were the strongest of the Japanese companies in computing, although they were continually jockeying for positions of dominance.

The second factor was that it was the same three companies—Fujitsu, NEC, and Hitachi—that were members of NTT's family of privileged suppliers. Under controlled competition, they enjoyed a long-term and stable relationship with NTT. Not only did this relationship give these companies access to NTT's substantial technical expertise, which NTT had accumulated as a sophisticated user and researcher of communications equipment and computers, it also gave them long-term and relatively certain access to NTT's lucrative market for computers. Although NTT is unwilling to release figures on the size of its procurement of DIPS computers, some indirect information can be gleaned from other data. In 1981, for example, NTT's total procurement budget came to about $2.7 billion (at then existing exchange rates). NEC's share of this procurement came to more than $500 million, constituting 12 per cent of NEC's total sales. This, together with the relative certainty of sales to NTT (at least until NTT's part-privatization in 1985), gives some idea of NTT's importance in keeping NEC, Fujitsu, and Hitachi in the computer market.

But these two factors, important though they were, were not the only reasons why Fujitsu, NEC, and Hitachi remained to continue the fight. Equally significant was the long-term strategic commitment that these companies made to the computer market. To illustrate this point, it is illuminating to compare them with one of the major casualties in the US computer market, RCA.

---

[37] Quoted in Fransman, *The Market and Beyond*, 161.

RCA and the Lure of the Computer[38]

RCA was formed in 1919 by General Electric, AT&T, and Westinghouse in order to develop radio technology and products. Before the Second World War, as the dominant company producing radios and vacuum tubes, RCA also created and operated a nationwide broadcasting network, NBC. After the war, RCA became the leader in the US black and white and later the colour television industry. By 1964 the company held a 43 per cent share of the US market for colour TV, followed by Zenith with 14 per cent.

RCA also made a major commitment to developing transistor technology after the transistor was commercialized by AT&T in 1948, and thereafter to integrated circuits. During the war RCA had developed an analog computer for the purposes of gun control, and the company followed this up after the war with work on military-related computers. In 1959 RCA introduced its first major commercial computer, a middle-sized transistorized computer, the 501, which was a reasonable financial success. It followed this with a larger and smaller model. At this stage RCA was a company twice the size of IBM. However, IBM was narrowly focused on computers, and the introduction of its System 360 in 1964 was a significant challenge to RCA. RCA responded by competitively upgrading its computers.

However, while RCA's R&D engineers were attempting to come to grips with the competitive threat posed by IBM, RCA's 'concept of the company' changed dramatically. Under the influence of Robert Sarnoff, succeeding his father David Sarnoff who had led RCA since its establishment, and with the support of Wall Street, RCA selected a strategy of unrelated diversification. From 1966 RCA acquired companies in diverse areas such as publishing, sports equipment, car rentals, frozen foods, and carpet manufacturing. By 1975, RCA's share of the US colour TV market had dropped to 20 per cent compared with Zenith's 24 per cent. In that year RCA's revenue from consumer electronics had dropped to 16 per cent of total revenue and many of the TVs which it sold were made by Matsushita.

Driven by a concept of the company in which calculations of rates of return rather than considerations of competence–compatibility ruled, RCA failed to sustain its commitment to computers when in 1970 IBM's System 370 signalled the increase in resources that were necessary to remain in the industry. Accordingly, in 1971 RCA, under the influence of what business historian Alfred Chandler has called 'the curse of the conglomerate', decided to exit from the computer industry. Reviewing this decision, one of RCA's senior executives later reflected, 'We shot a whole generation of research engineers on computers and starved the real cash-cow—color television—to do it.'[39]

---

[38] This section draws on an unpublished paper by Alfred Chandler given at a workshop in Vancouver in May 1994, entitled 'Japan and the Theories of the Firm'. The phrase 'the lure of the computer' used here is Chandler's.

[39] Quoted in Chandler, 'Japan and the Theories of the Firm'.

To complete the story, in 1985 RCA was sold to General Electric for $6.4 billion. Eighteen months later, GE traded RCA for Thomson's medical instruments division. Later, RCA's Princeton laboratories, which had been responsible for a large number of important innovations in consumer electronics and computers, were transferred to the contract research firm, Stanford Research Institute.

The comparison between RCA in consumer electronics and computing and ITT in telecommunications equipment, analysed in the last chapter, is extremely close. Both operated with a similar concept of the company. The contrast with the concept of the company held by Fujitsu, NEC, and Hitachi is striking. In these Japanese companies a long-term commitment was made to a set of competences which from the 1950s included computers that were competence-compatible with their other products. While, as we have seen, government assistance and the firms' relationship with NTT were important, their endurance in the global computer market also owed a great deal to their concept of the company and to the institutions in Japan—such as the financial system—which supported this concept.

Weaknesses of DIPS in the 1980s and the Multi-Vendor Integration Architecture

While DIPS computers suited NTT's data communications and information-processing needs in the 1970s and early 1980s, thereafter several important problems with the DIPS system became apparent. The most significant of these was that, with its unique operating system, NTT was unable to purchase hardware and software that conformed to other operating systems, such as IBM's. This meant, for example, that, if NTT wished to use other applications software, it had to be rewritten to run on DIPS computers. This raised computing costs for NTT, an important consideration in view of both the shortage of software engineers in Japan and the increasing pressure on costs that NTT confronted after it was partly privatized in 1985 and faced competition from the new common carriers (see Chapter 7 on the future of NTT).

Part of the difficulty arose from the fact that NTT's relationship with its supplying companies involved three distinct roles that at times conflicted. First, NTT was a co-operative researcher and developer of those inputs that it needed for its network and services, inputs that were not adequately available on the market. Secondly, NTT was a user of the inputs it had jointly researched and developed. Thirdly, in the case of computers, NTT was also a systems integrator and seller of integrated computer systems and services.

While NTT's first two roles were complementary and helped both NTT and its suppliers to innovate (using controlled competition to internalize learning-by-using economies), the third role was more problematical. The reason was that, as a seller of computer systems and services, NTT competed directly with its suppliers—Fujitsu, NEC, and Hitachi—and furthermore, in order to compete effectively and profitably, often had an incentive to procure hardware and software from outside this group of suppliers. For example, as a systems integrator NTT competed with Fujitsu, NEC, and Hitachi in selling computer systems to banks. NTT's systems used DIPS computers, jointly designed and developed by NTT and the three companies but manufactured by each of the companies using their own hardware technology and conforming to the DIPS operating system. The competing systems offered directly to the banks by Fujitsu, NEC, and Hitachi (in competition with one another) were based on their own hardware and software.

The competition between NTT and its suppliers meant that the latter soon lost the incentive to innovate in DIPS computers. Increasingly, it was NTT that had to assume responsibility for making the necessary innovations in DIPS computers as enabling technologies improved and new computing needs emerged. In the late 1960s and 1970s this was not so much of a problem, since the main aim of Fujitsu, NEC, and Hitachi was to improve the performance of their computers *vis-à-vis* IBM, and close co-operation with an R&D-sophisticated user—namely NTT—was seen as a good way of achieving this goal. By the mid-1980s, however, the situation had changed significantly as Japanese computers matched those of IBM. Just how much change had occurred is evident in the following account by a senior development engineer involved in DIPS work in one of the three suppliers:

The incentive for Hitachi, Fujitsu, and NEC to advise NTT to make improvements to DIPS computers was [by the mid-1980s] reduced. The firms did not have a great incentive because they did not want to compete with their own computers [i.e. the DIPS computers which they manufactured for NTT] in the free market [that is, outside NTT, e.g. in computer systems for the banks]. The main stimulus for innovation in DIPS computers therefore came from NTT itself. Accordingly, NTT did its own research and requested improvements from the three suppliers. Because NTT is an important customer, the suppliers have to comply.[40]

Furthermore, the strong competition between Fujitsu, NEC, and Hitachi meant that in some instances these companies were unwilling to share technical information, making further innovations to DIPS computers more difficult and costly:

Fransman: Given that DIPS is so close to your own general-purpose computers, and given that you are competing with the other two suppliers, has it been difficult for engineers from Fujitsu, NEC, and Hitachi to share ideas? Have they felt in danger of leaking information to competitors?

Informant: This is a problem, especially if a strategic technology is involved. In DIPS hardware meetings they have that problem. So sometimes they cannot have the meeting with all members present and only NTT's ECL engineers meet with one company's engineers. NTT does not have a manufacturing division, so the companies

---

[40] Author's interview with a senior engineer involved in the development of DIPS computers for one of the three major suppliers to NTT.

feel free to discuss with NTT. NTT will keep information confidential. However, in the case of software the problem is less serious, since much software is application-specific with fewer competitive implications.[41]

This suggests the hypothesis that within the DIPS system of controlled competition information flows between the competing suppliers were limited, while more flows occurred between each supplier and NTT. In order to test this hypothesis, I collected data on all computer-related patents granted to NTT between August 1985 and September 1986.[42] There were 41 patents in all. Of these, 15 were held by NTT/ECL alone. The remaining 26 patents were joint patents where the patent-holders came from more than one company: 17, or 65 per cent, of these patents were held by NTT/ECL and only one of the suppliers; 2 by NTT/ECL and two suppliers; 4 by NTT/ECL and three suppliers; and 3 by NTT/ECL and four suppliers. This suggests that, to the extent that joint patents are a satisfactory indicator of interfirm flows of knowledge, the hypothesis is supported.

NTT's Response: Incorporating IBM and DEC in MIA

In response to these difficulties, NTT did two things. First, it spun-off its Data Communications Division as a distinct wholly owned subsidiary. Secondly, it did what would have been unimaginable ten years previously, when together with Fujitsu, NEC, and Hitachi it worked so hard to rival IBM: in 1988 it established a new computer development programme, which included not only these three Japanese computer suppliers, but also IBM (Japan) and Digital Equipment (DEC). The inclusion of IBM provides a vivid indicator of the degree to which the ball game had changed!

In 1988 the NTT Data Communications Systems Corporation was established, with a capitalization of ¥10 billion and an initial staff of 6,000. Most importantly, this move allowed NTT to resolve its three conflicting roles as developer, user, and seller of computing systems by hiving-off the latter function. Through NTT Data, NTT was able to benefit financially from the computer systems integration competences it had developed. The subsidiary, with its distinct set of accounts, also allowed NTT to escape from the criticism that had been levelled against it that it was unfairly subsidizing its Data Communications Division from other parts of the company, to the detriment of fair competition in the computer services market. Finally, the change freed NTT Data from the NTT bureaucracy, allowing the company to pursue its business targets in a more flexible way.

In January of the same year, under the Track Three procurement provision for the development of new telecommunications-related equipment, NTT publicly invited companies in Japan and around the world to apply to join a new co-operative computer project. This project was aimed at developing a new computer architecture that would provide NTT with multi-vendor possibilities. In May and June of 1988, NTT selected its participants from among the

---

[41] Ibid.   [42] I would like to thank NTT officials for access to this patent data.

applicants. In addition to its usual suppliers—Fujitsu, NEC, and Hitachi—IBM (Japan) and DEC were chosen.

The objective of the Multivendor Integration Architecture Project (MIA), led by NTT and NTT Data, was to develop new architectural interfaces which in future would allow NTT to purchase both hardware and software from a large number of potential vendors. MIA was in line with the global trend towards so-called open systems ('open' in the sense that the hardware and software of different companies could be integrated), and NTT has attempted as far as possible to make MIA compatible with the other emerging international standards for open computing. MIA allowed NTT to overcome the problems with DIPS, which, as was seen, was a proprietary system limiting NTT's ability to purchase from a wide circle of suppliers.

Why did NTT make such a radical change to its computer strategy, opting for a co-operative development alliance with a group of companies that included not merely foreign companies, but the hitherto dreaded IBM? One factor certainly was the extreme pressure exerted, particularly by the USA, on the Japanese government and NTT to open imports and telecommunications procurement to US companies. (Europe was far less successful in applying similar pressure.)

But it would be incorrect to see NTT's incorporation of Western suppliers as simply a response to foreign pressure. We have seen in the case of DIPS that problems were already accumulating which limited the effectiveness of the old system of co-operative development and procurement. By incorporating sophisticated Western suppliers such as IBM and DEC—particularly in developing open, multi-vendor computer systems—NTT was able to increase its options beneficially. This was, however, to some extent at the cost of the old nationally defined ball game, according to which 'us' was NTT and its Japanese family of suppliers, while 'them' referred to Western rivals. But the old ball game in any event was collapsing. As was seen in Chapter 3, for example, NEC and Fujitsu are busily building bridges in the USA to the former Bell operating companies in order to supply them with telecommunications equipment. The Japanese computer companies are, of course, also heavily committed to the US computer market.

It is worth noting, however, that, despite the radical nature of these changes, NTT has not abandoned the principle of controlled competition, only transformed it by globalizing it. NTT still works with a closed group of companies in order to develop the equipment it needs which is not available on the market. The competition between the suppliers in this group is still controlled in much the same way as previously. Although there is now greater possibility of competition from outside firms at the procurement stage (since NTT is obliged to invite competition from any potential supplier), those companies that have co-operated with NTT in Track Three development programmes generally have an advantage; they have already developed the transaction-specific assets, standards, and competences needed for the equipment concerned. So controlled competition is alive and well, although transformed and globalized.

DEC and NTT[43]

Why have Western companies been willing to join their Japanese competitors in co-operatively developing equipment for NTT? How have these Western companies—sometimes alleged to be opportunistic, short-term-oriented profit maximizers—coped in one of Japan's longest-lasting examples of obligational co-operation? The case of DEC's involvement in MIA throws light on these important questions.

In 1957 the Digital Equipment Corporation was founded as a venture capital undertaking by Kenneth Olsen, an MIT researcher, and some of his MIT colleagues. In view of IBM's dominance discussed earlier, DEC soon developed one of the first 'downsizing strategies'. This involved competitively positioning itself through the development of so-called minicomputers which offered cost-effective processing performance to compete against IBM's lower range of mainframes.

Like Northern Telecom in the field of switching (discussed in the last chapter), DEC was attracted primarily by the prospect of large procurement orders from NTT. By the late 1980s, DEC was beginning to feel the pressures emanating from microprocessor-driven personal computers and workstations which began eating into its markets in much the same way that DEC had bored into IBM's markets from the 1960s. DEC realized that it had no option but to abandon its proprietary computer systems and make a commitment to open systems. NTT's MIA project was in line with this new strategic thinking in DEC. Furthermore, although DEC had already done business in Japan for twenty years, the company had decided that the rapidly growing Japan–Asia–Pacific region deserved high priority.

Despite these factors, however, a senior executive from DEC (Japan) recollected that 'I had great difficulty persuading company officials in the US that we would not be giving away our "crown jewels" by participating in MIA with NTT and the Japanese computer companies.' But was DEC not risking leakage of the strategic knowledge on which its competitiveness depended to Fujitsu, NEC, and Hitachi? 'In developing MIA with NTT, all of the companies offered some of their proprietary technology. The size of NTT's procurement offers a strong incentive to co-operate. But NTT has operated in a highly professional manner, particularly in ensuring confidentiality when this is necessary.'[44]

Interviews that I held with senior NTT officials involved in running MIA indicate that the relationship between NTT and DEC was perceived to be mutually very beneficial. NTT was particularly impressed with the degree of commitment and goodwill that DEC had shown. There were even indications that DEC had been willing to go further than some of the Japanese companies in offering its technical co-operation and knowledge. (Of course, it was the

---

[43] I would like to express my gratitude to a senior official from DEC (Japan) for numerous frank discussions of DEC's relationship with NTT, including the MIA project.

[44] Author's interview with DEC official referred to in fn. 43.

Japanese companies—particularly Fujitsu, which was thought to have received about 60 per cent of NTT's purchases of computers—that had most to lose from the relationship being forged between NTT and its new Western computer suppliers.) Indeed, it was suggested that on several occasions DEC went so far as to use what influence it had in Japan to assist NTT behind the scenes in its battle to avoid divestiture in 1990 (discussed in more detail in Chapter 7).

Despite its American roots, and the fact that the bulk of its business was still in the USA, in its co-operative relationship with NTT, DEC behaved in essential respects like its Japanese counterparts, taking a long-term view of the benefits of co-operation with NTT. However, NTT's *de facto* rules of controlled competition took some getting used to. Particularly daunting was the requirement that DEC would have to fund a substantial portion of the development costs of its participation in MIA (which I have estimated amounted to around $30 million). (Only if NTT commissioned special deliverables—such as particular software items over which it acquired proprietary rights—would NTT pay costs during the development stage of the project.) In line with NTT's past practice as well as the expectations of the Japanese suppliers, DEC anticipated that its development costs would be adequately compensated by NTT's subsequent purchase of MIA-compatible computers. But, in true Japanese spirit, there was no explicit obligation on NTT's part to do so, and in any event NTT is obliged to invite tenders for its procurement of equipment. In the meantime DEC had to put up with the cash-flow difficulties and the uncertainties involved in the implicit long-term obligational contract. However, although it is both a Western company unused to such obligational contracting, and a newcomer to the relationship with NTT, DEC is behaving in very much of a 'Japanese-like' way in its dealings with NTT.

Attempting to Break Out of the IBM Mould

Until the early 1980s, Japanese companies and government policy-makers, like many of their counterparts in Western countries which also adopted IBM's architecture of the mind, spent much of their time trying to keep up with the fast moving IBM. The Japanese predicament is illustrated by their activities in developing advanced integrated circuits.

The VLSI Projects of NTT and MITI

IBM's System 370/Models 135 and 145, announced in the autumn of 1970, were the first major commercial computers to use integrated circuit memories as their main memory device. Stimulated by this event, the Japanese companies began to develop integrated circuit memories for industrial purposes. By 1974 they had made some progress, capturing about 5 per cent of the world market for 1K random access memories (RAM).

In the summer of 1973, however, an event occurred that was to throw the Japanese involved in memory semiconductors into a state of panic. A senior NTT official, closely involved in the company's computer activities, tells the story. 'On a hot summer's day a senior employee from Fujitsu came to ECL in an extremely agitated state. In the US he had discovered that, as part of its secret Future Systems plan [referred to above], IBM was planning to develop very large-scale integrated (VLSI) memories. This was beyond the capability of any of the Japanese companies, and he requested NTT's help in developing similar VLSI technologies.'[45]

At about the same time, integrated circuit memories began to be used in electronic switches, although NTT had not yet carried out any research and development on large-scale integration. In response to IBM's move, NTT established a co-operative VLSI project with NEC, Fujitsu, and Hitachi which began in 1975 and was to last for two years. The aim of the project was to produce 64K bit VLSI semiconductors for use in communications, including computers and switches. A total of ¥10 billion was spent on this project, which was extended to two further projects in 1978–80 and 1981–4.

In view of its responsibility for computers, MITI also wanted to start a VLSI project. The NTT official just quoted had a friend in MITI who was given responsibility for launching the ministry's VLSI project. 'In order to justify the expenditure to the Ministry of Finance, we had to co-ordinate our activities. It was agreed that NTT would concentrate on VLSI for use in communications while MITI would deal with VLSI for general-purpose computers.'

MITI's VLSI Project 1976–80 has been analysed in detail elsewhere[46] and the analysis will not be repeated here. MITI's project, however, was quite different from NTT's. Coming a year later, it aimed at developing 256K bit devices. While Fujitsu, NEC, and Hitachi were also members of MITI's project, so were Toshiba and Mitsubishi Electric. There was some division of labour between the projects, with NTT's project focusing on telecommunications-related equipment and MITI's being more concerned with the development of semiconductor processing equipment. Although research was done on optical lithography, MITI's project also concentrated on the development of electron beam equipment in the belief, common at the time, that electron beams with their narrower wavelength than optical beams would be needed to produce submicron circuits. In the event, however, the belief regarding the limitations of optical lithography, widely held in the global semiconductor industry at the time, turned out to be incorrect. Through a remarkable process of incremental technical change, optical lithography was improved to such an extent that in the mid-1990s it was still the dominant technology.

What were the long-term effects of these projects? In the absence of such

---

[45] Author's interview with senior NTT official closely involved at the time with the company's VLSI project.

[46] See Fransman, *The Market and Beyond*, ch. 3.

projects, it is clear that the Japanese companies concerned would in any event have begun significant VLSI research and development; this technology was so central for their products that it had to be developed. Nevertheless, the NTT and MITI projects enabled them to make faster progress than they are otherwise likely to have made. Furthermore, the projects reduced the cost of their entry into VLSI technology. Cost reduction occurred not only as a result of the effective subsidy the companies received from NTT and MITI, but also from the economies that were realized from research co-operation. These included the avoidance of overlapping research, benefits from the blending of distinctive competences in the different companies, and the sharing of expensive equipment.[47] The most important effects of MITI's project resulted from the closer relationship that was developed between Japanese semiconductor equipment suppliers, such as Nikon and Canon (which went on to dominate the world market for optical semiconductor equipment), and the Japanese semiconductor manufacturers. By bringing the manufacturers together, clarifying their equipment needs, and mobilizing their knowledge of semiconductor manufacturing processes, and by bringing this knowledge together with that of the equipment suppliers, the project was able to internalize the benefits arising from learning-by-using.

By the early 1980s Japanese companies had achieved significant global success, holding about 70 per cent of the world market for memory LSIs. As noted, it would be wrong to attribute this solely, or even largely, to the NTT and MITI projects, despite the important contribution that they undoubtedly made. Neither was Japanese success the result of uniquely 'Japanese' characteristics, as was underlined by the dramatic entry in the 1990s of Korean companies into the global memory semiconductor market. By the early 1990s, for example, Samsung was one of the world's largest manufacturers of memories, demonstrating the significant progress that can be made through high rates of investment and patient efforts at incremental process improvements. (The Koreans do not have a strong national semiconductor equipment industry and depend largely on imports. However, a national co-operative semiconductor project, like that of MITI's, targeted largely at memories—organized by the Korean Electronics and Telecommunications Research Institute (ETRI)—played a similar role in assisting the Korean companies.)

With the Japanese semiconductor companies dominant in world markets, the VLSI project, which ended in 1980, was the last one organized by MITI and targeted at the production of final silicon semiconductors. In the early 1990s, however, a co-operative project organized and funded through the Japan Key Technology Center focused on the use of synchrotron-generated X-rays for the purpose of semiconductor production. (X-rays have far narrower wavelengths than optical beams and are expected to be used in the late 1990s.)

---

[47] See ibid. for further details regarding the economies of research co-operation.

Furthermore, in tune with the increasing tendency towards the globalization of research in the 1990s,[48] in 1994 MITI announced that it would attempt to establish a new project aimed at developing silicon wafers for 1 gigabit dynamic random access memories (DRAMs). The aim is to develop silicon wafers with a diameter of 40 centimetres (compared with the current 20 centimetres), which will allow more 'chips' to be produced on each wafer. The project is expected to begin in 1995 and to last seven years and cost ¥18 billion ($181 million). Although Japanese companies such as Shin-Etsu Handotai are globally dominant in the silicon wafer market, with a 70 per cent world market share, MITI invited Western companies to join this project. The project's eleven members—apart from Japanese companies such as Shin-Etsu, Toshiba Ceramics, and Showa Denko—include MEMC Electronic Materials of the USA and Wacker Chemitronics of Germany's Hoechst group.[49]

Apart from relatively small co-operative projects such as these, the main action in the field of semiconductors has moved to interfirm strategic alliances organized by the companies themselves without government assistance. In these alliances, significantly, the Japanese companies have allied themselves to Western companies, rather than to their main Japanese rivals. For example, Toshiba has an alliance with IBM and Siemens to develop 256 megabit DRAMs; Hitachi is co-operating with Texas Instruments; and NEC is working with AT&T and Samsung of Korea. These alliances reflect primarily the significant escalation in the R&D and plant and equipment investment costs in developing future generations of semiconductors. Increasingly, these costs are beyond the capability of individual companies, large though they are. But the allied partners remain competitors, or potential competitors, and accordingly, despite the co-operation, the companies ensure that competitively significant leakages of knowledge are minimized.

The examples of MITI's internationalized co-operative research project in silicon wafers and the global R&D alliances established by the major companies themselves illustrate how significantly the situation has changed since the 1970s and 1980s. The major information and communications companies still compete fiercely in global markets, and MITI is still concerned to enhance the competitiveness of Japanese companies and the growth of Japan (in addition to its concern to maintain harmony in Japan's international relations). However, these objectives are now pursued within the context of an increasingly internationalized set of relationships.[50]

---

[48] For a detailed analysis of the internationalization of Japan's co-operative research and development programmes, see M. Fransman, 'Is National Technology Policy Obsolete in a Globalised World? The Japanese Response', *Cambridge Journal of Economics*, 1995; also included in Fransman, *Visions of the Firm and Japan*.

[49] *Nikkei Weekly*, 25 July 1994: 2.

[50] See fn. 48.

Attempting to Out-IBM IBM

By the early 1980s, the frustrations of MITI's bureaucrats who were responsible for computer policy were evident. Until this time they felt they had little option but to assist the Japanese computer companies in their attempts to keep up with IBM. However, once the Japanese companies had caught up with IBM in terms of computer performance (although not in global market share, as a result of IBM's dominance in installed hardware and software), it appeared to the bureaucrats that the time was ripe to try and 'out-IBM IBM'.

Two strategies were pursued by MITI. The first involved an attempt to improve significantly on the performance of large computers through the development of new enabling technologies. The second strategy was to take a fundamentally different tack from IBM by developing a radically new kind of computer that would be substantially more user-friendly. The first strategy was embodied in the Supercomputer Project 1981–9, while the second strategy was the objective of the Fifth Generation Project 1982–91.

Both these projects have been analysed in detail elsewhere and the analysis will not be repeated here.[51] For present purposes, the significance of both these projects lies in the extent to which they indicate the internalization by MITI bureaucrats of IBM's architecture of the mind. In attempting to out-IBM IBM, these bureaucrats remained within the confines of the IBM mould. Just over a decade later, it would suddenly become apparent how MITI's computer strategy for Japan largely involved following IBM—or even trying to lead IBM—into a *cul de sac*. By then the kaleidoscope had rolled on, revealing fundamentally different beliefs regarding what computing was all about.

There were two key components to the Supercomputer Project. The first, in line with earlier Japanese attempts to compete with IBM through the development of advanced electronic devices, involved pushing new technology for new devices. Since the early days of the transistor, silicon had been the preferred material for electronic devices. (Some of the earliest transistors used germanium.) One school of thought in the semiconductor field was that silicon would continue to be the material of choice for most purposes. However, a second school believed that so-called III–V compound semiconductors, using materials such as gallium arsenide and indium phosphide, would become superior. The main reason was that electrons move faster within these materials, although there are fabrication difficulties that negate some of this potential advantage. The project aimed at developing these devices, which included field effect transistors (FETs) and high electron mobility transistors (HEMTs). Another device developed was the Josephson Junction (JJ), originally invented at Cambridge University. IBM had poured considerable sums into JJs, but eventually withdrew from this area of research.

The second component of the Supercomputer Project involved the development of parallel processing techniques. Since the time of the earliest computers,

---

[51] Fransman, *The Market and Beyond.*

architectures had been based on von Neumann principles which involved the sequential processing of information. Reasoning that processing speeds could be considerably increased if the computer's processors were allocated tasks which they worked on simultaneously, some mainly academic research had been done around the world on parallel processing. However, little of this research had become 'mainstream' research in the laboratories of the computer companies, including IBM. The aim of the Supercomputer Project, therefore, was to produce a computer that would be significantly faster than IBM's (measured, for example, in terms of operations per second, which is how the project's objectives were formulated).

The objective of the Fifth Generation Computer Project, in contrast, was to produce a fundamentally different kind of computer. While conventionally computers—including IBM's—were based on numerical or arithmetic processing, the Fifth Generation Computer would be based on logic processing (processing in logic). An important part of the project also involved the development of parallel processing.

The project was originally conceived by an ETL computer researcher, Kazuhiro Fuchi, who managed to sell it to MITI's Machinery and Information Industry Bureau which financed the project. Fuchi had become interested in logic programming, an approach to artificial intelligence pioneered mainly in Europe. In retrospect it is clear that the project was 'overhyped' as a result of the attempt to get it funded in Japan (something which later came back to haunt the project's leaders when the project terminated and Western observers on the whole gave it a lukewarm evaluation). Nevertheless, the Fifth Generation Project was formulated in the belief that, through the use of logic programming, computers could be made to become more 'intelligent', and therefore better able to do what the user wanted. This fitted in with an attempt to out-IBM by doing something fundamentally different from IBM.

With the benefit of hindsight, several conclusions concerning the significance of these projects are probably justifiable. The first is that it is likely that the participating Japanese companies used the projects to accumulate competences in technology areas that would not otherwise have achieved the same degree of attention and resources in their companies. This is because at that time the technologies were not mainstream commercialized technologies, but rather were technologies mid-way between the academic/basic research stage and the as-yet-unreached stage of commercialization. There was also a good deal of uncertainty attaching to the commercial viability of these technologies, with the result that the companies were prone to neglect them. Through these projects, therefore, the technological competences of the companies were widened beyond what would otherwise have occurred.

For example, all of the participating companies in the Fifth Generation Project were able to develop capabilities in logic programming that complemented and stimulated the other different approaches to artificial intelligence they were developing in their companies at the time (such as the use of the LISP language).

This was probably the main benefit of the Fifth Generation Project (a not-inconsiderable benefit, given the uncertainties surrounding appropriate approaches in artificial intelligence, a benefit missed by many Western 'analysts' who failed to understand that the objectives of the project were 'overhyped' for political and financial reasons). Another example is Fujitsu's development of competences in HEMT devices. While Fujitsu had already begun research in this area (using expensive molecular beam epitaxy (MBE) equipment), and would have developed this technology in any event since at that stage it put great faith in the potential of HEMTs in high-speed computing, the Supercomputer Project gave the company additional resources and its researchers in this area greater prominence. Furthermore, all the companies involved in parallel processing in the two projects derived some learning benefits in this area, a technology that is beginning to achieve commercial prominence only in the mid-1990s.

Nevertheless, despite these not inconsiderable benefits, it is clear that neither project took the Japanese companies much further along the road to out-IBMing IBM. Neither project had led by the early 1990s to new approaches that gave the participating companies important competitive advantages.[52] However, this turned out to be not very significant, because by this time it was becoming apparent that it was no longer really important to catch up with, keep up with, or even out-IBM, IBM. The reason was that the prevailing beliefs regarding what computing was all about were changing dramatically. As if to underline this, in the beginning of 1993 IBM announced the biggest loss in corporate history, and the company plunged into a deep crisis from which by the mid-1990s it had not yet fully emerged. The main reason for this crisis was the undermining of IBM's competitiveness, profitability, growth, and size by the microprocessor.

The Mighty Microprocessor and the Personal Computer

The Invention of the Microprocessor

By the early 1990s, the kaleidoscope had moved sufficiently to generate a fundamentally new pattern—a new set of beliefs, a new vision—of what computing is all about. If IBM's architecture of the mind was built around the

---

[52] For example, following the Supercomputer Project, Fujitsu invested hundreds of millions of dollars in the gallium arsenide-based HEMT in the hope of finding a superior electronic device that would replace devices such as the silicon bipolar device in high-speed computing. As things turned out, however—as in other cases, such as optical lithography for semiconductor production or radio as opposed to optical transmission in telecommunications—cumulative innovations in the 'old' technology were sufficient to allow it to compete with the 'new' technology. Despite some of the predictions of a decade earlier, silicon has remained the material of choice for most applications in electronics. (A notable exception is in optical applications, where the properties of III–V compounds such as gallium arsenide make this material superior for use in devices such as semiconductor lasers and light-emitting diodes (LEDs).)

importance of large, centralized mainframes, the new vision saw computing as a network of decentralized information processors. While some of these processors took the form of mainframes and server systems servicing distributed smaller computers, others were workstations, personal computers, and even new kinds of machines the design of which had not yet been agreed—such as personal digital assistants (PDAs) and teleputers (combining functions such as telephone, fax, television, and computing).

If any one causal element is to be singled out in the interrelated series of elemental changes that brought about the new vision of what computing is all about, it is the microprocessor. A microprocessor may be defined as a computer central processing unit that is contained on one or a few integrated circuit chips, using large-scale integration (LSI) technology.[53]

This device, which was to become a slow-motion timebomb, destroying the old vision of computing and creating the new one, had an inauspicious beginning. Indeed, even the inventors of the microprocessor, who announced the new device in 1971, failed to hear the ticking that in time would herald a new age in computing. The first microprocessor was invented in Intel, a semi-conductor company whose main product was memories. (The year before, Intel had invented the first dynamic random access memory (DRAM).) The proximate cause of the invention of the microprocessor was a request by a Japanese hand-held calculator company, Busicom, for wired logic circuits that would perform the calculator's functions. Ted Hoff, the engineer in Intel assigned to the job, came to the creative conclusion that he could meet Busicom's requirements by using Intel's knowledge of memory devices to store the necessary software instructions, while integrating sufficient logic circuits on a single silicon chip to perform the operations required by the instructions. In effect, this meant that a simple computer was created on a single chip. It is likely that Hoff's 'creative insight' was due at least partly to the knowledge he had already accumulated through his previous work in minicomputers.

Although Hoff was readily able to get permission from Intel's management to go ahead with his design, its benefits were not immediately apparent to Hoff, the management, or Busicom. Indeed, Busicom simultaneously commissioned its own design team to continue with the task of designing several interrelated chips. As Hoff's work continued, however, Intel realized that Hoff's new solution (albeit one built from 'old' elements) had potential commercial value, as is indicated by its decision to refund Busicom the $60,000 the company had paid for the design of the system in return for Intel's acquisition of the proprietary rights to the system. However, the first microprocessor had such limited processing capability that Intel at first thought its use would be restricted to applications such as calculators and traffic lights. This seemed to be confirmed by the significantly more powerful processors that were being developed at the

---

[53] *Chambers Science and Technology Dictionary*, Chambers, Cambridge.

time for military purposes, even though the latter involved the combination of several chips.[54]

However, as with the computer, the demand for which was at first expected to be satisfied by a few machines, so the performance of the microprocessor increased beyond all initial expectations. Every three years since Intel introduced its X86 family of microprocessors in 1979, their performance has increased four or five times. This 'trajectory' became known as Moore's Law, after Gordon Moore, one of the founders of Intel. Single microprocessors in the mid-1990s perform the functions of large computer systems of the late 1980s. The quantum increase in the performance, and reduction in the cost, of microprocessors has made possible the new vision of information processing referred to above.

The Japanese Response to the Microprocessor

It was in November 1971 that Intel anounced the first microprocessor. Five months later, in April 1972, NEC produced Japan's first microprocessor. The short time-lag that separated these two events was unsurprising in view of the underlying technologies which Japanese companies such as NEC had already mastered.

What is in need of further explanation, however, is the international success that Intel achieved through microprocessors compared with NEC, which lagged significantly behind in global terms in this particular semiconductor market. In 1982, NEC was the third in the world in terms of total semiconductor sales, after Motorola and Texas Instruments; Intel was in seventh place. By 1987, NEC had moved to first place and Intel had dropped to the tenth position. NEC's positioning reflected its strength in memory semiconductors, while Intel's indicated its weakening in memories before the company's sales of micro-processors had been able to compensate. In 1985 Japan's share of the world semiconductor market for the first time exceeded that of the USA, at just over 40 per cent, largely as a result of the country's strength in memories. In 1992 Japanese companies held 45 per cent of the US market for MOS (metal oxide silicon) memories and 57 per cent of the market outside the USA. In 1993, however, as a result of burgeoning microprocessor sales, Intel replaced NEC as the largest company in the world in terms of total semiconductor sales.

Only in microprocessors was the picture fundamentally different. In 1992, Intel held the overwhelming majority of the market for the then state-of-the-art 32-bit microprocessors. Intel's share of 73 per cent of this market ($3.18 billion) compared with Motorola's 8.5 per cent ($0.38 billion), Advanced Micro Devices' 8.0 per cent ($0.35 billion), and Texas Instruments' 1.9 per cent ($0.06 billion). NEC came fifth, with 1.1 per cent ($0.05 billion).

---

[54] R. N. Noyce and M. E. Hoff, 'A History of Microprocessor Development at Intel', *IEEE Micro*, 1(1981): 8–21.

Why are the Japanese Globally Weak in Microprocessors?

Why have Japanese companies performed so badly in global markets for microprocessors, in view of their strength in the technologies that underlie these devices (as indicated by the Japanese dominance of the memory market)? There are two related components to the answer to this important question. The first relates to the strength of Japan's US competitors in microprocessors, such as Intel; the second involves the specificities of the market for microprocessors in Japan to which the Japanese companies were responding. Both these factors will now be examined.

Intel

Intel was established in 1968, when Robert Noyce, Gordon Moore, and Andrew Grove left Fairchild Semiconductor to establish a new firm to manufacture memory semiconductors. (Fairchild Semiconductor itself was set up in 1957 when eight scientists left Shockley Semiconductor Laboratories after a dispute about company priorities. They wanted to concentrate on manufacturing processes rather than new devices. Shockley Semiconductor Laboratories was established in 1955 in Palo Alto, California, by William Shockley, one of the three inventors of the transistor in Bell Laboratories. It was Fairchild that developed the crucial planar process for semiconductor fabrication.)

Although Intel's main objective was memories, it had invented the microprocessor in 1969–70, the announcement being made in November 1971. This was the 4004, a 4-bit microprocessor (that is, capable of processing 'words' with a 4-bit—binary digit—length). In April 1972 Intel announced its 8008 and a little later the 8080 8-bit microprocessors. Very soon after Intel's breakthrough with the 4004, other companies announced their own microprocessors—including the biggest semiconductor manufacturer, Texas Instruments, which had simultaneously been working on ideas similar to those of Intel, and Motorola, which in 1974 announced its 6800. By July 1974, 19 different microprocessors had been announced, including NEC's.[55]

At first Intel hesitated to market its microprocessors, since its staff had technical rather than marketing capabilities and it was a company that had dedicated itself to memories. Then it decided to take the plunge. In retrospect, a crucial breakthrough occurred for Intel when in 1974 Ed Roberts, owner of MITS, a small company selling electronic goods including calculators, entered into a contract with Intel for the 8080 for use in the first microcomputer. This computer, known as the Altair, was in reality little more than a kit of electronic components linked to the microprocessor by a 'bus' of wires (which became known as the S-100 bus, one of the microcomputer industry's first compatibility standards). In January 1975, the Altair was memorialized with

---

[55] E. Braun and S. Macdonald, *Revolution in Miniature*, Cambridge University Press, 1982, 110.

a front cover story in the hobbyist magazine, *Popular Electronics*. The Altair soon became popular with hobbyists, such as the Homebrew Computer Club in northern California.

It was not surprising that Roberts chose Intel's 8080, since from 1972 to 1974 Intel's 8008 and 8080 were the only industry standard.[56] The 8080 was also used in the IMSAI 8080, the first Altair clone. (The IMSAI was developed by an entrepreneur, Bill Millard, who had been asked to develop a computerized car dealership system. Wanting to use the Altair because of its low price, but finding it unavailable because of order backlogs in MITS, Millard developed his own microcomputer. The IMSAI soon overtook the Altair in terms of sales.)

Intel's 8080 was given a further boost when Gary Kildall, founder of a company called Digital Research, produced an operating system for this microprocessor called CP/M. This system, controlling the activities of the computer, quickly became a standard, facilitating the rapid growth of applications software developed by independent producers. In turn, the increasing availability of software furthered the sales of microcomputers, providing additional reinforcement for the *de facto* standards that they embodied.

IBM's Choice of the Intel 8088.

By 1980 it had become apparent to IBM that it was missing out on a growing market in microcomputers. Although MITS and IMSAI soon dropped out, other start-ups were growing rapidly, including Apple, Tandy, Commodore, Osborne, and Atari. Part of the reason for the rapid growth was the development of the business market for microcomputers, largely as the result of the appearance of software such as spread-sheets.

IBM's chairman, Frank Carey, who in the 1960s had led the company into minicomputers and who believed that smaller computers would become increasingly important for the company, was behind the decision to move IBM into microcomputers (or personal computers—PCs—as they were increasingly being called). He chose William Lowe, head of IBM's Boca Raton Laboratory, to head a project charged with developing IBM's first PC by August 1981. It was this laboratory that earlier had developed the 5100, a desktop computer designed for scientific use.

When Lowe first met with IBM's Corporate Management Committee, he told them: 'The only way we can get into the personal computer business is to go out and buy part of a computer company, or buy both the CPU [central processing unit, incorporated into the microprocessor] and software from people like Apple or Atari—because we can't do this within the culture of IBM.'[57] Philip Donald Estridge, who soon succeeded Lowe, later elaborated: 'We were allowed

[56] Ibid. 111.

[57] J. Chposky and T. Leonsis, *The People, Power and Politics behind the IBM Personal Computer*, Facts on File, New York, 1988: 9; quoted in R. N. Langlois, 'External Economies and Economic Progress: The Case of the Microcomputer Industry', Department of Economics, University of Connecticut, March 1990.

to develop like a startup company. IBM acted as a venture capitalist. It gave us management, guidance, money, and allowed us to operate on our own.'[58]

In developing its PC, IBM made two decisions that were to have monumental implications for the future new patterns emerging in computing. The first was the choice of microprocessor, while the second was the choice of operating system.

For IBM's first PC, the Intel 8088, an improved version of the 8080, was chosen. The main reason for this choice was that it was compatible with the large amount of PC software that had been created, largely as a result of Kildall's CP/M operating system. Furthermore, some of the Boca Raton staff had used an earlier version of the 8088—the Intel 8085—for their 5100 desk computer. The decision, however, was not uncontroversial, as some of the staff had favoured Motorola's microprocessor.

IBM's Choice of Microsoft's MS-DOS.

It was assumed that the IBM PC would use Kildall's CP/M since it had become the standard for Intel-based computers. However, Kildall was slow in signing the agreement with IBM (for various conjectured reasons), and IBM then approached Bill Gates and Paul Allen of Microsoft. Apparently, 'Gates and Allen appreciated the opportunity little better than Kildall and agonised for some time before accepting the challenge.'[59] Although Gates and Allen had earlier developed their own operating system, part of the problem was the short time-horizon demanded by IBM. However, they knew of a company, Seattle Computing, that had developed an operating system that emulated the CP/M, called QDOS (for 'quick and dirty operating system'). Gates purchased the licensing rights for $25,000 and later exclusive rights for $50,000. This was to become Microsoft's MS-DOS, the operating system which became the global standard for PCs.

Intel's Initial Response to IBM's Decision.

With hindsight, we know that, in view of the huge immediate success of the IBM PC and the later success of IBM-compatible PCs, all of which used Intel microprocessors, IBM's decision was crucial for the future of Intel. At the time, however, this was not apparent to either Intel or IBM. According to one account, 'Gordon Moore, cofounder and chairman of Intel, recalls that, in Intel's view, IBM's choice of the 8088 was viewed as "a small design win". Intel's major business at the time was selling memory chips; IBM paid only about $9 a chip for the 8088, or, as Moore put it, "about the same as the solder on a PC circuit board". For both companies, understandably, it was just not a big deal.'[60]

    [58] *Business Week*, 'How the PC Project Changed the Way IBM Thinks', 3 October 1983, 86; quoted in Langlois, 'External Economies'.
    [59] Ferguson and Morris, *Computer Wars*, 26.
    [60] Ibid. 25.

Microprocessors in Japan

The growth of the microprocessor in the USA was very much tied to sales of personal computers. To some extent the same was true in Japan.

As mentioned earlier, NEC produced Japan's first domestically made microprocessor, the PD700, just five months after Intel's 4004. Like the 4004, the PD700 was a 4-bit microprocessor. The following year NEC produced an 8-bit microprocessor, like Intel's 8080. Interestingly, the PD700 was Intel-compatible, indicating that NEC, with its ever stronger competences in semiconductors, was following Intel closely. In 1977, with sales of micro-processors growing, NEC decided to use Intel as a second source for its microprocessors. However, as Koji Kobayashi, who became NEC's CEO in 1976, explained, 'as NEC's competitiveness increased and we began to compete with each other in the marketplace, the alliance became difficult to sustain'.[61]

NEC then made a decision which was to have a significant effect, not only on the future evolution of NEC's microprocessors, but also on the company's presence in global microprocessor markets: the company decided to switch to its own proprietary microprocessor design, which was incompatible with Intel's, the V series (for victory). It is doubtful, however, whether the decision led to victory for NEC, at least as far as presence in the global market for microprocessors is concerned, for that market was to become increasingly driven by Intel with its base in its *de facto* microprocessor standard for PCs.

Why did NEC make this crucial decision? It is likely that two considerations were responsible. The first was the difficulty of remaining Intel-compatible without infringing Intel's proprietary rights. (Indeed, despite NEC's switch to its own proprietary design, Intel brought a long-lasting lawsuit against NEC, alleging infringement of its microprocessor code.) The second consideration was that NEC's microprocessors were to be used in a wide range of its own products, which spanned virtually the entire range of products in the communications and computing field. Microprocessors developed with PCs in mind were not necessarily optimally adapted to the requirements of many of these products.

However, from 1973 NEC sold its microprocessors outside the company. This was in strong contrast to IBM, which took the decision to do so only in 1993. IBM has been heavily criticized for failing to sell its microprocessors externally. While this was done in an attempt to protect its computer products from the IBM-compatible clones, over time it meant that, by failing to interact closely with market forces, IBM, while strong in process technology, was not developing competitive competences in microprocessor design. When finally, in the early 1990s, IBM decided to launch a challenge to Intel's dominance, it had to do so in alliance with Motorola and Apple in developing the PowerPC RISC-based microprocessor. Although IBM's alliance partners were also chosen to try to consolidate a user support base for the PowerPC (and therefore to persuade other

[61] K. Kobayashi, *Rising to the Challenge: The Autobiography of Koji Kobayashi*, Harcourt Brace Jovanovich, Tokyo, 1989, 80.

users to come on board), the link with Motorola was also motivated by IBM's design weakness.

IBM was also criticized for failing to ensure a second source of supply inside the company to supplement Intel's microprocessors for the IBM PC. The decision to outsource to Intel in the first place, and Intel's subsequent sale of its microprocessors to PC clone producers, was clearly beneficial for the industry as a whole. It led to more rapid technical and design change, lower prices, and a more rapid rate of PC diffusion than would otherwise have occurred if IBM had kept its PC's microprocessor proprietary. However, IBM's failure to ensure a second microprocessor source within the company meant that it rapidly lost the competitive competences that it otherwise might have retained.

NEC's PC
We have seen that in the USA the development and diffusion of PCs occurred through a remarkable *market-mediated process* that brought together the competences that were needed but were housed in different firms. Specialist microprocessor producers emerged (in cases such as Intel, at first rather reluctantly) which supplied *juridically distinct* developers and sellers of PCs. Furthermore, software developers, which again were distinct from the producers of microprocessors and the developers and sellers of PCs, played a crucial role in the generation of demand for PCs.

In Japan, however, far more of the competences were housed within the large, vertically integrated computer and consumer electronics companies that produced the country's first PCs. NEC is of particular importance since this company quickly came to dominate the Japanese PC market. NEC's entry into PCs is analysed in detail in Chapter 6 within the context of the evolution of the company. The analysis will not be repeated here apart from several overall comments.

The first point to emphasize is that it was NEC's semiconductor group which developed and sold the company's first PC. It did so originally as a novel way of selling microprocessors to new groups of users. Secondly, NEC realized from the outset that it had to develop a *mini open system* if it wanted to generate a large market. Like the early successful American PC producers—including MITS, IMSAI, and Apple—NEC understood that what was important was not the PC itself, but its use-value, that is the uses to which it could be put. In turn, this required the generation of sufficient applications software. Furthermore, NEC realized that it could not itself possibly generate all the software that was needed. On the one hand, it did not have the personpower required; on the other, it could not conceive of all the possible applications that would find markets. Accordingly, again like its US entrepreneurial counterparts, NEC incorporated dependent and independent software producers by putting the technical specifications of its PC into the public domain. It was NEC's success in generating software applications for its PC more than any other single factor that explains its overwhelming market share—around 50 per cent of the Japanese market for

PCs in 1994—even though it was Hitachi that brought out the country's first PC a year earlier than NEC in 1976.

Thirdly, although NEC's PC was developed as a mini open system, it remained a *proprietary system,* with NEC's own proprietary operating system. This meant that applications software created for NEC's PC would not run on other companies' PCs, a factor that until the early 1990s (as is shown below) gave NEC a significant degree of *de facto* protection. Finally, it is worth noting that, apart from applications software, NEC provided in-house all the remaining competences that were needed for its emerging large PC business—a strong contrast with the major US companies involved in PCs, including IBM. Thus, NEC produced its own microprocessor for the PC, designed it and its operating system, produced it, and marketed and sold it. While novel marketing channels were developed for the PC's consumer market—through new shops such as the Bit-Inn and Miconshop—NEC's existing channels into the business market were mobilized for its PC.

The Japanese Language and the Diffusion of PCs in Japan

As in the USA, in Japan too it is clear that the development and diffusion of the microprocessor was closely tied to the development and diffusion of the PC. A crucial difference, however, stemmed from the impact of the Japanese language on the diffusion of PCs in Japan. Simply put, the large number of Chinese (*kanji*) characters in the Japanese language—about 5,000 are needed to read a newspaper—makes Japanese-language processing a difficult task. On the conventional PC, the word is keyed in on a keyboard containing the phonetic (*kana*) characters that in combination generate all the sounds in the Japanese language. The possible *kanji* characters that correspond to this 'sounded word' then come up on the screen (there may be many possibilities). The PC operator then has to identify the appropriate *kanji* characters which are then stored in the PC's memory. Clearly, the whole process is laborious relative to word processing in the English language. It is precisely for this reason that facsimile has been so widely diffused in Japan—the *kanji* characters can simply be written and the information transmitted—a factor understood early on by Thomas Edison which motivated his attempts to improve fax technology with Chinese-language-using countries in mind (see Chapter 3).

It is primarily these language-related difficulties that account for a significantly lower diffusion rate for PCs and networks of PCs in Japan compared with the USA and Europe, although the proprietary PC and network systems that proliferated in Japan helped to keep the cost of personal computing high, which also slowed diffusion. The differences in rates of diffusion are indeed remarkable, as is shown in Figs. 4.1 and 4.2.

The information provided in these figures speaks for itself. Furthermore, in terms of the networking of information receivers and information processors (the so-called Information Superhighway), Japan has been further disadvantaged

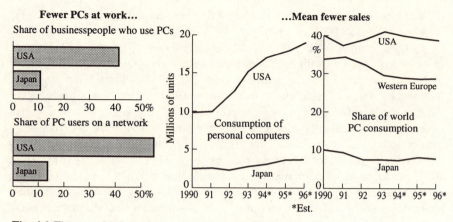

Fig. 4.1 The use of PCs in Japan, the USA, and Europe, 1990–1996
Source: NTT.

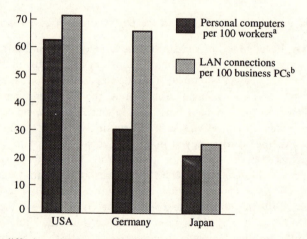

Fig. 4.2 The diffusion of PCs and PC/LAN connections in Japan, the USA, and Germany, 1993

[a] Based on 1993 employment data; includes home PCs.
[b] LAN = local area network.

Source: International Data Corporation; Merrill Lynch & Co.

by the conservative policies of the Japanese Ministry of Posts and Telecommunications (MPT). Partly in an attempt to protect the broadcasting interests under its jurisdiction, MPT restricted the activities of cable TV operators. As a result, in 1994 there were 11,075 cable TV operators in the USA, but only 149 in Japan. While most of the USA was networked by cable TV, little of Japan was: in 1994 there were 57.21 million cable TV subscribers in the USA compared with 1.08 million in Japan.[62] Although cable TV currently is a

[62] *Nikkei Weekly*, 16 May 1994.

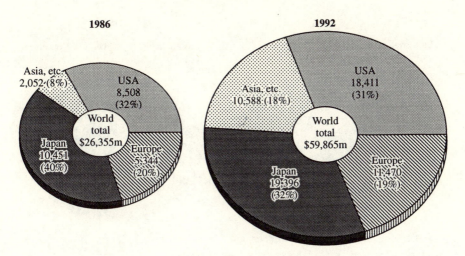

1986

1992

Asia, etc.
2,052 (8%)

USA
8,508
(32%)

World
total
$26,355m

Japan
10,451
(40%)

Europe
5,344
(20%)

USA
18,411
(31%)

Asia, etc.
10,588 (18%)

World
total
$59,865m

Japan
19,396
(32%)

Europe
11,470
(19%)

Fig. 4.3 World semiconductor market, by region, 1986 and 1992
Source: WSTS.

one-way point-to-multipoint service, at comparatively little cost cable networks can be upgraded to two-way networks providing interactive facilities. This is of obvious significance for Japan from the point of view of realizing the new vision for the 1990s and beyond of what computing is all about.

The Fundamentally Differing Demand Structures for Semiconductors in the USA and Japan

The lower rate of diffusion of PCs and networks of PCs in Japan compared with the USA is responsible for one of the distinguishing features of the different demand pattern for semiconductors in the two countries. Before examining this feature, however, the total size and country distribution of the world semi-conductor market is shown in Fig. 4.3. As can be seen, the size of the semiconductor market in Japan is larger than that in the USA, $19.4 billion in Japan (32 per cent of the world market) compared with $18.4 billion in the USA (or 31 per cent of the world market). Interestingly, however, in 1986 Japan had an even greater share of the market—40 per cent compared with 32 per cent for the USA. (The big gainer has been Asia, which in 1992 had 18 per cent of the world market, up from 8 per cent, compared with Europe's 19 per cent.)

However, although the total size of the semiconductor market in Japan and the USA is roughly similar, the composition of demand for semiconductors in the two countries is fundamentally different. This is shown in Fig. 4.4.

There are two distinguishing differences between the demand pattern for semiconductors in the USA and Japan. The first is the relatively large share of demand for use in computers in the USA, 62 per cent of the total compared with about half this—33 per cent—in Japan. One of the major reasons for this

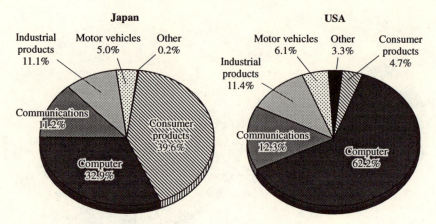

Fig. 4.4 Semiconductor market composition, USA and Japan, 1992
'Other' means government use, including the military and space sectors.
Source: WSTS.

difference is the lower diffusion rate of PCs and related networks in Japan, as already analysed.

The second distinguishing feature is the large share of demand for semi-conductors for use in consumer products in Japan. In Japan, 40 per cent of the demand for semiconductors comes from the consumer products industry, compared with only 5 per cent in the USA. The reason for this, in brief, is the collapse of the US consumer electronics industry (which is analysed further in the conclusion to this book).

Implications for Japanese Microcomputer Producers

We are now able to understand some of the paradoxes referred to at the beginning of this chapter, namely Japanese strength in computers but weakness in terms of global market share in computers-on-a-chip, or microprocessors; and Japanese weakness in microprocessors, but strength in memories.

Like their US counterparts—notably the case of Intel, which has been analysed in detail above—Japanese semiconductor companies have been tightly coupled with the semiconductor markets to which they have responded. The demand characteristics of their national markets, however, have been fundamentally different. As a result of the phenomenal global success of Japanese consumer electronics companies, the most important market for semiconductors in Japan has been in the production of consumer electronics goods. In the USA, on the other hand, computers, and particularly PCs, have constituted the most important market. In responding to the large consumer electronics market in Japan, Japanese semiconductor companies have developed strong distinctive competences in microcontrollers (which are similar to microprocessors but simpler, and are largely embedded in consumer products such as microwave ovens, video equipment, etc.). Indeed, NEC has become the world's largest producer of microcontrollers.

Furthermore, although the computer industry accounts for a relatively large source of demand for semiconductors in Japan, the proprietary nature of most of the computers produced by Japanese companies, together with the relatively low diffusion of PCs in Japan, has fragmented the market in Japan for microprocessors, while in the USA, with the surge in demand for PCs leading the way, Intel's microprocessors have become the *de facto* standard, creating a huge market for Intel. In Japan, the market for memories has been more homogeneous, creating a large 'commoditized' market for standardized memories. This demand for memories in the home market has benefited the main Japanese semiconductor companies.

While honing their distinctive competences largely to the demands in their home markets, Japanese and US semiconductor companies have used these competences in their attack on global markets. This is evident in Fig. 4.5. As can be seen, in the case of MOS (metal oxide silicon) micro devices—which include both microprocessors and microcontrollers—US companies have a 26 per cent share of the Japanese market, while Japanese companies have only a 6 per cent share of the US market. The reason for these figures is the significant market in Japan for microprocessors supplied by US companies, the high unit value of microprocessors relative to microcontrollers, and the small demand in the USA for microcontrollers arising from the small domestic consumer electronics industry.

In terms of market share in the rest of the world, however, the comparative advantage of the US companies in microprocessors shows up more clearly. While the US firms held 81 per cent of the rest of the world (RoW) market outside Japan in MOS micros (including the USA), Japanese companies had only 37 per cent of the RoW market outside the USA (including Japan). (Unfortunately, the data do not distinguish between microprocessors and microcontrollers in the MOS micro category.)

The Japanese comparative competitive advantage in memories shows up even more clearly in Fig. 4.5. While US companies had only an 11 per cent share of the Japanese market for MOS memories, Japanese companies held 45 per cent of the US market for these memories. While US firms held 23 per cent of the RoW market outside Japan for MOS memories (including the USA), Japanese companies had 57 per cent of the RoW market outside the USA (including Japan).

The distinctive competences accumulated by Japanese companies under these conditions are illustrated by the breakdown of semiconductor sales in NEC, Japan's largest semiconductor company. In 1992–3, NEC's total sales of semi-conductors came to $5.4 billion. Of this, dynamic random access memories (DRAMs) accounted for 28 per cent, microcontrollers for 22 per cent, custom integrated circuits (excluding general-purpose microprocessors) for 20 per cent,

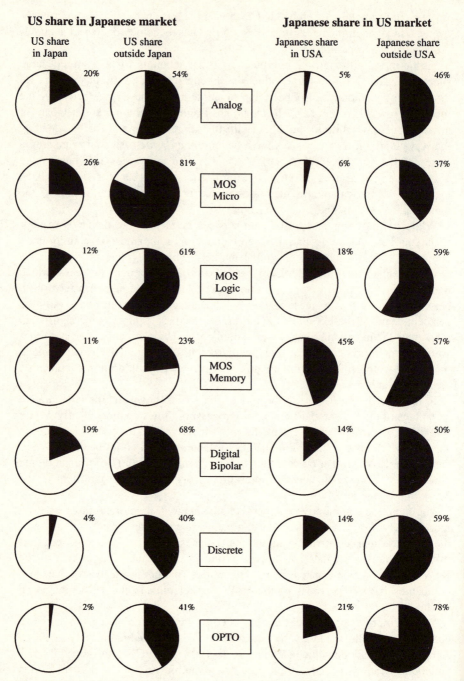

Fig. 4.5 US and Japanese semiconductor market shares, 1992
Source: Dataquest 1992.

LSIs (including general-purpose microprocessors) for 14 per cent, and other semiconductors for 16 per cent.[63]

Conclusion

It may be concluded that both US and Japanese companies have developed distinctive competences based on the specific characteristics of their home markets in microcomputers (including both microprocessors and microcontrollers). This has resulted in a comparative competitive advantage for US companies in microprocessors, and for the Japanese companies in microcontrollers. The case of memories, however, is different since there was a large demand in both the USA and Japan for memories. With memories, it is more the persistent effort made by Japanese companies in investing in, researching, and developing the following generations of memories that account for the Japanese distinctive competitiveness. By the early 1990s, however, Korean companies such as Samsung followed a similar path with equally impressive results as the Japanese and within a shorter timespan.

Global Alliances in Developing Microprocessors for the late 1990s

By the mid-1990s, Intel reigned supreme in the global microprocessor market as a result of its dominance of the *de facto* standard for PC-based microprocessors. At this time, however, several competing companies made bids to challenge Intel. Their challenges were based on a new technology for microprocessors—reduced instruction set (RISC)—which increases microprocessor speed by economizing on the instructions that need to be processed. While RISC was originally invented in IBM, the company failed to exploit it since its 'mainframe lobby' feared that RISC-based computers would eat into IBM's mainframe computer markets. In the mid-1990s, RISC microprocessors accounted for less than 10 per cent of all microprocessor units. The main problem for RISC microprocessors is that the software required is incompatible with the software for Intel microprocessors. While it is possible for compatibility to be emulated on a RISC microprocessor, this slows the processing speed, thus reducing the advantage of the RISC technology.[64]

The weakness of the Japanese semiconductors in this challenge is indicated by their position as supporting allies, rather than main challengers, in the battle with Intel. The main alliances are listed in Table 4.3. As can be seen, of the main Japanese semiconductor companies, NEC has allied itself with MIPS (which, together with Sun, was the first to develop RISC microprocessors); Toshiba is allied both with MIPS and Sun (which controls 38 per cent of the global market for workstations); Hitachi is allied with both IBM/Motorola/Apple and

---

[63] See Ch. 6 on NEC.
[64] 'Japan, US Firms Enter Microprocessor Pacts', *Nikkei Weekly*, 5 May 1994; 'Challenging the King of Chips', *Business Week*, 26 July 1993, 50–1.

Table 4.3 *Global Alliances in Microprocessors*

Microprocessor	Primary backers	Others in alliance
SPARC	Sun Microsystems	Fujitsu, Toshiba, Matsushita, Unisys, Texas Instruments
PA-RISC	Hewlett-Packard	Hitachi, Mitsubishi, Oki, Stratus Computers
MIPS	MIPS Technologies	NEC, Sony, Toshiba, Silicon Graphics, Siemens AG, Olivetti SaP
Alpha	Digital Equipment (DEC)	Mitsubishi, Kubota, Cray Research, Olivetti SaP
Power PC	IBM, Apple Computer, Motorola	Compagnie des Machines Bull, Canon, Hitachi

Source: *Nikkei Weekly*, 2 May 1994.

Hewlett-Packard; Fujitsu has an alliance with Sun (and is a major producer of Sun's SPARC microprocessor); and Mitsubishi Electric is allied with both Digital Equipment and Hewlett-Packard.

It must be stressed, however, that the Japanese weakness in global microprocessor markets has more to do with proprietary constraints than with technical competences such as the ability to design and fabricate microprocessors. One important indicator of Japanese technical competences is AT&T's decision to have NEC second-source its Hobbit microprocessor, which was developed in Bell Laboratories and is intended for use in communications products such as personal digital assistants (PDAs). A further indicator is the advanced microprocessors that Japanese companies have developed in conjunction with their Western allies. For example, in September 1993 NEC announced that it had developed a RISC microprocessor with MIPS, the VR4200, designed for hand-held PCs running Windows NT, an advanced operating system from Microsoft.[65] In May 1994 Fujitsu and Sun announced that they would jointly spend $500 million to develop a new RISC microprocessor for the workstation market.[66]

Transition from the Old World to the New

The Old World

IBM's Architecture of the Mind

By the late 1980s, Japan's computer industry reflected IBM's architecture of the mind. The mainframe was king. In 1988, for example, mainframes accounted

[65] *Nikkei Weekly*, 27 September 1993.   [66] Ibid., 2 May 1994.

for 27 per cent of Japanese computer production compared with 10 per cent for PCs.[67] As late as 1993, mainframes accounted for 65 per cent of Fujitsu's revenue,[68] and the situation in Hitachi was similar.

However, the mainframe market was fragmented into several 'domains', each of which was dominated by one of the large computer vendors. In 1993 Fujitsu ruled the biggest of these domains, with 25.1 per cent of the total Japanese mainframe market (including associated set-up software). Next came IBM Japan with 23.6 per cent, Hitachi with 17.8 per cent, NEC with 17.5 per cent (which accounted for 29 per cent of NEC total computer revenues, compared with 41 per cent for PCs); and Nihon Unisys with 10.2 per cent.[69]

The three major Japanese computer companies also developed super-computers. While the US firm, Cray, was dominant globally in this area, IBM had made the decision not to get involved in this specialist market niche. In 1992, of the total of 154 supercomputers sold in Japan, Fujitsu supplied 72 (or 46.8 per cent of the total), Cray sold 33 (21.4 per cent), NEC 26 (16.9 per cent), and Hitachi 21 (13.6 per cent). Supercomputers soon became an issue in the trade conflict that occurred between the USA and Japan.[70]

The relationship between the computer vendor dominating the domain and its customers, the computer users, tended to be long-term and mutually obligational. The computer systems sold by the computer vendor to the user tended to include both the hardware and the software that was needed. The computer system conformed to the computer vendor's proprietary architectures and designs. This made it costly for customers, once having purchased a system from a particular vendor, to switch to another vendor. In turn, this increased the costs of computer services and reinforced the long-term obligational relationships between vendor and user to which Japanese companies were in any event prone. In developing smaller computers, the vendors typically designed machines that complied with their proprietary architectures. This was the case, for example, with NEC-DOS, the operating system developed by NEC for its PC, and the EWS-4800, NEC's workstation, which gained 14 per cent of the Japanese market. It was also the case with Fujitsu's FMR-series, its PCs that were not particularly successful in Japan in view of NEC's dominance of the PC market.

Implications for the Japanese Software Industry

While the large computer users in Japan, e.g. banks and steel companies, worked closely with their particular computer vendors, they also developed strong in-house software competences. In developing software, both computer vendors and computer users subcontracted with software houses, which as a result were to some degree tied to the vendors and users. Some software houses, however, remained relatively independent of any particular vendor or user. Some of

---

[67] Ibid., 16 August 1993.   [68] Ibid., 13 September 1993.
[69] Ibid., 2 August 1993.   [70] Ibid., 5 April 1993.

the links are evident in the names of the top twenty-five Japanese software companies shown in Table 4.4.

This pattern of computer usage in Japan—with mainframes dominating, long-term obligational relationships between vendors and users, and proprietary computer systems—had important implications for the development of the Japanese software industry and the software market. Most importantly, it meant that a market for 'software commodities' was constrained. This was because most

Table 4.4 *The Top 25 Japanese Software Companies, 1991*

Rank	Name	Sales (¥bn)	Profits (¥bn)	Capital (¥bn)	Employees
1	NTT Data Communication Systems Corp.	395	5	10	7,721
2	Nomura Research Institute Ltd		6	10	2,849
3	Hitachi Information Systems Ltd	110	2	9	4,481
4	Hitachi Software Engineering Company Ltd	92	3	22	4,926
5	CSK Corporation	87	31	6	8,215
6	NEC Kofu Ltd	87	—	0.2	900
7	Japan Research Institute Ltd	81	0.2	2	2,507
8	Japan Steel Information and Communication Systems Ltd	70	0.3	2	2,657
9	Intec Inc.	68	2	18	3,145
10	Toyo Information Systems Company Ltd	66	1	18	2,364
11	NEC Information Service Ltd	58	—	0.2	988
12	Toshiba Information Systems (Japan) Corp.	56	0.6	1	2,911
13	Fujitsu Facom Information Processing Corp.	55	—	2	2,634
14	Daiwa Institute of Research Ltd	52	0.4	4	1,350
15	Yamaichi Computing Centre Company Ltd	48	0.04	0.4	559
16	FJSA	41	0.08	0.1	170
17	Ines Corp.	40	0.2	29	2,198
18	Japan Information Processing Service Company Ltd	38	0.4	1	1,631
19	Nikko System Centre Ltd	37	0.1	0.3	437
20	Sumisho Computer Systems Corp.	37	1	17	1,188
21	Fuji Research Institute Corp.	36	0.7	2	1,916
22	NEC Software	36	—	0.3	2,600
23	Hudson Soft Co.	35	1	0.04	318
24	NK EXA Corp.	35	0.2	1	1,608
25	TKC Corp.	33	2	6	1,281

Source: *Venture Japan*, 4(4).

software was customized (or 'bespoke') to meet a particular user's requirements, and therefore could not be sold, like any other commodity, on a market for software. (This is not unique to the Japanese software industry and is also the case in other industries, such as flexible manufacturing systems (FMS), which are configured to the requirements of a particular manufacturer.)

The distinctiveness of the Japanese software industry is dramatically illustrated in Table 4.5, which indicates the relative importance of customized and 'packaged' (or commoditized software, sold off-the-shelf) software in a number of OECD countries for 1985. In the USA, packaged software was significantly more important than customized software. This can be shown by the ratio of customized to packaged software. For the USA this ratio was 0.31, indicating that packaged software was more than three times as important as customized software. In European countries the relative importance of packaged software was a little less than in the USA, although packaged was still significantly greater than customized. In Germany, for example, the ratio was 0.61, while in the UK the figure was 0.67. For the four major West European countries the ratio was 0.88. This indicates the greater propensity to use packaged software in the USA.

It is striking that Japan was one of the few countries where customized software was more important than packaged software, and the only country where it was significantly more important: the ratio in Japan was 9.95! The only countries in this table for which customized software was more important than packaged software are France (with a ratio of 1.51), Turkey (1.16), and Finland (1.14). Japan, therefore, differed significantly from all the other countries in terms of its far greater propensity to use customized software.

In view of this fundamentally different pattern of software demand in the USA and Japan, together with the large size and sophistication of the US market for software, it is hardly surprising that US companies came to dominate the Japanese market for packaged software. Indeed, by 1993 US software firms, led by Microsoft, held more than 70 per cent of the Japanese market for packaged software.[71]

The other side of this coin is one of the paradoxes referred to at the beginning of this chapter. This refers to the strong international competitiveness of the Japanese computer vendors in software creation—measured in terms of software productivity and quality—co-existing with their failure to make much impact on the global market for packaged software. In 1990, one of the few quantitative studies of software productivity and quality in the USA and Japan concluded that 'Japanese software projects perform at least as well as their US counterparts in basic measures of productivity, quality (defects), and reuse of software code.'[72] However, in 1994 NEC, one of the largest Japanese computer vendors, reported that the previous financial year its sales of packaged software

---

[71] Ibid., 11 October 1993.
[72] Cusumano and Kemerer, 'Quantitative Analysis', 1384.

Table 4.5 *The Software and Computer Services Industry (including Hardware Manufacturers), 1985*[a]

| | Value-added marketed domestic revenues ($m) | | | | | | |
	Packaged software	Custom software[b]	Total software	Processing services[c]	Total services[d]	Total industry	Software share (%)
France	859.9	1,298.8	2,158.7	1,120.9	1,239.9	3,398.6	63.52
Germany	1,157.0	707.0	1,864.0	760.0	904.0	2,768.0	67.34
Italy	573.0	498.0	1,071.0	460.1	521.1	1,592.1	67.27
UK	1,093.7	737.2	1,830.9	687.9	814.9	2,645.8	69.20
Western Europe (4 countries)	3,683.6	3,241.0	6,924.6	3,028.9	3,479.9	10,404.5	66.55
Austria	113.0	75.0	188.0[e]	89.9	104.9	292.9	64.19
Belgium	173.2	127.1	300.3	214.2	236.2	536.5	55.97
Denmark	115.0	94.0	209.0	267.0	285.0	494.0	42.31
Finland	87.0	99.0	186.0	173.9	190.9	376.9	49.35
Netherlands	291.05	284.05	575.1	325.1	373.1	948.2	60.65
Norway	102.0	86.0	188.0	233.8	249.8	437.8	42.94
Spain	190.0	115.0	305.0	117.1	139.1	444.1	68.68
Sweden	195.0	149.0	344.0	301.9	329.9	673.9	51.05
Switzerland	195.0	146.0	341.0	245.0	270.0	611.0	55.81
Western Europe (13 countries)	5,144.85	4,416.15	9,561.0	4,996.8	5,658.8	15,219.8	62.82

Ireland	43.7	27.7	71.4	24.5	30.9	102.3	69.79
Portugal	15.1	9.9	25.0	13.2	17.2	42.2	59.24
Turkey	3.12	3.63	6.75	5.7	5.95	12.7	53.15
Western Europe (16 countries)	5,206.77	4,457.38	9,664.15	5,040.2	5,712.85	15,377.0	62.85
Greece	2.81	3.13	5.94	4.1	4.46	10.4	57.12
Western Europe (17 countries)	5,209.58	4,460.51	9,670.09	5,044.3	5,717.31	15,387.4	62.84
Australia[f]	324.5	175.2	499.7	137.4	175.9	675.6	73.96
Canada	388.9	208.7[g]	597.6	454.1	572.7	1,170.3	51.06
Japan	270.1	2,590.8	2,860.8	3,555.9	4,206.1	7,066.9	40.48
USA	12,602.0	3,944.0	16,546.0	10,479.0	14,012.0	30,558.0	54.15

[a] Data for the first 13 countries, based on *ECSA Report 1986*, have been revised by IOC Europa in accordance with additional information. Figures for 1985 have been recalculated by OECD adopting the corresponding IMF exchange rates. According to IOC Europa, these figures include software bundled with hardware by hardware manufacturers.
[b] Related consultancy included.
[c] Including facilities management.
[d] Excluding total software.
[e] Diebold Austria estimates the 1985 domestic software market at US$172.1 m. According to this source, packaged software account for about 80% but customized software which is provided for its adaptation is included in this value. Software bundled by hardware manufacturers in included and consultancy is excluded.
[f] Australian figures reflect unbundled software only. The value for custom software includes consulting and facilities management.
[g] Custom software development only.

Source: OECD, adapted from IOC Europa *EUROCAST*, June 1986, for the first 13 countries and IOC Europa for the *ECSA Report 1986* for Greece, Ireland, Portugal, and Turkey; IOC Australia; IOC Canada; IOC for Japan and the USA; US Department of Commerce.

came to only $152 million, less than 1 per cent of annual sales. Moreover, 'Its software exports have been negligible.'[73]

As in the case of microprocessors just examined, the absence of Japanese companies from the global packaged software market has little to do with technical competences, but is rather a reflection of the market for customized software in Japan and the lucrative opportunities that it offered. As will shortly be shown, however, this situation is rapidly changing in Japan as the transition is made from the old to the new order.

The Winds of Change

Forces for Change

What were the winds of change that began blowing, causing the old order to crumble and ushering in the new? Three forces of change may be identified as being particularly important. The first force was 'downsizing', whereby computer users gradually began substituting more powerful cost-effective smaller computers and distributed networks of these computers for mainframes. Downsizing was one of the major consequences of the development of more powerful microprocessors. Although, as was shown earlier, the downsizing process proceeded significantly more slowly in Japan than in the USA and Europe, this process nevertheless began under the old order.

In 1991 a second powerful force for change was unleashed when IBM (Japan), together with a consortium of NEC's competitors in the PC market, developed a bilingual operating system for personal computers called DOS/V. This operating system was compatible with Microsoft's Windows which was widely used abroad in IBM-compatible PCs. In May 1993, Microsoft introduced a Japanese-language version of Windows. DOS/V was rapidly adopted by other computer companies, including Compaq and Dell, the low-cost US PC makers. The significance of DOS/V was that it allowed the Japanese purchasers of DOS/V PCs to run English-language MS-DOS-compatible software at the same time as running DOS/V-based Japanese software.

The relatively low-priced DOS/V PCs posed a threat to NEC, the PC market leader. Its PC-98 series ran on NEC's proprietary operating system, NEC-DOS, which at that stage could not use DOS/V-based software. However, as was seen earlier, the success of NEC's PC-98 series had led to the creation of a substantial amount of Japanese-language applications software compatible with this series. On the other hand, while the diffusion of DOS/V machines increased the amount of Japanese-language software compatible with this operating system, NEC's PC-98-compatible software significantly outnumbered DOS/V Japanese-language software. At first, NEC made a point of stating publicly that it would not change its proprietary PC standard to accommodate DOS/V. It hoped

---

[73] *Nikkei Weekly*, 18 July 1994.

to rely on the relative abundance of Japanese-language software for the PC-98 series to ensure its continued dominance of the Japanese PC market. Eventually, however, as will shortly be seen, with the rapid sales of DOS/V PCs encouraged by their favourable price differential relative to NEC's PCs, NEC could withstand the tide no longer and made moves to accommodate DOS/V. The steady encroachment of the DOS/V standard into NEC's market is shown in Fig. 4.6, which also shows Apple's share based on its own proprietary operating system. Since this date NEC's market share has declined further.

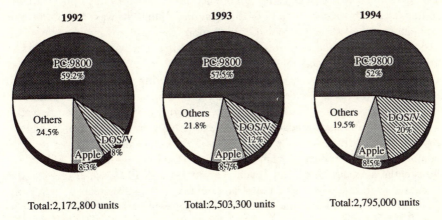

Fig. 4.6 Standards in the Japanese PC market, 1993
Source: Nikkei, 25 October 1993.

A third force for change, closely related to the other two, was the gradual move on the part of Japanese computer vendors from proprietary to so-called 'open' systems (open in the sense that users could integrate hardware and software sold by other vendors into their open computer systems, resulting in a multi-vendor environment). For example, one of the reasons for Fujitsu's acquisition of an 80 per cent shareholding in the British computer company, ICL, in November 1990 was the latter's expertise in UNIX-based open systems. (UNIX is an operating system developed in Bell Laboratories and used widely in smaller computers such as workstations.)[74]

---

[74] Fujitsu's relationship with ICL has been remarkable as a result of the unexpected degree of freedom that Fujitsu has given to the British management of ICL to continue with its activities in its own way. The acquisition at first caused waves of panic in Europe as a result of fears that ICL would become a European 'Trojan horse' for Fujitsu, and there were threats to exclude ICL from European computer research programmes such as those in ESPRIT. This panic, however, gradually subsided as it became clear that Fujitsu was content to have an arm's-length relationship with ICL (helped by ICL's remaining profitable, unlike the other European computer companies and even Fujitsu itself). Fujitsu has made it clear that it intends to sell up to 49% of ICL to European shareholders in order to further 'Europeanize' the Japanese-owned company.

Indicators of Change

One of the most dramatic indications that irreversible change had begun was Fujitsu's decision, announced in July 1993, that it would not license the 1993 version of IBM's mainframe software technology. After a dispute between IBM and Fujitsu over proprietary software rights, Fujitsu in 1988 had agreed to pay IBM 'hundreds of millions of dollars' for the right to use this technology.[75] Although it is likely that in making this decision Fujitsu was also influenced by its serious financial situation—the company was making its first losses since 1949—it reflected the decreasing importance of mainframes in Fujitsu's future business. At the same time, Fujitsu announced that it was recharting the company's future strategic course, giving more emphasis to smaller computers and software (in addition to its continuing strength in semiconductors— especially DRAMs—and telecommunications, the revenue from which gave Fujitsu, unlike IBM, some flexibility in restructuring the company). As far as the old order was concerned, according to which the Japanese computer industry was constructed in IBM's image, the writing was clearly on the wall.

A further important indicator of change was the growing production of PCs relative to mainframes. While in 1988 mainframes constituted 27 per cent of computer-related production compared with 10 per cent for PCs, by 1993 they were equal at about 20 per cent each.[76] From 1991 to 1994, while the average annual growth rate of sales of mainframe-related software increased by 7.2 per cent, that for workstations increased by 34.7 per cent and for PCs by 12.0 per cent.[77] Similarly, the growth in demand for packaged software far exceeded that for customized software, as is shown in Table 4.6. It can be seen that, as early as 1990, packaged software was becoming significantly more important. Between 1985 and 1990, the average annual growth in revenues from packaged software was 31.4 per cent compared with 15.5 per cent for customized software.

The New World in the Japanese Computer Industry

Just as IBM and its architecture of the mind, which had dominated the world of computing for over three decades, began to crumble under the force of the creative–destructive winds of change, so the old order in Japan, modelled in IBM's image, began to give way to the new. Although the process took longer to get underway in Japan as a result of the proprietary computer systems and long-term obligational relationships that were pervasive in the country, by the mid-1990s it was clear that similar changes to those occurring in North America and Europe were irreversible. In Japan too, the vision of what computing is all about had changed. Henceforth, computing would increasingly come to be seen not as a dominant 'continent' of mainframes, but in terms of decentralized and

---

[75] *Nikkei Weekly*, 13 September 1993.
[76] Ibid., 16 August 1993.
[77] JISA, 'Information Services Industry in Japan', Tokyo, 1993.

Table 4.6 *Software and Computer Services in Japan (including Hardware Manufacturers), 1985 (US$m)*

Market segments	Value-added marketed domestic revenues[a]		
	1985	1990	AAGR(%)
Packaged software	270.1	1,057.6	31.39
Custom software[b]	2,590.7	5,329.7	15.52
Total software	2,860.8 (40.5%)	6,387.3 (48.5%)	17.43
Processing services[c]	3,555.9 (50.3%)	5,699.6 (43.2%)	9.90
Total services excl. software	4,206.1	6,792.9	10.06
Total industry	7,066.9 (100.0%)	13,180.2 (100.0%)	13.28

[a] Figures for 1985 have been recalculated and extrapolated by OECD, adopting the relevant IMF exchange rate and the IOC-deflated growth rates. According to IOC Europa, these figures include software bundled with hardware by hardware manufacturers.
[b] Related-consultancy included.
[c] Facilities management and value-added network services included.

Source: OECD (IDC/C&L); additional information provided by IOC Europa.

distributed networks of information processors linked by high-speed communications channels.

One of the most important implications of this radical change is that, increasingly, the computing environment in Japan is becoming harmonized with that in the other industrialized Western countries. Previously the Japanese environment had been significantly different in a number of important respects. Proprietary domains, carved out by the major Japanese computer vendors, had given them a degree of protection. In a rapidly growing postwar economy, this had provided profits and growth. But these benefits for Japanese computer companies (unchallenged—or at least not opposed—by the country's policy-making bureaucrats) were had at a cost. The main cost was a very different computing environment in Japan compared with the main Western countries. This meant that in some important cases products, honed for the domestic market, could not, with only minor modification, be sold abroad. Unlike their Japanese counterparts making products such as TVs, video equipment, cars, and cameras, the Japanese producers of customized software and PCs could not immediately sell their products in the other major markets of the world. In microcomputers too, the different demand conditions existing in Japan—specifically, the large demand from consumer products—had an important impact, with the result that Japanese producers tended to concentrate on micro-controllers rather than microprocessors.

Where the environmental conditions in Japan were more similar to those in the major Western markets, Japanese companies tended to perform far better globally. Examples include memory semiconductors; flat panel displays (including thin film transistor liquid crystal displays which helped Japanese companies to achieve a dominant position in notebook computers); optical steppers for semiconductor fabrication (where Nikon has 60 per cent of the

Japanese market, Canon 30 per cent, and Hitachi 7 per cent);[78] silicon wafers (where companies like Shin-Etsu Handotai have a strong global position); and laser 'engines' for laser printers (where Canon, using its competences in optical technologies, enjoys a dominant position). Indeed, in some cases environmental conditions in Japan have been significantly better than in other Western countries, giving Japanese companies an important advantage. Instances include facsimile where, unlike in the case of PCs, the Japanese language has been a positive advantage, and optoelectronic devices such as semiconductor lasers, where the strong domestic consumer electronics industry has given Japanese companies an international competitive edge (incidentally, in research too).

However, in areas such as packaged software, microprocessors, and computers, environmental conditions in Japan, being sufficiently dissimilar from those in the major Western countries, have not bestowed similar advantages on Japanese companies—at least not yet. On the other hand, one of the main implications of the new order in the Japanese computer industry is that environmental conditions in Japan in this industry are becoming increasingly harmonized with those in Western countries.

A possible harbinger for the future is the highly significant moves by Fujitsu and NEC, first announced in 1994, into the global market for packaged software. In June 1994, for example, Fujitsu announced that it would market globally (in conjunction with ICL) several 'middleware' packaged software products. ('Middleware' is the area of software between operating systems and application software; it allows applications to be written and used on many different combinations of hardware and operating systems such as UNIX, Windows, Macintosh, and Sun.) According to Fujitsu's manager of global software product development, Yoshio Izumida, 'This will be the first case in which software products developed by Fujitsu will be exported.' According to *Nikkei*'s reporter, this 'marks Japan's possible emergence as a major player in a global software market that has always been dominated by American companies'.[79]

However, while it is clear that Fujitsu and its ICL subsidiary have the necessary software capabilities, its 'competences'—which include the whole value chain, from design and production to marketing, distribution, and sales—are more problematical. More specifically, Fujitsu currently lacks the marketing, distributions, and sales networks that are important for the sale of packaged software, something the company will try to remedy through alliances with American companies.

Also offering a portent for the future is NEC's decision to alter fundamentally its proprietary strategy in PCs. In June 1994, NEC announced that it would alter the architecture for some of its PC-98 series so that users can use IBM-compatible software applications such as Windows. Furthermore, by accepting IBM compatibility standards—such as the Peripheral Component Interconnect

[78] *Nikkei Weekly*, 18 October 1993.   [79] Ibid., 27 June 1994.

(PCI) bus architecture promoted by Intel—PC-98 users will be able to connect their machines to peripherals produced by other companies and will also be able to network with DOS/V compatibles. By broadening its standards in this way, NEC has eroded the 'proprietaryness' of its PC-98 series, contributing to an increase in standardization and openness in the Japanese PC market as a whole. However, NEC hopes that the fact that DOS/V users still will not be able to run Japanese-language applications software developed for the PC-98 series—and NEC still has the bulk of Japanese-language PC applications—will allow it to retain its market share.[80]

Equally importantly, in July 1994 NEC announced that it would end its proprietary software strategy and pursue a new 'multi-platform software strategy' that will allow it to develop packaged software not only for its own computers but also for others such as IBM and UNIX compatibles. According to Toru Shiozaki, senior manager of NEC's Application Software Division, 'Since the global software market has long been dominated by US firms such as Microsoft . . . Japanese firms have only been paying money to them. I think this is a good opportunity to use multi-platform software titles as a tool to break into overseas software markets.' In the case of workstations, for example, NEC's multi-platform strategy will allow more than 60 per cent of the packaged software originally developed for NEC's proprietary EWS-4800 workstations to run on either Sun's or Hewlett-Packard's workstations or on Windows-installed personal computers. While in 1993 NEC earned only ¥15 billion from packaged software, it plans to increase this figure to ¥50 billion by March 1998.[81] Of course, in overseas markets NEC faces the same competence problems of distribution that Fujitsu does.

It is clear from these details that the New World has arrived in the Japanese computer industry, leaving the Old World, modelled in the image of IBM's architecture of the mind, irreversibly behind.

Conclusions

The Evolution of the Japanese Computer Industry in Comparative Perspective

Fig. 4.7 presents a summary of the evolution of the Japanese computer industry in comparative perspective. More specifically, it shows some of the major landmarks occurring in the US computer industry, and the corresponding events (sometimes in direct response to happenings in the USA) in the Japanese computer industry. This evolution has been analysed in detail in the body of the present chapter.

---

[80] Ibid., 13 June 1994.   [81] Ibid., 18 July 1994.

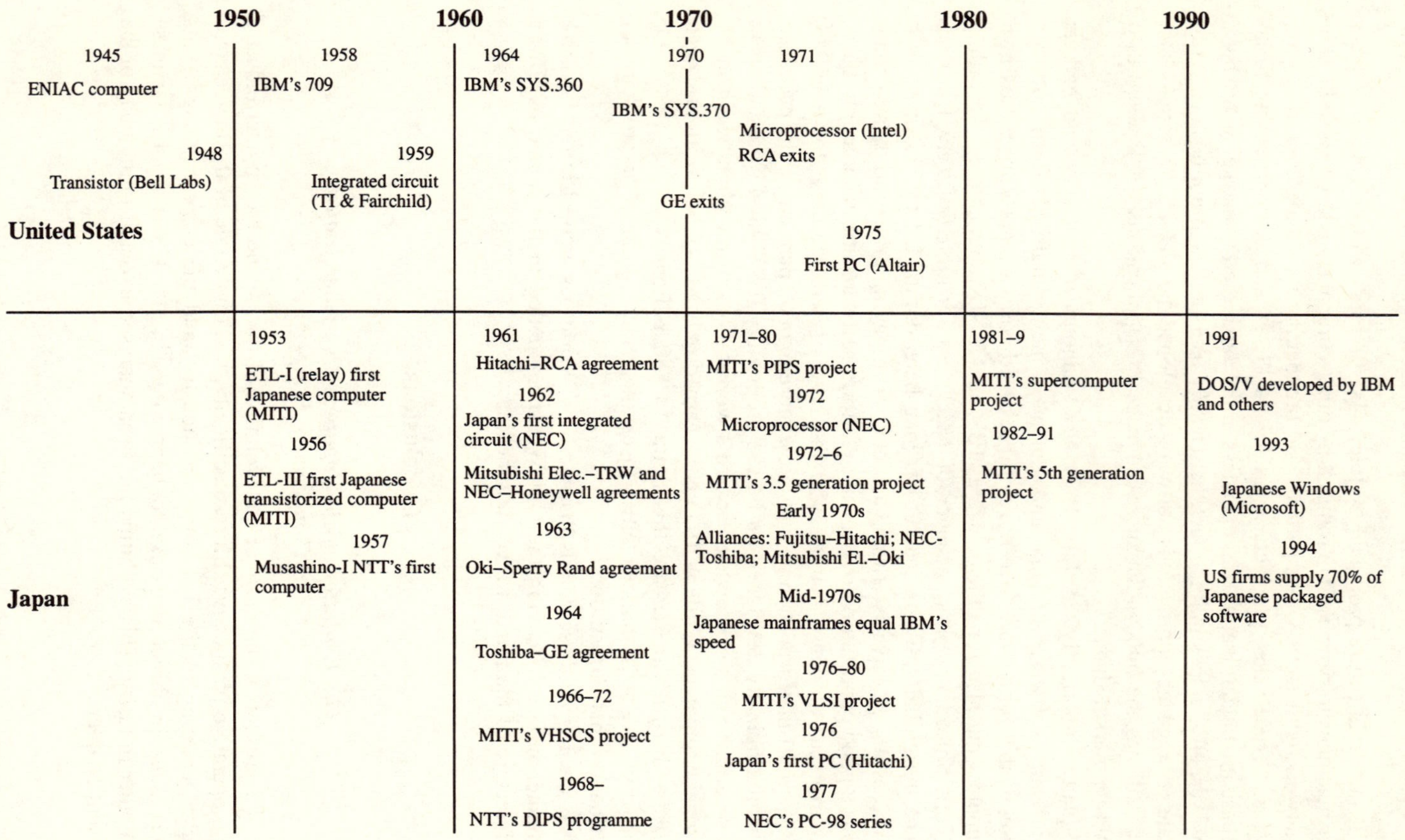

Fig. 4.7 The evolution of the computer industry, 1945–1994

Timeline (1945 – 1990):

United States
- 1945 ENIAC computer
- 1948 Transistor (Bell Labs)
- 1958 IBM's 709
- 1959 Integrated circuit (TI & Fairchild)
- 1964 IBM's SYS.360
- 1970 IBM's SYS.370
- 1970 GE exits
- 1971 Microprocessor (Intel)
- 1971 RCA exits
- 1975 First PC (Altair)
- 1991 DOS/V developed by IBM and others
- 1993 Japanese Windows (Microsoft)
- 1994 US firms supply 70% of Japanese packaged software

Japan
- 1953 ETL-I (relay) first Japanese computer (MITI)
- 1956 ETL-III first Japanese transistorized computer (MITI)
- 1957 Musashino-I NTT's first computer
- 1961 Hitachi–RCA agreement
- 1962 Japan's first integrated circuit (NEC)
- 1963 Mitsubishi Elec.–TRW and NEC–Honeywell agreements
- 1964 Oki–Sperry Rand agreement
- 1966–72 Toshiba–GE agreement
- 1968– MITI's VHSCS project
- NTT's DIPS programme
- 1971–80 MITI's PIPS project
- 1972 Microprocessor (NEC)
- 1972–6 MITI's 3.5 generation project
- Early 1970s Alliances: Fujitsu–Hitachi; NEC–Toshiba; Mitsubishi El.–Oki
- Mid-1970s Japanese mainframes equal IBM's speed
- 1976–80 MITI's VLSI project
- 1976
- 1977 Japan's first PC (Hitachi)
- NEC's PC-98 series
- 1981–9 MITI's supercomputer project
- 1982–91 MITI's 5th generation project

Competences of the Japanese Computer Companies

The theoretical approach adopted (for the most part, implicitly) in this book suggests that the analysis of 'competences' must lie at the heart of the explanation of industrial evolution. Competences refer to the activities and knowledge of the firm, relating to the entire value chain, which allow the firm to compete. What conclusions may be reached regarding the competences of the Japanese computer companies in the postwar period?

To begin with, it is clear that, just as in AT&T, the competences that the Japanese telecommunications equipment suppliers—NEC, Fujitsu, and Hitachi—accumulated before the Second World War in the area of telecommunications created the knowledge base from which they were able to move on into computers and semiconductors. In the prewar period, such competences were accumulated by these suppliers under conditions of controlled competition in co-operation with the Ministry of Communications (later to become NTT). From the beginning, it was these three companies that were strongest in the emerging field of computers.

The accumulation of competences by these companies, however, did not represent a smooth or automatic progression from telecommunications to computers. Both vision and company-specific effort played important roles. For example, in the case of Fujitsu, it was shown that this company's vision regarding the potential role of computers for its future was shaped by its *relative weakness* in telecommunications equipment. Since NEC dominated in the field of telecommunications equipment, Fujitsu's leaders eventually made the strategic decision, in the light of their vision of the future, to prioritize the emerging area of computers and extend their existing competences into this field. However, as was seen, this decision itself was a cause of controversy and conflict within the company, and it was only with a new leader, Okada, that a new strategic direction was decisively articulated and followed.

A different example of the discontinuity involved in the extension of competences from telecommunications equipment into computers is provided by Oki. In the prewar period, Oki was second only to NEC as a telecommunications equipment supplier. However, even then, Oki's relative strength was steadily eroding, and in the postwar period this company never made a major impact in the field of computing.

The remaining major computer companies, Toshiba and Mitsubishi Electric, were not key telecommunications equipment suppliers to the Ministry of Communications in the prewar years. This meant that they were unable to accumulate competences as strong as those of NEC, Fujitsu, and Hitachi on the basis of which to enter the emerging computer industry. Nevertheless, their competences in heavy electrical equipment, electronic components such as vacuum tubes, consumer electrical products, and, particularly in Toshiba's case, radio communications, put them in a favourable position to enter the computer industry. However, they remained in a distinctly second rank compared with

NEC, Fujitsu, and Hitachi. This was apparent in their position in the pecking order in the co-operative projects that MITI established up to the early 1970s. It was, therefore, no surprise that their relative weakness was confirmed when, despite the efforts made by MITI, they exited from the mainframe computer business in the mid-1970s in the wake of IBM's System 370.

Unquestionably, it was Fujitsu that was the big gainer from the new opportunities provided by computers. Fujitsu was able to transform itself from the second or third biggest supplier of telecommunications equipment at the end of the war to the largest Japanese computer company by around the 1980s. And the computer market had become far larger than that for telecommunications equipment. Hitachi also made substantial gains. As was seen earlier in this book, Hitachi was a comparatively late entrant into the telecommunications equipment business, although it was favoured from the late 1920s by the nationalistic Ministry of Communications, partly as a result of its decision not to depend on foreign suppliers of technology. Nevertheless, not enjoying the support that NEC and Fujitsu received from Western Electric and Siemens respectively, Hitachi remained relatively weak in telecommunications equipment. After the war, initially as a result of the reversal of its earlier technological self-reliance and its conclusion of a computer technology agreement with RCA, Hitachi made important advances in the Japanese computer industry.

Toshiba, after exiting from the mainframe business, was later able to re-enter the computer market on the basis of its competences in electronic components. Ever since it accumulated competences in vacuum tubes through its technology agreement with General Electric, Toshiba had been strong in electronic components. This facilitated its production of small computers, particularly lap-tops and notebooks in the 1980s, which in the early 1990s put Toshiba in tenth place in the global rankings in terms of total sales. Mitsubishi Electric and Oki, however, have remained relatively weak in computers (the latter in the 1990s using its competences in telecommunications to enter into a strategic alliance with Hewlett-Packard).

By the late 1970s, the leading Japanese computer companies were producing mainframes that equalled IBM's in terms of performance. That they were unable to make much inroad into IBM's markets outside Japan was more a reflection of the advantage that IBM derived from its global distribution networks and its installed base of hardware and software than of technological weakness on the part of the Japanese firms. But the Japanese companies were able to compensate for their global weakness by their strong positions in the rapidly growing postwar Japanese market. Accordingly, they consolidated their domains inside Japan, largely on the basis of proprietary computing systems in which customized software featured prominently. While they were able to do some important business in overseas markets—partly through acquisitions and alliances, such as Fujitsu's acquisitions in Amdahl and ICL and NEC's link with Bull in France—most of their sales of computers were in Japan. By around 1990, about 80 per cent of their sales of computers were in the Japanese market.

The story in computer commoditized components, as opposed to computing systems, was quite different. In fields such as semiconductor memories, flat panel displays, lasers, optical steppers for semiconductor fabrication, silicon ingots, and wafers, Japanese companies held dominant positions in global markets. A notable exception was microprocessors, where Japanese companies were relatively weak for reasons that were analysed in detail in this chapter. A further (though different) exception was packaged software, also analysed above. In the area of computer commoditized components, Japanese companies were helped by their ability (aided by their links with their related financial institutions) to steadily accumulate competences through increasing and stable (i.e. relatively immune to business cycle fluctuations) investments in plant and equipment and R&D, and manufacturing practices that resulted in continuous incremental improvements.

However, there were two major related problems with the competences (embodying the entire value chain) that the Japanese computer companies accumulated. The first of these was that their competences were very much made in IBM's image. This was particularly the case with Fujitsu and Hitachi, which most consciously followed in IBM's footsteps, only to fall over the same precipice. Like IBM, Fujitsu and Hitachi were eventually forced to come to terms with the limitations of a mainframe-centred computer strategy, although, as was seen, the global trends in computing took longer to make themselves felt in Japan. Unlike IBM, however, the Japanese companies had the advantage of market strengths in semiconductors and telecommunications equipment which helped them to restructure, reducing their dependence on mainframes while maintaining lifetime employment (although reducing overall employment significantly).

As stressed throughout this chapter, NEC was in a somewhat different position. NEC's vision of the role of computers in its future development was predicated upon its existing strength in telecommunications equipment. Computers were from the beginning, therefore, seen as part of information *and communications* systems. As a result of this vision, although NEC too partially embraced IBM's architecture of the mind and became heavily involved in mainframes, the company did not come to depend on them to the same extent as Fujitsu and Hitachi. Furthermore, its breakthrough into personal computers, which emerged from its competences in microprocessors, gave NEC strength in the smaller computers that would become important in the New World of computing.

A second set of problems emerged from the competences that the Japanese companies had accumulated in computers. These competences were accumulated in interaction with the selection environment existing in the Japanese computer market. More specifically, the mainframe-dominant proprietary computing systems sold by the major Japanese computer vendors to their customers meant that the computer companies accumulated competences in their proprietary systems and the related customized software. Competences in other areas that would become increasingly important in the New World of computing tended to be neglected. These included, for example, competences in open-systems architectures, smaller computers, and packaged software. As the Old World began to crumble in the mid-1990s, and conditions in the Japanese computer market began to harmonize with those in North America and Europe, Japanese companies began to realize that they had to increase their competences in these areas.

By the mid-1990s, however, it seemed clear that the Japanese computer companies still had far to go if they were to stamp their authority outside Japan, and outside the areas of commoditized computer components where they had already made their mark globally. In particular, Japanese companies would still have to work hard if they were to dominate the new 'architectural domains' that were coming to assume importance in the new world of computing. These domains include, for example, architectures and *de facto* standards for personal computers and workstations, networking of computers, personal digital assistants, multimedia equipment and services, etc. Companies such as Microsoft, Novell (in computer networking), and Intel have shown the benefits that can follow from the domination of such architectural domains. (In 1994, for example, Microsoft and Intel, with sales at 6 and 14 per cent respectively of IBM's sales, were valued by the stock market at 83 and 71 per cent respectively of IBM's valuation!)

In order to dominate these emerging architectural domains, however, Japanese computer companies will have to devote significantly more attention than they have done in the past to the international universe of computing. In this effort, they may be assisted by the changing characteristics of the Japanese computer market, which, as analysed in this chapter, are steadily harmonizing with those in North America and Europe. The increasing globalization of Japanese information and communications companies, a process that still lags behind that in comparable Western companies, will assist their attempts to respond to these emerging trends in computing.

The Role of MITI and NTT in the Evolution of the Japanese Computer Industry

The role of the telecommunications sector in Japan in facilitating the development of the Japanese computer industry has been seriously underestimated in much of the literature on this industry. One reason for this error is that most accounts of the Japanese computer industry begin after the Second World War. However, as shown in Chapters 2 and 3 above, and as stressed in this chapter, the telecommunications sector has in many ways been the seed-bed out of which the computer industry grew.

In the late nineteenth century, the government-owned factory originally established to produce telegraph equipment and the laboratories that were later added—all of which were subsequently taken over by the Ministry of

Communications—served as an incubator for the entrepreneurs and engineers who went on to establish and expand companies such as the predecessors of NEC, Fujitsu, Toshiba, Hitachi, and Oki. After the war these laboratories were split, one part becoming NTT's Electrical Communications Laboratories (ECL) and the other becoming MITI's Electrotechnical Laboratories (ETL). As we saw in this chapter, it was in these laboratories that the computers were developed which were to become the first commercial computers of the Japanese companies. It was only in the latter 1950s, as a more certain market began emerging for computers, that the companies made a firm commitment to the computer industry. From then, however, the action moved decisively to the companies.

From the latter 1950s, the heart of the Japanese computer industry—lying in the ability to design, develop, manufacture, market, sell, service, and maintain computers—was located in the Japanese computer companies. The role of the Japanese government was primarily a supportive one. But it was an important role, and it is doubtful whether the Japanese computer industry would have survived (or even started) had there been no government support at all, and if the Japanese companies had been required to exist under completely free-trade conditions with no subsidies. The quality, price, and performance of Japanese computers until about the latter 1970s simply would not have been competitive with those of imported computers in the absence of any government support. As shown earlier in this chapter, the US government also played a particularly important role in subsidizing the emergence of its computer industry.

As computer technologies and products became more sophisticated and the sunk costs in investment and R&D necessary for remaining in the computer industry increased substantially—coinciding with IBM's introduction of its System 370—so the costs of a strategic commitment to computers were significantly raised. In the USA, companies that had succumbed to the 'lure of the computer'—companies such as RCA and General Electric, which were larger and technologically more sophisticated than the Japanese companies—soon decided to exit. In Japan, the 'infant industry' protection and promotion that was given by the government to the computer companies was necessary for their survival.[82]

Nevertheless, despite government protection and promotion, only three of the six Japanese computer companies remained in the mainframe market. It was no

---

[82] This was given through measures such as quotas (*de jure* and *de facto*); tariffs, subsidized credit through government organizations such as the Japan Electronic Computer Company, which subsidized the use of Japanese-made computers; R&D incentives; and government-initiated co-operative R&D programmes. Interestingly, from the point of view of economic theory, most of these policies are second- or even third- and fourth-best in view of the distortions in the price mechanism that they cause. Nevertheless, they worked in so far as they kept in existence an industry that later learned and became more efficient, eventually becoming an 'adult industry'. However, whether the cost of protection and subsidization was eventually more than compensated by the advantages of an internationally efficient computer industry—that is, whether the Japanese computer industry passed the so-called Mill-Bastible test in economic theory—is rather more difficult to answer.

coincidence that these three—NEC, Fujitsu, and Hitachi—were also the three main telecommunications equipment suppliers. Not only did they enter the computer industry with the strongest competences as a result of the capabilities they had accumulated in producing complex telecommunications systems, they were also able to benefit from NTT's technical assistance (provided through ECL), from the economies of joint research and development provided through NTT's programmes with its suppliers, and from NTT's significant procurement of computers. In the present chapter, NTT's DIPS computer programme was analysed in detail.

Indeed, the fact that there were *three* companies that had these strong telecommunications-related competences in the first place was the result of the controlled competition adopted by the Ministry of Communications (the origins of which were examined in Chapter 2). It was controlled competition that gave Japan three major computer companies which also had strong competences in communications. This contrasts starkly with the situation in the USA, where AT&T's vertical integration meant that there was only one all-round telecommunications equipment company (Western Electric, a part of AT&T), and where the company's consent decree with the Justice Department meant that there were no US computer companies with competences in both computing and communications. (Whether the different combination of competences in the major Japanese information and communications companies—that is, in both computing and communications in addition to semiconductors—is a characteristic that can be put to their international competitive advantage is a question that will be examined in the conclusion to this book.) Nevertheless, it is this competence characteristic that is perhaps the most important legacy of the Japanese telecommunications sector for the Japanese computer industry.

Mighty MITI?

Several past accounts of the Japanese computer industry (including my own[83]) have stressed the importance of MITI's role in the development of the Japanese computer industry. However, these accounts were written in the late 1980s, at a time when Japan's computer industry was still unquestioningly modelled in the image of IBM's architecture of the mind. Still to come was the IBM débâcle in 1993, when the company declared what was then the largest loss in corporate history, revealing at the same time the fall of the mainframe and ushering in a new vision of what computing is all about. In the new climate—which some computer industry analysts have dubbed 'the post-IBM era'—it is necessary to reassess how well MITI bureaucrats have done for the Japanese computer industry, the industry which in the late 1960s they identified as the most important for Japanese growth.

With hindsight, several conclusions are justifiable regarding the evaluation of MITI's role in the development of the Japanese computer industry. The first

---

[83] Fransman, *The Market and Beyond.*

conclusion, it has to be said, is that MITI's bureaucrats, despite all their famous 'visions', failed to foresee the new computing world that was about to dawn in the early 1990s. At that time, Japan found itself with a computer industry structure that had several important weaknesses. These included the relatively low diffusion of smaller computers and networks of these computers (which was partly the result of the proprietary policies of the major computer vendors); little progress in the development of capabilities in open computing systems; weaknesses in the development, domestic sale, and export of packaged software compatible with the major international architectures; and the supportive, rather than leading, position of Japanese companies in the global market for microprocessors.

In this sense, therefore, MITI suffered from 'vision failure'. But why is this surprising? It is only because Western authors have mystified the process of vision formation in general, and MITI's ability to formulate correct visions in particular, that anyone could expect that MITI had a special purchase on the future. MITI and its bureaucrats did not. But then, neither did the experts in IBM, the company that massively dominated the global computer industry; nor did the analysts in the Wall Streets of the world and in the business schools. It was these analysts who supported IBM's architecture of the mind, as is evident from IBM's share price until the late 1980s and from the multitude of business books extolling IBM's 'excellence'. MITI's bureaucrats, subjected to the same problems of interpretive ambiguity and belief construction as anyone else, did little better.

But what about all MITI's co-operative research programmes, which struck fear in the hearts of Western policy-makers and their companies—compounded by Japanese international competitiveness in areas such as consumer electronics and motor vehicles—and prompted emulative programmes in the USA and Europe? What, with hindsight, is the legacy of these programmes?

It is useful to divide MITI's co-operative programmes in computing into two categories. The first consists of the earlier programmes, which may be labelled 'catching-up programmes'. The largest of these, e.g. the VHSCS and the 3.5 Generation programmes introduced in response to IBM's Systems 360 and 370 respectively, primarily involved giving the Japanese computer companies sufficient financial resources to launch the development projects that allowed them to improve their computers. Here MITI's role was mainly supportive, in the sense that it supported the competences of the companies, although ETL (and NTT's ECL) also provided some technical input.

The second category involved attempts to facilitate the creation of radically new technologies which, it was hoped, would significantly improve the competitiveness of the Japanese companies. In a few cases, these technologies were included in some of the catching-up projects, such as the inclusion of electron-beam technology in the VLSI project. Radical new technologies in some of the other programmes included pattern recognition and processing in the PIPS Project; gallium arsenide-based devices such as field effect transistors and high electron mobility transistors in the Supercomputer Project; and logic programming in the Fifth Generation Project.

It is likely that MITI's projects helped to strengthen the capabilities of the Japanese companies in new radical technologies such as these. It is also likely, however, that, if these technologies had turned out to be commercially significant, the Japanese companies, having grown significantly in size and competences largely as a result of the rapidly growing Japanese economy, would have developed them even without MITI's programmes. In the event, however, many of the radically new technologies selected in the MITI projects turned out to be of limited commercial importance. For example, electron-beam technology for semiconductor etching was delayed as optical technology was incrementally improved beyond all expectation to produce submicron semiconductors; similarly, silicon has proved far more effective as a semiconductor material than many had thought in the early 1980s, confining materials such as gallium arsenide (in which electron mobility is faster) to special uses such as lasers; logic programming has not become as important in general-purpose computing as MITI officials had hoped; etc. Indeed, one of the remarkable features of the electronics and information revolution is the durability of some of the key 'old' technologies under the influence of constant incremental improvement.

In retrospect, there are very few examples, if any, of MITI projects that can be directly credited with producing major, commercially important, breakthroughs by participating Japanese companies. However, this is not to say that MITI's projects did not help to strengthen the capabilities of Japanese companies. Furthermore, many of MITI's projects helped to develop future technologies that, in view of the uncertainty that surrounded them, might not otherwise have received the same degree of attention. And it is possible that some of these technologies will in the future turn out to be important. But then again, it would be unreasonable to expect that MITI's projects should produce such momentous results. As I have shown elsewhere,[84] MITI's total expenditure on science and technology was much smaller than that of either the Ministry of Education or the Science and Technology Agency, by far the biggest spenders in science and technology, and furthermore, MITI's expenditure on co-operative research and development was a very small proportion of its total expenditure.

It may be concluded, therefore, that the Japanese government played a primarily supportive but necessary role in facilitating the development of the Japanese computer industry, even though its co-operative R&D programmes on the whole failed to produce momentous breakthroughs. In the concluding chapter, the role of the Japanese government in the development of the information and communication industry as a whole is taken up once more.

---

[84] See Fransman, 'Is National Technology Policy Obsolete . . . ?'

5

The Evolution of the Japanese Optical Fibre Industry

CHAPTER OVERVIEW

The chapter begins with a brief, simplified account of the basics of optical fibre technology. A detailed analysis is then provided of the invention, innovation, and diffusion processes that led to, and subsequently followed, Corning's 1970 breakthrough in optical fibre. However, so as not to overload the reader with the complex details that are necessary for an explanation of the evolution of optical fibre technology, this analysis is presented in Appendix 2.

The main body of the chapter, acccordingly, continues from the point when Corning's breakthrough was announced in 1970. A detailed examination is then undertaken of the response of NTT and its family of suppliers—including Sumitomo Electric, Fujikura, and Furukawa—to Corning's result. How optical fibre knowledge was assimilated in Japan and diffused to the Japanese cable suppliers and how the Japanese companies managed to produce world-record-breaking low-loss optical fibres is then analysed.

The following section contains an examination of the process of innovation involved in the development of the Japanese VAD (vapour phase axial deposition) process for producing optical fibres. It was this innovation that allowed the Japanese patent office to refuse Corning's patent applications in Japan and facilitated the domination of the Japanese market by the Japanese cabling companies. How important was the VAD innovation? How did it differ from the process technologies used in the major Western companies? Does the VAD process have any competitive advantages over the other alternative technologies? How was the VAD technology diffused to three further Japanese companies—Hitachi Cable, Dainichi-Nippon Cable, and Showa Electric Wire and Cable—making Japan the most competitive market in the world for optical fibre? What role did AT&T play in diffusing optical fibre technology to Japan? These questions are examined in this section.

The legal battles between Corning and Sumitomo Electric are then analysed. The globalization of controlled competition is then discussed, as NTT in the early 1990s added Western and other Japanese companies to its group of suppliers developing new optical-fibre-related transmissions systems.

This chapter ends with an analytical section. The first analysis involves a detailed account of the way in which controlled competition worked in the case of optical fibre in Japan, throwing light on the strengths and, equally important, the weaknesses of this Japanese form of organization.

The second analysis contains critical reflections, based on the present study of optical fibre, on Joseph Schumpeter's view of the process of innovation. How meaningful, in the light of the evolution of optical fibre technology, is Schumpeter's concept of 'creative-destruction' and his distinction between invention, innovation, and diffusion? How does the approach to the firm developed in the present book fit into the Schumpeterian framework, particularly the notion of vision as a process of belief formation?

Introduction

Although some important early research was carried out in Japan in optics and optical fibre, the first optical fibres suitable for use in telecommunications were invented in Western countries in the late 1960s. In 1970 a crucial breakthrough was made by researchers in Corning.* From 1974, however, Japanese companies rapidly caught up in this key telecommunications technology. Indeed, in 1976 and 1979 Japanese companies produced world-record-breaking optical fibre with the lowest signal loss rates. Furthermore, in Japan a process technology was developed that allowed Japanese optical fibre companies not only to dominate the Japanese market for optical fibre, but also to challenge the leading US companies in the US market. By the early 1990s, Japan had the most competitive optical fibre market in the world with six producers of optical fibre.

How were these results achieved? How precisely did NTT and the major cabling companies—Sumitomo Electric, Furukawa, and Fujikura—respond to the advent of optical fibre in Western countries? What role was played by NTT's 'controlled competition' form of organization in the invention, innovation, and diffusion of optical fibre in Japan? What combination of factors allowed the Japanese companies to break world records in 1976 and 1979? How was the Japanese VAD (vapour phase axial deposition) process for the production of optical fibre developed and how does it differ from the corresponding processes used in Western countries? What was the substance of the legal battle that took place between Corning and Sumitomo Electric and what was the outcome? How in the early 1990s did NTT globalize controlled competition by including Western companies and how have these companies adjusted to this Japanese form of organization? These are some of the questions that are analysed in detail in the present chapter.

Further important questions arise in attempting to explain the global evolution of the optical fibre industry. In the USA, AT&T and Corning dominate the industry. In Japan, the market is shared largely by Sumitomo Electric, Fujikura, and Furukawa. In Europe, major players include Siecor (a joint venture between Siemens and Corning), STC, BICC (which also has a link with Corning), and Pirelli. The explanation of the global evolution of the optical fibre industry must

---

* The enthusiastic reader may want to begin by reading Appendix 2, which provides a detailed account of the circumstances leading to Corning's 1970 breakthrough.

in the first instance explain why it was Corning that made the key breakthrough in 1970, when it announced the development of an optical fibre that for the first time broke the 20 decibels per kilometre loss rate barrier. This loss rate enabled optical fibre to compete with other alternative transmissions technologies, such as copper cables and microwave radio including satellite communications. One key factor, of course, was that Corning possessed competences in the field of glass. But so did other glass companies—such as the UK's Pilkington Glass and Japan's Nippon Sheet Glass—which had also entered the research race in optical fibre for communications. Why it was Corning is answered in Appendix 2 through a detailed analysis of the innovation process in Corning that led to the crucial breakthrough.

The evolution of this industry must also contain an explanation of the successful entry of the other present-day incumbents in the industry. Apart from Corning, they are all companies with histories in telecommunications and telecommunications equipment—specifically copper cables—that significantly predate the optical fibre era. How did they manage to develop the competences that allowed them to enter and remain in this new industry with its new technologies? Why in some cases was entry through joint ventures? As noted above, particular attention is paid to the mode of entry of the Japanese companies.

A central issue in the evolution of the optical fibre industry relates to the role played by competition. The present chapter reveals that there were three very different forms of competition that were important: competition between the different companies; competition between 'technological regimes', i.e. optical fibre, copper cable, microwave radio, and satellite; and competition between 'product and process design configurations', specifically the IVD, OVD, and VAD processes (which are explained in this chapter). How important were these different forms of competition and what were their effects on the evolution of the industry?

Additional questions arise from the real-time, that is *ex ante*, analysis that is provided here of the evolution of the industry. An important set of issues relates to the kind of conceptualization of the firm that is needed in order to explain the roles and interactions of the firms that comprised the optical fibre industry. Following the theory of the firm used in this book, a number of questions emerge.

The first set of questions relates to the *competences* that were necessary for success in this industry. Three kinds of competences were crucial. The first was *technological competences*, more specifically, the knowledge of how to produce optical fibres with sufficiently low loss rates to be useful in communications systems. A study of the accumulation of technological competences in Corning shows that there was an important element of path dependency involved, in so far as, in producing its path-breaking optical fibre, the company was able to draw to a significant extent on prior knowledge which it had acquired in making glasses in the pre-optical-fibre years. However, equally important were the path independencies, the break with the past as new elements of knowledge were acquired which had to be integrated with the old knowledge in order to achieve the desired result. A similar combination of path dependencies and independencies was important in the process that led Japanese companies to break the world record for optical fibre loss rates in 1976.

The detailed analysis in this chapter shows that the process of technological competence accumulation can be understood as a process of belief construction. For example, a key contributor to Corning's breakthrough was the belief that impurities (dopants) should be added to the glass in order to obtain the differential in refractive indices that were necessary. (The technical aspects of this issue are elaborated in Appendix 2.) This belief contradicted the common-sense belief, held by researchers in many of the other laboratories, that such impurities, while they may produce a differential in refractive indices, would be self-defeating since they would increase the scattering of light in the fibre and thus increase its loss rate. On the basis of this belief, the latter researchers followed a different search-path, attempting to reduce loss rates by developing even purer glasses, rather than 'contaminating' them with dopants. Another example is the belief that Corning's researchers adopted in attempting to deal with the problem of the bubbles that formed between the core and cladding of the fibre when they tried to fuse the glass rod and the glass tube (each of which had different refractive indices). The belief was that a method common in the semiconductor industry could be used. This involved adding the second layer by depositing it in vapour form on the glass rod. Corning had already had experience in using this method, known as vapour deposition, in connection with earlier glass products.

Accordingly, as discussed in Appendix 1, technology can be understood as belief—belief about how to achieve particular ends—and the accumulation of technological competence can be thought of as a process of belief construction and the testing of beliefs. Furthermore, also as discussed earlier, this conceptualization of the process of technical change has the additional merit of allowing a link to be made to another key area of a firm's activity, namely the construction of a *vision* of what the firm should be doing and the direction in which it should move. Like technical change, vision construction is also based on a process of belief formation.

For example, as shown in this chapter, in the latter 1960s Corning formed a vision of a future in which telecommunications transmissions systems would be based largely on optical fibre. A significant contributor to this vision was information provided by the UK Post Office regarding the potential demand for video phones. The transmission of video images, however, required greater bandwidth than could be provided by existing copper cables, and this is where optical fibre came in. However, when Corning, having succeeded in producing low-loss optical fibre, went back to the UK Post Office, it was told that it would take a long time before there would be sufficient demand for video phones. The visions of Corning and the UK Post Office, evidently, had diverged significantly. In the event, it took seventeen years from the time Corning started research on optical fibre to when it started making a profit from this product! Clearly, there is a close similarity between the processes of technical change and vision formation, both of which involve the process of belief creation. The conceptualization of technology-as-belief and vision-as-belief provides the basis for a unified theory of the firm, whereby the same concept of knowledge is used to analyse both the interior and the exterior (environment) of the firm.

A second kind of competence was also crucial in the transformation of optical fibre knowledge into value. This consisted of *complementary competences* such as those needed to embody optical fibre into cables that could be used terrestrially and in submarine situations. These competences included splicing, connecting, coating, cabling, and repeater (used to boost signals over long distances) capabilities. It was Corning's lack of these competences that provided part of the company's motivation for joint ventures with copper cabling companies. However, a third kind of competence was also important. This was *competences relating to market access.* Here too Corning was weak, since it was a glass company without connection to the main telecommunications carriers. This provided a further motivation for joint ventures. This categorization of competences serves to underscore the point made throughout this book, that competences refer to activities and knowledge embodying the *entire* value chain.

The Basics of Optical Fibre Technology

An optical fibre serves essentially to guide a wave of light. As shown in Fig. 5.1, it is composed of two parts: a core and a cladding. The core has a higher refractive index than the cladding. As a result of this difference in refractive index, light remains in the core since there is total reflection at the boundary between the core and the cladding.

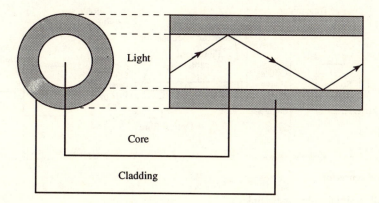

Fig. 5.1 The structure of optical fibre

The following features characterize the essence of optical fibre technology:

1. Protons (i.e. light waves) rather than electrons provide the basis of the communications signal.
2. The signal is transmitted through glass, rather than through the air or other material.
3. With the use of dopants such as germanium, impurities are added to highly pure glass in order to alter its refractive index and produce the core and cladding.
4. The manufacturing process involves essentially three different stages (although it is possible for these to be combined): (i) the use of vapour deposition to produce doped fused silica; (ii) drying and sintering; (iii) fibre drawing. Some of the different techniques for manufacturing optical fibre are analysed later.

In order to build an effective optical-fibre-based transmissions system, a number of complementary technologies are essential. These include a light source to send the light signal (usually a semiconductor laser or light-emitting diode (LED)), a light detector to receive the signal (usually PIN or avalanche photodiodes), coating to protect the fibre, cabling to combine and protect numerous fibres, splicers and connectors to join fibres, and repeaters to boost the signal over long distances (such as in the case of submarine cables).

A simple optical fibre link is shown in Fig. 5.2. Optical fibre has a number of important advantages over alternative transmissions media such as copper cable, microwave radio, and satellites, including the following:

1. *Broad bandwidth.* Optical fibre offers more potential bandwidth than any of the other alternative transmissions media, allowing a typical single cable to carry voice, data, text, and video while leaving extra capacity for later expansion of traffic.
2. *Immunity from interference.* Optical fibre is immune from electromagnetic

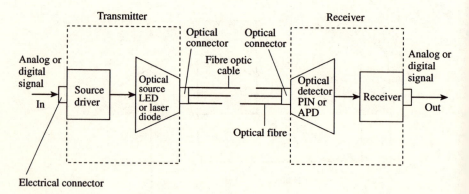

Fig. 5.2 A simple fibre optic link
Source: Datapro Research, McGraw-Hill, New York, 1980.

or radio frequency interference, providing a significant advantage over all three of the alternative media. This means that optical fibre can be run together with electric cables or in high-noise environments, such as alongside or above railway tracks or highways. Optical fibre is also suited for use within and between systems that use electricity and electronic components such as computing systems. As a result of this immunity, optical fibre provides extremely reliable signal transfer, measured by very low bit error rates.

3. *High security.* Since optical fibre emits no radiation, and since any signal loss can be detected almost immediately, this medium is virtually un-tappable. Any break in the fibre can be accurately pinpointed to within several centimetres. This has made optical fibre particularly well suited to applications requiring high security, such as in military and some business communications.

4. *Small size and low weight.* Optical fibres are thin and weigh very little. One kilometre of optical fibre weighs 13.6 kilograms, compared with 90 kilograms for traditional copper cable. Its small size means that optical fibres can be installed in places where space limitations preclude copper cables.

These advantages mean that optical fibre has for many applications become strongly competitive with the other transmissions media, particularly copper cable, but also microwave radio and satellite transmission. In some fields of application, however, such as areas where the laying of cables is costly or even impossible or where natural hazards such as earthquakes are a threat, microwave and satellite transmission may be preferred or used together with optical fibre. In other cases, such as where extremely long distances are required or where point-to-multipoint communication is necessary, satellites may be the preferred medium.

The Diffusion of Optical Fibre Knowledge to Japan

Japanese Knowledge in Optical Fibre before 1970

Research in the optical field has a long history in Japan. Before the Second World War a significant proportion of this research was undertaken in government laboratories, such as the communications laboratories under the control of the Ministry of Communications (see Chapter 3). For example, research in these laboratories on the use of quartz glass as an optical communications medium led to the filing of a patent application in November 1936 by Masao Seki (later Seimiya) and Hiroshi Negishi. This patent was granted in Japan in June 1938 as Patent No. 125,946, titled 'Improvement of Optical Communication Method'.

It was in the late 1950s and early 1960s, however, that Japanese research in the area of optics began to take off. This early research included work on the theory of the transmission of electromagnetic waves through dielectric materials (including, but not limited to, glass), such as the work of Tsuneo Nakahara of Sumitomo Electric.[1] In 1965 two academics from Tohoku University, S. Kawakami and J. Nishizawa, proposed that a graded index optical fibre (where there is a gradual change in refractive index within the fibre) might be used for high-speed optical transmissions.[2] This idea was taken up by two Japanese companies, Nippon Sheet Glass and NEC, both members of the Sumitomo group of companies, which succeeded in 1969 in making the world's first graded index optical fibres. These fibres were made using an ion-exchange process, rather than doping, to develop the refractive index gradient, and they were marketed under the brandname SELFOC (SELf-FOCusing glass fibre). However, they had an attenuation rate that was too high for long-distance optical transmissions, although they found use for optical communications terminal equipment, medical equipment, and short-haul laser optical transmission.[3]

By the late 1960s Japanese companies had also begun to turn their attention to the complementary technologies that would be required for the effective application of optical fibre transmissions systems. Here a major difficulty was presented by the fragility of optical fibre which limited its use. In order to deal with this problem, experimental work was done with thermoplastic resins such as nylon which were coated directly on to the SELFOC fibres. The incremental improvements that such work resulted in greatly aided the applicability of optical fibre technology.

In the latter 1960s NTT, like many Western companies, concentrated a good deal of attention on the development of millimetre waveguide technology. This involved sending electromagnetic signals through a tube which, like cable, could be placed underground. However, as in the West, research on millimetre waveguides was rapidly overtaken after 1970 by optical waveguides.

In the years following Maiman's development of the first laser, Japanese researchers became active in this field too. In 1968 researchers at NTT's Electrical Communications Laboratories proposed a long-term research project on laser optical transmission. This was accepted, and in 1969–70 NTT's Basic Research Laboratory at Musashino did a field trial in central Tokyo using a helium neon laser to send a communications signal through the atmosphere. However, as Alexander Graham Bell had discovered with his photophone, the air does not make for a very satisfactory transmissions medium, and rain, fog, and other kinds of interference limited the success of this Tokyo project. Nevertheless, Japanese researchers made more progress in other optical areas. For example, in 1970 Izuo Hayashi and M. B. Panish at Bell Laboratories

[1] T. Nakahara, 'Thin Dielectric-Membrane Surface Waveguide', mimeo, 1960; T. Nakahara *et al.*, 'Millimeter Waveguides with Applications to Railroad Communications', in L. Young (ed.), *Advances in Microwave Technology*, Academic Press, New York, 1969.

[2] S. Kawakami and J. Nishizawa, 'Propagation Loss in a Distributed Beam Waveguide', *Proceedings of the IEEE*, December, 2148–9.

[3] K. Kobayashi, *Computers and Communications: A Vision of C & C*, MIT Press, Cambridge, Mass., 30.

achieved continuous oscillation of double heterojunction semiconductor lasers at room temperature. Hayashi later joined the NEC Central Research Laboratories where related work on semiconductor lasers was being done by Yasuo Nannichi.[4]

On the basis of these prominent examples of Japanese optical research, it is clear that there were strong capabilities in the optical area in Japan that would facilitate a rapid assimilation of any breakthroughs made internationally. Indeed, as we shall see, this is precisely what happened after 1970 with Corning's breakthrough, resulting in a rapid diffusion of optical fibre knowledge to Japan fairly shortly thereafter.

Japanese Response to the Optical Fibre Breakthroughs of the Early 1970s

In 1970 there was only one research group in NTT working on optical fibre. This was a group under Mr Hirano (who later joined Aoyama Gakuin University), who was also responsible for strategy reports on the future of optical technologies in telecommunications. The group also included Dr Nobukazu Niizeki, who had worked on the helium neon laser transmissions project in Tokyo and in the group was doing research on single glass crystals. On hearing the news presented at the 1970 Conference on Trunk Telecommunications by Guided Waves that Corning's researchers had broken the 20 dB/km barrier, Niizeki later recalled, 'I was astonished!'.[5]

NTT rapidly formulated its response to this crucial breakthrough that was fundamentally to alter the future of optical communications. The first problem that its researchers faced, however, in common with other competing researchers around the world, was that Corning's 1970 announcement concentrated on the result of their research—namely the development of a fibre with an attenuation rate below the critical 20 dB/km level—without disclosing the product and process characteristics that facilitated this result. For competitive reasons, Corning's concealment was natural enough—the application for what was to become Corning's '915 patent was made on 11 May 1970, its conference announcement was made in October 1970, and the patent was finally issued on 2 May 1972. Competing researchers, however, were left in the dark until the issuing of the patent provided them with the detailed information that would aid their own research and innovation efforts.

Given this knowledge gap, NTT researchers at first continued along the same 'search path' that they, along with their colleagues in the international research community, had been following before 1970. Accordingly, in line with the teachings of Kao and Hockham,[6] and with the research being done in other venues such as the UK Post Office group, NTT researchers continued with the

---

[4] Ibid.   [5] This and the following quotations, unless otherwise indicated, are taken from the author's interviews with key people involved in the research and development of optical fibre.

[6] C. Kao and G. A. Hockham, 'Dielectric-Fiber Surface Waveguides for Optical Frequencies', *Proceedings of the IEEE*, 113: 1151–8.

attempt to purify various compound glasses which were then processed using the double crucible method. The advantage of this line of research was that the glass materials involved were relatively well understood; the disadvantage was that attenuation rates remained high relative to those achieved by Corning.

With the issuing of Corning's '915 patent on 2 May 1972, important new information became available to researchers around the world, including those working in NTT's Basic Research Laboratory in Musashino, Tokyo. In order to assimilate and begin to use this information, a second research group was established in the laboratory to work in parallel with the first group, which continued its research on compound glass materials and purification. Although also under Mr Hirano's direction, research in the second area was largely the responsibility of Dr Izawa, an electrical engineer who had graduated from the University of Tokyo. According to one of the senior researchers closely involved in this research at the time, 'Izawa obtained knowledge regarding the method [for producing the fibre] from Corning's patent. However, he wanted to devise a new method that was different in a patent sense from Corning's.' But Izawa had less choice when it came to the materials that were to be used (both the glass itself, fused silica, as well as the dopants), since these had proven to be the winning formula in terms of attenuation rate. Therefore, 'As far as the materials were concerned, Izawa had to follow Corning's ideas.'

Around the end of 1972 Corning sent Charles Lucy, an MIT electrical engineering graduate who had joined the company in 1952, to Japan to see whether a technical and marketing agreement could be established. As a senior Corning official who was closely involved at the time recalled, 'We decided that the telecommunications markets were national and monopolised, closed with few suppliers—in the US too. So we spoke to people in the industry and the PTTs (i.e. the telecoms carriers.)'

In Japan Corning offered the same standard agreement that it offered in other countries (which later led to agreements such as those with Siemens in Germany and BICC in Britain). In Corning these were referred to as 'joint development agreements'. Corning's motivation for these agreements arose from the fact that 'complementary knowledge and market access were both missing'. Under the agreement, the job of Corning's partner was to 'figure out how to make cable effectively with the fiber, feedback this information [to Corning], and carry the message [regarding the efficiency of optical fibre] to the PTT'. In return, the partner would be licensed to use Corning's optical fibre technology, including both its product patents and its manufacturing processes. The partner, however, would be required to pay royalties to Corning and also was restricted from exporting optical fibre and optical fibre cable to any other country where Corning, either directly or indirectly through other agreements, had interests.

In Japan Lucy went directly to NTT to propose an agreement. This effectively left NTT with two choices. On the one hand, it could, as it had done in the past, establish a joint R&D agreement with its three major cabling suppliers, Fujikura, Furukawa, and Sumitomo Ecletric, in the area of optical fibre. On the other hand, it could agree to, or even urge, its suppliers to establish agreements with Corning. Some compromise between these two positions was a further possibility.

In examining NTT's options, a number of background factors need to be analysed. First, it must be recalled that NTT had earlier embarked on research in the area of optical fibre in its Basic Research Laboratory, with the result that it already possessed significant capabilities which could facilitate a process of rapid assimilation and further development of the required technologies. Furthermore, as seen earlier, the Japanese cabling companies as well as others such as Nippon Sheet Glass and NEC had also accumulated relevant knowledge in this field. This effectively reduced the entry costs of the 'self-reliance' option. As a senior NTT research manager, closely involved in the decision-making at the time, put it, 'We believed then that in one or two years we could develop similar fibre in Japan. Perhaps the cost would not be so high.'

Secondly, it was also relevant that in making their choice NTT and the cabling companies had in mind their past experience when they had come to depend on foreign companies for the supply of copper coaxial cable. In order to reduce this dependence to some extent through dual sourcing, the Japanese had selected Western Electric of the USA and STC from the UK as their suppliers. This, however, presented problems. 'We had had bad experience earlier—paying very high prices to Western Electric and STC for co-axial cable. Sumitomo Electric got co-axial cable from STC; Furukawa from Western Electric. So in Japan there were two kinds of co-axial cable—S-type from STC and W-type from Western Electric. We had to pay a very high price for these licences.' This experience gave further weight to the 'self-reliance' option.

Thirdly, NTT was concerned with Corning's restrictions on the ability to export: 'Corning's insistence on preventing exports was a serious problem.' Without the ability to export optical fibre and cable, the Japanese cabling companies, having to share the Japanese market (which at that time was still of uncertain size, given the uncertainties that remained regarding the competitiveness of optical fibre), might have had to forgo important economies of scale and possibly scope, resulting in higher costs and prices. Furthermore, the possibility of 'learning-by-exporting' would also be forgone.

In the event, NTT decided to opt for a Japanese co-operative development of optical fibre and cable, while at the same time establishing some ties with Corning. Before elaborating on this decision, it is worth noting the similarity of NTT's choice and that of some other companies such as AT&T and STC. Like NTT, both AT&T and STC had also developed considerable capabilities in the optical fibre area. Indeed, AT&T had informed Corning, soon after it had been approached by the latter regarding the purchase of optical fibre, that it (AT&T) intended to develop its own technology in this field.[7] AT&T's endeavours in this area were assisted by the cross-licensing agreement that it had signed with

---

[7] I. Magaziner and M. Patinkin, *The Silent War*, Random House, New York, 1989, 275.

Corning which gave it some immunity to Corning's patents. Similarly, STC, on the basis of the research that Kao, Hockham, and others had begun in the 1960s, never purchased optical fibre technology from Corning, insisting on developing its own proprietary technology.[8]

In the autumn of 1973, NTT concluded a co-operative R&D agreement with Fujikura, Furukawa, and Sumitomo Electric.[9] The agreement was based on the understanding that the three companies would contribute resources to the joint research and development of optical fibre and cable, in return for which they would all get a share of the purchases that NTT eventually made. At the same time, NTT decided that Furukawa should be the company that would establish a formal agreement with Corning. According to a senior Corning official who was closely involved in the negotiation, Furukawa was offered one of Corning's joint development agreements.

Attached to the agreement was a form of licensing agreement which we promised we would enter into in the future. That is, [Furukawa] had an option, but the final form of the licence was negotiable. . . . The licensing agreement promised covered both patents and manufacturing know-how plus a stream of royalties to Corning. . . . In all the countries [we were dealing with] we had the same agreement. In Germany [for example], rather than a licence there was a joint venture company established [with Siemens] which itself was licensed.

However, NTT, in the light of the background considerations mentioned above, was anxious to ensure that any agreement between Corning and Furukawa would not unduly limit its own ability to develop, as far as possible, optical fibre capabilities, thus minimizing its dependence on foreign suppliers. NTT therefore wanted Furukawa to work with Corning in joint development while at the same time continuing to co-operate with NTT, Fujikura, and Sumitomo Electric in their joint effort in the development of optical fibre technology. Furthermore, NTT wanted Corning to give Furukawa the right to sub-license Corning's technology ro Fujikura and Sumitomo Electric. In the words of the Corning official, 'NTT exercised guidance over Furukawa and required some changes in the contract before any agreement was concluded. The significance was to permit Furukawa to work with the NTT laboratory [and the other two Japanese cablers] and to contemplate the possibility of sub-licensing.' In other words, 'NTT caused the relationship with Furukawa to take a form which suited them, to allow their NTT laboratory to work with Furukawa. NTT looked to *eventual* licensing to Furukawa and through sublicensing to the other [two companies]' (emphasis added).

---

[8] Based on an interview with a senior STC manager, 1989.

[9] Nippon Sheet Glass, which had made the important breakthrough in 1969 in graded-index fibre, was not invited to join the joint research group. One important reason was that the company was not a member of NTT's 'family' of suppliers. Furthermore, after its breakthrough Nippon Sheet Glass's optical fibre, relying on a different technology, failed to keep up with improving international best-practice. Another reason was that the company's process required a poisonous chemical, thalium chloride, which NTT did not want to use.

In this way, NTT wanted to ensure that Furukawa and the other two Japanese cable manufacturers retained the option of gaining access to Corning's knowledge in the future if they wished to. However, again according to the Corning official, 'NTT made it clear to Furukawa that they expected their own technology to be used in Japan, developed in their laboratories.' Although NTT was willing to see the three Japanese companies licensing Corning's fundamental patents, it wanted them 'to use the know-how [i.e. the manufacturing technology] that it (NTT) had developed with the Japanese companies. In other words, the manufacturing value added should be "Japanese", but NTT was willing to have Furukawa take out Corning's patents and sub-license them to Sumitomo Electric and Fujikura.'

This view of the matter was corroborated by a senior Furukawa official interviewed, who acknowledged that NTT wanted to secure the agreement with Corning as a 'safety net' which would provide cover in the event of its joint development with the three Japanese cabling companies failing: 'NTT wanted us (Furukawa) to have a link with Corning and therefore possible access to Corning's manufacturing technology if our own attempts at developing the manufacturing technology failed.' It is significant to stress, however, that NTT had no objection in principle to the licensing of Corning's patents, although, like AT&T and STC, its strong preference was to develop jointly its own optical fibre technology. NTT did not mind Japanese companies licensing Corning's fundamental patents, although it had a strong preference for the manufacturing technology, if possible, to be 'home grown'. This would limit NTT's dependence on foreign suppliers, thereby widening its options and ensuring that it would not be held hostage and subjected to high input prices. Or, as a senior manager from one of the three cabling companies put it, 'The three companies had a sense of duty to develop optical fibre capabilities in Japan.'

In the event, however, for reasons that will be more closely analysed later, the Japanese Patent Office refused to allow Corning's optical fibre patent applications. Nevertheless, Corning, having earlier entered into its joint development agreement with Furukawa, also concluded a licensing agreement with this company in 1977. Furthermore, Furukawa sub-licensed to Fujikura and Sumitomo Electric. However, partly because of the Japanese Patent Office's refusal and partly because of the capabilities that NTT and the three companies had established, Corning did not earn the royalties that it had hoped in Japan. As the Corning official recounted,

There was a licensing agreement with Furukawa in 1977. We asked Furukawa if they would be interested in a joint venture (like BICC [in Britain]). They did not ever indicate if they might have been interested. They said that it was NTT's policy not to buy from a foreign affiliated supplier. 'Foreign' referred to [a foreign company holding] 20 per cent or more equity, so a joint venture could not be discussed. . . . Furukawa sublicensed to Sumitomo Electric and Fujikura—so royalties were paid by all three [cabling] companies, but not as much as we had expected.

NTT, therefore, was strategically placed. It had itself accumulated fairly strong research capabilities in the area of optical fibre, thus creating the option, which it intended to exercise, of attempting jointly with the Japanese cabling companies to develop further capabilities in both the product and the process technologies. If it succeeded, dependence on foreign suppliers would be minimized and the Japanese cabling companies, with whom NTT enjoyed a mutually dependent relationship, accordingly strengthened. If it failed, there remained the alternative option of deepening the relationship with Corning, which would have left NTT little worse off than if it had linked closely with Corning in the first place. (The former 'self-reliance' option, it is worth noting, became available only as a result of NTT's direct and active involvement in the R&D process. Had NTT taken a more passive role, leaving it to the cabling companies to determine their level of involvement in this new and as yet uncertain technology, it is unlikely that this option would have been possible. In this connection it should be recalled that it was only in 1983 that Corning itself began to make a profit on its optical fibre activities.)

As things turned out, however, NTT's self-reliance option was soon to receive a substantial boost from a rather unexpected source—AT&T.

Enter AT&T

By mid-1974, NTT's two research groups working in the Basic Research Laboratories in Ibaraki had made some progress, although their performance, measured by attenuation rates, remained significantly behind the improving performance of Corning. The first group working on materials continued to purify compound glasses using the double crucible method to produce the fibre, while the second group carried on with its attempt to 'innovate around' Corning's manufacturing process.

In July 1974, however, an event took place that was to have a substantial impact on the Japanese R&D process in optical fibre. This began with an important paper given by MacChesney and his colleagues from Bell Laboratories at the Tenth International Congress on Glass organized by the Ceramic Society of Japan in Kyoto on 12 July 1974, entitled 'Preparation of Low Loss Optical Fibers Using Simultaneous Vapor Phase Deposition and Fusion'.[10]

However, before examining the significant impact of MacChesney and his colleagues on the international diffusion of optical fibre knowledge to Japan, it is necessary to analyse further the role of Bell Laboratories in optical fibre research at this time and its relationship with Corning. Although the critical 20 dB/km barrier was breached by Corning's researchers rather than by those of Bell Laboratories (for reasons that are closely analysed in Appendix 2), Bell Laboratories and AT&T generally had a close and obvious interest in optical

---

[10] J. B. MacChesney, P. B. O'Conner, E. V. Dimarcello, J. R. Simpson, and P. D. Lozay, 'Preparation for Low Loss Optical Fibers using Simultaneous Vapor Phase Deposition and Fusion', paper presented at the Tenth International Congress on Glass, no. 6, 'Optical Properties and Optical Waveguides', 12 July 1974, Kyoto.

communications which was heightened by the 'reverse salient' in transmissions referred to in Appendix 2.

For example, by January 1966, about five-and-a-half years after Theodore Maiman invented the first working optical laser, Bell Laboratories had allocated substantial resources to the adaptation of the laser for use in optical communications. Writing at this date, Mr Stewart Miller of Bell Laboratories noted that 'Today there are probably more physicists and engineers working on the problem of adapting the laser for use in communication than on any other single project in the field of laser applications.'[11] At the time Bell Laboratories employed about fifty engineers and physicists in laser research, while only six to ten were involved in transmissions media research.[12]

Before Corning's 1970 breakthrough, Bell Laboratories, in addition to some research in optical-fibre-related areas, also did research on other kinds of light-transmitting media. This research included work that followed up on an idea originated by William Wheeler of Concord, Massachusetts, in 1880. In that year Wheeler had applied for a patent on a way of distributing light around a building from a central source using pipes with inner reflective surfaces. Although Wheeler's proposals were not practically implemented (since the mirrored surfaces absorbed too much light), in the mid-1960s Bell researchers developed a gaseous lens system intended to guide light down a hollow tube filled with an inert gas. By heating the wall of the tube, a radial temperature gradient was created which in turn altered the refracted index of the gas, thus forming a converging lens. Bell also experimented with a system of hard lenses which were mounted inside a gas-tight pipe and were aligned by servo-mechanisms. Although the system worked under experimental conditions, this research was abandoned since it was too costly and difficult to maintain, and this 'search path' was soon eclipsed by that pioneered by Corning. NTT, following Bell Laboratory research as it often did, had also done work along similar lines.

While there was, therefore, an overlapping research interest in Corning and Bell Laboratories in the area of optical fibre communications, there was also a more formal arrangement between these two organizations in the form of a cross-licensing agreement. The rationale behind this agreement involved the exchange of knowledge in the areas of semiconductors and optical fibres. Corning had two consistent objectives which it attempted to realize through this agreement. First, it had taken the decision to diversify into the field of semiconductors (through a company, Signetics, which it later sold to Philips) and wanted to gain access to some of AT&T's knowledge in this area. Second, it wanted to generate further interest in AT&T in the area of optical fibre and it reasoned that, since this company had the monopoly in the area of telecommunications, it would in any event have to sell its fibre ultimately to AT&T. By exchanging its optical

---

[11] S. Miller, quoted in District Court, S.D., New York, *Corning Glass Works* v. *Sumitomo Electric USA Inc.*, Nos. 84 Civ. 9155 (WCC) and 85 Civ. 3156 (WCC), decided 13 October 1987, as amended 21 December 1987, 1548.   [12] Ibid.

fibre knowledge for AT&T's semiconductor knowledge, Corning thought it would be able to 'kill two birds with one stone'. As a senior executive from Corning put it, 'We looked at AT&T as a monopoly buyer. We had to interest them in the US. . . . We needed AT&T patents in the semiconductor area and we reasoned that we might as well license our optical fibre patents to AT&T in trade for [their] semiconductor [patents]. If AT&T never did anything [in the area of optical fibre], there would not be any business for us [in the US] anyhow.'

While Corning, therefore, had a close relationship with Bell Laboratories, so did the Japanese. The Japanese (in what was in 1952 to become NTT) had developed close links with AT&T immediately after the Second World War. This relationship included an agreement that NTT and the Japanese telecommunications companies would have access to AT&T's patents in return for royalties. In the 1970s this agreement was broadened to facilitate wider exchanges of knowledge between the organizations. This co-operative framework facilitated the diffusion of optical fibre knowledge to Japan.

This background provides an understanding of the important impact that MacChesney and his colleagues had in Japan during their visit in July 1974. The paper that they presented at the Tenth International Congress on Glass in Kyoto reported on the results that they had obtained in Bell Laboratories using the MCVD (modified chemical vapour deposition) process to produce low-loss optical fibres. While the MCVD process differed in some respects from Corning's IVD (inside vapour deposition) and OVD (outside vapour deposition) processes—in ways that will be clarified shortly—all of these drew to some extent on knowledge developed in the semiconductor industry in the area of vapour deposition and were similar in terms of the materials and the methods that were used to produce the fibre. Using the knowledge that Corning had contributed in breaching the 20 dB/km barrier (analysed in detail in Appendix 2), Bell Laboratories, protected from charges of patent infringement by the cross-licensing agreement with Corning, had gone on to develop their own version of the technology, namely the MCVD process, and had begun to accumulate associated patents.

After MacChesney and his associates presented their paper at the Kyoto conference, they were invited to visit NTT's laboratories. Both the paper presentation and the subsequent visit had a profound impact on the Japanese researchers who were working on optical fibre. Despite the knowledge that they had gleaned from the issuing of Corning's '915 patent in 1972 and related other publications, these researchers had continued their work on compound glasses and had not yet realized the significance of the MCVD (and the related IVD and OVD) process. As one NTT research manager, who at the time was a young member of NTT's research team, recalled, 'Researchers who were involved in cabling and the material side were shocked by the MCVD process.' Further details on the impact of the MacChesney visit were provided by Dr Nobukazu Niizeki, who became Director of the Components and Materials Research

Division in NTT's Ibaraki Laboratory and was closely involved in the optical fibre research:

[MacChesney] showed us the MCVD machine [they had used] in Bell Laboratories. We were astonished. He also discussed the manufacturing details—and experimental data—on how to manufacture low-loss fibre. It was a very frank discussion. Hearing his lecture, [NTT's] people decided to concentrate on pure silica fibre, throwing out the compound glass (which achieved a loss-rate of 6 dB/km at the lowest, in contrast to about 1 dB/km for silica fibre using the MCVD method). . . . We were astonished by the simple method and his results—1.0 dB/km at a wavelength of about 1 micron.

Commenting on the role played by Bell Laboratories in the international diffusion of optical fibre technology, a Corning executive rather ruefully explained that 'Bell Laboratories [also] worked on the optical fibre problem and then got some patents and published papers which gave guidance to the outside world on how to go about this area.' He acknowledged that some people in Corning had been 'angry' that Bell Laboratories had played a significant role in diffusing knowledge so widely regarding the MCVD process.

Development of the VAD Process

In February 1967, six months before he joined Corning, Peter Schultz tried to produce an optical waveguide fibre by depositing flame-hydrolysis-produced pure fused silica soot on the outside surface of a titania-doped fused silica core rod. In April 1968, however, he altered the process somewhat by coating the *inner* surface of a pure fused silica tube with a titania-doped fused silica soot, also produced by flame hydrolysis. For several months Schultz's work continued along the latter lines, and in August 1968, the same month that he joined Corning, he produced the first fibre with an attenuation rate of 250 dB/km which was also the first fibre with a loss rate that was low enough for short-distance communications. In this way, the *outside vapour deposition (OVD)* and *inside vapour deposition (IVD)* methods were born. Although Corning used the IVD method for some years after Schultz's 1968 breakthrough, the company later improved the OVD method, which continued to characterize its principal production method.

The IVD and OVD methods are depicted in Fig. 5.3. It can be seen that, with the IVD process, chloride vapours of silicon and the dopants, such as germanium, phosphorus, and fluorine, which control the refractive index, are oxidized *inside* a glass tube and the resulting oxide 'soot' is deposited layer by layer. The heat source for this oxidation process is a gas burner outside the tube (though radio frequency plasmas inside the tube can also be used simultaneously). Once the preform has been prepared in this way, it is heated to a taffy-like consistency, and a continuous filament of glass fibre is pulled from it. Companies that have used the IVD method include Corning, Bell Laboratories, Western Electric, ITT, Philips, and Thomson-CSF.

The OVD method uses the same materials and the same essential processes.

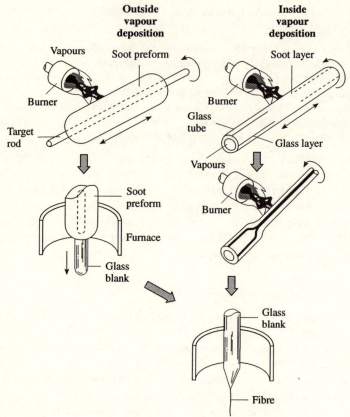

Fig. 5.3 Outside vapour deposition and inside vapour deposition
Source: IEEE Spectrum (1983): 36.

The main difference, as can be seen in Fig. 5.3, is that the soot preform is deposited on the *outside* of a rotating and traversing target rod or mandrel which is horizontal to the ground. The OVD method is used mainly by Corning.

The origins of the Axial Vapour Deposition method (VAD) developed by the Japanese lie in the work of the second research group which, as mentioned, was established originally in the Basic Research Laboratory of NTT at Musashino. With the publication of Corning's '915 patent in 1972, Dr Izawa, working in the Musashino laboratory, began to think of how a 'Japanese' manufacturing process might be developed for the production of low-loss optical fibre which would not infringe preexisting patents. As noted above, until the visit of Bell's MacChesney and his colleagues, the Basic Research Laboratory worked primarily on compound glasses rather than pure fused silica, which they attempted to purify.

In 1976 Dr Izawa was sent to Stanford University for a year. There he studied optical detectors, an area unrelated to his previous work on optical fibre process technology. On his return to Japan, he joined the Components and Materials

Research Division in NTT's Ibaraki Laboratory, which since 1976 had been under the Directorship of Dr Nobukazu Niizeki. Prime responsibility for the development of process technology for optical fibre was transferred from the Basic Research Laboratory in Musashino to the Components and Materials Research Division in Ibaraki from 1976. Dr Izawa headed a group of researchers here which by the end of 1976 numbered approximately thirty. All of these researchers were employed by NTT, none from the three Japanese cabling companies.

According to a senior research manager who was closely involved at the time in this optical fibre project, there were two main objectives: 'to make [NTT's] method different in a patent sense from Corning's, and to produce a longer preform than existing methods could produce [thereby facilitating a longer length fibre]'. In 1977 the first public announcement was made regarding the VAD method. This was at the Integrated Optics and Optical Communications Conference held in Tokyo.

The VAD method is portrayed in Fig. 5.4. This method uses the same materials as the IVD and OVD methods (fused silica, dopants such as germanium and fluorine) and the same basic process (flame hydrolysis). The main difference, as can be seen from comparing Fig. 5.4 with Fig. 5.3, is that the soot is deposited on the bottom (or axis—hence *axial* vapour deposition) of the preform which is rotated and moved upwards. Unlike with the OVD method, no target rod or mandrel is required.

As stated earlier, the VAD method was developed in the Musashino and, later, Ibaraki laboratories by NTT researchers working alone (i.e. without researchers from the three cabling companies). Unbeknown to NTT's researchers, however, researchers in Sumitomo Electric had independently, and without the knowledge of the other cabling companies, been working on a very similar approach. This resulted in a Japanese patent application on 18 December 1974, approximately three years before NTT's VAD process was made public. Patent application was made in the USA on 13 June 1977 and the patent was finally issued on 23 January 1979 as Patent No. 4,135,901 under the title 'Method of Manufacturing Glass for Optical Fibre' with Sumitomo Electric as the patent's assignee. Both the Sumitomo Electric and NTT processes operate in the axial direction. The main difference between them is that in the Sumitomo Electric case the burners are positioned at the top of the preform, which is moved downwards, while in the VAD process the burners are placed at the bottom. Later in Japan a patent was granted for axial vapour deposition under the co-ownership of NTT and Sumitomo Electric, Fujikura, and Furukawa.

It is probably best to understand axial vapour deposition as part of a process of incremental or experimental technical change (which may, nevertheless, have important consequences). Indeed, according to a senior official from Corning, the company had also experimented with a similar method which, however, had been rejected in favour of the horizontal OVD method. 'Unfortunately, we did not think to apply for patents on this.'

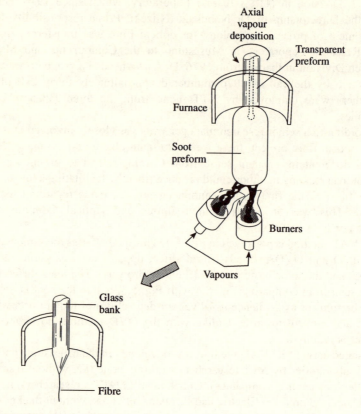

Fig. 5.4 Axial vapour deposition
Source: IEEE Spectrum (1983): 36.

Competitive Advantages

There are a number of advantages that follow from the positioning of the burners at the bottom of the preform as in the VAD method. The main advantages are that in principle longer preforms can be produced (since the preform is positioned vertically rather than horizontally) and the production process can be made continuous, with vapour deposition, drying and sintering, and fibre drawing following sequentially as part of the same process. Longer fibres mean that longer distances without connectors are possible. One of the Japanese cabling companies claimed that the 'VAD method is superior to the other fibre manufacturing methods in terms of high deposition rate [and] high conversion efficiency of starting materials. Also, the VAD method is the only method which makes possible the continuous formation of the glass preform. Therefore, the VAD method leads to low-cost fibres.'[13]

[13] Personal correspondence with the author.

Several points may be made in evaluating the competitiveness of the IVD, OVD, and VAD methods. The most important point is that the net relative benefits provided by these methods are too small to enable any one of them to eliminate competition from the other methods. As a result, all three of them co-exist and, unless any further process breakthroughs occur, will continue to co-exist. A further point is that there is some indirect evidence of the competitiveness of the VAD process. This comes from the decision of AT&T to purchase a majority stake in a US-based company owned jointly with Sumitomo Electric, Litespec, which produces optical fibre cable, the fibre being produced by the VAD method. Clearly, AT&T would not have entered into this venture if it had had doubts about the competitiveness of the VAD process.

Japanese World Records in Optical Fibre, 1976 and 1979

In 1976 and 1979 Japanese researchers broke world optical fibre records, establishing fibres with the lowest attenuation rates and demonstrating at the same time that their mastering of optical fibre technology had placed them on the frontiers of the technology. The story of the 1976 record is of interest, not so much as a result of any major breakthrough in knowledge, but rather because it provides an example of the integration of fragmented knowledge that was facilitated by Japanese co-operation between different organizations.

One of the main researchers in Fujikura was a chemist by the name of Osanai. In Japan at the time most optical fibre researchers had specialized in the area of either ceramics or glass. As a chemist, however, Osanai wanted to isolate the main causes of transmission loss in glass. His research led him to the conclusion that the level of water in the fibre in the form of hydroxyl (OH) ions was a major source of transmission loss.

Osanai's findings had also been made in Corning, where it was discovered that the flame hydrolysis method leads to the presence of unacceptably high OH levels. 'Several procedures had been tried at Corning for removing OH ions from optical fibre preforms, but these were not effective.' One procedure was to 'consolidate the soot preform in a gradient furnace containing a dry, inert atmosphere. This approach produced some drying but still left unacceptable levels of residual water.' An alternative approach was to 'consolidate the preform in a vacuum. This approach was more effective than a dry-atmosphere consolidation process, but was not economical.' In late 1972 or early 1973, Dr Robert D. De Luca, a researcher at Corning, tried another approach. This involved the 'dehydration of soot preforms by consolidating them in a chlorine-containing atmosphere. . . . This produced what was deemed a "startling" result. His initial attempt, in January 1973, yielded a water level which was about 2 per cent of the lowest attained previously.' De Luca's research resulted in a patent application filed on 22 April 1974 and issued on 20 January 1976 as Patent No. 3,933,454.[14]

---

[14] *Corning* v. *Sumitomo Electric*, 1564.

Osanai's experiments in Fujikura proved successful, and in 1976 he brought both his results and some of the optical fibre that he had produced to NTT's Ibaraki Laboratory. This showed the achievement of a 1 dB/km attenuation rate at a wavelength of 1.0 micrometres. It was at this stage that two complementary strands of knowledge, which had been evolving in Fujikura and in NTT's Basic Research Laboratory in Musashino, began to merge. At the Basic Research Laboratory, Dr Mizushima, a physicist, had been working on the effect of wavelength on attenuation rate. He predicted that the attenuation rate was a function not only of impurities, but also of wavelength. The OH level, he argued, absorbed light at certain wavelengths, thereby increasing the attenuation. Accordingly, Mizushima predicted, by varying both the OH level and the wavelength, lower losses could be achieved. Fujikura lacked the equipment to vary the wavelength of the light signal but this was done at Ibaraki, where researchers, alerted by Mizushima's theoretical predictions, tested the optical fibre that had been produced at Fujikura's laboratory. This research led to the announcement in 1976 by NTT and Fujikura that they had achieved a world record of 0.5 dB/km at a wavelength of 1.3 μm. In 1979 NTT achieved a further world record with a fibre recording 0.2 dB/km at 1.55 μm. After records such as these, it became known that 'windows' exist at 1.3 and 1.55 μm where loss rates are minimized. These 'windows', at wavelengths of around 1.3 and 1.55 μm, are shown in Fig. 5.5.

Subsequent Optical Fibre Developments in Japan

After AT&T began field trials of optical fibre systems in Atlanta and Chicago, NTT in October 1980 began a similar land-based trial. This involved a single-mode fibre (see below for an explanation of single versus multimode fibres), which ran for 76 kilometres from NTT's Musashino Laboratory, through Hachioji and Sagamihara in Western Tokyo, to the company's Atsugi Laboratory. This experiment was under the direction of Mr Yamaguchi, Chief Engineer of NTT, and Dr Oguchi, Director of NTT's Research Bureau (who later became an executive at Fujitsu). Up to this point NTT continued to back two technological horses: the MCVD process, which it originally received from MacChesney at Bell Laboratories, and the VAD process, developed at first in NTT's laboratories and independently in some of the companies. From around 1977, NTT established a co-operative R&D group together with Fujikura, Furukawa, and Sumitomo Electric to make further improvements to the VAD process. The understanding was that this research and development, financed partly by the three cabling companies, would be followed by significant purchases of optical fibre by NTT.

One of the objectives of the trial cable was to test the absolute and relative performance of optical fibre cable produced by the MCVD and VAD processes. At this stage the attenuation rate and strength of VAD-produced fibre were not

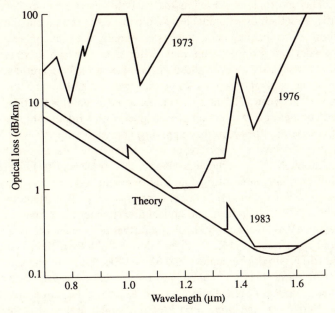

Fig. 5.5 Spectral loss data for silica fibres

Source: C. K. N. Patel, 'Lasers in Communications and Information Processing', in J. H. Ausubel and H. D. Langford (eds.), *Lasers: Invention to Application*, National Academy Press, Washington, DC, 1987.

yet up to the same standard as the MCVD method. In order to carry out the test, a small VAD section was installed. The results showed that the VAD-produced fibre was acceptable, although it did not yet perform as well as the MCVD fibre. In 1981–2 the three cabling manufacturers shifted their production process entirely to VAD, abandoning the MCVD method. The reason was that large quantities of cable were required for the new national trunk line that NTT had decided to install from Hokkaido in the north to Kyushu in the south. Economies of scale dictated that only one method be used. Furthermore, it was felt that the VAD method, with all the incremental improvements that by this stage had been made, was better for the production of long single-mode fibres than the MCVD method.

In 1978 Furukawa, which as was seen earlier had been involved in a joint optical fibre cabling agreement with Corning, decided to abandon Corning's technology. The main reason for this decision was (1) the royalty payments that would have had to be made to Corning in exchange for its technology and (2) the availability and efficiency of the VAD process. While NTT held most of the original patents on the VAD process, the VAD technology was actively transferred to Fujikura, Furukawa, and Sumitomo Electric. Engineers from these companies went to the Ibaraki Laboratory, where they studied the VAD equipment and process and were given further information by Ibaraki researchers. This information served as the basis for their own development of the VAD process in their own companies. While the VAD equipment and process developed in the three cabling companies is essentially the same, there are some significant design and process technology differences between the three firms. For competitive reasons, however, these differences are kept secret, and engineers in each of the companies do not know the precise details of the differences. The relationship between NTT and its suppliers has been characterized as one of controlled competition. The competitive aspect of this relationship, involving a degree of competition between the supplying companies for the NTT market, has served to generate some variety in the technologies developed by these companies. Although of an incremental nature, this process of technical change has been an important source of gradual improvement.

With the increase in demand for optical fibre in areas such as trunk lines, local area networks (LANs), computers, and optical measurement and control systems, NTT decided that VAD technology should be further diffused to the smaller NTT 'family' suppliers, Hitachi Cable, Dainichi-Nippon Cable (which has close links to the Mitsubishi group of companies), and Showa Electric Wire and Cable. NTT wanted to bring these three companies into the optical fibre age and wanted a larger number of optical fibre cable producers. Although the move was opposed by Fujikura, Furukawa, and Sumitomo Electric, which argued that they could extend their capacity to meet the required demand, NTT insisted on the additional diffusion of the VAD technology. However, the joint patents held by NTT and these latter three companies were not given to Hitachi Cable *et al.*, which were expected to develop their own technological capabilites in this field. Nevertheless, the basic VAD technology was transferred to these companies, with the NTT Technology Transfer Corporation (NTECH), established originally in 1976, playing an important role in the transfer.

Corning versus Sumitomo Electric

Having established its optical fibre production facilities in Japan, Sumitomo Electric, the largest of the Japanese cabling companies, was ready by the early 1980s to enter major export markets. The prime target was the North American market. Beginning in Canada, an agreement was concluded with Canada Wire and Cable which agreed to cable Sumitomo Electric's optical fibre. Although Canada Wire and Cable was a customer, Corning decided to enter into patent litigation in Canada. In early 1984 Corning won its case, and Sumitomo Electric was prevented from selling its fibre to Canada.

Sumitomo Electric next attempted to export optical fibre directly to the USA. Countering this move, Corning brought a case to the US International Trade Commission (ITC), charging that the dehydration and consolidation process which Sumitomo Electric used in Japan violated Corning's main optical fibre process patent (the '454 De Luca patent referred to earlier, which dealt with a method of making optical waveguides by flame hydrolysis). In 1985 ITC concluded that Corning's patent had been violated although it did not recommend the payment of damages as a result of Sumitomo Electric's very small market share. (Interestingly, the New York District Court judgment referred to below found, in contrast to the ITC, that Sumitomo Electric had not violated Corning's De Luca patent.)

Before the ITC delivered its judgment, Sumitomo Electric made the decision to start production in the USA in the North Carolina Research Triangle. Confronting the patent issue directly, the company's new American subsidiary, Sumitomo Electric Research Triangle Inc. (SERT), filed a complaint on 16 August 1984 arguing that Corning's '915 and '454 patents were invalid, unenforceable, and were not infringed by SERT. Production by SERT, however, was planned to begin after the ITC judgment in March 1985. On 19 December 1984 Corning counterclaimed that its '915, '550, and '454 patents had been willfully infringed by Sumitomo Electric. Judgment was eventually given by the New York District Court on 13 October 1987 (amended on 21 December 1987).

Essentially, Sumitomo Electric argued that the knowledge contained in these Corning patents existed in 'prior art'; that is, other sources were available before Corning's '915, '550, and '454 patents were filed (including other earlier Corning patents). This was the argument that the Japanese Patent Office had relied on in rejecting Corning's equivalent patent applications in Japan. The New York District Court accepted that much of the knowledge referred to in Corning's '915, '550, and '454 patents existed previously. For example, in its judgment the Court stated that 'At the time application for the '915 patent was filed, both germania and phosphorus pentoxide were known to be dopants which increased the refractive index of silica, and it was known how to produce fibers containing such dopants by sintering and drawing a soot deposited by flame hydrolysis.'[15] If knowledge so basic to the product and process inventions contained in Corning's '915, '550, and '454 patents was previously known, how could these patents be justified?

In reply, the New York District Court ruled that, although this crucial knowledge had existed before the patent application was filed, it was not 'obvious' from this knowledge how to produce an optical fibre that could be used effectively for communications. The Court accordingly concluded that:

A person of ordinary skill in the optical waveguide field in the late 1960s was a person having a degree in materials science, ceramics, physics or a similar field and familiar with the concepts of light transmission, material scattering and turbidity and the effect of composition on refractive index. He was also familiar with the phenomenon of glass transition and with devitrification, phase separation and cooling stresses in glasses.

The invention claimed in claims 1 and 2 of the '915 patent *was not obvious to such persons at the time* in view of any of the patents or publications relied on by Sumitomo, considered singly or in any combination.[16]

---

[15] Ibid. 1558.   [16] Ibid. 1556; emphasis added.

Similarly, the Court ruled that:

The validity of the Corning patents is confirmed by the presence and strength of all these objective criteria of non-obviousness. There was a widely-expressed desire for a glass fiber capable of long-distance telecommunications use to replace copper cables with their recognized disadvantages, and there was an intensive international effort to provide such a fiber. After years of unsuccessful search, when industry experts had all but despaired of reaching the goal, Corning had an unexpected 'breakthrough' which was immediately recognized as the long-sought solution and enthusiastically acclaimed. It literally created a new industry of substantial size.[17]

Therefore, as analysed in Appendix 2, although Corning's 'breakthrough' resulted more from the new combination of previously existing knowledge than from the creation of new knowledge, both the new combination of knowledge and the effect of this combination (the production of an optical waveguide with sufficiently low attenuation to permit communications) were not obvious to those possessing the general knowledge available in this field at this time.

Although Sumitomo Electric had made attempts to 'innovate around' Corning's patents, the Court ruled that these attempts were unsuccessful in avoiding the patents. These attempts included using germanium as a dopant in proportions different from those specified in the Corning patents, and substituting fluorine (added to the cladding to lower its refractive index) for germanium (which in Corning's patent was added to the *core* to *raise* its refractive index). The Court therefore ruled that, while one of the Sumitomo Electric's fibres did not literally infringe Corning's patent, it was nevertheless a 'functional equivalent' and for this reason infringement was held to have occurred. Although this fibre 'is not within the literal language of . . . [Corning's] . . . patent, it performs substantially the same function in substantially the same way to obtain the same result . . .'[18]

Ultimately, therefore, the Court found that Corning's two product patents, '915 and '550, were both valid and wilfully infringed by Sumitomo Electric. However, it found that Corning's '454 process patent was valid but not infringed. With regard to the latter patent, the Court concluded that 'there has been no literal infringement of claim 1 of the '454 patent. Nor has there been any infringement of claim 1 under the doctrine of equivalents. Both in the specification of the '454 patent and during the prosecution of the application therefor, the prior art was distinguished on the basis that it taught *separate* drying and consolidation steps, whereas the claimed invention involved simultaneously performing these steps.'[19] The implication, therefore, was that Sumitomo Electric avoided infringement by using a process involving separate drying and consolidation. Sumitomo Electric was ordered by the Court to stop the production of optical fibre at its North Carolina plant, and in a negotiated settlement it paid damages of $25 million to Corning.

This, however, was not the end of the story. After the judgment Sumitomo

---

[17] Ibid. 1569.   [18] Ibid. 1559.   [19] Ibid. 1570; emphasis added.

Electric divided its North Carolina plant into two separate companies. One, SEFOC (Sumitomo Electric Fibre Optics Company), producing optical fibre cable and related accesories such as splicing equipment, continued to be wholly owned by Sumitomo Electric. The other Litespec, producing optical fibre, was sold to AT&T, which acquired a 51 per cent share with Sumitomo Electric holding the remaining 49 per cent.

In an interview, a senior Sumitomo Electric executive claimed that the deal with AT&T was not motivated purely by the New York District Court's ruling. An important further consideration was the *strategic alliance* which was thereby established with AT&T. From Sumitomo Electric's point of view, this alliance not only provided the possibility of exchanges of technology, but also improved market access in the USA in view of AT&T's dominant market share.

From the point of view of our present concerns, the Sumitomo Electric–AT&T joint venture is of great significance since it represents a *de facto* vote of confidence in the VAD technology used by Sumitomo in Japan and in Litespec. Since intellectual property rights, as examined in this chapter, have prevented much head-on competition between the alternative MCVD, OVD, and VAD processes for manufacturing optical fibre, this joint venture is an important indication of the competitiveness of the VAD method as judged (implicitly) by AT&T. While some interaction between the MCVD and VAD processes is likely through the Litespec joint venture, the possibility of leakage of commercially sensitive know-how regarding VAD to AT&T is minimized by the sole control over process engineering which Sumitomo Electric has insisted on retaining. The company, however, like many others, retains its cross-licensing agreement with AT&T.

The Globalization of NTT'S 'Family'

After its part-privatization in 1985, NTT gradually began to widen the circle of its 'family' of suppliers to include both other Japanese and foreign companies. By the early 1990s, it had taken a number of important steps in this direction.

In early March 1991, NTT announced that under its Track III procedure it had selected four companies to develop a new optical fibre cable as part of its 'fibre-to-the-home' programme which is intended to replace copper cables with optical fibre in the subscriber loop, thus facilitating the delivery of broadband services to the home in the next century. While existing cables contained about 1,000 optical fibres, the aim of the joint development project was to produce a cable containing 4,000 fibres. Siecor, the joint venture between Corning and Siemens, and Sumitomo Electric were chosen to develop a high-density, small-diameter cable, while Furukawa and Fujikura were to develop connectors for low-loss, high-speed splicing. It was expected that the project would last five years.[20]

---

[20] *Wall Street Journal*, 3 March 1991.

In a related development, NTT shortly afterwards announced three joint projects to develop integrated fibre optic subscriber systems. The first, to develop a narrowband fibre optic subscriber transmission system, involved AT&T International, Fujitsu, and Hitachi. The second, developing a frequency division multiplexing fibre optic subscriber transmission system capable of carrying HDTV signals, included Fujikura, Fujitsu, Matsushita Electric, NEC, and Sumitomo Electric. The objective of the third was to develop a high-speed digital fibre optic subscriber transmission system operating at speeds up to several hundred megabits per second involving Hitachi and Mitsubishi Electric. These three projects were also under the Track III procedures.

An interview with a Corning executive revealed that the company, after its long conflicts in Japan, was satisfied to be included in NTT's R&D programme. It remained to be seen, however, what degree of sales and market share would ultimately emerge from Corning's involvement. Asked whether Corning was concerned that the process of joint development might carry the danger of significant leakages of knowledge to competing Japanese companies, the executive admitted that this issue 'has been exercising the minds of Corning's staff'.

Controlled Competition and the Diffusion of New Technologies

In this the concluding section, two issues have been selected for closer analysis.

The first is the form of organization—controlled competition—which in Japan has governed the assimilation, creation, and diffusion of new telecommunications technologies. As will be seen in detail, controlled competition enabled the three 'moments' of the evolution of technical change—invention, innovation, and diffusion—to be fused into one integrated process. Furthermore, by reducing the uncertain effects of technical change, controlled competition helped *all* of the Japanese cable manufacturers to make the difficult transition from copper to optical fibre technology. By so doing, the Japanese system was able to establish the most competitive market for optical fibre in the world, measured in terms of the number of suppliers of optical fibre cable.

The second area for analysis involves situating the evolution of optical fibre technology within the broader Schumpeterian process of creation–destruction which examines the effects of the creation and diffusion of new technologies in terms of their challenge to the old technologies. Of particular interest, emerging from this analysis, are the contradictory visions held by companies with varying interests in the new optical fibre technology and the different forms of competition that drove the process of creation–destruction.

Analysis 1: Controlled Competition in the Japanese Innovation System in Telecommunications: The Case of Optical Fibre

The present chapter has been largely concerned with the origins of optical fibre technology and with the diffusion of this technology to Japan and within Japan itself. The diffusion process, however, has been crucially shaped by the forms of organization that have evolved in Japan. The main aim of this section is to make more explicit the nature of these forms of organization through an analysis of the ways in which they have influenced the assimilation, creation, and internal diffusion of optical fibre technology in Japan.

Controlled Competition in Action

The way in which controlled competition works in the optical fibre field is shown schematically in Fig. 5.6. In order to see how this relates to reality in Japan, it is worth starting with an examination of Corning's invention, innovation, and diffusion of optical fibre. First, however, it is necessary to define more precisely what is meant by these three concepts and to examine some of the difficulties that arise in attempting to apply the definitions in the case of optical fibre.

As Freeman notes, 'An *invention* is an idea, a sketch or model for a new or improved device, product, process or system.'[21] As is implicitly clear from the account of the origin and development of optical fibre presented in this chapter and in Appendix 2, it is extremely difficult if not impossible to provide an unambiguous dating for the invention of optical fibre for communications. The reason is that optical fibre, even if defined narrowly as a glass fibre rather than broadly as a system for the transmission of communication signals, embodies not an idea, but rather an *interrelated system* of ideas. These include the idea of a medium which, as a result of differences in refractive index, serves to guide light; the idea of adding dopants to pure fused silica in order to produce the refractive index differential; the idea of developing the preform by adding the silica and dopants layer-by-layer by vapour deposition; the idea of producing the silica and dopant 'soot' by flame hydrolysis; etc. As is shown in Appendix 2, many of these ideas have a long history even before the late 1960s; some, indeed, go back to the nineteenth century. It was not the ideas in isolation, but rather their combination through experimentation and feedback, that resulted in the breaching of the 250 dB/km barrier in 1968 (which made short-distance optical fibre communications possible) and the 20 dB/km barrier in 1970 (which enabled optical fibre to compete with alternative transmission technologies). This poses problems with regard to the dating of the optical fibre invention. Should the date of the invention be taken to be 1968? If so, this would be a dating on the basis of the *consequence* of the ideas, namely the development of a practical short-distance communications medium, rather than on the basis of the *time of origin* of the ideas. However, if the latter basis were chosen for dating purposes, further

---

[21] C. Freeman, *The Economics of Industrial Innovation*, Pinter, London, 1982.

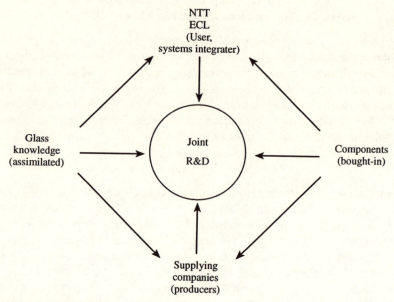

Fig. 5.6 Controlled competition in optical fibre

problems arise, since no single date is relevant but rather a number of dates. This follows since, as we have seen, optical fibre refers to an interrelated cluster of ideas. Furthermore, if dating is to be done on the basis of the consequence of ideas rather than the origin of the ideas themselves, then which is the correct date in terms of the significance of the consequences (for example, in the case of optical fibre, 1968 or 1970)? It is apparent that these problems are more complex than is often realized. Nor are the problems trivial, since the question of dating is often crucial in determining causal sequences.

Freeman defines innovation in the following way: 'An *innovation* in the economic sense is accomplished only with the first *commercial* transaction involving the new product, process, system or device, although the word is used also to describe the whole process.'[22] Once again, however, serious problems of interpretation and dating arise. When did Corning first 'commercialize' its optical fibre—when it first sold small quantities of fibre to telephone operating companies to be used on an experimental basis and tested, when it concluded joint development agreements and joint venture with cabling companies such as Siemens, BICC, and Furukawa, or when it first sold significant quantities of fibre to MCI and began, some seventeen years after the company started its research, to make a profit? If the latter, then the relevant criterion for innovation is not commercialization (selling) *per se*, but rather commercialization on a profitable basis.

<hr />

[22] Ibid. 7.

Nor is the definition and dating of Schumpeter's third 'moment' in the process of technical change—diffusion—any easier. In its broadest sense, diffusion refers to the 'spread' of the commercialized invention, a process that usually involves further invention ('children' of the initial invention). But in the case of optical fibre, does diffusion refer to the spread of the ideas (knowledge) 'underlying' the fibre, in which case the process of diffusion possibly began even *before* invention (depending on when invention is dated) as ideas spread through various channels to researchers in other laboratories? Or does diffusion refer to the spread of the optical fibre itself as it is adopted by users, in which case, following the usual sigmoid pattern, the diffusion process could be held to begin when fibre first began to be used (albeit for experimental purposes) followed by a more rapid rate of adoption as commercialized use began to occur? (A further problem arises, however, when diffusion is identified with adoption of the product for commercial use, since this, as we saw, was a key feature of the definition of innovation!)

However, if we stand back from the conceptual difficulties associated with invention, innovation, and diffusion, and refuse to become enmeshed in the complexities that undoubtedly exist with these concepts, a case can be made for their usefulness. In the context of Corning's experience with optical fibre, for example, it is illuminating (the difficulties notwithstanding) to suggest that invention occurred around 1968–70; that it was followed by innovation around the mid- to late-1970s when Corning established its pilot plant and then full-production plant and began to sell optical fibre in limited quantities; and that the diffusion process began to take off after 1983 with the first major adoption by MCI.

Following this periodization, several key features of the invention–innovation–diffusion process in Corning become apparent. The first is the sequential nature and separation of the three 'moments' in the process. To begin with, optical fibre was invented; then attempts were made to commercialize this invention, that is to innovate; even later the innovation began to become widely diffused. The second is the lengthy period of time taken from invention to diffusion, around thirteen years according to the present periodization. The third feature is that the process involved a number of different companies that were only loosely connected to each other through the possibility of commercial ties. Indeed, the invention itself took place in different companies, if account is taken not only of the optical fibre but also of the complementary inventions involved in areas such as coating, cabling, and connecting the fibre. 'Consolidating' the invention and attempting to transform it into an innovation involved a lengthy process, with Corning first attempting to master the complementary knowledge and then entering into a series of protracted negotiations with a number of cabling and telephone operating companies. This contributed to the time taken by the invention–innovation–diffusion process.

The invention–innovation–diffusion of optical fibre in Japan differed markedly with respect to these three features. However, it must be noted immediately that the differences are partly a reflection of the fact that Japan was a follower rather than originator of some of the key optical fibre inventions, and that the invention–innovation–diffusion process in other followers such as AT&T also differed from that in Corning.

The main difference is that in Japan the form of organization that governed the introduction of new technologies, namely controlled competition, fused the invention, innovation, and diffusion moments into a single integrated process. With NTT as the user–buyer deeply involved in the process and playing an active role in spreading the resulting technologies to several of its suppliers, any meaningful distinction between invention, innovation, and diffusion disappears. Thus, the invention process in Japan (acquiring and assimilating the new ideas regarding optical fibre and making changes and improvements so that existing patents were not violated) was at the same time an innovation (commercialization) process since NTT was the ultimate customer. Similarly, the knowledge acquired by NTT, for example through its invention of the VAD process, was immediately diffused, first to its three main supplying companies and then to a further three firms. Furthermore, the VAD process was developed by NTT initially with the manufacturing needs of the supplying companies in mind and later with their active support, therefore undermining further any distinction between invention, innovation, and diffusion. The intimate involvement by NTT, both as a user and as a developer of the new technology, therefore constituted one of the main differences in the technical change processes in Corning and Japan.

Co-operation and Competition within the 'NTT Family'

The introduction of optical fibre as a new superior transmissions technology posed a major threat as well as an opportunity to the copper cabling companies. Hitherto their competences, equipment, and routines had been based on copper and related cabling technologies. Now these technologies were beginning to be undermined by a new technology with advantages (analysed earlier) that would ultimately render copper cables obsolete. Under similar circumstances many other companies had previously proved unable to transform themselves sufficiently to adopt the new technology successfully. Examples in other fields include the transition from the vacuum tube to the transistor and from record-playing equipment to optical discs, where many incumbent companies eventually dropped out of the market for the new products. In the area of telecommunications transmissions, many Western copper cabling companies incorporated the new optical fibre technology through the establishment of joint venture agreements which gave them access to the new technology without their having to develop it internally. These companies included Siemens, BICC, and Pirelli, although companies such as AT&T and Western Electric and STC made the transition without resorting to such co-operative agreements.

In Japan all of the major copper cabling companies succeeded in making the transition to optical fibre technology, involving an area—glass—of which they originally had no knowledge. This remarkable feature of the Japanese innovation system in telecomunications requires further examination. Such an examination should begin with an analysis of the circumstances in the early 1970s surrounding the decision to invest in the new optical fibre technology. The main factor impinging on this decision was *uncertainty*. Although the 20 dB/km barrier had been broken in 1970, and although some of the important advantages of optical transmissions over electrical transmissions were beginning to be understood, a significant degree of uncertainly still attached to the new optical fibre technology. As was seen earlier, many problems still remained to be solved in the complementary technologies that would be needed for the development of effective optical transmissions systems. Furthermore, the sunk costs in copper cables constituted an additional hurdle for optical fibre. The importance of this uncertainty is evident in the internal debates that raged in Corning itself as late as 1975. As Magaziner and Patinkin record, 'By 1975, however, doubts at Corning grew. It had been five years since Donald Keck wrote "eureka" into his lab book [after recording the 1970 breakthrough]. And still all they were selling were samples. Some said it was time to stop wasting money and wait until the world was ready [for optical fibre]. But Amory Houghton, Jr, Corning's Chairman, still believed in the fiber's promise.'[23] If uncertainty played such a central role in Corning, the originator of the new optical fibre technology and the company most advanced in this emerging field, how could the Japanese copper cabling companies, novices in the area with a limited knowledge-base in optical fibre, cope with it?

The answer to this important question lies in the form of organization that governed the assimilation, creation, and diffusion of new telecommunications technologies in Japan. Without this form of organization, i.e. left to the 'forces of the market', it seems reasonable to hypothesize that the individual Japanese cabling companies would have hesitated before investing substantial amounts of their scarce resources in optical fibre technology. To begin with, there remained uncertainty regarding whether competitive optical fibre transmissions systems could be developed. For these uncertainties to be removed, substantial improvements were still required in production methods for optical fibre—in coating, cabling, connecting, and repeating technologies, and in light sources and detectors. Furthermore, even if these technological uncertainties were effectively removed, the individual Japanese copper cabling company would still have confronted the market uncertainty surrounding its ability to compete with other incumbents and new entrants in the optical fibre market. Under these circumstances, and with copper cable still the dominant technology, the failure of individual Japanese cabling companies to make a decisive and substantial commitment to the new technology would have been understandable (and perhaps even justifiable, under acceptable criteria for investment appraisal).

[23] Magaziner and Patinkin, *The Silent War*, 280.

In the event, however, the entry of the Japanese cabling companies into the field of optical fibre was facilitated by NTT's organization of controlled competition. Thus we saw that, as early as the autumn of 1973, NTT concluded a co-operative agreement with Fujikura, Furukawa, and Sumitomo Electric; according to the implicit and explicit terms of this agreement, the three companies would work closely with NTT in order to research and develop methods for the production of low-loss optical fibre, for the cabling of this fibre, and for its incorporation into optical communications sub-systems. Although the companies would do their share of the work initially at their own expense, their expectation was that they would all eventually be given significant purchasing orders from NTT at prices that would profitably compensate them. Under these circumstances, the degree of uncertainty that each of the cabling companies faced was far less than would have been the case under free-market conditions, where each company would act individually and would have to compete for its market share on the basis of winner takes all or most of the order for optical fibre cable.

One major advantage of controlled competition, therefore, was its uncertainty-reducing effect. Further significant advantages emerged from the economies of co-operative research and development that were facilitated by this form of organization (that is, lower costs of research and development and/or improved output from such research and development as a result of interfirm co-operation). These economies included:

1. avoidance of overlapping research and development;
2. sharing of information and knowledge;
3. fusing of firm-specific knowledge;
4. improvement in technological efficiency by directly incorporating user needs into the R&D process;
5. speeding of diffusion;
6. facilitation of standardization in order to create a multi-vendor environment.

These six economies of co-operative research and development will now be more closely analysed.

Avoidance of overlapping research and development
By working co-operatively, NTT, Fujikura, Furukawa, and Sumitomo Electric were able to avoid the wasteful duplication of research and development that is likely to have occurred to a greater extent had they worked independently. Co-operative work under controlled competition, however, also facilitated an important degree of *variety*, which is essential if a system is to adapt under conditions of uncertain change. To some extent this variety reflected the fact that, although the firms co-operated closely, they were simultaneously undertaking their own private research and development in areas deemed to be of strategic importance. Perhaps the best example of this is the research carried out in Sumitomo Electric on a process for the production of optical fibre which

was strikingly similar to the VAD process and was patented in the USA in 1974, three years before the VAD process had been officially announced.

Variety was also one of the objectives of the combined research group and was facilitated by the greater amount of resources that this group had under its command compared with what each would be able to command under independent research. Thus, the group worked simultaneously on both MCVD technology (originally developed in Bell Laboratories) and the VAD process (developed in NTT's Ibaraki Laboratory, but remaining inferior until as late as 1980, when it was tested together with MCVD in the experimental optical fibre cable built by NTT). The variety that was in this way generated decreased the risk of any company becoming wedded to a technology that would later prove to be inferior.

Sharing information and knowledge
Economies were also derived from the sharing of information and knowledge between NTT and the three supplying companies. This sharing, however, presents something of a puzzle as a result of the competitive relationship that existed between the three companies. As was seen, there was a degree of competition between the companies for the NTT market, even though this competition was controlled. Even more important was the competition, or potential competition, between the three companies in other parts of the Japanese market and in overseas markets. In time, the companies would compete in order to supply the new common carriers that were to contest the markets dominated by NTT and KDD. Furthermore, they would also compete in markets outside Japan. To what extent did this competitive relationship constrain the willingness of the three supplying companies to share information and knowledge? Did they not have an incentive to keep information and knowledge private in the hope of establishing a competitive edge over their rivals? Did this not, therefore, undermine the effectiveness and economies of co-operation under controlled competition?

The problems that the underlying competitive relationship posed for the process of co-operation in research and development emerged strongly in interviews that I conducted with senior research managers from the three companies. In developing optical fibre technology, engineers from NTT and the three supplying companies met together once a month at NTT's Ibaraki Laboratory. However, competition between the three companies influenced the information that these companies disclosed. As one manager put it, 'We met at NTT because NTT was neutral. In our companies we had prior meetings. How to exclude the know-how, while reporting the results of the research we had done—it was a very delicate issue. We needed to keep our own patents.'

It was clear that NTT played a crucial role in facilitating the sharing of information and knowledge between the three competing suppliers. A senior NTT manager, closely involved in the co-operative development of optical fibre in NTT, succinctly summarized the matter: 'NTT was neutral. This was one good thing. But NTT was also a big buyer.'

As a neutral leader and co-ordinator, NTT had an incentive to maximize flows of information and knowledge between the three companies in order to benefit the research, development, and production processes. The overall objective was to ensure that the companies produced substitutable optical fibre that was compatible with NTT's standards and specifications and met its cost–performance criteria. This did not require the sharing of all information and knowledge. In particular, the companies would insist on keeping their know-how private since it was on this that their competition largely depended. Private rather than shared know-how also produced the benefit of greater variety within the system as a whole, thus increasing the opportunity for innovation and reducing the risk of a firm becoming wedded to an inferior technology.

For their part, the companies trusted NTT to act in a neutral manner. Accordingly, as managers from the companies confirmed, where it seemed desirable, a company could discuss commercially sensitive information with NTT's engineers in the knowledge that it would not be passed on to the competing companies. The fact that NTT was not only neutral, but also a large procurer, the largest single customer for all of the companies, increased the incentive for firms to co-operate in this way. Furthermore, the companies had learned to co-operate through the long-term and stable relationship with NTT and one another. As a senior manager from one of the companies explained, 'NTT also showed us the goal and the final target. Our three companies [Fujikura, Furukawa, and Sumitomo Electric] had a long history of working together. We three companies were very intimate. However, there was also competition.'

On the basis of the discussion thus far, the following hypothesis can be put forward regarding the flows of information and knowledge between NTT and the three companies. Since NTT is a complementary/non-competing company, in contrast to the other supplying companies which are competing, knowledge flows are more likely between a supplying company and NTT than between it and one of the other supplying companies.

In order to test this hypothesis, I obtained information from NTT on all joint patents in the optical fibre area granted during the period end-August 1985 to beginning-September 1986, a time when a substantial amount of research was being carried out in Japan and elsewhere on optical fibre. A joint patent is defined as one held by the employees of more than one of the co-operating companies. The results are shown in Table 5.1 and Fig. 5.7.

As is clear from this figure, in the large majority of cases the joint patent is held by employees of one of the supplying companies together with staff of NTT's Ibaraki Laboratory. In only one case was there a joint patent involving all three of the supplying firms (a case concerning a method for connecting optical fibre). More specifically, sixteen out of the seventeen joint patents were held jointly by one of the companies and NTT: eight by Sumitomo Electric and NTT, five by Fujikura and NTT, and three by Furukawa and NTT. This,

Table 5.1 *Joint Optical Fibre Patents Granted Involving NTT and its Supplying Firms, September 1985–September 1986*

Companies	No. of patents granted
NTT (ECL Ibaraki) and Sumitomo Electric	8
NTT (ECL Ibaraki) and Fujikura	5
NTT (ECL Ibaraki) and Furukawa[a]	3
NTT (ECL Ibaraki) and Sumitomo and Furukawa and Fujikura[b]	1
Total	17

[a] One Furukawa joint patent is also with Showa Machine Tool.
[b] This patent concerns a method for connecting optical fibre.

Source: NTT, 'Report of Research Applications, Introduction of Patents, September 1985–September 1986' (Kenkyu Gitsuyoka Hokoku, Tokkyo Shokai); plus information given to the author by NTT.

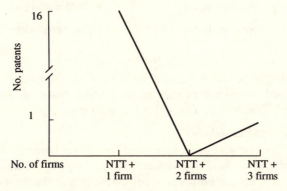

Fig. 5.7 Joint optical fibre patents granted involving NTT and supplying firms, September 1985–September 1986

Source: NTT, 'Report of Research Applications, Introduction of Patents, Sept. 1985–Sept. 1986' (Kenkyu Gitsuyoka Hokoku, Tokkyo Shokai); plus information given to the author by NTT.

therefore, tends to confirm the hypothesis (to the extent that joint patents are an adequate measure of knowledge flows that occur in the process of research and development).

In Fig. 5.8 an account is given of the importance of flows of information and knowledge between NTT and its supplier firms. The unbroken arrows represent substantial flows, while the dashed arrows indicate more restricted flows of information and knowledge.

On the basis of the argument and empirical evidence presented in this section,

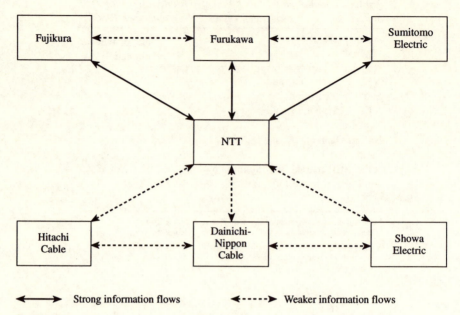

Strong information flows   Weaker information flows

Fig. 5.8 Flow of information between NTT and supplying companies

it may accordingly be concluded that NTT, as a neutral co-ordinator and large procurer, played an important role in facilitating flows of information and knowledge between the competing supplying companies.

Fusing firm-specific knowledge
The relatively free flow of information and knowledge between the members of the NTT 'family firms', and in particular between individual suppliers and NTT, created the possibility for further benefits deriving from the integration of firm-specific knowledge. One dramatic example is the breakthrough by NTT and Fujikura researchers which led to a world record-breaking low-loss fibre in 1976. As was seen, this emerged from the integration of knowledge developed by the chemist Osanai in Fujikura, who worked on ways of reducing impurities in optical fibre, with that produced by Mizushima in NTT, dealing with the effect of wavelength on attenuation. Such possibilities for the integration of knowledge fragmented across different companies constituted an important economy of co-operative research and development under controlled competition.

*Improving technological efficiency by directly incorporating
user needs into the R&D process*
A further economy of co-operative research and development under controlled competition resulted from the direct incorporation of user needs. As a technologically sophisticated user indirectly involved in shaping the research and

development of new technologies, NTT was frequently able to ensure that the needs of the telecommunications network were taken into account from the outset. NTT has always argued that this is one of the major benefits that it derives from its costly involvement with its suppliers in the R&D process. In the optical field, these advantages are most apparent in the effective operation of optical transmission sub-systems integrated into the telecommunications network.

Speeding diffusion
With its proprietary control over many of the key technologies, and supported by the power it wields as a substantial procurer, NTT has been able at times to ensure a rapid diffusion of new technology. Evidence of this emerged not only in the fast diffusion of VAD technology to Fujikura, Furukawa, and Sumitomo Electric, but also in the 'second wave of diffusion' to Hitachi Cable, Dainichi-Nippon Cable, and Showa Electric Wire and Cable, a move that was initially opposed by the former major three suppliers. Not only was NTT a beneficiary of this wider diffusion of optical fibre technology, since it was able to reduce further its dependence on individual suppliers and increase technological variety in the area of know-how, but other users of optical fibre were also able to benefit from the degree of competition that existed between the supplying companies.

Facilitating standardization in order to create a multi-vendor environment
A further economy of co-operative research and development under controlled competition followed from the greater degree of standardization that resulted as NTT ensured that telecommunications products from the different suppliers were inter-operable and compatible with the rest of the network. In turn, this facilitated the benefits of greater competition under multi-vendor conditions.

Increased Long-Run Competition under Controlled Competition

Somewhat paradoxically, there is evidence to suggest that controlled competition may lead to more competition in the long run. This emerges from data on market share by major companies in North America, Europe, and Japan, presented in Fig. 5.9. As can be seen from parts (*a*) and (*b*) of the figure, in North America AT&T and Corning between them held 83 per cent of the market, with AT&T accounting for 43 per cent and Corning 40 per cent. While the West European market as a whole might incorrectly appear to be more competitive, this does not take account of the dominance of individual country markets by few suppliers that are primarily national, such as BICC and STC in the UK or Siemens/Siecor in Germany. There is little doubt that the Japanese market is most competitive, to the extent that this is measured by corporate market share. As shown in Fig. 5.9(*c*), Sumitomo Electric had 35.0 per cent of the total market for optical fibre, Fujikura 21.5 per cent, Furukawa 20.6 per cent, Hitachi Cable 7.0 per cent, and Showa Electric 4.0 per cent.

The paradoxical result that controlled competition leads to greater competition as measured by market share is explained by NTT's allocation rule, which

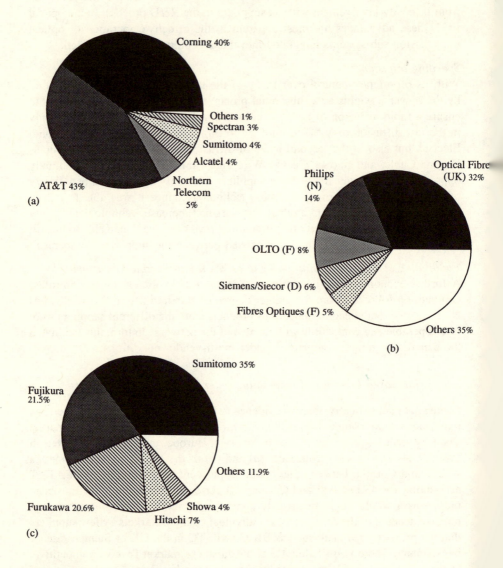

Fig. 5.9(*a*) The optical fibre market share, North America, 1987
Source: ElectroniCast Corporation, 1988.
Fig. 5.9(*b*) The optical fibre market share, Western Europe, 1987
Source: ElectroniCast Corporation, 1988.
Fig. 5.9(*c*) The optical fibre market share, Japan, 1989
Source: *Nikkei Shinbum*, 14 June 1990.

replaced market competition in the allocation of procurements, together with its policy on widespread diffusion. It seems reasonable to hypothesize that, under normal competitive conditions, where the winner, judged in terms of the cost–performance of its product, takes all or most of the market, a greater degree of market concentration would have evolved. This greater degree of long-run competition may turn out to be one of the most important benefits of controlled competition.

Seen from this perspective of lower market concentration, NTT's policy of paying its suppliers generous prices has a rationale based on competition. (NTT's price, it should be recalled, also compensated the suppliers under controlled competition for the uncertainty and costs borne in assisting in the research and development of new technology.) This puts NTT's pricing policies in a very different light when compared with international trade-related criticisms of these policies such as the following: 'Duke [from Corning] . . . points to what he calls a typical unfair trade practice: For a long time, Japan's state phone company bought fiber from local companies at three times international prices, allowing them high profits for investment and for selling the same fiber around the world below market prices.'[24] What appears as an 'unfair trade practice' from the American point of view may appear as a way of securing long-term suppliers under reasonably competitive market conditions from the Japanese viewpoint!

The Globalization of Controlled Competition

As we have seen, after 1985, and particularly after around 1990, NTT began increasingly to open its joint R&D projects to add foreign and other Japanese companies to its traditional family of suppliers. This has been done under its Track III procedure.

In general, it is important to stress that most of the benefits of controlled competition analysed in this section will remain. However, there are a number of important changes that will accompany the globalization of controlled competition. From NTT's point of view these changes are likely to be primarily positive. One of the main benefits of the new system for NTT is its ability to draw on the strengths and capabilities of these other foreign and Japanese companies in addition to those of its traditional suppliers. For example, the participation of both Corning and Sumitomo Electric, participating side by side with other suppliers in the NTT project referred to earlier, is not only remarkable in view of the previous conflicts between these two companies, but also highly beneficial for NTT in terms of the combined capabilities it is able to call on.

However, at least in the shorter run, until a new, satisfactory *modus vivendi* develops between NTT and the new companies on the one hand and between the old and new family members on the other, it is possible that this added availability of capability will be purchased at the expense of some flows of

[24] Ibid. 296.

information between the project members. Since the supplying companies are also competing, in some cases strenuously (in some global markets), caution regarding extra-company flows of information on the part of new family members would be understandable. It is true that strong inter-company competition was also a hallmark of interactions between the menbers of the old family, as emerged very clearly in the earlier analysis of joint patents. But the long-term and stable nature of the family relationship allowed the development of satisfactory practices, procedures, and trust which maximized co-operation in the face of the underlying competitive interactions. From the point of view of the new companies, however, there is a strong incentive to make positive attempts to develop similar co-operative modes of interacting. The size of NTT's purchases is sufficient to ensure this incentive. Nevertheless, it is to be expected that time will be necessary for the required adjustments to take place. The 'carrot' available for all family members at the end of the path is sufficiently attractive for all to make significant efforts.

Analysis 2: The Schumpeterian Process of Creative–Destructive Change: Optical-Fibre-Based Communications Systems

In this section optical-fibre-based communications systems are analysed in the context of Joseph Schumpeter's process of creative–destructive change. According to this analytical framework, optical-fibre-based communications systems constitute a 'new combination', or new innovation, which challenges older technologies and the organizations that bear them.

However, the Schumpeterian framework poses a number of crucial problems and puzzles relating to optical fibre. For example, how did this 'new combination' emerge, and what was the response of those who had vested interests in the older technologies? There were critical differences between the vision of those vitally affected by the new technologies, particularly with regard to the required time envisaged before the new optical fibre technology would be widely adopted. How are these differences in vision to be explained? Did not all the organizations concerned have access to the same information and knowledge and, if so, why did they see things so differently? What role did competition play in the process of creative–destructive change? These questions raise further issues of policy. For example, what lessons can be learned from the analysis of optical fibre regarding the conditions that are necessary for an innovative telecommunications system? What is the role of public policy in facilitating innovation? Finally, how were the gains from the innovation of optical fibre systems distributed, by company, country, and globally?

According to Schumpeter, capitalism is a process of change. Furthermore, it is a process of creative–destructive change. New innovations challenge, and in some cases destroy, the old. An understanding of the process of capitalist change, therefore, requires an analysis of the emergence of new combinations and their challenge to the old forms through their widespread diffusion and use.

Optical-Fibre-Based Communications Systems:
A Radical New Combination

The new combination that we have been particularly concerned with in this chapter comprises optical-fibre-based communications systems. These systems emerged, in ways that will be described below, to challenge the 'old' alternative forms or media of communications transmission, including copper cables, microwave radio, and communications satellites.

The first point to make about optical-fibre-based communications systems is that they constitute a radical new technology, offering significant, non-marginal, improvements under particular circumstances compared with the alternative technologies. This point is dramatically substantiated in Fig. 5.10, which shows the improvements in channel capacity that occurred since the 1890s when the first telephone lines were constructed. As can be seen from this figure, the improvements that occurred in relative information capacity in copper coaxial cables, microwave radio, and communications satellites from 1890 to the 1970s were all along the average slope shown in the diagram. Optical-fibre-based systems, however, represent a discontinuous improvement, with a relative information capacity significantly above the average slope. The main reason for this quantum jump, as mentioned earlier, is the far greater bandwidth capacity provided by optical fibre compared with the other media.

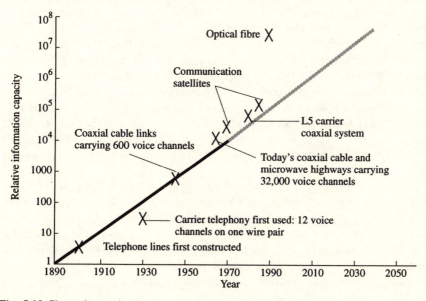

Fig. 5.10 Channel capacity improvement as a function of time, 1890–2030

Source: C. K. N. Patel, 'Lasers in Communications and Information Processing', in J. H. Ausubel and H. D. Langford (eds.), *Lasers: Invention to Application*, National Academy Press, Washington, DC, 1987.

It may be concluded, therefore, that optical-fibre-based communications systems constitute a radical, non-marginal, new combination (in circumstances that will be elaborated upon in greater detail below).

How Did this New Combination Emerge?

Schumpeter has observed that 'new combinations are, as a rule, embodied ... in new firms which generally do not arise out of the old ones but start producing beside them. . . . in general it is not the owner of stage-coaches who builds railways.'[25]

In the case of optical fibre, however, it was the 'stage-coach owners' (the telephone operating companies) and the 'stage-coach builders' (the telecommunications equipment supplying companies) that did some of the earliest research on optical communications. As was seen earlier, these companies included the UK Post Office (later BT), AT&T, NTT, Western Electric, STC, and Sumitomo Electric. Clearly, these companies had a *vision* which included a possible role in the future for optical communications.

However, while important contributions were made by researchers such as Kao and Hockham in STC, it was a newcomer, Corning, that first broke the 250 and 20 dB/km barriers, proving the feasibility of optical fibre communications. Significantly, the fact that Corning won this particular race was due not to fresh questions or directions pursued by a newcomer 'uncontaminated' by old routines and ways of thinking, but to the knowledge-base that it had accumulated, which proved particularly well suited to the requirements of low-loss optical fibres. More specifically, Corning had already accumulated significant knowledge in areas such as pure fused silica, flame hydrolysis, doping, and vapour deposition, which it was able to combine and modify to produce the successful fibres. Other glass companies, also potential newcomers to the field of optical communications (such as Pilkington and Nippon Sheet Glass) but with different knowledge-bases from Corning, pursued different search paths ultimately proved less successful. Also significant was the fact that it was one of the 'stage-coach owners', the UK Post Office, that first put Corning on to the idea of diversifying, on the basis of its existing competences, into optical fibre.

In terms of the stage-coach/railway analogy, therefore, it must be concluded that the new combinations that comprised optical-fibre-based communications systems emerged both from the organizations that were deeply involved in the 'old' technologies and from organizations that were new to the field such as the glass companies, and in particular Corning. However, the knowledge-base of the optical fibre that constituted a crucial part of this new combination came decidedly from outside the field of telecommunications.

---

[25] J. A. Schumpeter, *The Theory of Economic Development*, Oxford University Press, New York, 1961, 66.

Vison and the New Combination

Although the telephone operating companies, equipment suppliers, and Corning shared a vison of a future telecommunications system in which optical communications played an important role, there were crucial differences in their respective visions. In particular, they differed significantly in terms of the length of time they anticipated would be required before optical-fibre-based systems came into widespread use. Since by the mid-1970s these companies possessed similar knowledge and had access to the same kind of information in this area, the co-existence of visions that differed in important respects presents a puzzle that requires explanation.

First, however, it is worth noting that subsequent events proved all these visions to be wrong and so they accordingly had to be revised. In Corning's case the incorrectness of its vision began to become apparent as it tried unsuccessfully to sell its new optical fibre in great quantity. This emerges, for example, from one of the accounts of Corning's initial attempt to sell its newly invented optical fibre to the UK Post Office, the company that had first given Corning the idea of diversifying into optical waveguides. According to this account, Corning's

biggest disappointment was the British phone company, the people who'd started Corning on this in the first place. Now they told Lucy their biggest hope for waveguides had been for videophones, an idea that had been waiting for a new wire with more capacity than copper. Waveguides fit perfectly, but their latest surveys, they told Lucy, showed there wouldn't be much market for video phones until the next century. As much as Lucy believed in his product, he wasn't ready to wait that long.[26]

Clearly, the visions of the UK Post Office and Corning differed significantly in terms of the role that would be played by optical fibre in transmissions systems over the following ten years. (It is less clear, however, whether Corning would have made the same commitment of resources to optical fibre had it known in advance that the returns would be this long in coming. In this connection, a calculation of Corning's 'real' return on the capital that it invested in optical fibre, measured over and above what it could have earned on riskless interest-bearing assets, and the date at which this return became positive, would be highly illuminating.)

The visions of Corning and the other companies depended critically on the *interpretation* by their decision-makers of the information and knowledge they possessed. This information and knowledge, which was relatively clear in itself, left room for an important degree of interpretive ambiguity. Thus, Corning, mindful of the many advantages of optical fibre such as bandwidth and lack of interference, saw optical fibre cables as an economically superior technology which would soon outcompete the alternative transmissions technologies. This vision of the future was clearly influenced by the company's knowledge-base in the glass field, which affected its optimism for the new technology. However,

---

[26] Magaziner and Patinkin, *The Silent War*, 277.

with the benefit of hindsight, Corning's vision failed to interpret adequately information that was available, and which the company to a greater or lesser degree must have had, regarding the extent and significance of the sunk costs in, and therefore strength of commitment to, the old technologies. In time, this vision needed readjustment as Corning accumulated further information suggesting that it had been over-optimistic.

The vision of the telephone operating companies and the equipment suppliers, on the other hand, was crucially influenced, as far as timing was concerned, by the resources they had already accumulated in the old technologies, which constituted a sunk cost. These companies accepted that optical fibre was a potentially important future technology. However, their vision was also influenced by the belief that any advantage accruing from the new technology would have to be weighed against the costs of abandoning the old technology. This belief was responsible for the longer estimate of time before 'switch-over' to the new technology was likely.

However, this vision also had to be revised. In the USA important new information emerged with the decision of MCI in the new deregulated telecommunications market to install optical fibre cable. In order to remain competitive and offer similar services at a similar quality and cost (under the sanction of competitive pressure) it now became necessary to agree to write-off the investment in the old technology sooner than had previously been envisaged.

Selection Environment, Competition, and Vision Revision

In order to make decisions, companies have no alternative but to develop visions concerning the future. These visions emerge from beliefs and interpretations on the basis of incomplete information (no individual or even company can know all there is to know relating to a particular decision), and from expectations regarding future states of affairs, which cannot be predicted (even probabilistically) from past states. In other words, visions are held with uncertainty.

Corporate visions, however, interact with a 'selection environment' which, as in the biological world, provides feedback regarding which visions are viable and will lead to decisions that enable the corporation to grow, and which are unviable. In the light of this feedback, a process of vision–revision will occur which will result in further feedback; etc.

We have already seen that the process of competition was an important part of the selection environment which influenced corporate visions regarding the future role of optical-fibre-based communications systems. More specifically, in the USA it was in the first instance potential competition in the telecommunications sevices market from MCI, following the divestiture of AT&T and consequent increasing competition in this market, which challenged existing visions regarding the time-frame for the introduction of optical fibre communications. Accordingly, MCI's competitors, in view of the advantages of optical fibre over the other alternative technologies, were forced to take optical fibre cables more seriously and to write-off their sunk costs in copper cables more rapidly. In this way, competition between users of the new combination played an important role influencing the introduction and diffusion of the new technology. To put the matter differently, in the absence of increased competition between telephone operators who used the new technology, it seems clear that it would have taken even longer for optical fibre to occupy the position that it has come to enjoy in communications systems. In Japan, although NTT had decided in the late 1970s to introduce an optical fibre trunk running the length of the country, the decisions made in the newly liberalized markets in the USA served to underscore the importance of optical fibre.

Three other forms of competition were also important influences on the introduction and diffusion of this new combination: competition between producers of the new technology; competition between 'technological regimes', that is (in this case) between optical fibre cables, copper cables, microwave radio, and communications satellites; and competition between 'design configurations' within the optical fibre technological regime, for example between the OVD, MCVD, and VAD processes for the production of optical fibre.

While, as we have seen, competition between the users of optical fibre cables (beginning with MCI) was an important factor influencing the timing of the widespread introduction and diffusion of this new technology, competition between its producers was also important. Although much harder to document and measure (because of a lack of information), it is undoubtedly the case that competition between the companies producing optical fibre and optical fibre cable was an important influence on (1) the quantity of resources allocated to research, development, and production and (2) the speed of progress in this area. To take an example, Corning must have been influenced in its continuing work on optical fibre by the efforts it knew AT&T's Bell Laboratories were putting into this field. Similarly, the pace of development in Japan added further to the pressure that was on Corning to ensure that its initial technological lead was not undermined by subsequent improvements made by the Japanese.

The Importance of Competition from Japan

The question of the distribution of the gains from innovation in optical fibre, and particularly the issue of Corning's gains from its own inventions and innovations, is examined below. Here we are concerned more with the effect on the process of creation–destruction of competition from Japan.

There is enough evidence to suggest that the threat of competition from the Japanese influenced both the resources that Corning allocated to its R&D efforts in optical fibre and the rate of progress over time which it made. This, for example, emerges from an account of the impact on Corning of the competing work being done in Japan in the field of optical fibre. According to this account,

[David] Duke was somber as he flew home [from Japan in the early 1970s]. 'I remember coming back kind of shell-shocked,' he recalls. 'I'd seen what they'd done with cars, with consumer electronics—I was paranoid about the Japanese. I was scared to death of them.' But it only made him want to fight harder. At headquarters, Duke told his division chiefs what he'd found. The scope of Japan's waveguide plans left everyone alarmed. Corning was big—a $1 billion-a-year company at the time—but could it match [the Japanese effort]? . . . He went on to map out a new counterassault. This wasn't going to be another VCR story, Duke said, not another case of America giving away its inventions. Waveguides were Corning's. And the only way to keep them was to win on three fronts: the lab, the factory, and the market. In turn, that meant three priorities—lowest cost, highest quality, biggest volume.[27]

It is important to note that this story can be analysed at three fundamentally different levels and that at each level a substantially different meaning and significance emerges.

The first level involves competitive rivalry between companies. This rivalry can be viewed from two different perspectives. That of Corning has been well expressed in the last quotation. The picture that emerges is one of a company that has made the major breakthroughs in a field and now faces the threat of a rival attempting to make inroads into its newly established territory. Furthermore, Corning was concerned that the Japanese cable companies had the substantial support of NTT which was also the main user of optical fibre cable. The fact that Corning faced a very similar threat from another company, which also involved potential producers and users of optical fibre cable, and the fact that this company was American, namely AT&T, made little difference to the rivalry it expressed towards the Japanese. Nevertheless, the threat posed by AT&T was described in very similar terms to that presented by the Japanese. Indeed, the above quotation continues immediately in much the same tone: David Duke 'reminded everyone that it wouldn't work to merely stay even with the competition. Corning, he said, was smaller than its rivals, both here and in Japan. Look at AT&T, he said—it had more people, more money, and itself as a customer. When your competition's bigger, matching it isn't good enough. "I don't want to tie," he said. "If we tie, we lose." '[28]

The other perspective on inter-company competition is that of the Japanese. From their point of view, as documented earlier, the principal threat was one of technological domination by a foreign supplier and the corresponding problems of high price for technology and the absence of a closely co-operating supplier of optical communications systems that they felt would necessarily follow. As noted above, NTT had already experienced such a situation through its dependence on Western Electric and STC in the area of copper cable, a situation that it wanted, if at all possible, to avoid repeating. The effort that NTT and its closely related group of suppliers made in the area of optical fibre and the resources that they devoted were motivated by the desire to avoid this threat.

The second level of analysis is that involving competitive rivalry between the different countries. This rivalry, coming at a time of increasing trade-based

---

[27] Ibid. 283.   [28] Ibid.

competition between American and Japanese companies, was dressed in the terminology of trade conflict. From the perspective of the USA, this was another example of Japan placing 'unfair' barriers on the entry of American products and technology (in the case of the dispute over the recognition of Corning's patents in Japan) into the Japanese market. From the Japanese perspective, however, the issue was rather one of avoiding technological dependence and maintaining a close, long-term, co-operative relationship with trusted Japanese telecommunications suppliers.

It is the third level, however, that is of greatest concern from the point of view of the Schumpeterian process of creation–destruction. This level abstracts from rivalry between particular companies and their nation-states and the two-sided rhetoric that forms an inevitable part of this rivalry in order to focus more clearly on the process of creation–destruction itself. At this level, the issue of prime concern is not the corporate or national identity of the antagonists, but rather the creation of new combinations, the threat posed by these combinations to the old order, its structures and supporters, and the eventual replacement of the old by the new. From this perspective, 'progress' involved the emergence of a more powerful medium which facilitated the transmission, at lower cost and with less interference, of greater quantities of information than could be sent using the other alternative media, thus facilitating new telecommunications services in areas involving, and possibly integrating, voice, data, text, and images. Seen from this perspective, competition from the Japanese, and indeed from other rivals such as AT&T and STC, was significant only in so far as it facilitated the triumph of the new combination.

Technological Competition

It would be wrong, however to leave the discussion of the impact of competition at an analysis of competition between the users and producers of optical fibre cable. Competition between alternative *technologies* also played an important role. More specifically, competition between different 'technological regimes', such as optical fibre, copper, microwave radio, and satellite, and between 'design configurations' such as OVD, MCVD, and VAD, were also important.

Although competition between technological regimes has not been analysed in detail in this chapter and such competition therefore remains largely invisible in the present account of optical fibre, it is clear that this form of technological competition has been important. This emerges in a stark way, for example, in the definition in the 1960s of the 20 dB/km barrier as the target level of performance which the new technology of optical fibre would have to attain if it were to establish its viability. Those working on optical fibre and optical-fibre-based systems were very aware that there were alternatives to the technological solutions they were offering and that they had to keep up with the (improving) performances of the alternative technologies. This was important, for instance, in the competition between optical fibre and microwave radio. After the Second

World War, with the advances that had been made during the war in the area of radio, microwave radio emerged as an important technology for communications purposes. Furthermore, it was a technology that NTT strongly sponsored, and its main supplier (NEC) in particular, with NTT's support, developed strong capabilities in the field of microwave radio. Not only was this technology cost-effective in a situation where telecommunications cables had been destroyed in the war, it was also suitable in a mountainous, earthquake- and typhoon-prone environment. The developers of the new optical fibre technology were well aware that they had to match the performance of this and other alternative technologies.

Viewed through the prism of technological competition, however, the battlelines and combatants change markedly. In the case of Japan, for example, within NTT's Electrical Communications Laboratories there were groups working on each of the competing technologies, including communications satellites. A company such as NEC, while a user of optical fibre and producer of submarine optical fibre cable systems, was also a producer of microwave radio and communications satellite systems. Furthermore, it was NEC's 'sister' company, Sumitomo Electric, which was also part of the Sumitomo group (and which earlier had been a major founder and stakeholder in NEC), which became heavily committed to optical fibre. However, although the combatants and battlelines were very different for this technological competitive battle, it cannot be doubted that competition between those with a vested interest in the competing technologies also played an important role in influencing both the new combination itself and improvements in the challenged alternative technologies.

In this connection it is worth noting that, although substantial improvements have been made in optical fibre systems, these systems have not been able entirely to replace the alternative technologies. This is so for two main reasons. The first is the improvements that have been made in alternative technologies, partly as a result of the competitive response of their developers in the face of the challenge from optical fibre. The second is that the alternative technologies have proved to be superior in particular applications where optical fibre is too costly despite its more favourable characteristics such as greater information-carrying capacity and lower levels of interference (and therefore lower error rates).

These applications include entertainment broadcasting, where point-to-multipoint communications satellites have proved more cost-effective than laying numerous optical fibre cables to homes. In the case of some extremely long-distance communications, satellites have also proved to be superior in cost terms. Furthermore, microwave radio has proved to be advantageous in providing mobile communications with which optical fibre, as a result of its inherent inflexibility, cannot compete. Nevertheless, in many applications technological competition continues to exist and is an important influence shaping the further development of the alternative technologies. For example, in the broadcasting area, competition between companies using optical fibre cables and those using satellites (aided by new bandwidth compression techniques, which have markedly increased the carrying capacity of satellites) is significant and will become increasingly contentious as more cables are installed. (Bandwidth compression technology has also significantly increased the carrying capacity of the old copper cables, making them more viable.)

Technological competition between different 'design configurations' within the same technological regime has also been important. In the case of the optical fibre technological regime, it is clear that there has been a significant degree of competition between the MCVD, OVD, and VAD design configurations. This emerges clearly, for example, from the following (possibly partisan) account from Japanese authors with a vested interest in the VAD process:

On December 8, 1980, NTT in Japan announced the transmission loss of 0.2 dB/km and 0.35 dB/km at wavelengths of 1.55 micrometers and 1.3 micrometers, respectively, by using the VAD process. Corning Glass Works, seemingly influenced by this announcement, gave up the MCVD method and converted its production system to Outside Vapour Deposition (OVD) using flame hydrolysis, similar to the VAD process (the transmission loss of fiber then made at Corning Glass Works was 1.0 dB/km at 1.3 micrometers).[29]

Whether or not this account would be corroborated by those wedded to the alternative design configurations, it is clear that competition did exist between design configurations and that this competition had some influence on the evolution of optical fibre technology.

Policy Implications

What policy implications are to be drawn from this analysis of the process of creative–destructive technical change in the area of telecommunications transmissions?

The main conclusion to emerge is that the health and vitality of the global telecommunications system, measured in terms of its creation and use of new knowledge, is dependent on its ability to generate both a variety of competing new combinations and the conditions under which adopters will rapidly abandon less efficient combinations of knowledge in favour of new, more efficient combinations.

With regard to the first condition, the barriers to the emergence of new combinations constituted by the uncertainty of commercial reward must be acknowledged. True, Corning was remarkably persistent and patient in having to wait seventeen years before receiving substantial orders for its optical fibre. It is less clear, however, whether the company would have made the same commitment of resources had it known in advance that the returns would be this long in coming. One of the main advantages of the Japanese form of organization which governed the development and implementation of Schumpeter's new

---

[29] T. Nakamura, H. Shioyama, and T. Watamizu, 'Optical Fiber—From its Initial Development through Successful Production and Usage', *Sumitomo Electric Technical Review*, no. 26, 42.

combinations, namely controlled competition, was that it served to reduce significantly the effects of such uncertainty.

The second condition for health and vitality, namely an enabling environment under which rapid adoption of new combinations occurs, has more recently been addressed by the greater degree of competition, in both telecommunications service and equipment markets, that has increasingly emerged since the 1980s. The present analysis suggests, however, that attention needs also to be focused on competition between alternative technological regimes and between different design configurations within a technological regime. The supporters and opponents of these technological approaches tend to be defined on a basis that is different from the competing companies which produce and use the new combinations.

Distribution of the Benefits

Starting at the global level, it is clear that the users of telecommunications services have benefited from the new optical-fibre-based systems. The benefits they have received include lower costs and higher quality in the areas in which the application of optical fibre has proved particularly appropriate.

At the country level, all countries have benefited as *users* of these systems. Some countries, however, have also derived benefits as *producers* of optical fibre, notably the USA, Canada, Japan, the UK, Germany, France, and Italy.

At the company level, the main beneficiaries have been Corning (which made the initial breakthroughs) and its joint-venture collaborators in various countries, AT&T, STC (now part of Alcatel), and the Japanese companies Fujikura, Furukawa, and Sumitomo Electric.

6

The Evolution of NEC

CHAPTER OVERVIEW

How have NEC's competences evolved since the company was founded in 1899? The chapter begins by examining this question, showing how NEC advanced into competence-related technologies and new products. Particular attention is paid to those areas in which the company achieved international competitiveness. NEC's move into personal computers is closely examined. In this area the company held more than 50 per cent of the Japanese market in the early 1990s.

What are the major beliefs that underlie NEC's vision, and what were the main determinants of these beliefs? This question is tackled next, examining the creation of NEC's 'C&C Vision', that is its vision based on the convergence of communications and computing technologies. How important was this vision in influencing the evolution of NEC's competences, its forms of organization, and its understanding of its environment? Why is it that some of NEC's Western counterparts—such as IBM, Intel, and Ericsson—formed contradictory visions? What evidence is there to support the beliefs underlying NEC's C&C vision? These kinds of questions are examined in this section.

How has NEC's internal organization evolved since its founding? Specifically, how has the company organized and managed the large number of products, technologies, and markets in which it is involved? (NEC now produces more than 10,000 different products!) These questions are analysed in the following section, paying particularly close attention to the company's major reorganizations in 1965 and 1992. What factors motivated these reorganizations? What role was played by vision, competences, and selection environment? In this section a key organizational issue that is analysed in detail relates to the organization and management of research and development. How does NEC plan the R&D for 10,000 products? What role is played by NEC's core technologies programme? How does NEC's R&D network operate? How has the company's research and development been globalized?

How has NEC extended its competences through R&D, in the process developing new competences? This question is tackled next through a case-study of NEC's development of its automated fingerprint identification system (AFIS), which has captured about 60 per cent of the world market. The role of the company's vision and forms of organization in shaping the evolution of its AFIS is examined.

What has been the effect of NEC's selection environment on the company's evolution? This question is analysed in the final section. What impact has NEC's relationship with the Ministry of Communications and then NTT had? How important have been NEC's sales to organs of the Japanese government (including NTT), to the private sector in Japan, and to overseas markets? What do these sales reveal about NEC's international competitiveness? How important has the Japanese government generally been for NEC's evolution and growth? What role has been played in NEC's evolution by product market competition in Japan, by the company's corporate governance structure, by its strategic alliances with other companies, and by its globalization? These questions are analysed in this section.

How 'successful' has NEC been relative to other Japanese companies and globally? This question is taken up in the concluding chapter along with an analysis of the performance of the major Japanese IC companies and some of their main Western counterparts.

Introduction

In the last three chapters, the evolution of entire industries has been analysed by focusing on the way in which the firms that make up the industry have dealt with its specific products, technologies, and markets. In this chapter, the evolution of the individual firm becomes the unit of analysis. This allows a more detailed analysis of the inner workings of the firm than has been possible so far. More specifically, the *interdependence* and *co-evolution* of the four key dimensions that comprise the firm are examined: its vision, competences, organization, and selection environment. The focus on the individual firm, furthermore, requires taking into account how the firm deals simultaneously with the many products, markets, and technologies with which it is involved.

Why NEC? NEC is one of the key firms in the Japanese information and communications (IC) industry. The evolution of NEC is intimately bound up with the evolution of the Japanese IC industry. In the early 1990s, NEC was the only firm in the world to be in the top five in terms of sales in the three key parts of the global IC industry: computers, telecommunications equipment, and semiconductors. NEC is the largest Japanese telecommunications equipment firm; it dominates the Japanese personal computer market; until 1993 (when it was replaced by Intel) it was the largest semiconductor producer in the world; it is the largest producer of microcontrollers in the world.

How are NEC's achievements to be explained? What theory of the firm is needed for this purpose? In dealing with these questions, it is necessary to acknowledge that NEC shares many of the 'Japanese' characteristics (J-Firm characteristics) of other firms, such as Oki, which was founded at around the same time as NEC, was also a major supplier to NTT, and was a part of the same IC industry. These characteristics include the lifetime employment system and the rank hierarchy of employees that goes with it; relationship with Japanese banks; relationship with suppliers; etc. Yet it was NEC, rather than Oki, which went on to achieve top rankings. Why?

The answer requires an analysis of the interdependence and co-evolution of the firm's vision, competences, organization, and selection environment. These four dimensions are highly interdependent, and they co-evolve. For example, while NEC's vision was both shaped and constrained by its competences and organization, it was this vision that influenced the new competences and forms of organization which at particular junctures the company developed. Furthermore, although NEC's selection environment 'objectively' constrained what the company could do, the evidence in this chapter stresses the importance of NEC's *beliefs* about its environment. It was these beliefs that shaped the company's vision.

Examples of such co-evolution and interdependence, analysed in detail in this chapter, include NEC's diversification into competence-related areas such as radio communications, vacuum tubes, transistors, microprocessors, personal computers, digital switches, and automated fingerprint identification systems. Special attention is paid to the evolution of NEC's internal forms of organization, particularly the way in which the company organizes its research and development. It is shown that these forms of organization were closely influenced by NEC's vision, competences, and selection environment. The analysis of NEC's selection environment shows similar interdependence and co-evolution.

Background

Not only is NEC Japan's foremost telecommunications equipment company, it is also frequently held up as one of the world's most successful companies in the information industry.[1] In 1990, for example, *Business Week* titled a leading article 'Why NEC has US companies "shaking in their boots"'. The subtitle was 'The electronics giant [i.e. NEC] is fully integrated and positioning itself to take on IBM and AT&T.' In a 1990 article in *Harvard Business Review* that was to have a remarkable impact on those concerned with the analysis and practice of corporate strategy, Prahalad and Hamel began with NEC as a leading example of a company to emulate.[2] Until the early 1990s, NEC was the only company in the world to be in the top five in the three core areas in the information industry—computers, telecommunications equipment, and semiconductors.

This chapter deals with two major questions: (1) How is NEC's growth in

---

[1] This chapter is based primarily on a large number of interviews with many senior NEC executives, conducted by the author over a period of eight years. Particular mention must be made of several interviews with Dr Koji Kobayashi, who was then Chairman Emeritus of NEC. Dr Kobayashi has left his legacy in the form of a number of important books which are frequently quoted in this chapter. Extensive use has also been made of secondary sources on NEC, which are cited in the following footnotes.

[2] C. K. Prahalad and G. Hamel, 'The Core Competence of the Corporation', *Harvard Business Review*, May–June, 79–91.

these three core areas to be explained? (2) How successful is NEC? Both questions are far more complex than might at first sight appear. While many have described NEC's growth, few have explained why and how NEC came to achieve the position it enjoys in the 1990s. To provide one illustration of the complexity we are dealing with, NEC may be compared with Oki, another Japanese telecommunications company. Both NEC and Oki were founded in the late nineteenth century, and both companies were major suppliers of telecommunications equipment to the Ministry of Communications and later NTT. Both companies used 'Japanese' management and manufacturing practices. Yet it was NEC rather than Oki that became a leading international company. Why NEC?

Regarding the second question, it is necessary to challenge the assumption made by Prahalad and Hamel and others that a position in the world's top five in the three core areas of the information industry is sufficient for NEC to qualify as 'highly successful'. In the concluding chapter, NEC's performance is examined in more detail along with similar Japanese and Western companies.

NEC Today

NEC's main activities in computers, telecommunications equipment, and semiconductors are listed in Table 6.1, which also provides details on the relative importance of these three core areas for NEC and on the company's seventeen main product categories. As can be seen, communications systems and equipment accounted for 27 per cent of NEC's sales in 1993, down from 30 per cent in 1987. The five main product categories in this area are: digital switching systems; fibre optic and radio transmission systems; space electronics; mobile communications systems; and customer premises equipment.

Computers and industrial electronic systems were responsible for 51 per cent of NEC's 1993 sales, up from 43 per cent in 1987. The six product categories here are: supercomputers, mainframe computers, small business computers; personal computers; engineering workstations; and value-added network (VAN) information services.

In 1993, 17 per cent of NEC's sales were in Electron devices, down from 18 per cent in 1987. The five main product categories are: VLSI (very large scale integration) memories; microcomputers; ASICs (application specific integrated circuits); other semiconductors; and electronic components.

Although far smaller in consumer electronics than the Japanese specialist consumer electronics companies such as Matsushita, Sony, and Sharp, and the mixed Japanese companies with large consumer products divisions like Hitachi and Toshiba, NEC also produces consumer products. This area, together with the company's other operations, accounted for 5 per cent of sales in 1993, down from 9 per cent in 1987.

Table 6.1 *NEC's Products, 1987 and 1993*

Category	% of sales	
	1987	1993
I *Communications systems and equipment*	30	27
1. Digital switching systems		
2. Fibre optic and radio transmission systems		
3. Space electronics		
4. Mobile communications systems		
5. Customer premises equipment		
II *Computers and industrial electronic systems*	43	51
6. Supercomputers		
7. Mainframe computers		
8. Small business computers		
9. Personal computers		
10. Engineering workstations		
11. VAN information systems		
III *Electron devices*	18	17
12. VLSI memories		
13. Microcomputers		
14. ASICs		
15. Other conductors		
16. Electronic components		
IV *Consumer electronics and other operations*	9	5

Source: NEC's Annual Reports

The Evolution of NEC's Competences

How is NEC's relative international position in these areas to be explained?

At the heart of the explanation are the competences that the company has accumulated over the years. NEC's relative international position requires an explanation of the ways in which the company was able to accumulate these competences. The first step towards such an explanation requires a description of their evolution, a summary account of which is provided in Fig. 6.1.

The first products that NEC produced were telephones, telephone equipment, and switchboards, made primarily with Western Electric's technology. However, as Fig. 6.1 shows, it was the field of radio communications that was to provide NEC with its most important founding competence. On the basis of competences first accumulated in the radio area in the 1920s, by the 1950s and 1960s NEC was able to move into neighbouring areas such as transistors, electronic telecommunications switches, transistorized computers, and satellite communications. How did this process of competence accumulation occur?

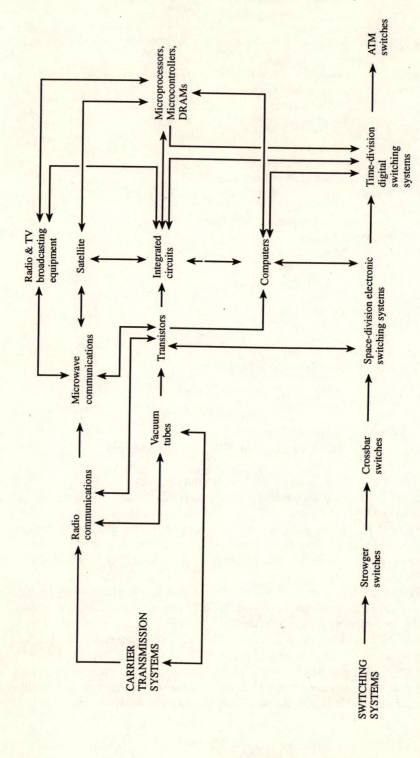

Fig. 6.1 The evolution of NEC's competences

Radio Communications

In the field of radio communications, significant efforts were made in Japan to modify and adapt imported technology and equipment in order to develop infrastructure that would be suited to the country's circumstances. As early as 1905, for example, the laboratories of the Ministry of Communications were involved in the development of indigenous wireless telegraph equipment. From the early 1920s, radio communications received a great boost when the Ministry embarked on a radio broadcasting programme.

Immediately after the great earthquake in 1923, the Japanese government passed laws regulating radio broadcasting. In 1924 Radio Japan was established, beginning operations in 1925 as the country's first broadcasting organization using radio equipment imported by NEC from Western Electric. In a 1926 reorganization Radio Japan was transformed into Nippon Hoso Kyokai (NHK).

At this stage in the transmissions field, NEC was focused primarily on the production of cable-based communications systems. The advent of radio broadcasting, however, the priority given by the Ministry of Communications to this medium, and the public investment that was to be committed to this area persuaded NEC's Japanese leaders Iwadare and Oi to diversify from cable into radio communications. The competences that had already been accumulated in cable communications facilitated to some extent the move into radio communications. In 1924 NEC established a small radio research unit in its Engineering Department. In 1930 it manufactured its first radio broadcasting transmitter, which was delivered to an NHK radio station in Okayama.

In 1935 NEC took the next major step in deepening its competences in radio when it began research on microwave communications. The accumulation of competences in microwave communications was to have a major impact on NEC's fortunes, since, as we shall see, it was in this area that the company established its first significant international competitiveness. Microwave communications remain a crucial competence to this day in areas such as land-based, satellite, and mobile communications. NEC's growing competences in communication transmissions soon became more important to the company than its capabilities in telephone equipment. By 1937, sales of radio equipment and carrier transmission equipment exceeded those of telephone equipment.

By the late 1930s two important, and related, events occurred that were significantly to deepen NEC's competences in radio and microwave communications. The first was the weakening of the technological ties between NEC and Western Electric, occasioned, as we saw in Chapter 2, by the growing nationalism expressed by the Japanese government. This forced NEC to strengthen its competences in all those areas in which it depended on Western Electric for technology, including radio. The second event was the rapidly growing demand by the Japanese military for radio-related military equipment such as radio and radar systems, radio locators, and acoustic equipment including echo-sounders and signal detectors.

In July 1939 NEC expanded its radio research unit into an independent research laboratory first located in the Tamagawa plant and in 1941 removed to a suburb of Tokyo. In addition, several radio development laboratories were established in some of the plants. By the late 1930s, some 40 per cent of the company's sales were to the military. By the end of the war this increased to 97 per cent.

Accumulating Competences: From Radio to Vacuum Tubes

The competences that NEC had begun acquiring in the radio area were to serve as a springboard for the accumulation of further competences in the related area of vacuum tubes. The decision to move into vacuum tubes, and afterwards into transistors, was to be crucial for the development of NEC, laying the foundations for the company's later attainment of its place at the top of the world semiconductor industry.

In the 1930s the production of vacuum tubes in Japan was dominated by the Tokyo Electric Company. This company, established originally in 1890, was to merge with the heavy engineering company, Shibaura Engineering (established in 1904). In 1978 the merged company was to be renamed the Toshiba Corporation ('To' from Tokyo Electric and 'shiba' from Shibaura). Tokyo Electric had a crucial technology agreement with General Electric from 1903, and by the 1930s had established a commanding presence in the Japanese markets for radio equipment and vacuum tubes and in several other areas such as light bulbs.

Within NEC in the 1930s there was growing pressure, coming primarily from technical leaders, to both widen and deepen the company's technological competences. There were mixed motives behind this pressure. On the one hand, there was the desire on the part of NEC's engineers, increasingly mastering the company's mainly imported technologies, to take up the challenge and extend the range of their experience and knowledge. On the other hand, these desires for more exciting learning opportunities intermingled with the nationalistic ideology of the day which decidedly favoured decreasing technological dependence on foreign companies.

In NEC a leading engineer who embodied both these motives was Yasujiro Niwa. He joined the company in 1924, having worked previously in the laboratories of the Ministry of Communications (further underscoring the point made earlier in this book regarding the important synergistic technological linkages that existed between the Ministry's engineering and research departments and the emerging telecommunications companies). In 1927 Niwa became head of NEC's Engineering Department. He fervently believed in the desirability, for both corporate and nationalistic reasons, of NEC widening and deepening its competences. One of the important organizational reforms that he introduced into the company, in pursuit of these beliefs, was the introduction of factory-level R&D, breaking with the inherited Western Electric tradition of confining research and development to specialist, separated laboratories. For Niwa, R&D ought to be pursued in both locations.

Under Niwa's leadership, pressure grew within NEC for a diversification into vacuum tubes. There were a number of strong arguments in favour of such a move. First, vacuum tubes, central not only in radio communications but increasingly also in other telecommunications equipment, could justifiably be regarded as a strategic core technology. It could reasonably be argued that as such it would be unwise to depend on external sources for this technology, particularly where a competing company—in this case Tokyo Electric—provided the technology. Secondly, the further argument could be added that by controlling vacuum tube technology itself NEC could not only ensure that this crucial input met the quality and reliability standards that its products required, but would also, through its research and development, be in a better position to shape the future development of this and related technologies. In this way NEC would be able to internalize the benefits arising from the synergistic development of vacuum tubes and the equipment using them.

Despite these persuasive arguments, however, NEC's leadership for a long time opposed diversification into vacuum tubes. Opposition came not only from the International Standard Electric Corporation (which inherited Western Electric's interests in NEC in 1925 when ITT was established, and which according to a 1932 agreement held 50 per cent of NEC's shares), but also from Sumitomo Honsha, which by this agreement increased its shareholding in NEC from 5 to 14 per cent. The reason for the opposition was the belief that NEC would not be able to accumulate the competences in the field of vacuum tubes that would allow it to compete successfully with Tokyo Electric. Accordingly, it was felt that NEC should continue to depend on this sophisticated supplier.

Opposition to the diversification, however, ceased some time after Fumio Shida became managing director of NEC in 1932. Shida, who, significantly, had been chief engineer of Sumitomo Densen Seizosho (the electrical cable manufacturing company of the Sumitomo *zaibatsu*), was eventually persuaded by Niwa's arguments. In this way, NEC moved into vacuum tubes.

In passing, it is worth observing—and we will return to this point later in this chapter—that the explanation of the evolution of competences cannot be separated from the analysis of 'vision' and the changing beliefs that underlie it. The extension of NEC's competences from radio-based communications into vacuum tubes, an extension that was to play an important role in the company's later ability to establish itself among the top five firms in the three crucial information areas, depended crucially on the new-found belief in NEC's ability to achieve competitiveness in vacuum tubes. This changing belief structure was the outcome of significantly conflicting views within NEC.

NEC's First Significant International Competitiveness: Microwave Communications

By the early 1930s, very few significant indigenous innovations had been made by Japanese engineers in NEC. A similar situation existed in the other Japanese electrical and telecommunications-related companies which also depended heavily on foreign technology. Indeed, Koji Kobayashi, a former chairman of NEC who was a young engineer in the company in the early 1930s, could identify only two 'technological breakthroughs' made up to this time by the company's Japanese engineers. These were a remote supervisory control system, and phototelegraph equipment, developed by Chief Engineer Niwa, which was used to transmit photographs to Tokyo of the ceremony in Kyoto at which Emperor Hirohito acceded to the throne.

Kobayashi recalls that, when a colleague asked his supervisor in NEC whether he could attempt to enlarge a three-channel carrier telephone system developed by Western Electric into a four-channel system, he was told: 'It is [too] risky to try something Western Electric hasn't already done.' Kobayashi remembers that 'We young engineers were far from happy with this situation', and he admits that he too 'was dissatisfied with NEC'.[3]

In the area of microwave communications, this situation was to change rapidly. In 1935, under the twin stimulations of decreasing technological dependence on Western Electric and increasing efforts made by the Ministry of Communications to deepen Japanese technical competences, NEC began its own research on microwave communications systems. While Japanese competences in microwave communications were to be further stimulated by the military demands of the war period, postwar reconstruction was to provide an additional boost. To some extent this was the result of the peculiarities of Japan's geography. According to one account, 'More than 80 percent of [Japan's] land consists of mountainous terrain, so the laying of cables is expensive and, moreover, installation is difficult and time-consuming. Given these factors, microwave links appeared to be the best solution for a quickly completed nationwide communications network, and pioneering efforts were made to utilize microwave systems.'[4]

In view of the advantages of microwave communications as a transmissions medium in Japan, the Ministry of Telecommunications decided in 1950 to use microwave communications systems for nationwide telephone and television relay networks. In order to develop these networks further, the Ministry's laboratories initiated a large R&D programme which equipment-supplying companies such as NEC were invited to join. This programme, complementing the R&D efforts that were being made inside the individual companies, played an extremely important role in helping the Japanese 'system' as a whole

---

[3] K. Kobayashi, *Rising to the Challenge*, Harcourt Brace Jovanovich, Tokyo, 1989, p. 16.
[4] K. Kobayashi, 'The Past, Present, and Future of Telecommunications in Japan', *IEEE Communications Magazine*, 22/5 (1984): 97.

(comprising the Ministry and the equipment suppliers) to accumulate new competences in microwave communications.

Significant practical achievements soon followed. In 1954, for example, a large-capacity microwave relay route was opened between Tokyo, Nagoya, and Osaka. The design, development, and implementation of such systems provided the Japanese companies with important learning opportunities, and, as a result, companies such as NEC were able to make several significant innovations.

Learning opportunities, however, are best consummated on the basis of growing production and sales. The learning process in the Japanese companies was boosted by the postwar reconstruction, which involved significant public investment in improving the country's infrastructure. At the same time, fuelled by a relatively high savings rate, the Japanese economy as a whole began to grow significantly, creating further demand for the goods and services of the country's private and public companies, which in turn provided more opportunities for communications equipment suppliers like NEC. In this way demand grew in Japan for independent microwave communications networks from organizations such as Japan National Railways and the electric power companies.

Although through learning by experience the competences of the Japanese companies were both widening and deepening, they still faced formidable competition from technologically superior Western suppliers. In 1953, for example, NHK began regular television broadcasts using microwave-relay-based equipment supplied by RCA. Japanese companies had an inbuilt bias in favour of imported equipment, preferring this option to taking the risk of using Japanese equipment that had not yet been adequately tested in the market-place. Nevertheless, the size and diversity of the Japanese market created openings for Japanese equipment companies that were willing to work hard enough. Thus, although NEC was unable to convince NHK or the Osaka TV Broadcasting Company to buy its broadcasting equipment, it was eventually able to persuade the smaller Chubu Nippon Broadcasting Company.

Informal personal networks could also, on occasion, be used by Japanese equipment companies once they had accumulated sufficiently competitive competences. NEC was particularly well placed in this connection as a result of its history as the largest supplier to the Ministry of Communications before the war and to NTT after 1952. NEC's link with Takeshi Kajii, the first president of NTT, illustrates this. Until 1938 Kajii was director of the Installation Bureau of the Ministry of Communications. In that year he became managing director of NEC and in 1943 became the company's president. In 1952 he became the first president of NTT.

Shortly afterwards, NTT decided to install a microwave circuit linking Tokyo and Fukuoka. NTT contemplated using a microwave system developed by the British company, Standard Telephones and Cables (STC). Hearing this, NEC mobilized its personal network. Koji Kobayashi, later to become chairman of NEC, tells the story.

The president of NTT at the time was former NEC president Takeshi Kajii. We asked him to give domestic makers a chance. He compromised by first having a domestically produced system installed between Tokyo and Osaka and then putting in an imported system between Osaka and Fukuoka. The Tokyo–Osaka circuit using NEC products was in operation two years ahead of the Osaka–Fukuoka link, to the great credit of supporters of domestic production.[5]

Supplying the Supplier—NEC Sells to ITT

There was no better indicator of NEC's growing technological maturity and increasing international competitiveness than its sale of technology to its erstwhile principal supplier of technology, ITT. In January 1962 the breakthrough came, with NEC supplying both over-the-horizon microwave communications systems and carrier transmission equipment to ITT. NEC's increasing technological strength also allowed it to loosen the restrictions that Western Electric and ITT had placed, as a condition of their sale of technology, on NEC's exports to third markets. This facilitated NEC's attempts to increase company growth by expanding into foreign markets. Here developing countries were particularly important, since the major industrialized countries tended to have their own equipment suppliers who monopolized these markets. NEC's first major export drive to developing countries began in the mid-1960s, with microwave communications systems which the company considered its most internationally competitive product.

By the late 1960s NEC was able to claim to be 'the world's leading exporter of microwave communications systems', winning orders in countries like Mexico, Brazil, India, Iran, and Australia.[6] Support for this claim came in 1968 when NEC won an important order for a microwave communications network linking US military radar stations between the USA's bases in the Kanto area around Tokyo. According to Koji Kobayashi, 'In the final analysis, the reason why we won the contract was that only we, NEC, had the technology that met US military requirements.'[7] In 1971, underscoring its success in this area, NEC supplied AT&T's New York telephone operating subsidiary with the USA's first digital microwave radio system.

From Terrestrial Microwave Systems to Satellite

The competences and knowledge-base that NEC had accumulated in microwave communications were to serve as a springboard for the company's entry into a completely different market and set of products, namely satellite communications.

[5] K. Kobayashi, *The Rise of NEC: How the World's Greatest C&C Company is Managed*, Blackwell, Oxford, 1991, p. 29.
[6] Ibid.
[7] Ibid. 60.

The knowledge that NEC had acquired in researching, developing, and producing over-the-horizon microwave communications systems was applied, with suitable modification and extension, in the first instance to base stations for satellite communications. Accordingly, what at the product and market levels looked like a discontinuous jump was, at the level of the underlying knowledge, a smoother extension into a closely related field.

NEC's move into the satellite area was prompted by a visit by Koji Kobayashi, then senior executive vice president of the company, to Hughes Aircraft, with which NEC already had business links. Lawrence A. Hyland, vice president of Hughes, proposed a strategic alliance to Kobayashi. This alliance would benefit from the complementarity of the knowledge-bases of the two companies, NEC's in microwave communications and Hughes's in satellites, an extension of the latter company's involvement in aircraft. This resulted in an announcement in August 1964 that the two companies would begin the joint development of a satellite communications system. This was the same month that the International Telecommunications Satellite Organization, INTELSAT, was established, a consortium to develop a global satellite communications system. In December 1965, NEC and Hughes succeeded in developing a system that allowed ground stations to communicate with one another via satellite at any time. Shortly afterwards, NEC became the world's biggest supplier of INTELSAT Standard A earth stations.

In May of the same year, NEC consolidated the space-related research that was being undertaken in its Communications Research Laboratory and its Radio Division into a new laboratory, the Aeronautics and Space Development Laboratory. In June 1967 this laboratory became the Space Development Division, a fully fledged and relatively independent operating division within the company. While NEC's efforts began in base stations, the company soon moved into electronic equipment used in the satellite itself. This included a joint effort with Hughes which resulted in the development of transponders for communications satellites.

In 1969 Japan's National Space Development Agency (NASDA) was established, and NEC and Hughes won their first contract for a weather satellite. However, although NEC was keen also to win the contracts for communications and broadcasting satellites, these went to Mitubishi Electric and Toshiba. Nevertheless, NEC's position in the satellite market was secured. By 1982 the company had received orders for 545 base stations from 73 countries.

Looking back, Koji Kobayashi has traced the origins of NEC's evolving competences in satellite communications:

NEC's timely entrance into the field of satellite communications was undeniably aided by several pieces of good luck, such as our relationship with Hughes Aircraft and the timing of the Tokyo Olympics; but the main reason for our success was that NEC already possessed the world's most advanced technology in the area of radio communications. Any detailed account of microwave communications technology at NEC would have to trace its development back to the war years and the immediate postwar period, but it would be safe to say that it had been primarily fostered during the construction of television relay lines throughout Japan in the 1950s.[8]

Mobile Communications

NEC's accumulated knowledge in radio and microwave communications was also extended into the field of mobile communications, currently one of the fastest-growing areas in telecommunications. In 1979 NTT began Japan's first commercial mobile communications service. NEC has since become a major international player in all four of the basic components of cellular mobile communications systems: mobile telephone switches (which switch calls between cells and between the mobile and public switched networks), base stations or cell sites (which, under the control of the mobile telephone switch, manages the radio channels at the site), the system interconnections, and the mobile phones.

From Vacuum Tubes to Transistors to Integrated Circuits

While there was a significant degree of continuity of knowledge (both know-how and know-why) in NEC's move from microwave communications to satellite communications, the move from vacuum tubes to transistors was far more discontinuous. However, the move from transistors, first to integrated circuits and then to large and very large-scale integration, was smoother.

Transistor technology diffused rapidly to Japan, aided on the one hand by the regulations governing AT&T, which prevented the company from turning the transistor into proprietary technology and appropriating maximum returns from it, and on the other by the high level of technical competence that had been attained in the Japanese electronics companies. This competence owed a good deal to the quality of engineering graduates turned out by the country's leading universities to government research laboratories. A flavour of the response in the Electrotechnical Laboratories of the Ministry of International Trade and Industry (MITI) to the invention of the transistor (and of the degree of interaction that existed at this stage between competing Japanese companies) is given by Makoto Kikuchi who was there at the time:

[Around 1950 in the US] there was already a mountain of information accumulating about transistors. . . . On countless occasions, the center director, Sakuji Komagata, would get together with my boss, Dr George Michio Hatoyama, with Dr Kubo from the University of Tokyo and researchers from NEC, Toshiba and other companies, to 'decode' this material.[9]

Soon Toshiba, Hitachi, and Mitsubishi Electric entered into an umbrella agree-

---

[8] Ibid. 28.
[9] M. Kikuchi, *Japanese Electronics: A Worm's Eye View of its Evolution*, Simul, Tokyo, 1983, p. 27.

ment with RCA purchasing transistor technology in return for royalties on all transistor-based products sold in Japan. In 1953, despite strong initial opposition from MITI (which controlled imports of technology through its control of foreign exchange allocations), Sony signed an agreement with Western Electric for transistor technology.[10]

In NEC, unlike in the case of its earlier entry into vacuum tubes, there was immediate consensus regarding the necessity for the company to accumulate competences in the new technology in view of the impact that the transistor was bound to make. However, there was internal dissention regarding both the timing of entry into transistors and the most appropriate way of acquiring the necessary competences. One reason was the substantial investment that had already been made in vacuum tubes. As Koji Kobayashi noted, 'at NEC there was serious hesitation about immediately beginning the mass production of transistors. NEC had already been manufacturing vacuum tubes.'[11] Another reason was disagreement over whether NEC should develop its own technology or, like the other major electronics companies, import the technology. According to Kobayashi,

Opinions at NEC were divided and the company was vacillating about the course we should take. Some felt we should develop transistors based on our own original technology, and our research people seemed quite confident of success. Although I couldn't fully agree with them, it was a new technology and I didn't have the confidence to voice a strong opinion of my own.[12]

Eventually, with MITI pressing NEC regarding its decision, the company decided on a technology agreement with General Electric which was agreed in December 1958, some five years after Sony's agreement with Western Electric.

Despite the slow move into transistors, NEC was to derive unforeseen benefits from the competences that it had previously accumulated in microwave communications. For its microwave systems, NEC had been involved in research and development on silicon diodes. While at this stage the other Japanese companies were using germanium for their transistors, NEC decided to change to silicon, becoming the first Japanese company to do so. The reason was that silicon could be used at higher temperatures and was a more reliable material than germanium, important characteristics for NEC, which was primarily a telecommunications equipment company. In the event, silicon was to become the material of choice for most semiconductors, even outperforming later materials that at one stage were thought to be preferable to silicon, such as

---

[10] Sony's acquisition of transistor technology is discussed in the following publications: *Genryu: Sony Challenges 1946–1968*, Sony, Tokyo, 1986, and A. Morita, *Made in Japan: Akio Morita and Sony*, Weatherhill, Tokyo, 1987.

[11] K. Kobayashi, *Computers and Communications: A Vision of C&C*, MIT Press, Cambridge, Mass., 1988, p. 32. NEC's move into transistors is also referred to in K. Kobayashi, 'The Making of NEC's Postwar Strategies', *JETS Papers*, no. 1, Institute for Japanese–European Technology Studies, University of Edinburgh, 1990.

[12] Kobayashi, *Rising to the Challenge*, 50.

gallium arsenide. By 1961 NEC's semiconductor output exceeded its vacuum tube production.

In 1960 NEC, utilizing the knowledge it had accumulated in the field of transistors, began the development of integrated circuits. In 1970 NEC began selling semiconductors to outside companies and in 1972 it developed Japan's first microprocessor. In 1974, just after the first oil shock, NEC, with support from its main banks, made the difficult decision to substantially increase its investment in semiconductors, despite the deepening recession which led its main rivals to decrease their investment. In 1984 NEC was rewarded for this decision by becoming the largest producer of semiconductors in the world, a position it held until 1993 when it was displaced by Intel.

From Integrated Circuits to Personal Computers[13]

One of the most important features distinguishing NEC from other companies in the information industry is the role played in NEC by personal computers (PCs). By 1990 NEC was the fourth biggest producer of PCs in the world. Its share of the world market was 5.7 per cent, compared to 12.9 per cent for IBM, 7.2 per cent for Apple, and 6.4 per cent for Commodore. Toshiba, the next Japanese company, came sixth with 3.1 per cent.

NEC holds a commanding share of the Japanese PC market, even though from the beginning of 1993 low-cost producers such as Compaq and Dell were starting to challenge NEC in the Japanese market on the basis of low prices. As shown in Fig. 6.2, in 1992 NEC sold no less than 53.4 per cent of the total number of PCs shipped in Japan, although this figure has since declined. This compared

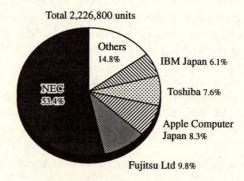

Fig. 6.2 PC shipments in Japan, 1992
Source: *Dataquest.*

---

[13] This subsection is based on the author's several interviews with staff in NEC who were closely involved in the evolution of the PC business in the company.

with 9.8 per cent for Fujitsu, the biggest computer company in Japan, 8.3 per cent for Apple, 7.6 per cent for Toshiba, and 6.1 per cent for IBM Japan. By the early 1990s PCs accounted for more than 10 per cent of NEC's consolidated sales.

NEC's success raises a number of important questions, including the following: How did NEC manage to establish such a strong position in PCs? Why is it that, although Hitachi brought its first PC to market before NEC, it was NEC that very quickly established a dominant position? How does NEC compare with IBM regarding the way in which they entered the PC market?

NEC's PC Story

NEC's PC story is important for a number of reasons. First, it illustrates very well how a company can extend existing knowledge into new areas, in the process creating entirely new knowledge and competences embodying the whole value chain. At the same time, the story underlines the value of analysing a firm as a bundle of competences, rather than as a bundle of products, a point made implicitly throughout this chapter.

Secondly, NEC's PC story illustrates important differences between NEC on the one hand and IBM and the main IBM-compatible Japanese computer companies, Fujitsu and Hitachi, on the other. The different composition of the computer output of NEC, Fujitsu, and Hitachi is shown in Fig. 6.3. We can see that, while sales of mainframe computers constituted about half of the computer sales of Fujitsu and Hitachi in 1991, they made up just over 30 per cent for NEC. On the other hand, PCs accounted for just under 50 per cent of NEC's computer sales, about 10 per cent of Fujitsu's sales, and only a negligible amount of

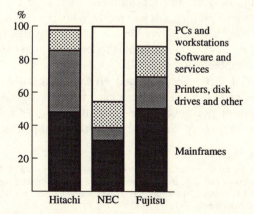

Fig. 6.3 Computer sales, NEC, Fujitsu, and Hitachi, year ending 31 March 1991
Source: *The Economist*, 11 January 1992, p. 68.

Hitachi's. In 1992/3, of NEC's total computer sales of $16.9 billion, PCs accounted for 41 per cent, mainframes for 29 per cent, office computers for 15 per cent, and workstations for 12 per cent.[14]

The Difference between NEC and IBM

The third reason for the importance of the NEC PC story is that it illustrates the significant differences that existed between NEC and IBM. While NEC's PC story will be related shortly, it is worth first outlining the major differences between the two companies in the case of PCs.[15]

Although NEC is also an important producer of mainframes (and, unlike IBM, of supercomputers), the 'mainframe lobby' was never able to rule the roost in NEC the way it did in IBM. There are several reasons for this. To begin with, as we have seen, NEC was primarily a telecommunications company, although computers and industrial electronics systems are now more important in terms of revenue. NEC is also an important producer of semiconductors. Furthermore, from the early 1980s PCs achieved a growing prominence in the company. The importance of all these interests has meant that NEC has never been unduly swayed by 'sectional' interests.

In IBM's case, the decision to introduce PCs was made from the top of the centralized company. Although Frank Carey, IBM's chairman, had long been convinced of the importance of smaller computers for the company—a conviction that underlay his leading IBM into minicomputers in the late 1960s—the company was rather slow to move into PCs. It was only after the growing market for PCs in the USA convinced IBM that it was missing an important opportunity that the decision was finally taken to produce an IBM PC. In the event, the PC was finally marketed in October 1981.

In NEC, as will shortly be documented, the entry into PCs came 'from below' in a more organic, flexible, and decentralized way, even though this mode of entry presented its own problems. It was partly in order to overcome the tardiness of a centralized, bureaucratized decision-making process that IBM in December 1991 announced its fragmentation into a 'federation' of relatively autonomous business and geographic units, which included a PC unit.

A further crucial difference was that NEC, unlike IBM, kept within the company the core competences and associated property rights necessary for the research, development, production, marketing, and sale of PCs. IBM, on the other hand, subcontracted two of the most important components—the operating

---

[14] Of the company's total semiconductor sales of $5.4 billion, dynamic random access memories (DRAMs) were responsible for 28%, microcontrollers for 22%, custom ICs for 20%, LSIs for 14%, and others for 16%. NEC's total telecommunications equipment sales in this financial year were $8.7 bn. (*Nikkei Weekly*, 1 November 1993).

[15] An informative recent account of IBM, on which the present section draws, is C. H. Ferguson and C. R. Morris, *Computer Wars: How the West Can Win in a Post-IBM World*, Times Books, New York, 1993.

system and the microprocessor—to outside companies. This, probably the most costly decision IBM ever made, gave birth to two major competitors, Microsoft and Intel, and, by indirectly reinforcing the power of the mainframe lobby in IBM, hastened the demise of the company. NEC ensured that these components came from within its own company. In part, NEC's different decision was the result of the history of the evolution of its PC, as we shall shortly see, but it was also a reflection of the company's philosophy, which always emphasized the importance of possessing in-house the crucial competences and property rights in the area of computers and communications.

Semiconductors: NEC's Springboard into PCs

It is the microprocessor, the 'computer on a chip', that lies at the heart of the structural changes that are sweeping the computer industry. The first microprocessor, the i4004, was produced by the American semiconductor company Intel in November 1971. Six months later, in April 1972, NEC made Japan's first domestically produced microprocessor. In 1973 the company began outside sales of microprocessors (something that IBM commited itself to doing in only 1993). In order to facilitate sales, NEC created the Microcomputer Sales Department in its Semiconductor and IC Sales Division in February 1976.

A major difficulty that faced the sale of microprocessors, however, was the unfamiliarity of potential users—mainly engineers and others with a technical background—with this kind of device. In order to help 'educate' its new potential customers, NEC created a training kit, the TK-80, which allowed the user to assemble the microprocessor. As the TK-80 gained in popularity, NEC opened a salesroom in Akihabara—Tokyo's popular electronics area—selling electronic devices. The salesroom was called the Bit-Inn. Soon enthusiasts flocked to the Bit-Inn, and over the weekends NEC engineers from the Semiconductor Division frequently went to the store to provide advice and assistance.

From their interaction with their new-found customers, the Semiconductor Division realized that what they really wanted was their own computers with software tailored to their own applications. This led to the development of NEC's first PC, the PC-8001, marketed in May 1979. Entire control over the PC-8001, from development through to marketing and sales, was given to the Electronic Components Group, and in April 1981, with sales far exceeding initial expectations, the Personal Computer Division was established in this group.

The manufacture of the PC-8001, however, was subcontracted to NEC's wholly owned subsidiary, NEC Home Electronics, to take advantage of its mass-production capabilities and in the belief that the PC would eventually become an item of home consumption. NEC Home Electronics then went on to develop its own PC, the PC-6000, intended specifically for the home and, like the PC-8001, an 8-bit machine. Sales of the PC-6000 series began in 1981.

When NEC's PCs began to attract a business market, a third part of the company, the Information Processing Group, which dealt mainly with larger computers, also became interested in PCs. In October 1982 it marketed its first PC, the 16-bit PC-9800 series, intended largely for the business market. The PC-9800 series was also manufactured by NEC Home Electronics and the microprocessors were supplied by the Electronic Components Group. It was this PC series that eventually took off and dominated the Japanese PC market.

This meant that three different parts of NEC had entered the PC business and were, to some extent, competing with one another, revealing the extent of the decentralization of decision-making in the company. With each of the three concerned with the performance of its own unit, however, significant conflicts of interest emerged. The decentralized nature of the company presented problems because no one had overall responsibility for PCs; for example, the Information Processing Group complained it was not getting the co-operation it required from the Electronic Components Group relating to the microprocessors for the PC-9800 series. In order to cope with these increasingly serious conflicts, a vice president was appointed to deal with the matter. This resulted in a Personal Computer subgroup being established in 1983 in the Special Projects Group, which acted as a single marketing channel for the three PC series. In the 1991 reorganization (discussed below), all personal computing was moved to the newly created Personal C&C Group.

Although NEC's first PC, the PC-8001, was introduced in 1979, Hitachi had introduced the first Japanese PC in 1978. Also in 1979 Sharp had introduced its first PC. How did NEC's PC come to dominate the Japanese market so overwhelmingly? There were several reasons. The first is that NEC's Semiconductor Division was prepared to confront uncertainty and 'take the plunge', introducing a completely new product, albeit one based on knowledge that the division had already accumulated in microprocessors.

Secondly, NEC was innovative enough to foresee the need for a completely new set of marketing channels. This underlines the point that a company's competence involves the *entire* value chain, including marketing and sales, and not only the technological ability to research, develop, and manufacture. The Bit-Inn, similar to the new outlets created by the fledgling computer companies in the USA, brought NEC into contact with a new kind of customer with new requirements. At the same time, this provided the feedback flow that the company needed to further improve its PC.

In order to consolidate this kind of innovative marketing channel, NEC persuaded many of its semiconductor dealers to open new sales outlets called the NEC Microcomputer Shop, referred to as the Micom Shop. The first one was opened in Hiroshima in 1978, a year before NEC's first PC was marketed, to sell the microprocessor self-assembly set, the TK-80. These Micom Shops, it must be stressed, represented a new concept in marketing for both NEC and its semiconductor clients, differing from the existing computer, communications, and home electronics outlets. The Micom Shops were also places where users could get expert technical advice. In 1994 some 70 per cent of NEC's sales were direct to the consumer, largely through outlets such as the Micom Shop; there were more than 300 Micom Shops in operation; and about 30 per cent of NEC's sales of PCs were through subsidiaries of NEC Home Electronics, its subsidiary.

Thirdly, NEC, helped by the sophisticated understanding of its customers' needs which it had acquired through the feedback received from these marketing channels, had the foresight to realize the central importance of *software applications*. NEC, more quickly than its rivals, understood that what its customers wanted were not PCs *per se*, but rather the ability to use PCs in particular *applications*. In other words, for most customers PCs were not an end in themselves but a means to solve application problems. NEC also understood more readily than its competitors that this implied that in order to sell its PCs it had rapidly to make available more software applications than it could provide itself. Furthermore, in order to help customers and potential customers use its PC effectively, user-friendly manuals were required.

NEC solved these problems in two main ways. Both involved enlisting the co-operation of independent but complementary firms that would assist NEC in providing value for its customers. These firms added new flexibility and opportunities for innovation to NEC's endeavours since they were independent and could respond in their own ways to the market without having to go through NEC's large-firm decision-making procedures. To improve the user's ability to use its PCs, NEC made freely available to publishers the proprietary technical information that would enable them to develop various kinds of manuals. To increase the availability of software applications, NEC provided independent software vendors with the technical details necessary for them to create new applications.

Further information is provided in Figs. 6.4 and 6.5 on the number of software vendors involved in producing applications for the PC-9800 and PC-8800 series, and the number of application software packages produced for the PC-9800 series.

In 1993, at a time when low-cost US computer companies such as Compaq, Dell, and Apple launched an attack on the Japanese PC market on the basis of low prices, NEC's defence, apart from lowering its prices considerably, consisted mainly in stressing the far greater number of Japanese-language applications that have been developed for its PCs. How effective this defence will be in the longer run, time will tell.

Fourthly, realizing the importance of software applications, NEC understood from the beginning that compatibility was needed across its different models so that the same software could be used. This meant that its customers' installed base of NEC software would help ensure loyalty to NEC's PC. This, however, was not understood as quickly by NEC's competitors, as is shown in Fig. 6.6, which examines the history of the change in PC architecture of some of the major Japanese PC companies. This figure clearly shows the architectural continuity

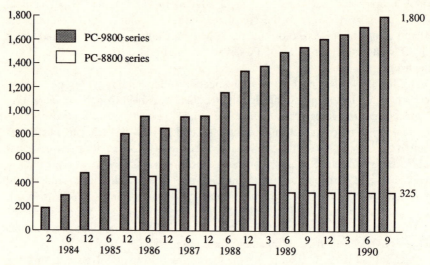

Fig. 6.4 The number of software vendors for NEC's personal computer, 1984–1990

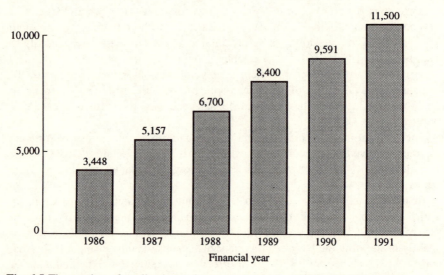

Fig. 6.5 The number of application software packages for NEC's PC-9800 series, 1986–1991

from the PC-8000 through the PC-8800 to the PC-9800 series and across the different versions of this series. The need for this continuity was recognized in NEC right from the beginning, when the Information Processing Group in developing the PC-9800 made the conscious design decision to establish software compatibility with the PC-8000 series developed earlier by the Semiconductor

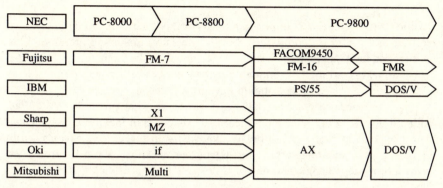

Fig. 6.6 The evolution of architecture in major Japanese PC makers

Division. The main reasons for this decision at the time were to take advantage of the 'reputation assets' that had already been accumulated by the company through customer satisfaction with the PC-8000, and to allow customers to use the software they had purchased for the PC-8000 with the PC-9800. However, the decision also had a further important advantage. It provided the architectural stability and continuity that was important for NEC's complementary collaborators, producing applications software and manuals for NEC PCs, to realize good returns from the investments they had made. Fig. 6.6 also shows the architectural discontinuities for NEC's competitors (indicated by the separated blocks).

Finally, NEC kept up with the times. For example, different NEC PCs use the major operating systems such as Unix, Windows, DOS, and OS/2. NEC has also differentiated its PC-9800 models including, for example, one designed specially for use in factories. In addition, the company has made use of its other competences in the computers and communications (C&C) area, for instance designing a cordless 9800 model with a radio antenna which allows it to connect with a local area network (LAN).

An important indication of the global standing of NEC's PCs is the agreement reached in September 1993 with AT&T/NCR whereby the latter will purchase NEC's IBM-compatible colour notebook personal computers and sell them under its own brand name in the USA. The reasons for NEC's strong international competitive position in notebook computers include its competences in precision manufacturing techniques, which facilitate miniaturization, and in thin-film transistor liquid crystal displays, which enable notebooks to provide high-resolution graphics without large and weighty monitors. The agreement on PCs extends an earlier strategic technological alliance which NEC's Semiconductor Group had established with AT&T's Microelectronics business unit. NEC is also the second source for AT&T's new microprocessor, the Hobbit, which will be used in AT&T's new personal communicators.

'Vision' and the Corporation

'Vision' has become a common (and overworked) term in modern parlance relating not only to companies but to decision-makers generally. Like motherhood and apple pie, 'vision' is assumed to be something good. All decision-makers, so the conventional wisdom goes, whether they be presidents of companies or of countries, should have a 'vision'.

What this parlance does not tell us, however, is what precisely 'vision' is. With a little reflection, it becomes clear that 'vision' is in fact more complicated than it appears at first sight to be. We know, for instance, that 'visions', with hindsight, are sometimes wrong, raising further questions about how they are formed, how they change, and how it is possible to detect quickly enough when they are wrong.

Digging a little deeper, we may become aware of some paradoxes relating to 'vision'. For example, a company with 'good' information may have 'bad' vision. IBM, an 'information company' *par excellence*, operated until as late as 1992 on the basis of a 'bad' vision which led it to believe that mainframes could sustain its size, profitability, and growth. This raises even more complex questions, such as the relationship between the information that a company processes and its 'vision'.

In the remaining part of this section we will examine NEC's core beliefs in greater detail.

The Evolution of NEC's Vision

In NEC's case we are extremely fortunate to have a number of excellent personal accounts of the formation of the company's vision by its main postwar architect, Dr Koji Kobayashi.[16] NEC's vision is summarized in the company's concept of 'C&C', a concept that refers to the convergence of computers and communications.

We have it on the authority of Peter Drucker, the management guru, that by July 1959, when he met him, Kobayashi 'surely already had the vision' of C&C.[17] The date is significant. In 1954 NEC, then primarily a telecommunications company, began research on computers. In 1958, with input from MITI's Electrotechnical Laboratories, NTT's Electrical Communications Laboratories,

---

[16] The discussion in this section draws heavily on personal discussions that the author has had on several occasions with Dr Kobayashi.

[17] Drucker's words are contained in the Foreword to Kobayashi, *The Rise of NEC*, p. xiii. Kobayashi himself has stated that 'Back in March 1959 I had published an article entitled "Digital Technology and the Advance of Automation" in a special edition of the Japanese journal *OHM*. In it I had argued that the introduction of digital technology would hasten the appearance of digital systems that would include electronic switching and data-processing equipment' (ibid. 122).

and Tohoku University, NEC produced its first computer, the NEAC 2201, which it claims was also the world's first fully transistorized computer.[18]

However, although there is evidence that Kobayashi was thinking about the implications of the coming convergence of computers and communications by the late 1950s, it was only in the late 1970s that he first referred publicly to his vision. The occasion was the INTELCOM'77 conference, held in Atlanta, Georgia, in 1977. In 1980 in an NEC publication Kobayashi elaborated on his vision in a diagram that has now become famous in the electronics industry, showing the evolution and gradual convergence of technologies in the areas of computers, semiconductors, switching, and transmission. This diagram is reproduced here as Fig. 6.7.

In the 1980s Kobashi reconceptualized his vision of C&C when he made an important addition: 'Human and C&C'. This addition took account of the increasing 'user friendliness' that computers and communications had achieved. It also recognized the fact that, in order to compete, electronics companies had increasingly to pay attention to the requirements of their customers, as well as improving the underlying technologies and the characteristics they provided.

Fig. 6.8 depicts in a more concrete way what the convergence of C&C in reality means.

Core Beliefs

NEC's C&C vision can be broken down into two core beliefs:

Belief 1: Convergence is occurring between computers and communications.

Belief 2: NEC must have *its own* knowledge and competences in all the core C&C areas in order to profit and grow as fast as its leaders believe it can.

These beliefs, it is important to note, are independent of one another. For example, it is possible to hold belief 1 without holding belief 2. A company, therefore, may accept that computer and communications technologies are converging while rejecting that it should possess all the core C&C knowledge and competences.

To be more specific, while NEC holds both beliefs, some of its major competitors do not. For example, although IBM for a time accepted both beliefs, which led it to purchase the telecommunications equipment company Rolm, it soon abandoned belief 2, selling Rolm to Siemens and remaining primarily a computer company. Another example is Ericsson, one of NEC's major competitors in telecommunications equipment, which appears to accept belief 1 but sold its computer interests and depends to a significant extent on outside semiconductor competences, much of which come from Texas Instruments. Of all the companies in the world, it is AT&T that is closest to NEC in its acceptance of both beliefs. Interestingly, NEC has had close ties with AT&T since NEC

---

[18] The early history of the Japanese computer companies is recounted in M. Fransman, *The Market and Beyond: Cooperation and Competition in Information Technology in the Japanese System*, Cambridge University Press, 1990, pp. 13–23.

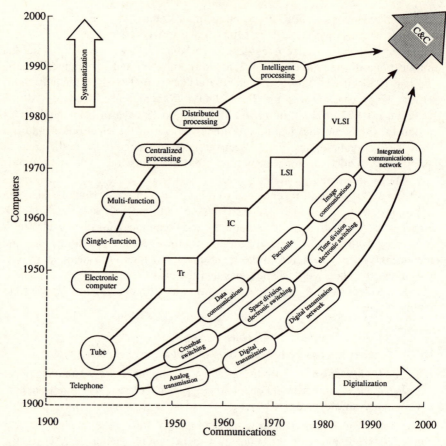

Fig. 6.7 NEC's general concept of C&C development

Source: K. Kobayashi, 'Information Society and Information Technology', *NEC Research and Development*, Special 30th Anniversary Issue, no. 96 (1990): 2.

was founded in 1899 as a joint venture with Western Electric, which was AT&T's wholly owned subsidiary.

The beliefs are also different in terms of the information on which they rest. While it may be argued that belief 1 rests on relatively complete information, this is not the case for belief 2. For example, belief 1 may be sustained by information such as that which indicates that digitization is becoming a common currency in both computers and communications switching and transmission; that switches have become computer-like; and that computers and communications increasingly depend on common technologies in fields such as semiconductors and software. However, the information that relates to belief 2 is more incomplete, leading to significant interpretive ambiguity. It is this interpretive ambiguity that has led IBM, Ericsson, and other companies to beliefs that differ significantly from NEC's second belief.

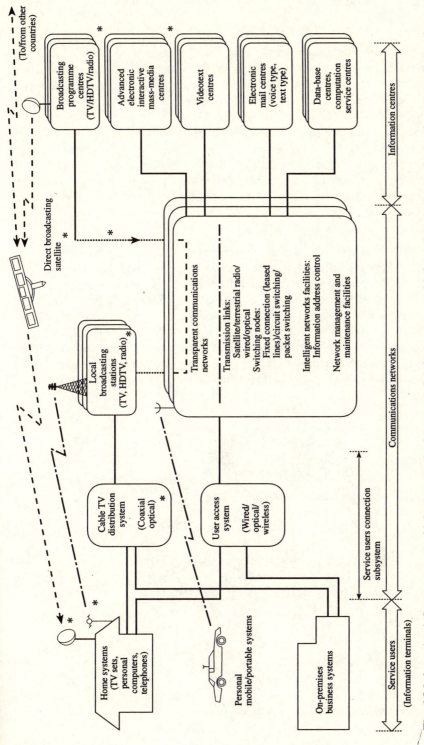

Fig. 6.8 Information infrastructures combining communications network infrastructures and information service centres, and corresponding end-user systems

Source: N. Shimasaki, 'An Overall View of the Information Technology Industry Complex', *NEC Research and Development*, 33 (1992): 547.

The Significance of NEC's Vision

Any company must deal with three important problems: (1) *how to establish boundaries* for the company's strategic decision-making, that is, how to decide which areas of activity are relevant, and which are not, for the company's strategies; (2) *how to co-ordinate the company's many activities* that require co-ordination—as Nobel Prize Winner Kenneth Arrow has pointed out, in companies limited use is made of the price mechanism for the purposes of co-ordination (although, with the increasing decomposition of large companies, greater use is now being made of this mechanism); (3) *how to inform stakeholders*—employees, customers, suppliers, bank-lenders, and share-holders—about what the company is doing, what its priorities are, and where it is going.

The NEC Tree

The 'NEC tree', a rendering of the company's C&C vision which embodies both of the beliefs identified above, has helped it to deal with all three of these problems. A contemporary version of the NEC tree is shown in Figure 6.9.

It was Koji Kobayashi who first conceived of the idea of the NEC tree, based on a model tree serving a similar purpose which he was shown in 1966 by Lawrence A. Hyland of Hughes Aircraft. It is worth reproducing Kobayashi's own account of the first version of the NEC tree, since to begin with, in tracing the growth of the tree over time, it makes clear his own understanding of the historical evolutionary path that the company has followed; and it also reveals

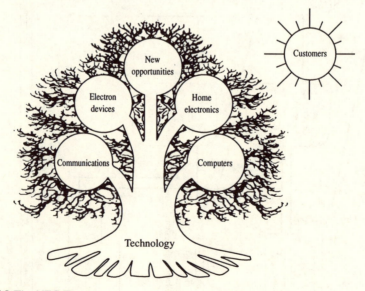

Fig. 6.9 The NEC Tree

Source: K. Kobayashi, *Rising to the Challenge*, Harcourt Brace Jovanovich, Tokyo, 1989, p. 7.

the difficulty that NEC has always had in finding an appropriate 'fit' for its home electronics activities:

The strong roots of the tree represent NEC's technological strength. From these roots the switching operations draw nourishment and send forth the first stout branch from the tree trunk. At about the same time another strong, independent branch forks off from the first branch: this represents our carrier transmission business. The next branch represents our radio division; it is followed by the branch for electronic devices, the basis for all our other business operations. Next comes the branch for electronic data processing—in other words computers. Finally, in order to suggest the growth of new branches, at the top of the tree is a branch labeled 'unknown' representing future divisions as yet unnamed.[19]

Kobayashi continues, expressing the ambiguities surrounding home electronics:

Sprouting from the earth as an offshoot of our technological roots is a young sapling depicting electrical household appliances. . . . (I did not feel that making household appliances a separate tree was necessarily appropriate, however, and we later changed its position.)[20]

Finally, Kobayashi deals with the role of customers:

In order for the tree to absorb nourishment from its roots and put forth branches and green leaves, it must receive light from the sun, which represents the marketplace—or, to put it another way, the needs of our customers.[21]

What Has NEC Been Offering its Customers?

An important part of a corporate vision is the conceptualization of the value that the company is offering its customers based on its competences. An example will make the importance of this conceptualization clearer. Casio used to conceive of a wristwatch, one of its most important businesses, as a time-piece attached to the user's wrist. A reconceptualization resulted in its thinking of a wristwatch as a source of information attached to the wrist. While this reconceptualization included time-keeping, it extended to other kinds of information such as blood pressure, heartbeat, and even communications functions such as radio paging.

The reconceptualization of the product that NEC was offering its customers has played an important role at various junctures in the company's evolution. One example is its redefinition of itself in the 1960s from a telecommunications equipment company to an information company contributing to the knowledge industry. As Kobayashi put it, 'the function of communications is to carry intangible *information*. That was the key word. . . . Computers processed information; communications equipment transmitted it. Even radio and television were no more than a means of receiving and reproducing information. . . . we were switching our sights from communications to information.'[22]

---

[19] Kobayashi, *The Rise of NEC*, 118. [20] Ibid.
[21] Ibid. 118. [22] Ibid. 31–2.

It is significant, however, that this reconceptualization of NEC's role was preceded by its move into computers in the late 1950s. In other words, in this case new competence preceded, rather than succeeded, the redefinition of the company's activities. In the mid-1960s, at a time when computers were firmly established as one of NEC's new product areas, Kobayashi's thinking about NEC's role was influenced by the writings of Fritz Machlup, an economist in the USA, and Tadao Umesao, of the Faculty of Science at Kyoto University, on the growing importance of the knowledge-related industry.[23] In 1966 this vision of the boundaries surrounding NEC's desirable areas of activity led the company to abolish its Nuclear Energy Research Laboratory. The reasoning was that nuclear energy was not centrally concerned with information. This facility was transferred to the Sumitomo Atomic Energy Company.

Computers and Digital Switches

Not only does a company's vision help it to define boundaries distinguishing those areas that it will deal with, its vision also assists it to *focus* on selected areas. This emerges clearly in NEC's case in computers and digital switches.

In line with its C&C vision, NEC's boundaries and focus have been competence-led rather than short-term-profit-led. This can be seen through a comparison of NEC and ITT, which inherited Western Electric's interests in NEC. ITT remained NEC's largest shareholder until 1971, after which its shareholding steadily decreased. But although both companies came from a similar background, rooted in the Bell system in the United States, in terms of technology, markets, and approach, from the 1970s the companies began to move in very different directions. The main reason for the divergence in their paths was the different corporate visions by which they were guided. At this time Harold S. Geneen led ITT in a conglomerate direction, where new business opportunities were pursued mainly on the basis of expected profitability, with scant attention being paid to the competence-compatibility of these businesses.

Since ITT was NEC's largest shareholder, when Kobayashi became president of NEC he regularly visited Geneen in New York to discuss his company's results. On these visits he was keen to understand ITT's approach and direction. In particular, he wanted to know how ITT was responding to the 'information age', an issue that was occupying a good deal of his attention. He was aware that ITT had acquired Avis Rent-a-Car and was also taking over hotels and food companies. Kobayashi recalls, 'I was at a total loss to understand how this was

---

[23] Ibid. 32. Interestingly, when Fujitsu, NEC's main Japanese rival in computers, first became involved in computers in the 1950s, there was strong opposition at board level to the company's diversifying from its traditional area of telecommunications into computers. The reason was the perceived uncertainty regarding likely returns in computers. NEC was slower than Fujitsu to make a decisive commitment to computers. All the Japanese computer companies at this stage received significant assistance from Japanese government laboratories, particularly MITI and NTT's laboratories, and from Japanese universities which facilitated their entry into the computer market. For further details, see Fransman, *The Market and Beyond*.

a response to the information age.' Kobayashi's approach, influenced no doubt by his engineering background and technical experience in NEC, was fundamentally different, despite the profitability that the conglomerate approach at the time seemed to be offering: 'though Geneen was certainly proving that this was a management strategy for high growth and good returns, I did not feel it was a direction I wanted NEC to take'.

NEC's vision determined that the company's boundaries and focus be competence-led, even if in the short to medium term this might be at the expense of a trade-off in terms of profitability. Explaining NEC's move into computers, Kobayashi noted that 'NEC took the orthodox route, perhaps. We decided to become a "billion dollar company" through internal growth built on our own traditional technological base.' Spelling out the guidelines for NEC's move into new business areas, Kobayashi observed that 'The criterion for pioneering new spheres was *not just their potential profitability*; they must share similar technologies, customers, and markets with our existing operations. Our entry into the computer field might be called diversification, but it was based on an area that was inextricably tied to our main line of business.'[24]

NEC's vision had effect not only in terms of the boundary conditions and focus that it defined, but also in terms of the substance of the technologies and markets within the business areas that would receive attention. This is apparent from the examples of computers and digital central office switches.

NEC entered the computer industry from a competence base in communications. This differentiated the company sharply from IBM, which came from a background in office equipment. As a result of its existing activity in communications, NEC's leaders were constantly concerned to ensure that its computer activities harmonized with its competences in communications.

Kobayashi's emerging vision of C&C had a number of important consequences for NEC's development of its computer business. Most importantly, the vision meant that NEC's computers were conceived from the start as being part of a broader C&C system. As Kobayashi has explained, 'My vision [in the late 1950s] of NEC was not simply one of a computer maker. The shape I had in mind integrated computers and communications—a communications network linking a number of computers, perhaps.'[25]

In turn, this vision meant that NEC soon began to think in terms of *distributed computing*, that is a distributed network of computers linked to one another through communications channels, rather than a large mainframe computer which would do most of the work. It was this concept that lay behind NEC's development of a distributed information processing network architecture, DINA, which was announced publicly in December 1976. As Kobayashi put it,

The thought gradually formed in my mind that instead of building a giant computer [as IBM was doing], it would be more efficient and more practical to have one of our small

---

[24] Kobayashi, *The Rise of NEC*, 49–50; emphasis added.   [25] Ibid. 111.

or medium-range systems 200, 300, or 400 . . . serve as a main or host computer to which some NEAC system 100 computers or other types of intelligent terminals could be connected as satellites in constellation fashion. This was the concept of DINA.[26]

This vision of NEC's involvement in computers had a number of important further consequences. First, it led to NEC's decision *not* to follow the IBM-compatible road that its main Japanese rivals Fujitsu and Hitachi, as well as a number of American companies, had chosen. This meant that NEC would develop its own computer operating systems independently. Secondly, this vision led NEC to focus mainly on small and medium-sized computers. It was in this area that NEC tended to concentrate in the co-operative research programmes sponsored by MITI and NTT. Thirdly, NEC's comparative strength in smaller computers led the company to sign its first major technological agreement in the field of computers with Honeywell in July 1962. Honeywell's large computers would allow NEC to complement its smaller computers, thus offering its customers a full family of computers. At the same time, it was hoped that Honeywell would also assist NEC in strengthening its software capabilities, an area that was becoming increasingly important. While NEC for these reasons went with Honeywell, Hitachi signed an agreement with RCA and Toshiba with GE. Fujitsu was alone among the emerging Japanese computer companies not to conclude a major technology agreement.[27]

NEC's early emphasis on distributed computing, therefore, was the result of its vision, which stressed the importance of a competence-compatible road to diversification. The company's existing competences were in the field of communications, and this, in the light of its vision, shaped its approach to computers. Although unforeseen by NEC's decision-makers in the early 1960s, by the early 1990s, with the growing replacement of large mainframes with ever more powerful smaller computers, it was becoming increasingly clear that distributed computing was becoming one of the most important trends in the computer industry. NEC is currently benefiting enormously from the evolutionary path which its vision fortuitously took it along from the early 1960s. IBM, Fujitsu, and Hitachi now have no option but to restructure and go along the same path.

The final example of the effect of NEC's vision on its evolutionary path is in the area of digital switching. Since this was discussed in detail in the earlier chapter on switching, only the broad outline will be repeated here.

By the mid-1970s, NEC had developed strong competences in the area of digital transmission but had not yet decisively entered the field of digital switching. The main reason was that NTT had not yet committed itself to this new switching technology and NEC had already invested heavily in the earlier analog electronic technology. Northern Telecom, however, having made the decision to enter digital switching sooner than most other switching companies, was a front-runner with its DMS switch. Nortel's president, Robert C. Scrivener,

---

[26] Ibid. 110–11.   [27] For further details, see Fransman, *The Market and Beyond*.

approached Kobayashi suggesting a strategic alliance between the two companies based on their complementary competences in digital transmissions and digital switching. However, although NEC had not yet begun to develop its NEAX-61 digital switch, Kobayashi turned the offer down. The main reason was that his C&C vision, and in particular the second belief underlying this vision (discussed above), dictated that digital switching was a core area in which NEC had to develop competences.[28] As we saw in Chapter 3, NEC is now in the process of trying to strengthen its position in the global switching market with its early entry into the next-generation ATM (asynchronous transfer mode) switch.

Sekimoto's Vision

Tadahiro Sekimoto, who assumed the NEC presidency in 1980, built on the C&C vision developed by Koji Kobayashi but, in building, transformed the vision. The crux of the transformation is an increased emphasis on the *human* aspects of C&C. While NEC's earlier vision stressed the need for C&C technologies to serve human needs, the emphasis was still more on the technologies and less on the human needs.

Sekimoto's approach is evident, for example, in the rather subtle change that NEC sometimes makes in describing C&C, transforming the nouns 'computers' and 'communications' into the verbs 'compute' and 'communicate', indicating the subordination of the technologies to the human activities. Sekimoto's emphasis on the human aspects of C&C is evident in his conceptual triad, his three related concepts of holonic management, individual mass society, and mesh-globalization.[29]

The concept of 'holonic management' is designed to deal with the contradiction that NEC faces as a result of its C&C vision: on the one hand, the realization of C&C systems requires that NEC *integrate* its competences in the underlying core technologies; on the other hand, efficiency requires that NEC *decentralize* its activities in order to avoid becoming too centralized, hierarchical, and bureaucratic. 'Holonic' is a synthesis of two Greek words—*holos*, meaning 'the whole', and *on*, meaning individual. According to Sekimoto, holonic implies 'harmonization and combination of these two opposites. Thus, "holonic" management means that while the individual, or each division or subsidiary, should develop its own business as an independent entity, it must also contribute to the development of the group [i.e. NEC] as a whole and in a harmonious way.'[30]

---

[28] The importance of the C&C vision in this context was stressed by Dr Kobayashi in one of his interviews with the author.

[29] Sekimoto's views have been reported in a number of articles in *Fortune*; see e.g. 1 August 1988; 31 July 1989; 30 July 1990; 29 July and 26 August 1991; and 27 July 1992. See also T. Sekimoto, 'Technological Innovation and Corporate Management for the 21st Century', Keynote Address at the IFIP TC 5 Conference on Computer Applications in Production and Engineering, 3–5 October 1989, Tokyo; reprinted in *Computers in Industry,* Elsevier, London, 1990.

[30] *Fortune*, 31 July 1989.

Greater 'individualization' is also evident in the trend that Sekimoto sees towards the development of 'individual mass society'. In this society products, aided by the increasingly flexible and small-production-scale nature of technology, will become increasingly tailored to the specific requests of specific customers. Individual mass society is therefore fundamentally different from mass-production-based society. According to Sekimoto, holonic management and organization constitutes an appropriate corporate response to this fundamental change in the business environment which electronic companies face.

'Mesh-globalization' is the corresponding principle that must be applied to corporate organization on a global scale. According to Sekimoto, globalization 'in the past, took place on a linear scale, meaning that all the foreign subsidiaries reported to headquarters in Japan. But from now on, they must intimately interact with one another, without depending entirely on headquarters.'[31]

Sekimoto's vision has been shaped not only by his experience in NEC as it evolved into a C&C company, but also by his academic background in both physics and engineering. Born in 1926, Sekimoto received a degree from Tokyo University's Physics Department in the Faculty of Science in 1948. In this year he joined NEC. He went on to receive his doctorate in engineering from Tokyo University in 1962. In 1965, the year that NEC's first Central Research Laboratories were established as part of a substantial corporate reorganization, he became chief of the Basic Research Department in the Communications Research Laboratory. In 1967 he became manager of the Communications Research Laboratory and in 1972 he became general manager of the Transmission Division. Sekimoto was elected to the board in 1974, becoming senior vice president and director in 1977, executive vice president and director in 1978, and president in 1980.

While Sekimoto's emphasis on the human aspects of C&C does represent a change of substance in NEC's vision, a significant degree of continuity with the past is also evident.

NEC's Corporate Organization

Competence, Vision, and Organization

A firm's competences, which determine its competitiveness, may be defined as the set of 'doings' and 'knowings' (activities and knowledge) that allow it to realize value. These competences relate to the entire value chain—from research, through development and manufacture, to marketing and distribution. The firm's accumulation of competences is influenced by its vision, by its beliefs which

---

[31] T. Sekimoto, 'Global Business Perspectives in the Information Age', paper presented at Washington University, St Louis, Mo., 30 September 1992, p. 5.

suggest how it should 'play its cards' given its existing circumstances as it sees and understands them. Competences, however, have to be organized. It is the attempts of the firm to change and improve its form of organization as its circumstances alter that explain the evolution of that firm's organization. But it is rarely possible to identify in advance the precise form of organization that will be most appropriate for the firm's circumstances from among the alternative forms that could be constructed. For this reason, vision—more specifically, the beliefs that underlie vision—also plays a crucial role in influencing the kind of organizational form that the firm creates. An explanation of the evolution of a firm's organization, therefore, must contain an analysis of the beliefs that have influenced the changes instituted in the firm's form of organization.

As shown in Fig. 6.10, the evolution of NEC's organization following the Second World War may be divided into three periods.

Fig. 6.10 The evolution of NEC's organization, 1945–1995

1945–1965: Plant-Based Organization

During the first period NEC's organization was essentially plant-based, even though several unsuccessful attempts were made to change this structure. Until August 1956, each plant in NEC was treated as an independent operating division with general functions such as administration, personnel, finance, and accounting concentrated in head office. By the mid-1950s the feeling grew that this organizational structure was inappropriate. Not only was there rapid technological change accompanied by the emergence of new products in NEC's traditional business areas, but the company was also becoming involved in a new generation of products and associated technologies including transistors and computers. Accordingly, in August 1956 NEC introduced what it called a 'product division system' and a total of five product-based divisions were created. The aim of this reorganization was to enable the company to focus more narrowly on particular product categories and to mobilize technological capabilities in support of the development of these products.

Despite this reorganization, however, the plants remained the centre of gravity in NEC. In April 1961 a further attempt was made to restructure the company according to relatively autonomous divisions defined by product. Once again, however, the reform was ineffective. Koji Kobayashi, who became President of NEC in November 1964, felt that 'Under the division system set up in 1961, the organisational reforms had been half-hearted and the respective status of the plants [relative to head-office] had not essentially changed.'[32]

1965–1991: Divisionalized Organization

On becoming president of NEC, Kobayashi identified two major shortcomings in the company's organization which he felt were impeding its progress. The first problem was that the company's existing form of organization demanded more attention from the president than he could be expected to provide.[33] In Kobayashi's words,

I had announced to the entire company that sole responsibility for management rested with one single person—me, the company president. But though I had become president I had not simultaneously been endowed with unlimited abilities to deal with any matter whatsoever. Herein lay a crucial dilemma. . . . the biggest problem of all was precisely the fact that all [the company's] levels of responsibility converged on one single point. If all the authority was concentrated in a single individual—the company president—how could he possibly perform the duties expected of him.[34]

A related problem with NEC's 'pyramid-shaped hierarchy' (often referred to as a unitary form of organization) was that it took 'too much time and effort for any information to reach the president's ear'. Furthermore, 'With a clearly de-fined authority figure on top, the lower echelons are all too often cowed into submission, and no one is willing to take the initiative. I had worked my way up from the lowest levels of such a hierarchy and knew only too well what it was like down there.'[35]

The second major problem that Kobayashi identified when he assumed office resulted from the separation of the marketing function from the division and its centralization in the head office.

---

[32] Kobayashi, *The Rise of NEC*, 17.

[33] This problem is well captured by the concept of 'bounded rationality' developed by Nobel Prize winning economist Herbert Simon. According to Simon, bounded rationality exists when the quantity of information required for a decision is great relative to the ability of the decision-maker/s to acquire and process that information.

[34] Kobayashi, *The Rise of NEC*, 8–9.

[35] Ibid. 58.

Because it did not do its own marketing, a division made products but had no responsibility for selling them. And because what the customer wanted could only be ascertained through marketing, the division was unable to recognize consumer trends rapidly enough and to respond accordingly. The barrier that existed between those who made the goods and those who sold them sometimes led to recriminations on both sides. I had experienced the problem at first hand [after the war Kobayashi became plant manager at the Tamagawa plant, one of NEC's main plants], and I believed that a solution was of the utmost importance.[36]

Kobayashi's Solutions

The need for a further reorganization was made all the more urgent by strong criticisms of its products which NEC received from two of its major customers, NTT and NHK, the state-owned broadcasting company. In his first presidential directive, given in 1965, Kobayashi attributed these and related problems in part to the 'partial paralysis of our organizational activities'.[37]

In order to deal with the first set of problems, Kobayashi set out to create what he called a 'horizontal' form of organization. He divided NEC into fourteen divisions, each defined according to product and related technology. The head of each division 'would have the same authority and responsibilities as the head of an independent company'.[38] The fourteen divisions, in turn, were aggregated into four groups representing NEC's four main product areas—telecommunications equipment, computers, semiconductors, and home electronics. 'Each group might be compared to a holding company with [its] division heads reporting directly to the executive in charge of [the group].'[39]

In conceptualizing his reorganization, Kobayashi used the metaphor of a disc, with himself as president occupying the central point. Each of the executives in charge of the four groups occupied part of the area of the disc and served as the president's *alter ego*. The Corporate Management Committee, on which the president and the group executives sat, served as a forum for the exchange of information. It also served to co-ordinate cross-group activities and to reconcile any conflicts that emerged between the groups. However, Kobayashi retained the traditional *ringi* system for final decision-making, according to which drafts are circulated for approval by appropriate senior management, though he reduced the number of managers involved in this process. In this way he dealt with the problem of information-overloading at the centre which had threatened to overwhelm him.

Kobayashi tackled the second major problem, which arose from the separation of the marketing function in head office, by giving each of the divisions responsibility for the function of engineering, manufacturing, and marketing. However, two distinct marketing divisions were retained to co-ordinate marketing, particularly to large customers such as NTT.

[36] Ibid. 17.   [37] Ibid. 12.   [38] Ibid. 19.   [39] Ibid.

Spinning-Off Semi-Autonomous Subsidiaries
In the late 1960s Kobayashi took the principle of decentralization one step further when he decided on a policy to establish semi-autonomous plants outside the greater Tokyo area. These plants were wholly owned subsidiaries and were incorporated into the organization of NEC's divisions which were responsible for the marketing of their products. Nevertheless, each plant was run as a relatively independent company with its own executive officers. In the 1980s this was extended to software activities with the establishment of a number of subsidiary companies dedicated to the creation of particular kinds of software. In this way NEC was able to take advantage of the greater availability and lower cost of labour, as well as the lower cost of land, which existed outside the Tokyo area.

1991–Present: Holonic Organization

As described in detail in the section on NEC's corporate vision, from the late 1970s, NEC, under Koji Kobayashi's leadership, increasingly began to articulate its C&C vision. This vision mapped out a future role for the company on the basis of the increasing convergence which it saw between computer and communications technologies. The problem, however, was that the C&C vision presented serious difficulties for NEC's existing form of organization.

To put it in a nutshell, NEC's organization after 1965 was based on the principle of decentralization, whereby decision-making power was partly devolved to divisions and to wholly and partly owned subsidiaries.[40] However, the convergence of computer and communications technologies implied a significant interdependence between the technologies of the four groups and the divisions in the groups. How could the benefits of this convergence be realized by an organizational structure based on relatively autonomous, decentralized units?

This organizational dilemma was well expressed by Kobayashi in a company directive of 30 July 1979. (In April 1976 Kobayashi resigned as president of NEC and became chairman.)

Because our company's business spans many different areas, it is extremely difficult for the chairman and the president to exercise constant control over what is going on in all our enterprises. The top management structure at NEC is therefore based on a division of labor, with each general manager of a division or group executive in charge of an operating group responsible for running the day-to-day business in his respective area. Under this division of labor a *centrifugal force* is at work as each division tries to choose the most suitable options for its particular business area *independently of what would be most suitable for the entire company.*[41]

---

[40] This decentralization, it is worth noting, was only relative, since the group structure provided for the executive in charge of each group to co-ordinate the activities of the divisions within the group as well as activities between groups. Their common membership of the Corporate Management Committee provided a further mechanism for inter-division and inter-group co-ordination.

[41] Kobayashi, *The Rise of NEC*, 136; emphasis added.

In order to secure the interests of the company as a whole, however, which are tied to the convergence of computers and communications, it is necessary that this centrifugal force be balanced by a countervailing force:

To maximize the efficiency of the technology, equipment and capital of the company as a whole, *and give maximum scope to the overall strength in the area of C&C*, a countervailing *centripetal force* is needed.[42]

Where was this centripetal force to come from? Kobayashi's answer in the same directive was that 'This centripetal force rests primarily in the coordination exercised by the group executives.'[43]

As time went on, however, two problems began to emerge that were to have important implications for NEC's organizational structure. First, the feeling grew that a stronger form of co-ordination was needed for NEC to realize the full benefits from C&C. Secondly, and closely related to the first point, under Sekimoto the conviction grew that, while NEC had traditionally been a technology-driven company, conditions in the 1990s required that it increasingly become market-driven. More specifically, with the widespread diffusion of many of the core information and communications technologies to new Japanese and Western entrants as well as to companies in countries like Korea and Taiwan, both competitiveness and profitability demanded far greater anticipation and responsiveness to consumer needs. (Sekimoto assumed NEC's presidency in June 1980 and moved into the company's driving seat after Kobayashi retired from the chairmanship in 1988.)

Sekimoto's Solutions
The response of Sekimoto and his team to these two problems resulted in a major reorganization of NEC, the most significant since 1965.[44] The substance of the reorganization is shown in Fig. 6.11.

The main thrust of the reorganization is the establishment of three new C&C groups and the consolidation of several previously separate groups under these three. The three groups are the C&C Production Technologies Group, which deals with telecommunications systems; the C&C Systems Group, which provides information-processing systems; and the Personal C&C Group, which deals largely with personal computers and other personal products. As a result of the reorganization, the ten groups that previously existed were replaced by seven new groups, as shown in the figure.

How does this reorganization solve the two problems referred to? The general answer is that, whereas the previous organizational structure emphasized individual products and their related technologies, the new structure is based on

[42] Ibid.; emphasis added.
[43] Ibid.
[44] I would like to express my deepest appreciation to the senior NEC staff who were closely involved in the 1992 reorganization, and who on numerous occasions explained in great detail to me the rationale for this significant change in the company's organizational structure. The information that they provided me with is made available here for the first time.

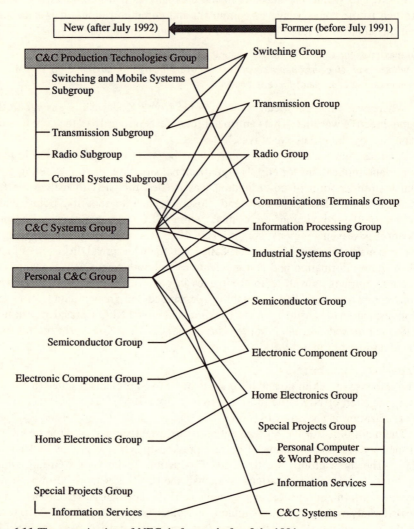

Fig. 6.11 The organization of NEC, before and after July 1991

C&C systems. For example, the C&C Production Technologies Group now incorporates the previously separate Switching, Transmission, Radio, and Communications Terminals Groups. Under the single executive in charge of the new group, co-ordination is far tighter than it was previously. Furthermore, the three new C&C groups are more rigorously focused on three groups of customers, namely the users of telecommunications systems, information-processing systems, and personal systems. These customers are interested in the *combined* characteristics and services they get from the systems they purchase. In order to serve the needs of these customers better, and therefore in this way to become more 'market-driven', it makes sense to combine the products and technologies that make up the component parts of the system into one group under a single executive. However, the distinctness of the individual products and technologies is still recognized in their separation into separate subgroups, as is shown in Fig. 6.11.

NEC's overall organization today is shown in Fig. 6.12.

NEC's Subcontractors

Not shown in NEC's organization chart but nevertheless a crucial aspect of the company's organization is its network of subcontractors. In 1993 NEC had about 150 core subcontractors, about half of which provided R&D-intensive inputs. Under the influence of the strong yen and increased competition in the Japanese market, NEC has accelerated its procurement of non-R&D-intensive inputs from offshore locations. This is the case, for example, with NEC's personal computer, which faces increasing competition in Japan from low-cost competitors such as the American companies Compaq and Dell.

Research and Development in NEC

NEC's evolution mirrors Japan's progression—not from science to research to development, production, and market, but in the reverse direction, starting from production and marketing and moving gradually into increasingly sophisticated development and then research. Whereas in the older industrialized countries engineering, as an area of systematic study, emerged from the field of science as a poor relative, in Japan engineering rapidly became an important field in its own right, quickly becoming equal to the pure sciences. At what is now Tokyo University, the Faculty of Engineering assumed the same status as the Faculty of Science soon after its establishment, an accomplishment that took many more years in the older industrialized countries.[45] Japan remains the only industrialized

---

[45] According to J. R. Bartholomew, *The Formation of Science in Japan: Building a Research Tradition*, Yale University Press, New Haven, 1989, 'When [Tokyo University] was founded in 1877 [from an amalgamation of several Tokugawa schools], its college of science had departments of chemistry, mathematics, physics and astronomy, biology, geology, and engineering all together on a basis of equality.' Engineering at Tokyo University was considerably strengthened in 1886 when it absorbed the Imperial College of Engineering, which had been established in 1871 by a young Glasgow engineer, Henry Dyer. Dyer was recruited by Hirobumi Ito, a chemist who was interested in the practical application of science and engineering. Ito had studied in the 1860s under Alexander W. Williamson, a theoretical chemist from Imperial College, London. Hugh Matheson of the Jardine Matheson Company arranged Dyer's appointment in mechanical engineering at Ito's request and on the recommendation of W. J. M. Rankine of Glasgow University. Williamson had close contacts with Glasgow University, being a friend of the physicist Lord Kelvin of the university.

Bartholomew states that Dyer's innovative engineering programme at the Imperial College of Engineering was modelled on Zurich's Polytechnic Institute. 'Dyer's four-year program included physics and chemistry, mechanical, civil, and mining engineering, and courses in the strength of materials. It relied almost entirely on a British teaching staff. . . . Only France and Switzerland had

[*cont. on p. 298*]

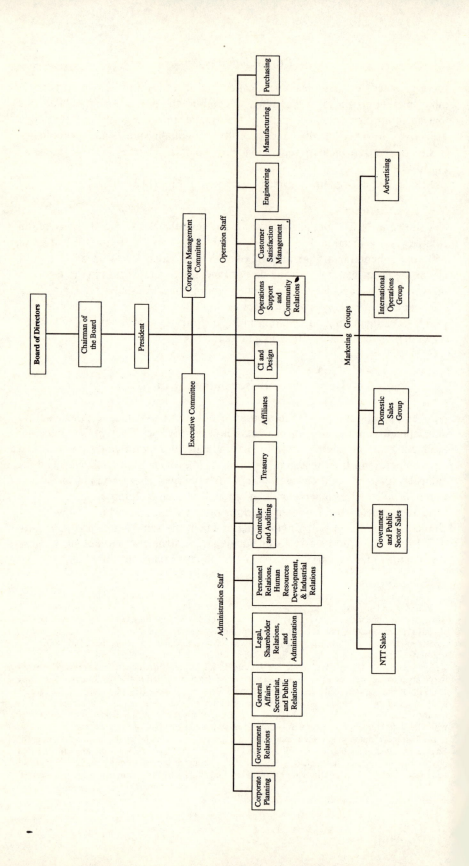

Board of Directors

Chairman of the Board

President

Executive Committee

Corporate Management Committee

Administration Staff

Corporate Planning

Government Relations

General Affairs, Secretariat, and Public Relations

Legal, Shareholder Relations, and Administration

Personnel Relations, Human Resources Development, & Industrial Relations

Controller and Auditing

Treasury

Affiliates

CI and Design

Operation Staff

Operations Support and Community Relations

Customer Satisfaction Management

Engineering

Manufacturing

Purchasing

Marketing Groups

NTT Sales

Government and Public Sector Sales

Domestic Sales Group

International Operations Group

Advertising

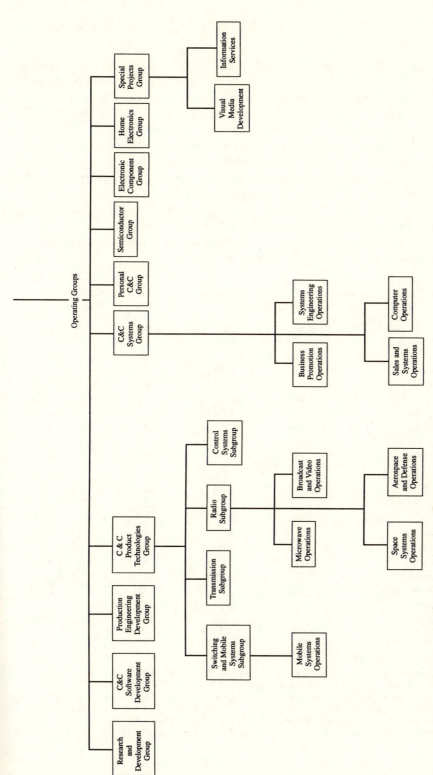

Fig. 6.12 The present organization of NEC's top management

country in which the proportion of engineering graduates is greater than that of science graduates. The first section of this chapter, which traced the evolution of NEC's competences, showed in graphic terms the important contribution made by the engineering graduates from many of Japan's engineering faculties.

As NEC increased its own competences, becoming less dependent on its foreign suppliers of technology, so research and development became more important for the company's survival and growth. By 1970 no less than 70 per cent of NEC's total annual consolidated sales came from products that were developed, increasingly with the company's own home-grown technology, in the previous five years. In 1993 NEC spent ¥275 billion on R&D, representing 8 per cent of net sales. In that year the company's total capital expenditure was lower than its R&D spending, at ¥231 billion.

NEC's R&D expenditure relative to other Japanese and Western companies operating in the same markets is shown in Table 6.2. When, in 1992, NEC spent

Table 6.2 *Research and Development in Japanese and Western IT Companies, 1993*

	R&D (US$m)	R&D/ sales	No. of patents, 1992	Patents/ sales
Japanese companies				
NEC	2,274	6.94	502	1.53
Fujitsu	2,947	9.13	443	1.37
Hitachi	3,907	5.55	1,165	1.66
Toshiba	2,392	5.54	1,176	2.72
Matsushita	3,144	4.77	732	1.11
Sony	1,809	4.86	446	1.20
Canon	794	4.44	1,118	6.26
Western companies				
IBM	5,083	7.88	842	1.31
DEC	1,754	12.59	223	1.60
Intel	780	13.35	75	1.28
Motorola	1,306	9.82	671	5.04
Northern Telecom	980	11.65	—	
Ericsson	1,170	17.90	53	0.81
Siemens	5,322	10.79	550	1.15
Alcatel Alsthom	2,625	8.73	222	0.74
GE	1,353	2.37	995	1.74
Philips	2,079	6.34	607	1.85

Source: *Business Week*, 27 June 1994.

comparable institutions. There was nothing like the college in Dyer's own country nor even in Germany before the Franco-Prussian War (1870–71)' (ibid. 91).

According to Bartholomew, 'Tokyo University was institutionally innovative in more than a Japanese context. Its inclusion of engineering . . . and agriculture . . . in the curriculum indicates a forward-looking policy rarely encountered in Europe. Engineering['s] . . . formal position in the academic system was higher than in Europe' (p. 93; see also pp. 65–6).

$2.3 billion on R&D, this put it fifth among the main Japanese information and communications companies, after Hitachi with $3.9 billion, Matsushita with $3.1 billion, Fujitsu with $3.0 billion, and Toshiba with $2.9 billion. NEC's total R&D expenditure was slightly less than AT&T's, which was $2.9 billion, but somewhat more than NTT's $2.3 billion. These Japanese figures are put into perspective by comparing them with the three highest R&D spenders in the world: General Motors, which spent $5.9 billion, Siemens with $5.3 billion, and IBM with $5.1 billion.

The table also examines the R&D intensity of these companies by making allowance for their size measured in terms of sales. NEC's expenditure of about 7 per cent of its sales on R&D was the second highest among the Japanese companies after Fujitsu's 9.1 per cent. Siemens' figure was 10.8 per cent while IBM's was 7.9 per cent. Some of the Western companies with a narrower product and technology range were significantly more R&D-intensive. This includes specialist telecommunications equipment suppliers such as Ericsson, which spent 17.9 per cent, and Northern Telecom, 11.7 per cent. It also includes the semiconductor company specializing in microprocessors, Intel, which spent 13.4 per cent, and the computer specialist, Digital Equipment, with a slightly lower figure of 12.6 per cent.

The Evolution of the R&D Function

Any large firm undertaking research and development must answer, explicitly or implicitly, at least four basic questions:[46]

1. What R&D should the firm undertake now in order to improve its current activities?
2. How can the firm prevent 'irrelevant' research?
3. Where should the R&D be done—in-house, or subcontracted to other companies?
4. What R&D should the firm undertake now so that it can anticipate future products and technologies?

This section will describe the evolution of NEC's research and development in terms of the efforts made by its R&D decision-makers to grapple with these questions. A summary of the R&D evolution in NEC is given in Fig. 6.13.

It was in the 1920s that research began to emerge in NEC as a distinct, specialized set of activities. This research started as a small bud on a tree, still only partly differentiated from the rest of the branch. At this time NEC's first small research unit was opened. In 1927, as we saw in the section on the evolution of NEC's competences, Yasujiro Niwa encouraged the development of factory-level R&D, believing that it would be more productive to have such activity located in the factory where it could interface easily with the other functions of

---

[46] Ch. 8, dealing with the comparison of NTT, BT, and AT&T, examines the way in which these four basic questions relating to R&D have been dealt with in each of these companies.

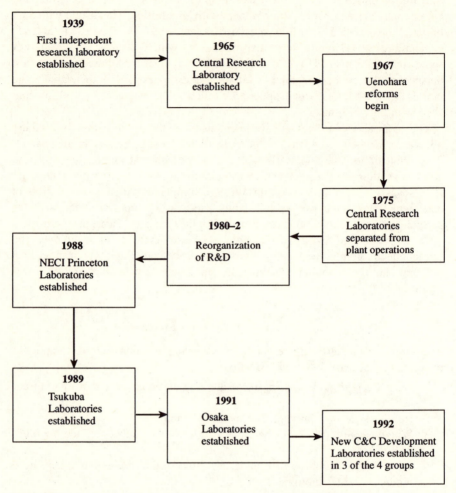

Fig. 6.13 The evolution of research and development in NEC, 1939–1992

production. This represented a departure from the prevailing practice in Western Electric, NEC's mother company and its major technology supplier, for which Bell Laboratories had already been designated as a central R&D facility in 1925.

At this stage the answers to the four questions were relatively straightforward. The answer to the first was that most of NEC's major R&D requirements were taken care of by Western Electric. This, however, still left the minor activities of adapting and modifying the imported technologies to suit the circumstances of NEC and Japan. As Koji Kobayashi, a young engineer in the company, noted, there were very few significant innovations that were made in NEC at around this time. Nevertheless, the incremental innovations that were made in the effort to adapt and modify, and the learning of the underlying technologies that occurred as a result, should not be underestimated, since they laid the ground for more substantial innovative activities later.

The second and fourth questions did not arise. There was no problem of preventing 'irrelevant' research since the company did so little research and what it did interfaced closely with production and marketing. Furthermore, NEC's future R&D needs were catered for by Western Electric. Niwa had already produced a satisfactory answer to the third question: research should be done as close as possible to the point at which it was needed, in this case the factory.

In the 1930s, however, a sea-change occurred, not only for the technological future of NEC, but for Japan more generally. As we have seen, the growing nationalism and militarism in Japan at the same time had the beneficial effect of reducing dependence on foreign technology while increasing indigenous capabilities. NEC's first independent research laboratory, established in July 1939, concentrated particularly on radio research as radio-based communications became increasingly important for both commercial and military purposes. The laboratory was established in the Tamagawa plant, which had been set up in 1936 to take care of the company's growing involvements (since the late 1920s) in radio communications and vacuum tubes.

The research that was begun in this laboratory created the basis for the accumulation of important new competences in the company. As NEC's official history acknowledges, its early postwar development of microwave communications and TV broadcasting equipment was possible largely as a result of the research done in this laboratory. It was in the area of microwave communications, it will be recalled, that NEC achieved its first substantial international competitiveness.

With NEC's technological capabilities growing steadily, stimulated by the company's postwar growth, the answers to the four questions began to change. NEC had increasingly to answer the first question itself, concerning what R&D should be undertaken in order to improve current activities. In most areas NEC could, and did, still resort to the import of foreign technology. However, this importation was complemented by ever more substantial in-house R&D. Furthermore, in the few areas such as microwave communications, where NEC was beginning to achieve international prominence, the company had increasingly to rely on its own resources.

The second question, however, how to prevent 'irrelevant' research, was still not a major issue. This was because NEC's laboratories were still located in the major factories and most of their activities were tightly coupled to the needs, problems, and puzzles thrown up by the operations of the factories. This factor also provided the answer to the third question, namely where should the R&D be done? It was with regard to the fourth question, however, that new policy problems were beginning to raise their heads: What R&D should be undertaken now to anticipate future products and technologies? Depending more than ever on its own technological capabilities, it was up to NEC to devise its own solutions to this question.

In 1961 a major boost was given to research and development as an increasingly differentiated set of activities. In that year NEC's research was reorganized, with activities being consolidated in five independent research laboratories: the Fundamental Research Laboratory (which included research on materials, etc.), Communications Research Laboratory, Electronics and Mechanics Research Laboratory, Nuclear Energy Research Laboratory (abolished in August 1966), and Manufacturing Techniques Laboratory.

For NEC, 1965 was a watershed year. This was the year in which a major reorganization of the company took place. A significant decentralization of decision-making was implemented, with a separation of the strategic function (made the responsibility of the Executive Committee) from day-to-day business functions (allocated to the product divisions). The company's five divisions were expanded into fourteen, each with responsibility for engineering, manufacturing, and marketing. These fourteen divisions were consolidated into four groups (now called 'basic business areas')—communications, computers, electronic devices, and home electronics—with an executive officer in charge of each group.

In 1965, as this decentralization was occurring in NEC, a part of the R&D function was centralized with the establishment, for the first time, of a *Central Research Laboratory*. This was achieved through the consolidation of the Fundamental, Communications, and Electronics and Mechanics Research Laboratories into the new Central Research Laboratories (CRL). The CRL remained in the Tamagawa plant. The primary function of the CRL was to undertake long-term fundamental research and development to provide the basis for entirely new kinds of products.

At the same time, three *development laboratories* (DLs) were established, positioned in the groups. These were the Computer Development Laboratory, the Switching Development Laboratory, and the Aeronautics and Space Development Laboratory. The role of these DLs was to undertake research and development in the service of medium-term objectives. Finally, the existing *engineering units* (EUs) were retained in each division with responsibility for the shorter-term development work needed in that division.

This gave NEC, in common with the other Japanese electronics companies, a *three-tiered R&D structure*. In the company's memorable terminology, the CRL would have responsibility for R&D for 'the day after tomorrow', and the DLs for 'tomorrow', while the EUs dealt with the needs of 'today'.

It was, therefore, only in 1965, sixty-six years after NEC was founded, that the company had its first Central Research Laboratory. It took another ten years, until 1975, for the CRL to be moved from the Tamagawa plant where it was situated to its present location in Miyazakidai, Kawasaki (in Tokyo), where it is physically separated from plant operations. The gradualism with which Japanese companies moved to establish R&D, not only as a specialized function, but as a physically separated function, marks a strong contrast with Western companies such as General Electric, AT&T, and Du Pont, which established centralized research facilities much earlier.[47]

Why was NEC's Central Research Laboratory established as a physically separated organization only in the mid-1960s? The main reason was that the company had reached the point in its technological development where it needed to delve more deeply into the technologies that underlay its various products. It also needed to carry out R&D in order to anticipate and adopt the technologies which in the future would become important in its numerous markets. Both of these factors were necessary for the company to maintain its competitiveness and growth. As Koji Kobayashi noted, it was only in the early 1960s that 'NEC finally freed itself from dependency on ITT'.[48] By the mid-1960s, NEC was starting to close the large technological gap that separated it from the Western leaders in the information and communications industries. This required increasing its indigenous R&D capabilities.

Although Hitachi established its central research laboratory in 1942, the 1960s was a period of rapid growth in corporate laboratories in Japan, a period referred to as *kenkyujō bu-mu*, 'research laboratory boom'. The reasons are not hard to find. Like NEC, many other Japanese companies were making similar progress in technological maturity. In 1961, for example, Toshiba established its central research laboratory. The rapid economic growth of the 1960s not only helped to increase the technological learning process in Japanese companies, but also provided the funding that was necessary to invest in new R&D facilities and capabilities. In 1960 the Ikeda government had launched its 'income doubling plan' (which reflected, more than caused, the rapid growth that Japan was experiencing). From 1965 to 1969, Japan's GNP growth rate averaged 15 per cent per annum. NEC's sales growth rate over this period was 22 per cent per annum.

The Uenohara R&D Reforms

There is enormous complexity in the set of R&D decisions that must be taken by a large company operating in markets characterized by rapid technical change. In 1994, for example, NEC was producing some 10,000 different products covering virtually the entire range of products and technologies in the field of information (including computers and semiconductors) and communications. Furthermore, these products and technologies are in a constant process of change under the pressure of domestic and international competition. Accordingly, inherent complexity, incomplete information, and uncertainty characterize the context under which R&D decisions are made.

---

[47] For an account of the origin and development of research laboratories in General Electric and AT&T see L. S. Reich, *The Making of American Industrial Research: Science and Business at GE and Bell, 1876–1926*, Cambridge University Press, 1985.

[48] Kobayashi, *The Rise of NEC*, p. xvii.

How does a company go about making its R&D decisions under these conditions? This question will be explored through an examination of the R&D reforms introduced in NEC by Dr Michiyuki Uenohara from the mid-1960s to the mid-1980s.[49]

Although Dr Uenohara worked closely with his colleagues in the company, he may be credited as the main architect of NEC's R&D system. This system began to take its present form with NEC's major reorganization in 1965 discussed earlier, which resulted in the establishment of the company's first Central Research Laboratory. However, as we shall see, the 1965 reorganization of R&D was only the starting-point. When Uenohara joined NEC in 1967, it was already apparent that further major changes were essential. It was Uenohara's efforts to deal with the problems resulting from the 1965 reorganization that were responsible for shaping the company's R&D system for the remainder of the century.

Uenohara graduated from the Department of Engineering at Nippon University in 1949. From there he went to Ohio State University from 1952 to 1956. On graduating from Ohio State he went to Bell Laboratories in 1957, becoming one of the first of a long line of well-known Japanese scientists and engineers to get their formative training in this famous laboratory.[50] Dr Uenohara remained at Bell until 1967 when he joined NEC.

Uenohara's experiences at Bell Laboratories, as for most of his other Japanese colleagues, were to prove extremely important in shaping his vision of the direction in which NEC should move in developing its R&D organization. Particularly important were the ideas of Dr Jack A. Morton, Uenohara's boss at Bell, who became vice president of Bell Laboratories in charge of electronics technology.

Dr Morton's Influence

Very fortunately, Dr Morton has left a rigorous account of his ideas on the organization of research and development in his book, *Organizing for Innovation*, published in 1971. In view of Uenohara's own account of the impact that Morton's ideas had on his thinking, it is worth examining some of the key features of Morton's book in order to identify both where Uenohara applied 'Mortonian thinking' and where he made his own departures.

The key to understanding Morton's thinking on the organization of innovation lies in the subtitle to his book, *A Systems Approach to Technical Management*. According to Morton, innovation must be understood as a *system* involving all

---

[49] This entire section on R&D in NEC is heavily influenced by numerous personal interviews conducted by the author over the last eight years with Dr Michiyuki Uenohara in particular but also with many of his colleagues in NEC's R&D organization.

[50] Uenohara's colleagues at Bell Labs included Dr Y. Takeishi, who later became head of Toshiba's ULSI Laboratories, and Dr Hiroshi Inose, the distinguished Tokyo University telecommunications professor, currently director-general of the National Centre for Science Information System in Japan.

the components of research, development, manufacture, and market. More specifically (and importantly, in view of the concerns of the present book) *innovation is a system, the essence of which is knowledge*. As Morton puts it:

In all the functions of the innovation process, the 'stuff' being processed is knowledge— relevant to its collective common purpose. Such knowledge is identified, created, and transformed into new patterns by creative people working independently and collectively as specialists. During most of the process, the knowledge is incomplete, unstructured, and of a hazy pattern. For the couplings of the process to work, the people in the process must engage in a good deal of interspecialist teaching–learning, constructive conflict, and tradeoff discussions and decisions. In short, specialized people can become a system only through coupling with each other—and effective interaction in the tough creative process of innovation can come only through facile two-way communications between people.[51]

Elsewhere, Morton adds: 'if specialists are to be coupled together for cooperative effort in the total process of innovation, they must be able to communicate with and understand one another. There must exist *overlapping understanding* at the interfaces between their specializations.'[52]

It is this kind of thinking that lay behind the introduction of a special function in Bell Laboratories, *systems engineering*, which absorbed a full 15 per cent of total R&D expenditure (compared with 15 per cent on research, 20 per cent on fundamental development, and 50 per cent on specific development and design).

Morton elaborates on the function performed by Bell Laboratories' systems engineers, emphasizing their coupling role in integrating knowledge of the possibilities emerging from R&D with knowledge of the needs of the rest of the Bell System and the needs of the market:

Through their professional and organizational activities, the R&D people at Bell Labs. . . . can know a great deal about scientific and technological potential. But know-ledge of communications-service limitations, needs, and opportunities must come from people in AT&T, the Operating Companies, and the general marketplace. *These areas of knowledge are complex, geographically dispersed, and greatly different in content from the specialized knowledge of R&D people.*[53]

It was in order to cope with this need for knowledge integration that Bell introduced the distinct function called 'systems engineering' which, Morton cautions, 'is not directly in the research–development–manufacture stream of information processing'.[54] According to Morton, systems engineers

are usually former specialists of considerable experience and judgment who have broadened their motivations and knowledge to include new disciplines, such as economics, sociology, and even psychology. In short, they are the interdisciplinary generalists of Bell Labs. One of their big jobs is to build information bridges connecting Bell Labs and

[51] J. A. Morton, *Organizing for Innovation: A Systems Approach to Technical Management*, 1971, p. 60.
[52] Ibid. 17; emphasis added.
[53] Ibid. 57; emphasis added.
[54] Ibid. 58.

Western Electric to AT&T, the Operating Companies, and the public—to relate service needs and opportunities to scientific possibilities and to weigh their priorities.[55]

Morton's view of innovation as a system of *knowledge* and Bell Laboratories' function of systems engineering had, as we shall see, a deep impact on Uenohara's thinking.

The Inital Problems

What was the situation that Uenohara confronted when he took on the organization of NEC's research and development in 1967?

In an interview, Uenohara identified two particular problems. The first related to the way in which R&D was planned and its relationship to the rest of corporate planning. The second problem pertained to the coupling of the R&D laboratories and the operating divisions in the company. In both areas Morton's ideas were relevant, although, as will be seen, they required considerable modification.

The first problem, in Uenohara's words, was that

There was no systematic analysis [in the planning of R&D]. Long term research was initiated quite independently [of the rest of corporate decision-making]. The leaders must have had their strategy, but it was not coordinated with the rest of corporate strategy, which was concerned primarily with developing new markets. The analysis of new markets was quite independent of current core research.[56]

Secondly, when he arrived in NEC, 'Technology from the central research laboratories was provided free to the operating divisions. Headquarters paid 100 per cent of the cost.' However, although Uenohara 'found that the operating divisions were quite ready, because of severe competition in the market-place, to contract with the central research laboratories for research, they were not serious enough to go ahead and make a serious commitment to developing further the technology that they received from the laboratories'.

Uenohara's Solutions

Uenohara's answer to the second problem was to introduce a practice commonly used in the USA, although *not* in Bell Labs, namely an internal market for R&D. According to this practice, the operating divisions, the demanders of internal R&D, commission *and pay for* research and development which is supplied by the Central Research Laboratories. The requirement that the divisions pay for their internal R&D creates the incentive, first, to demand R&D only when it is anticipated that it will add sufficient value to the division's activities relative to other possible uses of the resources, and second, actively to enhance the technology transferred from the research laboratories. From the point of view of the laboratories, the internal market for R&D creates an incentive to ensure that

---

[55] Ibid.

[56] This and the following quotations in this section come from the author's interviews with Dr Uenohara.

the commissioned research undertaken by the laboratories meets the needs of the internal customer, namely the division. In this way, the internal market for R&D helps to resolve the first and second questions posed above: What R&D should the firm undertake now in order to improve its current activities? and How can the firm prevent 'irrelevant' research?

Uenohara's introduction of an internal market for R&D proved successful (as it did in the other Japanese electronics companies). Currently some 30 per cent of NEC's Central Research Laboratories' funding comes from the divisions, leaving 70 per cent funded from central sources.

The first problem, however, was far more difficult. The reason was that it involved what may be referred to as the *Corporate Research Conundrum*: research must be relevant for the company's markets. (That is, in the modern corporation knowledge-creation is subordinated to value-creation.) But, because of the inherent time-lag involved, research must be undertaken *in advance* of the expression of market need through market demand. This raises a complex problem for the organization of R&D. For if market demand cannot 'lead' R&D, what principles or mechanisms should be used in answering the fourth question raised earlier, i.e., What R&D should the firm undertake now so that it can anticipate future products and technologies?

There were two dimensions to Uenohara's solution to the first problem. To begin with, he established two planning units, the Corporate Planning Office in NEC's headquarters, and the R&D Planning Office in the Central Research Laboratories. The activities of these two units were closely co-ordinated, and Uenohara, Director of the R&D Planning Office, became Deputy Director of the Corporate Planning Office. This helped to interface product with market and technology. This dimension was not particularly innovative or novel and corresponded to co-ordination mechanisms in other companies.

The second dimension, however, was far more daring and innovative. This involved the establishment of what NEC came to call its 'core technology programme'.

Uenohara's Core Technology Programme

Although, as we have seen, Morton conceived of AT&T's innovation as a system of knowledge, neither he nor the company made a rigorous attempt to define its *knowledge-base*. Uenohara's core technology programme, however, set out to do precisely this.

But why should NEC want to spend the considerable resources required to rigorously define its knowledge-base? For Uenohara there were several good reasons.

To begin with, a major problem confronting the planning of R&D in NEC arose from the large number of products produced by the company (currently 10,000) and the rapid changes occurring in these products. While the manufacture and marketing of these products was undertaken by the decentralized operating divisions in the company, and their development was undertaken by the development laboratories positioned in NEC's groups (containing a number of divisions) and engineering units placed in individual divisions, this left the problem of the technologies that the Central Research Laboratories should focus on for 'the day after tomorrow'.

The solution, according to Uenohara, is to focus on the underlying technologies rather than on the products. This has a number of important advantages. In Uenohara's words, 'knowledge is common to many products and changes much more slowly than products. Therefore long-term technology planning should be based on knowledge rather than products.' NEC's core technology programme accordingly aimed at defining systematically the main technologies that underlay its products. Furthermore, this enabled NEC to define its technologies in terms of an *interdependent system of knowledge, à la* Morton but taking his ideas one step further.

NEC's core technology programme started in 1970, but it took until 1977 before the programme began to have a significant impact on the company's R&D. Every three years the core technologies are updated so that there is a 'rolling' attempt to define those technologies that will be important for NEC over the following ten years.

How does NEC go about defining its core technologies? To begin with, the company's likely future 'C&C Products' (i.e. products in the converging areas of computers and communications) are identified. These products are bounded by the business strategy formulated by the Corporate Planning Office and the R&D strategy of the R&D Planning Office in the Central Research Laboratories. The multitude of technologies underlying these C&C products are then identified. It is worth noting that, by following this procedure, 'technologies' are defined not in purely technical terms, but by a product–market-technology matrix.

The underlying technologies are then distilled into a number of *core technologies*. At present NEC has about 30 core technologies. While the total list of such technologies remains confidential, in various places the company has mentioned some of them. They include digital communications, VLSI, optoelectronics, speech recognition and synthesis, image processing, pattern recognition, and software engineering. The core technologies are then further distilled into six 'strategic technology domains' or STDs. These are: materials and devices, semiconductor materials and devices, functional devices, communications systems, knowledge/information systems, and software.

What benefits does NEC derive from its core technologies programme? The first benefit, as Uenohara notes, is that by focusing on the knowledge underlying its many products—knowledge that changes relatively slowly and incrementally—NEC has developed an effective method of long-term R&D planning. This method helps the company to answer the fourth question regarding R&D referred to above.

Secondly, by focusing on an interdependent system of knowledge, NEC is able to couple and combine the many complementary elements in the set of knowledge comprising its knowledge-base. In this way it is able to integrate the elements of knowledge that are always fragmented by specialization and organizational barriers. This helps the company deal with the problem posed by Nobel Prize winning economist Friedrich Hayek, namely the problem of utilizing knowledge not known by anyone in its entirety. This knowledge integration is particularly important for NEC, since it conceives of most of its products as part of evolving C&C systems, systems that achieve their coherence as a result of the integration of the underlying knowledge-base (that is, the convergence of computer, communications, and device technologies).

By focusing on an interdependent system of knowledge, NEC is able to bring together the *people* possessing this knowledge, which, as Morton noted, is essential for an effective innovation process. This point is made more concretely in Fig. 6.14. As the figure shows, the identification of core technologies fa-cilitates the integration of the different knowledge sets of the researchers working within that core technology area both *within* a laboratory and *across* laboratories.

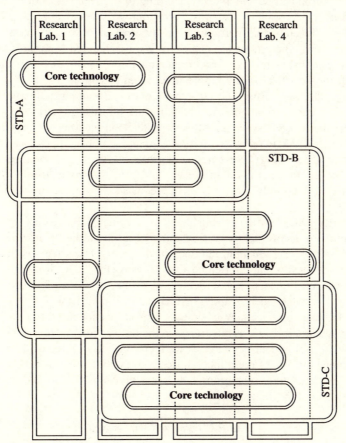

Fig. 6.14 NEC's core technology R&D organizational strategy
STD = Strategic Technology Domain

Furthermore, the identification of strategic technology domains performs the similar function of integrating the knowledge sets of those working in related core technologies. Note, significantly, that strategic technology domains overlap, thus achieving the 'overlapping understanding' that Morton argued is necessary for communication between knowledge-related researchers involved in an innovation process. In order to focus effectively on core technologies and strategic technology domains and to organize the inter-researcher and inter-laboratory interactions that are essential, NEC has designated specific research managers to be in charge of each core technology and strategic technology domain.

NEC's R&D in the 1980s and 1990s

As can be seen from Fig. 6.13, in 1980 there was a further reorganization of NEC's research and development. According to the company's official account, the aim of this reorganization was 'to encourage specialization and accelerate technology development, particularly in the area of basic long-term research'. To achieve this aim, production engineering was separated from the R&D Group with the establishment of a new Production Engineering Development Group. This left the new R&D Group more focused on research.

Within the new R&D Group, the Central Research Laboratories were reorganized into five laboratories covering the following areas: basic research, optoelectronics, C&C systems, software product engineering, and environmental protection. In 1982, in order to place even 'greater emphasis upon basic research', the Basic Technology Research Laboratories were reorganized into the Fundamental Research Laboratories and the Microelectronics Research Laboratories. Currently the R&D Group consists of nine laboratories and five research centres.

The latter 1980s saw the establishment of three new laboratories. The first was in Sagamihara; its official name, Sagamihara Liaison, indicates its role in linking research with the production activities in that area. The other two laboratories were more basic-research-oriented. These were the NEC Research Institute, established in Princeton, New Jersey, in 1988, and the Tsukuba Research Laboratories, established in the Tsukuba science town near Tokyo in 1989. In 1991 NEC established a new laboratory near Osaka for the study of compound semiconductors. In 1992, as mentioned in the last section on NEC's organization, new C&C development laboratories were established in three of the company's four groups; the aim of these laboratories is to facilitate the further development of C&C systems across the groups' different divisions. NEC's basic research is now considered in greater detail.

The R&D Process within NEC

Table 6.3 describes the R&D organization of NEC. It shares its three-tiered structure with the other Japanese electronics companies. On the first tier are the

Central Research Laboratories, which are organized as a distinct group. Their role is to do research for 'the day after tomorrow', and they receive approximately 10 per cent of the company's total R&D expenditure. Of this sum, about 20 per cent is allocated to 'oriented-basic research' (that is, 'fundamental' research which is oriented towards C&C systems), 50 per cent to applied research, and 30 per cent to 'developmental research'. About 70 per cent of the Central Research Laboratories' funds come from corporate sources, and the other 30 per cent is commissioned by the other groups and operating divisions.

The Development Laboratories, located in the groups, are responsible for about 20 per cent of total R&D. Their role is to do R&D for 'tomorrow'. It is the Engineering Laboratories, placed in the operating divisions, that undertake the bulk of the company's R&D, approximately 70 per cent. They respond to the current needs of the divisions. Accordingly, all of their funding comes from the divisions.

Table 6.3 *The Present Organization of NEC's Research and Development*

Kind of laboratory	Organization/ location	% of total R&D	Time scale of R&D	% funding from HQ
Central Research Laboratories *of which*:	A distinct group	10	'Day after tomorrow'	70
Oriented-basic research		(20)		
Applied research		(50)		
Development research		(30)		
Development laboratories	In groups	20	'Tomorrow'	—
Engineering laboratories/units	In operating divisions	70	'Today'	0

R&D Planning

As with other Japanese electronics companies, NEC's R&D planning process is both long-term and shorter-term-oriented. The core technologies programme discussed above plays a central role in NEC's long-term R&D planning. The Corporate Planning Office in the company's headquarters and the R&D Planning Office in the Central Research Laboratories agree the outlines of the long-term R&D plan. This provides the basis for the R&D Group's Medium-Term R&D Strategy Plan and for its annual planning cycle. The latter process is shown in Fig. 6.15.

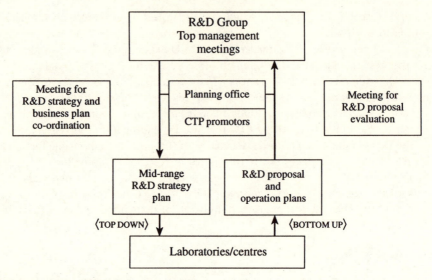

Fig. 6.15 NEC's R&D planning structure

As the figure shows, it is the meeting of the Corporate Planning Office and the Central Research Laboratories that provides for the co-ordination of R&D strategy and the company's business plan. This provides the context for the R&D Group's top management to develop a medium-term R&D strategy plan. In turn, this provides the context for the directors of the various laboratories and centres to plan the research that will take place over the forthcoming year in their areas.

The generation of specific research proposals within the R&D Group is both 'top-down' and 'bottom-up'. Top-down proposals are initiated by the R&D Group's management, while bottom-up proposals come from the researchers themselves. At the same time each year, these proposals are evaluated by the 'Meeting for R&D Proposal Evaluation', which also considers the R&D proposals that have emerged from the negotiations between the R&D Group and the other groups and operating divisions. The latter proposals include the internally contracted R&D agreed between the divisions and the Central Research Laboratories.

As in other Japanese companies, estimations of profitability are seldom decisive in determining whether a proposal is accepted. (This applies to the 70 per cent of the Central Research Laboratories' R&D that is centrally funded. The 30 per cent that is commissioned by the operating divisions will, of course, have to conform with the objectives of the divisions, which are treated as profit centres and therefore have to be profit-conscious.) Other criteria include contribution to the company's longer-term R&D goals, impact on company growth and market share, likely intellectual property rights, and contribution to academic knowledge (which helps the company to interact with universities and to buy its 'entry ticket' into the information networks in the various research communities).

Once the R&D Group has completed its annual R&D plan, this is discussed with the R&D Administrative Division in the company's headquarters in order to harmonize the proposed R&D activities with the suggested R&D in the other groups and operating divisions. This eventually results in the final annual R&D plan.

Coupling the R&D Engine to the Corporate Machine

The effectiveness with which a company's R&D activities are coupled to its other corporate activities is a crucial determinant of its innovativeness. Western companies have responded to the coupling problem in different, more or less effective, ways. For example, Intel, the world's largest semiconductor company dominating the global microprocessor industry, has elected not to have a central research laboratory. In other cases, Western companies have had excellent research laboratories which have produced more important results for other companies than for the parent. A notable case in point is Xerox's Palo Alto Research Center (PARC); this was a fount of innovations in the computer field which were exploited by other companies, many of them new start-ups.

How has NEC coupled its R&D engine to the rest of its corporate machine? A number of important coupling mechanisms can be distinguished.

Two of these have already been considered and therefore will not be discussed further here. These are internal contracted research and the core technology programme, both of which have proved to be effective coupling mechanisms.

Rotation of R&D Personnel

As was seen earlier, Jack Morton of Bell Laboratories stressed the importance of human resource development and management in order to achieve the coupling of different parts of the company's knowledge-base and the creation of new knowledge. Japanese companies such as NEC have been particularly fortunate in being able to rotate personnel across corporate boundaries. This has enabled them to establish effective networks of information flow, both formal and informal, which in turn have helped to integrate the sets of knowledge fragmented in different parts of the company. This has constituted an important input into the innovation process.

The practice of personnel rotation in Japanese companies is partly a by-product of the lifetime employment system. Since most personnel remain with the company for the duration of their working lives, the company is forced to treat them as fixed rather than variable costs. (That is, their salaries have to be paid irrespective of company output and profitability.) Personnel are therefore seen as given assets that must yield a satisfactory return for the company, rather than as inputs that can be hired and fired. This is one reason why Japanese companies spend relatively large sums on training; the practice is encouraged by the low level of staff turnover, which enables the company to appropriate the returns from training. It is also one reason why Japanese companies tend to rotate their staff relatively frequently across corporate functions. Such rotation broadens the skills and knowledge of personnel, thus increasing their flexibility, allowing them to be relatively easily redeployed in response to the opportunities and threats created by new technologies and competition. The employee's 'value'—i.e. the present discounted value of future earnings—is determined inside the Japanese company, rather than by the external market for specific skills. Accordingly, since the company values both the flexibility and the greater company-specific knowledge that rotation facilitates, the employee has an incentive to co-operate with rotation.

In order to give an idea of the relative importance of personnel rotation in Japanese companies, NEC's rotation of R&D personnel may be compared with that in AT&T's Bell Laboratories. In NEC, currently about 10 per cent of the R&D staff of the Central Research Laboratories are rotated annually to other groups and operating divisions. This figure is partly determined by the policy decision to keep the average age in the Central Research Laboratories at 32 years. With a total central research laboratory staff of around 1,000, this means that annually about 100 personnel are rotated. On average, researchers remain in the Central Research Laboratories for six years, after which they are transferred to the operating divisions.

The number of researchers transferred from AT&T's Bell Laboratories to the company's business units is shown in Table 6.4. Of Bell Laboratories' approximately 1,200 researchers (i.e. in Area 11), only 2 researchers were transferred in 1992. Furthermore, the number appears to be declining; in 1988, 11 were transferred while in 1989, 5 researchers were transferred. However, the managers of Bell Laboratories would like to see an increase in the number of researchers transferred in the future.

The incentive to rotate is also built into NEC's promotion rules. In order to be promoted to a managerial position in the Central Research Laboratories, it is necessary for a researcher to have had experience in an operating division. Transfer is negotiated with the division concerned, but the usual way, generally favoured by the division, is for the researcher to move with his project when it is ready to be transferred to the division. However, in order to ensure that the researcher keeps in touch with research, an internal rule states that researchers who are to return to the Central Research Laboratories should not be transferred

Table 6.4 *Transfer of Bell Laboratories Researchers (Area 11) to Business Units in AT&T, 1988–1992*

Year	No. transferred
1992	2
1991	1
1990	1
1989	5
1988	11

Source: Information supplied to author by Bell Laboratories, 1993.

to the operating divisions for more than two years. At times this process of temporary transfer leads to conflict when both the operating division and the Central Research Laboratory want to keep the researcher. Such conflicts are negotiated between the division and Central Research Laboratory, with the Personnel Office in headquarters as the final arbiter.

Cross-Group/Divisional Projects
A further way of coupling research is through R&D projects involving the Central Research Laboratories and members of more than one group or division. At present there are more than fifty of these kinds of projects.

Researchers in NEC are moved not only from the Central Research Laboratories to an operating division, but also *across* divisions within a group, and even across groups. This is made possible by the common knowledge-base that frequently underlies the products and processes of the different groups. Indeed, NEC's managers try to encourage such movement of researchers in order to help achieve the knowledge-integration necessary for the development of C&C systems.

Formal and Informal Meetings
A large number of formal and informal meetings held regularly helps to couple research and integrate knowledge. For example, there is a 'Technology Strategy Exchange Meeting' held annually between the R&D Group and leaders of the other groups. In addition, there are regular meetings of the 'Core Technology Forum', which brings together members of the research laboratories and the operating divisions. The R&D Group also holds regular exhibitions of its research in order to inform the operating divisions of the work being done in the laboratories. Informal gatherings also provide important flows of information. Once a month an informal gathering called the 'Plazza Sophia' is held in the company dining room with alcoholic beverages served! This promotes information exchanges between researchers from different areas of specialization and of different seniority.

M.Sc.s rather than Ph.D.s
In NEC's research laboratories, as in other large Japanese companies, most new recruits are hired with a B.Sc. or M.Sc. rather than a Ph.D. This practice is closely related to the lifetime employment system, which gives Japanese companies an incentive to train their staff. The reason is the expectation that they will remain with the company, with the result that the company will be able to appropriate the returns from its investments in training.

There are advantages in employing younger researchers with less university-based experience. One is that they can be more easily moulded to the specific routines and practices of the firm. Furthermore, they will not yet have acquired the 'professional' attitudes and values of the researcher who has been through a Ph.D. programme at a good university. These attitudes may emphasize the importance of contributing to the frontiers of knowledge and making what, in the eyes of the profession, is a contribution, even when this is at the expense of the company's priorities. In general, the employment of younger researchers can help a company to couple its R&D by helping to break down the walls of specialization that inevitably surround R&D activities.

Company-specific knowledge possessed by an employee is regarded as an important asset in NEC. It is one reason why NEC prefers to retrain employees whose knowledge has become obsolete rather than hire new employees. Company-specific knowledge allows an employee to fit into the company's formal and informal information networks, to learn how things are done in the company, and to make a contribution to the company on the basis of this knowledge.

An unintended consequence, however, of the practice of hiring M.Sc.s rather than Ph.D.s is the weakening of Japanese universities as locations for research. This corporate practice means that there is a high demand for good M.Sc.s, with relatively attractive pay. Research conditions are often also attractive with good research budgets, equipment, and availability of researchers in complementary areas. As a result, many good graduates leave university without going on to Ph.D. programmes, weakening the research base of the university.

Eleanor Westney notes that, while in 1985 US universities produced 7,651 Ph.D.s in science, Japanese universities produced less than 10 per cent of this number. In engineering, over 60 per cent of the Ph.D.s granted by Japanese universities have been to researchers from companies, who have carried out the research on which the Ph.D. is based in their companies.[57] While this practice may increase both the 'relevance' of Ph.D. research to the needs of Japanese companies and the strength of industry–university links, these advantages are to some extent purchased at the expense of the quality of university-based research.

'Cradle Research'

Like other Japanese electronics companies, NEC has the practice of allowing all researchers some time to follow their own interests, independently of their research projects which have been formally approved. In principle, about 15 per cent of a researcher's time may be allocated to projects done 'on the side', without the knowledge or approval of the research managers. In practice, a researcher's ability to do this research at any point in time—referred to as 'cradle research' in NEC—will depend on his or her current commitments to approved research.

Cradle research has a number of important advantages. It keeps the motivation of researchers high, since they are to some extent allowed to follow their own interests; it helps guard against the 'bounded vision' of research managers, who are not necessarily aware of all the research that should be prioritized; and in this way it creates a degree of flexibility in the research laboratories that otherwise would not exist. This flexibility can also assist the coupling of R&D

---

[57] D. E. Westney, 'The Evolution of Japan's Industrial R&D', in M. Aoki and R. Dore (eds.), *The Japanese Firm: Sources of Competitive Strength*, Oxford University Press, 1994.

to the firm's other activities. Once a 'cradle' project begins to show promise and require more resources, it must be formally proposed and approved in order to be continued.

NEC's highly successful automatic fingerprinting system, discussed in detail below, began as cradle research.

NEC's R&D Network

Up to this point, we have examined research and development within NEC's unconsolidated companies. In terms of flows of knowledge and information, however, which constitute important inputs into NEC's R&D, the company has a far wider R&D network. This network is represented schematically in Fig. 6.16.

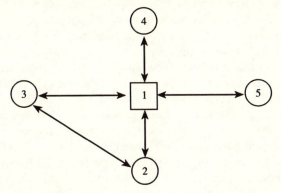

Fig. 6.16 NEC's R&D network

1, NEC Unconsolidated; 2, NEC's subsidiaries; 3, NEC's suppliers; 4, NEC's customers; 5, NEC's collaborative research partners.

Subsidiaries

Unlike some other Japanese companies, NEC's subsidiaries are integrated into its group-divisional structure. In terms of R&D, this means that the research and development done in the subsidiaries is included in NEC's overall R&D planning procedure outlined above. In this way there is a degree of co-ordination between the R&D undertaken in the subsidiary and that in the rest of the company.

Depending on the specificity of the subsidiary's activities, however, there may be only a small amount of overlap between the subsidiary's R&D and that carried out elsewhere in NEC. Nevertheless, there are projects jointly undertaken between the R&D personnel of the subsidiaries and those of other laboratories in the company, including the Central Research Laboratories. On occasion there is also the transfer of R&D staff from the latter laboratories to the subsidiaries. The subsidiaries, therefore, are an important part of NEC's R&D network.

Suppliers

As with other Japanese companies, NEC works closely with its suppliers and this includes R&D activities. One example is its co-ordination of R&D

activities with its subcontractors. Currently NEC has approximately 150 core subcontractors. About 75 of these operate in areas that are not particularly R&D-intensive. Approximately 20 of these 75 companies have subsidiaries operating outside Japan. The position of some of the remaining 55 companies is currently under threat as a result of the combined effect of the high yen and the recession in Japan. NEC has taken the decision, for example, to move a far larger proportion of its PC manufacture and assembly to offshore locations and to source a far greater amount of its components from these locations.

From the point of view of NEC's research and development, however, it is the remaining 75 more R&D-intensive subcontractors that are important. NEC has decided to keep these R&D activities and the subcontractors associated with them in Japan in order to facilitate effective co-ordination of R&D.

NEC's R&D-intensive subcontractors are an integral part of the company's R&D network. These subcontractors understand that, if they want their products to be part of NEC's new products and systems, then it is necessary that they co-ordinate their R&D activities with those of NEC at an early stage. This necessitates close interaction between the subcontractor's R&D engineers and those from NEC's development laboratories in the operating divisions and possibly even in the Central Research Laboratories. This interaction is usually initiated with the conclusion of a formal agreement between the subcontractor and NEC. According to senior NEC managers interviewed, NEC's R&D staff are often very demanding in terms of the research and development they require from their subcontractors. Accordingly, the subcontractors have little option but to treat the resources that they have to allocate to this purpose as part of the cost of entry into the new product or system.

The long-term relationship that exists between the R&D-intensive subcontractors and NEC, however, helps to ensure that the former eventually receive sufficient benefit to compensate for the interim costs. NEC generally operates a non-disclosure agreement with these subcontractors. In terms of this agreement, it is usually expected that the subcontractor will not supply to a third party for a minimum of six months. This time period is sufficient to give NEC a marketing lead which will enable the company to reap the benefit from its innovation. Thereafter, however, the subcontractor is usually encouraged to sell to third parties. In this way scale of output can be increased, costs can be reduced, and additional incremental innovations can be made, benefiting NEC as well.

Customers
NEC's customers are another important part of the company's R&D network. This is particularly the case with large, R&D-intensive customers who use NEC's C&C products and systems. First of all, these customers play an important role in specifying, perhaps even helping to develop, and implementing the products and systems they want. Secondly, these customers are also in a good position to provide NEC with feedback on the performance of its products and systems, thus providing an important input for further innovations. Thirdly, in some cases the

R&D capability of these customers constitutes an important input into NEC's own R&D process.

The best example of the importance of NEC's large customers in its R&D activities is NTT. The material provided in the present and previous chapters makes it clear that customers such as NTT—NEC's biggest single customer—are a crucial part of the company's R&D network.

Collaborative Research Partners

NEC's collaborative R&D activities, another important part of the company's R&D network, may be divided into three categories. The first is collaborations involving other private-sector companies which are neither suppliers nor customers. These include strategic co-operative R&D arrangements with competing, or potentially competing, companies. A leading example is the co-operation that occurs between NEC and AT&T's microelectronics business unit in the field of semiconductors.

The second category includes collaboration with public-sector institutions, such as universities and government research laboratories both inside and outside Japan. The third category includes hybrid private–public-sector collaborations, such as the co-operative R&D projects initiated by the Ministry of International Trade and Industry, which involve collaboration with competing companies as well as government research institutes and perhaps universities. Some examples, such as MITI's co-operative projects in the field of computers, were discussed in earlier chapters. (It is worth noting that some 5 per cent of NEC's total Central Research Laboratories' budget comes from MITI. This amount goes largely towards R&D with a more fundamental, longer-term, orientation.)

The establishment of NEC's first overseas research (as opposed to development) laboratory in Princeton, New Jersey, represented a significant step in the globalization of NEC's R&D network. Why was this laboratory set up? What are the benefits that NEC hopes will accrue? These questions are analysed in the following section.

The Globalization of NEC's R&D Network

In 1988 NEC established NEC Research Institute Inc. in Princeton, New Jersey, a $32 million research facility employing some fifty researchers with an annual budget of around $26 million. In setting up this research institute, NEC broke ranks not only with the other major Japanese electronics companies but also with NEC's American counterparts.

NEC Research Institute (NECI) undertakes research with a long-term horizon in the areas of physics, computing, and communications. It has a significant degree of autonomy in setting its research agenda and priorities—autonomy both from the rest of NEC's R&D network and from NEC's production facilities in the USA. NECI's autonomy, maintained despite the sharp fall in the company's profits during the Japanese recession in the early 1990s, stands in strong contrast to the trend in the major US information and communications companies.

In companies such as IBM and AT&T, there has been great pressure since the late 1980s to 'make R&D pay'. In IBM's case this pressure has been part of the response to the company's historic losses announced at the beginning of 1993. The result has been increased pressure on all research in IBM's laboratories to demonstrate results of commercial value to the company. In AT&T the pressure has come not so much from falling profits as from the reforms introduced by Chairman Bob Allen in 1988. These reforms also involved a 'cultural revolution' in Bell Laboratories where, under changes introduced by Arno Penzias, Vice President of Research, all research units now have to demonstrate that they are producing 'value' for customers inside the company.

NECI's mode of operation stands in strong contrast to this trend in the major US companies. According to Michael A. Harrison, a computer scientist from Berkeley University, NECI is now the 'only [corporate laboratory] devoted to unrestricted, undirected research in the US'. Richard A. Linke, a physicist employed at NECI who was formerly a senior research scientist at Bell Laboratories, believes that 'The rest of the world is very, very urgently trying to make research profitable. Its a national panic.'[58] He likens the research atmosphere at NECI to the 'glory days' at Bell Laboratories, before the post-1988 reforms, which gave Bell researchers a great amount of autonomy in deciding what research they wanted to undertake.

In establishing NECI, NEC was the first Japanese IC company to establish a research (as opposed to a design or development) laboratory outside Japan. Hitachi also has taken significant steps to globalize its research (as opposed to development) activities, establishing two fairly small research facilities in Europe, one at Cambridge University and the other at Trinity College, Dublin. These two facilities were set up by Hitachi's central research laboratories based in Kokubunji, in Tokyo, which sets their research agendas. The Hitachi laboratory that corresponds most closely to NECI in terms of its long-term orientation and autonomy from the rest of the company's R&D programme is the Advanced Research Laboratory, located in the greater Tokyo area.

This difference in R&D behaviour raises several questions. Why did NEC establish NECI, giving it so much autonomy? What benefit does NEC expect to get from NECI, now and in the longer term? How can NEC continue to justify the expenditure on NECI at a time of sharp decreases in the company's profits?

The Establishment of NECI

In the early 1980s Dr Uenohara proposed the establishment of a development-oriented laboratory in the USA. This was opposed from within NEC on the

---

[58] *Business Week*, 13 July 1992, p. 137.

grounds that the time was not yet ripe and that the returns would not be sufficient to justify the investment. As the 1980s progressed, trade-related tensions led to growing US–Japan conflict. Against this backdrop, in the mid-1980s Uenohara proposed that a basic research laboratory be set up in the USA. His reasoning was that such a laboratory would earn goodwill for NEC and therefore pave the way for the establishment of later development-oriented research and development in the USA. The Japanese had been criticized for drawing heavily from the world stock of knowledge in producing its products, while making little contribution to this stock. A basic research laboratory would enable NEC to contribute to the stock of knowledge in the USA. Although there was strong opposition in NEC to the idea because of worries regarding the profitability of this investment, Uenohara's proposal ultimately succeeded.

When the decision was made, Uenohara went to visit Bell Laboratories to explain NEC's plans. Uenohara, it will be recalled, had spent ten years at Bell as a researcher until the mid-1960s, and NEC, originally a joint venture with AT&T's Western Electric, had had long-standing and close ties with Bell. Bell Laboratories agreed to a free exchange of research ideas with NECI.

Uenohara, this time against opposition from NEC's Personnel Department, wanted all the staff, including researchers, at NECI to be either American citizens or green card holders. On the one hand, this would contribute an indigenous culture to NECI; on the other hand, it would avoid the criticism that NEC was sending Japanese researchers to extract US knowledge for commercialization in Japan. In searching for an appropriate person to head NECI, Uenohara eventually found Dawon Kahng, a Korean former pioneer transistor and memory semiconductor researcher at Bell Labs. Kahng, like Uenohara, had graduated from Ohio State University, and had been a close colleague of Uenohara's at Bell Laboratories. (Dr Kahng died in May 1992.) In discussion with Kahng, it was decided that NECI would initially have two departments, a Computer and Communications Science Department and a Physical Science Department.

How was the decision made to prioritize these areas? This was a question I put to a senior NEC executive researcher:

Fransman: How were these areas chosen?

Executive: Oh really, Dr Kahng decided on these two areas. Of course, he discussed with us—Dr Uenohara, me, and other people in NEC—but originally it was Kahng's proposal. He is from the physical science area but he considered that as a member of NEC he should also think of C&C. He then reached the idea that they should have two departments, one of which should relate to C&C [i.e. the Computer and Communications Science Department] and the other to physical science.

The Benefit to NEC from NECI

But what benefit will NEC, a profit-making company, get from NECI? I put this question to another NEC senior executive researcher.

Fransman: When does NEC expect to get *direct* benefits from NECI, in terms of ideas generated in NECI feeding into NEC's new products and processes?

Executive: In the twenty-first century. It cannot be rushed.

Fransman: Does this mean that NEC will have to wait a long time before benefiting from its investment in NECI?

Executive: We don't expect any direct benefit from NECI in the short to medium term. What I said to them was that if they can contribute to top-rank international conferences, I will be happy. [Laughter]

Fransman: To be the devil's advocate, let's say I am a financially minded person on NEC's board. I say, 'I am looking at the figures and this research looks very expensive. What's the return?' How do you answer such a question?

Executive: NEC is involved in highly complex future systems. Our customers critically evaluate our products. They want to know how long and how well the company will support its products. These are extremely expensive systems that must constantly be improved to meet future needs. If a customer has to invest in a completely different system, it is extremely expensive. Perhaps the customer will lose business opportunities. So our customers are extremely cautious about their suppliers. NECI will give strong support, and this will help the evaluation we get from our customers.

NECI also helps NEC's companies in the US recruit very capable engineers and researchers. Without NECI it would be very difficult even for NEC to recruit excellent engineers and researchers. Recruiting is a big future problem because we have to develop more and more new products, especially new architecture and software, tailored to the American market-place. We need excellent engineers. After establishing NECI we are getting more good engineers.

NECI in the Light of the Vision of NEC's Future Globalization

From my discussions, it seems clear that NECI's long-term role is envisaged in the light of NEC's vision of its future globalization. According to this vision, NEC will be a globalized company with one 'Culture', shaped by the concept of C&C, but with many 'cultures', determined by the nature of the societies and market needs in the different countries in which NEC operates. In the next century, NECI or its offshoots will continue to have an oriented-basic-research function, but the laboratories will also interface closely with NEC's other activities in the USA in much the same way that NEC's Central Research Laboratories interact with the company's other operations in Japan. In terms of Sekimoto's vision of 'mesh-globalization', discussed above, NECI will be part of NEC's relatively autonomous US operations which will interact 'horizontally' with the other parts of NEC's global system, rather than being 'vertically' subordinated to NEC's Tokyo headquarters.

The Creation of Competences through R&D:
NEC's Automated Fingerprint Identification System (AFIS)

In 1963, representatives of the FBI Identification Division in the USA approached scientists at the National Bureau of Standards to get advice regarding the feasibility of producing an automated fingerprint identification system (AFIS).[59] Ensuing research and development and government contracts led to the entry of several American firms into the AFIS market. In 1969 the Japanese National Police Agency (NPA) requested NEC to develop an AFIS. In the same year members from NPA and NEC visited the FBI to find out about the development of their AFIS. During the 1970s NEC developed its own system. By the early 1990s, NEC controlled about 60 per cent of the world market for AFISs with major systems installed in California, Australia, and Singapore.

This success story raises several questions. Why and how was NEC able to establish such a dominant position in this international market? How was NEC able to create the internationally competitive competences on which its dominant market position depends?

The Process of Competence Creation

Competences may be defined as the set of 'doings' and 'knowings' (activities and knowledge) that allow a firm to compete. The study of NEC's AFIS illuminates five key characteristics of the process of competence creation:

1. 'New' competences, and the products and services that they support, are usually an extension of existing competences, rather than competences created from scratch.

2. There are three crucial parts to the process of competence creation (although they do not necessarily occur sequentially, or in this order). First, knowledge of the user's requirements (or potential requirements) is obtained. Second, this knowledge is 'interfaced' with relevant knowledge (of both an explicit and a tacit kind) both within the firm and outside it. Third, emerging from these two processes, additional knowledge is generated in order to enable the user's requirements to be met.

A crucial part of the process of competence creation relates to the 'point' at

---

[59] I would like to express gratitude to Mr Kazuo Kiji, head of NEC Security Systems Ltd and one of the founders of NEC's AFIS, and his staff for the interviews and data on which the present study is based. Further information on automated fingerprint identification systems is to be found in: R. M. Stock, 'An Historical Overview of Automated Fingerprint Identification Systems', *Proceedings of the International Forensic Symposium on Latent Prints*, FBI Academy, Quantico, Va., 7–10 July 1987, pp. 51–60; K. R. Moses, 'A Consumer's Guide to Fingerprint Computers', *Identification News* (June 1986), 5–10; K. Kiji, Y. Hoshino, and K. Asai, 'Automated Fingerprint Identification System (AFIS)', *NEC Research and Development*, no. 96 (March 1990), 143–6; 'Taking a Byte out of Crime', *Time* (14 October 1985), 53; 'Massive IC Exercise to Start on June 3', *Straits Times* (Singapore) (16 May 1991); Kobayashi, *Rising to the Challenge*, 103–4.

which the characteristics of the firm's product or service 'meet' and 'match' the user's requirements. It is at this point that the *use-value of the competence* is determined. It is on the basis of the use-value of its competences that a firm competes.

3. The process of competence creation necessitates the integration of knowledge that is fragmented (in different people and in organizational segments), both within the firm and outside it. In turn, this necessitates solving the problem, noted by Nobel Prize winner Friedrich Hayek, of utilizing knowledge not known to anyone in its entirety.

4. Competences involve 'doings' and 'knowings' that relate to the *entire* value chain, that is from research, design, and development through production to marketing. Furthermore, competences must facilitate continual competitive improvements.

5. Competences (including new competences) have to be supported by appropriate *forms of organization* that will allow delivery to the user of competitive use-value. Over time, these forms of organization must also facilitate continual learning, innovation, and hence improvement in use-value.

Table 6.5 *Results of System Accuracy Tests for NEC's AFIS*

	NEC	Printrak
San Francisco Police Department		
Total number of latents[a] searched	51	51
Ten-print data-base	100,000+	100,000+
Correct respondent in no. 1 position	37	11
% in no. 1 position	72.5	21.6
Correct respondent in positions 2–10	5	6
% in top ten positions	82.4	33.3
California Department of Justice		
Total number of latents[a] searched	97	97
Ten-print data-base	300,000	240,000
Correct respondent in no. 1 position	65	18
% in no. 1 position	67	18.6
Correct respondent in positions 2–10	12	12
% in top ten positions	77	30
Calgary Police Department		
Total number of latents[a] searched	50	50
Ten-print data-base	300,000	100,000
Correct respondent in no. 1 position	47	23
% in no. 1 position	94	46
Correct respondent in positions 2–20	2	6
% in top twenty positions	98	58

[a] Latent prints are fingerprints found on the scene of the crime and are usually indistinct. Ten prints are collected formally, for example by police departments, and are clear.

Source: K. R. Moses, 'A Consumer's Guide to Fingertip Computers', *Identification News* (June 1986): 5–10.

The Significance of NEC's AFIS

Not only does NEC's AFIS illustrate the key characteristics of competence creation, it also illuminates some important features of NEC's firm-specific structure and functioning. More specifically, the development of the competences underlying NEC's AFIS illuminates an evolutionary path, beginning with 'cradle research' in NEC's Central Research Laboratories and ending with the spin-off of a separate organizational unit, NEC Security Systems Ltd. This company, a distinct cost centre in NEC, is run by people transferred from the Central Research Laboratories.

Furthermore, NEC's AFIS also shows C&C at work, in this case involving the synergistic combination of the company's competences in areas such as character recognition, image processing, dedicated LSI design and development, software, computing, and interfacing with broader communications systems.

The Puzzle: How Did NEC Achieve its Competitive Edge?

A puzzle is presented by the superior competitive use-value provided by NEC's AFIS. But before posing this puzzle, what is the evidence for the superiority of the NEC system?

In the mid-1980s, benchmark tests were done on two AFISs by five bodies: the San Francisco Police Department, California Department of Justice, Calgary Police Department, Alaska Department of Public Safety, and Suffolk County Police. Results for the first three bodies are given in Table 6.5; figures for the last two agencies are consistent with these. Two systems were tested, NEC's and the major American product, Printrak.[60]

Table 6.5 shows that NEC's AFIS was significantly more successful than Printrak in correctly identifying latent prints. In almost all cases, NEC's system was more than twice as successful.

The efficiency of NEC's AFIS was given great publicity in 1985 when, three minutes after California's AFIS, developed by NEC, was put into operation, it identified a latent print as that belonging to Richard Ramirez; Ramirez was arrested, and charged with one of fifteen murders attributed to the 'Night Stalker' serial killer (as reported in *Time* magazine, 14 October 1985). The following month NEC sold a second system to Alaska, and eight months later California decided to scrap its existing system in favour of NEC's AFIS.

The puzzle is: Why did NEC's system perform so much better, given that there was a similar starting-point for both systems in 1969? The proximate answer to the puzzle is that NEC was able to develop a superior method for the

---

[60] The research done into AFISs in the early 1970s by the FBI and National Bureau of Standards resulted in a pilot study being done by Calspan Inc. On the basis of this study, the FBI awarded the contract for its first AFIS to Rockwell International. Out of this evolved Rockwell's Printrak Series. In 1981, in the face of slack demand in the USA, Rockwell sold Printrak to Thomas DeLaRue Ltd of the UK.

identification of latent fingerprints. But this poses a further question, tackled in the next section: how was NEC able to develop a superior method, given the similarity in the conditions operating in fingerprinting departments in Japan and the USA?

The reason for the relative efficiency of NEC's AFIS is that the system makes use of more of the information that is available from a fingerprint than do competing systems. In turn, this requires greater computing power and software complexity. More specifically, fingerprint images are made up of lines called *ridges*. Ridges contain end-points and bifurcations that are called *minutiae*. The minutiae positions of every person are different. The systems developed in the USA were based on the recognition of minutiae.

NEC's AFIS, however, uses both minutiae and *ridge counts*. Ridge counts refer to the number of ridges that lie between adjacent minutiae. In the case of latent fingerprints found at the scene of a crime, the fingerprint is often distorted, with the result that the minutiae too are distorted. However, the ridge counts remain the same even in a distorted fingerprint. NEC's system, based on both minutiae and ridge counts, therefore produced a superior performance in the identification of latent fingerprints.

How Did NEC Produce its Superior AFIS?

A number of key factors were responsible for the different evolutionary path followed by NEC's AFIS.

The first factor had to do with a different demand specification by the major user in the USA and Japan. As mentioned above, beginning in 1969 and continuing into the 1970s, Kazuo Kiji and Yukio Hoshino, from NEC's Central Research Laboratories, frequently visited the FBI in the USA to discuss the development of the FBI's AFIS. According to Kiji in an interview with the author, 'Our impression from the visit [was that] the immediate intent of the FBI was to develop a system geared to identifying fingerprint data taken from inked tenprint cards.' The Japanese National Police Agency (NPA), however, 'intended to develop a system that identified fingerprint data using latent fingerprints, or fingerprints discovered at crime scenes. Since the quality of latent fingerprints is very poor when compared with that of tenprints, the NPA's intention represented the more difficult challenge.' From the beginning, therefore, NEC's system was geared towards the identification of latent prints. The superior ability of NEC's AFIS to handle latent prints was the main cause of its superior performance, as recorded in Table 6.5.

The second factor was that NEC's researchers, with the latent print objective in mind, were able successfully to mobilize *tacit knowledge* which existed outside NEC. In 1973 Kiji's team hired retired fingerprint experts from the Tokyo Metropolitan Police Department. In detailed discussions with these experts, conducted with the intention of acquiring their knowledge of how to identify latent fingerprints, it emerged that they were consciously aware of using minutiae (*tokuchō*, or characteristic points, in Japanese), and through detailed questions and answers it emerged that they also used ridge counts in differentiating between fingerprints; however, they were not consciously aware of using ridge counts, they did not themselves refer to ridge counts, and they had no term for ridge counts. In other words, this knowledge was not only tacit knowledge, but unconscious tacit knowledge.[61]

The third factor was that NEC had an existing stock of knowledge on which to draw in developing its AFIS. To begin with, the company already possessed knowledge in the key areas of pattern recognition and image processing. NEC's Central Research Laboratories had begun research on pattern recognition in the 1960s. Two groups working in this area were the Optical Character Recognition Group and the Voice Recognition Group.

The Optical Character Recognition Group had two objectives. The first was to use optical recognition in order to enter data into computers, while the second was to use this technology for mail-sorting. In 1967 NEC exported its first optical character recognition machine to Honeywell. In May 1968 the group completed its first test mail-sorting model which was supplied to the Ministry of Post and Telecommunications. It was members of the Optical Character Recognition Group under Kazuo Kiji who were designated to tackle the request from the Japanese National Police Agency to develop an AFIS.

Pattern recognition and image-processing capabilities in NEC were further strengthened by the research conducted inside the company as part of MITI's Pattern Information Processing System (PIPS) project, which ran from 1971 to 1980. This co-operative R&D project involved eight other major Japanese firms and MITI's Electrotechnical Laboratories. It generated a good deal of fairly fundamental knowledge that was to prove valuable in the longer run to the participating firms.[62]

In addition to NEC's existing knowledge in the areas of pattern recognition and image processing, the company also possessed key *supporting knowledge*. This knowledge was in areas such as dedicated LSIs (in this case, microprocessors) and software (which allowed for the development of the fingerprint-matching algorithms). It was this total stock of knowledge that gave Kiji and his team the confidence that they would be able to develop a system that could handle all the information required for the analysis of both minutiae and ridge counts.

---

[61] M. Polanyi, *The Tacit Dimension*, Doubleday Anchor, Garden City, NY, 1967. Polanyi is the *locus classicus* for the analysis of tacit knowledge. He defined someone as possessing tacit knowledge when they know more than they can tell. The present study, however, suggests that it is worth making a further distinction between tacit knowledge and *unconscious tacit knowledge*. In the latter case, a person does not even know that they know. Accordingly, in mobilizing unconscious knowledge, in the first step it is necessary to make the unconscious knowledge conscious. The second step—making the conscious tacit knowledge explicit—poses the same problems for both tacit knowledge and unconscious tacit knowledge.

[62] For further details on the PIPS project, see Fransman, *The Market and Beyond*.

The Development Process

The Three Sub-systems

NEC's AFIS is divided into three sub-systems. These are the Input Sub-system, into which the fingerprint data is put; the Matching Sub-system, which matches fingerprints with those held in the sub-system's data-base; and the Image Retrieval Sub-system, which allows the target fingerprint to be compared with the closest fingerprint in the data-base.

The chronology of the development process and the relationship with the Central Research Laboratories are shown in Table 6.6 and Fig. 6.17.

In 1955 Kazuo Kiji joined NEC's research laboratories. In the 1960s he

Table 6.6 *Chronology of the Development of NEC's AFIS*

Year	Stage of development
1969	National Policy Agency requests the system; Kiji visits the FBI
1971	Team formed in the research laboratory
1974	Project team set up in EDP Government System Division of the EDP Division
1979	Project team transformed into Fingerprint Identification System Department, in the EDP Government System Division
1983	NEC Security Systems Ltd set up in EDP Government System Division

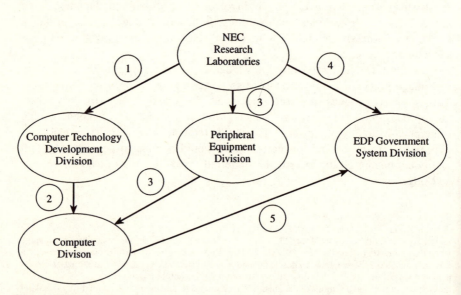

Fig. 6.17 The transfer of research on AFIS from NEC's research laboratories
TECHNOLOGY TRANSFERRED: 1, algorithms; 2, matching processor; 3, scanner; 4, software; 5, hardware. See text for further explanation

worked in the Optical Character Recognition Group. In 1969 the Japanese National Police Agency, which already had dealings with NEC, requested the company to develop an AFIS, and in the same year Kiji visited the FBI. (At this stage the NPA provided no funding for the project.)

In October 1971 a small research team was formed in NEC's research laboratory. At this stage the research was primarily 'cradle research', which occupied only a small proportion of the time of most of the researchers. Kiji, a manager in the laboratory at the time who was continuing with other research on optical character recognition and remote sensing, was designated as leader of the team. Yukio Hoshino, a supervisor in the laboratory who was also simultaneously working on other optical character recognition research, was the second member of the team, devoting about 10 per cent of his time to it. At this stage the only full-time member of the team was Koh Asai, a young researcher who worked on the development of the algorithms.

In 1974 a project team was set up in the Electronic Data Processing (EDP) Government System Division of the EDP Division. The members of this team were drawn both from the research laboratory and from the EDP Government System Division. However, most of the team members still worked only part-time on the project. There were 10 members of the team in all: one algorithm researcher (Asai); two people working on the development of the dedicated equipment (such as the scanner and processing equipment); three on the systems engineering (on how to organize the total system); and four on the hardware and software design.

In 1979 the project team was transformed into a department, the Fingerprint Identification System Department, in the EDP Government System Division. At this time Kiji was formally transferred from the research laboratory to head this department. Hoshino and Asai joined him.

In 1983 the Fingerprint Identification System Department became NEC Security Systems Ltd, with Kiji as its head, a 100 per cent NEC-owned company, treated as a distinct cost centre in the EDP Government System Division.

The role of the different co-operating divisions in NEC in the development of the AFIS is shown in Fig. 6.17. The algorithms developed by Asai (necessary for a processor dedicated to the matching of fingerprints) were transferred to the Computer Technology Development Division, a development laboratory located within the Computer Division. To facilitate the transfer process, Asai was moved to the Computer Technology Development Division although formally he remained a member of the research laboratory.

The work done by the project team on the scanner was transferred to the Peripheral Equipment Division in the Fuchu Plant. This division was responsible for developing new prototypes. Thereafter, the prototype scanner was transferred to the Computer Division, where it was manufactured together with other items such as the matching processor. It was the EDP Government System Division—and, after 1983, NEC Security Systems Ltd—that assumed responsibility for the total system design, for the software development (the initial software developed in the research laboratory was transferred here), for the testing of the final system, and for sales.

Post-Innovation Improvements

In order to retain its dominant share of the market, it has been necessary for NEC continually to improve its AFIS. The necessity for post-innovation improvements has been aided by the presence of Kiji and his colleagues, who began their working lives in NEC's research laboratories dealing with the technologies that underlie the AFIS. Kiji's words in an interview with the author are illuminating: 'I still think that I am doing research in my job as head of NEC Security Systems Ltd because of all the improvements we continually have to make.'

The following have been the most important post-innovation improvements made in NEC's AFIS:

* Improved accuracy—for example, improvement of the matching algorithm
* Improved processing speeds
* Easier operation
* Downsizing and reduced power consumption
* New features

As an example of the implementation of new features, beginning in July 1991, Singapore, using an NEC AFIS, required all 18-year-olds to carry an identification card with their fingerprints. The system requires the fingerprint to be put on glass; an optical scanner then reads the data which are then transferred to an optical disc where they are stored; from here they are printed on the identification card.

NEC is also involved in tracking the development of new technologies that may radically alter the way in which 'fingerprints' are identified. One example is DNA fingerprinting. At present, however, there are two major problems with this new DNA technology: first, it takes a long time to analyse the DNA; second, a huge data-base is required to store the genetic data. It is therefore likely that improved versions of the current AFIS will continue to be used until the next century.

NEC's Selection Environment

A firm exists within an environment that will influence its continued existence and growth over time. This environment, following the biological analogy, may be referred to as a selection environment since, for a population of firms, it selects which of these firms will survive and prosper. Unlike in the case of biological organisms, however, the individual firm, as with other social organizations, has a greater degree of freedom in responding to the external constraints imposed by its selection environment.

One of the major tasks of any firm, therefore, is to appraise its selection environment in order to understand the 'rules of the game' that this environment implies and, in the light of this understanding, to work out what should be done. This process of appraisal is intimately related to the *vision* of the firm's leaders, that is the set of beliefs that guide their understanding of their environment and therefore shape the strategies and tactics that they choose in deciding how the firm should act. The relationship between selection environment and vision, however, is not a one-way deterministic causation from the former to the latter. In other words, selection environments do not mechanistically determine beliefs and therefore vision. Within the same selection environment, different people may well arrive at different beliefs. This is a major cause of differences among firms. In turn, it is this variety, together with the selection process, that influences the evolution of the firms.

The selection environment is also closely related to the *competences* that the firm accumulates over time as well as to the *forms of organization* that it develops. The reason is simply that the firm's competences and forms of organization must be sufficiently well adapted to its selection environment to allow the firm at the very least to survive, if not to profit more than, and grow more rapidly than, the other firms in the selection environment.

For these reasons, the analysis of NEC must contain an appraisal of the company's selection environment. What have been the main features of this environment? How have these features changed over time? What influence have they had on the evolutionary path that the company has followed? More specifically, how has NEC's selection environment influenced its competences and forms of organization? And how, in turn, have these influenced the company's competitiveness and future prospects? These are the kinds of questions that will be examined in this section.

The Ministry of Communications and NTT

Historically, the Ministry of Communications and, after the war, NTT, have been among the most important features of NEC's selection environment. The Ministry and later NTT were an important source of demand and stability for NEC. Furthermore, as we saw earlier in this book, the practice of controlled competition introduced by the Ministry in the late 1920s and 1930s, a practice perpetuated by NTT, meant that NEC faced a degree of competition from the other telecommunications equipment companies, Fujitsu, Hitachi, and Oki, even though it remained the largest supplier. This controlled competition influenced both NEC's competences and its evolving form of organization. But not only were the Ministry and then NTT an important market for NEC; from the time of their establishment, both these bodies possessed important R&D facilities which transferred technologies to NEC and the other equipment suppliers, thus aiding their accumulation of competences in telecommunications-related areas.

Precisely how important were the Ministry and NTT for NEC? In a 1967 memo to his company's workers, Koji Kobayashi answered this question: 'Since NEC's founding the primary mission of our company has . . . been to make communications equipment for our number one customer, formerly the Ministry of Communications and now NTT. . . . Before the war almost three-quarters of our sales were to the Ministry of Communications. . . . Even today nearly half our sales are still to . . . NTT.'[63]

More specifically, NEC, Fujitsu, Hitachi, and Oki were beneficiaries of the many telecommunications expansion programmes launched by the Ministry and later NTT. These programmes reflected Japan's economic growth and were designed to improve the country's telecommunications infrastructure.

NTT's six five-year programmes, from the time of its founding until it became partly privatized in 1985, are set out in Table 6.7. As can be seen, the budget that was allocated for the first four programmes, spanning the twenty-year period 1953–1973, more than doubled in money terms on each occasion.

How did NEC's sales to NTT change over time? The answer to this question is contained in the information provided in Table 6.8. The table shows that, even through Japan's high-growth years in the 1960s and 1970s, sales to NTT were extremely important for NEC. As late as 1967, as Kobayashi noted, sales to NTT constituted almost 50 per cent of NEC's total sales. In the mid-1970s they still accounted for about one-third of NEC's total sales. Thereafter, however, these sales steadily decreased in proportional significance; by 1985, the year in which NTT was partly privatized, it accounted for only 13 per cent of NEC's sales. Although figures are no longer published, my own estimate is that NEC's sales to NTT account for between 5 and 10 per cent of total sales. This is still a highly significant amount and means that NTT remains NEC's largest single customer.

What has been the importance of the relationship with NTT for NEC's evolution? There are several components to the answer to this important question. On the positive side, NEC benefited from the relationship in a number of ways. The steadily increasing demand for telecommunications equipment from NTT, a by-product of the growth of the Japanese economy, gave NEC (and, to a lesser extent, Fujitsu, Hitachi, and Oki) steady growth in output and virtually guaranteed basic profitability. In this way the relationship with NTT provided

Table 6.7 *NTT's Five-Year Telecommunications Expansion Programmes, 1953–1985*

Period of expansion	Budget (¥bn)
Oct. 1953–Mar. 1958	302.1
Apr. 1958–Mar. 1963	725.5
Apr. 1963–Mar. 1968	1,787.5
Apr. 1968–Mar. 1973	3,819.8
Apr. 1973–Mar. 1978	—
Apr. 1978–Mar. 1985	—

[63] Kobayashi, *The Rise of NEC*, 35.

relatively stable and certain conditions, which were conducive for the accumulation of competences in NEC. As Koji Kobayashi acknowledged, 'doing business with NTT did not result in big earnings for NEC then, but it always guaranteed us a certain amount of profit. These assured profits contributed to NEC's business stability'.[64]

Furthermore, NEC's relationship with NTT had a number of other consequences that were to prove beneficial in the longer term. Although NTT's expenditure in the 1960s and 1970s increased steadily and grew faster than the growth of GNP, its growth rate was still significantly less than that for the manufacturing sector. At this time, growth in GNP was around 9 per cent while the manufacturing sector was growing at around 19 per cent; some of the companies involved in household electrical appliances were growing at rates of

Table 6.8 *Breakdown of NEC's Sales, 1939–1993 (%)*

	NTT/ government	Other domestic	Total domestic	Foreign
1939	~75			
1964			90.6	9.4
1965			91.9	8.1
1966			89.5	10.5
1967	~50		90.3	9.7
1968			81.0	19.0
1974	32	48	80	20
1975	32	47	79	21
1976	30	46	76	24
1977	25	49	74	26
1978	22	50	72	28
1979	22	52	74	26
1980	21	49	70	30
1981	20	50	70	30
1982	18	49	67	33
1983	16	50	66	34
1984	14	51	65	35
1985	13	53	66	34
1986			67	33
1987			72	28
1988			73	27
1989			75	25
1990			74	26
1991			77	23
1992			79	21
1993			77	23

Sources: NEC Corporation: The First 80 Years, NEC, Tokyo; K. Kobayashi, *The Rise of NEC*, Basil Blackwell, Oxford, 1991; NEC Annual Reports.

[64] Ibid. 41–2.

30 per cent per annum. Moreover, as a result of controlled competition, NEC had to share the NTT market with the other telecommunications equipment manufacturers, such as Fujitsu, Hitachi and Oki. These factors therefore constrained both NEC's growth and its size, to the extent that it remained highly dependent on NTT.

The Relative Importance of NEC's Sales to NTT, the Rest of the Domestic Market, and Overseas

At this time, however, according to Kobayashi, 'No one in his right mind would have considered a growth rate of only just over 10 percent [the rate of growth in NTT's expenditure] satisfactory for NEC. Our ambition in the early 1960s . . . was to maintain an annual growth rate of 20 percent.' This in turn, as Kobayashi noted, 'had obvious implications for our relationship with NTT. . . . Although from time to time I warned against underrating the importance of NTT in our eagerness to branch out into new areas, our main objective had to be cultivation of both the private sector and [the] overseas market.'[65]

How successful was NEC's strategy to use both the Japanese domestic market and the overseas market to fuel a growth rate faster than that provided by the growth in NTT's expenditures? Table 6.8 shows that, over the twelve-year period 1974–1985, sales to NTT decreased from 32 per cent of total sales to 13 per cent. However, over this period sales to the rest of the domestic market (i.e. excluding NTT and government) increased only slightly, from 48 to 53 per cent. During this period it was growing overseas sales, mainly to developing countries, that contributed most significantly to NEC's growth. These sales increased from 20 per cent of the total in 1974 to 34 per cent in 1985.

However, in the decade from the mid-1980s to the mid-1990s, it was primarily the other domestic market (i.e. not NTT or government) that fuelled NEC's growth. As Table 6.8 shows, from 1985 to 1993 NEC's total domestic sales increased from 66 to 77 per cent of total sales. Since we know that sales to NTT and government decreased proportionally during this period, it is clear that the rest of the domestic market became even more important in generating NEC's growth. Conversely, the proportional significance of foreign sales decreased substantially; while in 1984 they peaked, comprising 35 per cent of total sales, by 1993 this had fallen to 23 per cent.

These figures suggest that from the mid-1980s it was increasingly the domestic Japanese market, rather than the foreign market, that powered NEC's growth. This, in turn, raises other important questions. Was the same true for the other major Japanese information and communications companies? How did they compare with other leading sectors such as consumer electronics and motor vehicles?

The information provided in Table 6.9 throws some light on these questions.

---

[65] Ibid. 43.

This table shows the export ratio for Japan's leading companies in these three sectors, that is the company's exports as a percentage of total sales.[66] The table suggests two important things. First, the recent growth of all the major information and communications companies has been driven primarily by the Japanese domestic market. Second, the information and communications companies have been significantly more domestically oriented than their counterparts in consumer electronics and motor vehicles. In turn, this suggests that the Japanese consumer electronics and motor vehicle companies have enjoyed greater international competitiveness than the information and communications companies. In the conclusion to this book we will return to this significant point.

As Table 6.9 shows, NEC's export ratio was 18 per cent, the same as Mitsubishi Electric's, but higher than Fujitsu and Hitachi's, which were 14 and 16 per cent, respectively. Toshiba and the far smaller Oki had the highest export ratios—25 per cent each. However, the export ratios for all the information and communications companies were significantly lower than for all the consumer

Table 6.9 *Export Ratios of Selected Japanese Companies, 1992*[a]

	Export ratio
Information and communications companies	
NEC	18
Fujitsu	14
Hitachi	16
Toshiba	25
Mitsubishi Electric	18
Oki	25
Consumer electronics companies	
Matsushita Electrical Industrial	35
Sony	64
Sharp	45
Canon	78
Motor vehicle companies	
Toyota	36
Nissan	41
Mitsubishi Motors	48

[a] The 'export ratio' is the company's export as a percentage of total sales, and includes direct exports by the company and all exports through trading firms.

Source: Japan Company Handbook, Toyo Keizai Inc., Tokyo (1992): 29.

[66] The export ratio in Table 6.9 must be distinguished from the foreign sales ratio in Table 6.8. While the foreign sales ratio refers to total sales abroad, whether exported from Japan or sold from the company's plants abroad, the export ratio refers only to exports from production that occurs in Japan. The data in the two tables suggest that while 21% of NEC's total sales were to foreign markets, 18% of total sales went in the form of exports. This implies that 3% of NEC's total sales took the form of sales to foreign markets from the company's plants located abroad.

electronics and motor vehicle companies. In consumer electronics Canon and Sony had the highest export ratios of 78 and 64 per cent, respectively. Matsushita at 35 per cent had the lowest ratio among the consumer electronics companies, but even this was 10 per cent higher than the top exporting information and communications companies, Toshiba and Oki. In the case of the motor vehicle companies, Toyota had the lowest export ratio with 36 per cent, about the same as Matsushita's, while Nissan and Mitsubishi had higher ratios of 41 and 48 per cent, respectively.

NTT and NEC's Competences

As the first section of this chapter makes clear, the Ministry of Communications played an important role in assisting the company to develop its competences. Indeed, until the Second World War, all of NEC's competences—e.g. in transmissions, switching, and radio communications—were accumulated with the active assistance of the Ministry. Not only did the Ministry itself possess important technological capabilities in its research and engineering laboratories, it was also the most important *user* of these technologies, which were embodied in the equipment and other services which it purchased. As a technologically sophisticated user, the Ministry developed important knowledge about telecommunications technologies, and a significant proportion of this knowledge was transferred to NEC together with Fujitsu, Hitachi, Oki and the other suppliers such as the cable makers. In the early stages knowledge was transferred partly through the permanent transfer of technical staff from the Ministry to NEC, as documented above. But most important was the *joint learning* that took place as engineers from the Ministry and the supplying companies co-operated in research, design, and development activities. After the war, as we saw, NTT continued this role.

However, there was also a negative side to the impact of the relationship with NTT on NEC's competences. To some extent this negative impact was not on the technological capabilities *per se* that NEC developed, but on the way in which these technological capabilities were turned into valuable products. In other words, in some cases the negative impact was on the competences relating to the commercialization end of the value-chain.

Koji Kobayashi referred to some of these negative impacts when he frankly admitted that 'Because NTT had traditionally been NEC's chief customer . . . our dealings with the market for ordinary industrial or consumer use were weak.'[67] Kobayashi's insightful observation is extremely important because it points to the close interdependence that exists between a firm's selection environment and the kinds of competences it accumulates—in this case, inter-dependence between the demand characteristics of a firm's major customers and the competences which that firm develops in order to satisfy these demands.

[67] Kobayashi, *The Rise of NEC*, 33.

As a result of the overwhelming importance of NTT as NEC's biggest single customer, and the small number of similarly large telecommunications carriers in the company's other overseas markets, NEC failed to develop the competences, including marketing and distribution capabilities, that were needed to sell consumer electronics products effectively. As a result, NEC failed to make much impact on the consumer electronics market in Japan and abroad, despite the relative depth and sophistication of its competences in the underlying technologies relative to the major consumer electronics companies such as Matsushita and Sony. NEC has always been at something of a loss in deciding how to handle its consumer products division.

Other examples of the importance of the interdependence between selection environment—in this case the characteristics of customer demand—and the competences developed by NEC have been given elsewhere in this book. For instance, in Chapter 3 it was seen how NEC was slow to develop competences in digital switching as a result of NTT's belated decision to move into this new technology. It was only when NEC's US division began feeling the pressure from competitors such as Northern Telecom, which were offering digital switches, that NEC decided to develop its NEAX digital switch. However this meant, unlike in the cases of almost all other internationally successful Japanese products, that NEC had to develop a major export product *before* it had been tried, tested, and improved through use in the Japanese market. Partly because the NEAX switch did not first go through an initiation process in the Japanese market, partly because of NEC's late entry into the overseas digital switch market, and partly because of the company's problems in providing the software support needed to tailor the switch to the circumstances of the US network, NEC failed to establish a strong position in this market when it began liberalizing from the late 1970s.

Another example of NEC suffering from the negative influence (albeit unintended) of NTT is in the area of software competences. For strategic reasons, NTT has decided that it must possess strong in-house competences in the area of software engineering since these are crucial for the development of competitive new telecommunications services. For instance, as was seen in Chapter 3, NTT has decided that it will develop in-house some of the software-intensive layers of the new broadband ATM (asynchronous transfer mode) switch which will serve as the workhorse in the forthcoming multimedia age. This strategic decision of NTT's has deprived NEC and the other suppliers of switches, such as Fujitsu and Northern Telecom, of an important opportunity to strengthen their software competences. Although these companies will continue to develop their own competences in this area, necessary for their competitiveness in the emerging global broadband switching markets, NTT's decision, understandable though it is from its own strategic point of view, represents a lost opportunity, particularly for NEC as NTT's major supplier.

These examples of the negative impact of NTT on NEC raise a question of major importance: Has NEC's relationship with NTT, historically extremely important for the accumulation of NEC's competences, now outlived its usefulness? In short, has NEC's 'tail' (NTT, which now accounts for 5–10 per cent of NEC's sales) begun wagging the NEC 'dog', taking it in directions that will impede NEC's attempts to establish increasing global competitiveness?

Several preliminary points must be made in attempting to answer this question. As was explained earlier, the Ministry of Communications and later NTT played a crucial role in developing the initial competences that eventually allowed NEC to accumulate the further competences that now underlie its activities in computers, telecommunications, and semiconductors. At the present time, however, it is only in the area of complex telecommunications equipment, such as central office switches and transmissions, and related software, that NTT continues to exert a major influence on NEC competences. It is, therefore, only in this area that the 'tail and dog' analogy carries weight. Nevertheless, since complex equipment is an important market segment for NEC, the question remains pertinent.

Secondly, it is obvious that, however NEC might in the future want to modify its relationship with NTT, the latter, as the company's largest customer, will continue to carry weight. Accordingly, NEC, as NTT's largest supplier, will continue to focus on the specific needs of this important client. Having said this, it is interesting to note that there are at least some influential voices in NEC suggesting that now is the time for a fundamental reshaping of the company's traditional relationship with NTT. In the rest of this section, these arguments for change in the relationship will be analysed.[68]

Voices for Change

As discussed in various points in this book, since its part-privatization in 1985 NTT has continued its past practice, and that of the prewar Ministry of Communications, of jointly developing telecommunications equipment with a small group of suppliers. Under the Track 3 procedures, NTT has invited joint development where equipment that it considers important for the future development of telecommunications services is not available on adequate terms on the market. The main difference, however, from NTT's pre-1985 practice is that in principle any company—Western as well as Japanese—is now eligible for membership in the joint projects. In practice, this has meant that in most cases the traditional Japanese telecommunications suppliers—NEC, Fujitsu, Hitachi, and Oki—have been joined by other Western and Japanese suppliers in the Track 3 projects. The latter have included companies such as Northern Telecom, IBM Japan, DEC, Toshiba, and Matsushita.

How have the post-1985 changes affected NEC? Does the company still derive substantial net benefits from its relationship with NTT? In a frank interview with the author, a former senior vice president of NEC expressed the views of at least

---

[68] The following discussion is based largely on the author's interviews with a former senior vice president of NEC.

a few in the company regarding these questions. To begin with, as mentioned above, it was acknowledged that NTT is still NEC's biggest customer and therefore retains its overall importance for the company. Nevertheless, it was felt that the post-1985 changes have reduced the benefits to NEC of the relationship. The main reason, it was suggested, is that NTT, largely as a result of political pressures, is now forced to purchase equipment from Western and Japanese companies that are not necessarily the most competitive. More specifically, trade-related pressures from Western countries, in particular the USA, as well as political pressures from within Japan, are forcing NTT to introduce political considerations into its procurement and Track 3 joint development decisions. This means that NTT's traditional suppliers, such as NEC and Fujitsu, the companies with the strongest competences in telecommunications equipment—competences that are best adapted to the circumstances of the Japanese market—are forced to take a smaller cut of this market.

Before 1985, the *quid pro quo* involved the traditional suppliers committing resources to NTT's needs, partly through the joint development projects, in return for a reasonably lucrative share of NTT's procurement. Now, with the spreading of NTT's procurement beyond the traditional suppliers, the benefit side of the equation has been reduced. But the cost side, the commitment of resources to NTT, has not decreased similarly. Furthermore, resources committed to NTT are not necessarily in the best interests of NEC's global competitiveness.

One example is the case of the digital switches jointly developed for NTT—the D70 and D60. As shown in the earlier chapter on switches, NTT was late in developing digital switching, which in turn disadvantaged NEC and Fujitsu in their bid for a share of the US market for these switches. Moreover, the D70 and D60, when they were eventually developed, were optimized for the Japanese network and very few of them were ever sold abroad. Instead, NEC and Fujitsu were forced to develop an additional digital switch—NEC's NEAX and Fujitsu's FETEX—for sale outside Japan. The cost of supporting two different digital switches has been substantial and inefficient. In the words of the former senior vice president, 'We had to commit NEC's resources to NTT's projects, while at the same time developing our own equipment for sale on the global market.'

What are the implications of all this? In the opinion of the former senior vice president, the interests of both NTT and NEC would best be served by a radical transformation of the traditional relationship. In his view, NTT should move to a position closer to that of British Telecom. Accordingly, NTT should engage in fewer joint R&D projects and rely more on open competition in the telecommunications equipment market for its needs. This would allow NEC to compete more fairly and effectively for NTT's business while giving the company a freer hand in developing global strategies for the development and sale of its complex telecommunications equipment, allowing it to be less constrained by NTT's specific requirements.

This suggestion, it is clear, would involve a radical change in the relationship that NTT has forged with its suppliers. It must be said, however, that, although some in authority in NTT might agree with the direction being proposed—namely, those who are not convinced that the company's future lies in being a technology-driven company—this is not yet a dominant view in NTT. Nevertheless, it was clear from this interview that in the mid-1990s there is greater fluidity in the supplier relationships that characterize the Japanese telecommunications industry than at any time since the late 1920s and early 1930s.

The Role of Government

The discussion of the importance of the Ministry of Communications and NTT for NEC raises the broader question of the role of government in NEC's selection environment. How important has the Japanese government been for NEC's evolution and growth?

Part of this question was answered in the last section, to the extent that 'government' refers to the Ministry of Communications and, at least until 1985, NTT. It remains to clarify the role played by the Japanese government more generally in NEC's evolution and growth.

Protection and Promotion

Without doubt, one of the most important functions of the Japanese government has been to provide a protective environment enabling the infant communications and information industry to accumulate the competences that would eventually enable it to stand on its own two feet in a competitive way. As shown in Chapter 2, until the Second World War it was the Ministry of Communications that not only provided a protected market for the Japanese telecommunications equipment companies, but also actively promoted the development of their competences. In effect, foreign companies, denied the opportunity of exporting their equipment to Japan or supplying the Japanese market through wholly owned direct foreign investment, had no option but to sell their technology to the Japanese equipment suppliers.

In this way, for example, Western Electric supplied technology to NEC in its joint venture with Japanese entrepreneurs, and Siemens provided technology to the company that later became Fujitsu. The Ministry played a key role in assisting the transfer of technology to Hitachi (which before the war was alone in not having a major foreign technology supplier) some of which came indirectly from foreign companies. Under conditions of free trade and free inward capital movement, it is most unlikely that a significant infant communications industry would have emerged. Government protection and promotion was therefore a necessary condition for the development of the Japanese communications industry.

After the war, government protection and promotion also played a crucial role in enabling the Japanese communications companies to diversify into new emerging markets such as computers and semiconductors. However, although these markets were new, the competences on which they rested were derived from competences that the companies had already accumulated in the prewar period. In NEC's case, for example, computers were first developed in its Tamagawa plant. This plant was set up in 1936 and was responsible for radio communications and vacuum tubes. It was the transmission engineers in the Tamagawa plant who built NEC's first computers, in the process acquiring new knowledge on the basis of competences they had developed before the war.

The government helped the Japanese communications companies (together with Toshiba, which, though not one of the main telecommunications equipment suppliers, was from the prewar period deeply involved in radio communications) in two main ways. First, on the demand side, the government ensured that the domestic market, where possible, would be reserved for Japanese companies. Second, on the supply side, government institutions played a leading role in directly developing technologies and prototypes in computers and semiconductors and transferring them to the leading Japanese companies. Particular mention must be made here of the roles played by NTT's Electrical Communications Laboratories (ECL) and the Ministry of International Trade and Industry's Electotechnical Laboratories (ETL). NEC's first computer, for example, was based on the prototype transferred to the company from ECL's Musashino Laboratories. This initiating role played by the Japanese government was particularly important in facilitating timely entry by the Japanese companies into these new industries which at the early stage of their development faced significant uncertainty.

Government also helped by providing funding for R&D and organizing co-operative R&D projects involving the leading companies and government research laboratories. In addition, financial assistance was provided for the purchase of Japanese-made computers. It is worth noting that, by the late 1980s, in companies such as NEC about 5 per cent of total R&D expenditure came from Japanese government sources. However, this R&D funding was concentrated mainly in longer-term, more uncertain, areas and in these areas was of greater significance than the 5 per cent figure suggests.[69]

By the mid-1970s, the Japanese companies had successfully established themselves in the information and communications area and were by and large able to stand on their own two feet without great additional government support. Largely by taking advantage of the opportunities provided in the rapidly expanding Japanese market, they had grown to substantial sizes by international standards. As large global companies, they had their own significant in-house R&D capabilities and were able to tap international markets for their capital needs. In a real sense, they had outgrown the government that had nurtured them.

---

[69] A detailed analysis of the role of the Japanese government in the development of the Japanese computer and semiconductor industries is contained in Fransman, *The Market and Beyond.*

However, over the whole postwar period there is little doubt regarding the crucial facilitating role that the Japanese government played in creating the selection environment that encouraged the birth and growth of these companies.

Product Market Competition

A further crucial feature of NEC's selection environment was the competition that the company faced in its various product markets. Earlier parts of this book have stressed the importance of controlled competition, which governed the relationship between the Ministry of Communications and later NTT and their Japanese equipment suppliers. While this form of organization gave the suppliers longer-term stability, it also placed them under some degree of competitive pressure. Both these factors assisted in their accumulation of competences.

Outside its relationship with the Ministry and NTT, NEC faced strong competition from the other Japanese companies in the Japanese market. Anyone who has read the personal accounts by company leaders such as Koji Kobayashi of NEC or his counterpart and competitor Taiyu Kobayashi of Fujitsu cannot but be impressed by the intensity of the competitive battles that were waged.[70] Competitive pressure came not only from other Japanese companies. In the Japanese computer market, for example, IBM Japan, established in Japan since before the Second World War, provided a crucial source of competition, even if the Japanese government did its best to ensure that IBM did not overwhelm the Japanese companies with its superior technology.

Furthermore, Japanese companies faced strong competition in the foreign markets that they were entering increasingly from the 1960s on. In the 1980s and 1990s, the degree of foreign competition in the Japanese information and communications markets intensified greatly as the Japanese government, under mounting Western pressure, took steps to increase foreign access. Although controversy still surrounds the question of the degree of the openness of Japanese information and communications markets—and there have been vigorous debates regarding markets such as semiconductors, supercomputers, and mobile communications—there is no doubt that foreign competitive pressure on Japanese companies in Japan in these markets has become far greater. In NEC's case, for example, significant pressure has come in the early 1990s in the personal computer market, a market where NEC had enjoyed a more than 50 per cent market share.

From the point of view of an analysis of NEC's selection environment, it is crucial that the competitive pressure put in these ways on NEC and the other Japanese information and communications companies was a necessary complement to the protection and promotion measures taken by the Japanese government up to the 1980s. As a result of the competitive pressure, which

---

[70] T. Kobayashi, *Fortune Favors the Brave. Fujitsu: Thirty Years in Computers*, Toyo Keizai Shinposha, Tokyo, 1986.

increased significantly over time, the Japanese companies were forced constantly to hone their competences to suit their competitive environment.

Corporate Governance

A further crucial feature of NEC's selection environment is the link that the company has with the capital markets. This link has been an important determinant of NEC's behaviour through its influence on the company's corporate governance. Table 6.10 provides information on NEC's shareholders. It can be seen that financial institutions held 52 per cent of NEC's shares, other Japanese corporations held 16 per cent, Japanese individuals 24 per cent, and foreign investors only 8 per cent. A large proportion of the Japanese financial and other corporate shareholders, however, are what may be referred to as 'committed shareholders'. A committed shareholder may be defined as one that will 'stay and fight rather than switch', that is, will retain the shares rather than sell them even when a short-term gain is expected from selling and buying other shares. Why would a shareholder forgo the gain that could be made from selling? In Japan such shareholders are companies with a long-term stake in the company, for example banks and insurance companies which provide financial services to the company, or other companies which buy from or sell to the company.

Koji Kobayashi has acknowledged the significance of 'patient' shareholders and, indeed, has gone so far as to admit that 'it is doubtful whether the price of NEC stock met our shareholders' expectations until the late 1960s or early 1970s'. With shareholders such as these, it is less surprising that he was able

Table 6.10 *NEC's 'Committed' Shareholders, 1993*[a]

	%
Composition of shareholders	
Financial institutions	52
Other Japanese corporations	16
Japanese individuals and others	24
Foreign investors	8
	100
Major shareholders	
Sumitomo Life Insurance Co.	6.78
Sumitomo Bank	5.00
Sumitomo Trust & Banking	4.73
Sumitomo Marine & Fire Insurance	2.61
Sumitomo Electric	2.15
Sumitomo Corporation	2.15
	23.42

[a] 'Committed shareholders' will 'stay and fight rather than switch', even in the face of an unfavourable movement in expected share prices.

emphatically to declare that, 'Although profit is a necessary condition for the development of a corporation, *the ultimate objective of management is not profit, but perpetuating the business.*'[71]

Table 6.10 also lists those committed shareholders that are part of the Sumitomo group of companies. As can be seen, over 23 per cent of NEC's shares are held by this group of companies. (Interestingly, Sumitomo Trust & Banking, which holds 4.7 per cent of NEC's shares, also holds 2.8 per cent of Fujitsu's shares, NEC's main Japanese competitor.) In 1961, 38 per cent of NEC's shares were held by Sumitomo group companies.

In NEC, as in other similar Japanese companies, committed shareholders, while possessing detailed information about the performance and activities of the company in which they hold shares, have an arm's-length relationship with the management of the company, so long as it does not experience financial difficulties. If it does, committed shareholders will play an active role in the restructuring of the company.

This role played by NEC's committed shareholders is also evident in the composition of the NEC Board. In this connection it is worth noting that in 1992 the only outside director on the board was Kyonosuke Ibe, from the Sumitomo Bank; all the other directors were drawn from within NEC. (Sumitomo Bank was the second largest of NEC's shareholders, with a 5.0 per cent shareholding compared with 6.8 per cent for Sumitomo Life Insurance.) Until the late 1980s NEC usually had a former NTT employee as a board member but it has since ceased this practice. Fujitsu, on the other hand, still has one board member formerly from NTT.

It is also worth noting the composition of the NEC Board, since this affects the governance of the company as well as the substance of the decisions that it makes. Of the 38 directors of the Board in 1992, 60 per cent had a background in engineering while the remaining 40 per cent had backgrounds in areas such as law, marketing, and finance. Furthermore, 8 had backgrounds in research in the company, including Tadahiro Sekimoto, the president.

But is this form of corporate governance a positive or negative influence on NEC's long-term growth? On the positive side, it can be argued that NEC's corporate governance gives the company a stability that its Western competitors lack, allowing it steadily to accumulate the competences that will give it increasing international competitiveness into the twenty-first century. This is certainly one way of reading the nonplussed comments made in the financial press regarding NEC's behaviour under the influence of bad financial results, such as the following comments made in the *Financial Times*:

There is something almost quaintly old-fashioned in the optimism of Mr Tadahiro Sekimoto, the white-haired, bespectacled president of NEC. . . . Mr Sekimoto is exuberant about the future, even though his company just reported a 61.7 per cent decline in consolidated pre-tax profits in the year to the end of March. NEC's share price has dropped

---

[71] Kobayashi, *The Rise of NEC*, 103.

10 per cent in the past month; over 25 per cent since the start of the year. Capital spending this year is being cut by 19 per cent.

And Mr Sekimoto's response?:

Our Japanese-style management is not affected by the immediate results; we are not that short-sighted. We are looking at least five years ahead, sometimes 10 years ahead.[72]

It is, however, possible to give a less charitable interpretation to such responses. It could be argued that, while this mode of corporate governance is well suited to reasonably stable conditions in product markets and technology, and even is reasonably adapted to fairly wide fluctuations in the business cycle, it is not appropriate for radical changes in a company's environment. Where there are such radical changes, the argument might go, a board comprised almost entirely of insiders who have been appointed largely by the company's present leaders and who have imbibed their beliefs and prejudices is not equipped to deliver the changes in thinking and the pressure that is required to adjust to the new circumstances. Furthermore, although in the last resort the 'committed shareholders' can intervene to redirect the company, they are unlikely to rock the boat until they have to, and this may compromise the company's timely adjustment to the changes.

According to such thinking, from the 1990s conditions in the Japanese information and communications industry have altered radically. This is arguably evident in changes such as the following: unprecedented competition in the Japanese and global computer markets as a result of downsizing, open-systems, and the 'commoditization' of computers as the underlying technologies have been diffused to new, lower-cost, entrants; increased competition in telecommunications equipment markets as a result of the liberalization of previously closed national markets; greater competition in semiconductor markets, particularly memories, as a result of new entrants such as Samsung of Korea; more intense competition from both domestic and foreign companies in all the information and communications markets in Japan.

These changes, it can be argued, require the kinds of alterations in corporate behaviour that are sometimes so painful and threatening to consensus that only tough-minded 'independent' shareholders can push them through. These are the kinds of shareholders, it may be suggested, that are rapidly and effectively restructuring Western competitors such as IBM and AT&T, the companies that NEC will have to contend with in the increasingly globalized markets of the twenty-first century.

How convincing are these arguments? On the one hand, there is evidence that the 'independent' shareholder-driven corporate governance mode of Western companies is motivating significant corporate restructuring in the companies facing these radical changes. On the other hand, however, it is less clear whether the substantial costs of such restructuring, including the shake-up in corporate

[72] *Financial Times* (11 June 1992), 29

structures and morale, are justified by the longer-term benefits that will result. Regarding NEC, a major question is whether the company's leadership will be able to develop the new vision appropriate for the changed circumstances and whether it will have the muscle to force the necessary changes through in sufficient time. The answer to this question will only emerge in the future; the jury, it must be concluded, is still out on this important question of the appropriateness of NEC's—and Japan's—mode of corporate governance.

Strategic Alliances

What role have strategic alliances played in facilitating growth within the context of NEC's selection environment?

NEC's major strategic alliances from its founding in 1899 until the present time are listed in Table 6.11. Like the other main companies in the Japanese information and communications industry, NEC in the early stages of its development depended heavily on the technology provided by one of the companies that dominated the world in this industry at the time. The company concerned was Western Electric, the company that originally produced equipment for Western Union before it was taken over by the Bell system which was later to become AT&T. Similarly, Fujitsu allied itself with Siemens; Hitachi, after a prewar period of technological autarchy, linked with RCA; Toshiba with GE; and Mitsubishi Electric with Westinghouse.

The importance of Western Electric's initial supply of technology to NEC, the joint venture in which it owned a majority shareholding, cannot be overestimated. It allowed the fledgling company to enter the relatively new telecommunications industry and begin producing the equipment that this industry needed. While Western Electric contributed the technology to the joint venture, its Japanese entrepreneurial counterparts provided the 'political capital' that was also necessary, that is the contacts and connections that would allow NEC to become a major supplier to what would soon be the Ministry of Communications. The Ministry too would become an important source of technology for NEC and for this reason it is included as something of an 'ally' in Table 6.11.

Until the Second World War, NEC depended heavily on its technological alliance with Western Electric, although throughout this time it was steadily developing its own in-house competences through the knowledge acquired by its engineers involved in production, development, and, increasingly, research. In the postwar period, however, as NEC diversified into new emerging areas such as computers and semiconductors, it turned to other companies for the technology that would give it a 'leg up' into the new markets that were to become its major source of growth.

In 1958, for example, ten years after the transistor was invented in Bell Laboratories and five years after Sony had signed a licensing agreement for transistor technology with Western Electric, NEC, under pressure from MITI, signed its own transistor agreement with General Electric. Another five years

Table 6.11 *NEC's Strategic Alliances, 1899–1994*

Ally	Date	Area
Western Electric/ITT	1899–1970s	Telecommunications equipment
(Ministry of Communications/NTT)	(1899)	(Telecommunications and related equipment)
GE	1958	Transistor technology
Honeywell	1962	Large computers
Fairchild	1963	Semiconductors—silicon planar process (exclusive licence for Japan)
Hughes Aircraft	1964	Satellite communications systems
Intel	1977	Microprocessors
Honeywell-Bull	1987	Joint venture between Honeywell, Bull, and NEC to sell computers in USA
Groupe Bull	from 1980s	Joint development of mainframes; sale of components; marketing in Europe (NEC owns 4.3% of Bull)
AT&T Microelectronics/Bell Labs	early 1990s	Semiconductors, e.g. S-RAMs, gate arrays
MIPS	early 1990s	RISC microprocessors
Samsung	1994	256M D-RAM

later, in 1963, NEC concluded an agreement with Fairchild, one of the 'fathers' of the semiconductor industry in the USA, for the important planar process, signing an exclusive agreement covering the whole of Japan.

In the area of microprocessors, NEC concluded a short-lasting agreement with Intel in 1977. The agreement soon ended when NEC made the strategic decision to develop its own microprocessors. These eventually became the company's V-series. They were incompatible with Intel's microprocessors which eventually, through the influence of personal computers, became the global standard. Indeed, in the 1990s NEC's relationship with Intel was further bedevilled by the latter's litigation alleging that NEC had infringed Intel's microcode.

In order to assert its independence from the world-dominant Intel while taking advantage of new RISC (reduced instruction set) microprocessor technology, NEC concluded an agreement with the US company MIPS in the early 1990s. In 1993, NEC agreed to an alliance with MIPS and Toshiba aimed at developing a next-generation RISC microprocessor with the objective of competing to establish the new standard in microprocessors. In this way, NEC and its allies confronted head-on the other powerful players in this field, including IBM, Motorola, and Apple developing PowerPC; DEC and its allies backing the company's Alpha microprocessor; Sun Microsystems supporting the Sparc microprocessor; Hewlett-Packard and Hitachi; and Intel with its Pentium microprocessor.

In the area of memory semiconductors, NEC in March 1994 finally decided to join Samsung, the largest of the Korean companies involved in this market, to develop the next-generation 256M D-RAM. In doing so, the two companies were following the same logic, i.e. the logic of rapidly escalating development costs for next-generation memory technologies, that earlier had led companies such as IBM, Toshiba, and Siemens into a similar alliance for 256M D-RAMs. In the early 1990s NEC also concluded a number of agreements with AT&T Microelectronics and Bell Laboratories in the area of semiconductors, thus perpetuating the technology tie-up with Western Electric, the earlier incarnation of AT&T Microelectronics.

In computers, NEC signed a technology agreement with Honeywell in 1962. NEC's first computers were transferred to the company from NTT's Musashino Laboratories and from MITI's Electrotechnical Laboratories and provided the platform that allowed NEC to begin accumulating computer competences. The agreement with Honeywell, however, gave NEC, which had begun to acquire expertise in small and medium-sized computers, the opportunity to develop more sophisticated large computers. Honeywell's software knowledge was of particular value to NEC. At around the same time, Hitachi concluded similar computer technology agreements with RCA, and Toshiba with General Electric. Only Fujitsu did not enter into a major technology acquisition agreement.

The agreement with Honeywell led later to a joint venture between the two companies and Groupe Bull of France for the development and sale of computers in the USA. Honeywell eventually pulled out of this venture when it exited from the computer business, and NEC later acquired an equity holding of just under 5 per cent in Bull. At the same time, NEC cemented a marketing agreement with Bull involving the sale of computers in Europe, including Eastern Europe and the former Soviet Union.

Globalization

A qualitative change has been occurring in NEC's selection environment since it began to globalize its activities. Although, as stressed above, the overseas market has always constituted a relatively small part of NEC total sales—never amounting to much more than one-third of sales—conditions in this market have become an important part of the company's selection environment.

How is the globalization of NEC's activities to be explained? It is the competences that NEC accumulated which eventually allowed it to expand its activities, and therefore grow more rapidly, by entering foreign markets. More specifically, as NEC accumulated its competences, it emerged that some of these were such as to give the company a competitive edge in several international markets. Table 6.12 provides information pertaining to the beginnings of this process of NEC's globalization.

As the table shows, NEC made its first exports in the mid-1950s. Until this time its sales were almost exclusively to Japan (before the war including those

Table 6.12 *The Globalization of NEC*

	Year
First exports	
Microwave communications equipment	1956
Cable carrier systems	1959
First overseas sales companies	
Joint sales venture:	
Tung Cheng Dong, Taiwan	1958
Tatung, Taiwan	1966
First overseas sales office, Taiwan	1961
Sales office, Bangkok	1961
Sales office, New Delhi	1961
First overseas production (DFI)	
Brazil subsidiary (microwave, crossbar switches, carrier transmission)	1968
Mexico subsidiary (telecommunications equipment)	1968
Australian subsidiary (telecommunications equipment)	1969
Malaysian subsidiary (ICs)	1974
Ireland subsidiary (ICs)	1976

areas in Asia such as parts of China, Korea, and Taiwan that Japan had colonized). To some extent, the reason for this exclusivity was that NEC was still small, its resources did not give the company sufficient capacity to provide for foreign markets, and its competences were not yet strong enough to give it the necessary competitiveness. However, NEC's ability to export was also constrained by its technology agreements with Western Electric and its successor ITT, which limited exports. Indeed, it was only in 1965 that NEC was in a sufficiently strong position technologically to pressurize ITT into modifying the clauses that limited its ability to export. Significantly, it was three years earlier, in 1962, that NEC first sold its own technology to ITT, namely over-the-horizon microwave communications and carrier transmission equipment. In 1965 overseas sales constituted 8 per cent of NEC's total sales; by 1970 the figure had increased to 16 per cent and in 1979 it was 26 per cent.

Not surprisingly, as Table 6.12 shows, microwave communications equipment and cable carrier systems constituted NEC's first exports in the latter half of the 1950s, confirming the company's revealed internationally competitive competences in these areas. While these exports were primarily to developing countries, NEC's sale of similar equipment to ITT several years later merely underlined the competitive competences that NEC had accumulated. Significantly, NEC's other major products, such as telecommunications switches and consumer electrical products, at this stage lacked the same competitiveness. (Some of the reasons for NEC's strength in microwave communications and carrier systems were analysed in the first section of this chapter on the company's competences.)

Shortly after its first exports overseas, NEC began to open sales companies in foreign countries. The first one was a joint venture with a Taiwanese trading company, Tung Cheng Dong, in 1958. In 1966 this was replaced with a sales venture with the Taiwanese electronics company Tatung, which had more activities in common with NEC. The company's first wholly owned overseas sales office was started also in Taiwan in 1961 and was followed in the same year with offices in Bangkok and New Delhi.

It took several more years for NEC to open its first overseas production facilities through direct foreign investment. Interestingly, the company's first such plant was opened not in East Asia, NEC's 'natural' hinterland, but in Brazil. In 1968 NEC's first production subsidiary was started in Brazil producing microwave communications equipment, carrier transmission systems, and also crossbar switches. Brazil's import-substituting industrialization policies at the time provided the necessary incentive for NEC together with that country's nationalist sentiment which favoured broadening the source of telecommunications supplies beyond North America and Europe. Later the same year another NEC subsidiary was opened in Mexico and in 1969 one started up in Australia. However, it was only in the mid-1970s that NEC began producing semiconductors in overseas subsidiaries, revealing that it had taken longer for the company to establish internationally competitive competences in this field. In 1974 NEC's first overseas plant dedicated to semiconductors began operations in Malaysia and in 1976 another one began in Ireland.

By 1993 NEC had 22 consolidated subsidiaries in 10 countries. The company's 30 majority-owned manufacturing subsidiaries and affiliates (in which it had ownership interests of 20–50 per cent) operated a total of 31 plants in 15 countries, and had 68 marketing and service subsidiaries and affiliates in 27 countries. The company also had one overseas R&D subsidiary, NEC Research Institute in Princeton, New Jersey. By 1993, 23 per cent of NEC's sales were outside Japan.

Conclusion

In this chapter the interdependent evolution of NEC's competences, vision, forms of organization (including R&D organization), and selection environment have been analysed in detail. One key question remains: How 'successful' has NEC been? This question is reserved for the concluding chapter in this book, where NEC's performance is analysed together with those of the other Japanese information and communications companies.

7

The Future of NTT

CHAPTER OVERVIEW

The chapter begins with an analysis of NTT's vision, its set of beliefs regarding what the company should be doing and how it should be doing it. This vision is referred to as the 'NTT Way'. What is the NTT Way? A key feature is the belief that the company should be technology- or innovation-driven. This belief, in turn, accounts for NTT's increasing expenditure on R&D as a proportion of revenue and its continuation of controlled competition after 1985 under its Track Three joint R&D and procurement procedure. It is shown that this belief was important for NTT even before competition in telecommunications services was introduced in Japan after 1985, and that it accounts for the significant amount of innovation that occurred in the company before this date, leading to a substantial reduction in telephone tariffs. (The differences in vision between NTT and its US and UK counterparts—AT&T and BT—and the corresponding differences in their competences and innovation are examined by the author in a companion volume, *Visions of the Firm and Japan*.)

The rest of the chapter is devoted to a detailed analysis of the three winds of change buffeting NTT. The first is increasing competition. Where is this competition coming from and what impact is it having on NTT's financial performance? What role is being played by the Ministry of Posts and Telecommunications (MPT)—NTT's regulator? Do the competitive pressures mean that NTT will have to change its way and reduce the extent to which it is technology-driven?

The second wind of change is the threat of divestiture, that is the breakup of NTT similar to that of AT&T in the 1980s. The detailed examination of this issue reveals that NTT has been under the threat of divestiture since before it was partly privatized in 1985. However, with help from powerful allies, NTT has so far managed to avoid divestiture. In 1990, for example, although divestiture was proposed by MPT, the proposal was defeated. Who were the major protagonists and antagonists? Why did the attempt at divestiture fail? Divestiture is on the agenda again for 1995/6: is the outcome likely to be any different from before?

The third wind is globalization. Japan is the only major country in the world to separate domestic from international telecommunications services, the former the domain of NTT and the latter of KDD. As a result of this regulation, NTT has been unable to follow rivals such as AT&T and BT/MCI which have decisively entered the emerging markets for global telecommunications services. For those observers who see a Japan Incorporated, a well-oiled consensual machine bringing harmoniously together different interest groups in the country, this restriction on NTT appears to be an anomaly, something of an own-goal. Why has NTT been constrained in this way? To what extent has NTT been able to take part in global activities outside Japan? Do the restrictions mean that Japan will not have a serious contender in the new global markets for telecommunications services? Is there a new coalition of political interests in Japan strong enough to reverse this shackle on NTT?

Finally, what effect will these winds of change have on NTT's role in the Japanese information and communications industry? The answer to this question concludes the chapter.

Introduction

NTT—first in its incarnation as part of the Ministry of Communications, then as a public company from 1952 to 1985, and finally as a partly privatized company since 1985—has had a major impact on the evolution of the Japanese information and communications (IC) industry. NTT has been much more than just another company in this industry: it has been a 'mother' company, giving birth to and nurturing some of the leading companies in this industry.

But since 1985, NTT itself has been in the throes of radical transformation. The aim of this chapter is to analyse the winds of change in NTT's selection environment that are buffeting the company and will shape its evolution into the twenty-first century. Three major forces for change are identified: increasing competition, threatened divestiture, and globalization. What impact will these forces have on NTT's vision, competences, and organization? In short, what effect will these winds of change have on the 'NTT Way', that is, the way in which NTT, over the years, has come to play its role in the Japanese IC industry? These are the major questions that will be tackled.

Background

It is no exaggeration to say that NTT, and its whole approach to enhancing telecommunications services in Japan, is at a critical watershed, facing the biggest challenges in its entire history. These challenges stem from the new circumstances that have emerged since 1985 when NTT became partly privatized and when competition in some of NTT's most important markets became legally possible.

The magnitude of the difficulties NTT now faces was dramatically underlined when in August 1992 NTT's share price fell 7.6 per cent in one day, down 13.4 per cent on the week, pulling down the entire Nikkei index of 225 leading companies to a record low of 15,518. The original price of NTT's shares, which were first floated in early 1987, was ¥1.197 million and in the spring of that year the price of these shares reached a high of ¥3.18 million. In August 1992 the price stood at ¥509,000. Although this fall in NTT's share price was part of a generalized fall on the Tokyo Stock Exchange and cannot be attributed entirely or even mainly to the difficulties now facing NTT in the aftermath of part-privatization, it is likely that the price fall was to some extent a consequence of the uncertainties confronting the company.

This chapter identifies the three major uncertainties challenging NTT: increasing competition, divestiture, and globalization. Although, as the chapter carefully documents, the competition that NTT faces is still limited, it is increasing in intensity. One result is that NTT's profitability has suffered since 1988 while that of the new common carriers that compete with it has grown from strength to strength. The further effects of this increase in competitive intensity are analysed below.

In 1990 NTT was able, with the support of powerful allies, to get discussion of the proposal for its divestiture, put forward by the Ministry of Posts and Telecommunications (MPT), postponed until 1995/6. Why did MPT propose divestiture? Why was its proposal defeated in 1990? And, most importantly for the future of NTT, is the divestiture of the company a likely outcome of the 1995/6 review of NTT and Japanese telecommunications more generally? These questions are examined in this chapter.

The globalization of its activities is the third major challenge that NTT faces. While by law NTT's activities are confined to the Japanese domestic market, and international activities are the preserve of KDD (NTT's counterpart for Japan's international telecommunications), this chapter reveals that the legal status quo has not prevented a significant increase in the extent of NTT's globalization. It is also shown that, although currently there are important constraints inhibiting the pace of NTT's further globalization, these constraints are being increasingly challenged by an emerging coalition of forces which are likely to result in the more rapid globalization of NTT's activities in the medium term.

Increasing competition, divestiture, and globalization are, therefore, the winds of change that are buffeting NTT. But this chapter is also concerned with the approach that NTT has taken in formulating its vision for the future, establishing its priorities, and organizing its activities. This approach is referred to here as the 'NTT Way'.

Briefly, according to the NTT Way, NTT is seen primarily as an innovation-driven company which co-operates synergistically with a group of companies supplying telecommunications equipment and competing among themselves. The characteristics of the NTT Way are explored further in a companion book, in which the distinctiveness of this approach is illuminated by comparison with other major telecommunications carriers, particularly BT and AT&T.[1] Why has innovation been central for such a long time in NTT, even in the monopolistic era before competition was introduced into the domestic

---

[1] M. Fransman, *Visions of the Firm and Japan*, Oxford University Press, forthcoming.

Japanese telecommunications market in 1986? This question is answered below.

How are the challenges facing NTT likely to affect the NTT Way? Before attempting to answer this question, it is necessary to have a clear understanding of what is meant by the NTT Way.

The NTT Way

General Definition

Since the NTT Way is of central concern in this chapter, it is necessary to begin with a more rigorous definition of what is meant by the term.

Basically, the NTT Way refers to an *approach*, a way—indeed, what is seen as the most appropriate way—for NTT as an organization to exist and act in the world in which it finds itself. This approach permeates all aspects of the organization—the way NTT is structured and organized; the priorities that have been set within the organization; its allocation of resources; the relationship between NTT and other organizations, particularly other supplying companies and government bodies; and, finally, the vision of the organization and the 'mindset' of its leaders.

Evolution

It must be stressed immediately that the NTT Way, as an approach, has evolved as part of NTT's history, first as part of the Ministry of Communications (Teishinshō) and then, after 1952, as a semi-independent government corporation. It is important to stress the evolution of the NTT Way for the simple reason that this approach *is continuing to evolve*. Indeed, the primary aim of this chapter is to analyse the major forces currently influencing the NTT Way in order to understand the main changes that are likely to occur in this approach.

Before coming to an overview of the major forces influencing the NTT Way, however, it is necessary to delve more deeply into the evolution of this approach. At the heart of the NTT Way is the belief that NTT must be an *innovation-driven* organization. This belief emerged originally from the organization's mission, first when it was part of the Ministry of Communications and then, after the Second World War, when it was established as a distinct government corporation. This mission, reinforced by the pressures of the political process in Japan, was both to expand and to improve the telecommunications network and the services that it provided. From the outset, it rapidly became accepted that innovation was the major means through which this mission would be achieved. It was for this reason that NTT, like its predecessor, became an innovation-driven organization.

Monopolistic NTT

But is it not incorrect to argue that NTT, which after all was a gigantic monopoly until 1985, and which even now (as will soon be documented) is subject only to limited competition, has been an innovation-driven organization? Did not NTT's monopoly status obviate the need to innovate? It is important to know the answer to this question in order to understand the origins and evolution of the NTT Way and also the changes that are currently affecting this approach.

In the post-1985 era in Japanese telecommunications, which may be dubbed the 'pre-competition era', it is important to remember that, not only were there powerful pressures requiring innovation *before* 1985, but also, a significant amount of innovation occurred during this period when NTT (like its counterparts in the other major Western countries) was the monopolistic supplier of domestic telecommunications services. Indeed, practically all of the innovations under-lying the current revolutionizing of telecommunications services—services such as ISDN, mobile communications, satellite, and high-speed optical-fibre-based services—were produced during the era when throughout the world national telecommunications services markets were monopolized by a single carrier. These innovations were in areas such as telecommunications-related electronic devices and software, digital switching, and optical fibre. It is therefore clear that the monopoly era produced important innovations, and that any attempt to attribute the process of innovation in telecommunications to market competition is incorrect.

Forces Encouraging Innovation in NTT before 1985

What, then, were the forces that existed in Japan before 1985 which encouraged innovation and, by so doing, contributed to the emergence and perpetuation of the NTT Way?

The following forces may be identified as crucial. First, there was great pressure on the organization (originally as part of the Ministry of Communications and later as NTT) to expand and improve telecommunications services. In the period following the Second World War this pressure was expressed in the two major objectives that were set for Japanese telecommunications policy—in the official jargon, 'eliminating the installation backlog [of telephones]' and 'nationwide installation of direct dialing', objectives that were attained only in 1978 and 1979 respectively.[2] NTT's performance was measured, directly and indirectly, against these objectives. Failure to achieve these objectives, or slow progress in achieving them, would have resulted in the discontent of NTT's customers, which could have been expressed politically through a variety of channels. The result was real external pressure, which encouraged NTT to achieve these objectives through innovation.

---

[2] Ministry of Posts and Telecommunications, *Open Telecommunications Market of Japan*, Ministry of Posts and Telecommunications, Tokyo, 1992, p. 2.

Secondly, this pressure was complemented by the enormous advances in telecommunications technologies that were being made worldwide as the major carriers, responding to similar pressures, ploughed resources into innovation. These technological advances provided an effective means for the organization that became NTT to achieve its objective of expanding and improving services. In turn, this required the acquisition of technological knowledge from abroad, the adaptation of this knowledge to suit the circumstances of the Japanese telecommunications network, and eventually the improvement of the knowledge itself. In this book this process of technology acquisition, adaptation, and improvement has been examined in great detail in the cases of central office switches (Chapter 3), optical fibre (Chapter 5), and computers (Chapter 4). Until the mid- to late 1970s, this involved catch-up with the leading Western countries; in the 1980s and 1990s this was superseded by shared leadership in an increasing number of telecommunications technology areas.

Thirdly, it is important to stress that competition *was* a potent force for innovation even before 1985 (incredible as this may at first sight appear to those influenced by the ideology of the post-1985 'competition era'). However, this was not competition between various providers of telecommunications services in national markets, but rather competition of a more indirect kind—but competition nevertheless—between the carriers of the major countries to improve their technologies and services.

This competition took the form of a 'demonstration effect', whereby the introduction of a major new technology or service in one national system was rapidly emulated in other countries through the process of research and development. (More accurately, the onset of this demonstration effect and the international diffusion of technology that it implied often began at a much earlier stage, with discussion of the new technological ideas in conferences, technical journals, and more informal ways such as visits to the laboratories of other carriers, etc.)

Strong empirical evidence of this 'competition via the demonstration effect' in the Japanese case is provided elsewhere in this book, particularly in the areas of switching, optical fibre, and telecommunications-related computing. Readers of this material cannot fail to be impressed with the intensity of the efforts that were made in Japan through this demonstration effect to catch up with the leading Western carriers and their suppliers.

Pre-Competition Innovation in NTT and Falling Telephone Tariffs

Further evidence of the importance of these three factors encouraging innovation *before* 1985 (or 1986, when NTT first faced competition from the New Common Carriers, NCCs) comes from the analysis of changes in telephone tariffs. Fig. 7.1 provides the data that have now become commonplace in Japanese publications, showing the reductions that have occurred in NTT's and the NCCs' tariffs since 1986. The usual implicit (and sometimes explicit) message is that

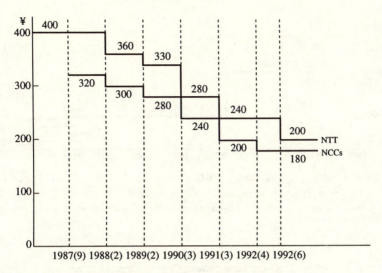

Fig. 7.1 Telephone tariffs of NTT and NCCs, 1987(9)–1992(6)

Note: based on a three-minute daytime telephone call from Tokyo to Osaka.

Source: S. Nagai, 'On the Competition of Telecommunications under Regulation in Japan', *Journal of International Economic Studies*, no. 4 (1990): 18.

these reductions have been *caused* by the competition between NTT and the NCCs in the services market in Japan since 1986.[3]

In view of this causal interpretation, it is worth comparing Fig. 7.1 with Fig. 7.2, which extends the tariff backwards to the beginning of 1980. As Fig. 7.2 shows, NTT's tariff dropped from ¥720 to ¥400 over about three-and-a-half years from 1980 to mid-1983, during the monopoly era, a fall of 44 per cent. This compares with a fall of 50 per cent over five years in the era of competition, from mid-1987 to mid-1992.

The figures clearly show that, whatever new forces for innovation and tariff reduction were unleashed with the introduction of services competition between NTT and the NCCs after 1986, these forces must be distinguished from the different forces that existed before this date and which also encouraged innovation and reductions in tariffs. A rigorous causal analysis of the effects of the post-1986 'competition era' would therefore have to separate out the *additional* effects of new services competition from the other *continuing* forces which also encouraged innovation and lower tariffs, including the three forces mentioned here. (In practice, however, this is obviously an extremely difficult task.)

---

[3] For example, in a Ministry of Posts and Telecommunications document, under the heading 'Rapid Decrease of Price of Telecommunications Services', it is shown that the price of three-minute long-distance calls from Tokyo to Osaka decreased from ¥400 in 1985 to ¥200 in 1991. It is stated that 'There has been a rapid decrease of price of telecommunications service *through competition*' (Ministry of Posts and Telecommunications, *Telecommunications Reforms in Japan*, MPT, Tokyo, undated, p. 3, emphasis added).

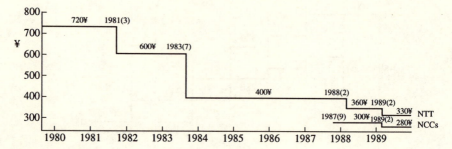

Fig. 7.2 The fall in telephone tariffs, 1980–1990

Note: based on a three-minute weekday daytime long-distance telephone call.

Source: S. Nagai, 'On the Competition of Telecommunications under Regulation in Japan', *Journal of International Economic Studies*, no. 4 (1990): 18.

NTT as an Innovation-Driven Organization

To return to our discussion of the NTT Way, it is clear that the organization that eventually became NTT the government corporation, and then NTT the partly privatized corporation, was always under significant pressure to innovate. From 1986, it is true, these pressures increased greatly with the introduction of new services competition which added to the pre-existing and continuing forces for innovation. The importance of these new pressures will be analysed in more detail later. For the moment, however, from the point of view of the emergence and perpetuation of the NTT Way, the point to stress is that this approach was forged under conditions that put a premium on innovation. It is for this reason that, as stated earlier in this chapter, 'at the heart of the NTT Way is the belief that NTT must be an innovation-driven organization'.

But what is understood, both implicitly and explicitly, in NTT by 'an innovation-driven organization'? It is crucial to understand that the phrase 'innovation-driven organization' means more than an assertion that innovation is important for the organization; indeed, the latter is a truism, since it is true for practically all organizations. Rather, the phrase signifies that NTT sees innovation as the most important necessary condition for its well-being.

Furthermore, 'innovation' in NTT is positively correlated with research and development.[4] Therefore, for NTT to be innovation-driven is for it to give high priority to R&D. This view has long permeated the entire company and accounts for the great influence (as those who are familiar with NTT know) wielded by engineer-leaders in the company with backgrounds in activities involving

---

[4] The comparison between NTT and BT in the author's companion volume, *Visions of the Firm and Japan*, helps to drive this point home. As shown, while the BT view is also that innovation is crucial, for BT this does not translate into the same commitment to R&D as conventionally measured as NTT has made.

research and/or development. Their influence has shaped not only the direction that NTT has taken, but also the vision that NTT has of its future.[5]

NTT and the Market

A further characteristic of the NTT Way must be clarified. This relates to the role played by the market as a causal influence on both the direction and the *modus operandi* of the company. While NTT currently believes that it should continually be improving the services that it provides to its customers, it does not believe that the market can be given sole responsibility for guiding the development of new services.

NTT does not believe this for one simple reason: generally speaking, the market is unable to articulate adequately a demand for new telecommunications services. It is only when these services are made available that the market can react—positively, for example, in the case of mobile services or more slowly and hesitantly with ISDN services. It is for this reason that technological innovation must drive the market for telecommunications services rather than the other way round, even though NTT as a for-profit organization must of course be highly sensitive to changing market demand and the emergence of new market segments and niches.

R&D

NTT's commitment to an innovation-driven approach as defined here has, if anything, deepened since its part-privatization in 1985. This is revealed starkly by the figures for its increasing R&D allocation as shown in Table 7.1, which reveals that R&D as a percentage of operating revenue increased from 2.7 per cent in 1986, immediately after part-privatization, to 4.6 per cent in 1992.

The extent of NTT's commitment to its innovation-driven approach has also drawn comment from Japanese analysts. In November 1992 the *Nikkei Weekly* rather bemusedly reported that 'NTT's financial position may be withering, but it is still bucking an industry trend towards slashing research and

Table 7.1 *NTT's Research and Development, 1986–1992*

	Financial year						
	1986	1987	1988	1989	1990	1991	1992
Amount spent (¥bn)	136.2	149.3	181.7	221.7	248.0	272.5	276.7
% of operating revenue	2.7	2.8	3.2	3.8	4.1	4.4	4.6

Source: NTT Annual Report 1991; information supplied to the author by Infocom.

---

[5] A vision that is analysed in Fransman, *Visions of the Firm*, comparing it with visions of AT&T and BT.

development budgets [in the existing climate of economic recession].'[6] According to this article, NTT President Kojima 'acknowledged that NTT's pretax profits for the current fiscal year will not reach the initial forecast of 267 billion yen, largely due to heightening competition from rival carriers'. However, the article also reported, 'Despite its declining business performance, the company says it has no plans to reduce its overall R&D budget of 290 billion yen, which represented 4.7% of its [projected] sales for the year ending March 1993.'[7]

NTT's Suppliers

The final characteristic of the NTT Way is the division of labour between NTT and its suppliers. In short, while NTT designs, develops, and operates the Japanese domestic telecommunications network, it also plays a proactive role in researching and developing new telecommunications technologies. To some extent, this R&D role is undertaken in co-operation with a group of competing suppliers who take sole responsibility for manufacture. While NTT engages in co-operative R&D with these suppliers, in most areas it takes a commanding lead in initial research into the main telecommunications technologies to be developed. This role of NTT has been exhaustively examined elsewhere in this book and therefore does not require any further elaboration at this point.

The Winds of Change Buffeting the NTT Way

The important degree of continuity in the NTT Way should not obscure the substantial forces for change that now impinge on the company. The main aim of the remainder of this chapter is to examine these forces, analysing how they are likely to change the NTT Way.

Three main forces have been identified which separately and together threaten to transform substantially both NTT and the NTT Way: competition in telecommunications services, divestiture, and the globalization of NTT's activities. How significant are these forces? How will they affect the NTT Way and its legal and organizational forms? These are the questions that will now be addressed, taking each of the forces in turn.

Competition

The Legal Basis for Competition and the Entry of the New Common Carriers

The proposal that NTT (and KDD) should face competition from new carriers with their own facilities was first seriously put forward in the discussions leading

---

[6] *Nikkei Weekly*, 9 November 1992, p. 8.   [7] Ibid.

to the 1982 report of the Provisional Commission on Administrative Reform. This report also recommended that NTT be privatized and, furthermore, divested into a company providing long-distance services and several companies providing local services. While this Commission proposed competition as an alternative to regulation, in which it did not have much faith, it stopped short of proposing competition in local services on the grounds that this might endanger universal service. It is worth noting, however, that the primary overall concern of the Commission was with ways of decreasing government expenditure in order to reduce the government debt.

In December 1984, new legislation was passed in the Diet, partly privatizing NTT and introducing the possibility of competition in both long-distance and local services. While the NTT Corporation Act dealt with the privatization of NTT, the Telecommunications Business Act set the ground rules for competition. According to the latter Act, different forms of regulation were established for two types of carrier: Type I carriers with their own facilities, and Type II carriers which provide services by leasing facilities from Type I carriers. Type I carriers are far more strictly regulated, requiring entry permission from MPT which also must approve tariffs. Type II carriers are divided into two categories: Special Type II carriers, which provide large-scale nationwide services and/or international services, and General Type II carriers. While the former must register with MPT before beginning activities and must report tariffs to the Ministry before implementing them, the latter are required to notify MPT only before starting business.

While by 1991 there were 68 Type I carriers, there are currently three major inter-city carriers which together comprise NTT's main source of competition. These are Daini Denden Inc. (DDI), Japan Telecom Company (JT), and Teleway Japan Corporation (TWJ) which started leased-circuit services in 1986 in the high-volume Tokyo–Nagoya–Osaka corridor.

One of the features distinguishing these three New Common Carriers (NCCs) from their counterparts which compete with the former monopolistic carriers in the USA and UK (e.g. MCI and Sprint in the USA and Mercury in Britain) is their large number of corporate shareholders. DDI has 225 companies as shareholders, the dominant ones being Kyocera with a 25 per cent holding and Sony with 5 per cent. DDI began leased line services in October 1986 and telephone services in September 1987 under the leadership of Mr Inamori, the chairman of Kyocera.

Japan Telecom, which has a total of 302 corporate shareholders, originally emerged from the former Japan National Railways (JNR) which was privatized and broken up in April 1986, one year after the privatization of NTT, also as a result of recommendation from the Provisional Commission on Administrative Reform. Before its privatization, JNR was in debt each year, and had a total outstanding debt amounting to $74 billion at the time of privatization. Currently, JR Eastern Japan holds 20 per cent of Japan Telecom while JR Western Japan has a holding of 15 per cent. Japan Telecom's entry as a Type I carrier was facilitated by the communications network that JNR had established in support of its railway activities. In May 1989 Japan Telecom merged its activities with the Railway Telecommunications Corporation (Tetsudo Tsushin), which after the privatization of JNR operated the communications network for the JR Group. Teleway Japan has 289 company shareholders, Toyota being the largest with a holding of 7 per cent of the company's shares. The company's entry was aided by its ability to install optical fibre cables alongside highways under the control of the Ministry of Construction.

While Japan Telecom and Teleway Japan benefited to some extent from their close links with the Ministries of Transportation and Construction respectively, Daini Denden, the largest and most aggressive of the three NCCs, originally lacked such connections. This was soon remedied, however, when former MPT officials took up two of the company's three executive vice president positions. Senior positions in Japan Telecom and Teleway Japan are also held by former MPT officials.

The Direct Impact of NCC Competition

Market Share

One measure that has often been used to determine the effect of competition is the share of calls that the NCCs have obtained along the important Tokyo–Nagoya–Osaka long-distance corridor. This is shown graphically in Fig. 7.3, which reveals that, for the financial year ended 31 March 1992, NTT provided 47 per cent of the calls in this corridor while the three NCCs together accounted for 53 per cent.

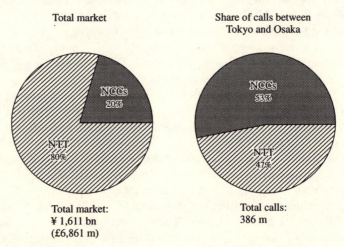

Fig. 7.3 Market share of long-distance telephone services, NTT and NCCs, 1 April 1991–31 March 1992

However, as an indicator of the degree of competition that NTT faces, this figure is misleading. To begin with, in terms of *number of calls*, the Tokyo–Nagoya–Osaka corridor accounted for only 5.1 per cent of the total number of inter-prefectural calls for the year ending March 1991. Furthermore, inter-prefectural calls accounted for only 18.4 per cent of the total number of calls, that is both intra- and inter-prefectural calls.

Revenue

A more accurate indication of the impact of the NCCs on NTT is provided by an examination of revenues.

First, revenue from local calls (i.e. *within* the 567 messaging areas) is 1.22 times as important as long-distance revenue (i.e. *between* messaging areas). For the 1991 financial year, the revenue figures for local and long-distance calls were ¥1,569.2 billion and ¥1,289.8 billion respectively. Since NTT still faces only very limited competition in local telephone calls, this means that the overall impact of competition in long-distance calls from the NCCs is accordingly muted. This is reflected, secondly, in revenue figures for telephone services, as is recorded in Table 7.2. In the 1991 financial year these services provided 80 per cent of NTT's total revenue; NTT earned 93.5 per cent of total telephone service revenues accruing to all Type I carriers, thus leaving all the NCCs with only 6.5 per cent of this revenue.

Thirdly, however, the overall impact of the NCCs in other newer services was more significant. In leased circuit services, for example, which accounted for 7 per cent of NTT's total revenue, the table shows that NTT controlled 86.4 per cent of the market, with 13.6 per cent going to the NCCs. The presence of the NCCs in cellular phone services was even more significant; in these services, which provided NTT with 3.8 per cent of its revenue, NTT had a 64.2 per cent share, leaving the NCCs with 35.8 per cent of this market. Fourthly, the greater presence of the NCCs in these non-telephone markets has resulted in these competitors to NTT gaining 9 per cent of the total Type I market for telecommunications services in the 1991 financial year. This shows a significant gain over the previous year, when the NCCs accounted for only 6.5 per cent of this total market.

From these figures it must be concluded that, while NTT faces growing competition from the NCCs, the impact of this competition in terms of NTT's share of total revenue is still fairly limited. Furthermore, if the revenue of the NCCs is disaggregated by company, it is clear that NTT remains the overwhelmingly dominant company (as is shown in more detail below).

Profitability

In terms of profitability, however, the NCCs have had a far greater impact on NTT. This is evident from the data provided in Table 7.3. A number of extremely important points emerge from this table.

Table 7.2 *Type I Domestic Telecommunications Revenue, 1991 and 1992 (¥bn)*[a]

Service	1990 financial year[b]			Annual growth rates (%)	1991 financial year[b]		
	NTT	NCCs	Total		NTT	NCCs	Total
Telephones	4,653.9 (95.3)	230.2 (4.7)	4,884.1	1.1	4,617.7 (93.5)	322.2 (6.5)	4,940.0
Leased circuit[c]	389.7 (89.0)	48.2 (11.0)	438.0	6.0	401.4 (86.4)	63.0 (13.6)	464.4
Cellular phones	176.1 (71.3)	70.8 (28.7)	247.0	37.5	218.0 (64.2)	121.7 (35.8)	339.7
Ship telephones	11.4 (97.1)	0.34 (2.9)	11.8	7.8	12.4 (97.5)	0.32 (2.5)	12.7
Radio paging	88.6 (70.8)	36.5 (29.2)	125.2	20.3	101.9 (67.7)	48.7 (32.3)	150.6
Other	335.3 (97.4)	8.9 (2.6)	344.2	17.8	394.3 (97.2)	11.4 (2.8)	405.7
TOTAL	5,655.3 (93.5)	395.0 (6.5)	6,050.4	4.3	5,745.9 (91.0)	567.4 (9.0)	6,313.3

[a] Excludes the revenues of the Railway Telecommunications Co., which provide telecommunications services for JR.
[b] Figures in parentheses are percentages.
[c] The leased circuits consist of standard circuits, high-speed digital leased circuits, and video communications circuits.

Source: Outline of the Telecommunications Business, MPT, November 1992, table C1, p. 11.

Table 7.3 *Revenue and Profits, NTT and the NCCs, 1985–1992 (¥bn)*

	1992 (est.)	1991	1990	1989	1988	1987	1986	1985
NTT								
Revenue	230,000		6,056,049	5,958,429	5,769,239	5,652,688	5,662,001	5,353,581
%[a]	15.1		1.6	3.3	2.1	− 0.2	5.8	5.1
Income before tax	25,000		352,850	414,326	484,728	425,901	496,736	357,956
%[a]	6.7		− 14.8	− 14.5	13.8	− 14.3	38.8	13.2
DDI								
Reveue	230,000	199,832	155,438	98,943	40,619	8,838		
%[a]	15.1	28.6	57.1	143.6	359.6			
Income before tax	25,000	23,432	20,679	17,529	4,477	− 6,439		
%[a]	6.7	13.3	18.0	291.5				
JT								
Revenue	211,000	173,380	119,397	77,155	26,907	7,152		
%[a]	21.7	45.2	54.8	186.8	276.2			
Income before tax	18,000	16,043	12,053	11,287	864	− 4,897		
%[a]	12.2	33.1	6.8	120.6				
TWJ								
Revenue	50,000	33,781	29,446	23,881	13,292	3,865		
%[a]	48.0	14.7	23.3	79.7	243.9			
Income before tax	0	− 7,099	− 1,416	435	− 4,285	− 6,748		

[a] Percentages represent the percentage increase in the figure above over the previous year.

Source: Calculated from data provided by Infocom.

First, in every year except one (1987) NTT's revenue has increased; the last recorded increase, 3.8 per cent for 1990–1, was the third highest since part-privatization in 1985. This supports the conclusion that competition from the NCCs has not had a major impact on NTT's revenue.[8] Secondly, while competition from the NCCs did not prevent a continuing rise in NTT's *revenue*, the same was not true for *profits*. Using gross income as the measure for profits, Table 7.3 reveals that, except for one year (1988), NTT's income before tax has decreased each year since 1987; in 1990–1 income before tax decreased by 2.6 per cent. Conversely, in the first year after part-privatization (1985–6), before competition from the NCCs had begun to bite, NTT's income before tax increased, by 39 per cent.

Thirdly, the profitability data for the NCCs is the mirror image of NTT's, reflecting the impact on NTT of the NCCs' greater competitiveness, measured in terms of their lower tariff *vis-à-vis* NTT's (as shown in Fig. 7.1 above). In every year since 1989 both Daini Denden and Japan Telecom increased their income before tax, although the rate of increase in each year fell markedly, reflecting the rise from an initial small base. Nevertheless, in marked contrast to the 2.6 per cent fall in NTT's revenue before tax in 1990–1, the figure for the same period for Daini Denden was a 6.7 per cent increase, while for Japan Telecom it was a 12.2 per cent increase.

Also notable is the fact that Teleway Japan is the odd one out among the three NCCs. While its revenue increased each year from 1987, in four out of the six years for which figures are shown income before tax fell and there was an estimated zero increase for 1992.[9]

Fourthly, Table 7.3 also provides an indication of the relative size of each of these companies. In terms of revenue, NTT in 1991 was 31 times larger than Daini Denden, 36 times larger than Japan Telecom, and 183 times larger than Teleway Japan. NTT's 1991 revenue was 15 times larger than the combined revenue of all three of these NCCs. Interestingly, Daini Denden's estimated revenue for 1992 fell a little short of KDD's 1991 revenue, i.e. ¥244 billion for the former compared to ¥253 billion for the latter. With KDD's revenues growing more slowly than Daini Denden's, their total revenues are currently about equal. This statistic provides a clear example of the favourable conditions that have enabled Daini Denden and Japan Telecom to grow very rapidly.

At the end of 1992 NTT announced that its pretax profits for the year ended

---

[8] NTT was able to increase its revenue while at the same time losing market share to the NCCs because of the growing size of the telecommunications market in Japan. In turn, this growing market size resulted partly from the growth of the Japanese economy during these years and partly from the substitution of telecommunications services for other goods and services (the substitution effect) as the real cost of these services, particularly telephone, fell.

[9] It is worth noting, however, that the greater 'competitiveness' of Daini Denden and Japan Telecom as reflected in their favourable increases in income before tax should not be taken as an indication of greater *efficiency*. The reason is that their performance is to a significant extent the result of the difference (in their favour) between their tariff and NTT's. This differential has been influenced by MPT's regulation.

March 1993 were expected to drop by 35 per cent from the previous year to ¥229 billion as a result of the cut in long-distance call rates and declining telephone use caused by the economic slowdown. Revenue was projected to be almost unchanged at ¥5.9 trillion.[10]

Profitability on Long-Distance and Local Telephone Services

In terms of profit, where is NTT 'hurting'? The overall picture is provided in Table 7.4.

First, it is telephone services that in the 1991 financial year accounted for no less than 96.6 per cent of NTT's operating income from the company's telecommunications activities (¥505 million out of a total of ¥523 million).

Secondly, however, there is a marked difference between the contribution

Table 7.4 *Breakdown of NTT's Revenue, Expenditure, and Income, 1991 (¥m)*

Service	Revenue	Expenditure	Operating income	
(a) Kind of service				
Telephone	5,084,170	4,579,703	504,466	
Telex	3,649	3,227	422	
Telegram	68,191	90,589	-22,397	
Leased line	407,784	331,403	76,381	
Digital data	48,728	40,898	7,829	
Paging	102,828	85,874	16,954	
Other	30,560	91,571	-61,011	
TOTAL	5,745,913	5,223,268	522,644	
	Operating revenue	Operating expense	Operating income	Income before tax
(b) Telephone services				
Telephone subscriber	4,247,275	3,578,871	668,404	528,496
Monthly rental	1,094,528	1,249,893	-155,364	-203,053
Local service	1,569,184	1,548,854	20,330	-55,673
Long-distance service	1,289,842	476,908	812,933	797,491
Other fees	293,719	303,214	-9,494	-10,267
Pay phone	314,932	329,728	-14,796	-23,381
Mobile (cellular)	219,063	184,844	34,218	29,072
Other mobile (Maritime)	16,233	18,995	-2,762	-3,323
Other	286,665	467,262	-180,597	-180,128
TOTAL	5,084,170	4,579,703	504,466	350,734

Source: Data supplied by Infocom.

[10] *Nikkei Weekly*, 23 November 1992, p. 25.

made by long-distance services and local services to operating income. Thus, long-distance services contributed ¥813 billion but total operating income was only ¥505 billion. The shortfall was accounted for by operating losses made on a number of items, the most important being rentals of telephones (¥155 billion loss), and pay phones (¥15 billion loss). Not shown separately in the table, but also an important loss-making item, was directory assistance service. Operating income from local telephone services amounted to only ¥20 billion, compared with ¥813 billion for long-distance services. In terms of operating revenue, it will be recalled, local telephone services contributed ¥1,569 billion compared with ¥1,290 billion for long-distance services.

Thirdly, still on the issue of the contribution of long-distance and local telephone services, while the former contributed ¥798 billion to income before tax, the latter accounted for a loss before tax of ¥56 billion. Telephone rentals were responsible for the biggest loss before tax of ¥203 billion, while pay phones accounted for a further loss of ¥23 billion.

The Question of Rate Rebalancing

As these figures show, NTT has been making profits on its long-distance telephone services while running a loss on local services. This amounts to a *de facto* cross-subsidization of local by long-distance services. According to NTT, this is the inevitable consequence of MPT's refusal so far to allow a sufficient increase in charges on some or all of the following items: local telephone services, telephone rentals, pay phones, and directory enquiries.

NTT argues that this is untenable in the longer run because of the increasing competition in long-distance services from the NCCs, and to remedy the situation the company intends proposing a 'rate rebalancing' which will allow it to raise tariffs on some or all of these items. The question of rate rebalancing, and the contrasting viewpoints of NTT and MPT, are examined later.*

Is There Now 'Excessive Competition' in the Long-Distance Market?

The policy concept of 'excessive competition' was made famous by the Japanese Ministry of International Trade and Industry (MITI). It was excessive competition that served as the rationale for MITI's attempts to consolidate growth industries such as steel, cars, and computers, as well as its efforts to form cartels in the face of economic recession or structural industrial decline. The concept implies that competition, normally a socially useful force, has become excessive, endangering the health of at least some of the corporate participants in the industry to the longer-run detriment of the society as a whole. Is there now excessive competition in the Japanese long-distance market?

In view of the impact of competition in the long-distance market by the NCCs

---

* In the financial year ended March 1995, after MPT allowed NTT to increase basic charges and directory assistance, NTT recorded the first growth in profits for 5 years.

on NTT's profits, an impact that was documented above, I interviewed a number of senior officials in MPT, asking them whether they thought there was now excessive competition in this market which was beginning to impede NTT's ability to operate effectively to the detriment of the whole Japanese telecommunications sector. My reconstruction of the argument put forward by these officials (which should not necessarily be taken as a reflection of MPT's official views) is first discussed; this is followed by my construction, on the basis of many interviews in NTT, of what I understand to be the position of many in authority in NTT.

MPT's Reconstructed Position

The general response of the MPT officials was that there is *not* currently excessive competition in the Japanese long-distance market. Three arguments were given in support of this position. The first was that the NCCs' share of the Tokyo–Nagoya–Osaka long-distance market, which in 1992 amounted to 53 per cent, was an inaccurate reflection of the state of competition in this market as a whole. In this connection, they pointed out that traffic along this corridor was only a small proportion of total inter-prefecture traffic. (Detailed data relating to this point were provided earlier in this chapter.) Furthermore, they noted that, while the NCCs' tariffs in this corridor are lower than NTT's, in many other parts of the country NTT's long-distance rates are currently beginning 1993) lower than the NCCs. This is reflected in NTT's own publicity material.

Secondly, it was argued that there was indirect evidence that NTT was not suffering under excessive competition. One example of this evidence is NTT's capital expenditures, which have increased at a reasonable rate since the introduction of competition, reflecting NTT's continuing ability to further enhance the Japanese domestic network. Thirdly, although NTT's profits have suffered in recent years, the company's profits performance is no worse than those of comparable Japanese companies.

Is there evidence to support the arguments of these MPT officials? Data on the first argument, as already noted, were provided earlier and will not be repeated here. They do confirm that market share statistics relating to the Tokyo–Nagoya–Osaka corridor do not adequately reflect the state of competition between NTT and the NCCs in the Japanese long-distance market generally.

Regarding the second argument, NTT's capital expenditures from 1987 (the first year when competition from the NCCs, which began competing in 1986, started showing up in the statistics) to 1991 are shown in Table 7.5. We can see

Table 7.5 *NTT's Capital Expenditure, 1987–1991 (¥bn)*

1987	1988	1989	1990	1991
1,613.2	1,796.7	1,764.4	1,831.5	1,935.4

Source: NTT Annual Report 1991.

that, with the exception of 1989, when it decreased slightly, NTT's capital expenditure (in money terms) increased every year.

In support of the third argument, MPT itself has produced data comparing NTT's dividend ratio (dividend per share) with those of a number of companies in four other sectors, i.e. electricity, gas, railways, and airlines. These figures are presented in Table 7.6; they show that, for the 1990 and 1991 financial years, NTT's dividend ratio has been higher than the average for the companies in these other four sectors.

Table 7.6 *NTT Dividends Compared with those of Other Public Corporations, 1990 and 1991 financial years* [a] *(%)*

	Electricity	Gas	Railways	Airlines	NTT
Dividend ratio [b]					
1990	10	10	8–10	10	12
1991	10	10	8–10	10	12
Dividend propensity [c]					
1990	85.5	54.5	75.1	47.8	36.1
1991	82.3	58.7	76.2	63.0	34.8

[a] Electricity: 9 corporations; Gas: 9 major corporations; Railways: 14 major companies; Airlines: JAL and ANA
[b] Dividend ratio: calculated from dividends per share and face-value on the securities report.
[c] Dividend propensities: from Nikkei Financial Analysis (Autumn 1990 and 1991).
Source: MPT, *Telecommunications Reforms in Japan* (undated), p. 22.

Other Evidence Supporting the MPT Argument

Two other factors are worth considering in this connection. The first is NTT's credit rating, which reflects an independent assessment of NTT's current financial state. The second is an overall evaluation of NTT's performance relative to that of other Japanese companies.

In October 1992, when NTT acknowledged that its pre-tax profits for the year ended March 1993 would not reach the initial forecast of ¥267 billion, Moody's Investors Service assigned an Aaa rating to NTT's Eurobond issuance worth $200 million. This clearly indicated that, despite NTT's profits squeeze, the company was thought to be in sound financial circumstances.[11]

In a survey undertaken by the *Nihon Keizai Shimbun* of the performance of 1,916 non-financial companies quoted on the Tokyo Stock Exchange, NTT was ranked eighth. In this study, growth (in net assets, capital, number of employees, and sales) was the most important component of 'performance', accounting for 35 per cent of a firm's overall score in the league table; profitability accounted for 26 per cent; managerial competence (measured by net worth to total capital, dependency on borrowings, and interest burden) contributed 24 per cent; while financial soundness (ratio of depreciation to sales, current expenditure to income, and cash in hand) had a 15 per cent weighting. The company with the highest

[11] Ibid., 9 November 1992, p. 8.

score was allotted 1,000 points and the others were rated relatively.[12] The results are shown in Table 7.7. It can be seen that NTT ranked eighth overall according to these measurements of performance with a score of 886, just after Toyota which had 909.

Table 7.7 *The 'Terrific Ten' Japanese Companies, Ranked by Performance, 1992*

	No. of points scored[a]
1. Nintendo	1,000
2. Seven-Eleven Japan	995
3. Tokyo Steel	986
4. Fanuc	968
5. Heiwa	927
6. Fuji Photo Film	925
7. Toyota	909
8. NTT	886
9. Ono Pharmaceutical	872
10. Taisho Pharmaceutical	869

[a] See text.

Source: Nihon Kenzai Shimbun; see The Economist, 22 August 1992, p. 60.

NTT's Reconstructed Position

How might NTT respond to this set of arguments claiming that it is not suffering from excessive competition? The following, based on numerous interviews with senior NTT managers, is the kind of counter-argument that I believe would be put forward by NTT.

For a start, NTT managers are likely to accept that, according to the kinds of measure discussed here, the company has performed reasonably, both absolutely and relative to other large non-financial Japanese companies. At the same time, NTT has been able to make progress on other fronts, such as decreasing its work-force by 56,000 since 1985 to 264,908 in 1991 and reducing its long-term interest-bearing debt by an average of ¥200 billion per annum, from ¥5 trillion in 1985 to ¥3.5 trillion in 1991. NTT's managers are therefore likely to agree that its Aaa credit rating is an accurate reflection of the financial health of the company.

Despite this financial health, NTT's managers are likely to argue that the pressure on the company's revenue and profits, underlying circumstances remaining constant, is likely to threaten NTT's longer-term performance. In order to analyse this argument further, it is necessary to return to a further consideration of the NTT Way.

[12] *The Economist*, 22 August 1992, p. 60.

NTT's commitment to innovation can be quantified by examining changes in two key variables: R&D expenditures and capital expenditures. These two variables constitute complementary parts of the innovation process. Broadly speaking, R&D expenditures help to produce the basis for new or improved telecommunications services, while capital expenditures help to ensure that this new potential is translated into the actual availability of better services.

Table 7.8 presents some performance ratios relevant to an examination of NTT's R&D and capital expenditures. The following points emerge.

First, as already noted in Table 7.1, since its part-privatization NTT has been allocating an increasing proportion of its available resources (measured by operating revenues) to research and development. In 1987 R&D accounted for 2.8 per cent of operating revenues; by 1991 this had increased to 4.4 per cent, and by 1993 it had risen to 4.7 per cent.

Secondly, it is significant to note that the proportion of available resources (operating revenue) allocated to capital expenditure has remained more or less constant during this period. Thus, while capital expenditure constituted 30.1 per cent of operating revenue in 1987, the figure was 30.4 per cent in 1990 and 31.0 per cent in 1991.

This implies, thirdly, that R&D has become more important over time relative to capital expenditures. NTT has therefore become increasingly R&D-intensive in a double sense: R&D has increased as a ratio of both operating revenues and capital expenditures. As Table 7.8 shows, while capital expenditures were 10.83 times as great as R&D expenditures in 1987, by 1991 they were only 7.09 times greater.[13]

Table 7.8 *Some NTT Performance Ratios, 1987–1991*

	1987	1988	1989	1990	1991
R&D:Operating revenue	2.8	3.2	3.8	4.1	4.4
Capital expenditure:Operating revenue	30.1	31.7	30.2	30.4	31.0
Capital expenditure:R&D	10.83	9.87	7.95	7.39	7.09
Net income:R&D	1.29	1.47	1.19	1.05	0.96

Source: NTT Annual Report 1991.

[13] As an unusually infrastructure-intensive company with a costly telecommunications network to maintain and upgrade, NTT still spends significantly more on capital expenditures than R&D, in sharp contrast to most of the large Japanese electronics companies which have a far lower capital expenditure-to-R&D ratio. In NEC, for example, the Japanese electronics company with the largest revenues from telecommunications products, the ratio of capital expenditures to R&D was 1.28 in 1991. In passing it is worth noting that in 1991 NEC, one of the most R&D-intensive of the Japanese electronics companies, spent slightly more on R&D in *absolute* terms than NTT, ¥279.5 billion compared to NTT's ¥272.5 billion. However, while NEC's revenue for the year was ¥3,769 billion, NTT's was ¥6,252 billion. The R&D data for NTT show, nevertheless, that the company is moving in the same direction in terms of its growing R&D intensity as the other Japanese electronics companies.

Can NTT's Growing Commitment to Innovation be Sustained,
and What Are the Consequences?

This question provides one way of approaching the earlier question of whether there is excessive competition in the Japanese telecommunications services market: namely, by analysing the ratio of NTT's net income to R&D expenditure. This will give some idea of the company's ability to sustain its growing absolute and proportional allocation of resources to R&D.

Table 7.8 provides the data. These show that the ratio of net income to R&D decreased steadily from 1987, when competition from the NCCs started to bite, to 1991, falling from 1.29 in the former year to 0.96 in the latter. In other words, in 1991 NTT spent more on R&D than its net income. This suggests that NTT's commitment to innovation, a central plank in the NTT Way, is unlikely to be sustainable in the future if the company's present circumstances continue.

How serious is this present state of affairs? As we have already seen, in terms of NTT's financial health it is not particularly serious. However, we have also seen that under current circumstances NTT is unlikely to be able to continue, at the same pace, its effort (in accordance with the NTT Way) to become increasingly innovation-driven.

Does this matter, for NTT itself and for the health of Japanese telecommunications more generally? This is an extremely important but difficult question because the answer depends on a number of contingencies. In the first place, it is necessary to assume that the status quo will continue, i.e. that NTT will continue to be restricted to providing domestic services only (with KDD playing the major international role) in competition with the NCCs. The question then becomes, what are the consequences for Japan's domestic telecommunications services if NTT is unable to maintain its current allocation of resources to innovation?

This hinges, in turn, on a further question, namely the extent to which the R&D requirements of the Japanese domestic network can be provided in sufficient areas by the telecommunications supplying companies (Japanese as well as foreign) rather than by NTT. In other words, to what extent is R&D by these suppliers substitutable for R&D by NTT? To the extent that it is substitutable, and that the supplying companies are actually willing to undertake the required R&D, the impact of NTT's reduced ability to innovate will not be particularly serious.

NTT's view on these questions, a view, it is worth noting, that is central to the philosophy underlying the NTT Way, is that the supplying companies cannot substitute adequately for NTT's research and development. This is because these companies, concerned mainly with their market shares and profits rather than with the development of the Japanese telecommunications network, tend to be incrementalist and rather conservative in their R&D and are therefore unlikely to make the same long-term commitment that NTT does to confront uncertainty and develop the future technologies that will transform telecommunications services. Furthermore, since 1985 there has been a tendency for NTT's R&D to shift from equipment to network planning, design, operation, and new services. To the extent that this has occurred, NTT's R&D and that of the companies are not substitutable. If NTT's reasoning is accepted on this point, then any reduced ability on the part of NTT to innovate will not be adequately compensated for by the supplying companies moving in to fill the gap. Conversely, of course, if NTT's reasoning is not accepted, and it is believed that, were NTT's ability to innovate reduced, the supplying companies would increase their commitment sufficiently to researching and developing future telecommunications technologies, then NTT's present plight is of less consequence for the health of Japanese telecommunications.

Is it possible to test the basis of NTT's reasoning? The short answer is that it is probably not possible to test and arrive at unambiguous conclusions for the simple reason that many sub-arguments could be put forward to support both the NTT view and its opposite. For example, we have seen that NEC, a major telecommunications supplier, spends more in absolute terms than NTT on R&D (even though not all of this is on telecommunications-related objectives). If NEC's commitment to telecommunications-related R&D is aggregated with that of the other Japanese and non-Japanese suppliers, it might be argued that collectively they could make up for any reduced ability to innovate on the part of NTT resulting from competition from the NCCs. Conversely, it might be argued that NTT, which probably makes a greater commitment to basic and long-term research than these suppliers, is currently performing a role which these companies are not in a position to undertake. (Currently NTT allocates about 10 per cent of its R&D to basic research.) At the same time, however, there may be some areas—in some electronic devices or software, for example—where any reduction of R&D activity by NTT could be adequately taken over by the suppliers.

The conclusion that follows is that whether or not the current squeeze that is being placed on NTT's attempt to increase its innovative capacity has detrimental consequences for Japanese telecommunications depends on the belief that is held regarding the ability of the supplying companies to substitute for NTT's research and development. This belief cannot be 'scientifically' tested. The result, unfortunately, is that room for disagreement remains.

The argument about the consequences of a reduced ability on the part of NTT to innovate, however, changes fundamentally once the focus is broadened to include not only Japanese domestic telecommunications, but also the global situation. Then the fundamental question becomes, who will be the major Japanese players in the global telecommunications markets and what role should NTT be playing in these markets? The issue of globalization is tackled later in this chapter.

The Question of Rate Rebalancing Once Again

The issue of the longer-term sustainability of NTT's increased commitment to innovation through R&D adds a new slant to the question of rate rebalancing referred to earlier. As we saw, NTT's general argument in favour of rate rebalancing rests on the supposition that there is a contradiction between MPT's policy of strong competition in the long-distance market (which has forced NTT to reduce its long-distance tariffs) and its insistence that NTT continues to provide universal service without (up to early 1993) raising local tariffs and charges. NTT argues that this contradiction makes it increas-ingly difficult to continue subsidizing its local services from its long-distance services. It is for this reason that NTT has argued that rate rebalancing is now essential.

A further argument for rate rebalancing, one that to my knowledge has not been officially made by NTT, is that this is also necessary if the company is to continue its innovation-driven approach, which is essential for the longer-term future of Japanese telecommunications. As already noted, this argument depends on the assumption that the supplying companies will not be able to fill effectively any gap that would be left if NTT were unable to maintain its commitment to innovation through R&D.

What is the response of MPT to these two arguments for rate rebalancing? I put this question to several senior MPT officials with regard to the first argument. Their answer was twofold. First, while they could see the underlying logic in NTT's argument, they wanted at this stage (end 1992) to reserve their position on the need for, and extent of, rebalancing pending the availability of more reliable data on NTT's costs and revenues relating to particular services. As mentioned in the following section on divestiture, from April 1992 NTT was required by MPT to segment its accounts so that these data can be made available. The officials argued that in 1993, on the basis of this segmented data, they would be able to form a judgement on the desirability and extent of any rebalancing. Secondly, one of the officials argued that NTT's local services remained 'inefficient', which is MPT-speak for 'overmanning'. According to this official, overmanning continues to exist in NTT despite an overall reduction in em-ployment levels, thus keeping costs high and contributing to the decline in profits.

How persuasive are these arguments? The expressed need for more accurate information is hard to object to, and it remains to be seen how long it will take before sufficient data are available and what ground-rules MPT will employ when deciding on the desirability and extent of rebalancing on the basis of this data. As far as I am aware, MPT has not been explicit, publicly or privately, regarding this point.

Neither, to my knowledge, has MPT been explicit regarding the implications of its second argument regarding NTT's alleged 'overmanning'. This would require some operational definition of 'overmanning' as opposed to 'acceptable manning'. From a policy point of view, this definition, if it is to serve as an adequate guideline for NTT's behaviour, would have to come to terms with the practice of lifetime employment, still deeply entrenched in most large Japanese companies. If the definition of 'acceptable manning' were to imply a violation of lifetime employment as presently practised by NTT, it is obviously important that the likely implications are spelled out and confronted.

The present discussion implies that there is a lack of transparency regarding the reasoning and rules that guide MPT's decision-making in this area (and possibly other areas). The frustration of the regulated is understandable, given the uncertainty about precisely what behaviour is being encouraged (regardless of whether the regulated intends to comply with the encouragment or not). (Without explicit criteria, the argument that 'NTT remains "inefficient"' runs the risk of being irrefutable.) But the lack of transparency is also likely to frustrate the regulator, by its failure to convey effectively an unambiguous signal to the regulated regarding the behaviour that is desirable. When this point was put to one senior MPT official he appeared to agree. Nevertheless, this and other discussions in MPT left the distinct impression that in the Ministry's view there is still sufficient 'fat' left in the NTT system for significant efficiency gains to be realized, thus improving NTT's financial position without a rise in tariffs.

The further possible argument for rate rebalancing—i.e. that it is necessary for NTT to pursue its innovation-driven approach—was not put to MPT officials. It is likely though that these officials would not accept that NTT needs to maintain its current commitment to innovation for the sake of the health of Japanese telecommunications.*

The Indirect Impact of Competition from the NCCs

Competition from the NCCs has had a further major impact on the NTT Way, but an impact that is more subtle than those that have been discussed so far. This impact has changed the way in which the prices of telecommunications services are formed and therefore the way in which revenue is determined. In turn, this has transformed the determination of the appropriate level of R&D expenditures.

In the monopoly era tariffs were in effect set on a 'cost-plus' basis. That is, tariffs were set by calculating the revenue that NTT needed in order to cover its given costs and make an allowable rate of profit. Legally, it was MPT and ultimately the Diet that had to approve the tariffs that were set in this way. Under this cost-plus system NTT's costs, including its R&D expenditures, were regarded effectively as 'fixed costs'. These costs were the 'independent variable' used to calculate the tariffs, which were the 'dependent variable'. In other words, the tariff was calculated on the basis of costs that were exogenously given and the direction of causation was therefore from costs to tariffs. Of course, this does not mean that NTT's managers were free to set any level of R&D expenditures, since there was some degree of scrutiny by the Ministry and Diet regarding the company's level of costs. Indeed, as we have seen, up to 1985 R&D was a significantly smaller fraction of operating revenues than it is now.

In the post-1985 competition era, on the other hand, this direction of causation has been reversed. Tariffs are now increasingly determined not by being 'built

---

* As noted above, in the financial year ended March 1995, after MPT allowed NTT to increase basic charges and directory assistance, NTT recorded the first growth in profits for 5 years.

up' from costs as previously, but by the market, albeit a regulated market. More concretely, NTT's long-distance tariff is now determined not by the level of its own existing costs, but by the tariff that MPT allows the NCCs to charge. The NCCs' tariff, in turn, is determined first by their level of costs, and secondly by the regulatory regime established by MPT (which, as we have seen, allowed the NCCs to achieve rapid increases in both revenue and, in the case of Daini Denden and Japan Telecom, profits, despite the regular decrease in the long-distance tariff, as shown in Figs. 7.1 and 7.2). In the competition era, therefore, the direction of causation is from the tariff determined in the (regulated) market to the level of costs that this tariff (via revenue) can sustain. The tariff, therefore, becomes the 'independent variable', with the level of costs becoming the 'dependent variable'.

Implications of the New Competitive Pricing Mechanism

The main implication of this new competitive pricing mechanism for the NTT Way is that R&D costs (like other costs) are transformed from a given fixed cost into an investment. While in the monopoly era it could be assumed that this given fixed cost would be covered by the politically authorized tariff, in the competition era R&D cost becomes an investment that *must* be justified by the additional return that it generates. If R&D expenditures do not generate an appropriate return, then the company will eventually discover that its cost structure is inappropriately high. (With R&D expenditures in NTT running at 4.7 per cent of operating revenues and one-seventh of the amount of total capital expenditure, it is clear that R&D is a significant cost item.)

The implication of this is that NTT's managers will increasingly have to ask what return they are getting, and are likely to get, from their R&D expenditures. While this is common practice in all companies subjected to market discipline, it involves a substantial break from NTT's past practice. In turn, a further implication is that the 'innovation through R&D' plank in NTT's approach will increasingly have to be subjected to the discipline of the market (albeit currently regulated), which will determine the kind of return that the company must get on its R&D expenditures in the light of market-determined tariffs and revenues. In the past this plank was for the most part an article of faith, unchallenged by market forces; this is no longer possible.

Conclusions

The following conclusions can be drawn regarding the impact of competition on NTT and the NTT Way:

1. While competition is having an increasing impact on NTT, its overall effect is still fairly limited.
2. More specifically, competition has not yet had a serious effect on NTT's overall market share in telephone services, even though the NCCs have

made significant inroads into segments of the market for these services, notably in the Tokyo–Nagoya–Osaka corridor.

3. The NCCs have had a greater impact on the market for newer services, most notably cellular phone services. At present, however, these newer services still account for a relatively small proportion of NTT's revenue and profit.

4. While NTT has been able to increase its revenue since 1985, as competition from the NCCs has begun to bite, so NTT has recorded falling profits (as measured by income before tax).*

5. However, these falling profits have not affected unduly the financial health and performance of NTT, as this is reflected in the company's continuing Aaa credit rating and its excellent corporate performance (as measured above) relative to other Japanese companies.

6. Since 1985 NTT has become increasingly R&D-intensive, relative to both operating revenues and capital expenditures. NTT's increasing commitment to innovation-through-R&D represents an important component of the NTT Way, which forms the basis of the company's vision and strategy.

7. There is evidence to suggest that, with the present circumstances of competition and regulation continuing, NTT will be unable to maintain its current level of commitment to innovation-through-R&D.

8. Whether or not this will have serious negative consequences for the Japanese telecommunications network depends on whether the telecommunications supplying companies would be able to take over NTT's commitment to R&D, including its dedication to longer-term and basic research. The question of rate rebalancing needs to be seen partly in this light.

9. The transformation of R&D expenditures from a fixed cost into an investment with the emergence of the competition era has important consequences for the NTT Way. This represents a marked break with the past for NTT.

10. In the longer run, NTT is likely to face a significant increase in competitive pressures as existing and new competitors enter the various telecommunications markets, in some cases on the back of new technologies. One example is Motorola's plan to build Iridium, a global satellite communications network costing $3.37 billion. This network will use hand-held, wireless telephones that communicate through a constellation of sixty-six low-earth orbit satellites. The network will offer subscribers voice, paging, facsimile, data, and radiodetermination satellite services (RDSS). Daini Denden and its main shareholder, Kyocera, have expressed interest in participating in Iridium.[14] To the extent that competitive pressure increases, the existing trends analysed in this section will be accentuated.

---

* This was reversed in the financial year ended March 1995

[14] *Financial Times*, 7 January 1993.

Divestiture

The second of the great uncertainties facing NTT and the NTT Way is the imminent possibility of divestiture. The issue of whether NTT should be divested is by no means new in Japan. Indeed, it was put firmly on the Japanese agenda after the decision was taken to divest AT&T in the USA. The Provisional Commission on Administrative Reform in 1982 recommended NTT's divestiture, but this recommendation was not implemented when NTT was part-privatized in 1985. In 1990, when the position of NTT was again reviewed, the Telecommunications Council of MPT proposed divestiture, and this proposal was taken up by MPT itself; once again, however, nothing further was done. Divestiture has again become an issue for 1995/6 when NTT's position will be reviewed, and this is the cause of some apprehension both for NTT and for Japanese telecommunications generally.

The 1989–90 Divestiture Debate: Background

The history of the debate on divestiture in Japan raises a number of important questions such as: Who has proposed or opposed divestiture and why? Why have the opposers managed so far to defeat the proposers? What does the battle over divestiture reveal regarding the political processes that influence major policy-making decisions in Japanese telecommunications? Will NTT be divested in 1995/6? And finally, what are the consequences of divestiture for NTT and the NTT Way? Answers to these questions will be sought in this section.

The 1982 report of the Provisional Commission on Administrative Reform, which recommended full facilities-based competition in long-distance services, also proposed that NTT be divested into one long-distance company and several companies providing local services. The main reason for this proposal was to promote competition. In order to prevent anti-competitive cross-subsidization, the Commission recommended further that NTT create a number of arm's-length subsidiaries that would keep their own distinct accounts.

In the debate that followed the Commission's report, which eventually led to the part-privatization of NTT in 1985, the divestiture proposal was temporarily dropped. The main reason was disquiet regarding the effects of divestiture on tariffs, universal service, and employment. There was also the feeling that the 1985 reforms (discussed in more detail earlier) made sufficient provision for competition without divestiture. Furthermore, the NTT Corporation Act provided for a re-examination of NTT's structure within five years, and this left open the possibility of divestiture should it be thought necessary to secure competition in the future.

Towards the end of the five-year period, in October 1989, MPT's consultative committee, the Telecommunications Council, brought out an interim report which recommended divestiture. In order to comprehend the heated debates that ensued, however, it is necessary to understand a little more about the backgrounds of the protagonists which influenced the positions that they took on the question of divestiture.

The Protagonists in the Debate

MPT

As we shall see, MPT supported divestiture. The official reason given was that divestiture was necessary in order to decrease NTT's still excessive monopoly and political power. MPT's stand on divestiture, however, was made against the background of a long power struggle with NTT that had intensified in the early 1980s with the work of the Provisional Commission which made the radical reform of Japanese telecommunications inevitable. MPT's policy-makers saw the inevitability of reform as opening up new opportunities to enhance the influence of their ministry. While they originally opposed the privatization of NTT, they soon took the view that privatization together with the introduction of facilities-based competition would enhance the policy-making powers of the ministry. This would follow both from the new forms and powers of regulation that would be required in an industry that would for the foreseeable future be dominated by one player, namely NTT, and from the formation of new telecommunications carrier companies which would fall under the ministry's guidance and influence. The Ministry of International Trade and Industry, which (with the Ministry of Finance) was one of the two most influential ministries, clearly demonstrated the political power that followed from the possession of a client corporate base.

It was for this reason that MPT soon changed its position and supported the privatization of NTT. But in the years that followed privatization in 1985, MPT remained aware that NTT, which as we shall see had some powerful political allies, was still a force to be reckoned with despite the Ministry's new regulatory powers. Divestiture, however, would be likely to bring about a significant shift in the power balance by significantly reducing NTT's influence.

NTT's Management

NTT strongly opposed divestiture. The main reason was that NTT's managers felt that divestiture constituted a major threat to the NTT Way, which pro-pounded the continued improvement of existing telecommunications services and the introduction of new ones through significant investment in the network and R&D. From this point of view, the division of the company into a long-distance division and one or more local divisions was artificial. Whether services were long-distance or local, they all depended to a large extent on similar technologies and competences. To divest NTT would be to destroy the coherence of the NTT Way. From the perspective of NTT's managers, the illogicality of the divestiture proposal was apparent in the dilemma that it raised regarding where to locate the company's Electrical Communications Laboratories (ECL); while MPT's divestiture proposal recommended that ECL would be attached to the divested company providing local services (on the grounds that these services comprised the bulk of NTT's business), this raised the question of the 'technological engine' that would drive the long-distance company. From a *technological* point of view, therefore, divestiture seemed to lack a coherent rationale.

From a *business efficiency* point of view, on the other hand, NTT's managers felt that privatization, together with the new pressures that would be created by competition after 1985, would create sufficient conditions for increasing efficiency. Divestiture, accordingly, was not seen as being necessary to achieve the required increase in business efficiency. Indeed, to go a step further and follow the technological point of view, divestiture was likely to *decrease* efficiency by impairing the innovative dynamic that lay at the heart of the NTT Way. In summary, privatization, which gave NTT's managers increased freedom to make businesslike decisions, together with competition, which pressurized the company to improve the cost and quality of old and new services, would suffice to bring about the necessary business efficiency.

Lastly, it must be said that NTT's managers opposed divestiture also on the grounds that it would weaken the political and economic influence of the company which to some extent was a function of its sheer size. Clearly, there was little incentive to endorse proposals that were likely to decrease NTT's power significantly without sufficient compensations—all the more so since as we have seen divestiture flew in the face of the logic of the NTT Way, a logic that NTT's managers wholeheartedly endorsed.

NTT's Union

NTT's union, the All-Japan Telecommunications Workers' Union, opposed divestiture, and their stand received the support of the main opposition parties which had close links to the Japanese unions. Since the Provisional Commission on Administrative Reform was concerned mainly with the size of government expenditure, and since the operating costs of NTT largely comprised personnel costs, the union had reason to be concerned that attempts to reform Japanese telecommunications would contain measures to reduce employment. (As late as fiscal 1991, after a decrease in employment of 56,000 since 1985, personnel costs were still by far the largest element in NTT's operating expenses, at 39.3 per cent of the total.)

For this reason, the union was sensitive to all proposals to increase 'efficiency', seeing in them possibly hidden attempts to undermine the existing position of NTT's employees. While the union eventually accepted the proposal that NTT be privatized, it was opposed to divestiture on the grounds that its position would be weakened by the fragmentation of its membership. It was also concerned about the possibility of increasing inequalities in pay and employment conditions in the different divested companies.

Ministry of Finance

The Ministry of Finance opposed divestiture. One important reason was that the Ministry was a major shareholder in NTT and it did not believe that the economic and financial rationale for divestiture was such as to benefit NTT's share price. (As late as 1994, the Ministry of Finance still held 66 per cent of NTT's shares.) Furthermore, the ongoing conflict between the Ministry of Finance and the Ministry of Posts and Telecommunications over the role and conditions of post office savings accounts, controlled by the latter, did little to improve co-operation between them. The net result was that the Ministry of Finance became one of MPT's main antagonists in the battle over divestiture.

MITI

Opposition to divestiture also came from the other of the two most powerful ministries, the Ministry of International Trade and Industry. Overall, MITI's concern in the area of telecommunications was to ensure that appropriate conditions were created in Japan for the development of the computer and information industries in particular and of the 'information society' more generally. It was this concern that led MITI in the early 1980s to confront MPT with the demand that greater liberalization of leased telecommunications circuits be permitted in order to encourage the growth of on-line computer services. This confrontation led to the so-called 'telecoms wars' between MITI and MPT in 1982 and 1983 over value added networks (VANs).[15]

In general, MITI, like the Ministry of Finance, was not convinced about the economic and financial rationale for divestiture. Furthermore, MITI, and in particular its Machinery and Information Industries Bureau, was concerned about the likely effects of divestiture on the strength and international competitiveness of the main Japanese telecommunications equipment supplying companies such as NEC, Fujitsu, Hitachi, Oki, Sumitomo Electric, Furukawa Electric, and Fujikura. While, as shown in detail elsewhere in this book, NTT and its Electrical Communications Laboratories had helped to develop the competences of these supplying companies over the years, MITI's fear was that divestiture would weaken NTT's relationship with these companies.

There was, however, a further dimension to the conflict between MITI and MPT. This arose from the threat to MITI's position from MPT's attempts to increase its policy-making influence through both increased regulatory powers and the incorporation of a more extensive corporate base. From MITI's point of view, MPT's greater regulatory powers might be used in ways that would have negative consequences for the information society or for Japan's international competitiveness. The fact that computers were increasingly being linked through telecommunications networks raised the possibility of the two ministries pursuing conflicting policies in an area where their responsibilities overlapped. For this reason, MITI generally pressed for increased competition as an

---

[15] The so-called Telecoms Wars between MITI and MPT have been illuminatingly analysed by C. Johnson, 'MITI, MPT, and the Telecom Wars: How Japan Makes Policy for High Technology', in C. Johnson, L. D. Tyson, and J. Zysman (eds.), *Politics and Productivity: How Japan's Development Works*, Ballinger, Cambridge, Mass., 1989. The motivations of MPT's bureaucrats is examined in more detail later in this chapter.

alternative to increased regulation in Japanese telecommunications. MPT's attempt to extend its corporate base also threatened boundary disputes with MITI, since many of the companies involved as shareholders in the New Common Carriers also fell under MITI's control in their other lines of business. This provided a further source of tension between the two ministries.

Telecommunications Equipment Companies

Those telecommunications equipment companies that had been part of NTT's traditional supplying group before 1985 (known as the Den Den Family) had an obvious vested interest in opposing divestiture. Although NTT had already begun opening its procurement to both foreign companies and other Japanese companies, the 'traditional' suppliers such as NEC, Fujitsu, Hitachi, and Oki retained close links with NTT and continued to provide a substantial proportion of NTT's equipment needs. Over the years, these companies had established effective routinized modes of interaction with NTT and had even established departments dedicated to their dealings with NTT. In some cases the practice of *amakudari* (whereby senior NTT personnel 'descended' on retirement to executive posts in the supplying company) further cemented this close productive relationship. Divestiture, by multiplying the research, development, and procurement interactions that would be necessary between the supplying company and the several divested NTT companies, and by increasing uncertainty regarding the winning of orders, would respresent a setback for these traditional suppliers. It is not surprising, therefore, that they opposed divestiture.

It is significant, however, that some of NTT's newer suppliers opposed divestiture just as vehemently. Indeed, one of NTT's new Western suppliers played a possibly influential behind-the-scenes role in support of NTT's opposition. This involved the informal lobbying of LDP politicians, arguing that divestiture was likely to have the effect of raising politically sensitive telephone tariffs. While this Western company believed that divestiture would have such an effect, it, like its traditional Japanese supplier counterparts, had a vested interest in ensuring that the links and channels that it had invested in establishing with NTT were not undermined by divestiture.[16]

Keidanren

The stand of Keidanren, the Japan Federation of Economic Organizations, on the question of divestiture was far more ambivalent than that of the ministries mentioned above and the suppliers to NTT. Among its important members, Keidanren had companies that were in both the pro- and anti-divestiture camps. The former included the large number of big Japanese companies that had shares

---

[16] For confidentiality reasons, the name of this company cannot be revealed. The significance of this example, however, is that this new Western supplier to NTT behaved in the same way as NTT's traditional Japanese suppliers in opposing divestiture. This, of course, is not surprising, since they had all become 'insiders' in so far as they had established longer-term trust-based relationships with NTT and did not want to see them disturbed by divestiture, which would increase uncertainty regarding the size and success probability of their sales to NTT.

in the New Common Carriers, while the latter included the Japanese suppliers to NTT and a large number of corporate shareholders in NTT. Furthermore, Keidanren also represented the corporate users of telecommunications services, who wanted cheaper and better services and saw competition against NTT as being a major vehicle for the delivery of these services.

However, there was sufficient uncertainty within Keidanren regarding the probable effects of divestiture to produce considerable caution within the federation in 1989–90 on the question of the breakup of NTT. As we shall see, it was for this reason that, while Keidanren was critical of the degree of monopoly power that NTT continued to exercise, it stopped short of support for divestiture, advocating instead a wait-and-see attitude.

A Blow-by-Blow Account of the 1989–90 Divestiture Debate

The Telecommunications Council's October 1989 Interim Report

According to the 1985 NTT Corporation Act, a review of NTT's structure was required within five years of part-privatization. This review was conducted in the first instance by MPT's consultative committee, the Telecommunications Council. In October 1989 the Telecommunications Council produced its interim report.

The 1990 membership of the Telecommunications Council, which was established on 1 October 1982, is shown in Table 7.9. The wide representation on the Telecommunications Council is a notable feature. Apart from Japanese organizations directly involved in telecommunications, there were representatives from foreign companies (e.g. Japan NCR and BMW), from Japanese universities, and from research institutes, as well as a journalist and a number of independent 'critics'.

Noteworthy too was the membership of Mr Eiji Toyoda from the Toyota company who was the Council's chairman. It will be recalled that Toyota is the largest shareholder in Teleway Japan, one of the three New Common Carriers which from 1986 began to compete with NTT. Toyota's shareholding in Teleway Japan was 7 per cent. (In Table 7.3 it was pointed out that Teleway Japan has in fact been the least successful of the three NCCs.) The Council's membership also included representation from the traditional equipment supplying companies, NEC (whose representative, Katsumi Soyama, was an ex-MPT under-secretary) and Hitachi, and from the Japan Trade Union Confederation.

The Council's October 1989 interim report was based on two overall explicit assumptions. The first was that the size of NTT was so great that its management was constrained in its effort to increase efficiency; accordingly, divestiture, by breaking the company up into smaller units, would result in an increase in efficiency. Secondly, NTT's dominance of the long-distance service and its monopoly of local services constituted a 'structural' impediment which frustrated

Table 7.9 *Telecommunications Council Membership, 1990*

Member	Affiliation
Eiji Toyoda (Chairman)	Toyota, Teleway Japan
Katsumi Soyama	NEC, ex-MPT undersecretary
Akira Arai	*Japan Economic Journal*
Kiyoshi Iijima	Critic
Mitsuharu Ito	Professor, Kyoto University
Hiroshi Inose	President, National Centre for Science Information System
Koji Kamaoka	President, INTEC (special Type II carrier)
Yasuchi Kosai	Japan Economic Research Centre
Riyako Godai	Critic
Takayuki Kondo	Japan Finance Corporation for Municipal Enterprises
Yuri Konno	Research Institute of Living Science
Mamoru Sakai	Long-Term Credit Bank of Japan
Atsuchi Shimokobe	National Institute of Research
Yoji Hamawaki	BMW
Hiroshi Hirayama	Professor, Waseda University
Sakae Fujiki	Mobil Radio Centre Inc.
Minoru Hounoki	Captain Service
Mitsuo Matsushita	Professor, Tokyo University
Katsushige Mita	Hitachi
Hironobu Mitsutomi	Japan NCR
Fumio Watanabe	Japan Airlines
Mitsuharu Waroshina	Japan Trade Union Confederation

efforts to secure fair and effective competition. This was because the NCCs that competed with NTT in the long-distance network were at the same time dependent on NTT for access to its local network.

While the Council acknowledged that there were important costs associated with divestiture, it argued that there were also benefits that would help to deal with these two problems. Furthermore, the Council noted that there were three possible kinds of divestiture that should be considered: one long-distance company and one local company; one long-distance and several local companies; several companies providing both long-distance and local services.

The Council concluded, however, that judgement as to whether divestiture was desirable or not would hinge on an estimate of the associated costs and benefits. The Council stated that its judgement would be made in its final report.

MPT's Final Report, 2 March 1990

On 2 March 1990 MPT published its final report based on the interim report of its Telecommunications Council. Although by then MPT had had the opportunity to respond to the opposition to the October 1989 interim report, its final report was very close to that report. The second section of the final report identified two 'problems in the telecommunications market'.[17] The first was that 'NTT has enormous influence on not only the telecommunications industry but also the whole economy and society, because of its vast size, overwhelming market share, and strong buying power among other factors.'[18] NTT's great influence was causally linked to a corresponding inability on the part of the New Common Carriers to become sufficiently efficient: 'Therefore, without a thoroughgoing streamlining of NTT's operations, the new common carriers (NCCs) will not achieve adequate levels of efficiency to compete effectively, and customers may be denied the true benefits of market competition.'[19]

The second problem in the telecommunications market was the alleged 'unique structure' of this market: 'The Japanese telecommunications market is unique in that the competitive conditions between NTT and the NCCs are structurally different, a situation that severely limits fair and effective competition in the market.'[20] In what way were the competitive conditions of NTT and the NCCs seen to be structurally different? 'NTT is solely operating both monopolistic local communications networks and competitive communications networks such as long-distance and mobile ones. The NCCs have no alternative but to depend on NTT's local networks in order to provide their services, because it would be extremely difficult for them to construct huge local networks by themselves.'[21]

In order to solve these two 'problems', MPT made the following main recommendations:

1. 'The long-distance communications business should be separated completely from NTT, and placed under the management of a separated and completely privatized company; in other words, it should be freed from the restrictions imposed by the NTT Law.'[22] (Long-distance communications were defined as being approximately the same as inter-prefectural communications.)

2. 'The local communications business which NTT is now operating should be operated by one company for the time being, and this situation should be reviewed in the future.'[23]

3. 'The mobile communications business should be separated from NTT and placed under the management of a separated and completely privatized company.'[24]

Regarding the proposal that NTT become a single company responsible for local communications, the report acknowledged that 'it would not necessarily be effective for NTT's current local business to be operated by one company after separating the long-distance business from it.'[25] Nevertheless, it was felt that this

---

[17] This and the following quotations come from Ministry of Posts and Telecommunications, *Summary of The Report on 'Necessary Measures to be Taken According to Article 2 of the Supplementary Provision of the Nippon Telegraph and Telephone Corporation Law', Submitted by the Telecommunications Council on March 2, 1990*, MPT, Tokyo, undated.

[18] Ibid. 1.   [19] Ibid.   [20] Ibid.   [21] Ibid.

[22] Ibid. 2.   [23] Ibid.   [24] Ibid.   [25] Ibid. 3.

proposal was justified for two reasons. First, 'There is an urgent need to solve the peculiar structure of the current telecommunications market.'[26] Secondly, 'If NTT's local business were divided into multiple regional companies in addition to the separation of the long-distance business, it would not be clear whether each regional local company would be profitable or whether each company would require different local telephone rates.'[27]

The report, furthermore, recommended that NTT, responsible for local communications under its proposals, be required to segment the accounts of its different regional divisions in order to 'eliminate abuses arising from NTT's [continuing] overwhelming size and its monopoly of the local market, and to promote a streamlining of its operations'.[28]

In view of the importance of NTT's R&D function, both for the Japanese electronics industry generally and for the telecommunications sector, it is worth noting the report's recommendations regarding R&D. The report observed that 'In many countries the telecommunications industry is looked upon as a strategic sector for the twenty-first century, and it is important for Japan to sustain and enhance the current level of R&D work on telecommunications, partly from the viewpoint of contribution to the international community.'[29] Without further justification or attempt to meet the obvious objections that might be raised, the report continued: 'Thus it is desirable that the local company should inherit NTT's existing laboratories and operate them as one body for the time being.'[30]

Finally, it is worth stressing that, while MPT's final report was unequivocally in favour of divestiture, and despite the fact that the Telecommunications Council's interim report stated that a decision on privatization should be made on the basis of an analysis of the costs and benefits involved, no such analysis was provided either in the final report itself or subsequently. As will be seen, this lack of 'supporting evidence' in favour of divestiture was to leave room for vigorous opposition to MPT's divestiture proposal.

The Response to MPT's Proposals

There was strong opposition both to the Telecommunications Council's interim report and to MPT's final report. As early as December 1989, that is some two-and-a-half months before MPT's final report of 2 March 1990, Keidanren issued its own report calling for a three-year suspension of any decision on the divestiture of NTT. While Keidanren's report admitted that because of' NTT's dominance fair competition in telecommunications did not exist, and while it acknowledged that divestiture could have the effect of increasing competition, it felt that further study was needed on the economic and financial consequences of divestiture. Furthermore, the Keidanren report proposed that any divestiture be delayed until NTT had completed the digitization of its network, on the

---

[26] Ibid.   [27] Ibid.   [28] Ibid. 4.
[29] Ibid.   [30] Ibid.

grounds that the NCCs would not be able to afford the huge investment costs of such modernization.[31]

Further vociferous opposition came from the Ministry of Finance. By February 1990 the Finance Minister, Ryutaro Hashimoto, had made it clear that he would veto any Cabinet authorization of the divestiture proposal. He argued that the proposal had depressed the price of NTT's shares, harming the interests of NTT's 1.6 million shareholders (to say nothing of the Ministry of Finance's own 66 per cent shareholding in NTT!), and had threatened to jeopardize the sale of government-owned shares in Japan Railways.[32] Strong opposition also came from MITI, from the All-Japan Telecommunications Workers' Union, from the main opposition parties, and from the main telecommunications equipment supplying companies, for reasons explained above.

In view of the stalemate between MPT on the one hand and the Ministry of Finance and MITI on the other, the matter was left to the Liberal Democratic Party to resolve. This led to a process of negotiation and compromise by the LDP's *zoku* ('tribes' associated with the interests of various ministries) most closely linked with MPT and the Ministry of Finance. While the postal *zoku* (*yusei-zoku*) were very influential within the LDP in view of the political significance attached to the appointment of post officers (particularly in the rural areas), the *zoku* associated with the Ministry of Finance also had substantial clout. The result was a compromise which was worked out and reflected in new Cabinet-agreed measures that were announced by MPT on 30 March 1990.[33]

The Measures Announced by the Japanese Government on 30 March 1990

With some irony, the preamble to the 30 March measures began by stating that 'the spirit of the recommendations . . . submitted by the Telecommunications Council to the Minister of Posts and Telecommunications on 2 March 1990' had been taken 'into consideration'.[34] In fact, in so far as the 'spirit' of the 2 March final report was to be identified with the proposal to divest NTT, the preamble was more an attempt to smooth the ruffled feathers of the MPT bureaucrats and the members of its Telecommunications Council than a reflection of the truth. Although, as we shall see, some of their recommendations were indeed implemented, the 30 March measures failed to propose that NTT be divested. Nevertheless, the main impact of these measures followed from the requirement that NTT segment its accounts for long-distance and local communications. This

---

[31] *Japan Times*, 12 December 1989.
[32] Ibid., 31 March 1990.
[33] This refers to the *Measures to be Taken in Accordance with Article 2 of the Supplementary Provisions of the Nippon Telegraph and Telephone Corporation Law*, issued by MPT on 30 March 1990 (unofficial translation).
[34] Ibid. 1.

requirement was imposed in an attempt to prevent NTT from cross-subsidizing its services and thus subverting competition from the NCCs.

The measures started from the 'Basic Idea' that, although 'some achievements' had been brought about, 'such as the entry of a large number of new . . . carriers and steady reductions in rates and charges', the fact remained that 'NTT still holds an overwhelming share in the market and that Japan lags behind the United States in terms of diversification of telecommunications services and digitization of networks'.[35] The measures went on to state that 'it is necessary to promote further reduction of rates and charges, as well as the sophistication and diversification of telecommunications services'.[36] Furthermore, if these goals were to be achieved, 'it is necessary to secure conditions for fair and effective competition and to improve NTT management by taking every possible measure to remove the disadvantage caused by NTT's hugeness and monopoly.'[37]

How did the measures propose to secure 'fair and effective competition'? Two main sets of requirements were stipulated. The first was that NTT introduce what was referred to as an 'independent division system',[38] consisting of a long-distance communications division and regional communications divisions. The accounts of these divisions would be segmented in order to make their costs and revenues transparent. Furthermore, NTT was required to provide separate revenue and expenditure data for the different types of telephone services in order to prevent cross-subsidization and thus promote competition. The second set of requirements related to measures to facilitate interconnection between NTT's network and those of the NCCs and in this way to secure openness. In addition, NTT was required to promote the 'positive disclosure'[39] of information that would assist competition.

In line with the recommendation of MPT's final report of 2 March, the 30 March measures stipulated that NTT's mobile communications business be separated from the rest of the company 'within about two years'.[40] Other measures included further study regarding the separation of NTT's terminal equipment sales business; measures to segment the revenue and expense data of NTT's satellite communications business; and the exhortation to NTT to speed the completion of its digitization.

The main measure proposed to improve NTT's management was the requirement that the company introduce 'a drastic rationalization plan'.[41] This implicitly referred to a plan to reduce employment levels. Furthermore, in acknowledgement of the interests championed by the Ministry of Finance, the MPT recommended that the 'government shall pay much attention to the return of profits to NTT stockholders planned by NTT'.[42]

A further feature of the measures proposed, which is of particular interest here in view of the concern with the NTT Way, was the attention given to NTT's R&D activities. Here it was stated that the 'government shall have NTT actively

---

[35] Ibid. [36] Ibid. [37] Ibid. [38] Ibid. 2.
[39] Ibid. 3. [40] Ibid. [41] Ibid. 4. [42] Ibid.

promote its R&D activities'.[43] However, 'In order to effectively disseminate NTT's R&D results, the government shall study systems to secure transparency of NTT's activities, such as the disclosure of its R&D results and the establishment of . . . codes [of practice] to allow manufacturers to sell products using joint R&D results.'[44] Furthermore, 'With a long-range perspective of the development of telecommunications in Japan, the government shall study the establishment of comprehensive R&D systems to vitalize R&D activities in Japan as a whole by various organizations, including national laboratories, universities, telecommunications carriers and manufacturers.'[45]

Divestiture in 1995/6?

In 1990 it was agreed that the structure of NTT would be reviewed yet again in 1995/6. The possibility of divestiture in 1995/6 has continued to cause uncertainty regarding NTT's future. So how likely is it that NTT will be divested?

In answering, the first point to make is that there is no consensus on this question, either in NTT itself or among the other interested parties reviewed earlier. In the large number of interviews that I conducted regarding this question, views about the likelihood of divestiture in 1995 differed sharply. Indicative of the lack of consensus was the view of a senior NTT executive who not only felt that divestiture in 1995/6 was likely, but favoured it on the grounds that it would increase NTT's dynamism and help it to globalize.

In examining more systematically the question of the likelihood of NTT being divested, it is worth beginning by posing a further question.

Is MPT Likely to Propose Divestiture Again?

In answering this question, it is necessary to understand why MPT advocated divestiture in 1990. The answer is that the Ministry wanted to weaken NTT *vis-à-vis* both the NCCs and the Ministry itself, thus increasing its control over NTT. That this is not mere conspiracy-theory-type speculation is evident from the second section of the final report of MPT's Telecommunications Council, published with approval by MPT on 2 March 1990. Here NTT's power, not only in the area of telecommunications services but also in Japan's economy and society more generally, is identified as a major 'problem': 'NTT has enormous influence not only on the telecommunications industry but also on the whole economy and society, because of its vast size, overwhelming market share, and strong buying power among other factors.'[46]

One consequence of NTT's influence, in the view of this report, was that, 'without a thoroughgoing streamlining of NTT's operations, the new common carriers (NCCs) will not achieve adequate levels of efficiency to compete

---

[43] Ibid. 5.   [44] Ibid. 3   [45] Ibid. 5.

[46] *Report* of the Telecommunications Council, Ministry of Posts and Communications, 2 March 1990.

effectively. . . .'[47] Unmentioned, but further implied, was that a 'streamlining' of NTT, i.e. NTT's divestiture as proposed in this report, would also have the effect of increasing MPT's influence relative to that of NTT.

Two further questions arise. Does MPT still feel that NTT must be further weakened? And, if the answer to the first question is yes, how does MPT assess the likely response to any moves on its part to divest NTT? These questions will now be tackled in turn.

Does MPT Still Feel that NTT Must be Further Weakened?

In dealing with this question, it is necessary to understand that NTT's position, relative to that of both the NCCs and MPT, has weakened significantly since 1990, even though NTT continues to be dominant in telecommunications services and equipment markets, and even though its political influence should not be underestimated. The following are important indicators of NTT's weakened position.

1. As documented in detail earlier in this chapter, NTT's profitability has suffered in absolute terms and relative to at least two of the three main NCCs with which it competes.

2. The increased transparency of NTT's accounting system, which requires a segmentation of its accounts by long-distance and local service, by region, and by type of telephone service, makes cross-subsidization by NTT difficult if not impossible, and therefore protects the NCCs from unfair competition from NTT. On 1 April 1992 NTT restructured its organization, complying with a government decision made in March 1991, following on the government's measures of 30 March 1990 that were analysed earlier.

NTT's restructuring involved the establishment of a Long-Distance Communications Sector offering inter-prefectural telephone, private leased line, and ISDN services. In addition, eleven Regional Communications sectors were set up (including Tokyo, Kanto, Shinetsu, Tokai, Hokuriku, Kansai, Chugoku, Shikoku, Kyushu, and Hokkaido). The latter provide intra-prefecture telephone, private leased line, and ISDN services, as well as public telephones, directory assistance, customer premise equipment, and phone directories within their regions.

Four other business units were also established: the Telegram Sector, Packet Communications Sector, Video Communications Sector, and Mobile Communications Sector. NTT has been required to prepare profit-and-loss statements and other financial data in accordance with new rules issued by MPT and to disclose a list of assets and liabilities for each of these sectors.[48]

3. The beginnings of serious decentralization in NTT through the spin-off of relatively autonomous subsidiaries has further eroded the company's effective centralized influence, even though NTT headquarters in Hibiya remains a potent force. NTT's 1991 Annual Report states that there were 146 specialized

---

[47] Ibid.   [48] *New Era of Telecommunications in Japan*, 1 April 1992, no. 157, p. 10.

subsidiaries and affiliates.[49] These include NTT International Corporation, established in October 1985, which provides engineering and consulting services for overseas telecommunications systems; NTT Data Communications Systems Corporation, set up in May 1988 to provide computer networking and systems integration services; and NTT's mobile communications subsidiary, NTT Mobile Communications Network, Inc., known popularly as NTT Docomo, which was established in June 1992.

4. Since the 'telecoms wars' with MITI in the early 1980s, MPT has succeeded in asserting its authority as chief regulator in the field of telecommunications. This is evident in NTT's cautious, if not deferential, handling of any issue which it feels might be sensitive for MPT. A case in point is the issue of globalization, which is considered in more detail in the following section.

For these four reasons, it is not clear that MPT would achieve a great deal more, in terms of a further weakening of NTT relative to the NCCs and the Ministry itself, if it were to achieve the divestiture of NTT. Nevertheless, in interviews that I conducted with several senior MPT officials, they made it clear that they were not abandoning the possibility of pressing for divestiture in 1995/6. They wanted to keep the divestiture option open while waiting to see how the other measures mentioned in this section worked. Needless to say, the implicit threat of divestiture in the run-up to 1995 could also serve to strengthen MPT's regulatory hand.

Regardless of whether MPT itself would wish to see NTT divested, the question remains regarding the political viability of this wish. In short, would there simply be a re-run of the 1990 scenario with the opponents of divestiture succeeding in crushing any move for divestiture? This raises the second question asked earlier.

What is the Likely Response to Any Move to Divest NTT?
It is likely that MPT realizes that NTT's allies in 1990, particularly the Ministry of Finance and MITI, do not have any obvious reason for changing their position on divestiture. In this connection it is important to note that no detailed estimates have been made by any of the major players in the divestiture debate regarding the likely economic and financial effects of divestiture, let alone the political effects. Against this background, it remains the case that the Ministry of Finance, which retains a 66 per cent shareholding in NTT and which is looking for an opportunity to sell more of these shares, is still concerned that divestiture might further weaken the price of NTT's shares at a time when the Tokyo Stock Exchange is performing badly.

Moreover, many policy-makers in MITI are known to be concerned that a further weakening of NTT will have negative consequences both for Japan's position as an international player in telecommunications and for the global strategic and competitive positioning of the Japanese telecommunications

[49] NTT *Annual Report*, 1991, p. 23.

equipment companies, who have still failed (partly for protectionist reasons) to make a major impact on telecommunications markets in the advanced Western countries in complex equipment.

There is another, though fortuitous, factor. As was seen in the discussion of MPT's final report of 2 March 1990, MPT depended on its *zoku* ('tribe') in the Liberal Democratic Party to negotiate a compromise with the Ministry of Finance primarily and MITI secondly. Even though MPT did not get its way with divestiture in 1990, it is clear from the government-agreed measures of 30 March 1990, discussed earlier, that many of MPT's suggestions have been faithfully incorporated. MPT's success in this respect was in no small measure due to the political influence of its *zoku*.

More specifically, MPT had the good fortune to have Shin Kanemaru as the leader of its *zoku*. Mr Kanemaru was an elder statesman in the LDP and was often referred to as a 'kingmaker' in view of the power that he wielded in mediating between the LDP's different factions. He was therefore able to stand up effectively to former Prime Minister Noboru Takeshita, who was regarded as the leader of the Ministry of Finance's *zoku*. When MPT and the Ministry of Finance were at loggerheads, Kanemaru and Takeshita negotiated a compromise.

At the end of 1992, however, the political power balance within the LDP between the MPT's and the Ministry of Finance's *zoku* changed dramatically when Kanemaru was forced to resign from the LDP for accepting an illegal political donation. The following incident reflects this significant change in power balance. On 11 December 1992, Prime Minister Kiichi Miyazawa's second Cabinet was installed with Junichiro Koizumi as the Minister at the Ministry of Posts and Telecommunications. While Mr Koizumi belonged to a faction which rivalled that of Mr Kanemaru (a faction under the leadership of Hiroshi Mitsuzuka, who was chairman of the LDP's powerful Policy Research Council), he was also a member of the Finance Ministry's *zoku*.

As if that was not enough, Mr Koizumi, one day after his installation, proceeded to break with past precedent, which required that incoming ministers implement the policies that had already been adopted by their predecessors. Accordingly, he declared his opposition to the plan to raise the tax exemption on postal savings held by senior citizens. The Ministry of Finance had long opposed MPT's attempts to raise this tax exemption. This challenge to the authority of MPT's bureaucrats led to the resignation of a senior official of this ministry in protest. According to the *Nikkei Weekly*, 'Koizumi himself admitted that he would not have challenged the exemption plan if Kanemaru were still head of the faction.'[50]

Conclusion

Since 1994 Japan has plunged into a period of extreme political instability, with rapidly shifting alliances both within and between political parties. Although

[50] *Nikkei Weekly*, 21 December 1992, p. 2.

there has been a far greater degree of continuity within the Japanese bureaucracy, the political uncertainties add a further element of unpredictability regarding the possibility of divestiture. Although the considerations mentioned in this section remain relevant, it remains to be seen whether MPT will push for divestiture in 1995/6 and, if it does, whether it will succeed.

Globalization

The major telecommunications carriers, e.g. AT&T and BT, are increasingly looking to global telecommunications markets as the major source of growth for the 1990s and for the early twenty-first century. A major question from the Japanese point of view is: which company or companies will represent Japan in these markets? As we shall see, it is this question more than any other that divides and confuses the major players in Japanese telecommunications.

The Globalization of Telecommunications Markets

In its 1991 Annual Report, AT&T states its three main 'financial objectives and strategies for the future':

- To achieve an average annual earnings growth rate of at least 10 per cent and a return on equity exceeding 20 per cent.
- To derive half our revenues from international activities by early in the next decade.
- To achieve long-term revenue growth that exceeds that of the information movement and management industry as a whole.[51]

In 1991, boosted by the merger with NCR, which derived some 60 per cent of its revenue from non-US sources, AT&T earned 24 per cent of its revenue from international sources—9 per cent from operations located in other countries, and 15 per cent from international revenues from US operations (comprising international telecommunications services and export sales).

BT has announced major new global projects. For example, BT's worldwide network, Project Cyclone, will provide facilities in twenty of the world's largest cities at a cost of $1 billion. This network, which will 'by-pass existing phone companies to provide intra-company services for multinational corporations', is expected to be fully operational in the year 2003 after getting the necessary government approvals.[52] BT also launched its project Synchordia, which 'will assume complete control of a client company's global telecommunications'.[53] As we shall see, an abortive attempt was made to persuade NTT to joint BT's

---

[51] AT&T *Annual Report*, 1991, p. 18.

[52] *Business Week*, 7 December 1992, p. 18.

[53] Ibid. At this date it was stated that 'Synchordia now manages networks for only four companies, including IBM Europe and BP', although BT naturally expected that this reflected the short time of Synchordia's existence and that the number of customers would rapidly grow (p. 18).

Synchordia consortium. The Germans and French, and the Dutch and Swedes have made similar global telecommunications alliances.

Why have the major telecommunications carriers begun to pay increasing attention to global telecommunications markets? To begin with, in countries such as the USA and UK the main carriers face increasing competition in their domestic markets. This has encouraged them to look to the international market for long-term growth and profitability. Secondly, large and medium-sized corporate customers have always been an important market segment for the major carriers. This is increasingly the case, as substantial demand comes from these customers for new telecommunications services which the carriers hope will replace the slowing demand for telephone services. These customers, however, are becoming ever more involved in international activities, thus encouraging the large carriers to cater for their international telecommunications needs.

Thirdly, the large carriers believe that they have acquired distinctive competences in the movement and management of information as a result of the large networks that they have designed, developed, and run. These competences, they believe, allow them to provide information services for multinational companies more efficiently than the companies themselves can deliver. This belief has led companies such as BT and KDD to offer companies the opportunity to outsource their telecommunications services.

For these reasons, there are powerful forces facilitating the growth of global markets for telecommunications services and encouraging entry into these markets by the large carriers. What role will Japanese companies play in these emerging global markets?

NTT as a Domestic Carrier

According to the NTT Corporation Act, article 1, NTT 'shall be a limited company whose purpose is to operate a domestic telecommunications business'; it is KDD that provides international telecommunications services. This *de jure* distinction, however, has not entirely prevented NTT from 'globalizing'.

How Has NTT 'Globalized'?

Despite these legal restrictions limiting NTT to the operation of 'a domestic telecommunications business', NTT has been able to 'globalize' in at least five important senses.

1. NTT has to a significant extent globalized its research, development, and procurement of telecommunications equipment, as has been described throughout this book. It has done this by including companies such as Northern Telecom, IBM Japan, DEC, Ericsson, and AT&T in its Track III joint development projects.
2. Through several of its subsidiaries NTT has been able to offer telecommunications consulting and engineering services outside Japan. Here the

activities of NTT International, established in October 1985, are noteworthy.

3. NTT has recently been able to draw on its competences to get directly involved in overseas operations in other countries. The outstanding example is the $1.62 billion contract that was awarded to NTT in July 1992 in connection with the Thai Telephone & Telecommunications Company.
4. NTT has also to some extent been able to help its Japanese customers take care of their international telecommunications needs by giving them advice and by leasing circuits from other international carriers for its customers' use. The Japanese legislation, however, has prevented NTT from owning and providing its own circuits linking Japan with other countries.
5. NTT has established several strategic alliances, including one with Microsoft.

Since the first kind of globalization has been discussed in detail earlier in this book, attention here will focus on the other kinds.

Sale of Consulting and Engineering Services Abroad

NTT International (NTTI) is one of NTT's major vehicles for the sale of telecommunications services outside Japan. For the year ended 31 March 1992, NTTI's sales were ¥13.07 billion and the company employed 394 people. NTTI's sales were about 0.2 per cent of NTT's sales and its employment was about 0.15 per cent of NTT's.

According to NTTI's publicity material, 'We primarily provide clients worldwide with access to NTT's vast managerial resources and superior capabilities in developing telecommunications infrastructures and advanced communications systems. . . . to provide services tailored to your specific tele-communications and data communications needs.' While most of NTTI's work is in developing countries, the company has also been involved in the construction of global information networks for private companies in countries such as the USA, UK, Switzerland, and Germany.

Direct Operations Abroad:
Thai Telephone & Telecommunications Company (TT&T)

NTT's deal with TT&T is by far its largest operation abroad and serves as a model for the future regarding this kind of globalization. But how did NTT come to win this deal against strong competition from international carriers such as France Telecom? What role will NTT play in TT&T? Why did MPT support NTT in Thailand on this occasion when it failed to provide such support in earlier cases involving Mexico and Brazil? These are the kinds of questions that we shall now consider.

Background to the TT&T Deal
As a rapidly industrializing country with a high growth rate, Thailand has

experienced an increase in demand for telephone services. With approximately 1.3 million telephone subscribers, only 2.3 per cent of Thailand's 55 million people own telephones. The Thai government therefore decided to aim to increase the number of subscribers by a further 3 million within a period of five years.

In order to speed the development of Thailand's telecommunications infrastructure and the diffusion of telephones, the Thai authorities, influenced by ideas of privatization, decided to authorize consortia of private companies to develop additional telecommunications facilities. Accordingly, the Telephone Organization of Thailand (TOT), the country's national telephone company, awarded two concessions, one for two million lines in the Bangkok area and the other for one million lines outside Bangkok. Thai companies were invited to form consortia and apply for these concessions, although they were required to include an international carrier in their consortium.

In view of the difficulties of installing lines in congested Bangkok, NTT decided that it would rather be involved with the concession taking responsibility for the area outside this city. It therefore entered into negotiation with a consortium bidding for this concession, namely Thai Telephone and Telecommunications Company (TT&T). (In the event, the consortium that won the bid for the two million lines in the Bangkok area was called Telecom Asia; it includes the American company Nynex as the international carrier involved in the consortium.)

There were four Thai companies involved in TT&T: Loxley, a trading company dealing in telecommunications, computer-related equipment, and defence; Jasmin, also involved in telecommunications, satellites and computers; Italthai, a joint Italian–Thai construction company; and Patratanakit, a securities company. The other international carriers that competed with NTT to join TT&T were France Telecom, US West, and the main carriers from Australia and New Zealand. In the event, it was NTT and France Telecom that turned out to be the main competitors.

Why Did NTT Beat France Telecom?

France Telecom was a strong competitor. Perhaps most importantly, France Telecom had the backing of the French government and was accordingly able to provide capital on attractive terms. France Telecom had also teamed up with the French telecommunications equipment company Alcatel, which agreed to provide the equipment that TT&T would require. Furthermore, the French already had defence-related connections in Thailand, something the Japanese lacked.

NTT's major weakness was that it was unable to get MPT's assistance in order to provide capital on concessionary terms. NTT did approach MPT for help but was told that the Ministry could not give favoured treatment to one carrier. In terms of the provision and costs of capital, therefore, the company was at a disadvantage. Nevertheless, NTT had other strengths which ultimately won the battle. Most significantly, as has been shown in detail in this book, NTT had learned to operate on a multi-vendor basis, buying, and in some cases jointly developing, telecommunications equipment from a number of equipment suppliers, including non-Japanese ones. From TT&T's point of view this was a major advantage, since it overcame the problem of dependence on a single supplier, which might have proved costly in the longer term.

However, if TT&T were to operate a multi-vendor bidding system in order to procure its telecommunications equipment, it would need strong in-house engineering capabilities. This followed since the equipment of different suppliers would need to be adapted to TT&T's network. Furthermore, equipment would have to be maintained when the original supplier, losing out to stronger competitors, ceased to supply TT&T. Here too NTT was well placed. The company had a strong reputation in Thailand for the excellence of its engineering capabilities and training. Furthermore, for thirty years NTT had operated an office in Thailand which was involved in various forms of technical assistance in the country. As part of the deal, NTT agreed to two programmes dealing with training. Under the first, key engineers from TT&T will go to NTT in Japan for training, while the second programme will involve NTT's engineers providing training in Thailand.

It was for these reasons that NTT succeeded in winning the contract with TT&T.

What Role Will NTT Play in TT&T?

Although NTT contributed more than one-fifth of TT&T's capital, it has a 20 per cent shareholding in the company. This compares with 25 per cent each for Loxley and Jasmin, 20 per cent for Italthai, and 10 per cent for Patratanakit.

NTT has entered into two main contracts with TT&T. The first deals with its shareholding in TT&T; the second involves its contract to design, construct, operate, and maintain TT&T's network. This second contract will make an important contribution to NTT's overall rate of return on the TT&T project as a whole. TT&T will be run by a board of directors consisting of sixteen directors drawn from the five member companies which will meet monthly. In addition, five executive directors, meeting weekly, will be responsible to the board.

Why Did MPT Support NTT in the TT&T Case but Not Others?

As mentioned earlier, MPT supported NTT by allowing it to participate in TT&T, although it did not go so far as to provide concessionary funding for the project. However, in two previous cases, the one involving a privatization project for a Mexican national telephone company in 1990 and the other, the privatization of a mobile telephone service in Brazil, MPT had refused to give NTT permission to participate. Why the change in policy in the case of TT&T?

According to senior NTT officials whom I interviewed, MPT bureaucrats felt 'nervous' about NTT's international involvements, fearing that they might lead to an undermining of KDD's position as the leading Japanese international carrier. But why was there less 'nervousness' in the TT&T case? The reason is a growing awareness in Japan about the importance of internationalization in the case of telecommunications.

There are several strands to this discussion, which also involves politicians and bureaucrats from other ministries such as MITI. To begin with, there is the awareness that Japan needs a major carrier (or carriers) in the emerging global telecommunications markets. Secondly, there is a growing feeling that the international success of Japanese telecommunications equipment companies is partly contingent on the success of Japanese carriers in global markets. Against the background of these widening discussions, MPT officials are becoming increasingly aware that there is a crucial international dimension to their telecommunications policies which hitherto have had primarily a domestic focus.

MPT's approach in the case of TT&T, therefore, is best seen as a reflection of new thinking in the Ministry regarding the international dimension of Japanese telecommunications. We shall return later to this important point in a broader discussion of the options that are open to MPT to increase the Japanese presence in global telecommunications markets.

Providing Japanese Companies with International Circuits

Although, legally, NTT is a 'domestic' carrier, it is nevertheless permitted under the law to lease circuits from an international carrier and to use these circuits to provide international telecommunications facilities for its customers. In this way NTT is able to compete with the other international carriers such as AT&T, BT, and France Telecom, who are touting for this kind of business in Japan and other markets.

How important is this kind of business to NTT? I was unable to get accurate data on the significance of these services (for example, in terms of their contribution to NTT's revenue), partly because the revenue appears under a variety of different headings and is difficult to disentangle. However, the NTT officials I spoke to suggested that NTT is able to provide this kind of service to a fair number of its largest customers and that the revenue earned is not insignificant. Nevertheless, it is clear that NTT operates under tight constraints in its international activities. The nature of these constraints will now be examined more closely.

Constraints on NTT's Globalization

While NTT can provide its customers with international facilities by leasing circuits from international carriers, it is not permitted to resell any excess capacity that remains after the customer's needs are fulfilled. This is a significant restriction, since it increases NTT's costs relative to those of the international carriers from which it leases circuits, accordingly decreasing NTT's competitiveness and/or profitability on these services. Furthermore, NTT's flexibility is reduced as a result of the constraints on its ability to allocate and reallocate capacity; for example, the restrictions make it more difficult and costly to provide a customer with back-up capacity in the event of line faults.

But perhaps even more important than these legal and technical limitations are the tacit regulatory constraints imposed by MPT on NTT's international activities. As already mentioned, there is a strong awareness in NTT that MPT is reluctant to give it much leeway to operate internationally. This reluctance, however, is often more implicit than explicit, with the result that NTT feels it confronts a significant amount of uncertainty in deciding precisely where MPT draws the boundary between acceptable and unacceptable international activities. A further source of uncertainty is that, wherever the boundary is currently, it appears to be in a state of flux, as MPT's change of mind in supporting NTT's involvement in TT&T shows. As a result of these uncertainties, NTT has tended to move with extreme caution in the international field.

Why Do these Constraints Exist?

The formal reason is the division of domestic and international telecommunications responsibilities between NTT and KDD, as already described. But it is necessary to ask why this division continues to be enforced, particularly since Japan is now the only country in the world where the main domestic carrier is not allowed to operate internationally in a relatively unimpeded way. (Until recently the situation in Canada, Australia, and New Zealand was similar, but the national carriers in these countries are now allowed to operate internationally.)

The answer to this question lies in the regulatory stance taken by MPT. Even before 1985, the Ministry saw KDD as one way through which to limit NTT's revenue and influence. The lucrative nature of international telephone calls, supported by CCITT regulations and practices, has now received widespread international attention as organizations such as the Financial Times have publicized the substantial excess of revenues over costs of these services. Companies like BT have benefited enormously from these international pricing practices, while NTT has been deprived of this source of revenue.

Indeed, so entrenched has KDD been in MPT's regulatory division of domestic and international activities that many in Japan commonly state that KDD is regarded by MPT as its 'child'. Accordingly, while post-1985 KDD also confronted significant competition from its own NCCs—IDC (partly owned by Cable and Wireless) and ITJ (which has established fairly close operating links with KDD)—it is often believed in Japan that KDD retains its 'favoured son' status *vis-à-vis* NTT in the regulatory eyes of MPT.

MPT's regulatory stance and the strong position enjoyed by KDD is well illustrated by the Synchordia saga.

Synchordia

As we saw earlier, as part of its globalization strategy, BT attempted to set up Synchordia as a global alliance of telecommunications carriers. The main aim of Synchordia is to outsource telecommunications services for large multi-national corporations. BT invited NTT to join Synchordia, and according to newspaper reports was willing to offer NTT a share of around 20 per cent in the project.

The Synchordia proposal provoked a good deal of discussion in Japan among the interested parties. The major problem was that the offer to NTT challenged MPT's relatively clear-cut division between the domestic activities of NTT and the international operations of KDD. One option that was considered involved a joint participation in Synchordia by both NTT and KDD. This, however, was rejected by KDD on the grounds that NTT would dominate the Japanese contribution. In the end, MPT proposed a compromise: NTT would be allowed no more than a 3 per cent stake in Synchordia. This NTT found unacceptable on the grounds that the stake was too small to justify the effort required. Confronted with MPT's refusal to compromise any further, NTT eventually rejected the offer.

Forces for Further Globalization

The Synchordia saga did not put the lid on debate about the further globalization of NTT. Indeed, a major contention of this book is that we are currently witnessing the early stages of the coalescence of new forces in Japan pressing for NTT to be allowed greater leeway in its international activities.

Why Globalize Further?

Increasingly in Japan, policy-makers in the bureaucracy, the political parties and companies are beginning to ask, 'In this new era of globalized telecommunications services and carriers, which Japanese players will be able to establish themselves as serious international competitors?' In short, which Japanese companies will be able to compete with companies such as AT&T, BT, and France Telecom? A number of key issues emerge in considering these questions.

To begin with, the question of size of company arises in view of the resources that are required to compete in global markets, although size alone is neither a necessary nor a sufficient condition for success in these markets and market niches. It is worth bearing in mind, however, that, with revenue in 1991 of ¥6,252 billion, NTT is twenty-five times as large as KDD, which in 1992 had a revenue of ¥253 billion. Secondly, it is clear that NTT's competences as carrier, researcher, and developer of information services have not been fully exploited internationally. Accordingly, there is room for the further exploitation of these competences although, as will be discussed further below, NTT would need to develop additional competences in order to become an effective global player.

Thirdly, the domestic and international NCCs are also, like KDD, seriously constrained by their size in becoming major global players. In this connection it will be recalled that DDI, the largest domestic NCC, is approximately the same size in terms of revenue as KDD. Fourthly, the opportunities open to the major Japanese telecommunications equipment companies—companies such as NEC, Fujitsu, Hitachi, Oki, Toshiba, Mitsubishi Electric, Matsushita, and Sony—may to some extent be linked to the global activities of Japanese carriers. As has been demonstrated elsewhere in this book, these companies have not been very successful so far in industrialized country markets for complex telecommunications equipment, although to some degree this has been the result of continuing protectionism.

Indeed, there are several signs that these kinds of issue are beginning to be seriously addressed in Japan. For example, of all the questions that I asked of senior MPT officials, it was clear that the greatest degree of uncertainty and ambivalence related to the issue of the globalization of the activities of Japanese telecommunications companies.

Furthermore, a study group in MPT has been considering whether the NCCs should be restricted to either domestic or international activities. In addition, discussions have begun between MPT policy-makers and their counterparts in MITI over the future process of globalization of Japanese telecommunications. Not only does MITI have policy control over the Japanese telecommunications equipment companies, with its international responsibilities it has long had more of an international perspective on Japanese affairs than MPT.

The Policy Options

The following are the main options:

1. Maintain the status quo.
2. Allow the current domestic NCCs (DDI, TWJ, JT) to operate internationally, either alone, in alliance, or through merger.
3(a). Allow NTT to operate internationally alone.
3(b). Allow NTT to operate internationally either alone or in alliance, or through merger.
4. Some combination of 2 and 3.

The advantages and disadvantages to each of these options:

Option 1 Advantage
The main advantage is continuity and an avoidance of the costs of reorganizing Japanese telecommunications.

Option 1 Disadvantage
The issue of the Japanese role in globalized telecommunications markets will not be adequately addressed.

Option 2 Advantage
This will create greater flexibility for the domestic NCCs, giving them the opportunity to operate internationally.

Option 2 Disadvantages

It is not clear whether this option will provide sufficient 'muscle' for Japanese companies to become major global players. Here the following points are relevant.

First, the domestic NCCs have been in existence for only a short time and have not yet completed the process of building up their domestic network and services. Secondly, new competences are required in the global market-place, competences that even AT&T and BT have not yet acquired, and it will still take a significant amount of time before the domestic NCCs are able to acquire them. Particularly important is the organizational ability to 'think globally', that is to understand the various markets and environments that exist in the major part of the world, and to be able to deliver services competitively in these markets. The difficulties of achieving these competences, even for carriers such as AT&T and BT which have traditionally had a domestic focus, should not be underestimated. Furthermore, there are also the difficulties of limited organizational attention span which may prevent the Japanese domestic NCCs from focusing effectively on international markets when they have not yet fully established themselves domestically.

Thirdly, alliances or mergers do not necessarily provide a solution to the problem of the size of company that is necessary in order to become a major global player. This is because of the difficulty of efficiently co-ordinating the allied/merged components of the organization; in short, the new whole may fall short of the sum of the old parts. Finally, and perhaps most importantly, the domestic NCCs lack technological capabilities—especially in R&D, systems engineering, and software—with the result that they are highly dependent on their suppliers. It is therefore unclear how they will achieve the *distinctive* competence necessary to underpin global competitiveness.

Option 3(a) Advantages

NTT has the 'muscle' to become a major global player in terms of size and telecommunications service capabilities, including systems engineering, software, and R&D. However, fundamental changes in attitude, approach, and 'culture' will be necessary if NTT is to become a fast, responsive, and innovative global operator. The difficulties for NTT, as a company that has traditionally led a sheltered existence in protected markets, to make these changes should not be underestimated.

Furthermore, NTT has forged a highly effective set of relationships with suppliers, some of which are non-Japanese companies, and has established a symbiotic *modus operandi* with them. This, together with its strong in-house capabilities in systems engineering, software, and R&D, should allow NTT to compete effectively with companies such as AT&T and BT. Although AT&T has in-house manufacturing capabilities which NTT lacks, NTT should be able to compensate adequately for this through the effectiveness of its relationship with its suppliers, which compete to some extent among themselves for NTT's business. In the early stages, however, both AT&T and BT will have a head-start in terms of having begun to think and organize globally.

By removing the constraints on its ability to operate globally, MPT will allow NTT to advance further down the 'global-telecommunications-service-providing learning curve', consolidating the early learning that has been achieved through activities such as those undertaken by NTTI, NTT Data, and now TT&T. This option is also likely to provide a boost for the Japanese tele-communictions equipment suppliers which have forged close, co-operative ties with NTT.

Option 3(a) Disadvantages
To the extent that NTT is 'liberated' to operate globally and begins to do so effectively, the danger, clearly uppermost in the minds of many MPT bureaucrats, is that NTT's global *and domestic* market power and influence will increase and will be used anti-competitively, to the detriment of both the NCCs (domestic and international) that MPT has so carefully nurtured, and Japanese telecommunications consumers more generally.

In addition, there seems to be the related worry, on the part of some in MPT, that, to the extent that NTT operates globally and profitably, the profits could be used to cross-subsidize its domestic long-distance activities to the competitive disadvantage of the domestic NCCs. However, the segmentation of long-distance and local accounts, which we saw earlier was imposed on NTT by MPT from April 1992, could be further used to segment the revenues from international operations, thus preventing cross-subsidization. Accordingly, the existence of this administratively feasible solution undermines the argument that the possibility of international–domestic cross-subsidization, with its anti-competitive implications, should stand in the way of removing the restrictions on NTT's global operations.

How real is the anti-competitive threat stemming from NTT's increased market power and influence as a result of its greater global activities? The most convincing answer would seem to be that in the short run, particularly where customers have limited alternatives to using NTT's services, there is a threat resulting from any increase in NTT's market power and influence. But in the longer run, it seems inevitable that the alternatives available to customers will become far more substantial. For instance, as was shown earlier in this chapter, competition to NTT from mobile communications is rapidly gaining in significance. Furthermore, satellite-based competition is also likely to grow in importance, an example being Motorola's Iridium consortium which, as noted above, may in the future be introduced into Japan with the assistance of one of the domestic NCCs. Other similar alternatives for customers are very likely to be introduced in Japan in the future. It seems reasonable, therefore, to conclude that in the longer run the anti-competitive threat resulting from NTT's increased market power and influence following its greater ability to operate internationally is likely to be negligible.

Option 3(b) Advantages

This option opens up a whole new range of possibilities that would allow NTT's muscle to be used not for its sole benefit, but, in conjunction with other partners, to the possible benefit of consumers, *provided that adequately competitive conditions prevail.*

For example, NTT's Long-Distance Division may be able to establish alliances of one form or another with KDD (where there is competence complementarity, even though KDD naturally fears being submerged in the relationship), or with IDC or ITJ. Since at present the global activities of all of these companies are fairly small, at least relative to companies like AT&T and BT, such alliances might facilitate economies of scale. Similarly, since global competences and experience are limited in Japan, the pooling of what is available might provide considerable benefit. For these reasons, this option may have the best chance of achieving the objective of getting one or more major Japanese players into the globalizing telecommunications markets.

Option 3(b) Disadvantages

However, it must be recognized that achieving the benefits of alliance or merger is never easy. Furthermore, alliance or merger also may pose a threat to competition, which has been discussed in connection with the other options. It is worth remembering, though, that this threat is reduced to the extent that competitive alternatives exist or could be brought into existence.

Likely Policy Decisions

It is highly unlikely that MPT will be able to, or will want to, maintain the status quo with its separation of international and domestic operations. The forces described in this subsection are likely to be too strong to resist.

Less obvious, however, is whether MPT will allow NTT to operate globally in a more unconstrained way, either alone or in alliance. MPT's regulatory stance has tended towards limiting the power of NTT, and giving the company greater leeway would amount to a significant shift in direction for the Ministry. However, if NTT is not allowed to operate more effectively globally, the Ministry will have to confront the possibility of failing to achieve a significant presence by a major Japanese competitor in the globalizing telecommunications markets.

In view of this, there seems to be a 'fair possibility' that MPT will eventually allow NTT greater flexibility to operate globally. However, in deciding whether to exercise this option, MPT may not be unconstrained time-wise. This is because, although the process of globalization is still in its early days, many of the 'windows of opportunity' that are now open, allowing for early entry on the part of the players, may soon begin to close as major players enter and consolidate their positions in the new markets. For this reason, MPT would be wise not to delay for too long the fundmental decisions that it will inevitably have to make regarding globalization.

Conclusions

This chapter has been concerned with the future of both NTT (the company) and the NTT Way. It has been shown that both are at a watershed in their history, facing the biggest changes they have ever confronted. In analysing the future of NTT and the NTT Way, particular attention has been paid to three 'winds of change', namely competition, globalization, and divestiture. The effects of these winds of change will now be summarized.

The most important structural change that NTT has undergone has stemmed from the introduction of facilities-based competition to the company from 1985. To date, competition has had only a limited impact on NTT, decreasing the company's profitability somewhat while decreasing only slightly its overall market share. However, in some market segments, such as the Tokyo–Nagoya–Osaka corridor, and in some services, such as mobile telephone communications, the NCCs have significantly eroded NTT's market share. Nevertheless, this has not deprived NTT of its Aaa credit rating, or affected its overall very satisfactory corporate performance compared with other Japanese companies.

In the longer run, however, it must be concluded that competition will increase substantially, partly from the existing NCCs and partly from new forms of competition that do not yet exist, such as international consortia of various kinds. This increased competition will create significant pressures which will change NTT's behaviour and even its form of organization. As a result, the NTT Way will also be transformed in important respects.

In general terms, increased competitive pressure will force NTT to become far more commercially oriented than it has hitherto been. Far more attention will therefore have to be paid to the competitiveness of the company's services and to the cost efficiency of its operations. New forms of organization will have to be developed to streamline decision-making, and to increase the focus, flexibility, and speed of response to market opportunities and threats.

While NTT has begun to feel the competitive winds of change, the culture and orientation of the company still largely reflect the pre-competitive era. Although I have been at pains to stress that during the pre-competitive era NTT was none the less an innovation-driven company and made many important innovations, the forces that created the need for innovation and the competences that were necessary to bring about this innovation were fundamentally different from the forces and competences that are now essential to deal with more competitive telecommunications markets.

More specifically, in the pre-competitive era innovation took the form of catching up, keeping up, and in a few cases overtaking the telecommunications carriers of other Western countries through NTT's own R&D and co-operative development with a group of competing supplying companies. Through this process, significant improvements were made to the Japanese telecommunications network and services. In the competitive era, however, new competences and forms of organization are required if NTT is to deliver competitive services to its customers in the face of competition from other carriers. Under these competitive conditions, factors such as focus, flexibility, and speed of response assume a significance that they did not have in the pre-competitive era. NTT still needs to make the transition from the old competences, which enabled it to innovate in the pre-competitive period, to a new set of competences that will enable it to compete successfully in the new era. The difficulties of acquiring these new competences, and the new forms of organization that they will require, should not be underestimated.

With regard to the NTT Way, it was stressed that the competitive era has brought about an important change which will have significant implications for the company's belief in the importance of innovation-through-R&D. While this belief has been a central part of the NTT Way and the company's vision, we have seen that increased competition will mean that it will increasingly be squeezed by the commercial realities of the market. Regardless of whether NTT is successful in achieving the kind of rate rebalancing that it wants in order to restore profitability, greater competition will force the company constantly to ensure that its R&D expenditures are adding value for the company in terms of increased revenue generated. Increasingly, therefore, NTT's managers will have to look upon R&D expenditures not as a *de facto* fixed cost to be covered by the tariffs and rate of profit authorized by the Diet as in the pre-competitive era, but as an investment which, like any other investment, must be justified by the return that it generates. This is an important change for NTT as a whole, and one that will require a reorientation in the company's approach to R&D.

Further fundamental changes in competences, organization, and approach will be required if NTT is to increase its degree of globalization. The section of this chapter that dealt with this topic showed that, although NTT has been limited to a role as a domestic rather than international carrier, this has not prevented it from beginning to globalize in several important respects. However, it was also shown that there are circumstances that may well provide NTT with the opportunity for significantly increased globalization in the future.

Most important of these circumstances is the new awareness that is beginning to emerge in Japan that telecommunications markets are beginning to globalize and that it is important for Japan to have one or more major contenders in these markets. Seen in this light, NTT remains a potent option for ensuring that Japan has a significant presence in these new globalizing markets. Weighed against this consideration, however, is the strong antipathy that MPT has traditionally shown to NTT's extending its 'international wings'. This antipathy emerged very clearly when the Ministry frustrated NTT's attempts to joint BT's Synchordia project.

Despite the strength of feeling in MPT that NTT should not be allowed to encroach on territory that is perceived as being the proper domain of KDD and the international NCCs, it has been argued in this chapter that a new coalition of interests is beginning to emerge in Japan concerned at the prospect that current regulatory policies may prevent the country from having a serious contender in the globalizing telecommunications markets. The options that are available to MPT to meet this concern were outlined and the advantages and disadvantages of each option analysed. Two of these options included a larger global role for NTT.

However, while the chance for further globalization represents an important opportunity for NTT, it must at the same time be stressed that the difficulties involved should not be underestimated. More specifically, NTT will need to develop new competences, forms of organization, and attitudes if the company is to be a successful global carrier. In many cases the company will have to abandon aspects of its previous culture which inhibit successful globalization. As the experience of carriers such as AT&T and BT, companies that have embarked far earlier than NTT on the global road, shows, the transformation that is required can be painful.

The possibility of the divestiture of NTT being passed in 1995/6 has also been examined. As background to this possibility, the history of the divestiture debate in Japan from the early 1980s to the present time was related. It is not clear whether MPT will push for divestiture. However, in the past MPT has seen divestiture as one important way to decrease NTT's power and influence, not only in the area of telecommunications but in Japan's politics and economics more generally. It therefore remains possible that divestiture will once again become an issue when the future of NTT and Japanese telecommunications is decided.

For the reasons mentioned, competition, globalization, and divestiture constitute significant winds of change that will transform both NTT and the NTT Way. Accordingly, NTT is now facing a watershed in its history. Although the company faces important threats, there are also new opportunities. Nevertheless, the challenges that will have to be confronted in the future remain substantial.

8

DDI: NTT's Main Competitor

CHAPTER OVERVIEW

The chapter begins with an examination of the origins and growth of DDI, then moves on to describe its growth and current performance. To what extent is DDI's impressive growth the result of the company's internal structure and strategy, and to what extent is it due to favourable external circumstances, such as a supportive regulatory environment created by the Ministry of Posts and Telecommunications (MPT)? What role was played by DDI's least-cost routing systems, which automatically selected the cheapest carrier for customers? How has DDI used the market for inputs into new services as a substitute for in-house R&D, and how effective has the company been in this respect?

The chapter continues with an analysis of DDI's vision for the future based on its beliefs regarding the sources of future growth and profitability. Here two issues are closely examined. The first is the personal handy phone system (PHS), a cheaper alternative to cellular mobile communications. The second is DDI's vision regarding the role that R&D will play in the company in the future.

Will DDI, with its far smaller size and quantity of resources, be able to compete with NTT into the twenty-first century? This is discussed in the final section by distilling the two companies' visions into the beliefs that support them.

Introduction

Since the introduction of competition into Japanese telecommunications services in 1985, Daini Denden (DDI) has emerged as NTT's major competitor. There are two reasons for including an analysis of DDI in this book. The first is to provide a better understanding of the competitive process in the Japanese telecommunications services market by analysing the structure and strategy of this major competitor to NTT. The second reason, closely related to the first, is to examine the contradictory beliefs that underlie the visions, and therefore the strategies, of DDI and NTT. This examination throws further light on an important theme that has threaded its way throughout the book, namely the ways in which corporate beliefs shape corporate vision, competences, and forms of organization.

At a more concrete level, this chapter is concerned with a puzzle: how can DDI, with a tiny force of engineers engaged in R&D and the provision of new services, hope to compete into the next century with NTT and its enormous army of scientists, engineers, and technicians?

Background

DDI (Daini Denden) is NTT's main competitor.[1] If NTT is Goliath, DDI is hoping to be David, a far smaller but highly potent challenger. Although still much smaller, DDI has grown impressively since it was founded in 1984; by 1993 it had revenues of about $2.4 billion compared with NTT's $56.1 billion. In that year DDI's revenues exceeded those of KDD (Japan's major international carrier) for the first time, making it the second largest carrier in Japan. DDI, moreover, was significantly more profitable than either NTT or KDD.

The competitive battle between NTT and DDI (as well as between NTT and the other two new common carriers, Japan Telecom, with revenues slightly less than DDI, and the far less successful Teleway Japan) raises an important question. How can DDI possibly compete into the twenty-first century with significantly smaller resources than NTT? For example, DDI has approximately 30 engineers involved in R&D and the development of new services; this compares with NTT's 8,500 employees in R&D alone. When to this is added the huge resources that NTT has in marketing, the puzzle deepens. How will David find the equivalent of the simple sling that will enable him to deal with Goliath?

In tackling this puzzle, three main questions are addressed in this chapter. How is DDI's performance up to 1993 to be explained? How might DDI build a competitive edge to allow it to compete successfully with NTT into the twenty-first century? Finally, what are the implications for NTT?

The Origins and Growth of DDI

Origins

DDI was first established in June 1984. It originally consisted of seven people. Dr Sachio Semmoto, senior vice president of DDI, recalled in an interview that, when NTT's leaders heard of this new group of would-be competitors, 'they laughed'. Whether or not the founding of DDI was a laughing matter, the new company had powerful backing. Its main shareholder was the Kyocera Corporation, a highly successful Japanese company with the largest market share in the world for ceramic packaging for integrated circuits, which held 25 per cent of DDI's shares. Dr Kazuo Inamori, chairman of Kyocera, became chairman

---

[1] The main source for this chapter is several interviews conducted by the author during 1993 with Dr Sachio Semmoto, senior vice president of DDI, and several of his colleagues.

of DDI, contributing his considerable managerial and organizational skills. Sony held 5 per cent of the shares, while Ushio, Secom, and Mitsubish Corporation held 2.5 per cent each. The Japan Development Bank provided the bulk of the original funding together with the Industrial Bank of Japan, the Long-Term Credit Bank of Japan, and the Sanwa Bank.[2]

DDI began by employing a small group of NTT's middle-level managers, which gave it the necessary competences in telecommunications with which to begin operations. Although in this way there were some similarities with Western start-ups spinning off from larger corporations, the fledgling DDI was decidedly the product of Japan's new regulatory structure in telecommunications and the country's business establishment. Included in the group of former NTT employees was Semmoto, whom Dr Inamori met in Kyoto in 1982 when the former was giving a lecture on NTT's future network vision, and Mr Sanshiro Fukada, who became DDI's general manager in charge of R&D. From the beginning, however, DDI has insisted on steering a course that is almost entirely independent of NTT.

Growth

DDI provides four main services: long-distance telephone, leased lines, cellular telephone, and customer premises system terminal equipment.

The growth of DDI has been spectacular, as Fig. 8.1 reveals. From revenues of $84 million in 1987, the company's revenues in 1993 reached nearly $2.4 billion. Profits grew to $238 million in 1993 from a loss of $61 million in 1987. Furthermore, DDI performed significantly better than Japan Telecom and better still than Telway Japan, which has been plagued by losses to the extent that its future is threatened.

By 1993, DDI and the other two new common carriers held more than 50 per cent of the long-distance market in the Tokyo–Osaka corridor. DDI's share of the total Japanese long-distance market now exceeds 10 per cent, while it holds more than 20 per cent of the cellular market.

Growth and Performance

On the basis of its growth and performance, DDI has been hailed outside Japan as a success story. Underlining this new-found reputation, the company now features in a Harvard Business School case-study,[3] and DDI executives are on the international business school circuit giving lectures on the success of their company. However, it is one thing to document the growth and performance of DDI but quite another to provide a rigorous *explanation* of why DDI has done

---

[2] A good source for background information on DDI is the Harvard Business School case-study, 'DDI Corporation', 9–393–048, February 1993. [3] Ibid.

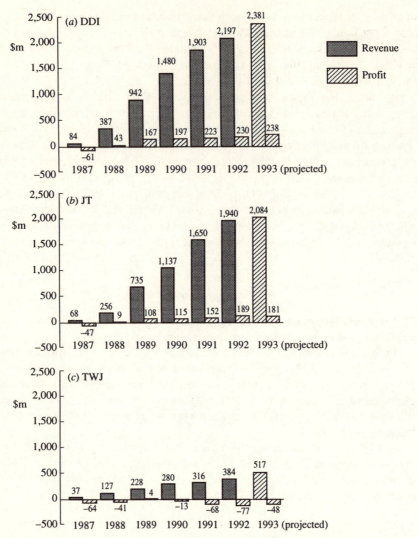

Fig. 8.1 Revenue and profit, DDI and competitors, 1987–1993 ($1 = ¥105)
Source: DDI Corporation.

as well as it has. To what extent is its success due to fortuitous external circumstances, and to what extent to its own innovative efforts? Furthermore, to
anticipate a question that will be asked later in this chapter, will DDI be able to
continue its success into the twenty-first century?

The Long-Distance Price Differential between DDI and NTT

In general, DDI's rapid growth in revenue has resulted from the significant price differential between its long-distance tariff and NTT's. (All the details regarding the movement of this differential over time are provided in Chapter 7.)

But how was this price differential achieved, and how has DDI been able to turn the differential to its competitive advantage? There are five elements in the answer to this question, two of which relate to favourable circumstances external to DDI and three of which are the result of DDI's own innovative efforts.

NTT's Long-Distance Tariff

The first element relates to the determinants of NTT's long-distance tariff (which were explained in detail in the last chapter). NTT kept this tariff relatively high, partly in order to cover the losses that it was making on the universal local telephone services that it provided (and was obliged by law to provide). NTT's cost structure was also influenced by the number of its employees and by its commitment to lifetime employment agreed with its labour union, the strongest in Japan. Although new technologies, such as automated exchanges and automated operator services, meant that total employment could be, and was, reduced, the constraints meant that NTT could do so only gradually. Conversely, as a new 'slim' entrant, with modern technology and a smaller work-force per unit of revenue, DDI inherited a competitive cost structure.

The Regulation of NTT

The second element deals with the regulation of NTT by the Ministry of Posts and Telecommunications (MPT). Through its regulation of telecommunications tariffs, MPT until 1993 prevented NTT from equalling the tariffs of the new common carriers (although it has sometimes denied this). Although the long-distance tariff came down in successive stages, MPT ensured that a significant price differential was maintained. From the Ministry's point of view, this discrimination in favour of the New Common Carriers (NCCs) was necessary in order to ensure an eventual 'level playing field' where NTT would be allowed to compete freely with sufficiently strong competitors.

These two elements, taken together, meant that NTT was relatively 'easy prey' for the NCCs.[4]

However, DDI's performance was due not only to fortunate external circumstances, as is suggested by the relative failure of Teleway Japan, which had the benefit of the same circumstances. Three further elements enabled DDI to turn the favourable price differential into rapidly growing revenue and profits.

---

[4] The main weakness of the Harvard Business School case-study referred to in fn. 2 is that it fails to examine the circumstances influencing the competitiveness of both DDI and NTT, including the government regulatory environment. By analysing DDI alone, the case-study erroneously attributes DDI's performance solely to its strategy and organization.

DDI's Least-Cost Routeing Systems

The third element relates to innovative new technology developed by DDI's own engineers. More specifically, DDI was able to turn the price differential with NTT to maximum advantage by developing a system, which at first it supplied freely to its business customers, which automatically selected the lowest-cost routeing. This system, installed in the customer's local telephone switch (PBX) or in a box attached to the customer's telephone, continually updated the tariffs charged on different routes by NTT and the new common carriers and selected the cheapest route. In the event of the same tariff being charged by DDI and NTT, the system selected DDI.

In this way, DDI was able to 'cream-skim' the long-distance market, the business market in particular. By 1992 it had 7 million subscribers, 85 per cent of which were business customers. The company wanted to strengthen its position in the residential market and also to take account of the trend towards the use of cordless telephones—by 1992 about 60 per cent of telephones sold in Japan were cordless.

In order to deal with these issues, Semmoto and Fukada decided to attempt to reduce the least-cost routeing system to a single chip set (containing a central processing unit, static random access memory, and other integrated circuits). This chip set, called the Alpha LCR2, could be installed directly into the cordless phone.

There were two dimensions to DDI's innovation. The first involved the development of the Alpha chip set. The second related to the way in which the chip set was diffused.

To begin with, the purpose and concept of the Alpha chip set were defined by Semmoto and Fukada on the basis of the earlier least-cost routeing system that DDI had developed. According to Semmoto, 'less than 10 engineers' from DDI were involved in the development of the Alpha chip set. They dealt mainly with the definition of the functionality of the chip set and with some of the key software required. The implementation of the chip set, involving the further development and manufacture of the dedicated microprocessor and associated software, was subcontracted to an unnamed electronics company. The chip set was then supplied by this company to Kyocera on an OEM basis. Kyocera in turn gave the chip set to the consumer electronics companies referred to below.

The example of the Alpha chip set is particularly important because it demonstrates how DDI was able to introduce an innovation which contributed significantly to its revenue and profits on the basis of a small in-house R&D team. This team was involved primarily in the conceptualization of the innovation wanted and in ensuring its compatibility with DDI's network and services. Most of the remaining R&D function, including most of the software development, was subcontracted. In this way DDI was able to get by with relatively few R&D engineers. (Whereas DDI allocates only about 1 per cent of its revenue to R&D, including the development of new services, NTT allocates approximately 4.5 per cent. We shall return later to the way in which R&D is organized in DDI.)

How did DDI ensure that the Alpha chip set was installed in a large proportion of the cordless phones sold in Japan? This required innovative distribution methods which were at least as important as the R&D of the chip set.

There were two dimensions to DDI's distribution strategy. The first involved persuading the major consumer electronics companies that dominated the Japanese market for analog cordless phones to include the Alpha chip set in their phones. This was done by giving them the chip set without charge, but the deal was part of a longer-term strategic alliance which DDI is establishing with leading consumer electronics companies (of which more will be said later). The companies included Sharp (which held about a third of the market for analog cordless phones), Sanyo (which had a further 20 per cent share), Panasonic, Kenwood, Mitsubishi, Pioneer, Victor, Sony (a major shareholder in DDI with about 5 per cent of this market), Kyocera, and Toshiba.

The second dimension involved giving a 'kickback' to retailers selling cordless phones with the Alpha chip set. This kickback amounted to 5 per cent of the income that DDI received from the phones it sold, a sum that could more than double the profit made by the retailer. By 1993, a large proportion of Japan's 66,000 electronics stores were participating in DDI's scheme.

Using the Market for Telecommunications Inputs

The fourth element in the explanation of DDI's performance relates to the company's use of the market for telecommunications inputs.

As is evident from the example of the Alpha chip set, DDI has been able to make effective use of the competences of its suppliers in developing its own services. In other words, DDI has been able to use *the market* for telecommunications inputs to competitive effect.

What are the main characteristics of DDI's relationship to its suppliers? In general, the company's decision-makers believe that, in the words of one of them, 'it is extremely important to develop a long-term relationship with suppliers which share the same goal and vision that we have'. However, in forging its relationship with its suppliers, DDI has attempted where possible to wield sufficient market power to be able to ensure that its needs are effectively satisfied.

The pursuit of this strategy has meant that DDI has tended to avoid using NTT's main suppliers on the grounds that they are beholden to NTT and, with NTT's significant purchasing power, are unlikely to side with DDI in the event of any conflict of interest with NTT. Accordingly, 'We did not want to deal with NTT's family [of suppliers]. NTT is their biggest customer. We could not influence them.' DDI therefore turned to DSC, a relatively small US producer, for its long-distance telecommunications switches, in preference to NEC, Fujitsu, and Hitachi, the main Japanese suppliers who supply NTT with most of its switches. DDI is DSC's second or third largest customer and this means that

'They listen to us very carefully!' DSC is also working with DDI on the personal handy phone, discussed in more detail later.

In the area of cellular communications, Motorola has been DDI's main supplier. In the field of cordless phones and, in the future, multimedia terminals, DDI is forging a number of strategic alliances with consumer electronics companies, believing that it is these companies, rather than the traditional telecommunications companies such as NEC, Fujitsu, and Hitachi, that possess the critical competences in production and distribution that will facilitate the creation of a mass consumer market for the future-generation phones that will provide future services such as multimedia.

How do DDI's beliefs regarding the supplier relationship compare with NTT's? On the one hand, there is a significant similarity in both their beliefs. Both believe that it is important to forge a long-term and stable relationship with suppliers that share their vision and objectives. Both believe that it is also important where possible to wield significant purchasing power over their suppliers, particularly where strategic inputs are concerned that affect their competitiveness. However, on the other hand, there is a crucial dissimilarity. NTT relies to a far greater extent than does DDI on in-house competences in areas such as design, development, and software. DDI is more willing to contract out these functions. It is this that explains the higher proportion of revenue allocated to R&D by NTT. We shall return later to consider the strengths and weaknesses of these contradictory strategic positions.

Creating an Efficient Organizational Structure

In explaining DDI's performance, the fifth and final element is the creation of an efficient organizational structure. As noted in the Harvard case-study, DDI is 'a flat, functionally constructed organization. Cost accounting and control [is] managed at a level of organization in which there [are] five to 100 employees. Transfers between these cells [are] at negotiated prices. The goal [is] to have each cell be cost conscious and therefore be a low cost provider.'[5] As already pointed out, DDI has been able to draw on the accumulated organizational knowledge of Kyocera in shaping the structure of its organization.

DDI's Vision for the Future

Profitability

As shown above, the main source of DDI's growth in revenue and profit until 1993 has been the differential between its and NTT's long-distance tariffs. At the end of 1993, this growth dynamic began to run out of steam. NTT announced

---

[5] Harvard case-study (see fn. 2), p. 4.

that on 19 October 1993 it would lower its tariff to be equal to or even lower than that of DDI and the other NCCs. This was greeted with the prompt response that DDI would reduce its tariff even further, in order to maintain a differential. This response came despite the recognition that such a move would eat substantially into DDI's profitability. DDI's executives were furious that NTT had taken this decision, arguing that NTT must have known that the NCCs would have to follow suit, and that NTT's move would only reduce its own profitability since MPT would not allow NTT to 'rebalance' its rates (i.e. increase its local rates). The DDI executives argued that the instability of the seven-party coalition that ruled Japan at the end of 1993 made any decision to raise local telephone rates too politically sensitive; therefore NTT had scored an 'own-goal', leaving all the carriers, itself included, worse off (although, of course, the users of long-distance telephone calls gained).

Why did DDI reduce its tariff to below that of NTT, despite the effect on profitability? Ironically, DDI's innovative technology, i.e. its least-cost routeing systems, *forced* it to take this decision. For DDI's tariff to remain above that of NTT is untenable, since the least-cost routeing systems, installed at DDI's expense, would automatically select NTT! For the tariff to equal that of NTT was also untenable (though less so), since DDI's customers have to use an additional four digits in making their calls and this is a sufficient disincentive to prevent a significant number of callers from using DDI.

Future Growth: the Personal Handy Phone System

A crucial question is raised by the demise of DDI's main source of growth up to 1993, i.e. the tariff differential: where will the source of DDI's future growth come from? Dr Semmoto speaks passionately in answer to this question. In short, he says, DDI's future growth will come from its development of the personal handy phone system (PHS).

Rationale for the PHS Vision

The PHS will offer customers a mobile telephone service that is far cheaper, in terms of both call costs and handsets, than the cellular alternative.

There are four aspects to DDI's rationale for the 'PHS vision'. The first is that the PHS answers the customer's emerging need for cheap communications 'anytime, anywhere, with anybody'. (The identification of this need is not particular to DDI and has become commonplace in the publicity material of all the major carriers such as AT&T, BT, etc.) The second aspect is that PHS provides DDI with a vehicle for attacking NTT in what it regards as NTT's 'Achilles' Heel', namely its residential customers. In 1992 NTT had 55 million subscribers, 32 per cent of which were business customers and 68 per cent residential. This compared with DDI's 7 million subscribers, consisting of 85 per cent business and 15 per cent residential. According to DDI, NTT, with its monopoly over local telephone services, has neglected its residential customers, thus leaving an opening for DDI.

The third aspect of DDI's rationale, closely related to the second, is that PHS provides the company with the opportunity to 'get close to its customers' and in this way win their loyalty. Indeed, DDI's main criticism of MCI in the USA (AT&T's main competitor), a company from which DDI learned a good deal when it first entered the long-distance market, is that MCI had failed to see the opportunity offered by mobile communications in general and by PHS (similar to the US PCS, personal communications services) in particular.

The fourth aspect is that PHS extends DDI's strong competences in the area of radio communications. From the beginning, DDI based its network on digital microwave communications.[6] From these beginnings, however, DDI has come to embrace the 'wireless ideology', believing it to offer important competitive advantages. PHS is in line with these beliefs (as is DDI's participation in Motorola's Iridium project, which will provide mobile services from 66 satellites).

The PHS Concept

The PHS is a mobile telephone that can be used within a 1,000 foot radius of a base station. Unlike cellular phones, where a call can be switched from one cell to an adjacent one and therefore the caller can move long distances without interrupting the call, in the case of PHS the call can be made only within this radius. DDI believes that this limitation on PHS is sufficiently compensated for by the significantly lower cost of this service compared with cellular. While users moving long distances during a call—such as those travelling in cars or trains—will be excluded from the PHS market, in DDI's view this still leaves the bulk of users who value mobility but whose calls take place within a single location, such as an office block or residential house. Besides, when moving outside the radius, it is possible to redial the call.

There will be a substantial difference in the cost of using PHS compared with cellular. In Japan cellular phones (which until April 1994 had to be rented) cost about $100 per month, while access charges were around $1.60 for three minutes. This compares with a monthly cost of $16.26 and $0.24 for three minutes for PHS. Part of the reason is the lower cost for the handset, which is simpler and therefore smaller than a cellular set. Another part is the lower cost of the base station (which does not have to switch calls to adjacent cells); while cellular base stations cost in the region of $3.0 million, it is estimated that PHS base stations could cost as little as $30,000.[7]

DDI is co-operating closely with NTT on an MPT committee setting standards for the Japanese PHS. These standards will ensure that users will be able to use

---

[6] This, however, was not DDI's medium of first choice, and microwave was chosen only after a series of negotiations by Inamori for rights of way for an optical fibre network were frustrated.

[7] *New York Times*, 18 November 1992.

the same handsets as they move from the network of one company to that of another. It is intended that this compatibility will greatly aid the diffusion of PHS in Japan. DDI also hopes that the same standards might be adopted in the USA and that this will allow it to begin operations in that country. The US equivalent of PHS is PCS (personal communications services), but the USA has been behind Japan in agreeing on the conditions under which PCS will operate.

PHS is in some respects similar to Telepoint, a relatively unsuccessful service introduced several years ago in Britain, and France Telecom's Bee Bop. According to Semmoto, Telepoint failed for several reasons: only outgoing calls could be made; there was little investment in the service, limiting its availability; there was no common standard for the different Telepoint systems, preventing users from moving from one to another. A major advantage of PHS is that it will interface with NTT's ISDN network, thus facilitating the development of innovative multimedia terminals (a development that DDI, with some of the consumer electronics companies, has already begun).

DDI is working with NTT and MPT in a field trial for PHS in Sapporo, where different base stations are being developed for use under various conditions (buildings, underground stations, etc.). DDI is co-operating with its supplier of long-distance switches, DSC, in developing five kinds of PHS base stations. It is also collaborating with Japanese consumer electronics companies (in preference to the traditional Japanese telecommunications suppliers) in developing new phones including new multimedia terminals.

R&D

What role does DDI envisage for R&D in the realization of its vision for the future, and how does it organize its R&D?

For DDI it is essential that the company possesses a small, flexible R&D team which concentrates primarily on the conception of the innovations required, including compatibility with DDI's network, while subcontracting much of the remaining R&D function. The case of the Alpha chip set discussed earlier showed this team at work.

But how can DDI hope to compete with its 30 engineers involved in R&D and the development of new services while NTT has 8,500 employees in R&D alone? There are two arguments in Dr Semmoto's answer to this question. The first relates to the strategic alternative that exists to doing R&D in-house, namely resorting to the market for R&D services. The second argument hinges on the disadvantages of a large, specialized R&D organization, that is, on diseconomies of scale and specialization in R&D.

According to the first argument, a telecommunications carrier does not need to do very much R&D in-house since it can contract out a large part of the R&D function. Sanshiro Fukada, DDI's general manager for its R&D Group, states: 'We have to be able to express *what we want*. It's the manufacturer's job to make it.' It is for this reason that DDI allocates only about 1 per cent of its revenue to R&D as opposed to about 4.5 per cent for the much larger NTT. Crucial to this argument, as we shall see later, is the assumption that the companies contracted to supply R&D inputs are able to supply them competitively in terms of price, quality, and timing, so that DDI will not be disadvantaged *vis-à-vis* competing carriers such as NTT. It is worth noting that this is an assumption that NTT, naturally enough, rejects.

In terms of the second argument, DDI believes that, while NTT's large and specialized R&D organization offers important benefits to the company, it also suffers from significant weaknesses. One DDI R&D engineer expressed great frustration in dealing with NTT over technical matters.[8] This is because there are so many specialized departments in NTT dealing with various aspects of any technical issue that it takes a significant amount of time to discuss and negotiate with these different departments in order to get agreement on the technical way forward. In DDI, on the other hand, with a smaller R&D team, all of whom are less specialized and are expected to cover a broader range of technical issues, decisions can be made much more rapidly.

He gave an example. 'DDI has only four engineers handling the ISDN interface for radio base stations. However, NTT has a large number who are specialized in different fields, such as radio engineers, ISDN specialists, etc. NTT has too many "best brains". It therefore takes too long to reach a conclusion. Everyone then becomes technically conservative and compromises to reach an agreement.' Semmoto adds, 'We can go anywhere—to universities, manufacturers—and insist on getting what we want.' He claims that this has allowed DDI to move far more rapidly than its competitors over PHS: 'We can continue maintaining our current growth rate with this number of R&D staff until the end of the century.'

For DDI, the crucial quality that is required in its R&D staff is vision regarding the company's future direction and the technical requirements that will aid it to move in this way. This is far more important than specialist knowledge in particular areas of telecommunications. Illustrating this point, Fukada gave the example of one of his R&D staff, Kishi, who was hired with a background in agriculture, rather than telecommunications or electrical engineering. According to Fukada, these kinds of recruits 'have wider views than specialists. We train them internally and they learn the requirements that DDI has. We don't mind their background. The key thing is our company philosophy!'

Competition with DDI: the Implications for NTT

One of the 'big questions' that arises in any analysis of DDI, a question that also arises in a comparative examination of MCI and AT&T in the USA or of Mercury

---

[8] Interview conducted by the author; see fn. 1 above.

and BT in the UK, is, can David co-exist with Goliath, even if he cannot slay him?

There are two very different answers that can be given to this question, each of which depends on a contradictory set of beliefs. The first, which could be given by DDI, is that DDI *will* be able to compete effectively with NTT, despite its smaller resources; the main reason is that the market for telecommunications inputs will work effectively so as to provide DDI with all the inputs it needs to compete. Indeed, the market may work so effectively that it will give DDI additional options compared with NTT, which, while it can also use this market, will be constrained in doing so by its commitment to use its internal capabilities. As Dr Semmoto put it, 'we can go anywhere we like for R&D'. To this may be added the advantages DDI derives from being a relatively small but highly focused organization, concentrating on only a small subset of the markets and technologies that occupy NTT's attention.

DDI could point to the way it is handling the PHS, which has been discussed in detail here, to support its answer; its main competitive edge emerges from its ability to move rapidly in developing and commercializing PHS services.

However, a second and contradictory answer to the question could be constructed by NTT. According to this, DDI will not in the longer term be able to compete. It is NTT that will gain a competitive edge through its substantial in-house R&D capabilities, including those in software, and the synergies that exist between its different areas of R&D competence. These will enable NTT to introduce new, competitive services before other suppliers are able to provide inputs to DDI for competing services.

In the light of the latter construction, the PHS story looks very different. From an NTT point of view, it could be argued that DDI lacks a convincing *source of competitiveness* in the longer run. While it is true that DDI can use the market for R&D, so can NTT; although NTT might feel obliged to employ its own internal R&D resources, if these do not provide the competences that allow it to compete, NTT has both the pressure and the incentive to go to the market. With its large purchasing power, it is able to have its needs effectively met in this market. Furthermore, under competitive pressure NTT will be able to find ways to integrate more effectively the different competences and knowledge possessed by its specialized R&D groups. Moreover, if the constraint comes from NTT's large, bureaucratized organizational structure, it is possible to decompose this structure further by spinning off relatively autonomous units, such as NTT has already done in the case of its cellular subsidiary, NTT Docomo.

According to this answer, while DDI lacks a convincing source of competitiveness, NTT's competitive edge comes from its *unique innovative competence*. Possessing competences in all the links of the value chain—from research through development to marketing, with the single exception of manufacturing—NTT is able to combine these competences in order to provide more innovative products and services more rapidly than DDI. Neither DDI nor its suppliers will be in a position to acquire or combine these competences as effectively. From this point of view, it is NTT, rather than DDI, that will establish the competitive edge in new services such as PHS in the longer run.

Which of these two answers has more weight? It depends on the validity of the *beliefs* underlying each of the answers. There are two key and contradictory beliefs which underlie the hypothetical arguments of DDI and NTT that we have constructed here. It is worth making these more explicit. They may be stated in the following way:

DDI Belief 1: The market for telecommunications inputs, including R&D, operates in such a way as to provide DDI with the inputs that will allow it to compete adequately with NTT.

DDI Belief 2: Small is beautiful. DDI, as a smaller organization than NTT (with around 3,000 employees compared with NTT's 242,000) is more focused, flexible, and rapidly responding. This will provide DDI with a competitive edge.

These are contradicted by NTT's two key beliefs (contained in our hypothetical construction):

NTT BELIEF 1: The market for telecommunications inputs cannot provide all the key inputs necessary for innovative and competitive new products and services. With its in-house capabilities, NTT will be able to provide the inputs necessary to give it a competitive edge quicker and/or better than other suppliers.

NTT BELIEF 2: Small may be beautiful in terms of focus, flexibility, and rapid response. However, a large organization can be made 'small' through decomposition into smaller, more autonomous, units. The reorganizations of AT&T, IBM, and several Japanese companies have shown how this may be done.

Conclusion

Which of these beliefs is 'correct'? The answer is that there is a good deal of interpretive ambiguity surrounding the assessment of each of them. This is because the 'correctness' of each belief is contingent on the complex circumstances that prevail at any point in time. And in view of the complexity of these circumstances, it is not possible to reach a definitive conclusion regarding which belief is 'correct'. The result is that DDI and NTT, as well as their shareholders and other backers, are able, for the time being, to continue clinging to their contradictory beliefs. With the passage of time, however, these beliefs will increasingly be tested in the hot flames of market competition. Then it will emerge more clearly which beliefs have more support.

9

Conclusion

What of the future of the Japanese information and communications (IC) companies and NTT? It is with this question that we end this book.

CHAPTER OVERVIEW

This chapter begins with an analysis of the distinctiveness of the Japanese IC companies. How do they compare with the Japanese motor vehicle and consumer electronics companies, with Western IC companies, and with one another? The performance of the Japanese IC companies is then examined: how well have they done in terms of technological performance, competitiveness in global markets, and financial performance? Attention is then turned to the prognosis for Japanese IC companies: are they likely to strengthen their international competitiveness in the future, or will they come under increasing pressure from their Western rivals?

Conclusions are next derived regarding the role of the various organs of the Japanese government—particularly MITI and NTT—in accounting for the performance of the Japanese IC companies. How important were government policies? Could the Japanese IC companies have achieved their present positions without the interventions of the government? How successful have the government's attempts been to strengthen the technologies of the Japanese IC companies?

We then consider future prospects for NTT. Will NTT be able to deal with the challenges of increasing competition in Japan, globalization, and threatened divestiture? What changes will the company have to make in order to survive and strengthen its position into the next century? The chapter ends with some comments on the limitations of the 'information revolution'. To what extent do the new information and communications technologies make the problem of decision-making in companies and government easier?

The Distinctiveness of the Japanese IC Companies

In order to consider the future of the Japanese IC companies, we need to understand their distinctiveness. Three sets of differences will be briefly examined here: the differences between the Japanese IC companies and motor vehicle and consumer electronics companies, the differences between Japanese and Western IC companies, and the differences among the Japanese IC companies.

Differences between the IC, Motor Vehicle, and Consumer Electronics Companies

Like the African lion, elephant, and giraffe, the Japanese IC, motor vehicle, and consumer electronics companies are quite different beasts. They have evolved in distinct ways even though they have some characteristics in common (e.g. the lifetime employment system, long-term relationship with a main bank, horizontal forms of information-processing, and co-operative relationship with subcontractors). But what are the main differences between these Japanese companies?

In retrospect (as Takahiro Fujimoto has emphasized), the key period in the evolution of the Japanese motor vehicle companies was the immediate postwar years. During this time the companies developed what later turned out to be radical organizational innovations for the design, development, and production of cars. Fujimoto has shown, however, that these innovations first emerged as piecemeal, iterative, solutions to piecemeal problems rather than as grand-plan blueprints for a radically different way of designing, developing, and producing motor vehicles. It is only with the benefit of hindsight, with the passage of a considerable number of years, that we are able to identify a different paradigm emerging in the Japanese motor vehicle industry—a different set of beliefs regarding how to do things.

As the efficiency properties of these organizational innovations slowly became apparent, so it dawned on the Japanese motor vehicle companies that they had (at first unwittingly) developed a set of distinctive competences that gave them an important international competitiveness. This competitiveness helped to give them a global perspective on their activities, backed up by their strong performance from the late 1970s in export markets.

The Japanese consumer electronics companies also developed a strong international competitiveness, at first in products such as radios, and then in televisions and videos. While their competitiveness was also assisted by organizational practices—including product development, manufacturing techniques, and co-ordinating the complementary activities of component suppliers—a key feature of their global selection environment turned out to be the rapidity with which their US competitors abandoned their efforts in consumer electronics. As noted in Chapter 1, a particularly important event for the Japanese consumer electronics companies was RCA's collapse and exit from the industry. Philips, their main European competitor, was encumbered by its decision to put its eggs in many baskets as well as by its slowness in bringing out advanced products. As Matsushita and later Sony overtook it in terms of sales, Philips realized that it had to focus its resources more sharply on the smaller set of competences in which it enjoyed distinctive international strength. The success of the Japanese consumer electronics companies in this global environment also gave them a strong international focus.

The evolution of the Japanese IC companies was different. As stressed in this book, their roots were sunk in the domestic telecommunications equipment industry. With the aid of close links with Western companies, the Japanese IC companies were producing reasonable telecommunications equipment by the early postwar years. However, unlike the Japanese motor vehicle and specialist consumer electronics companies, there were very few areas in which they had managed to establish strong internationally distinctive competences and competitiveness by the mid-1970s.

On the basis of the competences that they accumulated in developing and manufacturing telecommunications equipment, the Japanese IC companies entered the new electronics fields of semiconductors and computers in the 1950s. In semiconductors they steadily strengthened their competences, absorbing the new waves of technology as they rolled in from abroad, including the integrated circuit after 1959, the microprocessor after 1971, and very large-scale integration (VLSI) after the mid-1970s. Aided both by high rates of investment in plant, equipment, and process technology from the latter 1970s, and by constant incremental improvements which were cumulatively significant, from the late 1970s they came to dominate the world market for memory semiconductors. From the late 1980s, however, Korean electronics companies began to tread the same path.

In producing their semiconductors, the Japanese IC companies were responding in the first instance to the Japanese market. Buoyed by the rapid postwar economic growth rate, Japanese market demand for semiconductors rose steadily for use in products such as consumer electronics, computers, and telecommunications equipment. As noted, in the case of memories, production for the domestic market resulted in increasing international competitiveness from the latter 1970s. Similarly, in microcontrollers (simple microprocessors embedded mainly in consumer electronics products) the Japanese IC companies were helped by the substantial demand from the Japanese consumer electronics companies. Here too they managed to establish a strong international competitiveness.

However, the situation was different in microprocessors. Although NEC produced Japan's first microprocessor only five months after Intel announced the world's first microprocessor, the Japanese companies developed their own proprietary products largely for use in their other IC systems. In the USA, however, the evolutionary path for microprocessors was fundamentally different. Driven primarily by the exceedingly rapid growth of demand for personal computers, Intel was able to establish the *de facto* standard for the industry as a whole. In view of Intel's entrenched position, buttressed by its high rate of investment and rapid technical change, the Japanese IC companies—like their American counterparts Motorola, Texas Instruments, and Advanced Micro Devices—were pushed somewhat to the side. In this key part of the semiconductor industry, therefore, the Japanese IC companies were unable to establish a strong international position. Their efforts in microprocessors and microcontrollers remained driven primarily by the demands of the Japanese market.

In computers too, the efforts of the Japanese IC companies were oriented mainly to the domestic market, as emphasized in Chapter 4, an orientation that was reinforced by the overwhelming global dominance enjoyed by IBM from the early 1960s. This was a major difference in the global selection environment confronting Japanese IC companies compared with their counterparts in cars and consumer electronics, which did not face nearly so strong a competitor in foreign markets. The result was that the Japanese computer vendors tended to produce proprietary systems for their customers in Japan. These systems, however, unlike the Walkman or Japanese cars, were not readily marketable in Western markets, and this in turn further strengthened the domestic orientation of the Japanese IC companies.

This pattern of computer development and use also had knock-on effects for the development of the Japanese software industry. The dominance of proprietary computing systems resulted in a substantial demand for customized software and a correspondingly small demand for packaged software. The prominence of the large Japanese computer vendors (including IBM Japan) in the provision of these proprietary computing systems inhibited the growth of smaller, specialized, independent software houses and the growth of a vibrant software market. This structure in the software industry was further reinforced by the slow rate of diffusion of personal computers in Japan, largely a result of the difficulties associated with Japanese language processing. Accordingly, by the early 1990s, 70 per cent of the packaged software sold in Japan came from US companies, while the export of packaged software by the main Japanese computer vendors was negligible.

As a result of these evolutionary patterns, the Japanese IC companies were far more domestically oriented than were the Japanese motor vehicle and consumer electronics companies. In significant parts of the IC industry, they lacked strong international competitiveness. This was evident in the data provided in Chapter 1 on the competitive position of Japanese IC companies in various US markets and in the foreign sales ratios of these companies compared with the motor vehicle and consumer electronics companies.

Differences between Japanese and Western IC Companies

Japanese IC companies are also very different from their American and European competitors. Fig. 9.1 compares several major IC companies in terms of two dimensions. First, the extent to which they are vertically integrated distinguishes between companies that produce only components (such as microprocessors and memories), those that produce systems (such as computers or telecommunications equipment), and those that produce entire integrated systems, including the sub-systems and components (such as computer and communications systems). The second dimension deals with the technological range of the company, distinguishing between specialists, involved in a small number of technologies and products, and universalists, engaged in a large number.

As the figure shows, the main Japanese IC companies populate the north-east

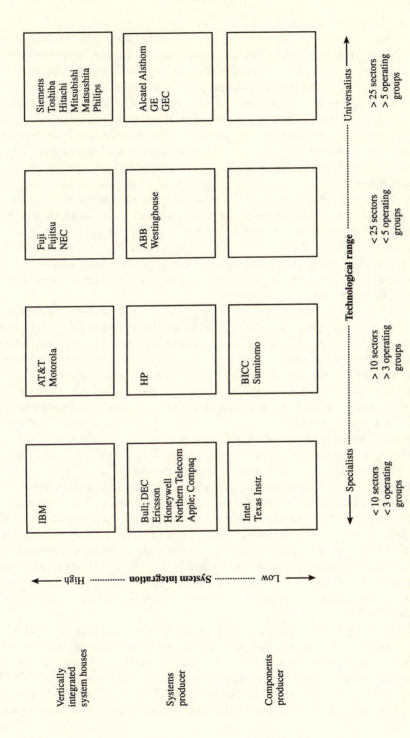

Fig. 9.1 Level of system integration and technological range of business, Japanese and non-Japanese companies

part of the graph. In other words, they are vertically integrated system houses and also universalists. In this respect, they are significantly different from their main North American competitors. In *computers*, for example, while their main competitor—IBM—is also a vertically integrated system house, the Japanese IC companies are involved in a far wider range of technologies and products. In the case of NEC, Fujitsu, Hitachi, and (to a lesser extent) Toshiba, these include telecommunications equipment, which gives these companies the ability to develop integrated information *and communications* systems. DEC and Hewlett Packard (HP)—two of the other US computer companies—are located in the central-west part of the graph, indicating that, although they design and produce many of their components, they are involved in a far more limited range of technologies and products than the Japanese companies. AT&T's location, more specifically its technological range, is explained partly by its acquisition of the computer company NCR. (However, by its own admission, AT&T still has not realized most of the synergies with NCR that motivated the acquisition.) The PC producers like Apple and Compaq are specialist, non-vertically-integrated companies which buy in most of their components. They are located in the central-west part of the graph.

In *telecommunications equipment*, the two main North American competitors to the Japanese companies are also located in the western part of the graph; that is, they are more specialized in terms of technology and product. The first is AT&T, which has a business unit that produces much of its microelectronic components; the other is Northern Telecom, which does not produce most of its own components. (In the area of telecommunications equipment, Motorola is involved mainly in radio-related equipment such as mobile communications equipment and terminals.)

In *semiconductors* the main US competitors to the Japanese are also in the more specialized western part of the graph. They include Intel and Texas Instruments, both highly specialized component producers, and Motorola, which as we have seen also produces radio-related telecommunications equipment.

Sumitomo Electric is shown as the only Japanese company in the western part of the graph, in *telecommunications transmissions*. It is the largest Japanese supplier of optical fibre cable and is also involved in other related areas such as optoelectronic devices. The other two major Japanese suppliers of optical fibre cable, Fujikura and Furukawa, not shown in Fig. 9.1, should probably be located with Intel and Texas Instruments as more specialized component producers. (BICC is the British optical fibre cable producer which also has interests in construction.)

Fig. 9.1 also shows that the European IC companies tend to be far more like their Japanese counterparts than the North American ones. Siemens is the obvious case in point, with its involvements in computers (through Siemens-Nixdorf), telecommunications equipment, and semiconductors, in addition to heavy electrical equipment and some consumer electronics. Siemens is closest to Toshiba, Hitachi, and (to a lesser extent) Mitsubishi Electric. Philips, however, should be seen as a consumer electronics company rather than an IC company, though it also has involvements in areas such as lighting and semiconductors; its relatively small activities in computers and telecommunications equipment means that it is more akin to Matsushita than to the other Japanese IC companies. However, both Siemens and Philips, like their Japanese counterparts, are universalist vertically integrated system houses.

One of the other major European telecommunications equipment companies, the French company Alcatel, is also located in the eastern part of the graph, although, like Northern Telecom, it does not produce most of its semiconductor components. It is categorized as a universalist as a result of its merger with the heavy electrical company, Alsthom. However, the other major European telecommunications equipment company, Ericsson, is, like Northern Telecom, a specialist producer of equipment which tends not to produce its own semiconductor components.

It is clear, therefore, that there are major differences between the Japanese IC companies and particularly their North American competitors. While in terms of the two dimensions discussed here, the Japanese companies appear to be closer to their European counterparts—particularly Siemens—a significant difference is that in Japan the market is contested by a relatively large number of domestic firms, while in Germany Siemens remains something of a national champion. In computers and semiconductors, however, two of the main IC product areas, Siemens is not as strong as its major Japanese competitors. In this book, the distinctive features of the Japanese were explained in terms of the role played by 'controlled competition', the form of organization developed by the Ministry of Communications and later NTT to develop telecommunications equipment.

Is the broader collection of technological competences possessed by the Japanese companies compared particularly with their North American rivals likely to be a source of competitive advantage in the future? We shall return to this crucial question later when we consider the performance of the Japanese IC companies.

Differences among the Japanese IC Companies

There are also important differences among the Japanese IC companies. Having to compete strongly in their major market—Japan—each of the companies has tended to specialize to some extent, achieving a relatively strong position in particular market segments: Fujitsu and Hitachi in large IBM-compatible computers; NEC in distributed networks of smaller computers; NEC and Toshiba in semiconductors; NEC and Fujitsu in telecommunications equipment.

Furthermore, there is an important difference between these companies regarding the range of their technologies and, more specifically, their products. This is evident in Fig. 9.1. Hitachi and Toshiba, like NEC and Fujitsu, are heavily involved in IC products which constitute their largest product category.

Their total sales of IC products in 1993 are shown in Table 9.1. However, Hitachi and Toshiba are also involved in heavy electrical equipment. They also produce consumer products to a greater extent than do NEC and Fujitsu. In 1993 power and industrial systems accounted for 31 per cent of Hitachi's sales, compared with 35 per cent for IC products. In the same year heavy electrical equipment provided 25 per cent of Toshiba's sales compared with 53 per cent for IC products. Hitachi's sale of consumer products was 11 per cent of the total. In Toshiba's case, 'consumer and other' products produced 31 per cent of total sales. NEC and Fujitsu, however, are relatively weak in consumer products.

Table 9.1 *Value of Information and Communications*[a] *Sales in Major Japanese Companies, 1993*

Company	¥bn
NEC	3,568
Fujitsu	2,871
Hitachi	2,860
Toshiba	2,439

[a] Includes: computers, telecommunications equipment, and electronic components.

Source: Company Annual Reports, 1993.

To some extent, however, these differences conceal different organizational histories. For example, Fujitsu began as a spin-off from Fuji Electric, and was set up as a joint venture with Siemens to produce telecommunications equipment. Fuji Electric is a large producer of heavy electrical equipment, although it is smaller than Hitachi and Toshiba in this field. In turn, Fanuc, the company manufacturing factory automation equipment including controls for computer numerically controlled machine tools, was a spin-off from Fujitsu. Furthermore, Furukawa is the company, closely associated with Fujitsu and Fuji Electric, that specializes in products such as optical fibre cable and transmission systems. Fuji Electric, Fujitsu, Fanuc, and Furukawa are regarded as being part of the Furukawa group. Similarly, Sumitomo Electric, also specializing in products such as optical fibre cable, is closely associated with NEC in the Sumitomo group. However, Hitachi Cable, which also produces optical fibre cable (though it is smaller than Sumitomo Electric and Furukawa), is part of the Hitachi consolidated group. It is clear, therefore, that the collection of competences housed in a company is to some extent a function of that company's organizational history. Nevertheless, even if the companies are grouped according to their financial and other links, the differences in specialization and market dominance noted above remain.

Performance of the Japanese IC Companies

Technological Performance

The technological strength of Japanese IC companies compared with their Western competitors is difficult to measure precisely. However, although there are problems with their use, patents may be used as an indicator of technological performance. Moreover, companies themselves often use patents as a measure of both their own and their competitors' R&D performance.

In this section some patent data will be examined in order to get an idea of the relative technological performance of Japanese IC companies. However, from the outset the limitations of these data must be stressed. To begin with, the broader point must be made that there is no necessary relationship between patent performance and market competitiveness. A company that performs well in terms of patents may steadily lose market share to another company that is better at delivering value to the customer. Secondly, it is not clear that all companies place the same stress on the importance of patents. There is evidence, for example, that until the late 1980s Kenneth Olson at Digital Equipment believed that patents provided little protection or other return, with the result that patents were not emphasized in that company.[1] In the case of IC products, technical change is so rapid that both products and processes quickly become obsolete, unlike in pharmaceuticals and chemicals, where several key patents may become the lifeblood of large companies for many years.

Thirdly, even if Japanese and Western companies agree that patents are important, it is not clear that their 'propensity to patent' is the same.[2] There may be different incentive structures within Japanese and Western companies which result in different propensities to patent.[3] Fourthly, in some cases a company may prefer to protect its intellectual property by *not* patenting, since patenting of necessity involves some degree of disclosure. In the case of some process technology, for example, which is not 'visible' outside the company, it may be felt wise not to patent. For all these reasons, care must be exercised in using patent data to indicate cross-company performance.

In Table 9.2, data are provided on the top ten companies in terms of number of patents taken out in the USA from 1987 to 1990. (Since patent regulations differ in the USA and Japan, and since the USA is the largest market in the world, patent comparisons are usually based on US data.) As can be seen, in

---

[1] *Business Week*, 9 August 1993, p. 49.

[2] The propensity to patent of two companies will be the same if, all other things equal—e.g. R&D expenditure, R&D staff and their qualifications, R&D strength and experience, and patent-related opportunities—both companies will produce the same number of patent applications.

[3] At a conference held in August 1994 in Stockholm, attended by senior management from several large companies including board members from Toshiba and Philips, there was discussion regarding possible differences between Japanese and Western IC companies in terms of the propensity to patent. The discussion was inconclusive. However, it emerged that some of the companies put a good deal of faith in patent measures to estimate their own performance relative to that of their rivals.

Table 9.2 *The Top Ten Corporations Receiving US Patents, 1987–1990*

1987		1988		1989		1990	
Company	No.	Company	No.	Company	No.	Company	No.
Canon	847	Hitachi	907	Hitachi	1,053	Hitachi	908
Hitachi	845	Toshiba	750	Toshiba	961	Toshiba	891
Toshiba	823	Canon	723	Canon	949	Canon	868
General Electric	779	General Electric	690	Fuji Photo Film	884	Mitsubishi Electric	862
US Philips	687	Fuji Photo Film	589	General Electric	818	General Electric	785
Westinghouse Electric	652	US Philips	581	Mitsubishi Electric	767	Fuji Photo Film	767
IBM	591	Siemens	562	US Philips	745	Eastman Kodak	720
Siemens	539	IBM	549	Siemens	656	US Philips	637
Mitsubishi Electric	518	Mitsubishi Electric	543	IBM	623	IBM	608
RCA	504	Bayer	442	Eastman Kodak	589	Siemens	506

Source: Data from US Patent and Trademark Office.

1990 the top four patent receivers were Japanese IC companies. However, the table does not provide sufficient information. For example, it does not give R&D expenditure or the size of the company. Further details are shown in Tables 9.3 and 9.4, which compare a sample of Western and Japanese IC companies. Column (3) in these tables provides the same data as in Table 9.2, namely number of patents received in the USA, except for 1992. It also shows that the top three Japanese companies—Toshiba, Hitachi, and Canon—outperformed the top three Western companies—GE, Motorola, and Philips. However, number of patents is also a reflection of the size of a company. In order to discount the effect of size, column (4) shows number of patents per unit of sales. In terms of this measure of patent performance, the top five companies from both samples are: Canon, Motorola (both of which had scores far exceeding those of the remaining companies), Toshiba, Philips, and GE.

A further problem arises from the fact that the companies have different R&D intensities (partly as a result of corporate strategy and partly following from different product mixes). Column (2) presents the R&D intensities. To correct for this, column (8) provides data for number of patents per unit of R&D expenditure, a measure of R&D productivity. According to this measure, the top five companies from both samples are: Canon (far above any of the other companies), GE, Motorola, Toshiba, and Hitachi.

Additional difficulties, however, result from the fact that patents differ in terms of their importance. It would be ideal to have a measure of the rate of return that a company earns from having a patent. In the absence of the data necessary to get this measure, an alternative is to measure the importance of a patent indirectly by the number of times it is cited in other patents. This can be used to generate two further measures of company patent performance: the company's 'current impact index' and its 'technological strength'. These measures are defined in the footnotes to Table 9.3. Tables 9.3 and 9.4 also provide data according to these measures for the sample companies.

As is evident from these two tables, the top five companies from both samples in terms of current impact index are: DEC, Intel, IBM, Canon, and Motorola. In terms of 'technological strength', which gives due influence to the number of patents a company has received, the top five are: Canon, Hitachi, Toshiba, IBM, and GE.

Tables 9.3 and 9.4 also show a 'science linkage' indicator. The five companies with the strongest science linkages are: DEC (significantly above the others), IBM, Alcatel Alsthom, Fujitsu, and Siemens.

While attention has focused thus far on the top five companies, figures are provided in Table 9.5 for the average for each of the samples. Row (1) in the table shows that the Western companies are significantly more R&D-intensive than the Japanese companies. This, however, is primarily a reflection of different product mix; for example, Hitachi and Toshiba also produce consumer electronics products and heavy electrical machinery, which tend to be less R&D-intensive than IC products. Row (2) shows that the Japanese companies have a

Table 9.3 *Research and Development in Selected Western Information Technology Companies, 1993*

	(1) R&D (US$m)	(2) R&D/ sales	(3) No. of patents (1992)	(4) Patents/ sales	(5) Current impact index[a]	(6) Technological strength[b]	(7) Science linkage[c]	(8) Patents/ R&D
IBM	5,083	7.88	842	1.31	1.77	1,488	0.82	16.57
DEC	1,754	12.59	223	1.60	1.92	429	1.37	12.71
Intel	780	13.35	75	1.28	1.88	141	0.41	9.62
Motorola	1,306	9.82	671	5.04	1.68	1,126	0.39	51.38
Northern Telecom	980	11.65	—		—		—	
Ericsson	1,170	17.90	53	0.81	0.96	51	0.42	4.53
Siemens	5,322	10.79	550	1.15	0.85	468	0.56	10.34
Alcatel Alsthom	2,625	8.73	222	0.74	0.80	177	0.71	8.46
GE	1,353	2.37	995	1.74	1.24	1,236	0.52	73.54
Philips	2,079	6.34	607	1.85	0.97	589	0.28	29.20

[a] *Current impact index*: how often a company's patents are cited in other patents: 1.0 rating = company's patents cited as often as overall average; 1.2 rating = patents cited 20% more than average.
[b] *Technological strength*: no. of patents × current impact index.
[c] *Science linkage*: no. of references per patent to journal papers and other scientific publications.

Source: Business Week, 9 August 1993.

Table 9.4 *Research and Development in Selected Japanese Information Technology Companies, 1993*[a]

	(1) R&D (US$m)	(2) R&D/ sales	(3) No. of patents (1992)	(4) Patents/ sales	(5) Current impact index	(6) Technological strength	(7) Science linkage	(8) Patents/ R&D
NEC	2,274	6.94	502	1.53	1.41	709	0.33	22.08
Fujitsu	2,947	9.13	443	1.37	1.57	697	0.67	15.03
Hitachi	3,907	5.55	1,165	1.66	1.45	1,688	0.43	29.82
Toshiba	2,392	5.54	1,176	2.72	1.29	1,514	0.37	49.16
Matsushita	3,144	4.77	732	1.11	1.27	931	0.36	23.28
Sony	1,809	4.86	446	1.20	1.26	560	0.21	24.66
Canon	794	4.44	1,118	6.26	1.76	1,971	0.24	140.81

[a] See definitions given in Table 9.3 footnotes.

Source: Business Week, 9 August 1993.

significantly higher average number of patents; this is mainly a reflection of their larger average size than the Western companies.

More comparable, however, are the indicators in rows (3), (5), and (6). Row (3) shows that on average the patents of the Japanese IC companies are cited (on a per-patent basis) 43 per cent more than the average for *Business Week*'s total sample of 1,000 companies from all sectors, compared with 34 per cent for the Western IC companies. Row (6) shows that patent productivity (patents as a percentage of R&D expenditure) was higher for the Japanese companies: 44 (or 27 if Canon, with its extremely high figure, is omitted) compared with 24 for the Western companies. Row (5), however, shows that the Western IC companies had a much stronger science linkage than their Japanese counterparts: 0.61 compared with 0.37.

Table 9.5 *R&D Performance in Japanese and Western Information Technology Firms, 1992*[a, b]

	Firms	
	Japanese	Western
1. R&D/sales	5.9	10.1
2. Average number of patents	797	470
3. Current impact index	1.43	1.34
4. Technological strength	1,153	634
5. Science linkage	0.37	0.61
6. Patents/R&D	44	24
	[27][c]	

[a] For definitions of terms, see Table 9.3 footnotes.
[b] Averages for the Japanese and Western firms referred to in Tables 9.3 and 9.4.
[c] Excluding Canon.

Conclusions

While, as noted, these figures must be treated with caution, to the extent that they provide a valid indication of technological capability, they suggest that at the very least the Japanese IC companies perform comparably to their Western counterparts. Indeed, Table 9.5 provides some grounds for suggesting that the Japanese companies may be performing slightly better than the Western companies in terms of patent performance.

What about 'business performance'? This question is examined in the following two sections.

Global Market Performance

The strengths and weaknesses of Japanese IC companies in global markets would appear to Western countries to have changed dramatically over time. For about a decade, from the late 1970s to the late 1980s, Japanese IC companies seemed to be presenting an increasingly serious threat to their Western rivals across the board—in computers, telecommunications equipment, and semiconductors. This period began with rapid and significant Japanese inroads into Western markets such as consumer electronics, memory semiconductors, cameras, cars, and numerically controlled machine tools.

By the early 1990s, however, the situation had begun to change. In Japan itself the 'bubble economy' burst, leading to a recession and with it the declining financial performance of major Japanese companies and banks. IC companies such as NEC and Fujitsu recorded their first postwar losses. At the same time, the crisis in IBM, which announced the largest loss in corporate history at the beginning of 1993, led to a reappraisal of what the world of computing was all about. In the wake of this reappraisal, it was the producers of the components and operating systems for distributed networks of smaller computers that came out on top—the Intels and Microsofts of the world—rather than the producers of large computing systems such as IBM, Unisys, DEC, Fujitsu, and Hitachi. Looking at the world of computing through a new set of beliefs, analysts came to discover that the Japanese had never made much of an inroad into the areas now considered as central—e.g. microprocessors, computer operating systems, packaged software, PCs, and workstations. What was earlier perceived as a Japanese threat has now turned into a perception of Japanese weakness.

The Revisionist Argument

But where precisely are the Japanese 'weak'? And what are the causes of their supposed weakness? In Appendix 3 one prominent 'revisionist' view of the Japanese IC industry is examined in detail. Here only the outlines of the argument are reproduced.

According to this argument, the Japanese IC companies have strong international competences only at the 'commodity' end of the IC market (such as memories, liquid crystal displays, and faxes). They achieve their competitiveness primarily by operating within the confines of existing architectures and standards, decreasing unit cost and increasing quality through high rates of investment and constant incremental innovation. However, the revisionists argued, the Japanese IC companies do not have the competences necessary to win 'architectural contests'; that is, they are unable to develop the *de facto* or *de jure* architectures and standards that dominate the commanding heights of information and communications systems. This is because they are weak in design and software activities, and their monolithic organizational structures prevent them from moving sufficiently quickly to put their standards forward as the common standard. It is for this reason, the revisionist argument states, that Japanese IC companies have made little headway against US companies like Intel and Microsoft.

As commodity implementers, however, Japanese IC companies are increasingly being caught in a low profit margin trap, owing to entry from other commodity implementers such as Korean and Taiwanese firms as well as from new US firms (like the PC producers Compaq and Dell) and reinvigorated older US companies. While new entry drives down the profit margins of the commodity implementers, the winners of architectural contests are protected by the *de facto* and *de jure* standards which they have established and maintained through rapid technical change. In this way they are able to earn economic rents.

The main problem with the revisionist argument, however, is that it fails to recognize the substantial competences that the Japanese IC companies have in designing and developing architectures and standards. As was noted in Fig. 9.1, the Japanese IC companies are vertically integrated *system* houses. The reason for the failure in their argument is that the revisionists have an 'Americo-centric' perspective, seeing only the US market. However, the competences of the Japanese IC companies in design, architecture, and standards have been developed and used mainly in response to the Japanese market. This is evident in the products and systems they have produced for this market, such as central office switches, proprietary computer systems, workstations, personal computers, customized microprocessors, and microcontrollers, all of which have tended to be sold primarily in Japan.

Nevertheless, despite the ill-informed basis of their argument, the revisionists are correct to point to important weaknesses in the global competitiveness of the Japanese IC companies. What is needed, however, is an explanation for these weaknesses. And to provide an explanation, it will be necessary to go beyond the 'commodity implementer–architectural winner' dualism of the revisionist argument.

Strengths and Weaknesses of Japanese IC Companies

Where precisely are Japanese IC companies strong and weak in terms of their global competitiveness? A summary is presented in Table 9.6. Many of the products referred to in the table have been analysed in detail in previous chapters.

Why is the global competitiveness of the Japanese IC companies high, medium, or low in these particular products? The explanation lies in the evolution of competences and products in these companies. More specifically, as shown earlier in this chapter, the Japanese IC companies, unlike their Japanese counterparts in motor vehicles and consumer electronics, failed until the early 1970s to establish a strong global competitiveness in many product areas. A striking indicator of the difference between the Japanese IC and consumer electronics companies in terms of international competitiveness is provided by the relative growth of NEC and Fujitsu on the one hand and Sony on the other. Together with the other consumer electronics companies such as Matsushita and Sharp, Sony soon after the war enjoyed substantial international competitiveness in its main products. NEC and Fujitsu were founded in 1899 and 1923 (though

Table 9.6 *Global Competitiveness of Japanese Companies in Selected Information and Communications Markets*

High	Medium	Low
Memory semiconductors	PBXs	Mainframe computers
Semiconductor equipment	Paper copiers	Workstations
Microcontrollers	Fibre optics (including	PCs
Microwave telecommunications	submarine cable	Central office
equipment	systems)	switches
Liquid crystal displays		Microprocessors
Laser printer engines		Packaged software
Facsimile		
Cordless phones		
Compound semiconductors		
Automated fingerprint identi-		
fication systems		

Source: Author's estimates.

they remained technologically dependent for a long time on Western Electric/ITT and Siemens, respectively, which limited their growth). Sony was founded in 1946. In 1994 Sony's net sales were $35.6 billion compared with NEC's $34.2 billion and Fujitsu's $30 billion.

The selection environment of the Japanese IC companies was therefore significantly more domestically oriented than that of the motor vehicle and consumer electronics companies, which from an earlier time played on a global stage. It was in interacting with this selection environment that, guided by their beliefs, the competences and products of the IC companies evolved. Fortunately, the Japanese economy, and with it the markets for IC products, grew rapidly and provided these companies with an important source of growth. (This was documented in detail in Chapter 6 in the case of NEC.) At the same time, the Japanese IC companies faced strong competition from one another, although their membership of broader financial and industrial groups on occasion gave them important entry opportunities.

In some cases, the competences that emerged from this evolutionary process were used to produce products that eventually (in most cases after the mid-1970s) gave the Japanese IC companies a global competitiveness. In other cases, however, in responding to their Japan-oriented selection environment, the IC companies moved down roads which led them in very different directions from their Western competitors, producing products and systems that were not easily marketable in Western countries. Equally importantly, in the latter cases their lack of an international competitiveness meant that they often were slow to build the facilities and networks to support the sale of their products and systems in the West, such as marketing, sales, and after-sale service networks. In turn, this reinforced the difficulty they faced in establishing a global competitiveness in these markets.

Distinction between Product Categories

Based both on the competences needed to become competitive in various kinds of IC products, and on the competences and products that evolved in the Japanese IC companies, it is possible to explain the latter's global competitiveness in terms of a distinction between three different kinds of product categories:[4]

1. Manufacturing-technology-intensive, investment-intensive products
2. Design-intensive, software-intensive products (where proprietary architectures and standards, and complementary marketing and sales 'assets', may also be important)
3. Specific-customer-requirement-intensive products and systems

Each of these categories will now be analysed in more detail.

Category 1: Manufacturing-Technology-Intensive, Investment-Intensive Products. Broadly speaking, the products in which Japanese companies have a 'high' global competitiveness as shown in Table 9.6 fall into this category. These include memory semiconductors, liquid crystal displays, microcontrollers, cordless phones, and facsimile. However, there are also some important exceptions, as will shortly be seen.

In these products, manufacturing competences are a particularly important determinant of international competitiveness, and frequently high rates of investment in both R&D and plant, equipment, and process technology are also necessary. A case in point is memory semiconductors. In Appendix 3, a graph is reproduced showing the increasing investment required as semiconductor circuit widths have fallen to submicron levels (see Fig. A3.1). Although design and software competences may also be necessary, their importance as a determinant of international competitiveness is subordinated to the significance of manufacturing competences. Similarly, proprietary architectures and standards, and complementary 'assets' such as marketing and sales facilities, while also necessary, are not major determinants of competitiveness. The products produced are relevant for a wide range of customers and therefore do not have to be tailored for multiple sub-segments of the market.

Category 2: Design-Intensive, Software-Intensive Products where Proprietary Architectures and Standards, and Complementary Marketing and Sales 'Assets', may also be Important. In these products, design and software competences are important determinants of competitiveness. The ability to develop proprietary architectures and standards and the possession of complementary assets—such as marketing, sales, and after-sale service facilities—may also be significant in establishing competitiveness. While manufacturing competences are also necessary, they are dominated by these other competences in terms of their importance in producing competitiveness. The products include PCs, workstations, PBXs,

---

[4] These categories are considered further in Appendix 2.

microprocessors, packaged software, and automated fingerprint identification systems.

In an important sub-category of these products, Japanese IC companies have put their competences to work in producing products that have been adapted to the specific circumstances of the Japanese market. This includes products such as PCs and microprocessors—such as NEC PC 9800 series and NEC's V series of microprocessors. However—unlike a Walkman, Toyota or Nissan—these products are not sellable outside Japan because of incompatible standards. The point (contrary to that of the revisionists) is not that the Japanese IC companies lack the competences to make these kinds of products, but rather that the products they have made have been adapted to the unique circumstances of the Japanese market.

The case of private branch exchanges (PBXs) illustrates the extent to which the competitiveness of products in category 2 may depend on access to complementary assets.[5] Figure 9.2 shows the value that users place on six characteristics that are associated with the consumption of the services provided by PBXs. The figure reveals that only two of the six categories thought to be important by PBX users relate directly to technological competences. These are the quality of the PBX and its price, thought to be the first and sixth most important characteristic respectively. The remaining four characteristics relate to what are referred to here as 'complementary assets': after-sale service, information and other assistance provided by the sales staff, degree of commitment to the customer, and training and documentation in the use of the PBX. It is clear from this figure that the

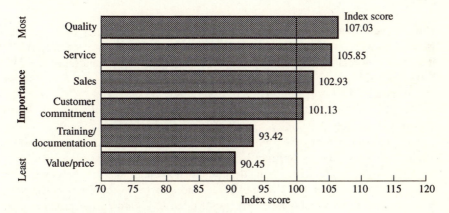

Fig. 9.2 Customer satisfaction regarding PBXs

Key indicator scores by importance, first half of 1992.

Souce: *Dataquest*.

[5] The competitiveness of Japanese IC companies in PBXs in the USA is analysed in detail in Appendix 3, based on data supplied by Dataquest.

latter four characteristics are important determinants of competitiveness. This underscores the point made continually in this book, namely that competences must be conceived in terms of the entire value chain, to include not only technological activities such as research, design, development, and production, but also marketing, sales, and after-sale services.

As shown in detail in Appendix 3, the Japanese IC companies dominate the PBX market in Japan, indicating that they possess all the necessary competences for competitiveness in this product in Japan, including the technological competences. (In Japan, the market for PBXs is open to international competition.) However, as also documented in the appendix, in the USA in PBXs the Japanese companies perform poorly relative to the three market leaders—AT&T, Northern Telecom, and Rolm/Siemens. Since it is unlikely that the Japanese companies are significantly weaker than their Western competitors in terms of technological competences, it is necessary to look elsewhere for an explanation for Japanese market share in the USA. Two likely candidates are: relative weakness in complementary assets, and relative weakness in adapting PBXs to both the US telecommunications network and the specific circumstances of customers.

Both these factors seem plausible. Since AT&T and Northern Telecom dominate the supply of complex telecommunications equipment in North America, it is likely that they have a competitive advantage in their possession of complementary assets and their ability to adapt their products to the requirements of this market. Correspondingly, just as the Japanese are weak in this area in the USA, so do AT&T and Northern Telecom for the same reasons tend to be weak in markets where they lack these assets and abilities, such as in Europe.

Category 3: Specific-Customer-Requirement-Intensive Products and Systems. Here the specific requirements of particular customers are of overriding importance in establishing competitiveness. Examples include central office tele-communications switches, and customized computing systems (such as those for interbank transactions or for airline reservations).

The case of central office switches was analysed in detail in Chapter 3. There it was shown that the ability to sell these switches to one carrier does not automatically transfer to the ability to sell to another. For example, it cost ITT $200 million to adapt its 'brilliant' digital switch, developed mainly in Europe, for sale in the USA. Even then, despite having undertaken these costs, ITT decided to pull out of the US market. In addition to the codified knowledge (made available by organizations such as Bellcore) regarding the requirements for adaptation, there is also a significant amount of tacit knowledge that is necessary. This contributes to the high cost of adaptation to specific customer requirements.

In Chapter 3 the reasons for the Japanese weak performance in digital central office switches in the USA have been analysed exhaustively, and the material will not be repeated here. Suffice it to stress that this kind of product is also quite different from the Walkmans, Toyotas, and Hondas referred to earlier which can be sold both in Japan and abroad far more easily and at lower cost.

Conclusions

As was seen in Fig. 9.1, the Japanese IC companies are vertically integrated system houses, with competences across the board in components, stand-alone systems, and complete integrated information and communications systems. Their collection of competences tends to be broader than their US competitors, although several European companies also have similar competences.

Unlike the Japanese motor vehicle and consumer electronics companies, which dominate Japan's international trade, the Japanese IC companies have tended to achieve a degree of international competitiveness in several product areas later. Furthermore, in many more IC product areas they are weak in terms of global competitiveness and have depended on the growth of the Japanese economy for their corporate growth. Their selection environment has accordingly tended to be more domestically oriented than that of their counterparts in cars and consumer electronics.

The products that the Japanese IC companies have been internationally strong in tend to be those that are both manufacturing-competence-intensive and investment-intensive. However, they have tended to be weak in two areas: first, where product characteristics and standards have evolved in Japan in a way that makes them incompatible with the requirements of the other major global markets and adaptable only at high cost; secondly, where product characteristics are highly customer-specific and the requirements of Japanese customers have diverged significantly from Western ones. Generally speaking, in relatively few areas have Japanese IC companies found the 'competitive edge' that has given them a substantial advantage *vis-à-vis* their international competitors, such as, for example, the just-in-time system or new innovative products like the Walkman or camcorder have given Japanese automobile or consumer electronics companies a decisive advantage. How internationally competitive Japanese IC companies are likely to become in the future is a question that is taken up later.

Financial Performance

Data on the financial performance of the same sample of Japanese and Western IC companies as discussed earlier are analysed in Appendix 4. The details will not be repeated here except for a brief summary of the main conclusions.

Generally speaking, financial performance data are inadequate as indicators of comparative corporate performance between Japanese and other companies. The reason is that the financial performance of Japanese companies is influenced by institutional and investor practices that are specific to Japan. Furthermore, macroeconomic factors—such as international capital flows, interest, and exchange rate differentials—affect overall share prices on a nation's stock exchange. This makes it difficult to compare performance between individual companies, or groups of companies, from different countries on the basis of share values.

This is apparent from the averages in Tables A.4.1 and A4.2. Return on equity is substantially higher for the Western IC companies—14.14 per cent compared with 1.6 per cent for the Japanese IC companies. Yields are also significantly higher—1.5 per cent for the Western companies and 0.7 per cent for the Japanese. However, price–earnings ratios are significantly higher for the Japanese companies—125 compared with 18 for the Western companies. As noted in the appendix, there seems to be some evidence to suggest that the Western companies received stronger rewards and punishments in terms of movements in their share prices in response to financial performance than did their Japanese counterparts.

The Future of Japanese IC Companies

On the basis of the arguments and data of this book, the following conclusions are put forward regarding the future of the Japanese IC companies.

Japanese IC companies have four important sets of potential advantages which may help them in the future in terms of global competitiveness. First, they possess a broader set of technological competences than their strongest Western competitors. This gives them the potential to realize important economies of scope.[6] However, there are also complexities and costs associated with the organization of such a broad range of competences, with the result that the translation of these competences into competitive advantage cannot be assumed. Indeed, thus far some of the main competition to the Japanese IC companies comes from smaller, more narrowly focused, and more competence-specialized companies—for example Intel, Texas Instruments, and Motorola in semi-conductors; Ericsson and Northern Telecom in telecommunications equipment; Microsoft in PC software; Sun, Apple, Compaq, and Dell in workstations and PCs. Organizational difficulties, which I have analysed elsewhere,[7] will have to be overcome if the broad collection of competences possessed by the Japanese IC companies is to be turned into greater global competitiveness in the future.

Secondly, Japanese IC companies are likely to be helped by the slow but steady globalization of their activities. Particularly important, as shown in this chapter, is the building up of the complementary assets that in the case of many IC products are necessary to support their technological strengths in order to achieve

---

[6] Economies of scope occur when a firm is able to produce several different products more cheaply within that firm than it could produce the same quantity of these products in different firms. To the extent that they are able to realize economies of scope, Japanese IC companies may be able to produce IC products and systems more cheaply and/or of higher quality than their more specialized competitors as a result of their in-house possession of competences in components, stand-alone systems, and integrated IC systems.

[7] M. Fransman, 'Different Folks, Different Strokes: How IBM, AT&T, and NEC Segment to Compete', *Business Strategy Review*, 5/3 (1994), 1–20.

market competitiveness. The globalization of their R&D, discussed in Chapter 6, will in time assist in their efforts to cater for the specific requirements of markets outside Japan. Japanese IC companies have been slower than many of their competitors in Western countries and than their Japanese counterparts in motor vehicles and consumer electronics to globalize their activities. In the case of products in categories 2 and 3 discussed earlier, the lower degree of globalization remains a source of weakness. However, steady efforts are being made by the Japanese companies in this area. One example, analysed in detail in this book, is the effort of Fujitsu and NEC to develop the support network needed in the USA to sell the new-generation broadband telecommunications switch, the ATM switch.

Thirdly, in an increasing number of IC product areas Japanese IC companies will be assisted by the greater degree of harmonization occurring with regard to standards and conditions in Japan and in the other major Western markets. To the extent that harmonization occurs, this will mean that Japanese products developed for the Japanese market will be more easily and at lower cost marketable in Western markets. Of course, it will also mean that Japanese companies are likely to face increasing competition from Western entrants into Japanese markets that were previously relatively closed by *de facto* standard differences. One example, analysed in Chapter 4, is the Japanese PC market before the development and diffusion of the DOS/V operating system. But this competition may help to strengthen the competences of the Japanese companies since they already have a solid foundation in Japan. In Chapter 4 the beginnings of harmonization in the case of the computer industry were examined. It was seen that the Japanese computer companies are increasingly adapting their products to international standards and for the first time are beginning to develop packaged software for the global market. It is likely that this is the forerunner of an important new trend in the Japanese IC industry.

Fourthly, Japanese IC companies, like their Japanese counterparts in many other industries, have a number of important forms of organization which over the long run are likely to be significant sources of competitiveness, particularly if the other conditions discussed in this section can be established. These forms of organization include the corporate governance system, which encourages a long-term emphasis on the accumulation of competences and growth; the lifetime employment system, which, despite costs particularly during times of recession, encourages co-operation and intrafirm sharing and integration of knowledge; and a dynamic, innovative, mutually beneficial long-term relationship with both suppliers and customers.

It must be stressed, however, that these four advantages remain *potential* advantages, and their translation into international competitiveness cannot be assumed. One of the main conclusions of this book is that, although the Japanese IC companies have come a long way since their founding, they still have some way to go if they are to emulate the success of their counterparts in motor vehicles and consumer electronics.

The Importance of the Government

The Japanese government has been an important direct influence in the selection environment of the Japanese IC companies and has also played a crucial indirect role in shaping this environment.

More specifically, from the beginning, organs of the Japanese government played an important role in nurturing the entrepreneurs and technicians who established the first IC companies. Particularly important in the late nineteenth century were the government-established factories and laboratories of the Ministry of Industry and later the Ministry of Communications. Out of these organizations emerged the individuals who went on to establish and develop companies such as NEC, Toshiba, Oki, Fujitsu, and Hitachi. Once these fledgling entrepreneurs and technicians had left the nest and set up their own firms, they continued to work closely with government organizations, slowly accumulating their competences as they produced equipment largely for government markets.[8] In this way, the Japanese government facilitated the entry of the first Japanese firms into the IC industry.

From the late 1920s to the end of the war, the Ministry of Communications, through its nationalistic procurement and technical assistance policies, required the Japanese IC companies to reduce their technological dependence on foreign companies. These policies, together with the technical learning experiences provided by the war, undoubtedly served to strengthen significantly the technological competences of these companies.

Furthermore, through controlled competition, the form of organization that it introduced in order to obtain telecommunications equipment, the Ministry of Communications shaped not only the core competences of the major IC companies, but also the structure of the entire Japanese IC industry. After the war, it was those companies that had been most closely involved with the Ministry of Communications in the development and production of telecommunications equipment that went on to develop significant further competences in both semiconductors and computers. More specifically, by the 1980s, partly as a consequence of controlled competition, NEC and Fujitsu were included among the world's top ten largest companies in telecommunications equipment, computers, and semiconductors, while Hitachi was in the top ten in the latter two industries. Although not one of the 'family' of major telecommunications equipment suppliers to the Ministry of Communications and later NTT, Toshiba also became one of the top ten in computers and semiconductors, although its position in computers is due largely to smaller computers, which in turn is mainly the result of strong competences in semiconductors.

In the postwar period too, until the latter 1970s, the Japanese government nurtured the IC companies through its policies of protection and promotion

---

[8] See M. Fransman, *Visions of the Firm and Japan*, Oxford University Press, forthcoming, for further details.

analysed in the various chapters of this book. At particular junctures these policies were especially important, helping to keep the Japanese companies in markets which, in the absence of government assistance, they otherwise might have had to leave. One example, analysed in Chapter 4, were the steps taken in the early 1970s by MITI and NTT in the wake of IBM's introduction of its System 370 series of computers. In the USA, on the other hand, IBM's move led to the exit of large companies such as General Electric and RCA from this industry. In other cases, organs of the Japanese government helped Japanese companies to enter new technologies and markets which, without this help, they might not have been able to enter. One instance, examined in Chapter 5, is the entry of companies such as Sumitomo Electric, Furukawa, Fujikura, and Hitachi Cable into fibre optics.

While the organs of the Japanese government were able through their policies to create a more conducive selection environment for the IC companies, how successful were they in picking and encouraging technology winners? In NTT's case, the technologies that it chose to develop jointly with the equipment suppliers were technologies that were required for the Japanese telecommunications network. While most of these technologies came eventually to serve their purpose, they did not always contribute to products that were competitive in global markets. As was seen in Chapter 3 on switches, in pursuing its own ends, NTT sometimes frustrated the efforts of its suppliers in international markets. Furthermore, by insisting on keeping some competences in-house, NTT on occasion indirectly constrained the accumulation of these competences in the firms of its suppliers. However, despite these problems arising from incompatibilities in objectives, it is likely that as a sophisticated researcher and user and as a large procurer, NTT generally helped the Japanese IC companies in their accumulation of technological competences.

MITI also attempted to encourage the development of particular technologies in the Japanese IC companies. It is worth distinguishing between two sets of 'technology accumulation' projects pursued by MITI. The first, followed until the late 1970s, involved the strengthening of 'mainstream' technologies in the Japanese companies, that is technologies which both these companies and their Western competitors were in any event using. Here MITI's projects were primarily supportive, providing the Japanese IC companies with financial resources and, less importantly, technical help from government laboratory researchers. On the whole, these projects tended to help the Japanese IC companies to catch up with their Western rivals.

The second set of projects, pursued mainly from the late 1970s, involved the identification of radically new technologies that were not yet in widespread usage, either in Japanese or Western companies. MITI's justification for these projects was sound—mainly on the grounds that, in view of the uncertainty attaching to these technologies, in the absence of government-subsidized projects the technologies would not receive the attention from the profit-seeking companies which they deserved. Furthermore, in many cases these projects succeeded in developing stronger competences in these technologies in the companies than would otherwise have occurred. Nevertheless, it is difficult in retrospect to point to many instances where MITI's projects made a significant difference to the Japanese IC companies, although they may have helped to some extent. In most cases it seems clear that the companies would have succeeded in developing the technologies without government assistance when it became clear that they were important enough.

MITI also attempted to influence the Japanese IC industry through its highly publicized visions for the future. MITI officials, working closely with Japanese industrialists and academics, can certainly be credited with quickly understanding long-term trends affecting the industry. A significant case in point is MITI's identification in the 1960s and 1970s of the coming importance of the 'knowledge industries'. In turn, this helped to create a consciousness regarding this issue among policy-makers in Japan. However, here too in retrospect it is doubtful whether MITI's visions can be credited with the production of beliefs in the Japanese IC companies which otherwise would have been fundamentally different. In general, it is more likely that the main function of MITI's visions was to generate an awareness and consensus beyond the IC industry regarding the pervasive importance of information and communications technology, and by so doing to create support for the Ministry's expenditure programmes in this field. The importance of this awareness, however, should not be underestimated, since it aided the diffusion of information and communications technologies in Japan.[9]

In some important cases, MITI's visions simply 'got it wrong'. In the case of the IC industry, perhaps the most important was the failure to understand the fundamental changes that were occurring in the global computer industry, as shown in Chapter 4. MITI, like most of the main Japanese computer companies, bought into IBM's 'architecture of the mind', which emphasized the centrality of large, mainframe computers. By the early 1990s, however, it had become clear that beliefs regarding what information-processing is all about had changed radically, a shift that MITI was no quicker to spot than the others who were also involved in the IC industry. But in its vision failure, MITI was in good company, sharing the same discomfort as IBM's main competitors as well as the financial and academic analysts who had also supported IBM's beliefs. However, MITI's shortcomings should not be surprising. Under conditions of interpretive ambiguity, no one is guaranteed to derive correct beliefs, not even MITI.

On the question of the role of the Japanese government in the Japanese IC

---

[9] In biotechnology, the Japanese government has since the late 1970s helped to speed the introduction of new technologies. To some extent this is similar to the role played by organs of the Japanese government in information technology in the 1950s and 1960s. For an analysis of the role of the Japanese government in biotechnology, see M. Fransman and S. Tanaka, 'Government, Globalisation, and Universities in Japanese Biotechnology', *Research Policy*, forthcoming. Also relevant is M. Fransman, 'Is National Technology Policy Obsolete in a Globalised World? The Japanese Response', *Cambridge Journal of Economics*, forthcoming.

industry, mention must be made, finally, of the Ministry of Posts and Telecommunications (MPT). MPT has frequently been criticized, both inside and outside Japan, with constraining the development of the country's communications infrastructure through its conservative policies. In Chapter 7, some of the major measures implemented by MPT and affecting NTT were examined and the rationale of the Ministry's policy-makers explained. In particular, the efforts made by MPT to constrain the development of NTT, both nationally and globally, in the interests of greater domestic competition, were stressed. MPT's policies, particularly *vis-à-vis* NTT, are considered in the next section.

NTT in the Future

NTT has been far more than merely one of the major companies in the Japanese IC industry; NTT (and its predecessor, the Ministry of Communications) has been a mother-company, giving birth to offspring (its suppliers) and nurturing them so that they could become strong sources of support. But NTT has not been a pampering mother, spoiling its children and letting them have their way without demanding an obligational *quid pro quo*. NTT has never lost sight of its overall commitment to running, expanding, and improving its network and the services that it provides to its customers. This commitment has at times meant that the 'children' have been forced to stay in line, often to their own cost, rather than being allowed to wander off in their own preferred directions.

By the early 1990s, however, as shown in Chapter 7, NTT's selection environment had begun to change radically. Three changes in particular were analysed in detail in this book: competition from new entrants, pressure for divestiture, and globalization, which have created both new threats and new opportunities for NTT. Furthermore, a combination of internal and external pressures—analysed in Chapters 3, 4, 5, and 7—forced NTT to modify its time-cherished form of organization, i.e. controlled competition, by broadening the circle of suppliers to include both Western companies and other Japanese companies.

All these changes have begun to force a reappraisal of the relationship between the mother and children (from all their points of view)—a reappraisal that has not yet been completed. From the mother's point of view, NTT has begun to realize that, although it was pressurized into loosening its ties with its children (the old 'NTT Family' of suppliers), important advantages have followed from admitting new adopted children into the fold. As shown in the chapters on switches and computers, the 'adopted children', e.g. Northern Telecom, Digital Equipment, and IBM, have brought new talents and knowledge into the family. From their point of view, the newly adopted children have been delighted at the opportunity to sup at NTT's plentiful table.

The genetically affiliated offspring, however, have greeted the changes with varying degrees of ambivalence. The ambivalence has been least among the hardiest of these children, the ones that not only are most able to stand on their own two feet in the face of a loosening or even cutting of the umbilical cord, but may even end up stronger as a consequence. Arguably, both NEC and Fujitsu can hold their own in a liberalized Japanese telecommunications equipment market and may even benefit by not being forced to follow NTT so closely, as a consequence becoming freer to focus on global markets in a more flexible and rigorous way. However, the weaker suppliers like Hitachi and Oki stand to lose more; while as a result of the changes they are likely to reduce their share of the Japanese telecommunications market, their global weakness in this area means that they are unlikely to compensate for this by stronger foreign sales.

But it is the mother herself, confronting significant environmental changes at a time when she has already become mature and fairly set in her ways, that faces the greatest challenges. Most important of these is the rapid increase in the liberalization and globalization of telecommunications services markets in Japan and abroad. Until now, as seen in Chapter 7, NTT has been able to retain most of its control over local telecommunications services, and even its total long-distance market has been subjected to only limited inroads by the new Japanese entrants. In the future, however, this is bound to change radically as competition comes from additional Japanese and foreign entrants. These are likely to include cable TV companies and new national and international suppliers of wireless communications, including global satellite-based consortia.

As a result, it is inevitable that in the future NTT will have to fight hard if it is to compete in the Japanese market. The same is true if NTT—like its counterparts AT&T and BT—is to attempt to take advantage of the emerging global opportunities (and be allowed by MPT to do so). But has NTT got what it will take to be competitive in Japan and globally? In tackling this question, it is necessary to acknowledge that NTT has accumulated its competences, forms of organization, and beliefs in adapting itself to a *domestically* oriented selection environment. In view of the radical changes that are occurring in this environment, will NTT be able to survive? To what extent will the company have to change its competences, forms of organization, and beliefs to do so?

Several points may be made in answering these questions. To begin with, NTT has already proved itself able to adapt some of its key forms of organization to the changing circumstances. One important example is the changes it has made to controlled competition by incorporating additional Japanese and, even more importantly, Western suppliers. NTT's success in this regard was documented in Chapters 3, 4, and 5. Another example is the company's ability to segment its activities through the spinning off of subsidiaries such as NTT Data and NTT Docomo (involved in information-processing and mobile communications respectively). These examples show that NTT's ability to adapt should not be underestimated.

However, there are at least two other areas in which NTT will be more severely tested. The first relates to NTT's ability to develop the competences necessary for it to operate successfully in foreign markets. In Chapter 7 it was seen that up to the time of writing MPT has been unwilling to abolish the regulatory division between NTT as a domestic operator and KDD as an international operator. However, it was also argued that it is likely that MPT will eventually be forced to abandon this distinction in the wake of increasing domestic pressure for Japan to put forward a global competitor capable of rivalling such global companies as AT&T, BT, France Telecom, and Deutsche Telecom. And it is clear that NTT is the only Japanese carrier that will be able, on the basis of its own competences, to spearhead a significant Japanese challenge in global telecommunications markets.

However, as was seen earlier in this chapter in the case of the Japanese IC companies, the competences necessary to be a successful global operator are significantly different from those required to be successful in Japan. In short, NTT will have to make significant changes to its structure, culture, and beliefs if it is to succeed internationally. The difficulty of making these essential changes should not be underestimated.

The second area relates to NTT's deeply ingrained belief that it must be primarily an R&D-driven company if it is to grow and compete in the longer term. While this belief is not unique to NTT—AT&T is closest to NTT in sharing the conviction—it is a belief that is challenged by other companies such as BT, MCI, and DDI. (The latter's position was analysed in detail in Chapter 8.) In contrast to NTT and AT&T, these companies believe that they can become more competitive by working closely with outside suppliers who can take on a significant share of the R&D burden. NTT and AT&T, on the other hand, believe that they must have strong in-house R&D capabilities if they are to establish a competitive edge. At the very least, as these beliefs are tested in the hot flames of competition, NTT must be open to the possibility of reassessing such long-held convictions.

Difficult as these issues will undoubtedly prove for NTT, it must be recognized that the company has a major set of assets in the competences that it has accumulated over more than a century in developing the Japanese telecommunications network and the services that it provides. As this book has shown in great detail, these competences should not be underestimated.

The Power of Belief and the Limitations of the 'Information Revolution'

It is appropriate that we should end a book on the information and communications industry with some comments on the so-called 'information revolution'. The main belief held by the proponents of the information revolution (who often have a vested interest in selling its ingredients) is that more, cheaper, information, made available anywhere and anytime, will help to bring about numerous improvements in our economy and society. In the area of decision-making, it is often argued, the information revolution will facilitate the making of better, more informed, decisions.

It is beyond dispute that the information revolution has had a radical impact, creating new solutions to old problems and making available powerful tools to tackle new ones. Less frequently discussed and analysed, however, are some of the inherent limitations of the information revolution. One of the main implications of the studies undertaken in this book is that there is a category of problems—problems that remain crucial to policy-makers in both companies and governments—that remain beyond the reach of the information revolution.

Two problems in particular may be identified. The first has been analysed by Nobel Prize winner Herbert Simon, who has pointed to the constraints that result from the need for *people*, co-operating in organizations, to *process* information in order to use it in their decision-making. The fact that people and their organizations are limited in their ability to process information, however, means that there will often be bounds on their 'rationality', no matter how plentiful or cheap the information. While the information revolution may shift the limits of the ability of people to process information, important limitations are always likely to remain. For this reason, Simon suggests that 'bounded rationality' will always be an important constraint in decision-making.

The second problem has been a major theme which has threaded its way through this book. This is that, under conditions which I have referred to as *interpretive ambiguity*, problems inevitably arise which are beyond the reach of the information revolution. Interpretive ambiguity exists where, no matter how plentiful and cheap the information, it still remains incomplete in the sense that it does not tell us all we ideally need to know in order to make a decision. Under these conditions, there is necessarily a loose coupling—or even an uncoupling—between information and knowledge/belief. Here, information, no matter in what quantity or how cheap, cannot generate unambiguous belief. Accordingly, beliefs, at least for a while, may become relatively autonomous from information. Different people may derive different—even contradictory—knowledge/beliefs from the same set of information.

The studies of the co-evolution of technologies, companies, industries, and national institutions presented in this book show that, far from being a remote theoretical possibility, interpretive ambiguity is part and parcel of the dynamics of industrial change as it unfolds in real time. Accordingly, more attention needs to be paid to the ways in which beliefs are constructed and how they are modified over time.

On this cautionary note I end this book as I began, not with a bang nor a whimper, but somewhere in between, with the words of T. S. Eliot:

> Where is the wisdom we have lost in knowledge?
> Where is the knowledge we have lost in information?

APPENDIX 1

The Firm and Industry in the Evolutionary Process of Economic Change

The aim of this appendix is to provide a summary of the theoretical approach to the firm and industry that has been used in this book. Further details are to be found in my companion volume.[1]

From the point of view of aggregate economic performance, it is the industry rather than the individual firm that matters. While the individual firm may expand, contract, or even die, it is the performance and growth of the industry as a whole that is of economic significance. However, an industry comprises a *population of firms*, and an industry's dynamics depends largely on interactions between its firms. At times, firms in other industries influence the dynamics of a particular industry. In order to explain the performance and growth of a population of firms, therefore, it is necessary to have a theory of the individual firm.

The Firm

What is a firm? What do firms do? Different authors, with different theoretical purposes in mind, have answered these questions in fundamentally different ways. Since the present purpose is to explain the performance and growth of the Japanese information and communications industry, an approach to the firm must be developed which will allow the attainment of this objective.

Competences

Perhaps the best-known approach to the theory of the firm in the context of Japanese firms is that developed by Masahiko Aoki. Since Aoki's approach to the firm has been analysed elsewhere by the present author[1], a brief summary will have to suffice here. Essentially, his approach is based on an analysis of the main characteristics of what he calls the J-firm. These characteristics include: what Aoki refers to as an 'internal rank hierarchy', according to which employees compete for faster promotion, which serves as the primary incentive device within the J-firm; the processing of information in a decentralized, horizontal, way; the tendency for J-firms to spin-off activities into independent subsidiaries

---

[1] M. J. Fransman, *Visions of the Firm and Japan*, Oxford University Press, forthcoming; see also M. J. Fransman, 'Information, Knowledge, Vision and Theories of the Firm', *Industrial and Corporate Change*, 3: 713–57.

and to use subcontractors for supplies; the main-bank system for the J-firm's financial needs; and the practice of cross-company shareholdings.[2]

While acknowledging the significance of all of these characteristics, the approach to the firm used in the present book differs in fundamental respects from that used by Aoki. The most important of these, as discussed below, is the approach to knowledge which is differentiated from information. For the purposes of this book, however, the major problem presented by Aoki's analysis of the Japanese firm is that his analytical concepts do not provide a way of explaining firm economic performance and growth. More concretely, while the Japanese firms in the motor vehicle, consumer electronics, information and communications, chemical, and pharmaceuticals industries are J-firms with J-firm characteristics, their performances (both within and between these industries), as shown above, have differed fundamentally. It is necessary that the theory of the firm used is able to explain these differences. Accordingly, in analysing the J-firm (or any other firm), it is necessary not only to examine its distinguishing characteristics, but also to link these characteristics with the firm's performance. In order to do this, it is proposed—following writers such as Chandler, Nelson, Winter, and Teece—that the concept of *competences* is necessary.

A firm may be defined as a *collection of competences* under the control of a decision-making structure. Firms grow primarily through their accumulation of competences. Competences refer to those activities and knowledge that have as their effect the ability of the firm to sell its output. Competences are not the same as inputs, since a firm that purchases inputs may not be able to transform them into saleable output under the prevailing market conditions. *Technological competences* refers to the technological know-how which allows the firm to commercialize its output. Competences do not necessarily include technological competences; for example, a firm's ability to sell its output competitively may depend on its distribution assets rather than its technologies.

Distinctive competences are those that give the firm a distinctive output, which may become the source of competitiveness and the earning for a while of an economic rent. The acquisition of distinctive competences are particularly important in Schumpeter's approach to innovation. *Core competences* refer to the subset of the firm's competences that underlie the key parts of its output. For example, as shown in Chapter 6 on NEC, competences in semiconductors are one of the important determinants of the company's commercial success in computers and communications equipment.

---

[2] See, *inter alia*, M. Aoki, 'The Japanese Firm as a System of Attributes: A Survey and Research Agenda', paper presented to the conference on 'Japan in a Global Economy: A European Perspective', Stockholm School of Economics, 1991; M. Aoki, 'The Participatory Generation of Information Rents and the Theory of the Firm', in M. Aoki *et al.* (eds.), *The Firm as a Nexus of Treaties*, Sage, London, 1990, pp. 26–53; M. Aoki, 'Toward an Economic Model of the Japanese Firm', *Journal of Economic Literature*, 28 (1990): 1–27; M. Aoki, *Information, Incentives, and Bargaining in the Japanese Economy*, Cambridge University Press, 1988. For a situating of Aoki's work within the context of various theories of the firm by economists, see Fransman, *Visions of the Firm*.

Competences emerge through using and extending the knowledge embodied in the inputs purchased by the firm, that is on the experience generated in the firm in carrying out its activities. It is difficult, costly, and time-consuming to accumulate competences. Competences therefore constrain what the firm can do at any point in time. Similarly, a firm's competences are difficult for other firms to imitate (although through reverse engineering it may be possible for a firm's product to be replicated).

While competences constrain what a firm can do, at particular junctures in the evolution of a firm competence-creating moments arise when a firm's decision-makers must decide whether to extend the firm's competences into new areas. These moments may have a critical bearing on the firm's performance and growth. An analysis of how firms make these decisions is therefore crucial. As will be seen later, the beliefs that firms construct play a central role in these decisions. Examples analysed in this book include Fujitsu's decision to enter the new field of computers, a decision that was hotly contested within the company but ultimately led it to the second position in the world in terms of computer sales; and NEC's failure to enter the new field of digital switching sufficiently quickly, which in turn contributed to its failure in the US market in the early 1980s.

Organization

In order to enable the firm to sell its output under existing market conditions, the activities and knowledge that comprise its competences must be organized. Oliver Williamson is therefore correct to insist that 'organisation form matters' and to lament the fact that 'Most recent treatments of the corporation [in economics] . . . accord scant attention to the [organizational] architecture of the firm and focus entirely on incentive features instead.'[3]

However, while a firm's forms of organization may be an important determinant of its performance and growth, it is frequently unclear to the firm's decision-makers how the firm should be organized. Furthermore, the selection process under which firms operate selects on the basis of output characteristics (particularly price and quality) and the correlation between these characteristics and forms of organization is often indeterminate. Accordingly, a major problem facing the firm relates to the forms of organization that it should implement. (Williamson's 'organizational imperative' that firms economize on bounded rationality and minimize the possibility for opportunistic behaviour does not take the firm far down the road in resolving its organizational problems.[4])

While the firm's internal incentive structures for its employees are important, a broader set of issues arises in trying to decide how the firm should best organize its innovation process. And clearly, innovation is a major determinant of the

---

[3] O. Williamson, *The Economic Institutions of Capitalism*, Free Press, New York, 1985, p. 281.
[4] See Fransman, 'Information, Knowledge' and *Visions of the Firm* for a critical examination of Williamson's approach to corporate organization.

performance and growth of firm, industry, and economy. Among the issues is the problem raised by Friedrich Hayek of how to utilize knowledge not known by anyone in its entirety, and how to create new knowledge. Chapter 6 on NEC and the comparison between NTT, AT&T, and BT (contained in the author's companion book, *Visions of the Firm and Japan*) pay particular attention to the way these kinds of issues have been tackled in these companies.

Selection Environment

Like biological organisms, populations of firms exist within *selection environments*, which influence their performance and growth over time. Unlike such organisms, however, firms cope with their selection environment largely through the construction of beliefs regarding what the firm should do in order to achieve its purposes under the constraints and opportunities that this environment provides. A crucial question relates to the way these beliefs are constructed and how they are revised over time. We shall shortly return to this question.

Like the concept of competences, the notion of a selection environment provides a crucial link between the internal structuring of the firm and its performance and growth. Firms with the same internal characteristics will perform differently in different selection environments. It is therefore necessary to analyse the relationship between the firm and its selection environment.

The competences and forms of organization that a firm develops must be adapted to the firm's selection environment since they allow the firm to continue to survive in that environment. For the firm, survival is contingent on its ability to sell its output; sale of its output enables the firm to purchase further inputs and thus renew its life cycle. Failure to sell in the absence of external subsidy will mean extinction. But selection environments may be more or less demanding or permissive in terms of the competences and forms of organization that they will allow. All this implies that the firm *per se* is not always an appropriate unit of analysis. This is so for the simple reason that what goes on inside the firm is dependent on what goes on outside in its selection environment. An analysis of the firm must therefore include an analysis of its selection environment. In earlier chapters, for example, it was shown that a major part of the explanation for Japanese 'failure' in microprocessors, packaged software, and complex telecommunications switches relates to the characteristics of the selection environment in Japan.

Four important features of a firm's selection environment are: the extent of competitive pressure; the impact of government interventions; the influence of capital markets; and the opportunities and constraints offered by new technologies. These features will be considered briefly.

Competitive pressure is a major determinant of a firm's behaviour and of the competences and forms of organization that it develops. The so-called 'new industrial economics', based on game-theoretic approaches, is largely concerned with the strategic moves that are available to the firm to restrict competition to its own advantage (for example to act so as to deter entry by a would-be new entrant).[5] The new industrial economics focuses on a category of competition-related issues that are of concern to the firm. However, the analyses in the present book of the evolution of parts of the information and communications industry—such as telecommunications switches, computers, and optical fibre— shows that the strategic questions relating to the creation and use of new technologies have been of far greater long-run competitive significance than those dealing with moves to limit competition. This is true both for the performance and growth of individual firms and for the long-term structure of industries. Furthermore, the uncertainty and ambiguity that usually surround the introduction of new technologies (which preclude the generation of agreed probability distributions and payoffs) means that game-theoretic tools are often not particularly helpful. The analysis of new technologies therefore requires different approaches. More will be said about this shortly.

Government intervention is an important aspect of the selection environment. Through means such as incentives, disincentives, information provision, co-ordination, exhortation, and direct control, government can influence the environmental conditions within which firms exist. Of course, there is no inherent reason why government interventions should have net positive effects for firms and industries: they may even fail to produce desired effects. But it is always the case that the interventions of government bureaucrats and politicians are rooted in the political processes of the nation. In order to explain why bureaucrats and politicians intervene in the ways that they do, it is often necessary to understand the specificities of the political process.

In the present book, for example, it is shown in Chapter 2 that the political circumstances of Japan in the late 1920s and 1930s had a crucial impact on the forms of organization and accumulation of domestic technological competences in the telecommunications sector. In turn, this affected the structure of both the information and communications industry and its firms in the postwar period. Also significant was the role of Japanese government laboratories in incubating the entrepreneurs and technologies that were important for the development of this industry, and the measures taken by the Japanese government to protect and promote the industry at various points in time.

However, just as in the case of firms, the beliefs that government officials constructed in order to guide their interventions were crucial. And at times these beliefs were subject to the same limitations as those influencing the firms. One case in point, analysed in detail in Chaper 4 on computers, was the impact that IBM's 'architecture of the mind' had on the beliefs of both Japanese government officials and the leaders of some of the country's major computer firms.

Another important link between firms and their selection environment is through the operations of the *capital markets*. As shown in Chapter 6 on NEC, the specificities of the Japanese capital markets have an important impact on the

---

[5] For a recent account of approaches in the new industrial economics, see G. Norman and M. La Manna, *The New Industrial Economics*, Edward Elgar, Aldershot, 1992.

way a corporation is governed, the way it responds to adversity, and its accumulation of competences. More specifically, the existence of 'committed shareholders' has been an important feature of the Japanese selection environment. ('Committed shareholders' may be defined as those who will retain shares in a company despite expecting that they could gain by selling the shares and using the proceeds to purchase other assets. They 'stay and fight' rather than switch since they have other interests in the company; for example, they may sell financial services or other products to the company, or they may depend on the company for inputs.)

The existence of an important cadre of committed shareholders in Japan contrasts with the environment in countries like the USA and UK, where 'arm's-length shareholders' are relatively more influential. The fact that the latter shareholders would rather switch in the face of expected potential gain than stay and fight (although they may put up some fight) has important implications for the constraints and pressures put on the management of firms. Whether these constraints and pressures are a positive or negative influence in facilitating the firm's adjustment to changed circumstances—such as the demands of the business cycle or changes in technologies and market conditions—is a question discussed in Chapter 6.

The *advent of new technologies* constitutes a particularly important change in the selection environment of firms. And, as many of the chapters in the present book show, new technologies constitute a significant influence on the dynamics of the evolution of firms and industrial structures. (Examples analysed in detail in the present book include the emergence of electronic switching in the wake of the invention of the transistor; the development of digital switching; the impact of the integrated circuit and microprocessor on the computer industry; and the transition from copper cable to optical fibre.)

In view of the importance of the interplay between new technologies and firm behaviour in determining the dynamics of industrial change, it is necessary to analyse how new technologies are created and how firms respond to their creation. Indeed, this is one of the major concerns of the present book, as is evident in all of the chapters.

From the point of view of the analysis of the firm's selection environment, however, the advent of new technologies raises in stark form the question of how firms appraise the significance of these technologies for their activities. One of the main contributions of this book is to show how much more complicated this process of appraisal is than is usually assumed in economic and other social scientific investigation. In order to clarify the complexities involved, it is necessary to delve briefly into the distinction between *knowledge, belief,* and *information.* While these concepts are examined theoretically here, various chapters examine them in different empirical contexts.

A Unified Theory of the Firm

A major departure in the present book follows from the proposal that a unified theory of the firm may be constructed on the basis of the concepts of knowledge, belief, and information. By a 'unified theory of the firm' is meant a theory that uses the same concepts to analyse both the firm's interior and its exterior, i.e. its selection environment. In order to clarify this proposal, it is necessary to consider the concepts of knowledge, belief, and information.

Knowledge, Belief, and Information

As the philosopher Dretske has noted, 'What is knowledge? A traditional answer is that knowledge is a form of justified true belief.'[6] But, as he also notes, this orthodox answer is unsatisfactory precisely because it is often unclear, either at a point in time or with the passage of sufficient time, when a belief is 'justified' and 'true'. The history of beliefs in any area of human thought provides examples of beliefs that were thought to be justified and true at some points but later came to be thought of as unjustified and untrue. Because of these difficulties, *knowledge* is defined here in terms of *belief*, whether or not this belief can be proved to be 'true'. In short, a firm's 'knowledge' consists of the set of its beliefs. A firm will act in terms of its knowledge/beliefs since it considers them to be true—or, at least, has more confidence in their truth than in the truth of an alternative set of beliefs.

Since beliefs may change over time, it is necessary to enquire into the causes of their change. One important possible cause of change is *information* received by the believer. Information may be defined as 'data relating to states of the world and the state-contingent consequences that follow from events in the world that are either naturally or socially caused'.[7] Information consists of a closed set of data in that there is a closed set of states and consequences. However, knowledge, equated with belief, is essentially open. In the light of the same information, beliefs can, and sometimes do, change. Knowledge may therefore often be thought of as in a constant process of becoming other than what it was.

What is the relationship between the information received and the beliefs held by the believer? In answering this question, it is necessary to distinguish between two polar cases. In the first, there is a 'tight' determinate coupling between information and belief. In short, received information determines belief. Belief, accordingly, is processed information.[8] It is this position that Dretske takes when

---

[6] F. I. Dretske, *Knowledge and the Flow of Information*, MIT Press, Cambridge, Mass., 1982, p. 85.

[7] See Fransman, 'Information, Knowledge, Visions and Theories of the Firm', p. 2.

[8] The questions as to why the believer received that set of information and no other, and the dependence of the belief on the set of information received, raise important difficulties. Clearly, if a different set of information had been received, it is possible that a different set of knowledge/beliefs would have been derived. This relates to Herbert Simon's concept of *bounded rationality*, which he defines as existing when the set of information relevant to a decision is greater than the set of information that can be acquired and processed by the decision-makers. See the references in fn. 1 above for a detailed critical discussion of the concept of bounded rationality.

he states that 'Knowledge is identified with information-produced (or sustained) belief.'[9] This is also the position taken in the Bayesian approach.[10]

In the second case, however, there is a 'loose' or indeterminate coupling between information and belief. A special case of a necessarily loose coupling between information and belief occurs under conditions that are referred to in this book as 'interpretive ambiguity'. Under conditions of interpretive ambiguity, information is 'incomplete' in the sense that there is insufficient information to generate unambiguous belief. Accordingly, under these conditions different individuals—or even the same individual at different points in time—may construct different, even contradictory, beliefs from the same information set.

A particular instance of interpretive ambiguity arises in the case of uncertainty. Here there is uncertainty regarding future states of the world and state-contingent consequences. Under these circumstances information, logically, cannot provide any assistance, since by definition data cannot be provided on future states and state-contingent consequences. In the future, things may be different from what they were in the past; but it is only in the future, when the data have been collected, that we can know whether things have changed or not. Accordingly, a probability distribution that is valid for the future cannot be derived. (It is only by making a continuity assumption, that is by assuming that the information available at the present time will continue to be valid in the future, that a probability distribution can be used for the future. But, under conditions of uncertainty, this assumption may be incorrect.) Under conditions of uncertainty, different individuals, or the same individual at different points in time, may arrive at different, even contradictory, beliefs on the basis of the same set of information.[11]

The significance of interpretive ambiguity for the evolution of firm and industry is studied empirically in several of the chapters in this book. Examples include: contradictory beliefs among competing telecommunications equipment companies regarding the appropriate timing for the introduction of digital switching; IBM's tenacious belief in the ability of the mainframe to sustain its

---

[9] Dretske, *Knowledge*, p. 86.

[10] The Bayesian approach may be defined in the following way: 'Proceeding from a definition of probability as a measurement of belief; considering statistical inference as a process of re-evaluating such probabilities on the basis of empirical observation', *Chambers Science and Technology Dictionary*, Chambers, Cambridge, p. 81.

[11] *A propos* of this decision-making situation, Frank Knight has the following to say: 'we do not react to the past stimulus [*read*: information], but to the 'image' of a future state of affairs. . . . We *perceive* the world before we react to it, and we react not to what we perceive, but always to what we *infer*. The universal form of conscious behavior is thus action designed to change a future situation inferred from a present one. It involves perception and, in addition, *twofold* inference. We must infer what the future situation would have been without our interference, and what change will be wrought in it by our action. Fortunately, or unfortunately, none of these processes is infallible, or indeed ever accurate and complete. We do not perceive the present as it is and in its totality, nor do we infer the future from the present with any high degree of dependability, nor yet do we accurately know the consequences of our own actions. In addition, there is a fourth source of error to be taken into account, for we do not execute actions in the precise form in which they are imagined and willed', F. Knight, *Risk, Uncertainty and Profit*, Houghton Mifflin, Boston, 1921, pp. 201–2.

profitability, growth, and size in the face of increasing amounts of information suggesting the contrary; the belief of financial analysts tracking IBM's performance, of many of IBM's rivals, of some of the major Japanese computer companies, and of MITI officials in IBM's 'architecture of the mind', namely the continuing importance of the mainframe; the belief of Corning regarding the speed with which optical fibre would be diffused; the belief of NEC and other information and communications companies regarding the importance of the convergence of computing and communications technologies.

The Interior and Exterior of the Firm. As argued above, two key concepts necessary for analysing the interior of the firm and explaining its performance and growth are *competences* and *organizational form.* Both competences and organizational form, however, are based on belief, and in this sense may be thought of as forms of knowledge. For example, a firm's technological competences consist largely of know-how, that is knowing how to achieve particular desired effects. But knowing how to achieve an effect is essentially a question of belief. With a change in belief, know-how (i.e. technology) changes. Knowing how to best transmit a signal is quite different in the ages of copper cable and optical fibre; knowing how to best store information is quite different in the ages of magnetic storage and optical storage; etc.[12] Chapter 5 contains a detailed analysis of the emergence of a new set of knowledge/beliefs regarding how best to transmit communications signals. It was this set of knowledge/beliefs that first allowed Corning to develop an optical fibre with a signal loss rate below 20 decibels per kilometre, thus making optical fibre superior to copper as a transmission medium. But this breakthrough—which not only transformed the telecommunications transmissions industry but also provided a crucial building-block for the so-called Information Superhighway—required the construction of new beliefs from the old beliefs that existed in both the glass and copper cable industries.

Similarly, as Alfred Chandler's discussion of the emergence and diffusion of the multidivisional form of corporate organization shows, changing organizational form is also essentially a matter of belief.[13] As shown in Chapter 6 on NEC, somewhat different beliefs emerged in Japan regarding how large corporations should be organized.

The issue of belief construction and change is also at the heart of the analysis of the exterior of the firm, namely its selection environment. How do the firm's

---

[12] Technological competences are also to some extent dependent on know-why, knowing why particular events have the effects that they do. Know-how and know-why may be independent; it is possible to know how to achieve an effect without knowing why that effect is achieved. However, know-how and know-why may be interdependent and may positively influence one another. Knowing why may assist in knowing how to produce a result; and knowing how may provide a useful input into the process of coming to know why.

[13] For an analysis of changing beliefs in IBM, AT&T, and NEC regarding the suitability of the multidivisional form of organization, see M. Fransman, 'Different Folks, Different Strokes: How IBM, AT&T and NEC Segment to Compete', *Business Strategy Review*, 5/3 (1994): 1–20.

decision-makers analyse their selection environment and, on the basis of this analysis, infer what they should be doing in order to achieve their objectives? The general answer is that they construct *beliefs* about their selection environment, and these beliefs shape their decisions. Following our earlier discussion, however, such beliefs may be tightly or loosely coupled to the information acquired by the decision-makers. Under conditions of interpretive ambiguity, these beliefs will necessarily be loosely coupled; it may be said with justification that the nature of the selection environment, like beauty, is in the eye of the beholder. The *opportunities*, *constraints*, and *threats* created by the firm's selection environment should therefore be seen as depending on the beliefs of the firm's decision-makers, rather than as 'objective' features of this environment.

More generally, the firm's vision of the future may be defined in terms of its set of beliefs regarding the shape of things to come. It is in the light of its vision that a firm's decision-makers construct their strategy and tactics. Strategy relates not only to how to act in the external world, but also to how to shape the firm's internal world, its competences and forms of organization.

Fragmented Knowledge, Tacit Knowledge, and Knowledge Creation.   Knowledge presents a major problem for the organization of the interior of the firm. To begin with, as shown in detail in the case of NEC in Chapter 6, it is difficult for the large, multi-product, multi-technology firm even to define its knowledge base (that is, the stock of knowledge that underlies its various products and processes). Furthermore, there is a good deal of interpretive ambiguity involved in deciding on how to categorize the various components of this knowledge-base. For these reasons, firms like NEC and Siemens, which have attempted to define their knowledge-base, have found the process to involve a great deal of time and much internal debate and even conflict.

Additional problems arise from the fact that a firm's knowledge stock is necessarily fragmented, stored in different individuals and divisions and embodied in different routines, practices, and equipment. Specialization and the division of labour, which increase the efficiency of firms, have as one of their costs the *fragmentation of knowledge*. However, activities such as innovation— e.g. the development of a new product—require the integration of different elements of the firm's stock of knowledge. Creating a new product, for instance, necessitates the integration of knowledge regarding the product characteristics desirable to customers, the design alternatives that are available, the materials and production processes that should be used to produce the product profitably, and the cost data that are needed to achieve efficiency—knowledge that resides in different people and functions within the firm. This raises, in the context of the firm, the problem that Friedrich Hayek saw in the economy as a whole: namely, the problem of how to utilize knowledge which no single person possesses in its entirety.

Further problems are raised by the difficulty and cost of communicating some forms of knowledge. Particularly complicated is the communication of what Polanyi called *tacit knowledge*, which he defined as existing when a person knows more than he/she can tell.[14] Yet various studies of the innovation process show that the mobilization of tacit knowledge and its conversion into expressable, more easily analysable, knowledge can provide an important source of innovation.[15] A particular instance of this is analysed in detail in Chapter 6, i.e. NEC's innovation in automated fingerprinting, which gave the company a dominant share of the world market.

In the present book a unified approach to the firm is adopted which analyses both the interior and the exterior of the firm in terms of the same theory of knowledge, belief, and information. In the body of this book this approach is used to explain the growth of the Japanese information and communications industry, which produced some of the largest companies in the world in computers, telecommunications equipment, and semiconductors. This approach is used to explain not only the strengths of this industry, but also its major weaknesses.

[14] The knowledge contained in tacit knowledge consists of beliefs. The problem posed by tacit knowledge lies in the communication of these beliefs. For example, the golf player's 'knowledge' of how to play golf is expressable in terms of beliefs regarding what should be done in order to achieve the desired objective, namely to get the ball in the hole with the minimum number of strokes. This knowledge is therefore the same as the know-how referred to earlier. The problem, however, lies in communicating these beliefs to another person. In Ch. 6, emerging from an analysis of NEC's development of its automated fingerprinting information system, it is suggested that some tacit knowledge may be unconscious; that is, the knower may not know that he/she possesses this knowledge. This emerged when NEC's researchers worked with members of the Japanese police who were not fully conscious of the knowledge they used in order to differentiate visually between fingerprints. In the case of unconscious tacit knowledge, there is the further problem of first making the unconscious tacit knowledge conscious, before attempting to communicate it.

[15] Ikujiro Nonaka, from a managerial perspective, has done fascinating work on how some Japanese companies have created new knowledge by organizing the mobilization of tacit knowledge within the company (see, *inter alia*, I. Nonaka, 'The Knowledge-Creating Company', *Harvard Business Review*, Nov.–Dec. 1991, pp. 96–104). Part of the process of creating new knowledge may necessitate the challenging or even destruction of old knowledge/beliefs. This explains the widespread use in companies like Sony of slogans such as the following, which at first sight appear irrational: 'Use unattainable dreams' (in creating innovations); 'Say okay before thinking about it'; 'Make the product before explaining the idea' (author's interviews in Sony).

The approach to the firm adopted in this book is summarized in Fig. A1.1.

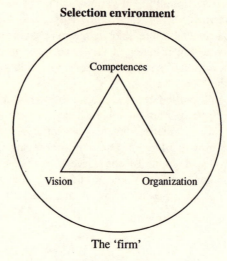

Fig. A1.1 Four key concepts for a theory of the firm

APPENDIX 2

The Evolution of Optical Fibre in Corning Glass

Introduction

This appendix contains a detailed analysis of the evolution of optical fibre technology in Corning. It explains why it was Corning that made the breakthrough in 1970 when researchers produced an optical fibre with a loss rate below 20 decibels per kilometre (dB/km), making optical fibre for the first time viable as a telecommunications transmissions medium. The analysis also examines the complementary technologies that were needed for optical-fibre-based transmission systems and discusses the further improvements made in optical fibre in the early 1970s.

Expected Payoffs to Research on Optical Fibre

In this section we go back to the mid-1960s, before the main breakthroughs in optical fibre for communications were made, in order to reconstruct the expected payoffs that potential producers and users of optical fibre thought might follow from their investments in research and development in this area. It is these expected payoffs that guided the allocation of resources to research on optical fibre in a context where functioning copper cable, microwave radio, and satellite systems provided viable alternative transmissions media.

Within the telecommunications network, transmissions constituted what T. P. Hughes has called a 'reverse salient'.[1] More than a simple physical constraint or bottleneck, transmissions technology was perceived by those building and operating telecommunications systems as a strategic weakness in much the same way that a military strategist might analyse a weakness in the battlelines (reverse salient being a concept drawn from a military context). Simply put, throughout the 1960s the demand for telephone lines increased rapidly, as did central office switching capacity, with the introduction of new electronic switching systems. The ability of the total telecommunications system to expand, however, was seriously limited by the transmission sub-system. Consisting largely of installed copper cables, the carrying capacity of this sub-system could not be readily and cost-effectively be increased, and as time went on new services such as data communications, facsimile, and video all demanded increasing bandwidth capacity. Accordingly, strategic attention was focused on possible

---

[1] T. P. Hughes, *Networks of Power: Electrification in Western Society, 1880–1930*, Johns Hopkins University Press, Baltimore, 1984.

ways of overcoming this reverse salient because of the high payoffs that would accompany a solution to the transmissions problem.

One effect of this attention was to increase the amount of research carried out on alternative transmissions technologies. In the late 1960s the search for such technologies in the area of waveguides took two principal forms. The first was the attempt to develop a millimetre waveguide system (based on electromagnetic rather than optical waves); the second was research on optical communications. Until 1970 the millimetre waveguide area received most attention. For example, at the September–October 1970 conference on Trunk Telecommunications by Guided Waves held in the UK, most of the papers were on millimetre waveguides. It was at this same conference, however, that a paper was read announcing that Keck, Maurer, and Schultz of Corning Glass had developed an optical waveguide that broke through the crucial loss barrier, establishing the viability of optical fibre. From then on, research attention in the leading telecommunications countries shifted sharply to optical fibre.

•

The Inherited Stock of Knowledge *c.* 1966–8

We now need to reconstruct the 'knowledge environment' that surrounded researchers working on optical fibre in the early 1960s, before the major breakthrough by Corning in 1970. In this section the knowledge that these researchers 'inherited' from the past in the area of optical fibre will be examined, while in the following section the 'new knowledge' that was required will be analysed. This will set the stage for an in-depth analysis of the contribution to knowledge made by Corning.

By the early 1960s some of the basic principles of optical communications in general and optical waveguides in particular were already well known. As early as 1880, Alexander Graham Bell had demonstrated that speech could be transmitted with the use of a lightbeam. This demonstration took the form of the 'photophone' which Bell developed just four years after he invented the telephone. The photophone used a beam of sunlight as the light source which shone on a mirror that was vibrated by sound waves (voice), thus modulating the intensity of the beam. The reflected light was focused onto a selenium rod which served as the light detector. The electrical resistance of the selenium rod varied as a function of light intensity. The rod was connected with a battery and a telephone receiver which reproduced the transmitted voice over a distance of 200 metres. However, as Bell quickly discovered, the atmosphere does not provide a very satisfactory medium for the transmission of light signals. His efforts in the field of optical communications were therefore overtaken by electrical signals conveyed through metal wires such as already existed in the telegraph.

The principle of total internal reflection was also long known. In 1870 the British physicist John Tyndall had demonstrated the phenomenon of total internal reflection when he showed how light could be guided around a corner. By opening a hole in the side of a tank of water and shining a light through the pouring water, Tyndall showed that the light described a parabola. This happened because the water guided the light, reflecting it back into the stream whenever it reached the boundary between the water and the air. Since the water had a significantly higher refractive index than the air, total internal reflection resulted.

In the late 1920s and early 1930s, the first patents were granted regarding optical image transmission using quartz glass fibre bundles. In 1927 British Patent no. 285,738, titled 'An Improved Method of and Means for Producing Optical Images', was issued to J. L. Baird. Related patents were issued to C. W. Hansell in the USA in 1930 and to H. Lamm in Germany also in 1930. In November 1936 Masao Seki (later Seimiya) and Hiroshi Negishi, who were working in the Electrical Communication Laboratory of the Japanese Ministry of Communications, filed a patent titled 'Improvement of Optical Communication Method', which suggested that quartz glass could be used as an optical communications medium. This application was published in August 1937 and the patent was granted in June 1938.[2] Seki and Negishi therefore anticipated a similar suggestion that was made much later, around 1963, by Elias Snitzer of the company American Optical.[3]

In the 1950s working-image-transmitting bundles of fibres were developed, for example by Brian O'Brien at the American Optical Company and by Narinder Kapany (sometimes referred to as the 'father' of fibre optics) in the UK. Further work was done on the improvement of performance by the addition of cladding on optical fibres. It soon came to be understood that, although air has a lower refractive index than glass and therefore light would be internally reflected within the glass, an unclad glass core does not perform satisfactorily as a waveguide since imperfections, scratches, or dust on its surface cause light to scatter rather than being refracted properly back into the fibre. In 1954 A. C. S. van Heel, in an article in *Nature*, proposed to increase resolution by putting a cladding on multi-component glass fibre. In 1959 Narinder Kapany produced the basic theory for cladded fibres. By the 1960s, therefore, image-transmitting bundles of fibres, used for purposes such as endoscopic probes, were usually of the cladded variety.

From the point of view of the feasibility of optical fibre transmission for communications, however, the major hurdle that remained was the high loss rates (attenuation) recorded by existing optical fibre, which rendered it unacceptable as a medium for long-distance communications. This problem came to be addressed by many researchers, including Dr Charles K. Kao and his collaborator George A. Hockham at (then) ITT's Standard Telephone Laboratories (STL) in Britain. Beginning their research in 1963, Kao and Hockham published an important paper in 1966 which summarized the 'state of the art' regarding the use of optical fibres for communications, outlined the problems that remained

[2] T. Nakahara, H. Shioyama, and T. Watamizu, 'Optical Fiber: From its Initial Development through Successful Production and Usage', *Sumitomo Electric Technical Review*, no. 26 (1987), 40–2.

[3] See D. A. Duke, *A History of Optical Communications*, Special Report, Telecommunication Products Department, Corning Glass Works, New York, 1983.

to be solved for the development of viable fibres, and proposed what they believed to be the most fruitful way forward. This paper had a significant impact on the international research community working on optical fibre, since it established a *de facto* research agenda.[4]

Kao and Hockham indicated that quartz glass was the most suitable material for use as an optical fibre transmission medium. They also argued that an important source of the high attenuation rates that had hitherto been achieved in such fibres was not the glass that had been used but rather the impurities that they contained, such as iron, which was responsible for absorption losses. Furthermore, they pointed to the significance of scattering losses caused by imperfections in the core–cladding interface. But it was perhaps their prediction that attracted most attention, not only in academia but also in industry: namely that with the removal of the impurities an attenuation rate of around 20 dB/km could be achieved, where 1 per cent of the light entering a fibre would emerge after a kilometre. This prediction, if realized, would make optical fibre competitive with the other alternative technologies such as copper cable.[5]

To what extent did the 1966 paper by Kao and Hockham contribute to the subsequent breakthrough that was made in achieving the 20 dB/km level? An opinion on this question was expressed on 13 October 1987 in the judgment of the District Court in New York in the case of *Corning Glass* v. *Sumitomo Electric*, in which Corning sued for a breach of its patents. According to this judgment, the Kao–Hockham paper 'offered no practical solutions to the problems it posed'.[6] More specifically, 'Although the Kao paper concluded that cladded glass fibers were possibly usable as optical waveguides, it expressly recognized that the feasibility of waveguides depended on the availability of suitable low-loss materials, and that this was a "crucial" and "difficult" materials problem which was yet to be solved.'[7]

The information presented thus far allows us to reconstruct the knowledge that was in the public domain and relatively easily available to a researcher in around 1966 working on optical fibre for communications. Such a researcher would have known that quartz glass was the preferred material for these optical fibres, although the optimal kind of quartz glass and its material characteristics remained

[4] C. Kao and G. A. Hockham, 'Dielectric-Fibre Surface Waveguides for Optical Frequencies', *Proceedings of the IEEE*, 113 (1966), 1151–8.

[5] 'The best optical fibers available in the mid-1960s had attenuation of 1000 decibels per kilometer, or equivalently, one decibel per meter. The decibel is a measure of the fraction of the signal which makes its way through a communication system. . . . To change decibels into the fraction of the signal which makes its way through the system, first divide the number of decibels by 10, then make the resulting number a power of (10XXX in the case of 100 decibels), and finally divide that number into 1. Thus, a loss of 1000 decibels per kilometer means that only 1 part in 10XXX of the light that enters a fiber can emerge after travelling through a one-kilometer length. That loss is far too much for optical communication systems, which typically can stand losses of no more than around 20 decibels/kilometer.' (Duke, *History of Optical Communications*, 4.)

[6] District Court, S. D., New York, *Corning* v. *Sumitomo Electric USA Inc.*, Nos. 84 Civ. 9155 (WCC) and 85 Civ. 3156 (WCC); Decided 13 October 1987; as amended 21 December 1987, 1545–71.

[7] Ibid.

unclear. Furthermore, he or she would also have known that the fibre required a core surrounded by a cladding with a lower refractive index. In addition (a point that will now be documented), by 1968 the researcher will have known, if he/she did not already know, that certain oxides could be added to the glass as dopants in order to change (increase or decrease) its refractive index. As the US District Court judgment noted, 'It has been known in the art at least since 1954 that the introduction of fluorine decreases the index of refraction of certain multicomponent glasses.'[8] Patents issued in 1967 and 1968 underscored the use of dopants as means of changing the refractive index of glass. In May 1967 US Patent 3,320,114 was issued to Schultz (of Corning Glass) for 'Method for Lowering Index of Refraction of Glass Surfaces'. This paper dealt with a 'method of making an optical fiber by treating the exterior of a silica fiber with a dopant which lowers the refractive index of the outer portion of the fiber'.[9] On 3 April 1968 UK patent 1,108,509 was published, 'teaching the use of . . . dopants to increase the refractive index of a fiber core', although it said 'nothing about the doping of fused silica'.[10] Interviews that I conducted with senior researchers in the British glass company Pilkington, who were closely involved in optical fibre research at the time, confirmed that the use of dopants to alter the refractive index of glass was well known to researchers working in this field in the mid-1960s.[11]

Inherited Complementary Knowledge

It is important to understand that optical fibre, like most other single technologies, does not exist in isolation but is part of an interacting system of technologies. Optical fibre, even in the laboratory, has to be manufactured, and this involves the use of other technologies. Once it is manufactured, a light source is needed (even if a light detector is not, assuming that the light passing through the fibre is visible to the naked eye). In an installed optical fibre transmission system, such as shown in Fig. 5.2, it is clear that a number of other technologies become important, such as fibre protecting, splicing and connecting, repeater, and cabling technologies. This illustrates the *knowledge interdependence* inherent in all technologies and in the process of technical change.

The concern of this subsection is the state of knowledge in the mid-1960s in some of the main technologies that complemented optical fibre. As will be seen,

---

[8] Ibid. 1551. [9] Ibid. 1556. [10] Ibid.

[11] Of course, it is a logically unjustifiable step to conclude, from evidence that knowledge was 'in the public domain' (through the publication of research papers and patents), that this knowledge was known by the majority of researchers working at the time. The knowledge that researchers possess at any time is partly a function not only of the cost of obtaining that knowledge, but also of prior knowledge regarding the places where relevant knowledge is to be found. The instant and relatively cheap on-line availability of patent data, for example, has greatly increased the dissemination of this kind of knowledge. A further complication arises from the *interpretation and meaning* that researchers give to the 'knowledge' they receive. As we shall see later in this chapter, the difficulties referred to here are more significant than is usually acknowledged.

these complementary technologies constrained and influenced the development of optical fibre, and, in turn, their own development was influenced by the capabilities and requirements of optical fibre technology.

The Laser.   The laser constitutes one of the central complementary technologies in optical communications systems. Serving as a light source, the laser emits a narrow, monochromatic beam of coherent light (that is, light waves that are precisely in phase with one another) at wavelengths that are consistent with low attenuation rates in optical fibre. The availability of working lasers in the late 1960s was undoubtedly an important condition facilitating the development of optical fibre as another crucial part of the emerging optical communications system. In turn, the development of the laser was also influenced by the requirements of such communications systems.

Essentially, the laser is a device that produces amplified light as a result of the stimulated emission of radiation. ('Laser' is an acronym for Light Amplification by the Stimulated Emission of Radiation.) In 1958 Charles H. Townes (then at Columbia University) and Arthur L. Schawlow (of Bell Laboratories) published a paper and patent application that provided the theoretical rationale for laser action. In 1964 Townes won a Nobel Prize for his work on coherent radiation, and in 1981 he shared a Nobel Prize with Schawlow for their research on laser spectroscopy. On 7 July 1960, Theodore H. Maiman of the Hughes Research Laboratories in Malibu, California, announced that he had developed the first working optical-frequency laser.

Some of the key concepts on which the laser is based can be traced back to the earlier twentieth century. In his 1964 Nobel Prize lecture, for example, Townes noted that:

already by 1917, Einstein had followed thermodynamic arguments further to examine in some detail the nature of interactions between electromagnetic waves and a quantum-mechanical system. A review of his conclusions almost immediately suggests a way in which atoms or molecules can in fact amplify. . . . Thermodynamic arguments can be pushed further to show that stimulated emission (or absorption) is coherent with the stimulating radiation.[12]

Since some of the essential ideas underlying the laser and its predecessor the maser (Microwave Amplification by Stimulated Emission of Radiation) had been known for a long time, the question arises as to why the laser was not invented sooner. Townes himself has stated that 'As I see it, lasers might well have been invented during . . . 1925–40 . . . '[13] Of the reasons that he gives for this delay, two are of particular concern in the context of the present book. The first is the fragmentation of knowledge that existed between two different specialized areas, physics and electrical engineering. In Townes's words:

---

[12] C. H. Townes, 'Production of Coherent Radiation by Atoms and Molecules', 1964 Nobel Lecture, *IEE Spectrum* (August 1965), 31.

[13] C. H. Townes, 'Ideas and Stumbling Blocks in Quantum Electronics', *IEEE Journal of Quantum Electronics*, QE-20/6 (1984), 549.

I believe whatever unnecessary delay occurred was in part because quantum electronics lies between two fields, physics and electrical engineering. In spite of the closeness of these two fields, the necessary quantum mechanical ideas were generally not known or appreciated by electrical engineers, while physicists who understood well the needed aspects of quantum mechanics were often not adequately acquainted with pertinent ideas of electrical engineering.[14]

Furthermore, physicists were constrained by the conceptual approach they took to light: 'physicists were somewhat diverted by an emphasis in the world of physics on the photon properties of light rather than its coherent aspects'.[15] An important factor overcoming this fragmentation of knowledge was the emergence after the Second World War of a new, practical field, namely radio and microwave spectroscopy (the study of interactions between radiowaves and microwaves on the one hand and molecules on the other): 'the real growth of this field came shortly after the burst of activity in radio and microwave spectroscopy immediately after World War II since this brought many physicists into the borderland area between quantum mechanics and electrical engineering'.[16]

Townes's own interests were in the area of spectroscopy with extremely practical applications in mind: 'My own scientific interests were primarily in the direction of new forms of spectroscopy and precision measurement.'[17] More specifically, 'it was primarily a strong desire to obtain oscillators at shorter wavelengths than those otherwise available that induced me to initiate experimental work on the maser'.[18]

The second reason given by Townes for the delay in the invention of the laser is the lack of practical applications foreseen at the time. 'In addition to conceptual stumbling blocks which affected the course of quantum electronics, in the early days there was also a limited appreciation of the potential of this field.'[19] Townes, however, was well aware of the practical applicability of research in this field:

A favourite quip which many will remember was 'the laser is a solution looking for a problem'. While an enthusiast myself, and aware of the potential for high precision measurements, monochromacity, directivity, and the high concentration of energy that optical masers would provide, I missed many potent aspects. The area of medical applications is one that did not occur to me initially as promising.[20]

However, Townes's beliefs were not immediately shared with the patent office in Bell Labs. According to Townes, 'Bell's patent department at first refused to patent our [laser] because, it was explained, optical waves had never been of any importance to communications and hence the invention had little bearing on Bell system interests.'[21]

While the lack of anticipated practical and commercial applications may

---

[14] Ibid. 547.   [15] Ibid.   [16] Ibid.   [17] Ibid. 550.
[18] Ibid. 547.   [19] Ibid. 549.   [20] Ibid. 550.
[21] Quoted in N. Rosenberg, *Exploring the Black Box: Technology, Economics and History*, Cambridge University Press, 1994, p. 223.

have limited research in the field of stimulated emission prior to 1958, by that year the situation had altered fundamentally. This emerged in the official address given by Theodore Maiman on receiving the Japan Prize in 1987: 'around 1958 . . . a number of scientists started to think about making coherent light. They knew that if coherent light could be achieved they could use it to convey 10,000 times more information than with any existing electromagnetic signal such as microwaves.'[22] At this time Maiman had been working on ruby masers at the Hughes Research Laboratories, and he decided to attempt to produce a ruby laser despite some published data which suggested that the ruby was unsuitable. Maiman recalls that:

At this very moment, one of the authors of the 1958 *Physical Review* article [i.e. Schawlow or Townes] announced at a professional meeting that ruby would never work. At the industrial laboratory where I was employed, my project was not popular and I received little support. But now as a result of these comments it was even more difficult for me to proceed . . . Nevertheless, I was so highly motivated by what I was doing I insisted on proceeding with my project, despite growing criticism from the administrators of the laboratory . . .[23]

On 16 May 1960, Maiman succeeded in generating 'the first coherent light in the form of a burst of deep red light from a small ruby crystal'.[24]

Soon rapid progress was made in developing new types of lasers, including the semiconductor laser which, operating successfully at the wavelengths at which optical fibre had low attenuation rates, was particularly useful for optical communications. Indeed, in 1970, the same year that Corning's researchers broke the 20 dB/km barrier, Hayashi and Panish achieved the first continuous wave operation of a semiconductor laser at room temperature. Several years later, with the demonstration that optical fibres with zero dispersion could be produced which operated at 1.55 micrometres, new semiconductor lasers were developed at this wavelength. In 1979 Yasuharu Suematsu and his colleagues at the Tokyo Institute of Technology reported a continuous-room-temperature semiconductor laser at 1.55 micrometres using a mixture of indium, gallium, arsenic, and phosphorus.[25]

As an integral part of optical communications systems, lasers have influenced, and simultaneously been influenced by, these systems in much the same way as the inventors of the laser have both shaped and been affected by the devices they have produced and also the uses of these devices. Out of this complex web of interactions has emerged the continuously evolving field of optical communications.

---

[22] T. Maiman, 'The Laser: Its Origins, Applications and Future', Japan Prize 1987 (official brochure), Tokyo, 15–16.

[23] Ibid. 16.

[24] Ibid.

[25] Y. Suematsu *et al.*, post-deadline paper presented at The Fifth European Conference on Optical Communications, Amsterdam, September 1979 (mimeo).

Cabling and Connecting Technology. Although cabling companies possessed relevant capabilities, their knowledge remained to be applied to the specific conditions of glass fibre. More specifically, major problems were posed by the brittleness of the glass fibre, increased by the high temperature at which it was processed, and the need to coat and therefore protect the fibre. Further difficulties were presented by the need to connect glass fibres, since their length was less than the distance between repeaters. As will be seen, important innovations occurred in the 1970s to deal with these problems, which together constituted essential technology complementing that of optical fibre itself.

Required New Knowledge

The knowledge that the researcher of the late 1960s 'inherited' from past efforts has now been summarized. The problems that still needed to be addressed were relatively clear.

1. What kind of glass with what purity was best to use for optical fibre?
2. How should the required refractive index differential between the core and the cladding be obtained? More specifically, while it was known that the refractive index could be altered by the addition of dopants, it was not yet known which dopants would achieve the desired aim in terms of refractive index while facilitating low loss rates.
3. What production processes would be needed to produce glass fibre of the desired characteristics? In particular, more knowledge was needed regarding the effects of alternative production processes. For example, would bubbles be introduced into the glass which would increase loss rates? What would be the effect of the production process on water (OH) levels?
4. A host of questions remained regarding the complementary technologies. For example, how could more reliable, longer-lasting, and cost-effective light sources and detectors be produced? Could light sources operating at higher wavelengths be developed so that the effect of wavelengths on attenuation rate could be examined? How could brittle and fragile fibre be protected so that optical fibre systems could be effectively implemented? What suitable methods could be developed for splicing and connecting the fibre? How could repeaters be developed which, given attenuation rates and the length of the cable required, would boost the fading light signal?

Breaking the 20 dB/km Barrier

By the late 1960s, Corning's researchers possessed most of the common knowledge available to researchers in this field. In addition, they possessed *company-specific knowledge*, based on the accumulated experience of Corning, which, as will be seen, played a significant role in their breakthrough invention.

More specifically, Corning possessed in-house knowledge in two important areas:

1. The manufacture of pure fused silica by the flame hydrolysis method, which produces soot which is then sintered to make fused silica
2. The doping of fused silica with substances that included titania

Corning's in-house knowledge of the flame hydrolysis method was contained in Corning's Hyde US Patent 2,272,342 for a 'Method of Making a Transparent Article of Silica', applied for on 27 August 1934 and issued on 10 February 1942.[26]

Corning's company-specific knowledge also included that derived from the experience gained from the company's invention in 1952 of a process that provided the purest fused silica (SiO_2) ever made, an invention that Corning includes among its 'key innovations'.[27] In the 1950s Corning began manufacturing pure fused silica glass in bulk in order to make products for early-warning systems for the US Department of Defence.[28] The company's specific knowledge also included knowledge of the doping of silica glass with titania (TiO_2).[29] Corning had also used alumina and zirconia for doping in order to change the properties of fused silica, although the results were not as good as with titania.[30] The aim of this doping was to reduce the coefficient of expansion of fused silica.

The opportunity for Corning to relate its accumulated knowledge in glass to new areas of application, thus making use of technological synergies in order to diversify into new (for the company) product markets, first presented itself through contact that one of its researchers, William Shaver, had with researchers in the UK Post Office. As was seen earlier, the Post Office in Britain since the mid-1960s had been working with a group of companies on optical fibres. As mentioned in a semi-official Corning history, 'The British Post Office mentioned its interest to many people, including a Corning scientist visiting Britain. He brought the idea back [to Corning], and it soon became one of several research projects assigned to a group headed by Robert D. Maurer.'[31]

Corning's researchers made significant use of the company's existing stock of knowledge and its associated competence and experience in their search for an optical fibre that would pass the 20 dB/km test. Most other competing researchers at the time had chosen to use so-called compound glasses which were made by melting at temperatures around 1,500°C and could be easily drawn into fibres. Furthermore, there were a large number of glasses that could be used, and this provided alternative options in the search for a fibre appropriate for long-distance optical communications. Compound glasses had been used in the

---

[26] *Corning* v. *Sumitomo Electric*, 1555.

[27] Corning, corporate brochure, 1989, p. 4.

[28] I. Magaziner and M. Patinkin, *The Silent War: Inside the Global Business Battles Shaping America's Future*, Random House, New York, 1989, p. 270.

[29] *Corning* v. *Sumitomo Electric*, 1549.

[30] Ibid. 1552.

[31] Duke, *History of Optical Communications*, 4.

short-distance image-transmitting fibre optics referred to earlier. Companies such as Pilkington and Standard Telephone Laboratories, working with the UK Post Office, were using a double-crucible technique for melting sodium silicate glasses.[32]

Significantly, however, Corning's researchers did not at the time know that many of their competitors were using compound glasses. This emerges in a history of optical communications written by Dr David A. Duke, who later became director of research at Corning. Duke states that 'The Corning Group did not know that others who had worked on the problem had chosen to use . . . "compound glasses".'[33] Instead, the Corning researchers began their work with pure fused silica, an obvious choice in view of the company's previous knowledge and experience with this material.[34]

There were, however, two major problems that followed from the use of pure fused silica. The first was that this glass had an extremely high melting point—2,000°C, more than three times the melting point of steel. This made it more difficult to draw the fibre. (In Corning's other applications that used fused silica, it was not necessary to draw the glass.) The second problem was that pure fused silica had the lowest refractive index of almost any glass. If both the core and the cladding were to be made of pure fused silica, it would be necessary to find a way of reducing the refractive index of the cladding even further.

While competing researchers, following the teaching of Kao and Hockham, were trying to purify the compound glasses they were attempting to use for the core, Corning's researchers decided to begin with the cladding, since they already had an extremely pure glass—pure fused silica—for the core. With this starting-point, the next logical question was how to raise the refractive index of the core. As noted earlier, it was widely known at this stage that the addition of dopants could have the effect of raising the refractive index. Such a step, however, carried the danger of increasing the signal loss rate of the fibre as a result of the addition of impurities. Nevertheless, perhaps as a result of the experience that the company already had in working with pure fused silica and with doping, Dr Maurer decided on 1 March 1967 to instruct the making and testing of a fibre with a titania-doped fused silica core and a pure fused silica cladding.

Maurer, a physicist rather than a glass specialist, who had graduated from MIT in the early 1950s, worked closely on this project with Peter C. Schultz, who joined Corning in August 1967 with a background in chemistry from Rutgers

[32] *Corning* v. *Sumitomo Electric*, 1548; and interview with senior Pilkington researcher.

[33] Duke, *History of Optical Communications*, 5.

[34] This lack of knowledge on the part of Corning's researchers provides an interesting twist to the usual (implicit) assumption behind discussions of 'bounded rationality' (H. A. Simon, *Administrative Behaviour*, Macmillan, New York, 1961), namely that more information is to be preferred to less. The present case, however, is an example of a situation where less information may have aided Corning's efforts to the extent that it encouraged the choice of an alternative 'search path' which ultimately proved to be more fruitful, albeit a path that was dependent on the company's previous knowledge and experience. In this way Corning's bounded rationality may have redounded to the company's advantage!

University. By the time he joined Corning, Schultz already had important experience in this field, having been issued with US Patent 3,320,114 for 'Method for Lowering Index of Refraction of Glass Surfaces' on 16 May 1967. Schultz's aim in doing the research on which this patent was based was to develop a fibre capable of transmitting light, and the patent described a method for producing an optical fibre by treating the exterior of a silica fibre with a dopant in order to lower the refractive index of the outer portion of the fibre.[35] In February 1967, six months before he joined Corning, Schultz had tried to produce an optical waveguide fibre 'by depositing flame hydrolysis-produced pure fused silica soot on the outer surface of a titania-doped fused silica core rod'.[36] Seen in the light, first, of Corning's inherited experience and knowledge and, secondly, of Schultz's prior research, it is hardly surprising that the company pursued the 'search path' that it did. This, as mentioned, involved using pure fused silica, which in turn, given the low refractive index of this material, suggested starting with the cladding and attempting, with the addition of titania dopants to the core, to raise the index of refraction of the latter. Corning's research strategy was, therefore, 'path-dependent' in the sense that it was heavily influenced by the prior knowledge of the company and its researchers.

Initially, Corning's method of producing the fibre, like that used in the manufacture of short-distance image-transmitting fibres such as endoscopes, involved producing a titania-doped pure fused silica rod for the core which was then surrounded by a pure fused silica tube for the cladding. The rod-in-tube was then heated, melted, and drawn. When this was done, however, it was discovered that small bubbles formed at the interface between the rod and the tube (core and cladding). These bubbles absorbed light and therefore increased the loss rate of the fibre, rendering it unsuitable for long-distance communications.

It was the solution to this problem that possibly constituted Corning's most important contribution to the state-of-the art in optical fibre for communications.[37] Nevertheless, the solution did not consist of entirely new knowledge specially created to meet the purpose at hand. Confronted with the bubble problem, the Corning research team

brainstormed ways to adapt every known glass-making process, but couldn't come up with anything. So Maurer told Schultz and [Donald B.] Keck [a physicist who had joined the Corning research team] to forget glass technology. If all you do is think about what the industry's doing, you're locked in mentally. He urged them to look at other, unrelated areas of science.[38]

Keck eventually reasoned that, since the air bubbles formed at the interface between the rod and the tube (the core and the cladding), the problem might be

---

[35] *Corning* v. *Sumitomo Electric*, 1556.

[36] Ibid. 1549.

[37] This, at any rate, was the view of a senior researcher at the British glass company, Pilkington, whom I interviewed and who was researching in this field at the time.

[38] Magaziner and Patinkin, *The Silent War*, 273.

overcome by looking for a different way of joining core and cladding. As a physicist, he had some knowledge of a method used in IBM for adding layers to a silicon substrate in the manufacture of silicon semiconductors and proposed that this method might be used to add 'core layers' to the inside of the cladding tube.

Schultz, with his background in chemistry and experience and knowledge in glass fibre manufacture, suggested a similar method to that used in the semiconductor industry, namely that the core layers be added by depositing vaporized silica containing the dopant on the inside of the cladding tube. This could be done by a well-known method called chemical vapour deposition (CVD) which Corning had already perfected for use in other areas. Once again, therefore, Corning was able to draw on the stock of knowledge that it had accumulated.[39]

In April 1968, Schultz tried to coat the inside of a pure fused silica tube with titania-doped fused silica soot produced by flame hydrolysis. On 1 August 1968 this research resulted in fibre 'measured to have an attenuation of approximately 250 dB/km. This marked the production of the first doped fused silica optical waveguide fibre with losses sufficiently low for short-range communication uses.'[40]

After this breakthrough, a process of incremental, experimental technical change took place in Corning with variations being made in some of the parameters (such as the proportional amount of titania dopant added to the silicon halide vapours). Fibres were then drawn and tested with a laser beam in order to measure the resulting attenuation rate. As a result of this process of incremental technical change, a gradual improvement in performance occurred, the cumulative significance of which was substantial. By early 1970 this improvement led to the development by the Corning research team of the world's first optical fibre with an attenuation rate below the crucial 20 dB/km barrier. This was a fibre with a pure fused silica cladding and a doped fused silica core containing around 3 per cent titania by weight. On 11 May 1970, an application was filed for what was to become on 2 May 1972 US Patent 3,659,915 (referred to in the rest of this chapter as '915) issued to Drs Robert D. Maurer and Peter C. Schultz and titled 'Fused Silica Optical Waveguide'. In autumn 1970 Maurer took one of these fibres to Bell Laboratories where a loss rate of around 16 or 17 dB/km was confirmed. Significantly, Corning, by showing the fibre to a potential rival organization, was not risking a significant leakage of knowledge since 'reverse engineering' of the fibre was not possible. 'Bell Laboratories considered Corning's achievement an important breakthrough which made long-distance optical telecommunications possible. Corning did not

[39] The vapour deposition method was the subject of the Mattmuller US Patent 3,334,982 for the 'Manufacture of Silica Glass'. The patent application was filed on 30 January 1962 and was issued on 8 August 1967. 'It discloses a method for the manufacture of silica glass by the decomposition of silicon halide vapors in the flame of an oxyhydrogen blowpipe and the direct vitrification of the resulting silica.' (*Corning* v. *Sumitomo Electric* (1987), 1555.)

[40] *Corning* v. *Sumitomo Electric*, 1549, 1550.

tell Bell how the fibres had been made and Bell and others were unable to duplicate them.'[41]

The Knowledge Contained in Corning's '915 Patent

The following is a summary of the main knowledge disclosed in Corning's '915 patent:

1. An optical fibre for use in optical communications systems has a fused silica core and a fused silica cladding
2. A dopant or dopants are added to give a differential in refractive index between the core and the cladding.[42]
3. The fused silica was made by the flame hydrolysis process as disclosed in Corning's Hyde US Patent 2,272,342 (discussed above).
4. The patent discussed two methods for making doped fused silica optical waveguide fibres: the rod-in-tube method and the inside vapour deposition method using the flame hydrolysis process (which was disclosed in a prior patent, US Patent 3,711,262). The fibre disclosed in the '915 patent used the latter method.

The question of the novelty contained in the '915 patent as distinct from 'prior art' is analysed later in this chapter in a discussion of the court case of *Corning v. Sumitomo Electric*.

Some Improvements

The success of the invention embodied in Corning's '915 patent encouraged greater involvement in optical fibre research in many companies around the world. The threat to its technological lead led Corning to increase further its own research activities, which in turn led to a number of important advances.

One of these advances occurred in connection with the dopants used to raise the refractive index of the core. While titania-doped fibres were used in the '915 patent, it was necessary to treat them at the high temperature of 700°C (in order to prevent TiO_2 from being transformed into Ti_3O_4). The problem, however, was that the heat treatment made the fibre too weak and fragile to use in practical applications.

There were at least two responses to this problem. The first occurred in Sumitomo Electric, which developed a technology in which liquid resin was

---

[41] Ibid. 1550.

[42] While the actual fibre referred to used a titania dopant to raise the refractive index of the core, the New York District Court judgment referred to concluded that 'the concept of the invention is clearly broad enough to include the use of dopants which decrease the index of refraction of silica to achieve the necessary differential between core and cladding. The inventors simply did not know of specific dopants that would decrease the refractive index of fused silica at the time the application was filed.' (*Corning v. Sumitomo Electric*, 1551.)

coated and baked on the fibre immediately after it was drawn and before it came into contact with any solid body. This coating served to protect the fibre against moisture and dust. A second resin coating was then applied which strengthened the fibre against external stresses such as compression, bending, and strain. This complementary technology played an important role in aiding the practical use of optical fibre.

The second response occurred in Corning, where experiments were undertaken on the use of dopants other than titanium. In the late 1960s, Schultz had attempted to use germanium as a dopant for optical fibre but had failed because of the volatilization of the germanium in the high-temperature furnace he was using. From late 1971, however, these efforts were revived in research done by D. L. Bachman and F. W. Voorhees under Schultz's direction. By mid-1972 this search path yielded fruit, with the development of a fibre with a germanium-doped fused silica core which had an attenuation rate of only 4 dB/km. In addition to the low attenuation rate facilitated by the use of germanium, other advantages included the elimination of the heat treatment step, which weakened the fibre, and the production of a higher numerical aperture (i.e. a wider angle of light acceptance). The higher numerical aperture was important because it allowed the use of a light-emitting diode (LED) as the light source. In view of the high cost and unreliability of lasers at the time, this was an important characteristic. On 4 January 1973, R. D. Maurer and P. C. Schultz filed application for a patent titled 'Germania Containing Optical Waveguide' which was issued on 20 May 1975 as Patent 3,884,550.

Advances such as these rapidly helped to improve the performance and cost of optical fibre. Other advances which are discussed in context later include the development of a method for reducing OH (water) impurities in the optical fibre and the use of light sources operating at higher wavelengths, both of which served to lower attenuation rates significantly.[43]

The Fragmentation/Distribution of Existing Knowledge

The elements of knowledge required to produce a practical optical fibre transmission system were identified earlier in this appendix. This knowledge, however, was fragmented and distributed unevenly among different companies. More specifically, it was a glass company that first breached the crucial 20 dB/km barrier, defined by the performance of other alternative technologies.[44]

[43] See Nakahara *et al.*, 'Optical Fiber', and *Corning* v. *Sumitomo Electric*, 1561–2.

[44] Other glass companies possessed many of the same elements of knowledge that Corning had and, with the knowledge disclosed in Corning's patent '915, would fairly easily have been able to produce similar optical fibre. In the event, however, as we shall later see, it was cabling companies, including some with close ties to telephone operating companies, rather than glass companies (with the exception of Corning) that eventually became established in the optical fibre market. The reason was that other glass companies were excluded by the Corning patents, which in all countries apart from Japan effectively protected Corning's position in optical fibre.

However, crucial complementary knowledge was in the possession of the cabling companies. The optical fibre itself had to be coated to increase its strength and to protect it, and bundles of fibre had to be consolidated into a cable. It was cabling companies rather than Corning or other glass companies that possessed the necessary prior knowledge.[45]

In the 1960s, when it was realized that optical waveguides might provide an effective communications transmission medium, several co-operative ventures were established to integrate the relevant knowledge which at the time was fragmented among the different kinds of companies. Thus, the UK Post Office (then in charge of telecommunications) set up a group which included Pilkington (one of the major British glass companies), Barr and Stroud, and British Titan Products. In Japan, acting, as was seen in Chapter 5, on a proposal made by researchers at Tohoku University, Nippon Sheet Glass and the telecommunications and electronics company NEC established a venture to produce a graded index optical fibre, eventually sold under the brand-name SELFOC.

Corning, lacking what has been referred to here as complementary knowledge, had the following options in its efforts to transform its optical fibre knowledge into value:

1. Sell optical fibre to the cabling companies, which would then coat the fibre and make it into cable. Under this option Corning would not be involved in attempting to acquire complementary knowledge.
2. License the cabling companies to use its optical fibre methods. Like the first option, this would not involve the acquisition of complementary knowledge. However, instead of the fibre itself being sold, the knowledge embodied in the fibre would be sold.
3. Establish a joint venture or other kind of partnership with one or more cabling company so that the contracting companies, by combining their distinctive knowledge sets, would be able jointly to reap value.
4. Vertically integrate 'forwards' from glass optical fibre technology into cabling technology. This option, unlike the other three, would involve Corning itself acquiring the complementary cabling technology. Corning had two further suboptions here: internally accumulating the complementary knowledge (for example through the training and/or hiring of staff in the cabling area); or acquiring the complementary knowledge by extending its boundaries through merger or acquisition.

In considering these options, Corning had a further complementary 'asset' to take into account and this was *access to markets*, both in the USA itself and abroad. Unlike many of the other glass-related markets in which it operated, the

---

[45] Although knowledge relating to optical devices such as light sources and detectors also constituted complementary knowledge, it did not present the same problems, since the devices containing the knowledge—such as lasers—could be readily bought in. However, a good deal of cabling-related knowledge was *tacit* and therefore was relatively difficult and costly to transfer between companies.

telecommunications market was relatively closed with national monopolistic telephone operating companies or PTTs acting as monopsonistic purchasers of telecommunications equipment. Furthermore, the PTTs had already developed long-standing and relatively stable relationships with preferred suppliers which included the major cabling companies. In deciding on the best way to transform its knowledge into value, therefore, Corning also had to consider how it might gain access to this particular complementary asset, namely access to relatively closed markets.

In making its decision, Corning could rely on the fact that it had secured a tight 'appropriability regime'[46] in so far as its patent gave it protection which could not readily be undermined by competitors. Therefore it did not have to worry about its knowledge leaking. This meant that Corning could consider options such as licensing and joint ventures without worrying that they might lead to the leakage of knowledge which would eventually enable its licensees and partners to become direct competitors. Despite the tight appropriability regime, however, Corning continued to allocate substantial sums to R&D in order to remain ahead, or at least on the frontiers, thereby ensuring that its current strong technological competitiveness, protected by its patents, would not be undermined by the future technological advance of competitors. Although Corning was the first to breach the crucial 20 dB/km barrier, strongly competitive research continued to be carried out in companies such as AT&T's Bell Laboratories and ITT in the USA, STC and Philips in Europe, and NTT and the major cabling companies in Japan. Indeed, Corning's breakthrough increased the intensity of competition from these quarters.

Transforming Knowledge into Value:
Creating a Market for Optical Fibre

As mentioned, the 20 dB/km barrier was widely accepted as the critical level of performance that optical fibre had to achieve if it was to compete with the alternative transmissions technologies such as copper cable, microwave radio, and satellite. By 1970 attenuation rates lower than this level had been achieved in optical fibre. By mid-1972, 4 dB/km had been attained. In view of the undisputed advantages of optical fibre over the competing alternative technologies, particularly its ability to carry greater quantities of information, Corning expected that a large market for fibre would rapidly develop.

In the event, however, Corning's expectations were seriously frustrated. Although the company had begun research on optical fibre in 1966, as late as 1976 it was selling only around $1 million worth of optical fibre. Only in 1983, seventeen years after research began, would Corning begin to make a profit!

A puzzle is therefore presented by the length of time that it took for optical fibre to be significantly diffused. To put the matter slightly differently,

---

[46] D. Teece, 'Profiting from Innovation', *Research Policy*, 15/6 (1986).

why was the global telecommunications industry locked into a set of older technologies?

The case of optical fibre was different from the phenomenon analysed by Arthur,[47] whereby a technology that is initially inferior establishes superiority by the dynamic improvements that follow from its widespread adoption. To begin with, the alternatives to optical fibre, particularly copper cable, were, at least before 1970, superior; even after 1970, although improvements occurred in the alternative technologies, these improvements were not sufficient to outweigh the advantages of optical fibre. The lock-in that benefited alternative technologies such as copper cable was rather the result of two factors. First, improvements were still needed in the complementary technologies such as optical fibre coating and cabling. The second factor was the sunk costs that had already been incurred by the telephone operating companies that had bought and installed the alternative transmission systems and the cabling companies that had invested in the resources and capabilities to produce them. In view of these sunk costs, although the telephone operators and their cabling suppliers were early entrants into research on optical fibre and indeed, in the case of companies such as the UK Post Office, STC and AT&T, had done pioneering work in this field, they were reluctant to invest rapidly and heavily in the new optical fibre technology. Of these two factors, the second was the more important. As we shall see, even when the problem of complementary technologies for optical fibre had been resolved, the established telephone operators and cabling companies still prevaricated, and it was a new entrant to the telephone operating market, unencumbered by the sunk costs of past investments, that was the first to make a significant commitment to the new technology by investing in a long-distance optical fibre network in 1983.

Indeed, when Corning, having first been alerted to the profitable potential in optical fibre by the UK Post Office, went back to this same company after it had achieved its 1970 breakthrough, it was told that no immediate demand was envisaged for optical fibre for telephone calls. The Post Office's research interest in optical fibres had been motivated by the possibility of establishing a videophone service which required a wider bandwidth than could be provided by copper cables. However, a demand for videophones was not expected before the next century. Corning got the same response from AT&T, which also made it clear that it intended to develop its own optical fibre technology with its supplier Western Electric. Similar approaches to other telephone operators and cablers in other parts of the world met with the same answer. Corning had come up with a solution to the 'transmissions reverse salient' analysed earlier, but having done so had failed to find a market for its product. Having won the battle, it seemed that the war had been lost. This pessimistic view was confirmed by a technology forecast study that Corning commissioned from one of the most

---

[47] W. B. Arthur, 'Competing Technologies: An Overview', in G. Dosi *et al.*, *Technical Change and Economic Theory*, Pinter, London, pp. 590–607.

prestigious consultancy companies in the USA. The demand for optical fibre for telephone systems was unlikely to be significant in the near future.[48]

Corning, however, did not give up. Driven by the vision of some of its senior executives of optical fibre networks meeting the capacity and speed requirements of the 'new information age', the company continued to allocate substantial resources to the new technology despite the poor prospects for short-term rewards. The immediate task that it faced was to create a market for its new technology. In order to do this, in view of the reluctance of the cabling and telephone operating companies spontaneously to develop the complementary technologies necessary to incorporate optical fibres into working optical transmission systems, Corning was impelled to play a more active role in the development of these technologies. In this way, it was hoped that the cabling and operating companies would come to show more interest in optical fibre and indeed might be motivated to do so by the threat of Corning's active promotion of the new technology and therefore its possible emergence as a new competitor.

In the mid-1970s Corning established a pilot cabling plant in order to produce optical fibre cables as sales samples and at the same time to begin learning more about the complementary technologies. In other words, the company began on an experimental basis to pursue the fourth option mentioned above, i.e. to integrate 'forwards' vertically from glass optical fibre technology into cabling technology. However, some three years later this attempt was abandoned, for two possible reasons. The first was the realization of the high costs of acquiring new knowledge which did not overlap with the company's existing knowledge-base. The second stemmed from Corning's need to access telecommunications markets with the assistance of cabling companies which were already firmly established as secure suppliers to the national telephone operating companies.

With the abandonment of the pilot cabling plant, Corning shifted its strategy to the third option, namely establishing a joint venture or other kind of partnership with cabling companies. The first and most important of these was established in 1977, when Corning and the German company Siemens set up a joint venture, Siecor. Other joint ventures included a company set up with BICC in Britain called Optical Fibres, which began production in 1983, and agreements with Pirelli of Italy, Ericsson of Sweden, and the French government in the form of a company called Fibre Optiques Industries. Under these agreements, Corning licensed its optical fibre technologies to the joint venture company while its partners contributed their cabling knowledge as well as their access to domestic markets. The agreements, however, restricted the joint venture companies to domestic or regional markets, and in this way Corning was able to avoid market conflict between its various partners while simultaneously ensuring access to relatively closed national markets.

While Corning was pursuing its joint venture strategy, interest in optical fibre

---

[48] This account of Corning's attempt to create a market for optical fibre draws heavily on Magaziner and Patinkin, *The Silent War*.

transmissions on the part of the telephone operating companies was slowly increasing. In 1976 Japan's Ministry of International Trade and Industry (MITI) announced plans to develop an experimental two-way interactive optical fibre-based information system called Hi-OVIS (Highly Interactive Optical Visual Information System). In 1977 Bell Laboratories and General Telephone in the USA installed prototype optical fibre systems. These and later experimental projects, however, generated only a limited demand for optical fibre, hardly justifying the decision that Corning made in 1978 to build a fully fledged optical fibre factory which came on stream in 1979. As late as 1982, Corning's sales of optical fibre were no more than $10 million a year, and this was due largely to its European joint ventures. Indeed, the company had to wait until 1983 to receive its first substantial commercial order, which was for single mode optical fibre. Significantly, this order came from a new entrant into the telephone operating business rather than one of the established companies. The company was MCI, which after the divestiture of AT&T in 1982 became a long-distance competitor to AT&T. As a new entrant, MCI did not already possess sunk investments in the old copper cable technology. This company's decision to install an optical fibre transmissions system marked an important shift in favour of the new optical fibre technology, and, significantly, from 1983, seventeen years after it began investing in research on optical fibres, Corning began to make its first profits.

The Strengths and Weaknesses of Japanese Information and Communications Companies: A Competence-Based Analysis

The Revisionist Critique of Japanese Information and Communications Companies

Since the crisis that hit IBM in the early 1990s, which coincidentally occurred at the same time as a major downturn in the Japanese economy, conventional wisdom has turned far more bearish regarding the future prospects for the Japanese information and communications (IC) industry. While previously conventional wisdom saw Japanese companies as posing an increasing threat to their Western rivals, now Japanese strength is often seen as confined to the 'commodity' end of the industry.

An example of this new conventional wisdom is one of the better of the popular books analysing the 'post-IBM world', Ferguson and Morris's *Computer Wars: How The West Can Win in a Post-IBM World.* According to these authors,

the computer wars are essentially a two-party contest between the US and Japan. But Japanese *computer* companies are not the primary threat to American firms. . . .The threat comes from Japanese component-makers. . . . While the Japanese control less than a quarter of the computer industry, they make well over half of its components. . . . The Japanese will drive to componentize and commoditize every sector of the industry so their great monolithic and lean manufacturing skills can define the industry's future.[1]

Ferguson and Morris argue that it is this same set of competences—which they refer to as 'commodity implementation'—that underlies Japanese international competitiveness in products such as faxes, liquid crystal displays, laser engines for laser printers, televisions, and memory semiconductors. In the case of faxes, they say:

The strategy for leading the world . . . is straightforward: learn the standard and engineer multiple products that provide a range of features within the single standard; be sure they look nice, are well made, and can be turned out in high volume very cheaply. Then manufacture zillions of them to drive down unit costs and keep price pressure on your competition. Plow your earnings back into improving manufacturing and tinkering with the product's features, so the cost keeps moving down.[2]

---

[1] C. H. Ferguson and C. R. Morris, *Computer Wars: How the West Can Win in a Post-IBM World,* Times Books, New York, 1993, pp. 220–1.　　　　　　　　　　　　[2] Ibid. 114.

However, the competences necessary to succeed in this strategy do not require an ability to develop architectures and standards:

But never challenge, or even enhance, the basic standard; for it is your skill in meeting it that is the secret of your success. This is a good description of the fundamental strategy that has kept Japanese companies on top in so many of the world's manufacturing industries. . . . [This] is precisely the same as the strategy that won [the Japanese] world dominance in television sets. Television standards are set by the government regulatory bodies that allocate airwave frequencies. The prevailing standards, the NTSC standard in the US and Japan, and PAL and SECAM in Europe, were established in the 1940s and 1950s, and the Japanese have been superbly successful in engineering high-quality products that meet them at a very attractive price.[3]

Even supposedly 'high technology' products such as dynamic random access memory semiconductors (DRAMs) fit the same pattern, according to Ferguson and Morris:

[I]n contrast to microprocessors, the basic design of DRAMs has been conserved from generation to generation, and future design directions are clear. Making better DRAMs has been primarily an issue of incremental design, process, and manufacturing improvements to reduce the size of devices and circuits and increase the memory capacity of a chip. For all their staggering challenges, competitive strategy in DRAMs is very much like that in televisions or faxes.[4]

On the basis of this reasoning, Ferguson and Morris conclude that:

Japanese companies . . . have succeeded . . . by being superb *commodity implementers* within well-defined, stable, open, nonproprietary standards. . . . [However] industries that are fast-moving, where standards are constantly evolving, and where the standards themselves are within the proprietary control of an individual company, are hostile environments for commodity implementers.[5]

According to Ferguson and Morris, while the Japanese IC companies have strong competences in commodities and components, they lack the ultimately more important ability (from a profitability point of view) to triumph in 'architectural contests'. The reason is that the competences and forms of organization required for strong competitiveness in commodities and components contradict those required to be good at establishing proprietary architectural standards:

[A]ll the companies . . . who control or are fighting for the control of proprietary architectural standards are American companies. . . . Japanese companies have not been comfortable playing in an architectural arena; *the set of skills developed as the world's best commodity implementers is simply not well adapted to architectural contests.* The only Japanese companies we can identify that have successfully established a proprietary architectural standard comparable to, say, Microsoft's, are Nintendo and Sega.[6]

Since in the 'commodity' area the Japanese face competition not only from Western rivals, but also from countries like Korea and Taiwan, Ferguson and

---

[3] Ibid.   [4] Ibid.   [5] Ibid. 113, 114.   [6] Ibid. 121; emphasis added.

Morris deduce that Japanese companies 'risk being squeezed into an unattractive high-investment, low-return industry, while architectural leaders in other countries reap the "sweet-spot" profits'.[7] On the basis of this conclusion, the authors criticize the policies and strategies of the Japanese computer-producing companies:

[T]he single-minded, thirty-year-long focus on IBM's position in mainframes has left the Japanese industry overcommitted to a commodity manufacturing and a mainframe strategy. Fujitsu and Hitachi are primarily IBM mainframe clone-makers in a shrinking mainframe market, while the other Japanese majors have been sliding into the position of commodity implementers of foreign architectures.[8]

How adequate are these arguments? In order to answer this question more rigorously, Ferguson and Morris's arguments will be distilled into two hypotheses:

HYPOTHESIS 1: The Japanese IC companies have strong competences in commodities and components.

HYPOTHESIS 2: The Japanese IC companies have weak competences in developing proprietary architectural standards.

Evidence for and against the Hypotheses

There is an important element of truth in the Ferguson and Morris arguments. In some areas that are investment-intensive, manufacturing technology-intensive, and incremental-learning-intensive, within clearly defined parameters, Japanese IC companies have performed well internationally. However, it is an 'Americo-centric' view—and one that shows little understanding of these Japanese IC companies—to confine their competences to those that are necessary for success in these areas.

The reason Ferguson and Morris fail to 'see' these competences is that their vision is bounded by the US IC markets. However, this is misleading. It is true that Intel and Microsoft have dominated in the USA in microprocessors and PC software respectively. But this dominance is partly an accident of history, buttressed by both *de jure* and *de facto* proprietary restrictions, in addition to the ingenious efforts made by these two companies. (Earlier in their book Ferguson and Morris show the historical accidents that led IBM to subcontract the microprocessor and operating system for its PC to Intel and Microsoft. It could easily have been other companies that ended up with these contracts that would later prove to be so lucrative.) The dominance of Intel and Microsoft in the US market has limited the room to manoeuvre of companies that also have strong technical competences in the same areas—companies such as IBM, Motorola, and AT&T. The Japanese IC companies have faced the same constraints.

It is incorrect (and ill-informed) to suggest that Japanese IC companies lack

[7] Ibid. 230.   [8] Ibid.

the competences necessary to develop proprietary architectural standards. One example where these competences have been developed (studied in detail in Chapters 4 and 6 above) is NEC's PC 9800 series. This product, based on a proprietary architectural standard, was developed and sold against strong competition in the Japanese market, not only from other Japanese companies, but also from IBM Japan. Another example is Fujitsu and NEC's development of digital time-division telecommunications switches and ATM switches, examined in Chapter 3. Similarly, all the major Japanese computer vendors have developed proprietary information processing systems for their customers in Japan, as stressed in Chapter 4. In the early 1990s, when Fujitsu decided that, owing to the decline in mainframe revenues, there was little to be gained from continuing to pay IBM for access to its software standards, the company was able to terminate its agreement with IBM immediately and turn its attention to developing networks of smaller computers. Clearly, Fujitsu would not have been able to do this without the necessary architectural competences.

These examples underline the competences that Japanese IC companies have accumulated in designing and developing the architectures and applications for complex IC products and systems. However, this book has stressed that these competences have been adapted largely to the needs of the Japanese markets. In some cases—such as proprietary computing systems, central office telecommunications switches, and NEC's PC 9800 series—this adaptation process has resulted in products and systems that have been incompatible with standards and conditions in markets in the USA or Europe. But these products and systems have been profitable for the Japanese IC companies, and more importantly, they have helped these companies to accumulate important technical competences.

It is clear, therefore, that Ferguson and Morris are incorrect to suggest that Japanese IC companies lack the competences to develop proprietary architectural standards. However, the weakness of these companies in many of the principal IC markets *outside Japan*—which was noted in the introduction to this book— does need to be explained. To do this, we require a more sophisticated categorization than the commodity-producer–architectural-standard-setter dual distinction used by Ferguson and Morris.

Puzzles to be Explained

There are two related puzzles that require explanation. Why have Japanese IC companies been so successful globally in products such as memory semiconductors, liquid crystal displays, cordless phones, and faxes? Why have they not been so successful globally (as documented in the introductory chapter to this book) in products such as mainframe computers, workstations, personal computers, and central office telecommunications switches?

In order to explain these puzzles, a tripartite classification of IC products is helpful.

Classification of IC Products

The products produced by Japanese IC companies may be divided into three categories, as shown in Table A3.1. The categories are designed to emphasize the competences that are particularly important in enabling a firm to compete. However, they do not represent watertight distinctions and to some extent they overlap one another. Moreover, the same product may be included in more than one category.

Table A3.1 *Categories of Information Communications (IC) Systems*

Mfg-, technology-, and investment-intensive products	Design- and software-intensive products[a]	Specific-customer-requirement-intensive products
• Memory semiconductors • Semiconductor equipment • Liquid crystal displays • Facsimile • Cordless phones • etc.	• Microprocessors • PCs • Workstations • Microcontrollers • Packaged software • PBXs • Automated fingerprint systems • etc.	• Central office switches • PBXs • Customized computer systems • Integrated IC systems • Application-specific integrated circuits • etc.

[a] Standards and 'complementary assets' may be important.

Category 1: Manufacturing-Technology-Intensive, Investment-Intensive Products. The first category consists of those IC products where manufacturing technological competences and substantial product-specific investments are particularly important determinants of competitiveness. Their importance dominates the other factors which also have a bearing on competitiveness, such as product design and software competences, and marketing and sales networks.

Products in this category include memory semiconductors, liquid crystal displays, faxes, and cordless phones.

Category 2: Design-Intensive, Software-Intensive Products (where Proprietary Architectures and Standards, and Complementary Marketing and Sales 'Assets' may also be Important). In the case of these products, design and software competences are important in determining competitiveness. However, proprietary architectures and standards as well as complementary 'assets' such as marketing and sales networks may also be significant. Other factors, such as manufacturing competences and scale of investment, may also be important, but are not sufficient to give the firm a competitiveness.

Products in the second category include personal computers, microprocessors, microcontrollers, and packaged software.

Category 3: Specific-Customer-Requirement-Intensive Products and Systems.
Competitiveness in these products depends crucially on the ability of a firm to
cater for the customer's specific requirements. Although other factors may also
influence competitiveness—e.g. product and process development competences,
software competences, scale of investment, and marketing and sales assets—it
is the ability to meet the specific needs of particular customers that is the main
determinant of competitiveness. There are usually high costs involved in adapting
these products and systems for other customer segments. For example, as shown
in Chapter 3, by 1986 ITT spent about $200 million in order to adapt its 'brilliant'
digital central office switch, developed mainly in Europe, for use in the USA.

Apart from central office telecommunications switches, this category also
includes private branch exchanges (PBXs), customized information-processing
systems, integrated computer and communications systems, and application-
specific integrated circuits (ASICs).

International Competitiveness of Japanese Companies in the Three Categories of IC Products

Category 1. Japanese IC companies have tended to be relatively successful
internationally in these products. An example is dynamic random access memory
semiconductors (DRAMs) used in products such as computers. DRAMs are
both manufacturing-competence-intensive and investment-intensive products.
Fig. A3.1 shows the increase in investment in R&D and facilities required to
produce integrated circuits with circuit widths of 1.5 microns in 1984 to 0.35
microns in 1994.

Japanese IC companies with strengths in semiconductors have been successful

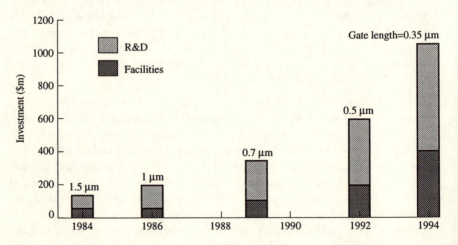

Fig. A3.1 Investment in research and development and facilities for LSIs

in designing the plant and equipment needed to produce new generations of increasingly integrated chips. Equally important, they have also been able to produce continuous post-investment incremental innovations which have resulted in increased productivity, quality, and profitability. One example is NEC, the largest Japanese semiconductor company, which has developed three key semiconductor plants in Kyushu, Japan, Livingstone, Scotland, and Roseville, California. New plant and process innovation is first introduced into the Kyushu plant and then transferred to Scotland and California. Important incremental innovations occurring in any of the plants are transferred to the others.

Category 2. Contrary to what is suggested by Ferguson and Morris, Japanese IC firms certainly have the competences necessary for products in this category. As noted, one example is NEC's PC 9800 series, which at the time of writing still has over 50 per cent of the Japanese PC market. Depending on NEC's proprietary architecture, this product is both design- and software-intensive. NEC not only had to develop the operating system software for the PC as well as the microprocessor, but also had to organize the important applications software that was produced largely by independent software companies. Moreover, in order to dominate the Japanese market, NEC needed strong complementary marketing and sales 'assets', as was shown.

In terms of the design and software competences required for its success, the PC 9800 series had a good deal in common with the games developed and sold by Nintendo and Sega. But NEC competences go significantly further than those of the latter two companies, including as they do the competences necessary for designing, developing, and producing the devices and components in the product as well as the competences to network the PC to broader IC systems.

However, unlike the games of Nintendo and Sega, NEC's PC 9800 series could not be sold in the USA. The reason had nothing to do with technical competences as such, but rather with *de facto* standards. While Nintendo and later Sega were able to create the *de facto* standards for games in Japan as well as the USA, in the case of PCs the standard was fundamentally different in the two countries. In the USA, as a result of IBM's size and reputation in computers, it was inevitable that the company would come to dominate the market for PCs when it finally entered. The *de facto* standard became that of IBM, Intel, and Microsoft (since IBM contracted out the microprocessor and operating system of its PC to Intel and Microsoft). NEC's PC 9800, on the other hand, designed for the Japanese market and to be compatible with NEC's other proprietary computing systems which it sold in this market, could not be sold in the USA. However, although NEC developed an IBM-compatible series of PCs (including notebook computers) for the US market, it did not possess the distinctive competences that would give it a competitive edge over its US rivals. Accordingly, although it supplies notebook computers on an OEM basis to companies such as AT&T/NCR, NEC has so far failed to make major headway in PCs in the USA against companies like Apple, Compaq, and Dell.

Category 3. Japanese IC companies also have the technical competences necessary to develop and produce products in this category. Examples include the central office switches produced by NEC, Fujitsu, and Hitachi; the proprietary computing systems (including customized software) produced by Fujitsu, Hitachi, and NEC; integrated information processing systems for use in applications such as interbank transactions, and airline reservations produced by companies such as NTT Data, Fujitsu, NEC, and Hitachi.

In these cases, however, the obstacle to exporting the system to the USA and Europe comes from customer specificity rather than from industry-wide *de facto* or *de jure* standards. In turn, this implies that there are large costs necessary to modify the system for other customer market segments.

A good example is the central office switches analysed in detail in Chapter 3. While the constraints imposed by customer-specific requirements limited the success of NEC and Fujitsu in the US market, the same constraints restrict the ability of AT&T and Northern Telecom—the companies that dominate the US market—to sell their switches in Europe.

The Case of Private Branch Exchanges (PBXs)

PBXs are an example of a system with features of both categories 2 and 3. They provide an illustration of the difficulties that Japanese IC companies have had in winning the same 'strong' market position in the USA that their Japanese counterparts in motor vehicles and consumer electronics have established (as documented in Chapter 1).

Table A3.2 provides a breakdown of Japan's imports and exports of telecommunications equipment in 1991.[9] As the table shows, Japan's exports of telecommunications equipment are dominated by terminal equipment. In the case of exports to the USA, the largest market outside Japan, exports of terminal equipment amounted to 89 per cent of total telecommunications equipment exports, while exports of network equipment came to only 11 per cent. The largest single product category was facsimile, which accounted for 61 per cent of total telecommunications equipment exports. Telephones came to 27 per cent. Exports to the USA of both central office switches and PBXs accounted for only 0.5 per cent of the total. Underlining the lack of Japan's international compe-titiveness in these products, imports from the USA of central office switches and PBXs were seventeen times as large as exports from Japan to the USA. These two product areas constituted about half of the total telecommunications equipment imports into Japan from the USA.

Facsimiles and telephones fall into category 1 in the classification proposed here, while PBXs fall between categories 2 and 3. Furthermore, faxes and phones are dominated not by Japanese IC companies (such as NEC, Fujitsu, Hitachi,

---

[9] I here record my appreciation to Dataquest Japan for the data given to me, including that on PBXs.

Table A3.2 *Japan's Imports and Exports of Telecommunications Equipment, 1991 (¥bn)*

	Exported to			
	North America	Europe	Others	Total
Telephone	51,088	26,239	39,318	116,645
Facsimile	113,571	103,298	52,034	268,903
Terminal equipment	164,659	129,537	91,352	385,548
COS/PBX[a]	993	2,339	53,019	56,351
KTS[b]	152	2,005	6,023	8,180
Tx[c]	20,542	3,649	18,497	42,688
Network equipment	21,687	7,993	77,539	107,219
Total	186,346	137,530	168,891	492,767
	Imported from			
	North America	Europe	Others	Total
Telephone	793	46	11,953	12,792
Facsimile			0	
Terminal equipment	793	46	11,953	12,792
COS/PBX[a]	17,578	251	1,349	19,178
KTS[b]			0	
Tx[c]	16,169	1,181	1,345	18,695
Network equipment	33,747	1,432	2,694	37,873
Total	34,540	1,478	14,647	50,665

[a] COS = central office switches; PBX = private branch exchanges.
[b] KTS = Key telephone systems.
[c] Tx= Transmission equipment.

Source: Ministry of Finance, *Dataquest* (December 1993).

and Toshiba), but by Japanese consumer electronics companies. In 1992, for example, according to *Nikkei* data, 16.2 per cent of the Japanese fax market was held by Matsushita, 16.1 per cent by Ricoh, 16.0 per cent by Canon, 11.2 per cent by Sharp, and 10.0 per cent by NEC. In the case of the Japanese cordless telephone market, 22.0 per cent was held by Sharp, 20.5 per cent by Sanyo, and 8.0 per cent by Sony. NTT—supplied by NEC, Fujitsu, and Hitachi—held 16.0 per cent. The Japanese consumer electronics companies were able to mobilize their competences in mass-producing high-quality and relatively low-cost products (competences originally accumulated through the production of products such as radios, TVs, and videos) for use in the production of faxes and telephones. Moreover, they were able to use their competences to market and sell these products in the USA, where they already had strong networks.

How does the case of PBXs differ? Tables A3.3 and A3.4 provide data on market share in the Japanese and US PBX markets. As shown in Table A3.3, the Japanese market for PBXs was dominated by the four Japanese telecoms equipment companies—NEC, Fujitsu, Hitachi, and Oki—with Toshiba also holding a significant share and coming fifth. In the USA, however, as can be seen in Table A3.4, Japanese companies were dominated by Western companies. While AT&T and Northern Telecom held the largest share of the US market (they held an even larger share of the US central office switch market, as shown in Chapter 3), Siemens, through its acquisition of the US company Rolm, was third; NEC, Fujitsu, Hitachi, and Toshiba *combined* held a smaller share than Siemens alone.

Table A3.3 *The Japanese PBX Market, 1990–1992*

	1990		1991		1992	
	Revenue (¥bn)	Share (%)	Revenue (¥bn)	Share (%)	Revenue (¥bn)	Share (%)
NEC	18.6	30.0	19.5	30.9	18.0	31.0
Fujitsu	17.4	28.0	18.3	29.0	16.8	28.9
Hitachi	10.6	17.1	10.1	16.0	9.0	15.5
Oki	8.1	13.0	7.6	12.0	6.7	11.5
Toshiba	4.3	6.9	4.4	7.0	4.1	7.1
Others	3.1	5.0	3.2	5.1	3.5	6.0
Total	62.1	100.0	63.1	100.0	58.1	100.0

Source: *Dataquest* Estimates (December 1993).

Why have these Japanese IC companies not achieved the same strong position as their Japanese counterparts in cars, televisions, videos, faxes, and telephones? The answer rests on the characteristics of products in categories 2 and 3 as defined above. Part of this answer is provided in Fig. 9.2 in Chapter 9, which gives a breakdown of customers' valuations of the key characteristics associated with PBXs.[10] The figure underlines the point that competences refer to activities and knowledge relating to the *entire* value chain, and not only to technical competences. As can be seen, technical competences relate primarily to product quality and price. These characteristics were rated first and sixth in the list of six characteristics seen as important by major users of PBXs; the other four characteristics had little to do with technology *per se*. And these four character-istics were very important, according to the users. After-sale service was almost as important as product quality (scoring 105.85 as opposed to 107.03). Sales (including information provided in selling the product), commitment to the customer, and training documentation scored 102.93, 101.13, and 93.42

[10] The data provided here come from a Dataquest survey based on a sample of 2,000 PBX users in the USA. The users were asked about their satisfaction with their PBX systems in six areas: quality, service provided, vendor's commitment to the customer, performance of the sales representatives, documentation and training provided with the PBX, and value for the price of the PBX.

respectively. Significantly, price was seen as being least important, with a score of only 90.45.

Figure A3.2 shows how the Japanese companies NEC and Fujitsu stacked up against the market leaders—AT&T and Northern Telecom—in providing the customers with these characteristics. The figure provides an 'intermediate' explanation for the market share figures given in Table A3.4, at least as far as these four companies are concerned. It shows that, according to the sample of users, NEC and Fujitsu were generally unable to provide the same characteristics

Table A3.4 *The US PBX Market, 1991 and 1992 (thousands of lines)*

	1991	1992	% change, 1991–1992	1991 market share (%)	1992 market share (%)
AT&T	1,323.2	1,292.1	− 2.4	27.9	28.1
Northern Telecom	1,099.4	1,225.1	11.4	23.2	26.6
ROLM/Siemens	873.6	710.2	− 18.7	18.4	15.4
NEC	296.6	298.9	0.8	6.3	6.5
Mitel	265.0	245.0	− 7.5	5.6	5.3
Fujitsu	160.0	168.9	5.6	3.4	3.7
InteCom	113.0	108.0	− 4.4	2.4	2.3
Hitachi	100.0	90.0	− 10.0	2.1	2.0
Toshiba	85.5	80.0	− 6.4	1.8	1.7
Others	420.5	385.5	− 8.3	8.9	8.4
Total	4,736.8	4,603.7	− 2.8	100.0	100.0

Source: Dataquest (June 1993).

as AT&T and Northern Telecom. Overall, Fujitsu slightly outperformed NEC, with a score of 96.64 as opposed to 96.32. However, they were both significantly outperformed by AT&T (with 102.15) and Northern Telecom (with 100.63).

However, performance on individual characteristics differed between Fujitsu and NEC. In terms of both quality and service, NEC (with scores of 106.10 and 104.63 respectively) outperformed Fujitsu (with 97.70 and 98.84). But in both these characteristics the Japanese companies lagged behind the industrial average score.

Wider Implications of the PBX Example

More difficult is the task of providing the 'ultimate' explanation for these scores. In the absence of the large amount of additional information that would be necessary for an uncontested explanation, the following may be suggested as a reasonable hypothesis.

The Japanese companies do not lack the technical competences that are needed to be competitive in PBXs. If they did, they would not be able to dominate the Japanese market; their customers, despite long-term obligational relationships

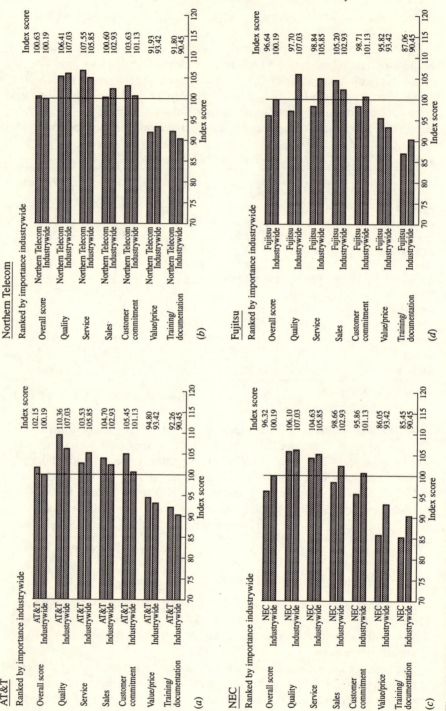

Fig. A3.2 Customers' valuations of PBX characteristics in the US market, 1992

Source: Dataquest.

with their suppliers, would soon turn to foreign companies if their Japanese suppliers lacked the necessary competences. The relatively weak performance in the USA is rather a reflection of two sets of factors: the need to adapt PBXs to the circumstances of both individual customers and the US telecommunications network, and the relatively weak 'distribution assets' possessed by these Japanese companies in the USA. Both these factors result from the emphasis that the Japanese IC companies have given to the Japanese market, a relative emphasis (as evident from foreign sales ratios provided in Chapter 1) that is far greater than that given by the Japanese motor vehicle and consumer electronics companies.

How might Japanese IC companies perform in the future in category 2 and 3 products such as PBXs? Two further factors are crucial. The first is the increasing globalization of Japanese IC companies. If these companies are able to increase their global presence in overseas markets—and correspondingly to reduce their focus (in some cases fixation) on the Japanese market—they may be able to win a greater share of the overseas markets. Particularly important in these two product categories are 'distribution assets' such as marketing, sales, and after-sale service competences, and the ability to tailor products and systems to national and specific customer requirements. As data show—e.g. the PBX survey figures given here and the foreign sales ratios—the Japanese IC companies still have some way to go in this regard.

Secondly, Japanese IC companies have a potential strength in the broad set of complementary competences which they possess, ranging from electronic devices through sub-systems to entire integrated computer and communications systems. While the figures just referred to indicate that the Japanese IC companies have not yet been able to realize this potential in the form of significant international competitiveness in many products in categories 2 and 3, in the future, with a greater global presence, they may be able to get greater leverage from their set of synergistic competences. This point is dealt with in more detail in Chapter 9.

APPENDIX 4

The Financial Performance of Japanese and Western IC Companies

Tables A4.1–A4.5 provide some indicators of financial performance for the selected sample of Japanese and Western companies used for comparative purposes in this book.

Table A4.1 *Profitability of Selected Western IT Companies, 1993*

	Market value (US$m)	Net sales (US$m)	Profits (US$m)	Profits/sales ratio	Return on equity
IBM	30,143	64,523	– 6,865		– 28.2
DEC		13,931	– 2,078		
Intel	23,205	5,844	1,067	0.1826	25.3
Motorola	21,416	13,303	576	0.0433	12.7
Northern Telecom	8,960	8,409	548	0.0652	12.9
Ericsson	9,283	6,535	67	0.0103	2.9
Siemens	21,328	49,346	1,128	0.0229	12.8
Alcatel Alsthom	16,328	30,085	1,312	0.0436	14.1
GE	79,341	57,073	4,305	0.0754	18.9
Philips	4,819	32,788	168	0.0051	2.0

Table A4.2 *Profitability of Selected Japanese IT Companies, 1993*

	Market value (US$m)	Net sales (US$m)	Profits (US$m)	Profits/sales ratio	Return on equity
NEC	14,370	32,764	422	0.0129	5.1
Fujitsu	12,780	32,297	– 304		– 2.8
Hitachi	25,842	70,382	719	0.0102	2.6
Toshiba	21,738	43,219	192	0.0044	1.7
Matsushita	25,031	65,901	355	0.0054	1.1
Sony	15,640	37,244	336	0.0090	2.5
Canon	10,116	17,866	335	0.0188	4.9

Table A4.3 *Average Profitability of Selected Western and Japanese IT Companies, 1993*

	Market value (US$m)	Net sales (US$m)	Profits (US$m)	Profits/sales ratio	Return on equity
Mean, Western firms	23,869.22	28,183.70	22.80	0.0561	8.16
Mean, Japanese firms	17,931.00	42,810.43	293.57	0.0101	2.16

How does the profitability of the Japanese and Western companies compare? The tables provide striking evidence of the significantly higher profitability of Western IC companies. While the mean ratio of profits to sales for the Western IC companies was 0.0561, the ratio for the Japanese companies was 0.0101. Similarly, while the return on equity for Western IC companies was 8.16 per cent, the figure for the Japanese companies was 2.16 per cent.

Further indicators of financial performance are provided in Tables A4.4 and A4.5 for 1994. These tables show that, while the mean return on equity for the Western companies was 14.14 per cent, the figure for the Japanese IC companies (NEC, Hitachi, and Toshiba) was just 1.3 per cent, while for the Japanese consumer electronics companies (Matsushita, Sony, and Canon) the figure was 1.6 per cent. While the yield for the Western companies was 1.5 per cent, that for the Japanese IC companies (including Fujitsu) was 0.9 per cent and for the Japanese consumer electronics companies, 0.7 per cent.

The relatively low profitability of the Japanese companies, however, was to some extent counterbalanced by a significantly higher price–earnings (P/E) ratio for these companies. While the P/E ratio for the Japanese IC companies was 188 and that for the Japanese consumer electronics companies was 125, for the Western companies it was only 18.

Why are the Japanese companies so much less profitable than their Western counterparts? One reason is that Japanese companies have tended to sacrifice profitability for greater market share and greater long-term growth in sales. This has been achieved through lower price and/or higher quality of their products, all other things equal, than their Western counterparts. It may be hypothesized, in turn, that this is partly a reflection of the importance of lifetime employment in the Japanese companies. The lifetime employment system implies that a greater weighting is given to long-term employment security relative to shareholder return in Japanese compared with Western companies.[1]

The data also imply that the performance of Japanese and Western companies cannot be compared validly through indicators that involve stock market values. The differences in institutional practice between the Tokyo stock market and its Western equivalents, as evident in the different rates of return on equity and P/E ratios on these markets, mean that variables such as these do not provide an adequate indication of 'real' performance differences. Furthermore, company stock prices in a particular stock market are also influenced by macroeconomic magnitudes such as capital flows and interest and exchange rate differentials. This further invalidates any attempt to compare the performance of Japanese and Western companies through stock-price-related variables.

---

[1] This reasoning is corroborated in H. Odagiri, 'Unravelling the Mystery of Low Japanese Profit Rates', *Business Strategy Review* (Summer 1990), and in E. Davis, S. Flanders, and J. Star, 'Who Are the World's Most Successful Companies?' *Business Strategy Review* (Summer 1991).

Table A4.4 *Financial Performance of Selected Western IT Companies, 1994*

	Net sales ($m)	Market value[a] ($m)	Yield[b] (%)	Return on equity[c] (%)	Price/book value ratio[d]	Price/earnings ratio	Net sales/ market value
IBM	62,716	36,673	1.6	negative	2.0	loss	1.71
DEC	14,371	2,976	0.0	negative	0.6	loss	4.83
Intel	8,782	26,125	0.4	29.9	3.5	12	0.34
Motorola	16,963	26,049	0.6	16.9	4.1	24	0.65
Northern Telecom	8,148	7,820	1.2	2.3	2.6	111	1.04
Ericsson	8,078	10,644	1.2	14.8	3.9	26	0.76
Siemens	49,664	23,500	2.7	11.7	2.1	18	2.11
Alcatel Alsthom	27,817	15,598	3.7	12.2	1.5	12	1.78
GE	60,562	84,938	2.9	17.1	3.3	19	0.71
Philips	31,918	9,130	1.0	8.2	1.4	17	3.50
AVERAGE	28,902	24,345	1.5	14.14[e]	2.5	18[f]	1.74

[a] Share price on 31 May 1994 × latest available number of shares outstanding.
[b] Latest 12 months' dividends per share as % of May 1994 share price.
[c] Latest 12 months' earnings per share as % of net worth per share or common shareholders' equity investment.
[d] Ratio of May price to net worth per share or common shareholders' equity investment.
[e] Excludes IBM and DEC.
[f] Excludes IBM, DEC, and Northern Telecom.

Source: calculated from *Business Week.*

Table A4.5 *Financial Performance of Selected Japanese IT Companies, 1994*[a]

	Net sales ($m)	Market value ($m)	Yield (%)	Return on equity (%)	Price/book value ratio	Price/earnings ratio	Net sales/ market value
NEC	34,208	17,515	0.8	0.8	2.3	277	1.95
Fujitsu	29,997	19,093	0.7	negative	1.8	loss	1.57
Hitachi	70,710	33,866	1.0	2.0	1.2	62	2.09
Toshiba	44,241	25,950	1.2	1.1	2.4	224	1.71
AVERAGE	44,789	24,106	0.9	1.3[b]	1.9	188[c]	1.83
Matsushita	63,255	36,647	0.7	0.7	1.1	157	1.73
Sony	35,641	22,212	0.8	1.2	1.7	152	1.61
Canon	17,545	13,281	0.7	2.9	1.9	66	1.32
AVERAGE	38,814	24,047	0.7	1.6	1.6	125	1.55

[a] Definitions: see Table A4.4.
[b] Excludes Fujitsu.
[c] Excludes Fujitsu.

Source: calculated from *Business Week.*

APPENDIX 5

The Performances of NTT, AT&T, and BT Compared

How does the profitability of these three companies compare? In Table A5.1 the data provided show that NTT is by far the largest company measured by market valuation. Indeed, NTT is the largest company in the world in terms of market valuation. However, the picture is very different in terms of sales, with AT&T slightly larger than NTT and both these companies about three times as large as BT. In terms of profitability measured by the profits–sales ratio, BT comes out on top, and its P/E ratio is more than three times that of NTT. In terms of return on equity it is AT&T that does best, with both AT&T and BT performing significantly better than NTT.

Table A5.1 *Profitability of BT, AT&T, and NTT, 1993*

	BT	AT&T	NTT
Market value (US$m)	40,701	82,400	140,521
Sales (US$m)	20,674	64,900	59,741
Profits (US$m)	1,952	3,850	1,783
Profits/sales ratio	0.0944	0.0593	0.0299
Return on equity	10.4	21.0	4.5

Further data on financial performance, this time for 1994, are given in Table A5.2. Most importantly, this table shows the huge price–earnings ratio of NTT compared with the two other companies. As shown in Appendix 4, this P/E ratio differential is typical of Japanese and Western companies generally.

Table A5.2 *Financial Performance of Selected Telecommunications Carriers, 1994*[a]

	NTT	AT&T	BT
Net sales ($m)	63,542	67,200	20,657
Market value ($m)	128,938	73,875	33,893
Yield (%)	0.6	2.4	5.8
Return on equity (%)	3.5[b]	31.8	14.4
Price/book value ratio	3.2	5.3	1.8
Price/earnings ratio	270	17	13
Net sales/market value	0.49	0.91	0.61

[a] Definitions: see Table A4.4.
[b] NTT Annual Report, 1993, p. 25.

Source: calculated from *Business Week*.

Table A5.3 provides data on technological performance for the three companies. As can be seen, the companies differ significantly in terms of their R&D intensity (R&D–sales ratio). The reason for this difference is analysed in Chapter 7.[1] In 1992 AT&T had by far the largest number of patents in the USA, and also performed best in terms of patents per unit of sales. However, in terms of current impact index (how often the company's patents is cited in other patents), it was NTT that did best. The 'technological strength' of AT&T (number of patents multiplied by current impact index) was by far the greatest, a reflection of the large number of patents which this company had in the USA; BT scored highest, however, in terms of the 'science linkage' indicator (number of references per patent to scientific journals). In terms of the patent–R&D ratio, a measure of R&D productivity, it was AT&T that did best, followed by BT. NTT came a long way behind according to this measure. However, as noted, this figure refers to patents in the USA and thus is not an adequate indicator of the overall R&D productivity of BT and NTT, which still are primarily domestically oriented carriers, particularly NTT.

Table A5.3 *R&D Performance of BT, AT&T, and NTT, 1992*

	BT	AT&T	NTT
R&D (US$m)	416	2,911	2,157
R&D/sales (%)	± 2.0[a]	± 7.0[a]	± 4.0[a]
Number of patents[b] (1992)	60	528	71
Patents/sales	0.29	0.81	0.12
Current impact index	1.34	1.81	2.05
Technology strength	80	955	145
Science linkage	3.02	1.57	1.23
Patents/R&D	14.42	18.14	3.29

[a] Author's estimate (see text).
[b] Patents in the USA.

[1] AT&T's ratio in Table A4.3 is higher than that in the published statistics. The reason is that AT&T's sales figure includes charges that have to be paid to the Bell regional holding companies for access to their local networks. It is my understanding that, if allowance is made for this, AT&T's 'real' R&D intensity amounts to around 7%.

APPENDIX 6

International Competitiveness:
NEC and Ericsson

In Table A6.1 data are provided on the sale of digital telecommunications switches by NEC and Ericsson in various global markets. These data provide an indication of the relative competitiveness of these two companies. See Chapter 3 for further relevant details.

Table A6.1 *Digital Switches Sold by NEC and Ericsson, 1990*

	NEC (NEAX-61)			Ericsson (AXE)		
	No. of exchanges	Local	Transit	No. of exchanges	Local	Transit
Asia/Oceania						
Australia	1	0	480	235	1,424,000	205,973
Bangladesh	5	0	8,200	—	—	—
Brunei	2	8,000	660	—	—	—
China	82	679,896	41,754	31	253,952	79,729
Cook Islands	1	2,000	0	—	—	—
Fiji	—	—	—	5	14,000	540
Hong Kong	7	83,660	810	2	0	38,912
India	99	58,988	0	—	—	—
Japan	10	5,700	5,684	—	—	—
Korea, Republic of	—	—	—	99	1,216,320	242,688
Macau	—	—	—	2	61,440	0
Malaysia	270	1,051,528	82,230	56	779,384	53,248
Maldives	1	10,000	0	—	—	—
Myanmar	4	12,800	0	—	—	—
New Zealand	213	890,008	395,660	—	—	—
Pakistan	1	0	0	3	30,000	3,072
Philippines	16	21,385	2,680	—	—	—
Singapore	7	171,000	67	—	—	—
Solomon Islands	4	3,000	0	—	—	—
Sri Lanka	16	18,996	7,949	—	—	—
Thailand	115	814,416	165,770	30	220,160	22,050
Tonga	—	—	—	5	2,304	314
Subtotal	854	3,831,377	711,944	468	4,001,560	646,526

Table A6.1 (cont.)

	NEC (NEAX-61)			Ericsson (AXE)		
	No. of exchanges	Local	Transit	No. of exchanges	Local	Transit
Europe/Middle East/Africa						
Algeria	—	—	—	9	73,472	57,856
Bahrain	1	2,000	112	4	48,384	26,000
Botswana	—	—	—	5	24,192	2,048
Cyprus	—	—	—	9	80,768	7,580
Denmark	54	114,000	7,033	98	635,408	337,472
Egypt	—	—	—	4	5,120	27,030
Ethiopia	—	—	—	13	58,088	7,872
Faroe Islands	—	—	—	1	14,592	2,560
Finland	—	—	—	48	261,324	166,144
France	—	—	—	70	913,571	0
Greece	2	40,000	60	2	0	15,513
Hungary	—	—	—	1	0	6,739
Iceland	—	—	—	9	38,656	2,048
Iran	2	12,620	0	—	—	—
Iraq	89	88,000	0	—	—	—
Ireland	—	—	—	20	279,040	66,644
Italy	—	—	—	92	1,348,736	137,760
Jordan	1	2,000	0	—	—	—
Kenya	—	—	—	1	0	1,024
Kuwait	2	25,000	57	20	358,144	46,092
Lebanon	—	—	—	1	0	6,656
Lesotho	—	—	—	9	14,592	4,608
Liberia	—	—	—	2	0	3,584

Country						
Libya	2	13,000	0	—	—	0
Malawi	—	—	—	1	4,096	0
Mauritius	—	—	—	—	—	—
Morocco	—	—	—	10	70,016	10,240
Mozambique	—	—	—	1	0	1,855
Netherlands	5	90,000	398	111	919,936	297,106
Norway	1	25,000	0	3	22,528	27,136
Oman	—	—	—	6	26,652	0
Poland	1	0	124	—	—	—
Portugal	1	0	0	—	—	—
Saudi Arabia	—	—	—	66	513,100	185,460
Seychelles	—	—	—	1	4,232	0
Spain	—	—	—	102	1,174,222	487,424
Sweden	—	—	—	122	2,174,678	235,884
Switzerland	—	—	—	58	275,096	87,648
Syrian Arab	3	100,000	0	—	—	—
Tunisia	2	3,000	0	13	119,808	10,742
Turkey	1	0	32	—	—	—
United Arab Emirates	1	5,908	627	15	146,048	29,184
United Kingdom	1	35,000	90	104	1,890,110	270,336
Yemen Arab Republic	1	0	0	—	—	—
Yugoslavia	—	—	—	52	298,496	76,631
Zambia	1	10,000	2,367	1	0	1,024
Zimbabwe	—	—	—	1	0	3,072
Subtotal	172	565,528	10,900	1,085	11,793,105	2,648,972
North and Latin America						
Antigua	1	0	0	—	—	—
Antilles (Neth.)	—	—	—	1	16,000	0
Argentina	37	193,161	144,971	7	50,560	18,432
Barbados	1	0	0	—	—	—

Table A6.1 (*cont.*)

	NEC (NEAX-61)			Ericsson (AXE)		
	No. of exchanges	Local	Transit	No. of exchanges	Local	Transit
Bermuda	1	0	0	—	—	—
Brazil	17	76,413	55,042	84	780,816	180,960
Cayman Islands	—	—	—	1	7,552	690
Chile	12	102,080	16,281	2	12,416	4,864
Colombia	97	105,565	23,162	43	426,136	88,968
Costa Rica	—	—	—	2	0	20,000
Ecuador	11	63,500	19,292	10	73,000	23,174
El Salvador	—	—	—	7	58,112	7,000
Guatemala	—	—	—	5	76,160	21,566
Guyana	2	0	223	—	—	—
Honduras	—	—	—	1	15,680	3,387
Jamaica	4	10,300	2,111	1	0	1,534
Mexico	—	—	—	144	781,632	641,824
Panama	6	37,500	2,500	9	71,608	3,460
Paraguay	1	0	0	—	—	—
Peru	18	150,000	8,396	—	—	—
Puerto Rico	36	271,690	96	—	—	—
Trinidad and Tobago	—	—	—	1	0	1,424
Uruguay	—	—	—	9	189,056	8,704
USA	142	617,296	440,283	32	111,085	72,654
Venezuela	10	44,000	4,000	20	105,070	21,600
Subtotal	396	1,671,505	716,357	379	2,774,883	1,120,241
TOTAL	1,422	6,068,410	1,439,201	1,932	18,569,548	4,415,739

APPENDIX 7

Market Share in Various Japanese IC Markets

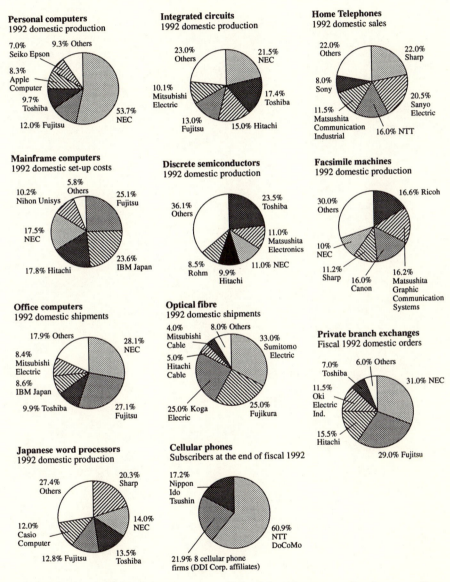

Personal computers
1992 domestic production

9.3% Others
7.0% Seiko Epson
8.3% Apple Computer
9.7% Toshiba
12.0% Fujitsu
53.7% NEC

Integrated circuits
1992 domestic production

23.0% Others
21.5% NEC
10.1% Mitsubishi Electric
17.4% Toshiba
13.0% Fujitsu
15.0% Hitachi

Home Telephones
1992 domestic sales

22.0% Others
22.0% Sharp
8.0% Sony
20.5% Sanyo Electric
11.5% Matsushita Communication Industrial
16.0% NTT

Mainframe computers
1992 domestic set-up costs

5.8% Others
10.2% Nihon Unisys
25.1% Fujitsu
17.5% NEC
23.6% IBM Japan
17.8% Hitachi

Discrete semiconductors
1992 domestic production

36.1% Others
23.5% Toshiba
11.0% Matsushita Electronics
11.0% NEC
8.5% Rohm
9.9% Hitachi

Facsimile machines
1992 domestic production

16.6% Ricoh
30.0% Others
10% NEC
11.2% Sharp
16.0% Canon
16.2% Matsushita Graphic Communication Systems

Office computers
1992 domestic shipments

17.9% Others
28.1% NEC
8.4% Mitsubishi Electric
8.6% IBM Japan
9.9% Toshiba
27.1% Fujitsu

Optical fibre
1992 domestic shipments

4.0% Mitsubishi Cable
8.0% Others
33.0% Sumitomo Electric
5.0% Hitachi Cable
25.0% Koga Elecric
25.0% Fujikura

Private branch exchanges
Fiscal 1992 domestic orders

7.0% Toshiba
6.0% Others
11.5% Oki Electric Ind.
31.0% NEC
15.5% Hitachi
29.0% Fujitsu

Japanese word processors
1992 domestic production

27.4% Others
20.3% Sharp
12.0% Casio Computer
14.0% NEC
12.8% Fujitsu
13.5% Toshiba

Cellular phones
Subscribers at the end of fiscal 1992

17.2% Nippon Ido Tsushin
60.9% NTT DoCoMo
21.9% 8 cellular phone firms (DDI Corp. affiliates)

Fig. A7.1 Who's who in Japan's markets: financial performances, fiscal year ending March 1993.

Source: *Nikkei*, 2 August 1993.

BIBLIOGRAPHY

Abegglen, J. C. and Stalk, G., 1985, *Kaisha: The Japanese Corporation*, Basic Books, New York.

Amsden, A. H., 1989, *Asia's Next Giant: South Korea and Late Industrialization*, Oxford University Press, New York.

Anchordoguy, M., 1989, *Computers Inc.: Japan's Challenge to IBM*, Harvard University Press, Cambridge, Mass.

Antonelli, C., 1994, *The Economics of Localized Technological Change and Industrial Dynamics*, Kluwer Academic, Boston.

Aoki, M. (ed.), 1984, *The Economic Analysis of the Japanese Firm*, North-Holland, Amsterdam.

——1988, *Information, Incentives, and Bargaining in the Japanese Economy*, Cambridge University Press, Cambridge.

——1990*a*, 'The Participatory Generation of Information Rents and the Theory of the Firm', in Aoki, Gustafsson, and Williamson (eds.), *The Firm as a Nexus of Treaties*.

——1990*b*, 'Toward an Economic Model of the Japanese Firm', *Journal of Economic Literature*, 28: 1–27.

——1992, 'The Japanese Firm as a System of Attributes: A Survey and Research Agenda', paper presented to the conference on 'Japan in a Global Economy: A European Perspective', Stockholm School of Economics, 1991.

—— and Dore, R. (eds.), 1994, *The Japanese Firm: The Sources of Competitive Strength*, Oxford University Press, New York.

—— Gustafsson, B., and Williamson, O. (eds.), 1990, *The Firm as a Nexus of Treaties*, Sage, London.

—— and Patrick, H. (eds.), 1994, *The Japanese Main Bank System: Its Relevance for Developing and Transforming Economies*, Oxford University Press, New York.

Arrison, T. S., Bergsten, C. F., Graham, E. M., and Caldwell-Harris, M., 1992, *Japan's Growing Technological Capability: Implications for the US Economy*, National Academy Press, Washington, DC.

Arrow, K., 1974, *The Limits of Organization*, W.W. Norton, New York.

Arthur, W. B., 1988, 'Competing Technologies: An Overview', in Dosi, Freeman, Nelson, Silverberg, and Soete (eds.), *Technical Change and Economic Theory*.

Asanuma, B., 1989, 'Manufacturer–Supplier Relationships in Japan and the Concept of Relation-Specific Skill', *Journal of the Japanese and International Economies*, 3: 1–30.

Baba, Y., 1985, 'Japanese Colour TV Firms: Decision-Making from the 1950s to the 1980s', D.Phil. dissertation, University of Sussex, Brighton.

Bartholomew, J. R., 1989, *The Formation of Science in Japan: Building a Research Tradition*, Yale University Press, New Haven.

Bertolotti, M., 1983, *Masers and Lasers: An Historical Approach*, Adam Hilger, Bristol.

Best, M., 1990, *The New Competition: Institutions of Industrial Restructuring*, Harvard University Press, Cambridge, Mass.

Branscomb, L. and Kodama, F., 1993, *Japanese Innovation Strategy: Technical Support for Business Visions*, Occasional Paper No. 10, Center for Science and International Affairs, Harvard University.

Braun, E. and Macdonald, S., 1982, *Revolution in Miniature*, 2nd edn., Cambridge University Press, Cambridge.

Bromberg, J. L., 1986, 'Engineering Knowledge in the Laser Field', *Technology and Culture*, 27/1: 798–818.

Brooks, J., 1975, *Telephone: The First Hundred Years*, Harper & Row, New York.

Business Week, 1983, 'How the PC Project Changed the Way IBM Thinks', 3 October: 86.

Calder, K. E., 1988, *Crisis and Compensation: Public Policy and Political Stability in Japan, 1949–1986*, Princeton University Press, Princeton.

——1993, *Strategic Capitalism: Private Business and Public Purpose in Japanese Industrial Finance*, Princeton University Press, Princeton.

Carlsson, B. and Jacobsson, S., 1993, 'Technological Systems and Economic Performance: The Diffusion of Factory Automation in Sweden', in Foray and Freeman (eds.), *Technology and the Wealth of Nations*.

Casson, M., 1987, *The Firm and the Market: Studies on Multinational Enterprise and the Scope of the Firm*, MIT Press, Cambridge, Mass.

Caves, R. E. and Uekusa, M., 1976, *Industrial Organization in Japan*, The Brookings Institution, Washington, DC.

Chaffee, C. D., 1988, *The Rewiring of America: The Fiber Optics Revolution*, Academic Press, Boston, Mass.

Chambers Science and Technology Dictionary, 1988, Chambers, Cambridge.

Chandler, A. D., 1969, *Strategy and Structure: Chapters in the History of the Industrial Enterprise*, MIT Press, Cambridge, Mass.

——1977, *The Visible Hand: The Managerial Revolution in American Business*, The Belknap Press, Cambridge, Mass.

——1984, 'The Emergence of Managerial Capitalism', *Business History Review*, 58: 473–503.

——1990, *Scale and Scope: The Dynamics of Industrial Capitalism*, The Belknap Press, Cambridge, Mass.

—— and Salsbury, S., 1971, *Pierre S. du Pont and the Making of the Modern Corporation*, Harper & Row, New York.

Chapuis, R. J. and Joel, A. E., 1990, *100 Years of Telephone Switching*, ii. *Electronics, Computers and Telephone Switching: A Book of Technological History,1960–1985*, North-Holland, Amsterdam.

Chposky, J. and Leonsis, T., 1988, *The People, Power and Politics behind the IBM Personal Computer*, Facts on File, New York.

Clark, K. B. and Fujimoto, T., 1991, *Product Development Performance: Strategy, Organization, and Management in the World Auto Industry*, Harvard Business School Press, Boston.

Clark, R., 1979, *The Japanese Company*, Yale University Press, New Haven.

Cole, R. E., 1971, *Japanese Blue Collar*, University of California Press, Berkeley, California.

Coopersmith, J., 1993, Facsimile's False Starts, *IEEE Spectrum*, February: 46–9.

Corning, 1989, *Facts about Corning*, Corning, New York.

Cusumano, M. A., 1985, *The Japanese Automobile Industry*, Council on East Asian Studies, Harvard University, Cambridge, Mass.

——1991, *Japan's Software Factories*, Oxford University Press, New York.

—— and Kemerer, C. F., 1990, A Quantitative Analysis of U.S. and Japanese Practice and Performance in Software Development, *Management Science*, 36/11: 1384–1406.

Cutler, R. S. (ed.), 1989, *Science in Japan: Japanese Laboratories Open to U.S. Researchers*, Westview Press, Boulder, Colo.

—— (ed.), 1991, *Engineering in Japan: Education, Practice and Future Outlook*, Westview Press, Boulder, Colo.

—— (ed.), 1993, *Technology Management in Japan: R&D Policy, Industrial Strategies and Current Practice*, Westview Press, Boulder, Colo.

David, P. A., 1986, 'Understanding the Economics of QWERTY: The Necessity of History', in W. N. Parker (ed.), *Economic History and the Modern Economist*, Basil Blackwell, Oxford.

——1988, 'Path-Dependence: Putting the Past into the Future of Economics', Technical Report 533, Economics Series, Institute for Mathematical Studies in the Social Sciences, Stanford University, Palo Alto, Calif.

Davis, E., Flanders, S. and Star, J., 1991, 'Who are the World's Most Successful Companies?', *Business Strategy Review*, Summer: 1–33.

De Nero, H., 1990, 'Creating the "Hyphenated" Corporation', *McKinsey Quarterly*, No. 4: 153–73.

Dertouzos, M. L., Lester, R. K. and Solow, R. M., 1989, *Made in America: Regaining the Productivity Edge*, MIT Press, Cambridge, Mass.

District Court, S.D. New York, *Corning Glass Works* v. *Sumitomo Electric USA Inc.*, Nos. 84 Civ. 9155 (WCC) and 85 Civ. 3156 (WCC), decided 13 October 1987, as amended 21 December 1987, pp. 1545–71.

Dodgson, M. and Rothwell, R. (eds.), 1994, *The Handbook of Industrial Innovation*, Edward Elgar, Aldershot.

Dore, R., 1973, *British Factory–Japanese Factory: The Origins of National Diversity in Industrial Relations*, Allen & Unwin, London.

——1983a, *A Case Study of Technology Forecasting in Japan: The Next Generation Base Technologies Development Programme*, Technical Change Centre, London.

——1983b, 'Goodwill and the Spirit of Market Capitalism', *British Journal of Sociology*, 34: 459–82.

——1984a, *Education in Tokugawa Japan*, Athlone Press, London.

——1984b, 'Technological Self-Reliance: Sturdy Ideal or Self-Serving Rhetoric', in Fransman and King (eds.), *Technological Capability in the Third World*.

——1986, *Flexible Rigidities: Industrial Policy and Structural Adjustment in the Japanese Economy, 1970–80*, Athlone Press, London.

—— and Sako, M., 1989, *How the Japanese Learn to Work*, Routledge, London.

Dosi, G., 1982, 'Technological Paradigms and Technological Trajectories: A Suggested Interpretation of the Determinants and Directions of Technical Change', *Research Policy*, 11: 147–63.

——1990, 'Finance, Innovation, and Industrial Change', *Journal of Economic Behavior and Organization*, 13: 299–319.

—— Freeman, C., Nelson, R., Silverberg, G. and Soete, L., 1988, *Technical Change and Economic Theory*, Pinter, London.

Doz, Y. and Lehmann, J. P., 1986, 'The Strategic Management Process: The Japanese Example', *Bonner Zeitschrift für Japanologie*, 8: 263–83.

Dretske, F. I., 1982, *Knowledge and the Flow of Information*, MIT Press, Cambridge, Mass.

Drifte, R., 1986, *Arms Production in Japan: The Military Applications of Civilian Technology*, Westview Press, Boulder, Colo.

Duke, D. A., 1983, *A History of Optical Communications*, Special Report, Telecommunication Products Department, Corning Glass Works, Corning, New York.

Eliason, G., 1990, 'The Firm as a Competent Team', *Journal of Economic Behavior and Organization*, 13: 275–98.

Eto, H., 1993, *R&D Strategies in Japan: The National, Regional and Corporate Approach*, Elsevier, Amsterdam.

Ferguson, C. H. and Morris, C. R., 1993, *Computer Wars: How the West can Win in a Post-IBM World*, Times Books, New York.

Flamm, K., 1987, *Targeting the Computer: Government Support and International Competition*, The Brookings Institution, Washington, DC.

——1988, *Creating the Computer: Government, Industry, and High Technology*, The Brookings Institution, Washington, DC.

Florida, R. and Kenney, M., 1990, *The Breakthrough Illusion: Corporate America's Failure to Move from Innovation to Mass Production*, Basic Books, New York.

—— ——1991, 'Transplanted Organizations: The Transfer of Japanese Industrial Organization to the U.S.', *American Sociological Review*, 56: 381–98.

—— ——1992, *Beyond Mass Production: The Japanese System and its Transfer to the U.S.*, Oxford University Press, New York.

Foray, D. and Freeman, C. (eds.), 1993, *Technology and the Wealth of Nations: The Dynamics of Constructed Advantage*, Pinter, London.

Fransman, M., 1982, 'Learning and the Capital Goods Sector under Free Trade: The Case of Hong Kong', *World Development*, 10/11: 991–1014.

——1984, 'Promoting Technological Capability in the Capital Goods Sector: The Case of Singapore', *Research Policy*, 13: 33–54.

——1986a, *Technology and Economic Development*, Wheatsheaf, Brighton.

—— (ed.), 1986b, *Machinery and Economic Development*, Macmillan, London.

——1986c, 'International Competitiveness, International Diffusion of Technology and the State: A Case Study from Taiwan and Japan', *World Development*, 14/11.

——1992a, 'Controlled Competition in the Japanese Telecommunications Equipment Industry: The Case of Central Office Switches, in C. Antonelli (ed.), *The Economics of Information Networks*, North-Holland, Amsterdam.

——1992b, 'Japanese Failure in a High-Tech Industry? The Case of Central Office Telecommunications Switches', *Telecommunications Policy*, 16/3: 259–76.

——1993, *The Market and Beyond: Information Technology in Japan*, Cambridge University Press, Cambridge.

——1994a, 'The Japanese Innovation System: How it Works', in Dodgson and Rothwell (eds.), *The Handbook of Industrial Innovation*.

——1994b, 'Economics and Innovation: The Knowledge-Based Approach to Japanese Firms and the Relevance of Economic Thought', in O. Granstrand (ed.), *Economics of Technology*, Elsevier, Amsterdam.

——1994c, 'AT&T, BT and NTT: A Comparison of Vision, Strategy and Competence', *Telecommunications Policy*, 18/2: 137–53.

——1994d, 'AT&T, BT and NTT: The Role of R&D', *Telecommunications Policy*, 18/4: 295–305.

——1994e, 'Different Folks, Different Strokes: How IBM, AT&T and NEC Segment to Compete', *Business Strategy Review*, 5/3: 1–20.

——1994f, 'Information, Knowledge, Vision and Theories of the Firm', *Industrial and Corporate Change*, 3/2: 1–45.

——1995, 'Is National Technology Policy Obsolete in a Globalised World? The Japanese Response', *Cambridge Journal of Economics*, 19: 95–119.

—— 1996, *Visions of the Firm and Japan*, Oxford University Press, Oxford.

—— and King, K. (eds.), 1984, *Technological Capability in the Third World*, Macmillan, London.

—— Roobeek, A., and Junne, G. (eds.), 1995, *The Biotechnology Revolution?*, Blackwell, Oxford.

—— and Tanaka, S., 1995, 'Government, Globalisation and Universities in Japanese Biotechnology', *Research Policy*, 24: 13–49.

Freeman, C., 1982, *The Economics of Industrial Innovation*, Pinter, London.

——1987, *Technology Policy and Economic Performance: Lessons from Japan*, Pinter, London.

——1988, 'Japan: A New National System of Innovation?', in Dosi, Freeman, Nelson, Silverberg, and Soete, *Technical Change and Economic Theory*.

——1992, *The Economics of Hope: Essays on Technical Change, Economic Growth and the Environment*, Pinter, London.

—— Clark, J., and Soete, L. L. G., 1982, *Unemployment and Technical Innovation: A Study of Long Waves in Economic Development*, Pinter, London.

—— and Soete, L. L. G. (eds.), 1987, *Technical Change and Full Employment*, Blackwell, Oxford.

Fruin, W. M., 1978, 'The Japanese Company Controversy: Ideology and Organization in Historical Perspective', *Journal of Japanese Studies*, 4/2.

——1983, *Kikkoman: Company, Clan, and Community*, Harvard University Press, Cambridge, Mass.

——1992, *The Japanese Enterprise System: Competitive Strategies and Cooperative Structures*, Clarendon Press, Oxford.

—— forthcoming, *Knowledge Works*, Oxford University Press, New York.

Fujimoto, T., 1994, 'The Origin and Evolution of the "Black Box Parts" Practice in the Japanese Auto Industry', Research Institute for the Japanese Economy Discussion Paper Series, Faculty of Economics, University of Tokyo.

——1994, 'Reinterpreting the Resource-Capability View of the Firm: A Case of the Development-Production Systems of the Japanese Auto Makers', Research Institute for the Japanese Economy Discussion Paper Series, Faculty of Economics, University of Tokyo.

Fujitsu, 1977, *The History of Fujitsu*, Fujitsu, Tokyo (in Japanese).

Gerlach, M. L., 1992a, *Alliance Capitalism: The Social Organization of Japanese Business*, University of California Press, Berkeley.

——1992b, 'Twilight of the Keiretsu? A Critical Assessment', *Journal of Japanese Studies*, 18/1: 79–118.

Gibbons, M., 1987, 'Contemporary Transformation of Science', in M. Gibbons and B. Wittrock (eds.), *Science as a Commodity*, Longmans, London.

Godet, M., undated, *From Anticipation to Action: A Handbook of Strategic Prospective*, UNESCO, Paris.

Gordon, A., 1985, *The Evolution of Labor Relations in Japan: Heavy Industry, 1853–1955*, Council on East Asian Studies, Harvard University Press, Cambridge, Mass.

Goto, A., 1981, 'Statistical Evidence on the Diversification of Japanese Large Firms', *Journal of Industrial Economics*, 29/3: 271–8.

Harris, R., 1966, 'Electronic Telephone Exchanges: An Introductory Review of Development', *POEEJ*, 59/3: 211–19.

—— and Martin, J., 1981, 'The Evolution of Switching Systems Architecture', *POEEJ*, 74: 187–93.

Harvard Business School, 1993, *DDI Corporation*, Case Study 9–393–048, Harvard Business School, Boston, Mass.

Henderson, R. M. and Clark, K. B., 1990, 'Architectural Innovation: The Reconfiguration of Existing Product Technologies and the Failure of Established Firms', *Administrative Science Quarterly*, 35: 9–30.

Hills, J., 1984, *Information Technology and Industrial Policy*, Croom Helm, London.

Hirschmeier, J. and Yui, T., 1975, *The Development of Japanese Business, 1600–1973*, Allen & Unwin, London.

Hitachi, 1970, *The History of Hitachi's Totsuka Works I*, Hitachi, Tokyo (in Japanese).

Hobday, M., 1994, 'Innovation in Semiconductor Technology: The Limits of the Silicon Valley Network Model', in Dodgson and Rothwell (eds.), *The Handbook of Industrial Innovation*.

Hughes, T. P., 1984, *Networks of Power: Electrification in Western Society, 1880–1930*, Johns Hopkins University Press, Baltimore.

Imai, K., 1990, 'Japanese Business Groups and the Structural Impediments Initiative', in K. Yamamura (ed.), *Japan's Economic Structure: Should it Change?*, Society for Japanese Studies, Seattle.

—— and Itami, H., 1984, 'Interpenetration of Organization and Market: Japan's Firm and Market in Comparison with the US', *International Journal of Industrial Organization*, 2: 285–310.

—— Nonaka, I., and Takeuchi, H., 1985, 'Managing the New Product Development Process: How Japanese Companies Learn and Unlearn', in K. B. Clark, R. H. Hays, and C. Lorenz (eds.), *The Uneasy Alliance: Managing the Productivity–Technology Dilemma*, Harvard Business School Press, Boston, Mass.

Inose, H., 1979, *An Introduction to Digital Integrated Communications Systems*, University of Tokyo Press, Tokyo.

—— Nishikawa, T., and Uenohara, M., 1982, 'Cooperation between Universities and Industries in Basic and Applied Science', in A. Gerstenfeld (ed.), *Science Policy Perspectives: USA–Japan*, Academic Press, Tokyo.

Inoue, T., 1990, *NTT: Kyoso to bunkatsu ni chokumensuru johoka jidai no kyojin* (NTT: a giant in the information-oriented age facing competition and partition), Otsukishoten, Tokyo.

Itoh, H., 1987, 'Information Processing Capacities of the Firm', *Journal of the Japanese and International Economies*, 1: 299–326.

Itoh, M., 1990, *The World Economic Crisis and Japanese Capitalism*, Macmillan, London.

Japan Company Handbook, Toyo Keizai Inc., Tokyo.

Japanese Technology Evaluation Program, 1986, *Telecommunications Technology in Japan*, Panel Report, Science Applications International, La Jolla, Calif.

Johnson, C., 1989, 'MITI, MPT, and the Telecom Wars: How Japan Makes Policy for High Technology', in Johnson, Tyson, and Zysman (eds.), *Politics and Productivity*.

—— Tyson, L. D. and Zysman, J. (eds.), 1989, *Politics and Productivity: How Japan's Development Strategy Works*, Ballinger, New York.

Kagono, T., Nonaka, I., Sakakibara, K. and Okumura, A., 1985, *Strategic vs. Evolutionary Management: A U.S.–Japan Comparison of Strategy and Organization*, North-Holland, Amsterdam.

Kamata, H., 1982, *Japan in the Passing Lane*, Penguin Books, New York.

Kaneko, H., 1990, *NTT no mirai aratana jigyotenkai to bunkatsu no shogeki* (The Future of NTT), Toyokeizai shinpo, Tokyo.

Kao, C. and Hockham, G. A., 1966, 'Dielectric-Fiber Surface Waveguides for Optical Frequencies', *Proceedings of the IEEE* 113/7: 1151–8.

Katzenstein, P. J. and Okawara, N., 1993, *Japan's National Security: Structures, Norms, and Policy Responses in a Changing World*, Cornell University East Asia Program, Ithaca, NY.

Kawakami, S. and Nishizawa, J., 1965, 'Propagation Loss in a Distributed Beam Waveguide', *Proceedings of the IEEE*, December: 2148–9.

Kawasaki, S. and McMillan, J., 1987, 'The Design of Contracts: Evidence from Japanese Subcontracting', *Journal of the Japanese and International Economies*, 1.

Kester, W. C., 1991, *Japanese Takeovers: The Global Contest for Corporate Control*, Harvard Business School Press, Boston, Mass.

Kiji, K., Hoshino, Y., and Asai, K., 1990, 'Automated Fingerprint Identification System (AFIS)', *NEC Research and Development*, No. 96: 143–6.

Kikuchi, M., 1983, *Japanese Electronics: A Worm's Eye View of its Evolution*, Simul, Tokyo.

Kilby, J. S., 1976, 'Invention of the Integrated Circuit', *IEEE Transactions on Electronic Devices*, ED-23: 648–9.

Kitahara, Y., 1983, *Information Network System: Telecommunications in the Twenty-First Century*, Heinemann, London.

Knight, F., 1921, *Risk, Uncertainty and Profit*, Houghton Mifflin, Boston.

Kobayashi, K., 1984, 'The Past, Present and Future of Telecommunications in Japan', *IEEE Communications Magazine*, 22/5: 97.

——1988, *Computers and Communications: A Vision of C&C*, MIT Press, Cambridge, Mass.

——1989, *Rising to the Challenge: The Autobiography of Koji Kobayashi*, Harcourt Brace Jovanovich, Tokyo.

——1990a, *The Making of NEC's Postwar Strategies*, JETS Paper No. 1, Institute for Japanese–European Technology Studies, University of Edinburgh.

——1990b, 'Information Society and Information Technology', *NEC Research and Development*, Special 30th Anniversary Issue, No. 96: 2.

——1991, *The Rise of NEC: How the World's Greatest C&C Company is Managed*, Blackwell, Oxford.

Kobayashi, T., 1986, *Fortune Favors the Brave: Fujitsu: Thirty Years in Computers*, Toyo Keizai Shinposha, Tokyo.

Kodama, F., 1991, *Analysing Japanese High Technology*, Pinter, London.

——1992, 'Technology Fusion and the New R&D', *Harvard Business Review*, July–August: 70–8.

Koike, K., 1988, *Understanding Industrial Relations in Modern Japan*, Macmillan Press, London.

Komiya, R., Okuno, M., and Suzumura, K. (eds.), 1988, *Industrial Policy of Japan*, Academic Press, San Diego.

Kono, T., 1984, *Strategy and Structure of Japanese Enterprises*, Macmillan, London.

Landau, R. and Rosenberg, N. (eds.), 1986, *The Positive Sum Strategy: Harnessing Technology for Economic Growth*, National Academy Press, Washington, DC.

Langlois, R. N., 1990, 'External Economies and Economic Progress: The Case of the Microcomputer Industry', mimeo, Department of Economics, University of Connecticut.

Langlois, R. and Robertson, P. L., 1995, *Firms, Markets and Economic Change: A Dynamic Theory of Business Institutions*, Routledge, London.

Lastres, H. M. M., 1994, *The Advanced Materials Revolution and the Japanese System of Innovation*, Macmillan, London.

Lazonick, W., 1991, *Business Organization and the Myth of the Market Economy*, Cambridge University Press, Cambridge.

Lehmann, J. P., 1993, 'Japan 20: The West 1—Reversing the Scorecard', *Business Strategy Review*, 4/2: 59–92.

Lillrank, P. and Kano, N., 1989, *Continuous Improvement: Quality Control Circles in Japanese Industry*, Center for Japanese Studies, University of Michigan Press, Ann Arbor.

Lundvall, B. (ed.), 1992, *National Systems of Innovation: Toward a Theory of Innovation and Interactive Learning*, Pinter, London.

Lynn, L. H., 1982, *How Japan Innovates: A Comparison with the U.S. in the Case of Oxygen Steelmaking*, Westview Press, Boulder, Colo.

——1986, 'Japanese Research and Industrial Policy', *Science*, 18/July.

—— and McKeown, T. J., 1988, *Organizing Business: Trade Associations in America and Japan*, American Enterprise Institute, Washington, DC.

MacChesney, J. B., O'Conner, P. B., Dimarcello, E. V., Simpson, J. R., and Lozay, P. D., 1974, 'Preparation of Low Loss Optical Fibers using Simultaneous Vapor Phase Deposition and Fusion', *Tenth International Congress on Glass, No. 6 Optical Properties and Optical Waveguides*, 12 July, The Ceramic Society of Japan, Kyoto.

Maddison, A., 1991, *Dynamic Forces in Capitalist Development: A Long-Run Comparative View*, Oxford University Press, Oxford.

——1995, *Explaining the Economic Performance of Nations: Essays in Time and Space*, Edward Elgar, Aldershot.

Magaziner, I. and Patinkin, M., 1989, *The Silent War: Inside the Global Business Battles Shaping America's Future*, Random House, New York.

Maiman, T. H., 1987, *The Laser: Its Origin, Applications and Future*, Japan Prize 1987 Official Brochure: 12–17.

Malerba, F. and Orsenigo, L., 1995, 'Schumpeterian Patterns of Innovation', *Cambridge Journal of Economics*, 19/1: 47–66.

March, J. G., 1994, *A Primer on Decision Making: How Decisions Happen*, The Free Press, New York.

Marshall, A., 1962, *Principles of Economics*, Macmillan, London.

Mason, M., 1992, *American Multinationals and Japan: The Political Economy of Japanese Capital Controls, 1899–1980*, Harvard University Council on East Asian Studies, Harvard University, Cambridge, Mass.

Matsushita, K., 1988, *Quest for Prosperity: The Life of a Japanese Industrialist*, PHP Institute, Tokyo.

Merz, J. L., 1986, 'The Opto-Electronics Joint Research Laboratory: Light Shed on Cooperative Research in Japan', *Scientific Bulletin*, 11: 1–30.

Metcalfe, J. S., 1995, 'Technology Systems and Technology Policy in an Evolutionary Framework', *Cambridge Journal of Economics*, 19/1: 25–46.

—— and Gibbons, M., 1989, 'Technology Variety and Organisation: A Systematic Perspective on the Competitive Process', *Research on Technological Innovation, Management and Policy*, 4: 153–93.

Meurling, J., 1985, *A Switch in Time*, Telephony Publishing Co., Chicago.

Milgrom, P., and Roberts, J., 1988, *Economics, Organization and Management*, Prentice-Hall, Englewood Cliffs, NJ.

Millman, S. (ed.), 1983, *A History of Engineering and Science in the Bell System: Physical Sciences (1925–1980)*, AT&T Bell Laboratories, Murray Hill, NJ.

—— (ed.), 1984, *A History of Engineering and Science in the Bell System: Communications Sciences (1925–1980)*, AT&T Bell Laboratories, Murray Hill, NJ.

Ministry of Posts and Telecommunications, undated(*a*), *Telecommunications Reforms in Japan*, MPT, Tokyo.

—— undated(*b*), Summary of the Report on *Necessary Measures to be Taken According to Article 2 of the Supplementary Provision of the Nippon Telegraph and Telephone Corporation Law*, submitted by the Telecommunications Council on 2 March 1990, MPT, Tokyo.

——1990, *Measures to be Taken in Accordance with Article 2 of the Supplementary Provisions of the Nippon Telegraph and Telephone Corporation Law*, issued on 30 March 1990, MPT, Tokyo (unofficial translation).

——1992*a*, *Open Telecommunications Market of Japan*, MPT, Tokyo.

——1992*b*, *An Outline of the Telecommunications Business*, MPT, Tokyo.

Miyazaki, K., 1995, *Building Competences in the Firm: Lessons from Japanese and European Optoelectronics*, Macmillan, London.

Molina, A., 1990, 'Building Technological Capabilities in Telecommunications Technologies: Development and Strategies in Public Digital Switching Systems', paper presented to the International Telecommunications Society Conference, Venice, 1990.

Morgan, K., 1987, 'Breaching the Monopoly: Telecommunications and the State in Britain', Working Paper Series on Government–Industry Relations No. 7, University of Sussex.

Morita, A., 1986, *Made in Japan*, Dutton, New York.

——1987, *Made in Japan: Akio Morita and Sony*, Weatherhill, Tokyo.

Morris-Suzuki, T., 1989, *A History of Japanese Economic Thought*, Routledge, London.

——1994, *The Technological Transformation of Japan: From the Seventeenth to the Twenty-First Century*, Cambridge University Press, Cambridge.

Morton, J. A., 1971, *Organizing for Innovation: A Systems Approach to Technical Management*, McGraw-Hill, New York.

Moses, K. R., 1986, 'A Consumer's Guide to Fingerprint Computers', *Identification News*, June: 5–10.

Mowery, D. C. and Rosenberg, N., 1989, *Technology and the Pursuit of Economic Growth*, Cambridge University Press, Cambridge.

—— and Teece, D. J., 1992, 'The Changing Place of Japan in the Global Scientific and Technological Enterprise', in Arrison, Bergsten, Graham, and Caldwell-Harris (eds.), *Japan's Growing Technological Capability*.

Murakami, Y., 1987, 'The Japanese Model of Political Economy', in K. Yamamura and Y. Yasuba (eds.), *The Political Economy of Japan*, i, Stanford University Press, Stanford, Calif.

Mytelka, L. K. (ed.), 1991, *Strategic Partnerships: States, Firms, and International Competition*, Pinter, London.

Nagai, S., 1990, 'On the Competition of Telecommunications under Regulation in Japan', *Journal of International Economic Studies*, 4: 15–32.

Nakahara, T., 1960, 'Thin Dielectric-Membrane Surface Waveguide', mimeo, Sumitomo Electric, Tokyo.

—— et al., 1969, 'Millimeter Waveguides with Applications to Railroad Communications', in L. Young (ed.), *Advances in Microwave*, Academic Press, New York.

—— Shioyama, H. and Watamizu, T., 1987, 'Optical Fiber: From its Initial Development through Successful Production and Usage', *Sumitomo Electric Technical Review*, No. 26: 40–2.

——1983, *Economic Growth in Prewar Japan*, Yale University Press, New Haven.

Nakatani, I., 1984, 'The Economic Role of Financial Corporate Groupings', in Aoki (ed.), *The Economic Analysis of the Japanese Firm*.

——1988, *The Japanese Firm in Transition*, Asian Productivity Organization, Tokyo.

Nakayama, S., 1991, *Science, Technology and Society in Postwar Japan*, Kegan Paul, London.

Nelson, R. R., 1977, *The Moon and the Ghetto*, Norton, New York.

——1980, 'Production Sets, Technological Knowledge, and R and D: Fragile and Overworked Constructions for Analysis of Productivity Growth?', *American Economic Review*, 70: 62–7.

——1981, 'Research on Productivity Growth and Productivity Differences: Dead Ends and New Departures', *Journal of Economic Literature*, 19/3: 1029–64.

—— (ed.), 1993, *National Innovation Systems: A Comparative Analyis*, Oxford University Press, New York.

—— and Winter, S. G., 1974, 'Neoclassical vs. Evolutionary Theories of Economic Growth: Critique and Prospectus', *Economic Journal*, 84: 886–905.

—— ——1977, 'In Search of Useful Theory of Innovation', *Research Policy*, 5: 36–76.

—— ——1982, *An Evolutionary Theory of Economic Change*, Belknap Press, Cambridge, Mass.

Nonaka, I., 1991, 'The Knowledge-Creating Company', *Harvard Business Review*, Nov/Dec: 96–104.

Norman, G. and La Manna, M., 1992, *The New Industrial Economics*, Edward Elgar, Aldershot.

Noyce, R. N. and Hoff, M. E., 1981, 'A History of Microprocessor Development at Intel', *IEEE Micro*, 1: 8–21.

NTT, 1953, *Twenty-Five Years of Japan's Automatic Telephone Switches*, i–iii, NTT, Tokyo (Jido Kokanki 25 Nen Shi).

——1972, *A History of Japan's Carrier Telephone Technology Development*, NTT, Tokyo (in Japanese).

Odagiri, H., 1985, 'Research Activity, Output Growth, and Productivity Increase in Japanese Manufacturing Companies', *Research Policy*, 14: 117–30.

——1989, 'Government Policies Toward Industrial R&D: Theory, Empirical Findings, and Japan's Experience', in M. Neumann (ed.), *Public Finance and Performance of Enterprises*, Wayne State University Press, Detroit.

——1990, 'Unravelling the Mystery of Low Japanese Profit Rates', *Business Strategy Review*, Summer.

——1992, *Growth through Competition, Competition through Growth: Strategic Management and the Economy in Japan*, Clarendon Press, Oxford.

—— and Iwata, H., 1986, 'The Impact of R&D on Productivity Increase in Japanese Manufacturing Companies', *Research Policy*, 15: 13–19.

—— and Yamawaki, H., 1986, 'A Study of Company Profit-Rate Time Series: Japan and the United States', *International Journal of Industrial Organization*, 4: 1–23.

Okimoto, D., 1989, *Between MITI and the Market*, Stanford University Press, Stanford.

Okimoto, D. I., Sugano, T. and Weinstein, F. B., 1984, *Competitive Edge: The Semiconductor Industry in the U.S. and Japan*, Stanford University Press, Stanford.

Owen, G. and Harrison, T., 1995, 'Why ICI Chose to Demerge', *Harvard Business Review*, March–April.

Patel, C. K. N., 1987, 'Lasers in Communications and Information Processing', in J. H. Ausubel and H. D. Langford (eds.), *Lasers: Invention to Application*, National Academy Press, Washington, DC.

Patel, P. and Pavitt, K., 1991, 'The Innovative Performance of the World's Largest Firms', *Economics of Innovation and New Technology*, 1.

Patrick, H. (ed.), 1991, *Pacific Basin Industries in Distress: Structural Adjustment and Trade Policy in the Nine Industrialized Economies*, Columbia University Press, New York.

—— et al. (eds.), 1986, *Japan's High Technology Industries and Industrial Policy*, University of Washington Press, Seattle.

—— and Rosovsky, H., 1976, *Asia's New Giant*, The Brookings Institution, Washington, DC.

Pavitt, K., 1987, 'The Objectives of Technology Policy', *Science and Public Policy*, 14: 182–8.

——1990, 'What Do We Know about the Strategic Management of Technology?', *California Management Review*, 32: 17–26.

Pempel, T. J., 1987, 'The Unbundling of "Japan Inc": The Changing Dynamics of Japanese Policy Formation', *Journal of Japanese Studies*, 13/2: 271–306.

Penrose, E. T., 1955, 'Limits to the Growth and Size of Firms', *American Economic Review*, 45/2: 531–43.

——1959, *The Theory of the Growth of the Firm*, Basil Blackwell, Oxford.

Penzias, A., 1989, *Ideas and Information: Managing in a High-Tech World*, W.W. Norton, New York.

Polanyi, M., 1967, *The Tacit Dimension*, Doubleday Anchor, Garden City, New York.

Porter, M., 1967, *Competitive Strategy*, Free Press, New York.

——1990, *The Competitive Advantage of Nations*, Free Press, New York.

Prahalad, C. K. and Hamel, G., 1990, 'The Core Competence of the Corporation', *Harvard Business Review*, May–June: 79–91.

Primot, D., 1992, 'France Telecom: Options for ATM', mimeo, Theseus Institute, Sophia Antipolis.

Reich, L. S., 1985, *The Making of American Industrial Research: Science and Business at GE and Bell, 1876–1926*, Cambridge University Press, Cambridge.

Rosegrant, S. and Lampe, D. R., 1992, *Route 128: Lessons from Boston's High-Tech Community*, Basic Books, New York.

Rosenberg, N., 1969, 'The Direction of Technological Change: Inducement Mechanisms and Focusing Devices', *Economic Development and Cultural Change*, 18: 1–24.

——1976, *Perspectives on Technology*, Cambridge University Press, Cambridge.

Rosenberg, N., 1982, *Inside the Black Box: Technology and Economics*, Cambridge University Press, Cambridge.

——1994*a*, *Exploring the Black Box: Technology, Economics and History*, Cambridge University Press, Cambridge.

——1994*b*, *The Emergence of Economic Ideas: Essays in the History of Economics*, Edward Elgar, Aldershot.

Rosenbloom, R. S. and Abernathy, W. J., 1982, 'The Climate for Innovation in Industry: The Role of Management Attitudes and Practices in Consumer Electronics', *Research Policy*, 11/4: 209–25.

Sakakibara, K. and Westney, D. E., 1985, 'Comparative Study of the Training, Careers, and Organization of Engineers in the Computer Industry in the United States and Japan', *Hitotsubashi Journal of Commerce and Management*, 20/1: 1–20.

Sako, M., 1990, 'Buyer–Supplier Relationships and Economic Performance: Evidence from Britain and Japan', Ph.D. thesis, University of London.

——1992, *Contracts, Prices and Trust: How the Japanese and British Manage their Subcontracting Relationships*, Oxford University Press, Oxford.

Samuels, R. J., 1987, *The Business of the Japanese State*, Cornell University Press, Ithaca, NY.

——1994, *Rich Nation, Strong Army: National Security and the Technological Transformation of Japan*, Cornell University Press, Ithaca, NY.

Saxenian, A., 1994, *Regional Advantage, Culture and Competition in Silicon Valley and Route 128*, Harvard University Press, Cambridge, Mass.

Saxonhouse, G. R. and Yamamura, K. (eds.), 1986, *Law and Trade Issues of the Japanese Economy*, University of Washington Press, Seattle.

Scherer, F. H., 1992, *International High-Technology Competition*, Harvard University Press, Cambridge, Mass.

Schumpeter, J. A., 1954, *History of Economic Analysis*, Oxford University Press, New York.

——1961, *The Theory of Economic Development: An Inquiry into Profits, Capital, Credit, Interest and the Business Cycle*, Oxford University Press, New York.

——1966, *Capitalism, Socialism and Democracy*, Unwin, London.

Sekimoto, T., 1990, 'Technological Innovation and Corporate Management for the 21st Century', Keynote Address at the IFIP TC 5 Conference on Computer Applications in Production and Engineering, 3–5 October 1989, Tokyo, reprinted in *Computers in Industry*, 1990, Elsevier, Amsterdam.

——1992, 'Global Business Perspectives in the Information Age', paper presented at Washington University, St Louis, 30 September.

Sheard, P., 1989, 'The Main Bank System and Corporate Monitoring and Control in Japan', *Journal of Economic Behavior and Organization*, 11: 399–422.

——(ed.), 1992, *International Adjustment and the Japanese Firm*, Allen & Unwin, St Leonards.

Shimasaki, N., 1992, 'An Overall View of the IT (Information Technology) Industry Complex: A Structure Alignment Trial in a Cubic Framework', *NEC Research and Development*, 33/4: 547.

Shimokawa, K., 1994, *The Japanese Automobile Industry: A Business History*, Athlone Press, London.

Shockley, W., 1950, *Electronics and Holes in Semiconductors, with Applications to Transistor Electronics*, van Nostrand, New York.

Sigurdson, J., 1982, 'Technological Change, Economic Security, and Technology Politics in Japan', Technology and Culture Occasional Report Series No. 4, Research Policy Institute, University of Lund, Sweden.

——1986, *Industry and State Partnership in Japan: The Very Large Scale Integrated Circuits (VLSI) Project*, Research Policy Institute, University of Lund, Sweden.

—— and Anderson, A. M., 1991, *Science and Technology in Japan*, 2nd edn., Longman, London.

Simon, H. A., 1961, *Administrative Behaviour*, 2nd edn., Macmillan, New York.

——1962, 'The Architecture of Complexity', *Proceedings of the American Philosophical Society*, 106: 467–82.

——1969, *The Sciences of the Artificial*, MIT Press, Cambridge, Mass.

—— Egidi, M., Marris, R., and Viale, R., 1992, *Economics, Bounded Rationality and the Cognitive Revolution*, Edward Elgar, Aldershot.

Smitka, M. J., 1991, *Competitive Ties: Subcontracting in Japanese Manufacturing*, Columbia University Press, New York.

Sony, 1986, *Genryu: Sony Challenges 1946–1968*, Sony Corporation, Tokyo.

Sowell, T., 1980, *Knowledge and Decisions*, Basic Books, New York.

Steinmueller, W. E., 1994, 'Basic Research and Industrial Innovation', in Dodgson and Rothwell (eds.), *The Handbook of Industrial Innovation*.

Stinchcombe, A. L., 1990, *Information and Organizations*, University of California Press, Berkeley.

Stock, R. M., 1987, 'An Historical Overview of Automated Fingerprint Identification Systems', *Proceedings of the International Forensic Symposium on Latent Prints*, FBI Academy, Quantico, Va., 7–10 July.

Suematsu, Y. *et al.*, 1979, Post-deadline paper presented at Fifth European Conference on Optical Communications, Amsterdam, September, mimeo.

Sugiyama, C., 1994, *Origins of Economic Thought in Modern Japan*, Routledge, London.

Suzuki, Y., 1991, *Japanese Management Structures 1920–80*, Macmillan, London.

——1992, *The Japanese Financial System*, Clarendon Press, Oxford.

Swedberg, R., 1991, *Joseph A. Schumpeter: His Life and Work*, Polity Press, Cambridge.

Takenaka, H., 1991, *Contemporary Japanese Economy and Economic Policy*, University of Michigan Press, Ann Arbor.

Tanaka, M., 1991, 'Government Policy and Biotechnology in Japan: The Pattern and Impact of Rivalry between Ministries', in Wilks and Wright (eds.), *The Promotion and Regulation of Industry in Japan*.

Tanaka, S., 1986, 'Post-War Japanese Resource Policies and Strategies: The Case of Southeast Asia', Cornell University East Asia Papers No. 43, Cornell University, Ithaca, NY.

Teece, D. J., 1980, 'Economies of Scope and the Scope of the Enterprise', *Journal of Economic Behavior and Organization*, 1: 223–47.

——1982, 'Towards an Economic Theory of the Multiproduct Firm', *Journal of Economic Behavior and Organization*, 3: 39–63.

——1984, 'Economic Analysis and Strategic Management', *California Management Review*, 26/3: 87–110.

——1986, 'Profiting from Technological Innovation', *Research Policy*, 15/6.

——1993, 'The Dynamics of Industrial Capitalism: Perspectives on Alfred Chandler's *Scale and Scope* (1990)', *Journal of Economic Literature*, 31.

Teece, D. J., Rumelt, R., Dosi, G., and Winter, S., 1994, 'Understanding Corporate Coherence: Theory and Evidence', *Journal of Economic Behavior and Organization*, 23: 1–30.

—— Pisano, G. and Shuen, A., 1994, 'Dynamic Capabilities and Strategic Management', mimeo, University of California, Berkeley.

Thurow, L., 1992, *Head to Head: The Coming Economic Battle among Japan, Europe, and America*, Morrow, New York.

Townes, C. H., 1965, '1964 Nobel Lecture: Production of Coherent Radiation by Atoms and Molecules', *IEEE Spectrum*, August: 30–43.

——1984, 'Ideas and Stumbling Blocks in Quantum Electronics', *IEEE Journal of Quantum Electronics*, QE-20/6: 547–50.

Toyota Motor Corporation, 1988, *Toyota: A History of the First 50 Years*, Dainippon Printing, Tokyo.

Trevor, M., 1988, *Toshiba's New British Company*, Policy Studies Institute, London.

Tsuru, S., 1993, *Japan's Capitalism: Creative Defeat and Beyond*, Cambridge University Press, Cambridge.

Turner, L., 1987, *Industrial Collaboration with Japan*, Royal Institute of International Affairs, London.

Tyson, L. D., 1992, *Who's Bashing Whom? Trade Conflict in High-Technology Industries*, Institute for International Economics, Washington, DC.

Uekusa, M., 1987, 'Industrial Organization: The 1970s to the Present', in K. Yamamura and Y. Yasuba (eds.), *The Political Economy of Japan*, i, Stanford University Press, Stanford, Calif.

Van Wolferen, K., 1989, *The Enigma of Japanese Power*, Basic Books, New York.

Vogel, E. F., 1979, *Japan as Number One*, Harvard University Press, Cambridge, Mass.

Von Hippel, E., 1988, *The Sources of Innovation*, Oxford University Press, Oxford.

Watanabe, C., Santoso, I., and Widayanti, T., 1991, *The Inducing Power of Japanese Technological Innovation*, Pinter, London.

Waverman, L., 1990, 'R&D and Preferred Supplier Relationships: The Growth of Northern Telecom', paper presented to the International Telecommunications Society (ITS) Conference, Venice, 1990, mimeo.

Westney, E., 1987, *Imitation and Innovation*, Harvard University Press, Cambridge, Mass.

——1994, 'The Evolution of Japan's Industrial Research and Development', in Aoki and Dore (eds.), *The Japanese Firm*.

Whittaker, D. H., 1990, *Managing Innovation: A Study of British and Japanese Factories*, Cambridge University Press, Cambridge.

Wilks, S. and Wright, M. (eds.), 1991, *The Promotion and Regulation of Industry in Japan*, Macmillan, London.

Williamson, O. E., 1975, *Markets and Hierarchies: Analysis and Antitrust Implications. A Study in the Economics of Internal Organization*, The Free Press, New York.

——1981, 'Modern Corporation: Origins, Evolution, Attributes', *Journal of Economic Literature*, 19: 1539–44.

——1985, *The Economic Institutions of Capitalism*, The Free Press, New York.

——1992, 'Strategizing, Economizing, and Economic Organization', *Strategic Management Journal*.

—— and Winter, S. G., 1993, *The Nature of the Firm: Origins, Evolution, and Development*, Oxford University Press, New York.

Womack, J. P., Jones, D. T. and Roos, D., 1990, *The Machine that Changed the World: The Story of Lean Production*, Macmillan, New York.

Wood, J. C. (ed.), 1991, *J. A. Schumpeter: Critical Assessments*, i–iv, Routledge, London.

World Bank, 1993, *The East Asian Miracle, Economic Growth and Public Policy*, Oxford University Press, Oxford.

Wray, W. D., 1989, *Managing Industrial Enterprise: Cases from Japan's Prewar Experience*, Harvard University Press, Cambridge, Mass.

Yui, T. and Nakagawa, M. (eds.), 1989, *Japanese Management in Historical Perspective*, Fuji Business History Conference XV, University of Tokyo Press, Tokyo.

Yuzawa, T. (ed.), 1994, *Japanese Business Success: The Evolution of a Strategy*, Routledge, London.

Zysman, J., 1977, *Political Strategies for Industrial Order: State, Market, and Industry in France*, University of California Press, Berkeley.

——1983, *Government, Markets, and Growth: Financial Systems and the Politics of Industrial Change*, Cornell University Press, Ithaca, NY.

INDEX